AMERICAN NOVELISTS OF TODAY

BY THE SAME AUTHOR

NOAH WEBSTER: *Schoolmaster to America* (1936)

THE AMERICAN MIND: *Selections from the Literature of the United States* (with Ralph H. Gabriel and Stanley T. Williams, 1937, revised 1947)

SKETCHES OF AMERICAN POLICY BY NOAH WEBSTER (1937)

AMERICAN LOCAL-COLOR STORIES (with G. Harrison Orians, 1941)

OF THE PEOPLE (with Elizabeth W. Manwaring, 1942)

THE RHAPSODIST, AND OTHER UNCOLLECTED WRITINGS BY CHARLES BROCKDEN BROWN (1943)

CUENTISTAS NORTEAMERICANOS (with Herschel Brickell and D. G. Poore, 1946)

AMERICAN COLLEGE ENGLISH: *A Handbook of Usage and Composition* (with Ernst G. Mathews and John C. Bushman, 1949)

THE DEMIES: *A History,* 1899–1949 (1949)

CHARLES BROCKDEN BROWN: *American Gothic Novelist* (1949)

AMERICAN NOVELISTS OF TODAY (1951)

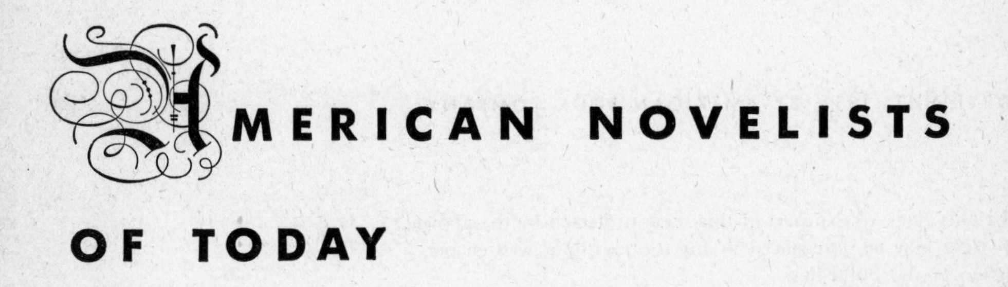

AMERICAN NOVELISTS OF TODAY

Harry R. Warfel

AMERICAN BOOK COMPANY
New York Cincinnati Chicago Boston
Atlanta Dallas San Francisco

Warfel: *American Novelists of Today*
V.B.P. 1 Made in U.S.A.

PREFACE

THIS BOOK CONTAINS 575 factually accurate informational sketches of the life and writings of contemporary American novelists. Every effort has been made to include accounts of those writers who have published two or more serious novels, one of them in the last ten years, and who in 1951 were at work upon a long piece of fiction. A few authors of distinguished first novels have been included. The object has been to give as complete a record as possible of the decade of the 1940's. Because of the difficulty of obtaining information about the writers who pseudonymously compose mystery, detective, and "western" fiction, all authors whose work has been entirely in these fields have been omitted.

Although there is some literary criticism in this volume, the main purpose has not been to criticize the artistic aims or to evaluate the literary merits of these writers. Rather, this survey is designed to present factual information for the benefit of readers who wish a guide through this extensive body of imaginative prose writing. No one reader can pass judgment satisfactorily upon so many books or upon so many authors within the time available for the compilation of an up-to-date reference work.

Each sketch is authoritative, for it has been reviewed either by the person whom it discusses or by a person whose knowledge of the life and work of the novelist gives authenticity to the statement. Many authors have kindly supplied information on their aims or philosophy, and most of these views are presented as direct quotations. No other book has ever included as equally complete a representation of the work of living American novelists.

The plan of each sketch is this: first, there is a brief biography; second, the works other than fiction are listed and sometimes briefly annotated; third, the author's leading theme, purpose, intention, style, aesthetic principle, or philosophy is stated; and, finally, a brief description of each novel is given. In a few instances there are statements about representative novels, but, in general, every novel by an author has been summarized by its theme or by its main narrative movement.

The length of each sketch has been determined by the amount of pertinent biographical data available and by the number of published novels. Length is not to be construed as a measure of aesthetic or popular success nor as a measure of a writer's final position as a contributor to the history of the American novel.

Novelists have been chosen for representation in this book because of the wide popular appeal of this form of writing. No other type of literature entertains as many readers, short stories in magazines excepted. Book sales, both in original and reprint editions, and library borrowing indicate that millions of copies of novels are read annually by an ever-increasing audience. A novel is more than a work of entertainment, however; the novel is a primary social record, a direct impression of life recorded by a sensitive and often poetically gifted writer. From these novels it is possible to construct a picture of contemporaneous American life in almost all its geographic areas and its economic levels; therein portrayed are American characters' psychological and social problems and their philosophic and spiritual attitudes.

Yet many writers describe events and personalities in foreign lands and in distant times. The absence of parochialism and narrow nationalism marks American fiction today, and it is through these books about faraway lands and bygone days that the persistent striving of men and women becomes as real for readers as it was for the participants.

The complete history of American fiction today would involve much information which the scope of this book does not include. Many of the novels mentioned in this work have been turned into dramas, radio plays, musical comedies, and motion pictures, but space limitation has required the omission of nearly all information of this type. Similarly, data about translations have been omitted, for almost every novel of significance has been published abroad in one or more foreign languages. Some of these books have become best sellers with immense influence. In general, however, it has been necessary, regretfully, to pass silently over this information. Many of the novels mentioned in this book have been published in other English-speaking countries. Although the titles in some instances have been changed, the American title alone has been given. Likewise, the new titles assigned to novels in reprint editions in the United States have not been included. Almost every author has contributed short stories and essays to magazines; this information has been omitted because it can be taken for granted. Serial publication of novels in magazines also has seldom been mentioned. Each entry is made under the pen name currently used by each writer. Because some married women published novels under their maiden names, an index to this information, as well as to known pseudonyms, is given.

For those readers who wish to gain further information about the authors and the books mentioned in this work, convenient reference works are available in most general libraries. *Book Review Digest,* a monthly publication which is cumulated annually, contains summaries and brief statements from reviews of books published since 1905. *Fiction Catalog* has been published periodically since 1908 to list, with brief annotations, "the best works of fiction for library use." Otis W. Coan and Richard G. Lillard's *America in Fiction* (Third edition, 1948) similarly records titles, together with brief annotations, "to help readers understand their country better." Books about individual authors or groups of authors are numerous; these can be located by consulting *Cumulative Book Index.* Magazine articles by and about authors are listed in *Readers' Guide to Periodical Literature* and *International Index to Periodicals.* Sources of biographical information since 1946 are given in *Biography Index.*

It is a pleasure for me to express appreciation to the novelists, publishers, literary agents, and literary critics whose assistance made possible the completion of this work. Hundreds of persons have cheerfully answered questions and supplied information. In a sense the excellence of the book is owing to their helpfulness. My wife assisted me daily in the immense bibliographical task required by this work; her cheerful co-operation is a constant source of inspiration to me.

Harry R. Warfel

UNIVERSITY OF FLORIDA
GAINESVILLE

TABLE OF CONTENTS

AMERICAN NOVELISTS OF TODAY

ABBOTT *to* ASCH

JANE (LUDLOW DRAKE) ABBOTT

Artist:
F. R. McGreerie

was born in Buffalo, New York. For generations her family has been connected with shipbuilding and commerce on the Great Lakes. She counted as lost any childhood vacation that was not spent on the water between Buffalo and Duluth. Her writing career began at Cornell University, where she served for two years on the editorial staff of the undergraduate newspaper. Marriage to Frank A. Abbott, a Buffalo attorney, and later maternal chores for their three children confined Mrs. Abbott's literary efforts for a time to newspaper features and plays for children. She soon fixed up a workroom on the third floor of the Abbott house and went to work on a book for girls. Later she turned to adult fiction. "I don't think my husband and children ever felt neglected," Mrs. Abbott has said. "I tried out on them everything I wrote, shared their interests, and took my writing time mostly from the time I did *not* spend on teas, bridge parties, women's clubs, department stores, and crowded streets."

Besides some twenty books for boys and girls, Mrs. Abbott has written fifteen romances. *Kitty Frew* (1931) concerns a girl who marries Gar Frew and refuses to allow his parents to direct the young couple's life. *The Silver Fountain* (1932) shows how Andy Keep has married Mollie, an invalid, for money to help his bankrupt father. When Virginia appears, Andy says he really wants her, but friends help him to a wise decision. *Miss Jolley's Family* (1933) is about a maiden aunt who has acted as a governess to the three motherless daughters of Adrian Daggett. Now that they are grown she must decide what to do; meantime, she pilots them over perilous shoals of marital difficulties and in the end finds romance.

Benefit Street (1936) portrays the selfish invalid, Amy Barron, who dominates her sister Anna until Kathie, Amy's daughter, comes home from college and a woman with a past returns from abroad. Then Amy gains freedom. In *To Have, To Keep* (1939) Diane and Bill Arden are married, and the problem is to keep the wealthy, fun-loving girl happy while the poor, proud lawyer is advancing in his profession. *Lorrie* (1941) carries a girl to success as a dancer because she refuses to be imprisoned in unhappiness. *Yours for the Asking* (1943), set in the Kentucky mountains, analyzes the conflict in the marriage of John Carter, a young, thoughtful preacher, and his pretty, red-headed wife, Darragh, who is drawn toward the impudent Leaf Garrick.

Mary Patten's Daughters (1945) describes the unwillingness of Charie and Flo Patten to be governed by their domineering mother, a successful business executive. *The Outsiders* (1948) brings Eliza Forrestall to New Hampshire to ownership of her grandfather's mill, which she modernizes with the help of a young visiting preacher, Chris Cameron. *River's Rim* (1950), set on the Niagara frontier in the War of 1812, places Quint Darby, the hero, under suspicion because his wealthy, snobbish father and brother sympathize with the British. Quint runs away from home to be with the American patriots.

SAMUEL HOPKINS ADAMS

Blackstone Studios

was born in Dunkirk, New York, on January 26, 1871. At Hamilton College, from which he graduated in 1891, he introduced football, played tackle on its first team, and won the intercollegiate tennis championship. From 1891 to 1900 he was a reporter and special staff writer for the New York *Sun,* and then for five years was associated with Samuel Sidney McClure as managing editor of McClure's Syndicate, advertising manager of McClure, Phillips & Company, and member of the staff of *McClure's* magazine. His "muckraking" articles on public-health topics in *McClure's* led to the "Great American Fraud" series which he did for *Collier's* and which acted powerfully as a lever in the passage of the Pure Food and Drug Act of 1906. His first book, *The Flying Death* (1902), was a mystery story about a prehistoric monster; his second, written with Stewart Edward White, was *The Mystery* (1905). In addition to essays and novels, Mr. Adams has produced three biographies: *The Godlike Daniel* (1930), a life of Daniel Webster; *The Incredible Era* (1939), a life of Warren G. Harding; and *A. Woollcott, His Life and His World* (1946), which won the Critics' Award. Mr. Adams lives at his lakeside farm, "Wide Waters," near Auburn, New York, not far from the Erie Canal, which is the setting of several of his novels.

His interests as a writer have varied widely. Perhaps it would be more accurate to say that the angle of his interest has swung almost around the circle. That is another way of stating that he has been interested in almost everything that has come within his horizon—as a good reporter should be, and he is a good reporter. "I shall never get over my newspaper training; nor do I want to!" he has said. "A good newspaper man knows instinctively what is interesting. If he cannot write well enough to make it interesting to others, that limitation will debar him from becoming a successful novelist."

Concerning his recent books Mr. Adams has stated: "Of late years I have had an ambition to recreate a vitally important part of our country—important historically—which has been too little written about, central New York. The 'York State' of a hundred years ago was a fascinating region, settled by the finest type of Americans. What I am trying to do is to show those people in their daily lives; not the big, historical figures, but the common folk of the street and store and office."

In his books Mr. Adams often contrasts intelligence and honesty with scheming self-seeking, chicanery, and incompetence. After writing three more mysteries and a fictionalized lecture on health, he published *The Clarion* (1914), which deals with the themes of quackery in medicine and dishonesty in journalism. Hal Surtaine, son of a patent-medicine millionaire, buys a newspaper, *The Clarion,* and soon must decide whether to print the truth about "Certina" or abandon his principles. There followed *Little Miss Grouch* (1915), a slight tale of love and laughter on an Atlantic voyage. Tribute is paid to the United States Public Health Service in the romantic tale, *The Unspeakable Perk* (1916). Short stories about his neighbors in an East Side park in New York City fill *Our Square and the People in It* (1917) and *From a Bench in Our Square* (1922). One aspect of American loyalty during World War I is dealt with in *Common Cause* (1919), a romantic novel set in a community with pro-German sentiments; a young reporter and his sweetheart fight for a clean press and for clean politics. A spoiled, unhappy, unhealthy girl is transformed through physical culture and athletics into a radiant, captivating woman in *Wanted, a Husband* (1919).

Success (1921) deals with newspaper publishing, and centers in the love affair of a publisher and his chief editorial writer, in the framework of a romance of a young New

York society girl and a station agent in the Southwest. The antagonism between a tyrannical Victorian dowager, Augusta Ruyland, and a modern girl comes into the open during a strike in *Siege* (1924). In *The Piper's Fee* (1926) Aunt Augusta befriends a girl from the gully in a mill town and sends her to art school in New York.

A public sensation was created by *Revelry* (1926), a contemporary historical novel about the oil scandal and other incidents in Washington during the Harding administration. A second historical novel about Washington during President Jackson's term of office, *The Gorgeous Hussy* (1934), was based on the career of Peggy O'Neale Eaton, a tavern-keeper's daughter, who charmed Washington society for a time and then disappeared. *Night Bus* (1936), a novelette, became the record-breaking motion picture "It Happened One Night." In *The Perfect Specimen* (1936) Jerry Wicks, who has been sheltered from the world by a high fence because a kidnapper once collected fifty thousand dollars for his return, becomes a willing slave to pretty Mona Verbeck when she decides to make a man of him. *Maiden Effort* (1937) concerns motion-picture people and recounts the solution of a star's and her lover's difficulties in the midst of a flood. *The World Goes Smash* (1938) prophesied war between communism and fascism in Europe in 1940 and a ruinous rebellion by gangsters and corrupt politicians in America.

Both Over Twenty-One (1939) is a romance of an heiress posing as a secretary and a millionaire posing as a milkman on a trip to Bermuda. The influence in 1891 of the girls who worked in Fred Harvey's restaurants during the development of the West is portrayed in *The Harvey Girls* (1942). In *Tambay Gold* (1942) an ex-carnival queen establishes her trailer-diner in the Carolinas and gives aid and counsel to a beautiful girl with a past.

Canal Town (1944) tells of a young physician who sets out to overcome prejudice and ignorance and to clean up the sanitary conditions of Palmyra, New York, during the 1820's when the Erie Canal was being constructed. *Banner by the Wayside* (1947) portrays a strangely assorted group of young and old members of a theatrical troupe who tour the Erie Canal country in the 1830's and become observers of the westward expansion of the United States. *Plunder* (1948) looks ahead into the year 1950 to examine the career of a grafter, Martin Strabo, who tries to gain control of a scientific formula and then meets his match when he tries to "fix" an Army-Navy football game. *Sunrise and Sunset* (1950) describes factory life in New York state in the 1830's.

PAUL (FASSETT) ADER

was born October 20, 1919, in Asheville, North Carolina, and spent most of his early years in piedmont or western North Carolina, where his father was a Methodist minister. By the age of fourteen, when Mr. Ader was attending Reynolds High School in Winston-Salem, he had determined to make his mark in the world as a writer of fiction. He graduated from Duke University in 1940, and produced in four very busy months following his freshman year his first novel, still unpublished. Following a year of reporting and feature writing for North Carolina newspapers, Mr. Ader joined the army air force as a private, emerging five years later as a captain in the radar section of a heavy-bomb squadron. In 1948 he entered upon graduate study at the University of North Carolina.

During two years' service spent in England he wrote at odd moments in the corner of a busy radar shack, producing his first published novel, *We Always Come Back* (1945). This book, published under the pseudonym "James Allen," concerns a bomber crew on a raid over Hamburg, Germany, with flashbacks to the life of American soldiers in England. *The Leaf Against the Sky* (1947) relates the growing pains and troubling experiences of two dissimilar boys—John Perry, a Methodist minister's son, and Milton Silverstein, a Jewish lad of great ability whose youth and power were destroyed by cynicism and defeat. The setting is North Carolina in the 1930's.

MARTHA ALBRAND

Trude Fleischmann

(Mrs. Katrin Holland Loewengard) was born on September 8, 1911, in Rostock, Mecklenburg, Germany. Her ancestors were ministers, farmers, and army officers, following an old rule under which a family gives one son to the Church, one to the land, and one to the military service. Her great-grandfather was a missionary in America, teaching the Chippewah Indians, among whom her grandmother was born. In her youth Miss Albrand lived with relatives in Germany, England, Switzerland, Italy, France, and Sweden. She is now an American citizen, having migrated to America in the 1930's. The many changes in environment, schools, and associates, she has stated, were among the factors which dictated her choice of a writing career. The meaning for Americans of events and personalities in Europe following World War I has been the major theme of her work.

No Surrender (1942), Miss Albrand's first book to appear in America, was written to tell Americans about the Dutch and to stress the significance of the German oppression; it is the story of the quiet heroism demonstrated by members of the underground movement in Holland as they resisted the Nazi invaders. *Without Orders* (1943) is a murderless mystery story about a young American, a prisoner in Africa in 1943, who awakens one day to find himself in a sanitarium in Rome. *Endure No Longer* (1944) pictures the particular clique of German officers whom Miss Albrand has always regarded as dangerous; the story is that of Frederica, the daughter of a Prussian officer, who futilely attempts to carry on alone when her Jewish husband is killed by Nazis, but in the end she leaves Germany in defeat.

None Shall Know (1945) portrays love and intrigue at work in neutral Switzerland in World War II, when Antonio and Julian smuggle French children through the underground. *Remembered Anger* (1946), set in Paris as it gropes its way back to normal life, is about an American paratrooper who is betrayed by a fascist. *Whispering Hill* (1947) pictures a son breaking away from his rich, domineering mother when she objects to his attachment to the daughter of a woman whom her late husband had loved. *After Midnight* (1949), a novel with an Italian background, points out the differences in mentality and tradition among nations. *Wait for the Dawn* (1950), with its setting in Europe, is about a sensitive girl married to a powerful financier.

BESS STREETER ALDRICH

was born in Cedar Falls, Iowa, on February 17, 1881. Her grandfather, Zimri Streeter, his wife, three sons, and seven daughters moved by team from Illinois to Iowa in 1852. Two years later her mother's family also arrived in Iowa by wagon. She graduated in 1901 from Iowa State Teachers College at Cedar Falls and taught in the public schools of her home state for five years. For one year she taught in Salt Lake City, Utah, and for another at her alma mater. In 1907 she married Charles S. Aldrich, a banker, who died in 1925. Four children were born to this union. Mrs. Aldrich wrote under the pseudonym of "Margaret Dean Stevens" from 1911 to 1918, but since that time she has employed her own name.

Mrs. Aldrich has formed her stories from the first-hand accounts of pioneering life related by her numerous relatives and by other early settlers. She includes in her novels the whole pattern of normal lives: love, marriage, childbirth, spinsterhood, work, and play. Her characterizations of ordinary people reveal the average person's joy in work, in duty, in self-sacrifice, and in family friendships. A kindly philosophy, a pleasant good humor, and an intense feeling for nature in all of its numerous and manifold phases brighten all her books.

Her first novel, *Mother Mason* (1924), concerns the prosperous Mason family, whose pleasures and problems mirror ordinary and normal American experience. Wholesome small-town life in Nebraska serves as a background for the romance of two pioneers in *The Rim of the Prairie* (1925). *The Cutters* (1926) portrays Ed and Nell Cutter, who symbolize in their daily round of trivial activities the average happy American family.

Wide popular success was accorded *A Lantern in Her Hand* (1928), a novel which pays tribute to pioneer mothers; Abbie Deal moves from an Iowa log cabin to Nebraska, where she shows sturdy courage in bringing up her family. *A White Bird Flying* (1931) tells the love story of Laura Deal and Allen Rinemiller, two members of the younger generation of pioneer settlers of Nebraska, and describes the courage and contentment of German and Scottish settlers on the plains. Ella Bishop in *Miss Bishop* (1933) teaches English for fifty years in a midwestern college, cares for her mother, loses two lovers, brings up other people's children, and surrenders her own hopes in a mood of courage and unselfishness. Four generations of two German-American pioneer families who moved into Nebraska in covered wagons provide in *Spring Came On Forever* (1935) a full picture of the settlement of the West.

Fourteen narratives in Mrs. Aldrich's favorite setting are collected in *The Man Who Caught the Weather* (1936). *Song of the Years* (1938) recounts Wayne Lockwood's arrival in pioneer Iowa in 1854 and his association with Jeremiah Martin, the father of seven daughters and two sons. In *The Drum Goes Ahead* (1941) a bank cashier seeking to recapture his lost faith in Christmas energizes a whole community to accept its responsibilities. *The Lieutenant's Lady* (1942) tells how Linnie Colsworth, the young wife of an army lieutenant in the Indian wars, traveled the Missouri River and endured a harsh winter. *Journey into Christmas* (1949) is a compilation of Mrs. Aldrich's Christmas stories.

The Bess Streeter Aldrich Reader (1950) contains *A Lantern in Her Hand, A White Bird Flying,* and short stories from *The Man Who Caught the Weather.*

NELSON ALGREN

Robert McCullough

was born on March 28, 1909, in Detroit, Michigan, of working-class parentage. He was brought up on Chicago's Northwest Side and attended Chicago's public schools. While selling Watkins Products from door to door in New Orleans in 1931, he fell in with another transient who claimed ownership of considerable properties in the Rio Grande Valley. Subsequently Mr. Algren found himself sharing an abandoned Sinclair gas station, between Harlingen and Rio Hondo, Texas, with the Owner of Considerable Properties. This Owner was approximately the same height as the station and also owned a trepanned skull, a combination which caused Mr. Algren to resort to paper and pencil instead of to direct rebuke when the partners began to have misunderstandings about the division of labor incident to their occupancy of the station. The paper-and-pencil method of rebuke ultimately resulted in a short story, "So Help Me," which was published in *Story* magazine in August, 1933.

Shortly after the publication of his first novel, *Somebody in Boots* (1935), which sold 757 copies in the United States and one copy in Canada for a total of 758, Mr. Algren made a decision: "I decided to get married and go to work. I decided I could be just as poor working around a downtown gymnasium as I could by skipping rope with a typewriter ribbon. But in 1941 I went back to writing and now it looks as though the work will be steady for some time." In 1942 Mr. Algren was inducted into the army as a private. He was honorably discharged in December, 1945, still a private, and has yet to earn his good conduct ribbon. He has received awards from the American Academy of Arts and Letters and from the Newberry Library of Chicago.

"I have almost no interest in the Literary Life as such," he has stated. "The only literary events I attend are under duress and I sweat the whole time. Outside the great Russians, almost the only books I read are those undertaken for reviewing purposes. My politics tend to the left. But since they don't always tend directly and with a sufficiently unwavering faith, they have been found unacceptable to the orthodox left. My friends, therefore, are men and women who never go to literary occasions and who seldom read a book and have no politics other than the politics of how to stay out of jail. And the more I see of literary and politically developed people, the deeper my trust becomes in those who have not had opportunity for such development. In fact, the more I see of those below, the more I say the hell with you squares on top."

Somebody in Boots (1935), his first novel, deals with the wild boys of the road during the depression years after 1929. *Never Come Morning* (1942) pictures a Northwest Side hoodlum who wants to escape from his environment by becoming a great fighter. *The Neon Wilderness* (1947), a volume of short stories, is largely concerned with the lives of men and women of whom our civilization has disposed by the simple expedient of putting up "No Trespassing" signs. *The Man with the Golden Arm* (1949), named by *Time* magazine the best novel of the year, is the story of a stud-poker dealer who is a veteran of World War II and a graduate of Chicago's backstreets as well. Frankie Machine, the man with the golden arm, attempts to escape from his environment through morphine. His own experience as a stud-poker dealer on Chicago's Northwest Side furnished Mr. Algren the authentic working background for this novel, of which Ernest Hemingway said, "Mr. Algren can hit with both hands and move around, and he will kill you if you are not awfully careful."

HERVEY ALLEN

was born on December 8, 1889, in Pittsburgh, Pennsylvania, where he attended public and preparatory schools. In 1910 he entered the United States Naval Academy, but injuries and illness forced his withdrawal. For a few months he worked for the Bell Telephone Company in the statistical and commercial engineering department of the Pittsburgh office. In 1915 he was graduated with honors from the University of Pittsburgh School of Economics. During his college years he wrote both prose and verse.

During service as a second lieutenant with the Pennsylvania National Guard on the Mexican border in 1916, he wrote verses of a popular Kiplingesque-Masefield character. From the Mexican campaign his regiment moved almost immediately into action in World War I and experienced heavy fighting from the Marne to the Vesle in 1918. In August he was wounded at Fismettes, but he returned to participate in the Argonne-Meuse drive. An account of his experiences is to be found in *Toward the Flame* (1926).

After the war he taught English in Charleston, South Carolina, where with Dubose Heyward and others he founded the Poetry Society of South Carolina, the first faint stir of interest in the southern scene. For two years after 1925 he taught at Columbia University and Vassar College. For a time he and his wife and two daughters lived in Bermuda, where he began *Anthony Adverse*. He died at Miami, Florida, on December 28, 1949. His books of poetry include *Wampum and Old Gold* (1921), *Carolina Chansons* (with Dubose Heyward, 1921), and *Sarah Simon* (1927), a long narrative. *Israfel* (1927) is a detailed biography of Edgar Allan Poe.

The vogue for historical fiction in the United States was nearly at an end when Allen's poetically sensitive account of Anthony Adverse, which has sold some two million copies, opened anew the vistas of the romance inherent in America's past. His stories contain vivid pictures of ordinary and extraordinary incidents in the life of the average person, such as soldiering, housekeeping, eating on forced marches, wig curling, the beauty of a snowfall in the pathless woods, and the comfort of an inn fire after a long day's march. Thrill-packed plots bind together these insights into social conditions of the past.

Anthony Adverse (1933), his first novel, recounts the extraordinary and heroic adventures of a resourceful foundling in Europe, Africa, and America from his lowly birth in an Alpine village in 1775 to his death in America's Southwest in 1825. *Action at Aquila* (1938) describes through the experiences of Colonel Franklin, a Pennsylvania cavalry officer, the feelings generated by the War between the States.

One of America's longest historical romances was undertaken by Mr. Allen in *The Disinherited*. The first of the five proposed novels is *The Forest and the Fort* (1943), the story of Salathiel Albine, who is captured as a child by the Indians and reared by them; he plays a leading role in the siege of Fort Pitt and the march to Bedford Village. The second, *Bedford Village* (1944), continues the adventures of Albine, now a ranger with the "Mountain Foxes," and also describes the life of this frontier town in 1763. The third, *Toward the Morning* (1948), recounts a journey over the wagon trail that connected Fort Bedford and Boiling Springs in Pennsylvania in 1764 and some weeks of wintering in the latter village.

The City in the Dawn (1950) contains these three books, edited as a continuous story and completed with a final section written before the author's death.

MARGUERITE ALLIS

was born in Ludlow, Vermont. Her grandfather and father were country editors: she was born with the smell of printer's ink in her nostrils. Before she was fifteen she had written reams of youthful poetry. When both journalists died, she drifted into music. For ten years she studied voice in New York and in France. For seventeen years she sang in church quartets in New Haven, Connecticut, and taught singing there and in nearby cities. During a summer at the American Conservatory at Fontainebleau, France, the old urge to write returned with compelling force. In the ancient library and gardens of the palace she wrote a history of the place designed for other American students there. This book never saw print, but served as an introduction to the publishers of subsequent works from her pen.

Miss Allis' first three books were based upon careful historical research into the background and the lives of pioneer New England settlers. *Connecticut Trilogy* (1934) narrates events in the settlement of the first three Connecticut towns: Hartford, Saybrook, and New Haven. A six-months' visit to England provided material for *English Prelude* (1936), an account of the English homes of some of the twenty thousand English men, women, and children who came to New England between 1620 and 1640. The story of the three-hundred-year history of the Connecticut River Valley is told in *Connecticut River* (1939).

Not Without Peril (1941), Miss Allis' first novel, is founded on the life and adventures of Jemima Sartwell, one of the first settlers of Vermont. This book was praised by Rose Feld for "the feeling for the land, for the river, the understanding of Indians, the variety of characters who walk its pages, the pageantry of the historical scene, the consistency of manners and customs and language," qualities which mark all her books. *The Splendor Stays* (1942) is the story of the seven daughters of Captain Elisha Hart of Saybrook, Connecticut, in the early years of the nineteenth century. Ann became the wife of Isaac Hull, captain of the *Constitution*. Jeannette, the dark, tempestuous one, nearly married Simón Bolívar, the South American liberator. *All in Good Time* (1944) details the married life of Job Hubbard, an enterprising young clockmaker, to Elvira Stone. These two meet hostility from grasping Gideon Leete and his daughter in the village of Horeb in the Litchfield Hills of Connecticut.

Charity Strong (1945) tells of the daughter of a die-hard conservative Connecticut Yankee in the early 1800's; she is determined to be an opera singer, marries unfortunately, goes to New York where she fails to achieve her ambition, and returns home with some hesitancy to find an understanding welcome from her father. In *Water Over the Dam* (1947) the fluctuating fortunes of Titus Todd, an orphan boy who clerks in a general store, parallel and intertwine with events in the building of the Farmington Canal in Connecticut in the 1820's. *Law of the Land* (1948) has as its basis the Connecticut laws of the 1840's which reduced women to the status of chattels. When Arabella Barlow inherits her father's stocks and mortgages, her brother Saul betroths her to weak-minded Ben Snow to gain control of them under the law that gave title to a married woman's property to her husband. She joins a group of women demanding civil rights and attends a meeting in Rochester, New York, in 1848.

The Bridge (1949) is the story of the Air Line Railroad between New York and Boston which depended on bridging the Connecticut River for success. Powerful steamboat interests opposed any such obstruction to navigation, and fought against it so successfully in the legislature that for thirty years the project was frustrated. The Lord family, purely imaginary, and its later divided loyalties provide the theme for this historical novel.

DAVID ALMAN

Walter Rosenblum

was born on March 29, 1919, in New York City. His parents are Ethel Friedberg Alman, a millinery worker, and Gabriel Alman, a man of a number of occupations. Both had been, before their marriage, active on the Yiddish stage. All his ancestors were workers and craftsmen of one sort or another. He graduated from Seward Park High School in New York City in 1936, went to New York University for some six weeks, and quit out of boredom with the school program.

His interest grew in anthropology, the study of which he pursued six hours a day in New York's libraries; he was introduced to that subject by an accidental reading of the first few pages of Robert Briffault's three-volume work, *The Mothers*. His interest remains as great today as it was then. He considers the anthropological refutation of Freudian and semi-Freudian concepts of "inherited" or "racial" instinctual behavior patterns or drives to be indispensable to any writer's understanding of human behavior.

He held minor positions in social-work agencies for a while, then became a machinist and remained one for some four years, working particularly in shipyards in the South and North. At the end of the war he returned to social work and became acting headworker of Grosvenor Neighborhood House. He left that to become a New York state parole officer, and resigned a year later to complete his first accepted novel, *The Hourglass*. In 1940 he married Emily Arnow, also a writer; they have two children.

Of his writing he has said: "I feel very strongly about the state of the world, and particularly about the state of our country. I have experienced the direst poverty, and have seen others in the same predicament. I have lived through violent prejudices and all sorts of exploitation, and I have felt the censor's authority. I have searched for those attributes which make our people, though not always our government, a democratic one."

The Hourglass (1947) deals with the aftermath of the rape of a Negro woman by three white men in the deep South. One, a young, embittered attorney, finds himself in a situation in which he can either confess his guilt or doom himself to live his life within the meanest and pettiest and most loveless set of values spawned by a Jim Crow South. "If I had it to do over again," Mr. Alman has said, "I would have made it more convincing that he chose to confess, and I would have also revealed those elements in his community from whom he could draw his courage." *The Well of Compassion* (1948) concerns the intermarriage of Negro and white in the North. Since it is likewise a story of artists and art, it makes many observations about that medium.

World Full of Strangers (1949) is the saga of a veteran who returns to find that during his absence and since his return many things have changed: his girl has been seduced by a social worker turned policeman, decisions affecting his life and welfare are still being made for and not by him, and any attempt on his part to break away from prescribed behavior, politics, and attitudes is treated as an abomination. He learns, too, that in waiting too long to make a decision in respect to his girl, he has permitted life itself to make a decision with which he is not in accord. The theme is that, as individuals and as persons, people must do what they believe to be right and necessary, regardless of the abuse they may suffer for it, and that they must do so on time. The scene is the lower East Side of New York, quite close to the area where Mr. Alman was born and raised. He intends, in his habitation and literary work, to remain there.

BARBARA ANDERSON

was born September 27, 1894, in Mansfield, Massachusetts, but comes from a family long established in the South. She was educated at Smith College. Her first essays in the literary field were magazine articles about historic houses and gardens in the South. These essays were published under her maiden name, Barbara Madison Tunnell, as were a number of poems. For a period of about five years she wrote only advertising copy for a Louisville agency. She is the wife of Dwight Anderson, dean of the school of music at the University of Louisville.

Mrs. Anderson writes about social conditions in the South as they affect the lives of young people. Her work is notable for its evocation of mood and its faithful yet restrained naturalistic pictures of heart-rending episodes.

The Days Grow Cold (1941), her first novel and a Literary Guild selection, concerns the impact of life on a sensitive child in a changing southern town. Living in a mansion, Lucinda tries to understand the pride of her parents, the poverty of the Negroes, and the conservative social opinions expressed by the people who visit her home. *Southbound* (1949) tells the story of a gifted illegitimate quadroon girl, Amanda Crane, who was born in Alabama. Abandoned by her mother, Amanda is taken to Ohio to live with a white family. Not until the age of eleven does she learn her color. After studying in Paris, she returns to her home in the South to teach Negro children, and there finds happiness.

ROBERT HARDY ANDREWS

was born Charles Robert Douglas Hardy Andrews in Effingham, Kansas, on October 19, 1903. At the age of eleven he began newspaper work for the Hiawatha, Kansas, *World.* In 1915 the Kansas City *Star* nominated him for "poet laureate of Kansas." At fifteen, while still attending school, he was night city editor of the Aberdeen, South Dakota, *Daily American.* Later he worked for newspapers in Kansas City, Sioux Falls, Utica, New York, Philadelphia, and other cities. At twenty-one he was city editor, and later he was special writer and book and art critic, for the Minneapolis *Journal.* In 1928 he founded, and during its entire existence edited, *Midweek,* the literary magazine of the Chicago *Daily News.* The first daytime radio serial was his creation, and subsequently over a period of fifteen years he originated and wrote twenty-nine nationally broadcast radio serials. James Thurber declared in *The New Yorker* and in his book, *The Beast in Me* (1949), that Mr. Andrews has "written more dialogue than any other writer in history—at least forty million words." Under his own name and pseudonyms Mr. Andrews (who says he believes "A writer's business is to write") has published a hundred short stories and articles, two book-length collections: *The Truth About Artists* (1926) and *The Truth About Pirates* (1927), and nine light novels, including *Three Girls Lost* (1929), which later became one of fifty-two produced motion pictures written by him under the name of Robert D. Andrews.

Windfall (1930), his first serious novel—since republished under its motion-picture title, *If I Had a Million*—stresses the theme that unearned riches are a destroying evil. *Burning Gold* (1945), an historical novel, contains the result of years of research into the lives of Daniel Defoe, William Dampier, Dr. Thomas Dover, and other authentic English historical personages. It undertakes to trace accurately the work of a pioneer medical scientist in Queen Anne's time, when England's merchant princes were seizing control of cultural and democratic progress from the post-Elizabethan nobles. *Legend of a Lady* (1949), a modern novel, studies a career woman whose field of success and tragedy is the advertising business and especially the so-called "soap opera." *Great Day in the Morning* (1950) is an historical novel of Colorado just before the War between the States. It is the story of Owen Pentecost, a virile type of gambler, and his part in the Pike's Peak gold rush, the settlement of Denver, and "The Georgia Conspiracy" to make the state secessionist.

BENJAMIN APPEL

Pinchot

was born on September 13, 1907, in New York City, and lived in the area which was known as "Hell's Kitchen" until he was seventeen years of age. It was in those years a tenement district bounded on the east by the glitter of Broadway and the theatrical district and on the west by the docks and piers of one of the world's greatest seaports. His parents were Polish immigrants descended from well-to-do families with a tradition of learning and culture. They were determined that their children should go to college. Their oldest son, Benjamin, was shielded from the worst influences of the neighborhood, but it was impossible for any sensitive human being not to learn of life in the university of the streets.

Benjamin Appel studied at the University of Pennsylvania, New York University, and Lafayette College, from which he graduated in 1929. Since that time, except for odd jobs as a tenement-house inspector in the depression years, as an aviation mechanic in the first year of the war, and as a government worker in Washington and Manila, he has been a full-time writer. *The People Talk* (1940) is a documentary narrative.

The world of "Hell's Kitchen" provided the basis for his most important fictional work, the *Brain Guy* trilogy: *Brain Guy* (1934), *The Powerhouse* (1939), and *The Dark Stain* (1943). It is a work of over a thousand printed pages and runs to almost five hundred thousand words. It is a thorough story of the *whys* of crime in the United States and shows the relations between vice and society, not in a single facet, but in all its ramifications. *Brain Guy* traces the connection between poverty and lawlessness. Bill Trent, a college graduate, loses his job in the depression of the 1930's; he is the "brain guy" who shakes down speakeasy proprietors, and realizes that "success" can be attained only through organization, through "the mob." In *The Powerhouse* he moves with his gang into big-scale crime, into prostitution and labor racketeering. Petty crime becomes murder, the tenement delinquents become mobsters and labor spies; a world of gunmen, gangsters, and procurers are protected by detectives and politicians; crime has become a parasitic industry on the body of society. In *The Dark Stain*, the "brain guy" operates against society directly in the final and most terrible offense of all, the fascist crime. The killing of a crazed Negro by a policeman in Harlem creates the conditions for fomenting a racial riot.

Three short novels also illustrate Mr. Appel's concern over the fundamental needs and aspirations of the common people. *Four Roads to Death* (1935) is the story of an imaginary expedition and is described by the author as "a metaphysical examination of values, set in the Taklamakan Desert in Asia, an area I have not visited." It is a story of greed. *Runaround* (1937) exposes the nasty corners of American politics as seen in Danny Englander's struggle "for the right to live like a man, to have a job, and to support a wife and kids" and was based on Appel's experiences in New York with the Fusion movement led by the late Fiorello La Guardia. *But Not Yet Slain* (1947) relates the story of Matt Wells, a young idealistic government official in Washington in the turbulent and uneasy years following the death of President Franklin D. Roosevelt.

ELLIOTT ARNOLD

was born in New York City on September 13, 1912. His father was an opera singer. At the age of seventeen Elliott started work as a copy boy on the Brooklyn *Times*. He subsequently became a reporter and in 1933 transferred to the New York *World-Telegram*. He covered everything, starting with the "lobster trick" at police headquarters. In 1938 he went to Europe and traveled through Scandinavia, Russia, and Germany. In 1942 he left the *World-Telegram* and enlisted as a private in the army. He was discharged honorably as a captain, after having been twice overseas in North Africa and Italy, and in the South Pacific from Australia through New Guinea to Leyte. General MacArthur awarded him a bronze star. Upon his discharge Mr. Arnold made his home in Tucson, Arizona, and became interested in the Indians; he has been active in efforts to improve their status. His non-fiction books include *Finlandia* (1941), a biography of Jean Sibelius for young people; *Nose for News: The Way of Life of a Reporter* (1941); and *Deep in My Heart* (1949), a biography of Sigmund Romberg.

Two Loves (1934), his first novel, shows the effect of the depression on Ted Hughes, a reporter. *Personal Combat* (1936) traces the links between crime and law-enforcement agencies in the story of Terry Donaghue, a boy who begins as a petty thief and ends as a dishonest policeman. *Only the Young* (1939) portrays the career of Robert Martin, a New York reporter, who adopts the American way while friends turn communist and fascist.

Four books reflect Mr. Arnold's wartime experiences and interests. *The Commandos* (1942) is the dramatically intense story of an American leader of a surprise assault group in World War II. An attack on the Norwegian coast is aided by a beautiful Norwegian widow, a leader in underground activities. The American is captured and tortured by the Nazis, but later escapes. More than fifty true stories of the human side of aerial warfare are narrated in *Mediterranean Sweep* (with Richard Thruelsen, 1945), an official Air Force history. *Big Distance* (with Donald Hough, 1946), another official history, tells of the creation of air power in the Pacific. Out of his experiences in Italy he framed *Tomorrow Will Sing* (1945), the story of an American airman serving at a base near Foggia in 1944 and of the establishment of a farm co-operative which resulted in the improvement of relationships between Americans and Italians.

On his return from military service Mr. Arnold wrote *Blood Brother* (1947), a fictionalized history of the Southwest from 1856 until the end of the Indian wars in 1874; the episodes involve Cochise, the chief of the Chiricahua Apaches, and Tom Jeffords, an Indian agent and peacemaker. The novel stresses the belief that men of all races are brothers. *Everybody Slept Here* (1948) deals satirically with life and love in wartime Washington as a background for a tale of the difficulties encountered by a civilian with temporary army rank in adjusting himself to the attitudes and concepts of the professional military mind. *Walk with the Devil* (1950), set in wartime Italy, concerns an Italian-American with a gangster brother who was deported from this country before the war. The moral issues of attaining military victory form the theme.

HARRIETTE SIMPSON ARNOW

Lee F. Redman

was born in Wayne County, Kentucky, on July 7, 1908, a descendant of Revolutionary soldiers who settled in the Cumberland River country before the War of 1812. She received her education in Burnside, Kentucky, at Berea College, and at the University of Louisville, from which she graduated. Though she had scribbled in prose and verse since her grade-school days, she loved science and planned to be a teacher of mathematics and general science. After six years of depression teaching in Pulaski County, Kentucky, and a short time in Louisville, she quit, went to Cincinnati, rented furnished rooms close to the main branch of the public library, and began to do what she had long contemplated: try to write and at the same time learn more about the art of fiction through much reading and study of the novel, particularly translations of the European novelists of the nineteenth century.

She supported herself by odd jobs as a waitress, clerk in a lending library, and assistant for a time on the Federal Writers' Project. During these five years she published a novel and various shorter pieces, one of which, "The Washerwoman's Day," is perhaps best known, since it appeared in Brooks, Purser, and Warren's *An Approach to Literature* (1939), a widely used college textbook. In 1939 she married Harold Arnow, a newspaper reporter; they bought a farm in the Cumberland National Forest and lived there for five years as writers and farmers. They and their two small children now reside in Detroit, but think of their home as being on the farm at Keno, Kentucky.

As a writer Mrs. Arnow considers herself a realist; she believes that beauty is as real as ugliness, and that good is as real as evil. She says that the most important things on earth are not the things people make, such as atom bombs and "isms," but the people themselves. To her the prime function of language is to communicate, and the main thing about writing is to have something to say and to say it as clearly as possible.

Mountain Path (1936), her first novel published over her maiden name of Harriette Simpson, is the story of a college girl, a would-be career woman in chemistry, who because of unexpected financial difficulties is forced to quit school and teach in the only opening offered—a backwoods community on the Cumberland River in Kentucky. Teaching much against her will, and determined to be an observer only and take no part in the somewhat primitive life, she finds herself unexpectedly enjoying such things as molasses-making and Christmas with homemade candles, and still much against her will becomes emotionally entangled in a neighborhood feud.

Hunter's Horn (1949) is the story of Nunnely D. Ballew, his family, his farm, and his neighbors in the Cumberland River country during the three years preceding Pearl Harbor. The characters know the hard work, poverty, and troubles of many subsistence farmers in the hills: pain, birth, and death are never far away; but laughter, hope, and peace are theirs at times. Most of these people have dreams of a better future. For Milly, wife of Nunn, the dream is mostly of heaven; for her daughter, Suse, the dream is earthly, centering in her hopes of going to high school. Nunn, "a lover of children and lambs and sprouting clover," has two dreams, one of making his farm as fine as it was in the old days, and the other of catching the big red fox, King Devil, whose tricks have earned the hatred of every hunter and farmer in the country. Nunn pursues him as fiercely as any man could pursue a dream, and the long hunt leads to many things, until over all—wife, children, farm, and himself—the shadow of the red fox falls. The New York *Times Book Review* listed this novel among the ten best books of 1949.

SHOLEM ASCH

was born at Koutno, near Warsaw, Poland, on November 1, 1880. He received rabbinical training, but decided that the ministry was not his profession. This instruction was of value, however, for it created a lifelong interest in religious thought and inspired the novels and stories devoted to an interpretation of Judaism and Christianity. At sixteen he went to work. His interest in authorship bore fruit in 1900 when his writings began to appear in two Warsaw journals. Short stories were soon followed by short novels and dramas. His first book was *Bilder aus dem Ghetto* (*Ghetto Pictures,* 1907). In 1910 he came to the United States and acquired American citizenship. Using Yiddish as his language, he wrote for *The Jewish Daily Forward,* a newspaper, and produced a number of plays and several novels of Jewish-American life.

In 1925 he returned to Europe, living in Paris and spending much of his time in Berlin. There he saw at first hand the desperate period of inflation, the suffering of the middle class, the rising hostility to the Jews, the conflict of the ideas of socialism and communism, and the other forces which brought Hitler to power. After several years in Europe, Sholem Asch returned to this country. "I originally left the United States for two reasons," Mr. Asch has said; "first, the high cost of living and, second, the terrific tempo of American life, particularly in New York. It was much worse in the 1920's than it is today. Such pressure makes it difficult for the creative impulse to survive. Now I have come back to the country of my adoption because it has become a center of world literature."

His non-fiction books include *What I Believe* (1941) and *One Destiny: An Epistle to the Christians* (1945), an appeal for unity among the inheritors of the Judeo-Christian faith. His books of short stories include *In the Beginning* (1935), a retelling of the narratives in *Genesis; Children of Abraham* (1942); and *Tales of My People* (1948).

Mr. Asch is one of the foremost interpreters of the Hebrew spirit and ambitions. His novels portray the sufferings of Jews in the modern world, the aspirations of Israel to achieve independence and economic well-being, and the history of the Holy Family and the early days of Christianity. He has urged reconciliation of the Jews and the Christians through mutual understanding.

The first book by Mr. Asch to be published in America was *Mottke the Vagabond* (1917), which was reissued in 1935 as *Mottke the Thief*. It is the story of a boy who grows up in a Jewish village in Russian Poland and becomes a terror before he moves on into the underworld of Moscow, where he is betrayed by a woman. *The Mother* (1930) portrays the emotional depths of Jewish motherhood in a story of two generations of a family which moves from Poland to New York's East Side.

Three Cities, A Trilogy (1933) recounts the history of three tense periods in twentieth-century Russia as seen in St. Petersburg after 1905, Warsaw before 1914, and Moscow during and after the revolution of October, 1917. The Jews are divided into two groups: the wealthy ones who pay for protection from a hostile society and the laboring class who strive for a classless proletarian state.

The first of Asch's books in English translation to reveal his special knowledge of Jewish religious history and feeling is *Salvation* (1934), the story of Jechiel, a saintly rabbi in Warsaw in the nineteenth century, whose life represents the ideal of humane service. *The War Goes On* (1936) is a social novel portraying the tragedy of the Jewish religious faith in Germany after World War I in the wealthy banking family of Bodenheimer. Three early short tales, written between 1916 and 1923 and descriptive of the adjustment of Jews to the American environment, were issued as *Three Novels: Uncle Moses, Chaim Lederer's Return, and Judge Not—* (1938). *Song of the Valley* (1939) portrays the efforts of a small group of city-bred Jews to transform a desolate, swampy valley in Palestine into a habitable, economically sound community.

The Nazarene (1939) tells the life story of Jesus and represents Him as the last of the Hebrew prophets. The events and the interpretation are presented from three different viewpoints: a Polish Jewish scholar reports the statement of the Roman military governor of Jerusalem, Judas Iscariot writes a "Fifth Gospel," and a young Jew, a reincarnation of a disciple of the Pharisee rabbi Nicodemus, tells what he "remembers." *The Apostle* (1943) opens seven weeks after the crucifixion of Jesus and tells the story of the heroic leadership of Paul, the Apostle, in the early days of the Christian Church. Paul is a vigorous young man with great learning in the laws of both the Jews and the Gentiles and with an eager desire to spread a gospel of hope among all oppressed people in the Roman Empire. Mr. Asch expresses the traditional Jewish opinion that Paul is the real author of Christianity.

East River (1946), a narrative of contemporary American life, tells the story of the Davidowsky family in the Jewish neighborhood of Forty-eighth Street in New York City in the early 1900's. The father becomes heartbroken when his younger son marries a Catholic girl. Vividly pictured are tenement life and the cutthroat competitive practices of the dress industry.

Mary (1949) completes the trilogy begun in *The Nazarene* and *The Apostle*. The events concern the life of Mary and Joseph from the time of their marriage to the crucifixion and resurrection of Jesus. It is a story of a mother's great love and of the Son's fulfillment of His mission.

BABSON *to* BUSHNELL

NAOMI LANE BABSON

was born and brought up on Cape Ann in Massachusetts. After having taught in several rural New England schools, she attended Radcliffe College. In 1922 she went to China to teach in a university in Canton. She made her home there for a number of years, both before and after her marriage. One of her novels and many of her short stories reflect this period of her life. Miss Babson has said, however, "I think of myself as a New Englander who has lived for a long time in China." At present, Miss Babson lives in Bozeman, Montana, but some day she hopes to settle down on a farm in Massachusetts with her husband, Paul A. Grieder, and their son. Although Miss Babson admits she never learned to like baked beans, she still believes that when God thought of Paradise he made Cape Ann first.

Her first novel, *The Yankee Bodleys* (1936), chronicles the family history from 1858 to 1935 of Horatio Bodley, a fisherman in Massachusetts, and his descendants, each of whom gets into some kind of trouble which shows a deterioration of quality. *All the Tomorrows* (1939) describes the effect on Canton in South China and on Hong Kong of the invasion of the Japanese in this account of the Chinese family of Felix Lo, a financier, from 1862 to 1937. *Look Down from Heaven* (1942), set in a Maine village in the early years of the twentieth century, portrays the growth into noble womanhood of Mary, a daughter of a poor Finnish woman, from the age of eight to her marriage. The quiet details about everyday affairs are especially attractive. The style has elements of lyric feeling and poetic grace.

DOROTHY DODDS BAKER

was born on April 21, 1907, in Missoula, Montana. Her childhood was spent in California, where her father was in the oil business. She was graduated in 1929 from the University of California at Los Angeles and in 1930 from Occidental College in Los Angeles. While living in Paris in 1930 she married Howard Baker. In 1933, after their return to the United States, she earned her master's degree in French at the University of California in Berkeley. Thereafter for three years she taught Latin in a private school. This experience formed the basis for a short story called "A Glance Around," which was published in 1934 in *The Magazine*. After publishing several short stories, she decided to abandon the teaching profession in order to devote all of her time to writing. In 1937 she held a Houghton Mifflin fellowship. At present she is living on an orange grove in California with her husband and their two daughters. Her books are notable for stylistic charm and psychological insight.

Her first novel, *Young Man With a Horn* (1938), had its inspiration in the career of Bix Beiderbecke, the "swing" musician, and traces the rise and fall of a jazz player. *Trio* (1943) is about a decisive moment in the lives of Pauline Maury, a university teacher of French, and Janet Logan, her graduate-student assistant, when Roy Mackenzie unexpectedly appears and brings love and conflict. This book received the gold medal of the Commonwealth Club of California for the best novel published by a Californian in 1943; it was dramatized with the assistance of her husband and produced at the Belasco Theatre in New York City in 1944. *Our Gifted Son* (1948), a short psychological novel, is the story of a summer in the life of a wealthy young musically inclined Mexican at home on vacation from an American college. Implicitly, it is a close examination of the moral and aesthetic values inherent in the life of an artist.

LOUISE (MAXWELL) BAKER

was born in Upland, California, on May 18, 1909. She spent her early childhood in a small California town, moving to Los Angeles at the age of thirteen. After attending the public schools, she graduated in 1930 from Pomona College in Claremont, California. Subsequently she studied further at Columbia University. There followed a period of newspaper reporting; later she taught English and arts and crafts in a boys' boarding school, and became co-director of a summer mountain camp for small boys. She wrote publicity for the Chicago World's Fair and worked for Scripps College in Claremont, California. For two years she was a member of the staff of the Samuel S. Fels Research Foundation at Antioch College in Ohio. Following her marriage to Cecil Sherman Baker, Jr., Mrs. Baker became a free-lance writer, combining the roles of housewife and author. For a number of years she wrote short stories for the women's magazines. Mrs. Baker serves as a trustee and member of the executive board of the National Society for Crippled Children. She has lived in the East, the Middle West, and the Southwest, and has traveled abroad, but in spite of a tendency to wander, she returns periodically to California and still calls it home.

Her first novel, *Party Line* (1945), although set in "Mayfield," California, is a story of the small-town life of America. The New York *Times* said, "Small towns can be cruel as well as friendly, and Mrs. Baker is to be commended for giving a complete picture." *Out on a Limb* (1946) is essentially the autobiography of Mrs. Baker. It is a light, humorous account of life on crutches, a subject well-known to the author since she is an amputee and has used crutches for thirty-two years. One reviewer said of *Out on a Limb,* "Rollicking humor—but more than a lightly written book . . . a whole philosophy."

FAITH BALDWIN

was born in New Rochelle, New York, on October 1, 1893. Her father was a famous lawyer, and her mother was a schoolteacher before her marriage. When Faith was seven, the family moved to Brooklyn, where she received her early education at the Packer Institute and at Brooklyn Heights Seminary. She also attended the Ossining, New York, School for Girls, the Leetverein in Berlin, Germany, and Mrs. Dow's School at Briarcliff Manor, New York. On November 10, 1920, she married Hugh H. Cuthrell; they separated in 1929. They have two sons and two daughters; the younger two, a boy and a girl, are twins. Miss Baldwin lives in New Canaan, Connecticut, in a sprawling white farmhouse, "Fable Farm," surrounded by ancient elm and apple trees.

She began to write when she was a child

of six. Her first published work was poetry for magazines and newspapers. After a few short stories, she wrote her first novel, *Mavis of Green Hill* (1921), while doing war work. Her first magazine serial, *Garden Oats,* appeared in 1927. She has written seventy books, and her work has been immensely popular. In all editions, including reprints, the total number of copies distributed in the United States by the fall of 1949 was approximately ten million. Overseas editions, translations, and sixteen early titles are not included in this figure. She has written two serious "period" books, *American Family* (1935) and *Woman on Her Way* (1946), and a book of poems, *Signposts* (1924).

Miss Baldwin writes a type of light romance which does more than merely give a happy ending after the lovers have surmounted obstacles. She chooses real-life problems, presents accurate pictures of locale, and portrays characters with mixed qualities of strength and weakness similiar to those seen in one's everyday business and social acquaintances. Her books stress the social history of the last thirty years, for she describes fashions of dress, furniture, houses, and ideas. She emphasizes in her books, too, that persistent yet sometimes misdirected striving for happiness upon which so much true romance is based. Though possessing the power of a satiric writer, she does not use the destructive weapon of laughter against struggling individuals who deserve the comfort of sympathetic, helpful understanding. "I am interested in people," Miss Baldwin has said. "I try to make my romantic themes as valid as possible by being sincere in presenting characters with whom my readers can identify themselves." Plots have always presented difficulties, and action *per se* does not much interest her. She is more intrigued by the motives of her subjects than by their deeds.

Mavis of Green Hill (1921) is the story of a semi-invalid who has fallen in love with her favorite poet, "Richard Warren," the *nom de plume* of the doctor whom she detests. The heroine of *Laurel of Stoneystream* (1923) is a homely woman whose tale of love and youth and adolescence is set in a small Berkshire town. *Magic and Mary Rose* (1924) is a story for young girls. *Thresholds* (1925) describes the marital difficulties which ensue when two sisters marry men of differing character and temperament. *Those Difficult Years* (1925) delineates the difficulties in adjustment of a young married couple. A study of a grandmother dominating her daughter-in-law and grandchild until the inevitable moment of revolt is presented in *Three Women* (1926). *Departing Wings* (1927) concerns the difficult first years of marriage; for David marriage means clipped wings, and for Sylvia, the loss of glamour in the care of house and baby. The love affairs of four people become extremely involved in *Alimony* (1928), which was followed by *Betty* (1928) and *Rosalie's Career* (1928). In *Garden Oats* (1929) a young couple separate because they have advanced theories about marriage, but they are brought together again in old-fashioned wedlock. Julie, the heroine of *The Incredible Year* (1929), attempts to cast off her North Woods background and conform to the "flapper" type she meets in New York society, but Bruce, the man she is trying to impress, prefers her in her true character.

In *Broadway Interlude* (with Achmed Abdullah, 1929) a playwright and actress survive the failure of their production and face the future resolutely together. *The Office Wife* (1930) is concerned with the conflicts between business and matrimony, and reaches the conclusion that the only career for a young and pretty woman is marriage. The heroine of *Make Believe* (1930) plays at marriage, cures a veteran of shell shock, and then becomes his wife. A juvenile, *Judy, A Story of Divine Corners* (1930), was followed by *Skyscraper* (1931), which is the love story of two young people who work in a New York office building. In *Today's Virtue* (1931) the heroine refuses to marry the father of her child because she discovers he is unworthy of her love. This novel was followed by three more of the "Divine Corners" stories: *Babs*

(1931), *Mary Lou* (1931), and *Myra* (1932). The difficulties which beset a young couple when the wife continues her career after the wedding are solved in *Week-End Marriage* (1932).

District Nurse (1932) portrays the problems of working girls, the double standard of sex morality, and the sadness of poverty. A successful New York business woman marries and finds she must sacrifice her career in order to be a good wife in *Self-Made Woman* (1932). *Beauty* (1933) and *White Collar Girl* (1933) are studies of a business woman in love. *Love's a Puzzle* (1933) carries two love stories side by side to happy endings. *Innocent Bystander* (1934), although thoughtfully treated, is an entertaining picture of superficial American life. In *Honor Bound* (1934) Laurie and Hank are not in love but marry for friendship after both have been involved in unhappy affairs of the heart. *Within a Year* (1934) is a collection of four novelettes dealing with New Yorkers in 1933.

American Family (1935), which contains much of Miss Baldwin's family history, is the story of Tobias Condit, his son David, and their respective families; it is chiefly concerned with their missionary work and family life, and is set alternately in New York state and China. *The Puritan Strain* (1935), the sequel to *American Family,* recounts four years in the life of David Condit's eldest daughter, Elizabeth. *Men Are Such Fools!* (1936) presents the struggle between the demands of marriage and a career. A slippery sidewalk unceremoniously propels the pretty heroine of *That Man Is Mine* (1937) into a bookshop—and romance. *The Heart Has Wings* (1937) details the reactions of three nice people in a romantic tangle. *Twenty-Four Hours a Day* (1937) is the story of the survival of the marriage of a dress designer and a department-store manager. The showy side of metropolitan life with its sentiment, cynicism, and melodrama appears in *Manhattan Nights* (1937).

Enchanted Oasis (1938) is the story of the adjustment of an English girl to life in the sophisticated society of a western American resort. Two women, a pretty school teacher and an ex-senator's daughter, help a young doctor struggling to establish himself in *Rich Girl, Poor Girl* (1938). *Hotel Hostess* (1938) considers the career of Judith and describes the effect of her love affairs upon her job. *The High Road* (1939) is the story of Jill, who at twenty-five has held almost every position a girl may fill. *Career by Proxy* (1939) is a story for white-collar girls. In *White Magic* (1939) the lives of an heiress, a young secretary, a German nobleman, a ski instructor, and several others are intertwined in Sun Valley during the winter season. A panoramic view of a gay crowd of sophisticates is presented in *Station Wagon Set* (1939). *Rehearsal for Love* (1940) is a story of New York life and reaches a climax during the hurricane of 1938.

Something Special (1940) describes marriage and divorce among sophisticate New Yorkers. A young lawyer succeeds in taming his pretty, wealthy client in *Letty and the Law* (1940). A New York hospital is the background for numerous love affairs in *Medical Center* (1940). *And New Stars Burn* (1941) is a triangle love story with a tropical setting. *Temporary Address: Reno* (1941) realistically describes women in the divorce capital. A separated couple working in the same publishing house are reunited in *The Heart Remembers* (1941). The lush background of a Florida estate provides the setting for a love story with four angles in *Blue Horizons* (1942). *Breath of Life* (1942) narrates the fight of a young doctor's wife to regain her health and sanity. Short accounts of femininity make up *Five Women in Three Novels* (1942). *The Rest of My Life With You* (1942) is a romance. *Washington, USA* (1943) is a collection of six short stories about young women in wartime Washington. The heroine of *You Can't Escape* (1943) is jilted in New England and flees to New York, where she finds a more lasting love. *He Married a Doctor* (1943) presents a thoughtful study of a marriage problem. *Change of*

Heart (1944) is a story of conflict between a selfish mother and a clever daughter. *Arizona Star* (1945) is a collection of short stories, the characters in which are visitors and natives of an Arizona vacation resort. In *A Job for Jenny* (1945) the heroine solves the difficulties of her married sister who has become emotionally involved with another man. *Woman on Her Way* (1946) is the success story of Meg, a dressmaker who became a fashion designer after a struggle of almost four decades. The love story of a young nurse and a doctor is told in *Sleeping Beauty* (1947). *Give Love the Air* (1947) and *Marry for Money* (1948) deal with problems of marriage. *They Who Love* (1948) is a collection of novelettes. *The Golden Shoe String* (1949) brings together two well-connected but poor youngsters whose ambition it is to marry for money and who learn to face love's responsibilities. *Look Out for Liza* (1950) concerns a girl with numerous friends who attempt to protect her until they discover, to their very great surprise, that they must safeguard themselves from this young, ingenuous widow.

MARGARET CULKIN BANNING

Nellys

was born March 18, 1891, in Buffalo, Minnesota. She graduated from Vassar College in 1912. In 1914 she married Archibald Tanner Banning, by whom she had four children. Her second husband, to whom she was married in 1944, is LeRoy Salsich, a mining and construction engineer. Mrs. Banning has traveled widely in Europe: she was in London during the war in 1914; in the hotel in San Sebastian which was the first to be fired upon when the civil war in Spain broke out in 1936; in Paris when the first mobilization took place in 1939; and in England during World War II. Subsequently she made trips to Europe for UNRRA and for personal observation. Mrs. Banning lives in Duluth, Minnesota, where she is active in many community groups.

Mrs. Banning's writing appeals to American women; it deals with the many problems they face each day. She has written, on the average, a book a year for thirty years. Her non-fiction books include *Letters to Susan* (1936), an analysis of the problems of young girls; *The Case for Chastity* (1937); *Salud!* (1941), a travel diary with comments on political conditions in South America; *A Week in New York* (1941); *Women for Defense* (1942), an account of war service; *Letters from England* (1943), a record of travel; and *Conduct Yourself Accordingly* (with Mabel L. Culkin, 1944), a study of American conduct.

Her first novel, *This Marrying* (1920), deals with the problems of a young woman who breaks away from middle-class respectability because she considers it awkward and dated. In *Half Loaves* (1921) a young and devoted wife, educated to an abhorrence of man's human nature, separates from her husband, but loneliness leads to a new start in marriage on a less illusory basis. *Spell Binders* (1922) studies real women without the aura of romance and sex. A bourgeoise heroine experiments in marriage and finds it to her liking in *Country Club People* (1923). *A Handmaid of the Lord* (1924) portrays a woman who marries a man whom she does not love; in striving for emotional adjustment she comes to the realization that she can neither cheat life nor control it.

A psychological study of the part played by insanity in heredity is presented in *Women of the Family* (1926); this is the one of her books which Mrs. Banning likes best. *Pressure* (1927) criticizes the structure of society in the small cities of America. *Money of Her Own* (1928) tells what befalls the marriage of a young couple when the wife inherits her uncle's fortune. The results of a week-long plunge into Long Island society by a young midwestern girl are told in *Prelude to Love* (1930).

Mixed Marriage (1930) deals with the problems of marriage between Catholic and Protestant, particularly with the question of birth control. *Path of True Love* (1933) is the story of a woman who holds fast to her faith and forgives when her husband falls in love with her close friend. *The First Woman* (1935) is the story of an American girl who learns of the difficulties which beset a woman in politics. *The Iron Will* (1936) shows the human side of a legal battle over back taxes.

In *Too Young to Marry* (1938) a youthful marriage nearly breaks up because of the influence of relatives and bad economics, but everything straightens out when the husband finds a position and learns that his wife is pregnant. *You Haven't Changed* (1938) provokes stimulating thought on the marriage-versus-career question for women. In *Out in Society* (1940), a novel of society and politics, two well-planned lives are disrupted by a man without background and a girl recently graduated from business college. *The Clever Sister* (1947) is a story contrasting the lives of two sisters in a midwestern town: one works outside her home and one does not. *Give Us Our Years* (1950) is a study of the impasse between middle age and youth in a tale about a wealthy woman in Chicago.

ELSIE OAKES BARBER

Solari

was born in western Massachusetts on September 6, 1914. She was educated at Turners Falls High School and at Tufts College, where she was elected to Phi Beta Kappa and was graduated *summa cum laude* in 1936. Working on a fellowship, she received her master's degree in history at Smith College and continued her graduate studies at Northwestern University. The following year she married Robert H. Barber, a young minister. They have had parishes in Scranton, in New Haven, and in Lawrence, Massachusetts. At present they are living on Boston's famous Beacon Hill while Mr. Barber teaches at Tufts College. When she was in college, Mrs. Barber suffered an attack of poliomyelitis. The consequent lameness does not interfere with her numerous activities, which embrace domestic chores, a heavy schedule of church duties, lecturing, and writing.

The Wall Between (1946), her first novel, describes the growth of a young woman, unprepared for her task as a minister's wife, who learns slowly and sometimes painfully to express her love for her husband. *The Trembling Years* (1949) tells of the devastating change infantile paralysis makes in the life of a young college girl. It describes vividly the bitterness, the psychological aftermath of physical incapacity, and the gradual readjustment to living which time and love bring about. *Hunt for Heaven* (1950), a selection of the Family Bookshelf, concerns Pastor John Bliss and his utopian colony in Pennsylvania in the 1880's.

CARMAN BARNES

Nellys

was born on November 20, 1912, in Chattanooga, Tennessee. Her father was James Hunter Neal. Her mother, whose maiden name was Mills, was well known throughout the South as a lyric poet and writer of mountain folklore under the name of Diantha Barnes, and her second stepfather, Dr. George Pullen Jackson of Nashville, is the leading authority on the Negro-white spiritual. She took the name of Barnes from her first stepfather, Wellington Barnes, of Chattanooga. She was educated at Girls' Preparatory School in Chattanooga and at the Ward-Belmont School for Girls in Nashville.

When Carman Barnes was sixteen years old she published her first novel, *Schoolgirl*, which became an international best seller;

with Alfonso Washington Pezet she dramatized the story, and it was produced on Broadway on her eighteenth birthday. Miss Barnes was taken up in liberal circles as exemplifying a new realistic approach to American education, and was included as a subject for discussion in *The New Generation,* a weighty psychological tome prefaced by Bertrand Russell. Clarence Darrow came to see her, and Theodore Dreiser corresponded with her. She went on to the writing of other books about her contemporaries, and published in all four novels before she was twenty-two years old. For a year she was in Hollywood as a writer-actress with Paramount-Publix Pictures Corporation, but she never wrote or acted in a film.

Then came a period of rest and "growing up" in which she examined a great many things but wrote nothing. She studied art and mathematics with the American writer and architect, Claude Bragdon, who gave nineteen lectures on these and other subjects under her auspices. She introduced the Russian philosopher and mathematical physicist, Peter Demianovich Ouspensky, author of *A New Model of the Universe,* to his first New York audience in her studio in 1941, and subsequently worked with him for three and a half years. She is a student of Indian thought and of American history. She is the wife of Hamilton Fish Armstrong, writer and editor of *Foreign Affairs.* Together they wrote *A Passionate Victorian,* a play about Fanny Kemble, the English actress, who married Pierce Butler of Philadelphia in 1834.

Schoolgirl (1929), her first novel, is an account of the extracurricular activities of teenage youngsters in this frank tale of Naomi Bradshaw, a headstrong child of sixteen, who tries to elope and therefore is sent to a southern boarding school. There the girls smoke, use bad language, fall in and out of love, and experiment with sex. *Beau Lover* (1930) examines the problem of Glory, a young girl, who wants to select from a group of eligible men the right lover. She almost marries a forty-year-old sculptor. *Mother, Be Careful!* (1932) is a light satire on Hollywood.

Young Woman (1934) is the story of a southern girl of good family who goes to New York to earn a living. It is a realistic account of the depression years and of the economic and psychological problems of a young woman of the generation which came of age between World Wars I and II, a generation caught between an old and a new way of life. *Time Lay Asleep* (1946) pictures a large southern family dominated by a tyrannical old lady, Grandmother Wickham, who brings culture to a Tennessee valley as the nineteenth century turns into the twentieth. A regional novel, it deals in a new form with certain philosophical ideas of place and time.

LARRY (LAURENCE BREVOORT) BARRETTO

Erich Hartmann

was born in Larchmont, New York, on May 30, 1890. Although the name Barretto is of Portuguese origin, he is of old New York ancestry on both sides; his mother, Laura Brevoort, was of Dutch descent. One of his paternal ancestors, Lewis Morris, was a signer of the Declaration of Independence, and one of his maternal forebears, irascible old Henry Brevoort, was responsible for the wide bend which Broadway in New York takes to the west at Fourteenth Street. Brevoort refused to permit the surveyors to cross his land and sat there with a shotgun until the by-pass was completed. From 1902 until 1907 Larry Barretto attended the Hoosac School at Hoosick, New York. In 1917 he enlisted in the ambulance service of the United States army, served in France and Belgium, and was honorably discharged on April 20, 1919. He was decorated with the French Croix de Guerre. In 1920 he became assistant editor of *Adventure* magazine (a job previously held by Sinclair

Lewis), and retained this position until 1924, when his first novel was published. On October 20, 1923, he married Anna Appleton Flichtner of South Orange, New Jersey. During his writing career he has been theatrical critic for *The Bookman* and has written scenarios in Hollywood. He has traveled extensively in Europe, Asia, Africa, and in South and Central America. For many years he lived in New York. In World War II Mr. Barretto was an enlistment officer for the American Field Service, a volunteer ambulance corps. Later he served as a war correspondent in the Caribbean area and the China-Burma-India theater. He now resides in Carmel, California. His books include *Bright Mexico* (1935), an account of travels, and *Hawaiian Holiday* (with Bryant Cooper, 1938), a juvenile; both books were illustrated by Mrs. Barretto.

In *Pleasures of the Jazz Age,* William Hodapp points out that "Larry Barretto is the eternal veteran trying to find in peace the reason for man's wars against himself. He is mystically seeking through his protagonists the answer to life and death." His novels concern themselves with morals and manners, especially with the impact of a changing world on the *mores* of people whose pattern has already been set. Largely psychological in content, these stories portray men and women who find it difficult to adapt themselves to an era which moves with ever-increasing speed. Although this theme was begun by Mr. Barretto in a comparatively stable period of American society, it is now so inclusive as to embrace practically everyone.

His first novel, *A Conqueror Passes* (1924), is the story of a veteran of World War I who solves his problems of adjustment and regains his self-confidence by marrying the girl he had left behind and by taking his old job after exorcising his ghosts by revisiting the battle areas. *To Babylon* (1925) illustrates the results of vaulting ambition; it is the story of what a young westerner gains and loses by going to New York, discarding his ideals, and climbing to the top. *Walls of Glass* (1926) is the record of the painful experiences of a widow who, in seeking courageously to provide for her little son, is forced by the press of trying circumstances to accept the equivocal position offered her by a man. In *Old Enchantment* (1928) a brother and sister rebel against the tyranny of Aunt Ellen Portland, a proud New York aristocrat. World War I provides the background for *Horses in the Sky* (1929), which presents the psychological reactions of four American ambulance men to their experiences.

The Indiscreet Years (1931) is the story of Helena Fane, who tries to live down her amorous past with five men in Europe before returning to America and settling down with a respectable husband on Long Island. *Children of Pleasure* (1932) analyzes the mentality of the people who led the United States into the stockmarket crash of 1929 in an account of Linda Gault, who rose from genteel poverty through a good marriage to great wealth and aristocratic position. The effect of the crash is seen also on the servants who made investments on the basis of tips overheard in dinner-table conversations; they lost all their savings. *Three Roads From Paradise* (1933) is the chronicle of three generations of a New York family and a house. *Tomorrow Will Be Different* (1936) is the story of a family, victims of the collapse of business in 1929, who adapt themselves to village life in New England.

The chilling fear of a new war appears in *Journey Through Time* (1940), in which a couple who met in France during World War I return in 1939 with their nineteen-year-old son to visit old scenes and incidentally to try to prevent the boy's participation in war, which no longer seems to them a romantic adventure. *The Great Light* (1947) is the story of a group of men seeking mental peace in a materialistic world; in its metaphysical undertones the novel suggests that the plane of the spirit has hardly been touched in contemporary thinking. The central character is Dirck Ericson, whose quest is made clear through the explanations of a novelist and a psychiatrist.

SARA WARE BASSETT

Bradford Bachrach

was born on October 22, 1872, in Newton, Massachusetts, in a family which traces its descent from the Pilgrims who landed from the *Fortune* at Plymouth in 1621. She graduated from the Lowell School of Design in 1894 and the Symonds Kindergarten Training School in Boston in 1897. She also studied at Boston University and Radcliffe College. For twenty years, from 1897 to 1917, she was a teacher in the public schools of Newton, Massachusetts. Her first books were a series of stories for boys and girls based on some of the great inventions and industries. The first of these was *The Story of Lumber* (1913).

Miss Bassett has written most of her romances against the background of the imaginary village of Belleport on Cape Cod in Massachusetts, which she pictures with a lively accuracy of detail. Her people have the amusingly peculiar characteristics which have made Cape Codders a subject of interest for many generations. A pleasant humor graces the romantic actions of youngsters in and out of love.

The Taming of Zenas Henry (1915), her first novel, pictures the adjustments made by Zenas and Abbie Henry to ensure the success of their marriage. *Wayfarers at the Angel's* (1917) brings Ann to nurse one of three bachelors whose house has a ship's figurehead of an angel over the door; she is persuaded to remain as the real angel in the house. In *Harbor Road* (1919) Aunt Deborah becomes the first person to take in summer boarders, an act which leads to complications when a niece, Tressie, falls in love. *Wall Between* (1920) pictures the feud of four generations of two New England families over a wall dividing their farms and the resolution of the difficulty when love leaps the barrier.

Flood Tide (1921) concerns an inventive genius with no technical training whose patent rights are protected by his housekeeper's nephew, a graduate of Boston Tech. *Granite and Clay* (1922) brings complications to a young Cape Cod couple who find after exchanging promises that they are not in love. *Bayberry Lane* (1931) tells how the three Miss Snows of a Cape Cod village share the large estate they inherit with their neighbors as a sort of community center. *Twin Lights* (1932) concerns two quarreling Cape Cod sisters who divide their cottage lengthwise; at night, lamps in the front windows provide "twin lights." The story is about their attempts to befriend the son of the man each woman had loved.

Shifting Sands (1933) involves an attractive widow, Marcia Howe, her niece, Sylvia, and a young man who appears unexpectedly. *Turning Tide* (1934) pictures Cynthia, who is freed from the domination of her invalid mother and must break through her timidity to decide between two lovers. *Hidden Shoals* (1935) describes the changes wrought in the Phinney family by an automobile accident. *Eternal Deeps* (1936) brings the inhabitants of Belleport into amusing relationship with some newcomers from New York. *Shining Headlands* (1937) shows how three suitors, two natives and a visitor, try to bring Thurza Bowne around to seeing that she should not live alone in her grandfather's big white house. *New England Born* (1938) tells of the mysterious bond between Abel Warren and Mary Carver, a tie which is explained by the arrival of Anne Armitage.

A Son of the Sea (1939) brings romance to a tired New York magazine publisher who returns to his native Cape Cod town to recuperate. *An Ocean Heritage* (1940) brings back to Belleport a native son after a ten years' absence in California. *Cross Currents* (1941) shows how an injustice is corrected. *Sea Magic* (1942) is set in the home of Aunt Melissa, who keeps house for a professor who is writing a book on sea shells. *Anchorage*

(1943) concerns Zinetta Harmon, who married the writer, Martin Royce, and learned that a good husband must be more than a cheerful dancing partner and a spendthrift. *Heart's Haven* (1944) concerns Sally Chase's establishment of an unofficial canteen for soldiers and the romance that comes to her. *Silver Moon Cottage* (1945) is the story of a Cape Cod house which has been kept up for thirty years by a man whose bride-to-be had disappeared on a trip to Boston to buy a dress.

The Beacon (1946) is about Jessie Gale, an orphan, who turns out to be quite capable of taking care of herself. In *Head Winds* (1947) a gentle Cape Cod spinster tries to help a young couple patch up their marriage. *Within the Harbor* (1948) is the story of a group of people in a Cape Cod boarding house as told by a retired college professor. *White Sail* (1949) concerns two strangers who meet in a Cape village and find their lives closely intertwined.

HAMILTON BASSO

was born on September 5, 1904, in New Orleans, Louisiana. He was educated in New Orleans public schools and attended Tulane University from 1922 to 1926. Leaving the university before he graduated, he went to New York to make a literary career for himself and ended, as he says, "by working in a print shop, trucking freight, and selling in a department store—one of the worst experiences I ever had." Returning to the city of his birth, he became a reporter for the now-defunct *Tribune,* and later worked for the *Item* and the *Times-Picayune.* Following his marriage to the former Etolia Simmons in 1930, he moved to the mountains of North Carolina, where he lived intermittently until 1941. He also spent considerable time in South Carolina, in the Southwest, and in Europe. He and Mrs. Basso lived for a year in a little village in southern France and also traveled in England and Italy, returning to the United States in the late summer of 1939. Mr. Basso was associate editor of *The New Republic* from 1935 to 1937, a contributing editor of *Time* magazine in 1942 and 1943, and after 1943 an associate editor of *The New Yorker,* a position he still holds. He has published a number of profiles in *The New Yorker,* for which magazine he has also been literary critic. The Bassos, who have one son, live in Weston, Connecticut.

His non-fiction books include *Beauregard, the Great Creole* (1933), a biography of the general, and *Mainstream* (1943), a collection of biographical essays presenting a character study of an average American named John Applegate. Mr. Basso's only theory of fiction, he insists, is to try to say what he means, and to mean what he says.

Relics and Angels (1929), his first novel, is a study of the maladjustment of a young southerner who wants to be a bacteriologist but works in the family factory. The locale is a city similar to New Orleans. *Cinnamon Seed* (1934) concerns Dekker Blackheath, whose father's suicide has sent him into the world at fourteen. Set in Louisiana, the characters include Kingfrog, a demagogue. *In Their Own Image* (1935) contrasts northern rich people in Aiken with some of the local workmen and shows the clash of two opposing ways of life. *Courthouse Square* (1936) concerns David Barondess, a novelist, who returns to Macedon, South Carolina, because of boredom with pseudo-intellectual life in New York, only to discover that the ills of the world, including intolerance and injustice, are everywhere.

Days before Lent (1939) shows the importance of casting one's lot with those who are upbuilding a community. Jason Kent, a bacteriologist, must decide at the Mardi Gras in New Orleans. *Wine of the Country* (1941) deals with the same theme in the life of Tait Ravenswill, an anthropologist. *Sun in Capri-*

corn (1942), a novel of the struggle between common decency and a lust for power, shows a Yale graduate being destroyed by Gilgo Slade, a power-mad politician who batters down every worthy opponent who stands in the way of his achieving the Presidency. *The Greenroom* (1949) tells the story of an associate editor of a publishing house who goes to the French Riviera to call upon his firm's most important author, a supposedly gracious lady.

SYLVIA CHATFIELD BATES

Von Behr

was born in Springfield, Massachusetts. After graduating from Elmira College, she did graduate work at Radcliffe College. At one time fiction editor of *The Woman's Home Companion,* she has been a teacher of English in New York state schools and at New York University. Now she lives in an old house at West Tisbury on Martha's Vineyard, Massachusetts, and devotes her time to writing.

Her first novel, *The Geranium Lady* (1916), is set on an island between Penobscot Bay and Barnegat. June Carver, a beautiful girl who wears a red geranium in her hair, is slow in explaining her presence to Miles Hawthorne, a former lieutenant in the United States Navy. *The Golden Answer* (1921) deals with the writer Amos Fortune, his ward Harmony, and the woman he marries, Christina. Their poverty causes Christina to depart for a long visit with an aunt; she reconsiders and returns.

Andrea Thorne (1925) concerns a brother and a sister in a cultivated home. In her senior year in college Andrea falls in love with Dan Cotsmur. When her brother Stephen's remonstrances are unheeded, he simulates an interest in Myrtle Cotsmur and brings about an unexpected climax. In *That Magic Fire* (1928) Lucia Fleming and Anthony Barr loved each other since childhood, but she married Albert Morgan to gain security. Anthony's return ignites the old love feeling. *I Have Touched the Earth* (1934) portrays the forces creating a neurotic personality, for Stella Donne's father rules her sternly. She goes away to Colorado, but returns at her mother's death. *The Long Way Home* (1937) traces a family of remarkable women from Colonial days in Connecticut to the 1930's, with the focus on Ellen Bowen Swain, who prospers as a New York real-estate operator. *The Floor of Heaven* (1940) portrays the fear of Johanna for her husband, Ben Fair, and how Piers April rescues her.

The folklore of the Indian town of Gay Head on Martha's Vineyard motivates the action and establishes the characters in *The Weather Breeder* (1948), a novel which brings under scrutiny the unwitting way in which American treatment of minorities—Indian, Negro, and Jewish—breeds disaster. Noepe Sanctuary, a sensitive, well-educated girl of mixed Indian descent, is able to conquer "the evil" symbolized in the lore of her people by making use of her rich heritage.

FLORENCE MARVYNE BAUER

was born in Elgin, Illinois, and educated in the public schools of that city. During her high-school years she developed an ambition to be a monologist, but her mother feared the influence of the stage. Florence, therefore, attended and graduated from the Church School of Art in Chicago, and went to North Carolina to teach in Chowan College. One year convinced her that teaching was not her forte. In World War I she enlisted as a student in the Army Nurse Corps and arrived in Camp Grant, Illinois, just after the armistice. Here she met Dr. William W. Bauer, and they were married on February 8, 1920. They now have two sons and a daughter: John, Erminie, and Charles; their first son died in infancy.

After their marriage they settled in Idaho, where Dr. Bauer practiced general medicine, but in 1922 they moved to Milwaukee, where he became epidemiologist in its health department. In 1924 he accepted a position as health commissioner of Racine. Here Mrs. Bauer became seriously interested in writing. She and her husband had found common interests in dramatics and painting, and now they turned these talents to health instruction. They developed educational pamphlets, Dr. Bauer doing the writing and Mrs. Bauer the illustrating, and they wrote and produced dramas on a local radio station.

It was not until Dr. Bauer took a position as head of the American Medical Association's Bureau of Health Education that either husband or wife attempted a book manuscript. Then it was Dr. Bauer who pioneered, with his wife reading, suggesting, and criticizing. Gradually she began to try her pen, first in writing one-act plays, then in magazine articles and radio scripts. Husband and wife collaborated on *Eat What You Want* (1942), a book on diet.

In her youth Mrs. Bauer had entertained the desire to write a novel of Biblical times. A year as proofreader in a Sunday-school publishing company fed this hope. She welcomed every opportunity to learn about Bible history and doctrines, archaeology, and orientalisms. For many years she taught a Bible class. In November, 1943, she experienced a need to escape from her own environment. Her older son was with General Chennault in China. A close friend was dying of cancer. Housework, never pleasant to her, seemed unendurable. One gloomy Thursday afternoon she sat down at her typewriter and began *Behold Your King* (1945). The story is that of Jonathan, nephew and potential heir of wealthy Joseph of Arimathea, and his stay in Palestine when Jesus of Nazareth was disturbing the authorities. The friendship of the two young men is set against a vividly pictured background.

To supplement her knowledge for the background of her second novel, Mrs. Bauer went to Philadelphia to the University Museum, which had worked with Sir Leonard Woolley in excavating the site of Ur of the Chaldees in the late 1920's and early 1930's. *Abram, Son of Terah* (1948) is the story of the patriarch Abraham of Genesis during his childhood and youth in the famous metropolis on the Euphrates River.

VICKI BAUM

Lotte Neustein

was born on January 24, 1896, in Vienna, Austria, the daughter of Herman and Mathilde Baum. At the age of eight she entered the Vienna Conservatory of Music, where she concentrated for six years on the harp. On July 17, 1916, she married Richard Lert, by whom she had two sons. She then went to Germany and for three years taught in the musical high school of Darmstadt. In Berlin in 1926 she edited magazines issued by Ullstein, then the largest German publishing house. After her second marriage, Miss Baum gave up music as a profession and turned to writing. She came to America in 1931 to see the dramatization of her famous novel, *Grand Hotel,* and then remained. She was naturalized in 1938. Miss Baum's first story was published in 1909, and her first book in 1914.

Miss Baum's novels usually contain a large number of characters whose lives are unexpectedly intertwined through a startling incident which provides a basis for an interpretation of human motives. Fast action and historical pictures are combined.

Her first novel to be published in the United States, *Grand Hotel* (1931), became immensely influential on other writers. It relates the actions and thoughts of people in a large hostelry in Germany after World War I. All wish for happiness: a bookkeeper with a few weeks to live wants desperately to see life; an aging dancer tries to find love; and a baron turns thief for a moment's thrill. *Martin's Summer* (1931) pictures Puck Dobbersberg, a baron's daughter, and Martin Heil, a chemical engineer, whose life she saves. *And Life Goes On* (1932) explores the secret places in the hearts of a physician, his wife, a film actress, and a wealthy manufacturer when an accident unites them at Lohwinkel.

Secret Sentence (1932) portrays the remorse of Joachim Burthe, a Berlin law student, who murders a statesman and escapes. *Helene* (1933) examines the economically restricted lives of German university students in the story of a girl chemist who makes a suicide pact. *Falling Star* (1934) pictures the love of Oliver Dent, a fading Hollywood star, and a Rumanian actress, Donka Morescu. *Men Never Know* (1935) has a judge look into an insurance murder. *Sing, Sister, Sing* (1936) is a romantic tale of Doris Hart, a waitress, who rises to stardom as a singer. *Tale of Bali* (1937) is an historical story from the Balinese viewpoint of the conquest of this South Sea island by the Dutch in 1904–06. The central character is Pak, a peasant, who stands in contrast to the nobles hastening the defeat of the natives.

Shanghai, '37 (1939) tells the life stories of nine people killed when Japan bombed the city in 1937. The detailed background explains the hostility between the Chinese and Japanese peoples. *The Ship and the Shore* (1941) recounts the lives of six passengers on a boat which stops at a South Sea island. *Marion Alive* (1942) tells the story of the political disturbances in Europe from 1900 to the fall of France in 1940 as a background for the life story of a woman of great vitality and buoyancy. *The Weeping Wood* (1943) is a history of rubber in terms of the people affected by the industry. The many tales range from gruesome to romantic.

Hotel Berlin, '43 (1944) takes place in a large hostelry which entertained German officialdom during World War II. Martin Richter hides there, and the pursuit provides the basis for sketches of many people who reflect the disillusionment following four years of a war that is leading only to defeat. This book was a Literary Guild choice. *Once in Vienna* (1945) concerns the love affairs of Hannes Bassiem, a Danish-born singer in the Vienna opera in the years before World War I. *Mortgage on Life* (1946) is a tale of the theater about a girl who helps another. *Headless Angel* (1948) begins in Goethe's Weimar in eighteenth-century Germany and concerns a romance between the poet's married friend Clarinda and a Spaniard. They go to Mexico and have many adventures.

MARGUERITE FARLEIGH BAYLISS

was born on June 27, 1895, in Norton, New Jersey. Her father was a Methodist minister, Rev. Richard Francis Bayliss, who was called "Cathedral Bayliss" because of his fame as an orator. Her mother, Josephine Farlee, was a professor of English literature and an authority on literature for children.

Marguerite Bayliss studied under the direction of her mother and spent a total of only five years in school. After passing examinations, she entered high school at the age of twelve and completed the course in less than three years. When she came to consider college, she discovered that she had already exceeded the requirements of most college courses in her specialty, and so again she turned to tutors. Her fields of specialization were anthropology, zoology, biology, paleogeography, and English language and literature. At sixteen she was an advisor on animal heredity to a cattle club, and she was already writing. For a year she practiced anthropology in the State of New York, where she did research in the prison system on the heredity of criminals, and then she entered her permanent field of work as a specialist in the heredity of the high mammals, especially horses.

For twenty years she was immersed in that job, eventually on a world-wide basis, and served as consultant to breeders and animal societies. She also wrote extensively. For a decade she edited the late J. W. Waring's *Official Horse Show Blue Book,* and that gave her acquaintance with thousands of show horses. At the same time research for the Jockey Club brought equal contact with race horses. She wrote a technical monograph, *The Matriarchy of the American Turf* (1931), the classic in its sphere, which traces the inheritance of the American Thoroughbred through female lines. Subsequent genealogies of the Thoroughbred have followed the pattern of this book.

The next three years she devoted to an analysis of the pedigrees of one hundred and sixty thousand horses. For relaxation she read fiction occasionally. Since she had read widely in the classics, she turned to modern novels. The more she sampled them, the less she liked them. In desperation she turned to the typewriter one day and started to write a novel in line with her ideas. Between sessions with astronomical numbers of horses she wrote along on the novel. The result was *Bolinvar* (1937), which was published in a limited de luxe edition in two volumes; later it was serialized in abridged form in *The Ladies' Home Journal* and in 1944 was issued as *The Bolinvars* in a trade edition. The work became a modern classic; it was translated into many languages, and in England it headed the best-seller list. Publishers pursued her for more novels, and vainly she explained that she is not a novelist. "There are moments," she has said, "when my sole philosophy of the novel is flight from it." Yet occasionally she writes fiction, and has other novels which she will prepare for publication as she has time. Meanwhile she is completing *The Splendid and Renowned Breed of Morgan Horses.*

Her philosophy of the novel is stated in *Romans* XII, 21: "Be not overcome of evil, but overcome evil with good." More specifically she has written: "The novel should not merely depict life; it should reciprocally create life. It should not only show us where we are; it should also show us where to go.

"Ever since World War I the trend has been toward the exposition of characters who are frustrated, and we are undergoing a large, drawn-out cult of the frustrated. These people know neither where they are in life, nor how they got there, nor how they are to get out, nor where they wish to go. It is the attitude toward frustration to which I object. These characters should be treated sympathetically; they should not be abandoned in the wilderness in which they are lost. The author should either help guide them to safety or stay there with them.

"Instead, the majority of the War Era writers stand aside objectively, looking on and reporting—too often cynically reporting. It is a proper task of the novel to play sun and stars to the frustrated ones, in and out of the novel. But that's the end of its responsibility. From there on it's out of the novelist's hands. He can't force crazed lost ones to believe that he knows which way is East. But at least the sun must shine, must shine from East to West. It has been a long spell of cloudy weather in fiction."

The Bolinvars (1944) is a romantic story full of the derring-do of the early nineteenth century in America and England, together with love of horses in the noble tradition. Hugo Bolinvar's past holds a mystery which clouds his name and prevents his marrying Nellie Farleigh until the blemish is cleared away. Devereux Bolinvar, a Princeton man, is a gentleman and heart-free. The two cousins meet and their paths take them to England, and there their lives come together to weave a pattern of beauty.

Earth Eagles (1947), a prose poem, is a very simple tale of two horses and an old Irish trainer. The setting is Kentucky where the two horses race. One is primed for winning and alive as an electric spark; the other is crippled, unable to race, and dead of a broken heart. Touched with mysticism, this is a religious story expressed in the language of the sporting field.

CEDRIC BELFRAGE

was born in London, England, on November 8, 1904. He describes himself as the descendant of a long line of penurious parsons and well-to-do brewers. He went to Cambridge University but left without a degree when offered a job after two years of study. Having early acquired a fascination for motion pictures, he crossed the Atlantic in 1926 and obtained employment in New York as a scenario reader for Universal Pictures. A year later he moved to Hollywood as a commentator on screen productions for newspapers and "fan" magazines. Returning to England in 1930, he became a film and theater critic. In 1945 he was one of the SHAEF psychological warfare team which set up the first post-Nazi German newspapers in Aachen, Frankfort, and other cities, and he received a Guggenheim fellowship to make a literary record of the work done in reviving a democratic press in Germany. He married the author-journalist Molly Castle; they have two children and live in upstate New York. He is the editor of the news weekly, *The National Guardian.* His books include *Away from It All* (1937), about his trip around the world in 1934, and *They All Hold Swords* (1941), a contrast between England's caste system and American democracy.

Promised Land (1938), his first novel, is a fragmentary historical tale about Hollywood and the California land boom. *South of God* (1941) is a fictionalized biography of Claude Williams, a Presbyterian minister among southern sharecroppers and miners. This book was enlarged in *A Faith to Free the People* (1944). *Abide With Me* (1948) describes the undertaker business and satirizes the mechanics of the trade to show that commercialized bad taste accompanies funerals.

JAMES WARNER BELLAH

Willard Stewart

was born in New York City on September 14, 1899. During World War I he was a pilot with the Canadian air force. From 1919 to 1922 he was a student at Wesleyan University in Middletown, Conneticut; his senior year was spent at Columbia University, where he received his bachelor's degree in 1923 and where for three years thereafter and in 1936 and 1937 he was an instructor in English. In 1927 and 1928 he was a foreign correspondent in Europe and Asia. The first reserve officer called to general staff duty with the First Infantry Division on October 7, 1940, he served as intelligence officer of the Eightieth Infantry Division and later was the American deputy to the British chief of staff for information and civil affairs with Admiral Mountbatten in the Southeast Asia command. He also experienced combat with General Stillwell and Colonel Philip Cochran. At the end of World War II he entered Georgetown University at Washington, D.C., and in 1945 received a master's degree in history. A year later he matriculated at the University of Pennsylvania to study for a doctorate in political science. Mr. Bellah is an internationally known fencer, a crewman on Corinthian ocean-sailing races, a noted deep-sea fisherman, and a veteran Hollywood screen writer.

Stories and sketches are published in *Sketch Book of a Cadet from Gascony* (1923), *Gods of Yesterday* (1928), and *Irregular Gentleman* (1948).

These Frantic Years (1927), his first novel, concerns John Sassoon, Jr., a wounded aviator, and his rehabilitation after World War I.

Sons of Cain (1928) has Major Murray Petching fall in love with Freda Seleyce, a married woman with a husband who hates her. *Dancing Lady* (1932) traces the rise of Janie Barlow as a dancer from a roadhouse to Broadway and then, again poor after 1929, back to small places. *White Piracy* (1933) tells about a rich Marylander who builds a roadhouse for his two sons and a daughter. *The Brass Gong Tree* (1936) portrays westerners, including an American journalist, suspected of assassinating a Japanese statesman. *This Is the Town* (1937) shows against the gaudy theatrical section of New York a southern girl succeeding as a dancer.

Seven Must Die (1938) portrays a group of tourists in Honolulu on an adventure cruise. They hunt pearls; a quarrel creates tension. *The Bones of Napoleon* (1940) is about a New York reporter's strange experiences on inheriting an historic estate on the Eastern Shore of Maryland, where the last remains of Napoleon supposedly rest. *Ward Twenty* (1945) details a twenty-four-hour cross section of life in a veterans' hospital, where the price of war is talked over by wounded men and their nurses. Joe Keenan is the most alert, and there is Halpern, blind and armless, whose despair gives a Brooklyn boy a desire to help. A suicide is prevented.

FRANCIS RUFUS BELLAMY

Conway Studios

was born in New Rochelle, N.Y., on December 24, 1886. After study at Williams College and Cornell University, he engaged in farming from 1907 to 1911. For four years he was a book salesman. During World War I he was Washington editor of the American Red Cross magazine, and then in 1918–19 he served as a foreign correspondent. After 1927 he was an editor, successively, of *The Outlook, The New Yorker, Fiction Parade,* and *Scribner's Commentator.*

The Balance (1917) is the story of a popular playwright with a socially conscious sweetheart who is disappointed in her fiancé's shallow drama and who breaks off relations until he sees as she does and employs his talent to dramatize her ideas. *The Flash of Gold* (1922) has Nancy van Wyck marry a physician who devotes his life to the poor in the slums; she almost turns to a country-club career with her father's business associate, but she realizes that happiness can come only through forgetfulness of self. *Spanish Faith, A Romance of Old Mexico and the Caribbean* (1926) is an account of the daring adventures in 1816 of Roger Buchanan of New York. *Blood Money* (1947) is an historical account of United States Treasury secret agents' counter-espionage work during World War II. *The Strange Blooming* (1948) concerns Julian Cortwright who is unable to persuade his wife to agree to a divorce, and so goes to Mexico to avoid "the easy deceit of a social marriage" and to achieve freedom to marry a gorgeous redhead.

SAUL BELLOW

was born in Lachine, Quebec, Canada, on July 10, 1915. Most of his life has been spent in Chicago, where he studied at the University of Chicago. He earned a Bachelor of Science degree at Northwestern University in 1937 and later studied at the University of Wisconsin. He holds a degree in anthropology and has taught that subject. His stories and reviews have appeared in the little magazines and major book reviews. In 1938 he taught in a Chicago teachers' college, and from 1943 to 1946 he was connected with the editorial department of *The Encyclopaedia Britannica.* Since 1946 he has taught English at the University of Minnesota. In 1948 he was awarded a Guggenheim fellowship.

Mr. Bellow is a writer of psychological stories which delve into states of mind created by unusual circumstances. *Dangling Man* (1944) reports the reactions of a young man who waits restlessly to be inducted into the army. *The Victim* (1947) tells of a young Jew, Asa Leventhal, who runs afoul of a Gentile, Kirby Allbee, and nearly goes mad under the impact of Allbee's constant and leechlike adherence.

LUDWIG BEMELMANS

Fred Stein

was born on April 27, 1898, at Beran in the Austrian Tyrol. His father, a Belgian, was a painter, and his mother was a daughter of a well-to-do Bavarian brewer. Because of the father's frequent absences, the boy grew up under the influence of his mother's family. At the Lyceum in Regensburg, Ludwig Bemelmans proved to be unwilling to obey the rules, and so he was sent to a private academy in Rothenburg, where his conduct did not alter. Withdrawn from school, he was sent to work under an uncle who owned resort hotels in the Tyrolean Alps. His unsatisfactory behavior led to an ultimatum that he choose between a reform school or immigration to America. He chose the latter and arrived in New York in 1914. After some difficulty he got a job in a dining room in an exclusive hotel, memorably pictured in *Hotel Splendide,* where in the course of three years he worked up to the position of waiter. He drew constantly and took a few art lessons, but soon gave up modeling his work on others' ideas because of an unwillingness to surrender his originality. In 1918 he was naturalized.

Mr. Bemelmans enlisted in the army in World War I and served at Camp Gordon; this experience was described in *My War with the United States* (1937). After being demobilized, he returned to New York and to work in hotels and restaurants. His pictures and sketches began to attract attention. He decorated Jascha Heifetz's studio and illustrated books. In 1933 he opened his own restaurant. His first book, *Hansi* (1934), a juvenile, was an instant success and led him to devote most of his time to writing and drawing. In 1937 and 1940 he made trips to Ecuador, a country which has supplied background for several of his books. In 1935 he married Madeline Freund; they have one daughter.

A gentle humor with a quality of understatement pervades the books of Mr. Bemelmans, and most of his writings are illustrated with his inimitably funny and original drawings. Much of his writing can be classed as informal essays, the lyric kind of prose expression in which the feelings and experiences of the author mingle in pleasant conversational and autobiographical style.

The juveniles by Mr. Bemelmans include *Hansi* (1934), *The Golden Basket* (1936), *The Castle Number Nine* (1937), *Quito Express* (1938), *Madeline* (1939), *Fifi* (1940), *Rosebud* (1942), and *A Tale of Two Glimps* (1947). His books of autobiographical sketches include *My War with the United States* (1937); *Life Class: Biography* (1937), an account of his youth and his first years in the United States; *The Donkey Inside* (1941), about his experiences in Ecuador; and *I Love You, I Love You* (1942), sketches about far-away places he has visited. His short-story collections include *Small Beer* (1939), *Hotel Splendide* (1941), and *Hotel Bemelmans* (1946).

Mr. Bemelmans' first novel was *Now I Lay Me Down to Sleep* (1943), the adventures of an elderly and wealthy Ecuadorian general who leaves his villa in Biarritz to return with his retinue to his home in South America. *Dirty Eddie* (1947) has for its hero in this comic story of Hollywood a small black pig which plays an important role in a motion picture and earns an enormous salary. The animal nearly ruins the picture but in the end provides the cause for its success. *Eye of God* (1949) pictures the villagers in Aspen in the Tyrol just below the triangular rocky summit of the same name. The Nazis occupy the community in World War II, but in spite of their suffering the people refuse to surrender their ancient freedoms. *Sunshine* (1950) portrays a gentle music-school teacher who outwits a Scrooge-like landlord.

(JOHN) BARRY BENEFIELD

Fabian Bachrach

was born in Jefferson, Texas, on the border of Louisiana. He graduated from the University of Texas in 1902 and immediately became a reporter on the Dallas *Morning News*. After ten years of journalism—in Dallas, Brooklyn, and Manhattan—he decided that he had skimmed the cream of newspaper experience and was getting down to pale blue milk. For four years he wrote short fiction, and then turned to a salaried job in the book-publishing business. As part-time or full-time editor, he remained in that field until 1947.

His writings are whimsical and touched with fantasy, and are generally and sympathetically concerned with victims of social injustice. He is entirely aware, he has said, that "not every underdog is a good dog," but he believes that every underdog is entitled to a generous probationary period of reasonable doubt.

The Chicken-Wagon Family (1925), his first novel, tells the story of a Louisiana peddler of Gallic descent who, replying to the demands of his wife to stop drifting and to settle in a town for the sake of their young daughter, determines to drive on to the biggest town in America. They migrate to New York, reversing the old route of the wagon pioneers and settling first in an abandoned fire-engine house just off lower Broadway. The experiences of the family and a wandering student they have picked up on the way comprise the story. *Short Turns* (1926) is a collection of fourteen short stories. *Bugles in the Night* (1927) deals with a former Confederate soldier who enters a soldiers' home, but almost immediately leaves to act as protector and counselor to a hopeless, apathetic, declassed girl who must be taken to different and distant surroundings if she is to find an opportunity for happiness. *A Little Clown Lost* (1928) is about a girl who, thinking she is a burden to her young student husband, leaves him to become a circus performer. The story also involves the husband's second wife.

Valiant Is the Word for Carrie (1935) is primarily concerned with a handsome young woman who lives alone on the edge of a Louisiana town and is suspected of immorality. Into Carrie Snyder's high-fenced back yard strays an unusual, self-invited guest one hot summer day—a ten-year-old boy. In time she adopts him and a younger stray girl. The influence of this "family" on Carrie's character is the main theme of the book. *April Was When It Began* (1939) is a fantasy of existence in a New York publishing house and in a slum district, and involves a sober-faced young editor with a strange imagination, a retired and absorbed college professor investigating the question of life after death, his motherless twelve-year-old daughter who desperately needs a friend, and a formerly famous Italian medium who is the professor's housekeeper, cook, and maid-of-all-work. In *Eddie and the Archangel Mike* (1943) a grim Texas copy-desk newspaperman sets out in his broken-down car for New York with the intention of becoming a playwright. He wants no more newspaper work and no encumbrances. On the way he unwillingly picks up a prim, reserved little woman who is fleeing from an intolerable domestic situation. Neither expects nor wishes their ride together to last more than a few miles. Their fighting existence, together, in the big city is the heart of the story.

KONRAD BERCOVICI

was born on June 22, 1882, in Braila, Rumania. In youth he learned to weave baskets, play the violin, and speak Caló, the language of the gypsies, as well as German, French, and Greek. After a private education at home, he went to Paris—where he worked for a clockmaker and as a painter on the Eiffel Tower—to study music and to perfect himself as an organist. In 1916 he came to the United States to make a concert tour. A broken wrist suffered in ice skating ended his organ-playing.

While recuperating, he began to write in his native language and then taught himself English mainly through two books, the Bible and Samuel Butler's *The Way of All Flesh.* For a time he worked in New York on *The World* and *The Post.* In 1920 he traveled with a gypsy caravan from New York to Chicago. From this experience, as well as from his knowledge of gypsy life in his homeland, grew many of his short stories and novels. Mr. Bercovici is a musical composer and has been a teacher of harmony. His autobiography is *It's the Gypsy in Me* (1941).

Mr. Bercovici's earliest books were two collections of short stories, *Crimes of Charity* (1917) and *Dust of New York* (1919), about social injustices experienced by poor immigrants in New York City. With *Ghitza* (1921) he found a new vein in romantic tales about gypsy tribes of the Danube area in southern Europe; thereafter he became known for his colorful short stories giving accounts of the customs of the Romany people in *Murdo* (1923), *Ileana* (1924), and *Singing Winds* (1926). *Peasants* (1928) deals with immigrants in New York City and in Minnesota.

His non-fiction books reflect an interest in immigrants and in the Balkans: *Around the World in New York* (1924) describes fourteen distinct foreign settlements in the metropolis; *On New Shores* (1925) pictures the color and romance of old-world customs retained in immigrant colonies in the United States; *Nights Abroad* (1928) sketches in a single incident the unique quality of each of a dozen famous cities; *The Story of the Gypsies* (1928) contains many legends and stories of the nomadic people; *The Royal Lover* (1931) narrates the life of Queen Marie of Rumania and of her amorous son, King Carol; and *The Incredible Balkans* (1932) analyzes those countries and their people's condition in the years after World War I. *Costa's Daughter* (1924) is a play about gypsies.

Marriage Guest (1925), his first novel, portrays the German quarter of New York City in the leisurely days of the 1890's and the changes wrought by industrial enterprise. Anton Zwenge, a violin-mender, represents the old order and his busy wife symbolizes the new. *For a Song* (1931) pictures Maria Caponi, an Italian-American, aspiring to become an opera star to vindicate her father's failure to achieve similar success. *Main Entrance* (1932) concerns Hirsh Aaron, a Russian Jew who migrates to Chicago in 1890 and later rises to be a wealthy merchant in New York. He grows unhappy as his children desert Jewish traditions. On the way home from Europe he secretly murders his youngest son.

The Exodus (1947) is a fictionized biography of Moses and a retelling of the story of the departure of the Israelites from Egypt and their journey to the Promised Land. *Savage Prodigal* (1948) recounts the life of the French poet and adventurer, Jean Nicholas Arthur Rimbaud. In childhood he showed a violent temper toward his stingy mother and sympathetic teacher; in Paris he became famous as a writer and associated with Verlaine; and in his last years he was a businessman in Africa, where he delayed having a surgical operation which would have prolonged his life. The almost untranslatable poetry is clarified by being set against the background of Rimbaud's strange studies.

ELLIN BERLIN

Pach

was born on March 22, 1903, at Roslyn, Long Island, New York, a daughter of Clarence H. Mackay and a granddaughter of John W. Mackay, an Irish immigrant who became rich in Nevada in 1872. Her father was president of the Postal Telegraph and Cable Company. In 1925 she wrote for *The New Yorker* two satirical articles on débutante life and the folly of débuts. On January 4, 1926, she was married to Irving Berlin, America's most successful writer of popular songs, and to her he dedicated the song "Always." Miss Mackay, a Roman Catholic, and Mr. Berlin, of the Orthodox Jewish faith, were married by a city clerk. Four children have been born to them—three daughters, and a son who died in infancy.

Her first novel, *Land I Have Chosen* (1944), tells the story of a spoiled Long Island society girl who steals the husband of a charming German actress. The time is the period of the depression in the late 1920's and the early 1930's. The dominant idea is political, for, in choosing a Nazi husband, the girl provides a basis for a discussion of fascist tendencies at the time of Hitler's rise to power. *Lace Curtain* (1948) deals with the tragic problem of Veronica Reardon, the daughter of a rich and devout Catholic family, who falls in love with a Protestant. The story concerns the difficulties she faces in her mixed marriage. It appears that tolerance and an avoidance of prejudice can save these marriages from disaster.

ALINE BERNSTEIN

Louise Dahl-Wolfe

was born in the heart of New York City on December 22, 1880. She received her education in public schools, Hunter College, and the New York School of Applied Design for Women, where she worked until she married. As soon as her two children were able to walk, she began to study painting with Robert Henri. Through her father, Joseph Frankau, one of America's leading actors of the 1890's, Mrs. Bernstein became acquainted at an early age with the theater, front and back. Her father also gave her an excellent discipline in literature; she was required to learn most of the female Shakespearean roles before she was fourteen. When some friends built the Neighborhood Playhouse, she began in 1915 her successful career of scenic designing, an art in which she holds a foremost position. She remarks that "it has been hard work, but a wonderful life." Her autobiography, *An Actor's Daughter* (1941), describes her sensitive childhood and youth at the end of the last century among New York theater people. In 1949 her many activities included a position as instructor and visiting lecturer in the drama department of Vassar College and consultant to the experimental theater there; president of the Costume Institute of the Metropolitan Museum of Art; and chairman of the educational committee of the United Scenic Artists Local 829 of the American Federation of Labor.

Mrs. Bernstein's first book was a slender volume of short stories, *Three Blue Suits* (1935). *The Journey Down* (1938) contains nine scenes in the relationship of a sensitive woman of forty to a young writer; the events begin at their first meeting and end with her illness after he has abandoned her. *Miss Condon* (1947) is about Jennie, the orphaned daughter of a portrait painter, who at seventeen marries Charlie Ames, a theatrical producer twice her age. Five years later she bigamously marries Zachary Earle.

ALVAH BESSIE

was born in New York City on June 4, 1904. He graduated from DeWitt Clinton High School and from Columbia College in 1924. After four years as an actor and stage manager in New York, he ran the gamut of occupations, including bookstore manager, publishing-house editor, translator from the French, newspaper researcher, and rewrite man in Paris in 1928. His first short story was printed in that city. Following his return from abroad, he published many short stories, several of which were reprinted in the O'Brien collections and other anthologies. He also wrote innumerable articles of criticism for many magazines on drama, literature, and the motion picture. Mr. Bessie has served as drama and Sunday magazine editor for the Brooklyn *Daily Eagle,* and as dramatic critic, motion-picture critic, and feature writer for *The New Masses.* He held a Guggenheim fellowship in creative writing in 1935. In 1938 Mr. Bessie went to Spain, where he joined the Lincoln Battalion (XV International Brigade) of the Spanish Republican army; *Men in Battle* (1939) is a narrative of his experiences. Since 1943 he has written picture scripts in Hollywood.

His first novel, *Dwell in the Wilderness* (1935), is the story of three generations of a middle-western family from 1876 to 1925. Eben Morris fails as a grocer, and his wife takes charge. Four children show the effect of family disunity: Roger moves away; Manley becomes bossy like his mother; Dewey devotes himself to theatrical work; and Martha unites in herself the qualities and problems of the family. *Bread in the Stone* (1941) pictures Ed Sloan after a youth of juvenile delinquency gladly marrying a good woman; for her and her small daughter he tries to go straight. An unskilled worker, he loses ground steadily and commits murder to get food.

HERBERT BEST

George Philip Sauter

was born on March 25, 1894, in Chester, England. In August, 1914, he enlisted in the English army and served as a signal officer with Indian, Australian, South African, and New Zealand troops. For twelve years he was a colonial administrator in Nigeria, Africa. While at home on leave recovering from the tropical climate, he met Miss Erick Berry, an American writer and illustrator. Three years later she went out to Africa; his next leave brought him to the United States, where they were married. They write together, farm together in summer, and go goggle-fishing together at their winter home in Jamaica in the West Indies. At their farm home in New York state he became interested in the dialect and customs of early settlers in that region.

"My literary theories are few," Mr. Best has stated. "There is too much writing by people who 'just love to write.' There is too much synthetic writing by people who derive their ideas from other fiction. The result of all this derivative writing is an inverted pyramid of fiction, the base of which makes little more than partial contact with solid reality. It would be better for most of us writers, and for the reader, if we knew at first hand something of that real hunger, real thirst, mud, rain, heat, cold, triumph, danger, hate, love, fear, courage, loyalty, treachery, glory, and despair which are the ingredients of our stories."

Mr. Best's first book was for boys, *Garram the Hunter* (1940). It was followed by three other swift-moving tales of Africa. His first novel written in the United States was *The Twenty-Fifth Hour* (1940), a story which is too gruesome for comfortable minds. Both sides in a war, occurring sometime in the future, seek to destroy the civilian population. *Young'un* (1944) tells of the fur-trading days along Lake Champlain shortly after the end of the Revolutionary War, and of three children who are abandoned when their mother dies and their father runs away following the burning of their home. The courage and ingenuity of the three form the basis for a tale colored with much authentic early American dialect. This novel was a selection of the Book-of-the-Month Club.

Border Iron (1945), a juvenile, is the story of Tod Randall, who with his white sheepdog solves a border dispute over Massachusetts iron ore destined for New York in the 1740's. *Whistle, Daughter, Whistle* (1947) is also set in the Lake Champlain country just after the Revolutionary War. Strong-minded Grandma Tuttle steals a stagecoach, saves a sailor, gets drunk, defies the town supervisor by managing a tavern, and above all helps bring about her granddaughter's love for the right man. *The Long Portage* (1948), a juvenile, describes the adventure of a young New York "dock rat" who, against odds, works his way into the French and Indian Wars and takes part in the Battle of Ticonderoga, learns woodcraft, tracking, fighting, and earns a place in Rogers' Rangers.

ARTHUR RAYMOND BEVERLEY-GIDDINGS

was born in England and educated for the army. He is a descendant of the Count de Beverlac who founded the town of Beverley, Yorkshire, in 1125. Mr. Beverley-Giddings resigned his commission in the early 1920's and came to the United States. He began his writing career with short stories which appeared in leading magazines here and abroad. His primary interest, however, was in novels, and after some years of magazine writing, during which he felt he was serving an adequate apprenticeship for the task to come, he turned to long fiction. His intensive study for years of tidewater Maryland and Virginia is reflected in his books in the accuracy of locale, detail, and atmosphere.

Larrish Hundred (1942), his first novel, pictures the attractive life of a Virginia plantation contemporaneous with the year when Sarah Larrish is in love with Sile, a troublesome neighbor. *Broad Margin* (1945) tells of Page Nugent, who comes home to the comfortable tidewater section of Virginia in 1943 after volunteer service in the English Royal Air Force. His health has been shattered, but among friends and familiar scenes in fields and woods he recovers. *River of Rogues* (1948) is a romantic tale of life on the Eastern Shore of Maryland in 1820, covering a period and events little touched heretofore in fiction, when David Innes marries Jeanne, a New Orleans woman who is a confidante of slave kidnappers whom her husband tracks down and disperses. After her death, David marries Prudence Foxall, a quiet Quaker girl whom he has always loved.

ARCHIE BINNS

Pinchot

was born on July 30, 1899, in Port Ludlow, Washington. He grew up on the family farm near Shelton, within sight of the Olympic Mountains. His grandfather, a cotton-blockade runner during the Civil War, died at sea off the Cape of Good Hope at the age of thirty-one. Archie attended the district school which his father established, and later the Shelton High School. Then he spent nine months on the lightship near Cape Flattery, and once remained there for one hundred and sixty days without coming ashore. He knows the northwest country as only a person can who has lived and worked and vacationed in it—and who loves it.

In 1918 he enlisted in the army and later was commissioned an officer in the Field

Artillery reserve. Alternating seafaring and college, he graduated from Stanford University in 1922. He sailed on a freighter by way of the Panama Canal to the East Coast, and was next heard from at the nation's capital, where he served as a newspaper reporter and Washington correspondent. Moving to New York, he became editor of a small publishing company. In 1931 he collaborated with Felix Riesenberg on a sea novel, *The Maiden Voyage.* His non-fiction books include *Northwest Gateway, The Story of Seattle* (1941), a history of the giant young metropolis, with vivid pictures of the landing of the Seattle Pilgrims in 1851, the Indians' siege of the infant city, the railroad troubles, the anti-Chinese riots, the great fire of 1889, and the Yukon gold rush. *Minnie Maddern Fiske* (1949) is a biography of the famous actress. *Radio Imp* (1950) is a fantasy for juveniles about a second-hand radio that plays what it wishes and brings good fortune to the Tompkins children on the East Side in New York City.

In all of his works Archie Binns strives to present an authentic picture of American civilization, past and present.

Lightship (1934), his first novel, is a story based upon the author's youthful experiences; it concerns the nine members of a lightship crew and their views on work, philosophy, religion, and love. The ship and its men serve as a miniature world for the examination of civilization. The vessel goes adrift in a hurricane; in a dramatic climax the crew members struggle heroically to save the ship and their own lives. One episode—the story of two sailors on a voyage up the Columbia River—was reprinted separately as *Backwater Voyage* (1936).

In *The Laurels Are Cut Down* (1937) two Pacific Northwest brothers who are in love with the same girl enlist to fight the Germans in World War I, and are sent instead for service to Russian Siberia. One is killed; the other returns disillusioned, to find the girl he loves already married, though still in love with him. This book was awarded the Prix Femina Américain and was a selection of the Literary Guild. *The Land is Bright* (1939) is based on a diary kept by a young woman in a wagon-train party that followed the Oregon Trail in the great migration of 1852. The novel pictures the hardships of the overland route, the emigrants' troubles with the Indians, their clashes among themselves, and the great cholera epidemic of that year. From the book also emerges a sense of the vastness of the country from the Mississippi to the Pacific, its contours, and its beauty.

Mighty Mountain (1940) might be called the spiritual sequel to *The Land Is Bright;* here, however, the voyage to the Northwest is by sea. It is the story of Elmer Hale, a young New Englander, who sails in the 1850's to see the world and who jumps ship when he sees the Puget Sound country in Washington. There he marries, takes part in the Indian War, and learns how to tame the wilderness to provide his needs. *Timber Beast* (1944) is the story of Charlie Dow, the hard-fisted logging operator who must struggle to hold his business when a deceitful partner tries to appropriate it. His other troubles include his young second wife's love for his own son Paul, and a conflict in philosophy between father and son. A secondary theme involves the violent clash between the "Wobblies" and the logging operators. This novel was a selection of the Book League.

You Rolling River (1947) is set in the early 1890's, the heyday of the great fleet of sailing ships carrying grain from the inland empire of the Northwest to the countries of Europe. It is the story of life along the lower Columbia River, from Portland to the treacherous bar; of the jaunty young pilot who knows that bar as few others do, and his beautiful wife who is jealous of his devotion to the sea; of the two brothers who wish to become sailors, but whose father wants them to enter staid professions; of the boy who wants to become a lawyer and the girl who loves him; and of the majestic Columbia, whose deep current shapes their lives.

MICHAEL BLANKFORT

RKO Radio Pictures, Inc.

was born on December 10, 1907, in New York City. A graduate of the University of Pennsylvania, he taught psychology at Bowdoin College and at Princeton, where he earned his master's degree. After several years spent in producing, writing, and directing plays in New York, he wrote his first novel. During World War II he was a captain in the Marine Corps; during off hours at Camp Pendleton he wrote *The Widow-Makers. The Big Yankee* (1947) is a biography of Brigadier General Evans F. Carlson, the New Englander who brought religious and democratic principles into the organization of his famous Gung Ho Marine Raiders. Related in full are Carlson's adventures as a soldier in Nicaragua, as a navy intelligence agent with the Chinese Red armies, and as a beloved leader of men on Makin Island, Guadalcanal, Tarawa, and Saipan.

Mr. Blankfort has lived in Southern California since 1938, where he writes, in addition to his novels, an occasional motion-picture scenario. He has traveled widely, his most recent trip being to the new state of Israel, which serves as the background of a novel now in preparation. Of all his works, he is most proud of his two daughters; and the only virtue to which he will confess is his love for, patience with, and understanding of all human beings below the age of twenty-one.

I Met A Man (1937), his first novel, is a study of loyalties against the background of the first use of poisoned gas in World War I. *The Brave and the Blind* (1940), one of the first American novels to deal with the inner life of fascists, is an account of the defense of the Alcazar in the Spanish civil war. *A Time to Live* (1943) is the story of Ernie Cripton, whose life reaches a crisis the day Pearl Harbor is attacked. Through his memory of his dead wife, his loneliness, his loss of friends, and his resistance to the future are revealed the conflicts, tensions, and indecisions of the 1930's. *The Widow-Makers* (1946) is the story of three orphaned children who are innocent victims of the international intrigue leading to the preparation for World War III. Torn by their affection for a man and a woman who are enemies of each other, they are enabled to chart their proper course through their understanding of the heart and mind of their murdered father. They hide the secret paper accounting for his death.

JEAN BOLEY

Ilse Mayer

was born in Bayonne, New Jersey, on May 25, 1914. She attended Sweet Briar College in Virginia and graduated from Barnard College of Columbia University. For many years she made her home in Buenos Aires. She now lives in California, where she writes humorous stories for *The New Yorker* and other magazines.

The Restless (1946) is a psychological story of Emily Hollin, an American living in Argentina, who reaches a critical moment in becoming aware that there is no one permanent answer to the restlessness that besets the human spirit. Satiric pictures of American businessmen and their families in South America supply background in *The Baby Lamb* (1948) for the story of Mary Buttonfield, a young woman who realizes that there is something better than the mean lives which the majority of people live; she exhibits, however, a lack of courage and certainty which would enable her to find and remain on this upper level. Her final marriage is simultaneously an outward triumph and an inner disaster.

ISABEL BOLTON

Leja Gorska

is the pseudonym of Mary Britton Miller, who was born in August, 1883, in New London, Connecticut, where her parents had taken a summer cottage. Her father was a distinguished lawyer in New York City; her mother came from Springfield, Massachusetts. When Mary was four, both parents died within an hour of each other, leaving five children. She was a twin and the youngest, for she was born a few minutes after her sister. They were identical twins, and her relationship to her sister remains the most important experience of a long lifetime. Following the death of the parents, the children were sent to Springfield, where their grandmother resided in a very lovely old house. She presently died, and the care of the Miller children was taken over by rich relatives. All this Mary Britton Miller has described in her first novel. "The position of poor relative was shared with my twin sister," writes Miss Miller "and this extraordinary experience of twinship remains for me the answer to almost every question that I can ask myself as to why I became at last a novelist possessed of a great deal that I am still determined to say. My sister was drowned when we were fourteen years old. Those early years with her are my treasury, I may say, of swift and accurate response to human behavior, of a queer sense of seeing into and through the human beings who accompany me through life.

"I had a silly education—private schools and uninspiring instruction and environment. Little that was important for the development of the spirit was offered. Much, however, was mine to observe. I read a great deal, discovering my own favorite authors and learning from good books the delight in confirming the truth and accuracy of my own observations. There was great tragedy in the lives of my brothers and sisters. Grief came to me early. Now that I am old and see others passing through great sorrows, I have the curious sense of having passed through the profound experience of grief—of tragedy, indeed—at an earlier age than most people."

Her first books were volumes of poetry: *Songs of Infancy* (1928), *Menagerie* (1928), *Without Sanctuary* (1932), *Intrepid Bird* (1935), and *The Crucifixion* (1944). It was not until 1940 that she began to think of writing prose fiction. Her first novel is autobiographical, and she originally intended to follow it with other tomes of self-revelation and confession. This idea was abandoned, however, and because of the break with her literary past in her second novel she adopted the *nom de plume*, "Isabel Bolton."

In the Days of Thy Youth (1943), her first novel, pictures satirically the socially prominent Augustus and Sarah Russell of Massachusetts in the 1880's. Rachel, a sister of Augustus, and her husband die and leave five young children to be reared. Sarah dictatorily assumes command for ten years. *Do I Wake or Sleep* (1946) is a novel with an allegorical meaning and is written in a modified stream-of-consciousness style. It portrays several levels of thought and feeling in the conversation of a few New Yorkers in 1939 during the World's Fair. The opinions, which are reported by Millicent Munroe, relate to the plight of the times as they impinge upon the tribulations of a woman whose child is in Nazi Austria.

The Christmas Tree (1949) is an allegory of the world going to smash in the way Larry Danforth's life comes to an assured end in the electric chair after he pushes to death his wife's new husband. The story portrays three days of increasing emotional excitement in December, 1945, when Mrs. Danforth reviews her unhappy life as she plans a Christmas tree for her grandson. Her son, Larry, showed homosexual tendencies which gave her a sense of guilt and led Anne to divorce him.

CHARLES BONNER

was born in Brooklyn, New York, on October 14, 1896. His forebears were identified with the financial growth of the city as bankers and members of the New York Stock Exchange. His maternal grandfather, a native of North Carolina and an officer on General Lee's staff during the War between the States, later became president of the New York Cotton Exchange.

Mr. Bonner's family encouraged his early revolt from the business tradition, and a novel, produced at the age of eleven, was printed. Educated at the Storm King School at Cornwall-on-Hudson, New York, and at Williams College, he graduated in 1919, interrupting his college career for eighteen months to serve as a second lieutenant in the infantry in World War I. At Williams he edited various undergraduate publications. He turned to newspaper work for his literary apprenticeship and worked as a reporter on the Springfield *Republican,* the New York *Sun,* and other newspapers, and as a correspondent for the Foreign Press Service in Spain. Returning to this country, he formed the publicity firm of Riis and Bonner, and engaged in that business for several years.

Meanwhile he had devoted his leisure time to a study of creative writing. In 1932 he gave up his business interests to devote all his time to authorship, and soon his short stories, dealing mainly with the problems of human relationships, began to appear in the popular magazines. During World War II he served with the Office of War Information, the Foreign Economic Administration, and in Africa for the Office of Strategic Services.

In his novels Mr. Bonner argues that effectiveness in life is achieved only through selection of a goal and adherence to it. It is better, he says, to make mistakes than not to act. To achieve happiness, it is important to avoid cerebral sclerosis, to keep the always-open mind.

The Fanatics (1932), his first novel, sets the pattern for much of his later work by describing the family unit as the social microcosm of most significance in the American scene. *Bull by the Horns* (1937), which strikes a lighter note, portrays the fortunes of a college professor who resigns from the tedium of academic life to plunge into a world of action for which he is ill-prepared. *Legacy* (1940), perhaps the best known and loved of Mr. Bonner's novels, is the sympathetic story of a widowered father struggling to rear his sons in the American tradition of loyalty and patriotism. *Angel Casey* (1941) describes the battle of a vital and unconventional western girl to win a place in the snobbish culture of the East. *Ambition* (1946) deals with false standards of success. *The Last Romantic* (1949) examines the difficulties facing a crusader in this materialistic age.

ARNA BONTEMPS

was born on October 13, 1902, in Alexandria, Louisiana. His father was a stonemason at the time, his mother a public-school teacher. The name Arna, which has given him a great deal of trouble despite the fact that names like Alva, Asa, Numa, and Ilya have accustomed people to the *a* ending on masculine names, is probably the result of dropping the last two letters from the name Arnaud. Of his ancestors he says as little as is customary for colored Americans to say when their roots are deep in French Louisiana, but there were Frenchmen, Spaniards, Indians, and free-born Negroes among them. Taken to California at the age of three, he was educated in the schools of that state, including San Fernando Academy, the

University of California at Los Angeles, and Pacific Union College at Angwin. He received a bachelor's degree in 1923.

Much later he attended the University of Chicago long enough to earn a master's degree in the Graduate School of Library Science. Meanwhile he held several minor teaching posts in New York, Alabama, and Chicago. For a time he was a supervisor on the Illinois Writers' Project, and in 1943 he became chief librarian at Fisk University in Nashville, Tennessee. Twice he was granted fellowships by the Julius Rosenwald Fund and once, in 1949–50, by the John Simon Guggenheim Foundation. He has six children, and has written extensively in the juvenile field: *Popo and Fifina* (1932), *You Can't Pet a Possum* (1934), *Sad-Faced Boy* (1937), *Golden Slippers* (1941), *The Fast Sooner Hound* (1942), and *Slapper Hooper* (1946); the last two were done in collaboration with Jack Conroy. *We Have Tomorrow* (1944) and *Story of the Negro* (1948) might be called in-between books. In 1946 the musical, "St. Louis Woman" by Arna Bontemps and Countee Cullen, was produced on Broadway; it was based on Bontemps' novel *God Sends Sunday*. He collaborated with Langston Hughes in compiling the anthology, *The Poetry of the Negro* (1949).

Mr. Bontemps' central theme is the effort of suppressed or enslaved people to free themselves. His examples thus far have been Negro people who try to emancipate themselves from bondage of one kind or another. He has preferred to deal with this struggle from a certain historical distance, which emphasizes his preoccupation with the past. *God Sends Sunday* (1931) was called by one critic "a blues song itself." It was described by others as the last novel of the Harlem Renaissance; it was in fact the last book written out of that literary ferment, but it was not related to Harlem. The author was trying to break away from the current vogue in the treatment of Negro materials. The novel dealt with an undersized jockey who acquired with horses the authority he lacked with people and who tried to free his cramped spirit through gaudy living.

Black Thunder (1935) takes the tone and mood of a Negro spiritual. It details an actual slave uprising in Virginia in 1800 under the leadership of a tragically heroic coachman named Gabriel Prosser. Slave life is described with all its longings for freedom at a time when the air is filled with rumblings of the French Revolution. The organization and effort of the slaves of the region toward revolt is the main substance of the novel. *Drums at Dusk* (1939) treats a successful attempt by slaves at armed emancipation; it deals with events leading up to the outbreak of the Haitian revolution. As in the earlier novel, the author stresses the soil and climate in which the dream of freedom dissolves into bloody reality. *Chariot in the Sky* (1950) is based on the adventures of the Fisk Jubilee Singers, who introduced the Negro spiritual to the musical world of America and Europe.

BURKE BOYCE

Velie

was born in St. Louis, Missouri, on June 19, 1901. He attended eight schools, three private and five public, before entering Harvard, where he received his bachelor's degree in 1922 and his master's a year later. For two years he taught at Harvard and also lectured at Radcliffe College. Later on he taught in the Department of Adult Education at New York University, and twice, for brief periods, at Storm King School at Cornwall-on-the-Hudson, New York, to help out in the war emergency. On leaving Harvard, after he had competed in the Olympic matches in Paris as a member of the American fencing team and made a trip around the world, he worked on the staffs of Ivy Lee and John Price Jones.

Mr. Boyce joined the National Broadcasting Company soon after its formation, and for eight years was editor of the script department, writing, buying, and blue-penciling radio drama. Exclusive of the radio interim, he has been writing fiction since leaving college. *The New Yorker* magazine ran two long series of his poems for several years: "Downtown Lyrics" and "Pavement Portraits." During World War II he was busy as Red Cross disaster chairman and member of the county war council from his vicinity. He is married and has two children, and makes his home about ten miles above West Point, near the Hudson, in Orange County, New York.

Interest in the Revolutionary history of the Hudson valley (he is a member of the Board of Managers of the Historical Society of Newburg Bay and the Highlands) led to the writing of his first novel, *The Perilous Night* (1942). This is a study of the problems and conflicts that confront a peaceable, settled county family when the consequence of making a decision between war and peace sweeps its turmoil into the valley.

Miss Mallett (1948) portrays a public-school teacher in the first thirty years of this century, whose devotion and ideals lead her to dedicate her life to the profession in spite of discouragements, drawbacks, aging loneliness, and the obstacles of politics and forced poverty. *Cloak of Folly* (1949) is a biographical novel about Edward de Vere, 17th Earl of Oxford, the dazzling, contradictory, and mysterious man who acted as propaganda minister for Queen Elizabeth in preparing the minds of Englishmen to withstand the onslaught of the Spanish Armada, and who is thought by many Elizabethan students to hold the solution to some of the unsolved riddles of Shakespeare. This novel was selected as a choice of the Book League of America.

KAY BOYLE

was born on February 19, 1903, in St. Paul, Minnesota. Since she left there at the age of six months and never returned, it can scarcely be called her home. Philadelphia, Atlantic City, Washington, and Cincinnati, in all of which she attended school, were the places she knew best, while some early years spent in the Pocono Mountains of Pennsylvania gave her a taste for the country, for hills, and for horses which she has never lost. The family traveled frequently to Europe; she visited England and Scotland, but for some reason did not go to Ireland, the home country on her father's side.

"In my childhood," says Miss Boyle, "I thought of my family as quite a usual American family, but obviously we were not, for we had no fixed dwelling place, and my father had neither a profession nor a trade. My grandfather, Jesse Peyton Boyle, was trained for the priesthood in England, but became, instead, a lawyer and the founder of the West Publishing Company of St. Paul. He was the life-force of our family as well as the provider. He was one of the few charming reactionaries whom I have ever met, and I have written a great deal about him. I loved him as I never did my father, but his rule was a rigid one, as my sister and I learned as we grew up. He insisted that the lives of those about him be of his making.

"With the devotion of a liberal mother to encourage us, we left Cincinnati for New York with our drawings and manuscripts in our portfolios, and with great faith in each other and in what we were going to do. We had always written and painted, for our mother's passionate interest in the creative artists of our time stirred us from our earliest years. We had done volumes of poetry, written novels, illustrated every book we admired, and issued a magazine which our grandfather had had mimeographed every month. In

New York I did freelance reviewing for *The Dial* and other magazines and papers; I wrote poetry which was printed by Harriet Monroe in *Poetry* magazine; and I served as secretary to a fashion writer. Then followed a job on the magazine *Broom;* and in 1922 I married Richard Brault, a French engineering student who had graduated from Cincinnati University, and we went to France to live.

"It would be impossible to say when I started to write, or that I decided I wanted to be a writer. I simply knew that my mother loved reading what I wrote, and I did it for her. It seemed as logical and natural as going for a walk, or playing cards, or reading a book. In fact, after nearly forty years of it, I feel slightly guilty if I am not writing, and impatient if I see nothing but interruptions ahead."

In 1931 she married Laurence Vail, an American artist and writer. She continued to live in France, then in Austria, then in England, eventually returning to settle in France in 1937. As she had not returned to America since leaving New York in 1922, her books and stories were about the people of the countries in which she lived, and revealed a growing interest in their political aspects. In 1941 she returned to America. She is now married to Joseph M. Franckenstein, a former professor and an Austrian refugee whom she had known for some years in Europe and who became an American citizen in 1943. They have two children, both born in New York while he was serving with the ski troops in the American Mountain Infantry. She has four children from previous marriages. In 1950 her home was in Germany, where her husband was with the American Military Government.

Miss Boyle was awarded a Guggenheim fellowship in 1934. A year later "The White Horses of Vienna" won the O. Henry Memorial prize award for the best short story of the year, and again in 1941 she won the prize with "Defeat." Her collections of short stories include *Wedding Day* (1930), *The First Lover* (1933), *The White Horses of Vienna* (1937), and *Thirty Stories* (1946). *Glad Day* (1938) is a book of poems, and *The Youngest Camel* (1939) is a children's story.

Miss Boyle is a modernist with a poetic style which inclines to obscurity in the earlier stages and which is highly romantic. She has written of love in all of its possible phases. The themes of the imminence of death and of sexual relationships reflect her aim to report all things, however perverted, however strange, however low. She has written of all people and all their virtues, their sins, their crimes, their loves. There is also a deep love of nature, of mountains, snow, and forests. Even in stories the theme of which may be marital maladjustment, the devotion to the country in which the drama is played exceeds the author's concern with the drama itself. A preponderant part of her writing is descriptive, although she does not conceive of scenery merely as background. In her character portrayals a kind of compassion permits Miss Boyle to enter into the life of others with an intensity as violent as if the life were her own. This compassion gives a moving quality to her skillful portrayals of the blight of Nazism and fascism in Europe.

In Miss Boyle's first novel, *Plagued by the Nightingale* (1931), an American girl married to a Frenchman decides not to have children in order not to transmit a blood taint existing in his family; Nicholas is a dependent and money will be provided only if there is a child, and so Bridget reaches an unpleasant decision and acts upon it. *Year Before Last* (1932) concerns Hannah, likewise an American girl married to a Frenchman: she leaves her husband to be with Martin, a young poet and editor, who is hopelessly ill and soon to die. Their love binds them together even when his wealthy aunt withdraws support from them. They live in cheap, sordid hotels until the inevitable end. *Gentlemen, I Address You Privately* (1934) is a story of wandering Lesbians and of seduction, treated with restraint. In these first novels, as in others which followed, the stories are a part of the ever-recurring themes of betrayal and loyalty.

My Next Bride (1934) is the story of expatriates in Paris and especially of Victoria John, a midwestern girl, whose common sense soon disappears in a strange colony of utopians. Though in poverty, she falls in love with a married man, a man of wealth as well as a poet, seeks escape through promiscuity, becomes pregnant, and finally comes to a realization of fundamental values through her friendship with the married man's wife. *Death of a Man* (1936) recounts the meeting of a young, neurotic American girl with an English husband and an Austrian Nazi sympathizer, Dr. Prochaska. Because of her love for the doctor, she sends her husband away, but the doctor's devotion to the cause eventually separates the two lovers.

Monday Night (1938) is the story of two Americans in Paris who become involved by accident in the hunt for a French murderer. *The Crazy Hunter* (1940) contains three short novels. The title story concerns an English girl's love for a blind horse; "The Bridegroom's Body" brings two frustrated women together through the battling of swans; and "Big Fiddle" tells of an innocent American jazz player accused of a murder in Paris.

Primer for Combat (1942) relates through the diary of an American woman in France the blighting influence of Nazism on conquered territory. More anti-Nazi data is contained in *Avalanche* (1944), the story of a French-American girl who returns to France in the early days of the French resistance to seek the man she loves. *A Frenchman Must Die* (1946) traces a young American engineer's escape from a German prison camp, his membership in the French Maquis, and his activity as a hunter of collaborationists. These two novels, both *Saturday Evening Post* serials, have been termed "elegant potboilers," but they served the author's stated purpose in writing them as purveyors of a sympathetic explanation of the spirit and life of a country in which she had lived for nearly twenty years.

1939 (1948) tells of the outbreak of war in Europe, of an Austrian skier who has lived for some years with a Frenchwoman in the alpine country of France, and of his ultimate decision to offer his services to the French army. *His Human Majesty* (1949) describes the life, the tragedies, the hopes, and the dreams of a band of ski troopers recruited from many nations and joined under one flag in the mountains of Colorado in wartime 1944. In this novel the dual themes are loyalty and betrayal.

GERALD WARNER BRACE

was born on September 23, 1901, in Islip, Long Island, New York, the descendant of an old Connecticut family. His great-grandfather and grandfather were writers. Gerald grew up in Dobbs Ferry, New York, and in New York City. He attended the Loomis School in Windsor, Connecticut; Amherst College, from which he graduated in 1922; the Harvard School of Architecture; and the Harvard Graduate School, where he received his master's degree in 1924 and achieved his doctorate in 1930. As a teacher he has served at Radcliffe, Williams, Dartmouth, Mount Holyoke, and Amherst, and at present is professor of English in Boston University. His hobbies include painting, mountain climbing, skiing, and boating; he has designed many boats, including a thirty-one-foot sloop which he now sails. He does most of his writing during summer vacations, which he spends with his wife and three children at Deer Isle in Penobscot Bay, Maine.

"My original impulse to write," says Mr. Brace, "was more a matter of feeling than idea. Probably my first novel should have been a poem. I was in love with the North and with the people who had learned to adapt themselves to the northern necessities of place, climate, and the physical arrangements that control so much of behavior. I try to tell the truth simply, for what is most commonly true about people is overlooked in favor of the unusual and the extreme. The artist's main job is to create with validity and insight. He makes life. Primarily it is not his business to argue with it or denounce it or turn it into propaganda. It is his task to create life in all its forms and colors and sounds and smells by using his imagination above all his other faculties."

Mr. Brace's first novel, *The Islands* (1936), grew out of a vivid impression of the Maine scene and environment, and this feeling, which is romantic and transcendental in a Wordsworthian sense, gives richness to the landscape pictures in this and later books. The story is that of a Maine lad who is adopted by a wealthy Boston spinster and sent to Harvard, but who returns to his own people and to the comforting simplicity of his native seacoast fisherfolk. *The Wayward Pilgrims* (1938) brings together at a Vermont railroad station a college teacher and a young lady who has lost her money; this quiet plot is decorated with beautiful landscape pictures. Another Vermont story, *Light on a Mountain* (1941), pictures the unpleasant disruptive force of Marjie, wife of Morton, in the Gaunt household. She wants to move to town and have gayety instead of drabness. The others like life on the farm. *The Garretson Chronicle* (1947) pictures three generations of the Garretson family in a village not far from Boston through the life stories of grandfather, father, and son. This chronicle is concerned chiefly with the differing concepts of each generation. *A Summer's Tale* (1949) is a light, half-real, half-fantastic story, the action of which takes place on an island far off the Maine coast.

HOUSTON BRANCH

John E. Reed

was born on March 5, 1903, in St. Paul, Minnesota, where his family had settled in territorial days. During school vacations he worked as a farm hand in the North Dakota harvest fields, as a tuna fisherman in California, and as a tool dresser in the Tampico oil fields. The struggle to combine night police reporting with schooling led him to give up the latter in his first year in college. As a newspaperman he worked through the South and Middle West, finally joining the staff of the San Antonio *Express,* where as political editor he inadvertently helped elect the first Republican congressman from Texas since the Civil War. Through Tex O'Reilly, a newspaperman and soldier of fortune, he was admitted to the inner circles of a Mexican revolutionary junta, an experience which led to the writing of his first play, *Dona Maria* (1922). The play was a failure but it gave him a taste for the theater. He became a theatrical press agent, handling the transcontinental tours of Sousa's Band, the San Carlo Opera Company, and a circus. When several of his short stories attracted the attention of Hollywood, he moved to the film capital. He is the author of more than a hundred screen plays. Mr. Branch is highly respected in the field of public relations, and is consulted by many major industrial corporations. During World War II he wrote propaganda and training films for the army. For the past decade he has been director of the American Library Foundation and has advocated federal aid for rural-school libraries.

As a novelist Mr. Branch considers himself primarily a storyteller. He is interested in odd and singular phases of individual free enterprise in our past. Thus, the fact that a pleasure boat's visit was once more important to the economic existence of some of our cities than a railroad led to the writing of *River Lady,* and the discovery that a Confederate cabinet member understood modern military logistics resulted in *Diamond Head.*

River Lady (with Frank Waters, 1942), his first novel, deals with free-lumber rafting on the Mississippi and describes a river pleasure boat whose mistress, Sequin, had a great deal more to do with the founding of several river towns than local historians will admit. *Diamond Head* (with Frank Waters, 1948), an historical romance of a naval officer and a whaling captain's daughter, has for a background the exploits of the Confederate cruiser *Shenandoah* which pursued the New England whaling fleet into the waters of the North Pacific. Its victorious assaults occurred after the surrender at Appomattox.

MILLEN BRAND

Lotte Jacobi

was born on January 19, 1906, in Jersey City, New Jersey. About 1912 his father bought a farm near Long Branch, New Jersey, and here Brand rode a plow horse, dug grubs from peach trees, raised potatoes, and attended a country school; he also took his younger brother, Earl, on long exploring expeditions through the pine woods country. The Brand and Myers families both had farm and country lineages; on the Myers side, Brand is descended from a private in the Revolutionary War. His parents later moved to Montclair, New Jersey, where he graduated from high school in 1924. He went to Columbia University on a scholarship and received the degrees of Bachelor of Arts and Bachelor of Literature in 1929. He edited *The Columbia Varsity* magazine and won four writing prizes in his senior year, including the Van Rensselaer Prize for lyric poetry. For eight years after his graduation, he was a publicity and advertising writer for the New York Telephone Company and, using his leisure during this time, slowly made a reputation as a poet and short-story writer. His work has appeared often in "little magazines" and anthologies.

During World War II Mr. Brand worked as a writer for the Office of Civilian Defense in Washington, handling many important campaigns for its fourteen million volunteers. He also edited service, operation, and repair manuals for a navy torpedo bomber. In 1946 he was called to Hollywood to collaborate with Frank Partos on the script of Mary Jane Ward's *The Snake Pit,* a picture which spearheaded many campaigns for the improvement of the care of the mentally ill. Brand lives at present on a farm in Pennsylvania, where he is working on a book of poems, *Local Lives.*

Mr. Brand's style of writing is clean and economical. Working without sentimentality, he never overplays emotional situations, however tender, glowing, or bitter they may be in substance.

The original draft of his first novel, *The Outward Room* (1937), was written in two and a half months. Mr. Brand then spent two and a half years rewriting it. This widely known forerunner of the present-day psychiatric novel tells the story of a young woman's cure and return to her rightful place in society after seven years in a mental hospital. The novel was a Book-of-the-Month-Club choice and was dramatized by Sidney Kingsley as *The World We Make. The Heroes* (1939) goes behind the scenes in a soldiers' home, picturing George Burley's experiences as a veteran who lost an arm, learned cabinetmaking, and then in the great depression lived in the home, where the quiet day-to-day isolation from normal life affects the spirits of the inmates. In a poignant struggle, Burley is able to fight his way back to a position in his own community. *Albert Sears* (1947) depicts the interconnected fate of a white Indiana frontiersman who had come east to a large city and a Negro, Thomas Manhurst, who moved into the house next to him during a real-estate feud. The threads of motivation which, in spite of prejudice, cause Sears to ally himself temporarily with Manhurst are shown sensitively and honestly.

MARC BRANDEL

Gloria Hoffman

was born in London, England, on March 28, 1919, the son of J. D. Beresford, the English novelist. He was educated in France and Switzerland, at Repton in England, and spent a year studying English literature at Cambridge University. At the age of eighteen, fed up with the artificial constrictions of a caste society, he left England for good and settled in the United States. In America he worked at a number of jobs from New York to California and spent a year at Westminster College in Fulton, Missouri. He was in the Merchant Marine during World War II, and at one time and another he has traveled over most of Europe, in Africa, India, Persia, and over a great part of North and Central America.

His main interest as a writer has always been in the enigma of free will, which he has explored from different points of view in each of his novels. He has little concern as a novelist with the examination of the fabric of society as it exists, believing that that fabric is merely an ever-changing symptom of certain much deeper and more permanent problems.

Rain Before Seven (1945), his first novel, is a frankly satirical approach to the problem of free will and shows what might happen if a young man, believing absolutely in predestination, were to come to accept the idea that it is his destiny to be the cause of a number of innocent people's deaths. The protagonist, making no attempt to escape his fate, finds himself at the end forced into wholesale murder by his lack of belief in his own power to act freely.

The Rod and the Staff (1947) explores the subject of free will from what might be termed a viewpoint of the Kierkegaardian idea of "subjective truth." The novel is concerned with a revolution in South America which fails to achieve its ends, less because of the abstract ideals involved than because of the relentless subjective reasons that have led certain kinds of men to embrace them without conscious decision or choice.

The Barriers Between (1949) concerns a young man, blindly driven to it by certain psychological compulsions in himself, who comes to believe that he has committed a murder. In the course of his flight and through helping a girl even more unhappy and confused than he is, he begins to understand some of the motives behind his act and realizes at the end that he need not have done it—that he is possessed of free will in his action, if not in his impulses, so long as he is prepared to examine his own motives at each turn, and that he now is free to choose what to do with the rest of his life.

The Choice (1950) satirically deals with the enigma of free will with special reference to the dispassionate man. The setting is New York City's Greenwich Village.

ROBERT BRIGHT

Lotte Jacobi

was born on August 5, 1902, in Sandwich, Massachusetts, the son of Edward Bright, a scholar, and Blanche Denio Bright, a daughter of Ebenezer Kellog Wright, President of the National Park Bank of New York City. When Robert was six months old, the family went abroad, and he did not return to this country until he was thirteen. His early schooling was in Göttingen, Germany, a university town where his father was studying. He continued his education in America at the Sandwich public schools, at Browne and Nichols in Cambridge, and at Andover, and completed it at Princeton University with a bachelor's degree in 1925. His major study was English, and his chief extracurricular activity was writing for newspapers, including the New York *World,* the Boston *Transcript,* and the Philadelphia *Ledger.*

His first job was as reporter on the Baltimore *Sun.* He left there to join the editorial staff of the Paris *Times.* Returned to America, he joined Condé Nast Publications, and from there went into advertising. He had never been able to think of creative writing as anything but a luxury he could not afford. This attitude was hardly relieved after he married Katherine Eastman Bailey and had two children. Yet it was his wife who finally convinced him to take the chance. In order to live cheaply, they moved to California. Within a year he had written a short story that was accepted by *Esquire* magazine.

But his interest was in novels because he wanted to create little worlds, not incidents. He wrote two novels before he wrote one that was published. By this time he had moved to New Mexico and bought an adobe house in a small village, Rio Chiquito, inhabited almost exclusively by Mexicans. His first published novel was the outcome of his love for this village and its people. As a relaxation, and to amuse his children, he wrote and illustrated two successful picture books for young children, *The Travels of Ching* (1943), the story of a Chinese doll, and *Georgie* (1945), the story of a small, bewildered ghost.

"In my writing," Mr. Bright has stated, "I strive for lucidity and simplicity. My best writing is invariably spontaneous. I achieve form not by careful planning but by means of an original situation illustrated by long-thought-out characters. These persons are mostly entirely invented except as they have sometimes mingled traits of various living people or, more frequently, of myself. Once my characters are alive, the story almost writes itself. I can't rewrite without losing life. While each of my books is markedly different from the others, they all propound the idea that human beings are masters of their fate only in a most limited sense and that to imagine otherwise makes a man ludicrously presumptuous or pathetically and sometimes cruelly cynical. My strongest characters are those who have made their peace, innocently or wisely, with the inevitable—that is to say, with death, or with the fact that life is at best a noble or dignified tragedy."

Mr. Bright's style is marked by lightness of touch and delicate verbal texture; a quiet humor reflects tenderness and tolerance. Especially notable is his capacity to dramatize the emotional quality of his characters, particularly as they awaken from childhood into the realities of adult responsibility.

The Life and Death of Little Jo (1944) tells the story of a boy, José, from the time he is born until he leaves his New Mexico village to go to war. The style is simple and lyrical, and the story funny and sad—like the people it describes. Superficially it is a regional novel; basically it is universal, timeless, and classical. It has been made into an opera by the composer, J. Donald Robb, and had its first performance at Albuquerque. *The Intruders* (1946), a *tour de force,* is the story of intolerance toward a white Negro doctor in a southwestern town. The plot is close-knit and grimly dramatic, but the story is more passionate than humanly warm. It is essentially an allegory and so the characters have a certain fixity. They do not change or grow but remain wholly in character. This book has been called the pioneer of a cycle of novels dealing with the white-Negro problem. *The Olivers* (1947) is set in France during the 1920's and tells the story of a charming hedonistic American painter, his bewildered midwestern schoolteacher wife, and their adolescent daughter, the heroine. She has the difficult problem of adjusting her normal, passionate, and maturing affections to an irresponsible and childlike environment. The picture of the simple peasants in the seacoast community serves as a foil to the strange Bohemianism of the family, whose emotional turmoil, arising from the artist's philandering tendency, leads the husband and wife to consider separating.

MYRON BRINIG

was born on December 22, 1900, in Minneapolis, Minnesota, the son of Rumanian parents. Both his father and mother came to America in the late 1880's. At first the father was a farmer, but about 1900 he moved to the copper-mining town of Butte, Montana, and opened a clothing store. In Butte, Myron, the youngest of seven children, grew up, attended public schools and high school, and read most of the novels in the public library. His first seventeen years brought acquaintance with many odd characters and a knowledge of mines, strikes, theaters, and the extraordinary physical aspects of Butte and the surrounding country. At seventeen he went east to study at New York University. After two years he transferred to the University of Pennsylvania, but illness forced his withdrawal. Later at Columbia University he began to write stories which he sold to popular magazines. In 1926, after selling stories for three years to *Munsey's Magazine,* he went to Europe, where he wrote *Singermann.* While this book was under consideration in a publishing house, he wrote and published *Madonna Without Child.* His broad interests are reflected in the diverse characters and social themes embodied in his novels.

Madonna Without Child (1929) portrays the need for fulfillment in life in the story of the unmarried stenographer, Mary Dunston, who at forty joyously takes charge of her boss's daughter and then suffers when the child goes away to school. *Singermann* (1929) is a detailed, impressive family chronicle of the Rumanian immigrants, Moses and Rebecca Singermann, and their seven children in Silver Bow, Montana. *Anthony in the Nude* (1930) is about a young man from Portland, Oregon, who destroys his chance for success in New York. *Wide Open Town* (1931) is a tale of an Irish miner who comes to Silver Bow, Montana, and experiences romance against a background of labor troubles in the mines and of the "white and eternal" mountains.

This Man Is My Brother (1932), a sequel to *Singermann,* recounts the return of the youngest son, Michael, now a successful novelist, and of his awareness of a change in the town and the family. *The Flutter of an Eyelid* (1933) concerns a Boston novelist in California who sees the story unfold of an elderly murderess and her youthful lover. *Out of Life* (1934) describes Sam Baggott's joy in becoming a father. *The Sun Sets in the West* (1935) is about Jim Hewitt's part in a labor war in 1932–33 in Copper City, Montana. *The Sisters* (1937) pictures three daughters of a druggist in Silver Bow and their marital ventures from 1904 to 1910. Louise, the bright one, marries a sports writer and goes to San Francisco; Grace, endowed with common sense, stays home with her banker husband; and Helen, who marries a copper king, has affairs with other men. *May Flavin* (1938) is a biographical novel about a Chicago policeman's daughter who marries Mike Flavin, a carefree drifter, and resourcefully raises her family alone.

Anne Minton's Life (1939) tells about a girl who stands on a window ledge of a Los Angeles hotel and reviews her life before falling to her death. *All Their Lives* (1941) describes two midwestern girls whose lives cross and recross in the years from 1900 to 1920. *The Family Way* (1942) satirizes New York City Bohemianism through the DeForests who are about to separate. *The Gambler Takes a Wife* (1943) is a melodramatic tale of Montana in the 1880's. *You and I* (1945) reunites in maturity after a long separation a boy and girl who are not related but who were reared as brother and sister. They now are prepared to understand each other.

Hour of Nightfall (1947) tells through the eyes of a neighbor the story of a beautiful woman whose egoism nearly spoils several lives. *No Marriage in Paradise* (1949) deals with the involved marital and love relationships of the Alexander family in Hawaii and in San Francisco. *Footsteps on the Stair* (1950) is a lusty, nostalgic story of two different families—one Irish, the other Jewish—and their robust life in rough-and-tumble Montana.

GWEN BRISTOW

was born in Marion, South Carolina, on September 16, 1903, the daughter of a preacher. She began to write as a child, and at Judson College, Marion, Alabama, from which she graduated, she wrote a play produced by the students. To earn her way through the School of Journalism of Columbia University, she was a nursemaid to rich women's children, wrote rags-to-riches biographies of businessmen for trade journals, and was secretary to a Central European baroness who had come to America after World War I. As a reporter from 1925 to 1933 on the New Orleans *Times-Picayune,* she competed for exclusive stories with Bruce Manning, then a newspaper reporter and now a motion-picture producer in Hollywood. They were married on January 14, 1929. Both were writing novels, and one Armistice Day she suggested the plot of a mystery novel based on the desire to murder a neighbor who persisted in playing his noisy radio. Together they wrote four such stories between 1929 and 1932. For a time after the Mannings went to Hollywood in 1934, she repressed her desire to write. Eventually, however, she planned three novels, each complete in itself, about typical families living in Louisiana from the time of the colonial settlement until the twentieth century.

Deep Summer (1937), the first of the Louisiana trilogy, describes the creation of the great plantation estates out of the wilderness as a background for the romantic tale of a Carolinian, Philip Larne, who elopes with Judith Sheramy, a fifteen-year-old Connecticut girl whose family has come to take up a royal grant bestowed by King George III. *The Handsome Road* (1938) is set in the period from 1859 to 1885 and portrays two women of the Larne and Upjohn families at opposite ends of the social scale. *The Side of Glory* (1940) continues with the Larnes and Upjohns to the end of World War I.

Tomorrow Is Forever (1943) tells of Elizabeth Herlong and her journey to California after word arrives that her husband has been killed in World War I; while building a new life, she comes face to face with her husband. *Jubilee Trail* (1950) is a story of California in the years from 1844 to 1848, just before the discovery of gold. It tells about Garnet Cameron, a New York girl who marries a western trader and goes to Los Angeles, at that time a Mexican village of about a thousand people.

LOUIS BROMFIELD

Blackstone Studios

was born on December 27, 1896, in Mansfield, Ohio, of pioneering stock which migrated to Ohio at the end of the eighteenth century from Virginia, Maryland, and New England. His father was a farmer. Louis attended the local public schools, and at an early age was aware of a struggle between the desire to write and the wish to farm. After a year at Cornell University College of Agriculture, he attended for a year the Columbia University School of Journalism. In 1917 he enlisted in an ambulance unit, served with the French Army, and was awarded the Croix de Guerre. On returning to America in 1919, he worked for the New York City News Service and the Associated Press. The idea of farming was not abandoned, but put forward into the future. During the next few years he was foreign editor and music critic with *Musical America,* assistant to a New York theatrical producer, and writer of art, theater, and book criticism for *The Bookman,* a magazine. For a brief space he was one of the original staff of *Time* magazine.

He married Mary Appleton Wood in 1921; they have three daughters. For a large part of the time thereafter until 1939 he resided abroad. He speaks three languages. His favorite sports are swimming, fishing, and skiing. He paints occasionally. In 1939 on the eve of the war he shifted his center of operations from France to the county of his birth. Here he purchased a farm and entered upon the enterprise of developing a modern farm community. He has devoted much time to agricultural problems and has written and lectured widely on this subject. His books on this theme include *Pleasant Valley* (1946), *A Few Brass Tacks* (1946), *Malabar Farm* (1948), and *Out of the Earth* (1950), all concerned with the world's crying need for food, with the shameful neglect and misuse of the soil, and with the need for more efficient and intelligent agricultural methods.

Beginning in 1919 he wrote novels steadily. After voluntarily suppressing four novels, he published the fifth, which therefore was his "first" novel. It was called *The Green Bay Tree* (1924) and is the story of a beautiful, rebellious, and unconventional woman set in the background of changing social and economic conditions in a big middle-western steel town and in Paris. *Possession* (1925) pictures a young Ohio woman who weds a devoted yet dull husband to achieve a musical career in New York. In *Early Autumn* (1926), which won the Pulitzer prize, a warm and spirited woman yields to her husband's family tradition, only to have a vivid stranger challenge her to escape. *A Good Woman* (1927) pictures the tragic influence of selfish, domineering Emma Downes upon her son and daughter-in-law. These four novels comprise a series named *Escape;* some of the characters reappear, as do the themes which show Mr. Bromfield's growing absorption in the social aspects of American life.

A very different novel followed, *The Strange Case of Miss Annie Spragg* (1928), which analyzes the effect on a dozen people in Brinoë, Italy, of the death of an elderly American lady with the stigmata of the crucifixion on her body. *Awake and Rehearse* (1929) contains thirteen short stories dealing with deaths or funerals. *Twenty-Four Hours* (1930) is a story of the New York of the 1920's, ranging from the waterfront through speakeasy life to fashionable Park Avenue and conservative Murray Hill. *A Modern Hero* (1932) describes an attractive but unprincipled adventurer who begins life as the illegitimate son of a leopard trainer and a German banker and ends as a murderer. *The Farm* (1933) is a semi-fictional account of an Ohio farm owned by the author's family from 1815 to 1915, and a history of the manners and social life of four generations of the family. *Here Today and Gone Tomorrow* (1934) contains four short novels about the 1920's, "a gay and senseless period," says Mr. Bromfield, "colored by booming prosperity and bootlegging, singularly confused and barren." *The Man Who Had Everything* (1935) has Tom Ashford regain assurance from his widowed French sweetheart of World War I. A successful playwright with a fine family and many friends, he became unhappy and unable to write. *It Takes All Kinds* (1939) contains nine short stories.

Two novels had their setting in India. *The Rains Came* (1937) portrays the efforts of Indians, Europeans, and Americans to raise the living standard of India, a land of floods and famine. *Night in Bombay* (1940) presents the drinking, gambling, intriguing, hating, and love-making of sophisticates at the Taj Mahal Hotel in Bombay, together with the tangled love story of three Americans. There followed a romantic novel about the New Orleans of the Civil War, *Wild Is the River* (1941), of which Mr. Bromfield has said, "All my life I wanted to write a wide-open unqualifiedly romantic novel, and in this book I realized that ambition." A short novel concerning the German occupation of Paris, *Until the Day Break* (1942), tells the story of an American dancer, her manager, and her French lover who engage in underground resistance activities.

Mrs. Parkington (1943) describes a fabulously rich eighty-four-year-old lady born in Nevada and still more energetic than her descendants. *What Became of Anna Bolton* (1944) relates the dissatisfaction of a girl who becomes rich and who then finds contentment in a life of altruistic self-sacrifice. *The World We Live In* (1944) is a collection of nine short stories. *Kenny* (1947) contains three stories, "Kenny," "Retread," and "The End of the Road." *Colorado* (1947) is a novel of Silver City in the 1880's in something of the old melodramatic style. *The Wild Country* (1948) describes the growth of thirteen-year-old Ronnie, a sensitive boy who is bewildered by the base elements in some people's lives and who breaks through his self-centered existence to a satisfactory relationship with adults.

RICHARD BROOKS

J. Balkan

was born in Philadelphia in 1912. He studied at Temple University and wrote sports news for the Philadelphia *Record*. Later he went to New York and took up radio work, becoming successively a news commentator, a director of radio shows, and a script writer for several important dramatic programs. When a screen writer in Hollywood, he enlisted in the United States Marine Corps. While he was a Marine sergeant, he wrote his first novel which stirred up considerable controversy and brought praise from Sinclair Lewis. After his discharge from the service Mr. Brooks returned to motion-picture writing.

Mr. Brooks' first two novels realistically and somewhat melodramatically portray the ugly aspects of anti-Semitism and political corruption. His indignation emerges in a shock technique which in machine-gun impact and frank language is similar to that of James M. Cain. Mr. Brooks indicates that the solution of social wrongs is to be achieved through the application of true democratic principles.

The Brick Foxhole (1945), his first novel, describes the conduct of Jeff Mitchell, a Marine, whose inactivity in camp drives him to indulge in a frenzied week end in Washington, D.C., and to find that his excesses have led to a charge of murder being placed against him. *The Boiling Point* (1948) portrays the bone-crushing fight between two political factions in a southwestern state. Both wish to enlist the support of Roy Nielsen, a war veteran and a sharecropper's son, but in the end he decides to stand with his own people. Wealthy Marge Kirby revolts against her class and helps Roy, her lover.

HARRY (PETER M'NAB) BROWN

was born on April 30, 1917, in Portland, Maine. He was educated in its public schools and was graduated from Portland High School in 1933. Until he entered Harvard University in 1936 he worked on a woman's penal farm in Connecticut. At the end of his first year in college he left to take a trailer trip across the continent, but returned in 1938 for an additional year of study. Then, his formal education ended, he went to New York, where his first job was that of office boy for *Time*. In 1940 he was on the staff of *The New Yorker*. He entered the engineer corps of the army in July, 1941, joined the staff of *Yank*, the army newspaper, upon its organization in May, 1942, and went to the British edition early in 1943 as an associate editor. During this period he created Artie Greengroin, the fictional Private First Class whose adventures delighted thousands of soldier readers of *Yank*. These sketches are collected in *Artie Greengroin, pfc* (1945). For a year he was with the Office of War Information in London, and during the last year of his army career he worked in the Anglo-American film unit, making "The True Glory," an official army film of the operations from D-Day to the final surrender of Germany. Following his discharge from the army, he moved in January, 1946, to Hollywood to work on films.

Mr. Brown's first work was poetry. At Harvard he was Pegasus or literary editor of *The Advocate* and a member of the Signet Society. While there he won the Lloyd McKim Garrison award for poetry, and in 1939 he shared the Shelley prize. With Dunstan Thompson in 1940–41 he edited the poetry magazine, *Vice Versa*. His first pamphlet of poems, *The End of a Decade* (1940), was followed by *The Poem of Bunker Hill* (1941), a verse description of the warm June day "when the nation was born." *The Violent* (1943) contains new poems; some of them show traces of Ransom, Auden, and Eliot. *Poems, 1941–1944* (1945) and *The Beast in His Hunger* (1949) are volumes of poetry. "A Sound of Hunting" (1946), a three-act play, pictures the activities of a group of soldiers in Italy and their attempt to rescue a comrade who fails to return from a scouting trip.

A Walk in the Sun (1944), his first novel, is a short, dramatic narrative of American soldiers in action for a few hours in Italy; a platoon lands on the beach, loses its lieutenant and three sergeants in quick succession, and then a corporal takes over and accomplishes the mission.

JOE DAVID BROWN

was born on May 12, 1915, and reared in Birmingham, Alabama. At twenty he was a police reporter for the *Post*. A year later he was city editor of the Dothan, Alabama, *Eagle*. From there he explored the country, working on newspapers in Atlanta, Chattanooga, and St. Louis, as press agent for a Mississippi River showboat, and as a guide and game warden. In 1939 he finally landed in New York and joined the *Daily News*.

When war came, his writing career consisted of signing up with the paratroopers. He was among the first twenty men to parachute down on France, was awarded the Purple Heart and the French Croix de Guerre with palm, and commissioned a second lieutenant in the field. For fifteen months after he was wounded, he made "a grand tour of military hospitals in France, England, and the United States." The only good thing about it, he says, was that he met his future wife who was an army nurse at Halloran Hospital.

His first short story appeared in *The Saturday Evening Post* and was later included in the *Best Post Stories* of the year. The day after it appeared, a publisher called him to ask if he would like to do a book based on its central character, the Parson. By the time he had sold his next story to *Collier's* and built up a backlog of seven assignments for the *Post,* he and his wife moved to Maryland, settled down in the middle of a 275-acre farm, and went to work. *Stars in My Crown,* his first novel, was the result.

It has been said of Mr. Brown that he is the only best-selling novelist to make a début since World War II who has not followed or attempted to broaden the road toward "realism." Asked about this statement, Mr. Brown replied: "To be blunt, I think the current rabbit-warren writing is pretty disgusting, and I think too many writers confuse 'realism' with sensationalism. Call me a clean writer, and I'll be happy. Or call me a story-teller, because basically that's what I want to be."

Stars in my Crown (1947) is the story of Parson Gray, a minister in a small southern town, who guided his life by the Golden Rule. He solved his community's problems, both large and trivial, by common sense and the application of Christian principles. The narrator is the preacher's adoring grandson. *The Freeholder* (1949) concerns Horatio Tench, born in an English prison, whose life was motivated by a search for freedom. To him the noblest poem he ever heard was the preamble to the American Constitution. Fired by the promise it contained, he finally killed a demoniac ropemaker who had adopted him and fled to the United States as a bonded servant. After a hard struggle, he finally won wealth, friends, and personal freedom—only to discover with the beginning of the Civil War that personal freedom was not enough, and that a man's beliefs must sometimes be defended on a national scale.

NANCY BRUFF

Sparta Photo

was born in Fairfield, Connecticut, a descendant of old Yankee stock. She was educated at various Connecticut schools, at the Nightingale-Bamford School in New York City, and at the Sorbonne. After four years in Paris, she returned to America, traveled about from east to west, and wrote with dogged, unrewarded constancy for ten years. In 1937 she was married to Thurston Clarke; they have two children. Her poems were collected in *My Talon in Your Heart* (1946).

The central theme in her work is man's perpetual search for his own salvation and, in a philosophical sense, his relation to his God. Nancy Bruff is growing and so are her books; this is the most important fact in her writing. In her opinion growth and change should be the first concern of a writer. She says: "It is easy to repeat a success. When you have mastered a soufflé, you can always concoct others of various heights and puffiness. But it is hard to develop new themes and ways of writing them,—hard but good for the author and essential to the vitality of his work."

The Manatee (1945), her first novel, is the story of a sadistic sea captain and his obsession by the figurehead on his ship. It was written in a semi-poetic style. *Cider from Eden* (1947) is again a psychological study, this time dealing with the effect of a mother's desertion of her husband and three sons. The book is concerned with the destiny of the three boys handicapped by this childhood scar. It is their story, and the mother enters into it rarely. *The Beloved Woman* (1949) is the story of the love of a colored porter in New York's Grand Central Station for a delicate and friendless white girl. The book quietly attempts to point a moral about injustice by stirring the reader's heart.

KATHARINE BRUSH

was born in Middletown, Connecticut, the daughter of Charles S. Ingham, headmaster of a private school for boys. She grew up in Washington, Baltimore, and Newbury, Massachusetts, and was graduated from Centenary Collegiate Institute at Hackettstown, New Jersey. A prolific writer even in youth, she served on the staff of the Boston *Traveler* from 1918 to 1920. On her marriage in 1920 to Thomas Stewart Brush, a newspaper publisher, she moved to East Liverpool, Ohio. They had one son. In 1923 she began to publish light verse and short stories, her first sales being to *College Humor*, a magazine. In 1927 she and her husband moved to New York City; a year later they were divorced. In 1929 she married Hubert

Charles Winans, the banker and economist.

Her pungent, deftly etched, satirical stories and novels became very popular, and the story "Night Club" is frequently reprinted as an example of ironic portraiture. Prosperity filled her life with clothes, European trips, and social activity. In a disarmingly frank autobiography, *This Is On Me* (1940), she tells of the effect of her new life and the paralysis of production her writing suffered in spite of an agonizing six or eight hours of daily effort. She recaptured her former verve, did movie scripts, and conducted a syndicated weekly newspaper column, "Out of My Mind." In 1941 she divorced Mr. Winans. In 1949 she was writing a weekly short story in the late Mark Hellinger's spot in the Hearst Sunday papers, and she was working on a very long novel which will require six years to complete.

Miss Brush is a red-haired woman with a love of clothes, jewelry, the theater, and ocean voyages. She writes painstakingly and intensely for five hours each day, taking a month for a short story and at least a year for a novel. She calls herself "the world's slowest writer." Her short stories are collected in *Night Club* (1929) and *Other Women* (1933). *Out of My Mind* (1943) contains thirty-five short pieces of opinion on persons, places, and foods.

Her first novel, *Glitter* (1926), tells of a young lad's college days and his experiences with a variety of attractive girls. *Little Sins* (1927) moves into the area of spoiled youngsters and shows that one society girl's modern ways bring her to grief while a virtuous working girl steadily gains in happiness. *Young Man of Manhattan* (1930) tells of the hasty marriage of Toby McLean, a sports writer, and Ann Vaughn, a movie columnist. *Red-Headed Woman* (1931) portrays an Ohio stenographer who marries a rich man and then divorces him for a cash settlement.

Don't Ever Leave Me (1935) takes place during one night at a country-club dance and describes the events resulting in tragedy and the people who love and hate the glamorous and beautifully dressed Mrs. Billy Cunningham. *You Go Your Way* (1941) describes the married life of Connie, a rich and whimsical girl, and the husband with whom she maintains a mood of continuous courtship. The period between the two world wars is bridged in *The Boy from Maine* (1942), a story of an awkward Maine boy, Hobey Hadley, who at seventeen joins the navy, becomes a master of ceremonies in a night club, attains fame on the radio, and marries a twice-divorced rich girl. *This Man and This Woman* (1944) contains four novelettes about young women who are either divorced or about to be divorced.

ARTHUR HERBERT BRYANT

was born in 1917, in Alexandria, Virginia. He attended the Episcopal High School of Alexandria and the University of Virginia from 1936 to 1939. In 1940 he entered the navy as an ensign and saw fifty months of service overseas in PT boats and destroyers. He was discharged from active duty with the rank of lieutenant commander. Since his discharge he has devoted his time to writing. He wrote a novel of World War II, but this he has not published.

"My burden as a writer," he has stated, "is to synthesize the emotional and intellectual aspects of experience, and above all to express the poetic truths of the inner life. My ambition as a writer is to transcend the category of the purely contemporary."

Double Image (1947), his first published novel, is a Greek tragedy set in a lonely tourist camp on the bleak seacoast of northern Florida, observing the unities of time and place, and involving the characters in an inevitable chain of unfortunate events, culminating in disaster. The narrative moves to its conclusion on several levels—of action and human relations, of deep mental horror and pathos—achieving physical and psychological suspense. The theme is the value of the inner lives of those caught in an uncompromisingly tragic circumstance.

The Valley of St. Ives (1949) is a study of infantile emotional relationships in the ostensibly adult world of a fox-hunting community somewhere in the East. The protagonist, an inhibited teacher at a boys' preparatory school, marries a member of the wealthy hunting set; the conflicts of this *mésalliance* are explored beyond the surface aspects of money, social position, and interest in horses, and are concerned with love and personal destiny in the timeless realm of the myth, where unconscious interrelationships motivate the action in the world of apparent reality. The final evocation is of hope through tragedy.

PEARL SYDENSTRICKER BUCK

Elizabeth Colman

was born in Hillsboro, West Virginia, on June 26, 1892. Her father's forebears came to America before the Revolutionary War, and her mother's, the Stultings, somewhat later, having left Holland and Germany in quest of religious freedom. They settled in the South, where many of her father's family, the Sydenstrickers, became distinguished in the professions. Her paternal grandfather made it a principle to hire both colored and white men and to pay them equal wages. "From my ancestors," Pearl Buck has said, "I have the tradition of racial equality."

Her parents were missionaries in the interior of China, but because they were home on furlough in 1892 their daughter was born in America. In China she grew up much alone in Chinkiang, a city on the Yangtse River. She learned to speak Chinese before English, although when the time came to read and write she studied English rather than Chinese characters. The first direct literary influence upon her was her Chinese nurse, who told tales of magic from Buddhist and Taoist sources. The Buddhist stories were about wonderful daggers that a man could make small enough to hide in his ear or in the corner of his eye, but which, when he fetched them out again, were long and keen and swift to kill. The Taoist tales were of devils and fairies, and of all the spirits that live in tree and stone and cloud, and of the dragons that were in the sea and in the storm and wind. Pearl's father went on frequent journeys into remote parts, and he brought back tales of his own adventures, some of which took him close to death. Her mother talked to her for long hours, mostly about her own childhood in West Virginia, about music and art, and about the beauty of words and their use. Under her mother's tutelage Pearl wrote something almost every week. Soon some of these writings were published in the Shanghai *Mercury,* an English-language newspaper.

When she was fifteen she was sent to boarding school in Shanghai, her first formal education, and at the age of seventeen went home to America to enter Randolph-Macon Woman's College at Lynchburg, Virginia, where she became president of her class. She wrote for the college paper and in her senior year won two literary prizes, one of which was awarded for the best short story. On returning to China she found her mother ill and spent two years in caring for her. She married a young American and, her mother having recovered, the young couple went to a town in North China and remained there five years. Here she went freely among the Chinese people and gained the closest and most intimate knowledge of their lives. Famine and attacks by bandits gave an exciting quality to her experiences. For some years she busied herself with the cares of home, children, and parents and with the teaching of English literature in the University of Nanking and in Chung Yang University.

In 1922 she wrote an article for *The Atlantic Monthly,* and thereafter prepared other essays. On a ship bound for America in 1925 she wrote the story "A Chinese Woman Speaks," which was published in *Asia* magazine; five years later this story developed into her first novel. Upon her return to China in 1926, after a year of study for her master's degree at Cornell University, she began to write constantly and in earnest, working on a history of the Chinese novel and on a novel of her own. But in March, 1927, the Nationalist soldiers entered Nanking, looting and killing foreigners. She escaped with her family by the narrow margin of ten minutes. For thirteen hours they hid in a tiny hovel. Sounds of hideous shouting and the crashing in of gates and doors dinned in her ears. She had the terrifying experience of facing death because of her color. Her house was gutted by fire, and the manuscript of that first novel was destroyed. Her observation of this and other scenes in the revolution are in *The First Wife, and Other Stories* (1933).

In 1929 she left China for a hurried business trip to America. Upon her return she wrote in three months *The Good Earth* (1933), which was acclaimed by critics and awarded the Pulitzer prize. In July, 1932, she moved permanently to the United States. In 1933 she published a translation of one of China's most famous novels, *Shui Hu Chüan,* under the title *All Men Are Brothers.* In June, 1933, Yale University bestowed upon her the degree of Master of Arts. On June 11, 1935, she married Richard J. Walsh, the editor of *Asia* magazine and president of a publishing firm, The John Day Company. In November, 1935, she was awarded the William Dean Howells medal by the American Academy of Arts and Letters. In 1938 she received the Nobel prize for literature, the first American woman to be so honored by the Swedish Academy, not for one book, as is sometimes mistakenly said, but for the whole body of her work. Besides novels on Chinese and American themes, she has written stories for children, essays on minority rights, and reports on conversations with foreign-born friends about problems at home and abroad. She speaks and writes passionately in favor of equality for the "colored" peoples of the world. *Exile* (1936) and *Fighting Angel* (1936) are character studies of missionaries, based respectively upon the author's mother and father. *Today and Forever* (1940) and *Far and Near* (1947) are collections of short stories. *The Child Who Never Grew* (1950) discusses problems facing parents with mentally retarded children.

East Wind: West Wind (1930), her first published novel, contrasts eastern and western civilization in present-day China through the marriage of two young Chinese aristocrats. The husband is a physician with a western education, and the wife cherishes ancient Chinese teachings, but they grow in wisdom and understanding through intelligence and love.

In *The Good Earth* (1931) Wang Lung greatly loves his piece of land, and for a time he enjoys prosperity. With O-lan, his faithful, plain wife, he suffers poverty and famine. Yet he retains the land, eventually becomes wealthy, and takes a second, pretty wife. The children are a disappointment, for they do not love the soil, and at Wang's death they plan to sell the property and move to the city. This novel reflects the mood of the world depression of the late 1920's when the social systems of many countries were breaking down. Wang Lung's passionate devotion to his land met with sympathetic understanding in every country. *Sons* (1932), a sequel, is about Wang Lung's three sons: a merchant, a rich man, and a "good" war lord. The theme follows that of the "good bandit" in Chinese literature. *The Mother* (1934) narrates the sorrows of an unnamed impoverished Chinese woman whose joy in life is destroyed when her husband deserts her and her five children; she regains her former happiness when a grandchild is born. *A House Divided*

(1935) pictures the difficult situation facing young men and women enmeshed in the Chinese revolution. Yuan, grandson of Wang Lung, returns to China after studying in America and with his aristocratic wife sets out to teach modern methods of agriculture to assist Young China to prosper. The trilogy is collected in *The House of Earth* (1935).

Pearl Buck's first story with an American setting is *This Proud Heart* (1938), which tells of Susan Gaylord, an unusual woman, who has ability to do many things and who manages to have love, a home, and her work as a sculptor. *The Patriot* (1939) details twelve years in the life of a young Chinese patriot who joins the communists, visits Japan and marries a Japanese girl, and eventually returns to his homeland to fight under Chiang Kai-shek. *Other Gods* (1940) concerns Bert Holm, an American, whose mountain climbing wins him a hero's acclaim and a talented, wealthy wife.

Dragon Seed (1941) traces the effect of the Sino-Japanese war on the family of Ling Tan, whose first palsied horror at the looting following the fall of Nanking soon impels them to participate actively in guerrilla warfare. *The Promise* (1943), a sequel to *Dragon Seed,* shows the effect of Japan's ruthless conquest of Rangoon, Burma, through the story of Lao San, the third son of Ling Tan, who fights under Chiang Kai-shek. Mayli, Lao's wife, heads the corps of nurses.

Portrait of a Marriage (1945) describes the "impossible" but successful marriage of a wealthy Philadelphia artist to the uneducated yet worthy daughter of a Pennsylvania farmer. *Pavilion of Women* (1946) is a symbolic story of the intellectual woman, in the person of the beautiful forty-year-old Madame Wu. *Peony* (1948) is a study, in the form of an historical novel, of the Jews in China. *Kinfolk* (1949) is a novel of China today, with the scene laid partly in the United States. Dr. Liang and his American-educated family provide the theme.

HENRIETTA BUCKMASTER

Marcus Blechman

was born in Cleveland, Ohio. Her father was a newspaperman in Ohio until his removal to New York City to become foreign editor of the *Herald.* Her education was entirely in private schools, including the Brearley School in New York and others in Europe. She began writing when she was a small girl and at twelve had her first story published in *Child Life* magazine. By the time she was eighteen, she was writing book reviews for the New York *Times,* and subsequently she completed similar chores for other newspapers and magazines. In 1944 she held a Guggenheim fellowship, and in 1945-46 she was in Europe as a magazine correspondent, concerned with the problems of women and children.

Shortly after she left school she became deeply interested in the problems of the Negro, and most of her writing and activities since that time have concerned themselves with the problems of minorities. Her ancestors settled in the South in the early eighteenth century and remained there until, as small landowners, they felt they had greater opportunities in the newly opened West. This aspect of American history—the non-slaveholding southern whites as well as the antislavery and reform movements of the nineteenth century—has furnished the themes of two novels and of *Let My People Go* (1941), a history of the underground railroad and the antislavery movement.

"My writing concern," Miss Buckmaster has stated, "is with spirit and motivation. Above all, my interest is in characters who endeavor to fulfill some affirmative and dynamic progression of spirit as exemplified in some particular love of freedom. To me, writing is the most intensely creative of all the arts, for it discloses more bluntly than any other art the individual's meager or abundant attitude toward life, and demands a maturity of purpose which cannot be glossed over in any way."

Tomorrow Is Another Day (1934), her first novel, pictures the confident faith of young people in an affirmative attitude toward life. Rebecca Starr, the daughter of a famous novelist, runs off to New York and with the help of Christian Holm gets an opportunity to write book reviews and then to achieve literary recognition. *His End Was His Beginning* (1936) deals with the theme of the individual's need to adjust himself spiritually to a new era in society. The scene is Vienna before and after World War I. The story concerns Count Paul von Holenburg, whose love of his sister's children's nurse is contrary to custom. He adopts democratic views.

Deep River (1944), an historical novel laid in Georgia in the late 1850's, shows the conflict between the slave-holding plantation owners and the freedom-loving mountaineers. The story portrays the marriage of Savanna, a girl reared on a plantation, to Simon Bliss, an upland man, who fights slavery. *Fire in the Heart* (1948) traces the life story of Fanny Kemble from the time of her début as an actress in London's Covent Garden until her divorce from Pierce Butler, an American owner of slaves. Fanny's humanitarian zeal to free the slaves is the "fire in the heart."

JOHN D. BURGAN

was born in 1913 in Vintondale, Pennsylvania, about seventy-five miles east of Pittsburgh. He graduated from the University of Pittsburgh in 1934. He did newspaper and public-relations work in Rochester and Albany, New York, before the outbreak of World War II. During the war he served for four years in the navy as an enlisted man and as an officer. His last two years were spent in the Pacific, first with a mobile radar unit and later with Admiral Nimitz's staff.

His first novel, *Even My Own Brother* (1942), portrays the career of an American fascist in Lang Taylor, a garage mechanic, whose discontentment at his lowly position leads him to enter politics. *Two Per Cent Fear* (1947) describes the terror of combat troops in contact with the enemy and their boredom when inactive in the Pacific. *The Long Discovery* (1950) concerns the people who live in and are shaped by the small town of Beautyburg, Pennsylvania. Young John Riddell, son of the mine superintendent, falls in love with Rose, the ambitious daughter of a Russian coal miner. The whole town watches and speculates on the outcome.

FIELDING BURKE

is the pen name of Mrs. Olive Tilford Dargan. She was born in Kentucky into a school-teaching family. When she was ten, the family moved to Grayson County, Missouri, and again to the foothills of the Ozarks. There her father founded a successful academy. Olive Tilford received a year of training from her father, and at the age of fourteen took charge of a school of her own, where her pupils included some older than herself. At sixteen she entered George Peabody College for Teachers in Nashville. After graduation and two years of teaching in San Antonio, Texas, she went north for special study at Radcliffe College. Here she met Pegram Dargan, a brilliant young South Carolinian, then in his senior year at Harvard. They were married and moved to New York City. Mrs. Dargan's first two books, *Semiramis and Other Plays* (1904) and *Lords and Lovers and Other Dramas*

(1906), were written during the six years they lived looking out across the Hudson to the Palisades. *The Mortal Gods* (1912) contains three poetic dramas. Her volumes of lyrics include *Path Flower* (1914), *The Cycle's Rim* (1916), *Flutter of the Gold Leaf* (with Dr. Frederic Peterson, 1922), and *Lute and Furrow* (1922).

Mrs. Dargan has lived in many places, east, south, north, and west in her native country, and in Canada and Europe. Her favorite spot of anchorage, however, is the friendly mountain region of western North Carolina. In 1915 tragedy overtook her when her husband was drowned on his way to Cuba. She returned to the highland farm which they had purchased in the Great Smokies. The high ridge fields, weather-washed and worn, unfortunately made life hard for the three mountain families dependent on them. Feeling a challenge from her pioneer ancestors, who had loved and helped make fruitful the Kentucky wilderness, she undertook to restore the high slopes to production. It was a difficult task, with problems unknown to the lowland farmer. Mrs. Dargan became so involved and interested that writing was almost forgotten. An occasional poem appeared. The mountain people around her, with their strong, dramatic appeal, inevitably became her subject, and their stories were collected and published in *Highland Annals* (1925) and *From My Highest Hill* (1942). When she gave up life on the peaks, she settled in Asheville, and wrote proletarian novels under the pen name of "Fielding Burke."

In trend sociological, Fielding Burke's novels are "purpose" novels, if one may use that word in connection with indubitable art. They record the growth of concentrated power in conflict with modern man's evolution, and its effect on all human life today within its touch. Mrs. Dargan achieves her effects through vital human beings, not "symbolical distillations." She handles doctrinal substance easily with no bulging threat to the narrative. Her most supercilious objectors admit that she is "always the artist."

Call Home The Heart (1932), her first novel, is the story of industrial conflict which takes place in the hill country of North Carolina. The central character is a young woman who rebels against her life as a poor white and runs away to work in a mill, later to become a labor organizer. *A Stone Came Rolling* (1935) concerns a North Carolina town where the mill owners experience feelings of uncertainty as the workers unite to strike. The locale of *Sons of the Stranger* (1947) is the town of High Grampian in the ore-rich Montes de Sol range of the West where the story of Dal MacNair begins. His boyhood is spent among the miners, but he leaves High Grampian to fulfill the ambition of his young manhood. This is a notable portrayal of the evolution and development of a fighting liberal. His deep and complicated love for Fai Barnett survives scandal, heartbreak, and misunderstanding in the midst of strikes, militia, scabs, murders, and jailbreaks.

BEN LUCIEN BURMAN

was born on December 12, 1895, in Covington, Kentucky. In high school he edited the student paper. He left Harvard in his senior year to enlist in World War I. Severely wounded at Soissons, France, he returned to the United States to receive his degree in 1920 at Harvard. That year he became a reporter on the Boston *Herald*, in 1921 he was assistant city editor of the Cincinnati *Times Star*, and in 1922 he was a special writer for the New York *Sunday World*. After a short period of work with the Newspaper Enterprise Association and the Scripps-Howard newspapers, he returned to Covington to write fiction.

Covington was a steamboat town, and it seemed to him that the river was the proper background for fiction. Because editors were not interested in narratives set in this locale, he wrote detective stories under a pseudonym until 1926, when his first river story was published in *The Pictorial Review*. Thereafter his writings made America conscious of the Mississippi. He has lived close to his characters, even to the extent of becoming an amateur "hoodoo doctor" in order to observe Negro life at close range. *Big River to Cross* (1940) is an anecdotal account of the Mississippi: its people, legends, folklore, and boats.

In 1941 he went to Africa to investigate the Free French movement; he was the first writer to reach the capital at Brazzaville, French Equatorial Africa. For months he was America's sole source of information about the Free French; often he and his wife, Alice Caddy, were the first non-military white persons ever allowed to visit the mysterious areas of the interior. His novel *Rooster Crows For Day* is a direct outgrowth of these experiences, as is *Miracle on the Congo* (1942), which describes the political and social situation of the Free French during the early months of America's participation in World War II. The French government decorated him with the Legion of Honor for his writing during the war.

The basic theme of Mr. Burman's later books has been the childishness of the human race, a theme that he has invested with humor. In 1948 he created great interest in the state of American literature by publishing an essay, "Wanted: New Gods," in *The Saturday Review of Literature*. "Most American writing," he declared, "has lost all pretensions to artistry, and has substituted nonsense or dullness or flippancy. For depth, it has substituted formlessness or propaganda or a shallow egotism. As an artist, I protest against ugliness for the sake of ugliness. We need a new set of gods, a new literary religion. There must be art, there must be beauty. For when we have lost beauty, we have lost the world."

Mississippi (1929), his first novel, depicts the feud between Captain Lilly, a steamboat owner and pilot, and the nomadic, illiterate shanty-boat people whose home is on the Mississippi River. An adopted son, the child of shanty-boaters, goes back to his own people, marries a girl of this group, and comes to hate Captain Lilly. A flood brings the captain to the rescue and sends the boy back to piloting and eventual understanding. *Steamboat Round the Bend* (1933), set against the poverty and superstition of the river people, is a whimsical tale about an elderly "Doctor John," who sells an Indian herb remedy and who buys a steamboat to be a captain like his father. He woos Miss Robbie, a spinster who paints butterflies on china. His nephew, the murderer of a worthless man, comes to the boat with a runaway swamp girl. The doctor persuades the boy to surrender, and then tries to keep the lad from the gallows. *Blow for a Landing* (1938) pictures Ingenious Willow Joe, an unlettered yet noble youth, who produces music on jugs, cigar boxes, and a guitar. His ambition is to play a steamboat calliope. He loves the river, but his mother wants him to move with her to a farm. *Rooster Crows for Day* (1945) is an ironic novel of an American abroad who tries to take the ideas of his own small town with him around the world, no matter how inappropriate these may be under different circumstances. The story concerns a young Mississippi River pilot's journeys to beautiful and mysterious Africa, where he finds adventure on the Congo, in the jungle, and on the Sahara Desert. Racked by fever, he goes to a hospital and eventually returns home, finally achieving membership in the Cotton Valley Boosters Club. *Everywhere I Roam* (1949) is an ironic novel of the South and of America. A Kentucky mountaineer and his children seek peace and happiness on a trip by trailer through the South. They look for a place "where people's still nice, and living the way they used to do." Although the journey ends in disappointment for Captain Asa, the three youngsters learn much about America and about themselves.

W(ILLIAM) R(ILEY) BURNETT

Charles Bell

was born in Springfield, Ohio, on November 25, 1899. He was educated in the local grammar and high schools and at the Miami Military Institute at Germantown, Ohio, from which he graduated in 1919. He then enrolled in the College of Journalism of Ohio State University, but he attended irregularly for only one semester. His principal interest at the time was athletics. At his marriage when twenty-one he had made no choice of a profession. For a while he worked in a factory as a shop clerk, sold insurance, and then for six years did statistical work in Ohio's Department of Industrial Relations; he spent his week ends and evenings writing furiously, producing at this time scores of short stories, five novels, and a play, all of which he stored in a trunk. While living in Chicago he wrote his first published book, *Little Caesar,* which was an immediate best seller. The novels which followed are set in various localities. His style is derived from a study of translations of stories from the French of de Maupassant, Merimée, and Flaubert; the Spanish of Pió Baroja; and the Italian of Giovanni Verga.

Little Caesar (1929), which established the vogue of the gangster novel in America, tells in clipped-sentence style the doings of Rico, who was born Cesare Bandello, Sam Vettori, and other underworld characters in Chicago at the time of Al Capone. The story begins with Sam planning a holdup. Rico, a rat-like destroyer who hates life and yet wants to live, fights Sam successfully for leadership and becomes dictator of the gang. In a holdup he kills a policeman and is shot down by another. *Iron Man* (1930), about the fight racket, portrays the career of Coke Mason, a middleweight boxer, whose unfaithful wife on whom he dotes leads to a split with Regan, his manager, and to the loss of the championship title.

Saint Johnson (1930), set in frontier Arizona in the 1880's, deals with the problem of law enforcement. Wayt Johnson wants to be a good officer as United States Marshal in Alkali, but everytime he achieves peace his youngest brother Jim commits an act that stirs trouble. A Mexican kills Jim, whose death Wayt tries to avenge. *The Silver Eagle* (1931) portrays the aspirations of Frank Harworth, a restaurant-chain owner, to respectability and the way the gangster Molina enters his life. *The Giant Swing* (1932) pictures Joe Nearing's rise from a piano player and singer in a dance hall in Middleburg to a composer living in a new world in New York City.

Dark Hazard (1933), about dog racing, takes its name from a greyhound that Jim Turner wants to own. Jim marries Marg, a religious woman, and tries to live up to her standards, although his love of gambling persists. *Goodbye to the Past* (1934) gives six scenes in inverse order of the life story of William Meadows, an eighty-year-old Ohio industrialist, who grew up in the West. *The Goodhues of Sinking Creek* (1934) is a novelette about a family in a small Ohio town in the early 1860's. A feud arises with the Bristowes over the slavery question, and Jim Goodhue is murdered for expressing abolitionist sentiments. His son Clay kills the murderer. *King Cole* (1936) shows Read Cole, the Republican governor of Ohio, campaigning demagogically for re-election in the hope that victory will bring the nomination for the Presidency. Gregg Upham, an editor, thinks that Cole has fascist leanings and opposes him.

The Dark Command (1938) is a tale of Kansas at the time of the Kansas-Missouri War in 1860–62. Mary McCloud's love for two men provides the plot. *High Sierra* (1940) has Roy Earle, a criminal who at thirty-seven had a life sentence commuted, participate in a holdup of an inn. *The Quick Brown Fox* (1942) describes the dishonest social and political aspirations of Brant Harding to show how a fascist-minded person can lie and cheat to get himself elected to office. *Nobody Lives*

Forever (1944) pictures the trickery of a confidence man in the relationship of Jim Farrar to the wealthy widow, Gladys Halvorsen. *Tomorrow's Another Day* (1949) goes behind the scenes of horse-race fixing and stud poker-playing in a story of Lonnie, a gambler, and his wife, Mary. *Romelle* (1946) portrays a faded café singer looking for a husband and getting connected with an illegal business. *Asphalt Jungle* (1949) concerns a manhunt in a midwestern city with police, lawyers, and crooks engaged in a struggle for survival.

JOHN HORNE BURNS

Loring Studios

was born on October 7, 1916, in Andover, Massachusetts, into a numerous family in which, he recalls, "each individual was permitted to develop along his own lines of genius or mania, but was never allowed to conflict with the interests of the group or with the others." After four years at Phillips Andover, he went to Harvard where he played squash and sang in the glee club. Upon leaving Harvard, Mr. Burns taught English in a boys' preparatory school for several years. World War II came, and in January, 1942, he entered the infantry as a private. He became a corporal and then attended officers' school. In 1943 he went overseas as a second lieutenant and served for a year in Casablanca and Algiers as a military intelligence officer with Allied Force Headquarters. The next year and a half he spent in Italy, returning to the United States and to his school in February, 1946. He left teaching to devote full time to writing in 1947. He lives in Boston, Massachusetts.

Mr. Burns has said: "The theme of my two published novels and the others yet to come will be that widest and most illusive reach of experience, American life. Nothing is worth writing about except America, for we have the power to *be* the future, whereas everything else in the world is either standing still or looking into the past. I see no point in historical novels nor in those which seek to dose with aspirin the reality of the present. It may be a very noble reality if people will look it straight in the face, and that is one of the functions of the new American writer. The priests are outdated, and the scientist can only give more material goods (or death) to the people."

The Gallery (1947), his first novel, sketches in a shock technique the behavior of some Americans in 1941 who act as pitiless conquerors of lonely, frustrated, but grateful Italians. The pictures of Italy and North Africa vividly recreate some of the unpleasant social aspects of war. *Lucifer with a Book* (1949) describes life intimately and somewhat disconcertingly at an exclusive private boys' school.

KATHARINE NEWLIN BURT

was born at Fishkill-on-Hudson, New York, on September 6, 1882. Educated by tutors and at private schools in America, she also attended a kindergarten course in Munich, Germany. Her first stories, written for children, were published in England. At Oxford she met Maxwell Struthers Burt, whom she married in 1913. They returned to America, where Mr. Burt had homesteaded and desert-claimed a ranch in Wyoming in 1912. Many of her romances portray the backgrounds of the Rocky Mountain country or of western North Carolina where the Burts have their winter home. Others revert to the country of her youth in New York state or to her husband's family neighborhood of Philadelphia. The central theme and motive in her books is the importance of courage in facing life.

Mrs. Burt's first novel, *The Branding Iron* (1919), was written when a winter snowstorm imprisoned the Burt family in its log cabin. The story tells of Joan Carver's change from a mountain girl to a New York actress under the tutelage of a rancher and an author. *Hidden Creek* (1920) tells how an eastern artist's penniless daughter is aided by a western hotel keeper and how she, a barmaid, is befriended and ultimately married by the half-drunk yet poetically sensitive son of the hotel man. *The Red Lady* (1920), a mystery story, has Janice Gale not only come face to face with a ghostly counterpart of herself, but also solve the enigma and in the end marry the detective who suspected her of murdering a child. In *Snow-Blind* (1921) a murderer has sheltered and cared for a snow-blinded girl whom he found in the woods after she had wandered away from a group of snowbound actors. She regains her sight, realizes that her protector has a base character, and falls in love with his younger brother.

Q (1922) retails the story of a cowboy who, in a few weeks of direct physical action, frees a group of easterners from inhibitions that have imprisoned and injured their lives for three times as many years. *Quest* (1925) has three cousins searching after God: Nicholas as a mystic, Little John as a lover standing in fear of God, and Stephen as an agnostic. *Cock's Feather* (1928) brings Sophie Copley to an understanding of the self-sacrifice of David Cray. *A Man's Own Country* (1931) shows Micah MacKael yielding to a woman who for a time seems to prove that the West is not a man's country. *The Tall Ladder* (1932) takes a wealthy New York divorcée to Wyoming, where on her ranch she seems about to make another mistake. *Beggars All* (1933) finds a young southern aristocrat in the power of a racketeer returning after an absence to find his home occupied by a northern woman, the daughter of this gangster. *This Woman and This Man* (1934) contains romantic action contrasting the West and East. In *Rapture Beyond* (1935) Jocelyn Harlowe becomes engaged to Felix Kent to please her mother, but loves a man in the world of thieves and gangsters. *The Monkey's Tail* (1936), written under the pseudonym of "Rebecca Scarlet," shows the essential and profound pagan "happiness" of a woman's original nature.

Four daughters of an actress visit wealthy members of their father's family and bestow benefits on all in *When Beggars Choose* (1938). *Men of Moon Mountain* (1938) is a western story of a feudal cattleman who tries to hold his range against the advance of civilization. *Safe Road* (1938) discloses how Sally Keyne solves the problem of the Crewe estate and gets a husband in Roger Ashe. *If Love I Must* (1939) shows Crystal Jayne being groomed for a man by a beauty culturist and her divorced mother. In *No Surrender* (1940) Jed and Cathryn are reunited after years of hatred for each other. The danger of pulchritude is described in *Fatal Gift* (1941), the story of a Philadelphia girl whose unbelievable beauty causes trouble when her father brings home a second wife.

Captain Millett's Island (1944) shows a Nazi officer who almost succeeds in controlling an island off the Carolina Coast. *The Lady in the Tower* (1946) is a mystery story about how "love casteth out fear" in the determination of a young girl to clear her mother of a murder charge. *Close Pursuit* (1947) shows how closely the Old World pursues the freedom of the New. Three women try to escape: one from the dissolute treatment of aristocracy; one from the gallows; and the third from an enforced marriage in order to join her first and only love. *Still Water* (1948) is a tale of suspense set in the Great Smoky Mountains. *Strong Citadel* (1949) portrays an aristocratic Philadelphia mother who tries to mold her children according to her heart's desire and is saved from wrecking their lives by the intervention of her son's wife, a Russian-Polish peasant girl of immigrant stock.

(MAXWELL) STRUTHERS BURT

though born in Baltimore, Maryland, on October 18, 1882, is in reality a Philadelphian; his parents were only temporarily in Baltimore at the time of his birth, and he grew up in Philadelphia. He was educated in private schools and at Princeton, from which he graduated in 1904. At college he edited *The Tiger* and wrote two Triangle Club shows; he also was a reporter on the Philadelphia *Times*. After a year of study at the University of Munich and a year and a half at Oxford University, he returned to Princeton as an instructor in English. In 1908 he settled in Jackson Hole, Wyoming, and in 1912 he homesteaded and desert-claimed the Bar BC ranch, which he held until its sale in 1938. In 1913 he married Katharine Newlin, who also is a novelist.

In 1921 Mr. Burt's story, "Each in His Generation," won the O. Henry Memorial award. His poetry has been collected in *In the High Hills* (1914), *Songs and Portraits* (1921), *When I Grow up to Middle Age* (1925), and *War Songs* (1942). His non-fiction books include *The Diary of a Dude Wrangler* (1924), essays and sketches about ranch life; *The Other Side* (1928), essays on the good qualities of the United States; *Escape from America* (1936), essays on loyalty; *Powder River* (1938), a volume in the "Rivers of America" series; and *Philadelphia: Holy Experiment* (1945), a history. *They Could Not Sleep* (1928) contains ten short stories.

Mr. Burt's stories and novels contain well-devised plots, much description of western scenery and of Philadelphia, and many sage, witty, and challenging remarks upon life.

The Interpreter's House (1924), his first novel, concerns Julian Eyre, who at the age of thirty-five seeks to quiet the vague restlessness surviving from his wild youth and war years by asking whether beauty and certainty can be found in this life. *The Delectable Mountains* (1927) tells about a Philadelphian of good family who marries a Broadway chorus girl and takes her to his ranch in Wyoming; they part, learn in separation a more correct evaluation of life, and reunite.

Festival (1931) concerns Dorn Griffiths, a wealthy retired Philadelphia broker who surrenders his quiet retirement to rescue his daughter, who is unhappily married to an Italian prince. *Entertaining the Islanders* (1933) is a love story of two modern people who vow to be sensible but who feel the dizzying effect of love on the romantic West Indies island of St. Birgitta. *Along These Streets* (1941) presents a picture of the conventional and reactionary life of Philadelphia, the traditions and wasted opportunities, and the customs and strange club life as a background for the tale of a scientist required by his uncle's will to live in the city a portion of each year.

NIVEN BUSCH

was born on April 26, 1903, in New York City. His father, Briton Busch, was a stockbroker, real estate operator, and in his later years a motion-picture executive. Niven Busch attended St. Bernard's School in New York City and the Hoosac School in Hoosick Falls, New York. After spending two years at Princeton University in the class of 1926, he went to work for *Time* magazine, then in its infancy. He amplified his income by writing for *Collier's* and *The New Yorker*, becoming an associate editor of the latter publication in 1926. In 1931 he was put under contract by Warner Brothers as a motion-picture writer, a trade which he practiced for the next eight years, writing and producing numerous feature pictures, one of which, "In Old Chicago," was nominated for the Academy award for the best screen story of 1937.

In the field of the novel he has been successful in selling much of his work to picture companies, although he maintains that this is not his objective. "I write about things and people that interest me," he says. "And having learned my trade at the film-maker's bench, I am influenced to some extent by this background. The function of the motion picture and the novel is basically the same; that is, to reflect life in terms of the emotions. I feel that the two crafts are so closely allied that one may practice both together without detriment to either."

The Carrington Incident (1941), his first novel, is the story of an American college teacher, Bertha Carrington, who is engaged to teach Italian to Hitler. Through her eyes is given a portrait of Nazi Germany just prior to World War II. On the outbreak of war she is caught in a plot, betrayed, and subsequently sent to a concentration camp from which she escapes at the end of the war. *They Dream of Home* (1944), though written in a wartime period, was actually one of the first successful post-war novels. It presents the problem of a group of discharged servicemen who fight together in the Pacific and try to carry over their comradeship into civilian life. The central figure of the story is a young Marine, Cliff Harper, who goes straight from high school into the Corps, from which he emerges cynical and disoriented. He finds within himself the road to rehabilitation, dispensing with dependence on the comrades from whom he is now separated.

Duel in the Sun (1944), one of the first contemporary novels to apply highly modern story techniques and characters to the age-old form of the "western," has as its central figure Pearl Chavez, an orphan of Indian blood, who is accepted as a pensioner in the home of a cattle baron in the Southwest of the 1880's. Becoming the mistress of this man's outlaw son, Lewton, she eventually reaches the conclusion that she cannot exist as a woman as long as he is alive. The climax of the book is a duel to the death between these two, fought in the blazing sun on a mountain range.

Day of the Conquerors (1946) takes place within the twenty-four hours of V-J Day. The location is San Francisco where the United Nations is about to hold its first organizational meeting. The conclusion which Busch presents from a shifting panel of characters—a conclusion most unpalatable to the public at the time the book was written—is that the United States had won the war but lost the peace. The central figure is Mark Gregory, a newspaper correspondent, who returns from the war in the Pacific to discover that his wife has betrayed him. *The Furies* (1948) pictures a cattle baron who disinherits his two sons in favor of his daughter, but who incurs her hatred and in the ensuing quarrel finds her more than a match for him.

ADELYN BUSHNELL

was born in Thomaston, Maine, on September 29, 1894. Her father, Dr. Jerome Bushnell, trained her mind in a way unusual for those days. At the age of seven she was familiar not only with Dickens, Shakespeare, Thackeray, and Tom Paine, but she was also allowed to read *The Decameron.* This background of reading enabled her to graduate from high school at an early age. She remembers with pride that she dashed through Caesar, Cicero, and Virgil, and went on in her senior year to read Ovid "because she had nothing to do in Latin." The same held true with her French.

In 1908 Miss Bushnell entered the Leland Powers School in Boston. One of her teachers was George Riddle, at that time also a

Harvard professor. He became interested in her, and she became his private pupil in English literature and the Greek drama. Through his influence she went on the stage in November, 1910, with a stock company in Paterson, New Jersey. In January, 1911, she married the company's character actor, George Manning, who died three years later; they had one son. In 1911 she obtained her first leading role in Paul Wilstach's *The New Code,* and thereafter she starred in many dramas. In 1925 she married Marshall Bradford.

In 1926 she lost her voice due to excessive overwork. Her friend, Kathleen Millay, suggested that she "stop moping around about it and start to write something." Miss Bushnell did so, and found herself launched in the business of writing and directing headline vaudeville one-act plays. Her last appearance as an actress was as star in *Phantom Cargo* in 1933. She then engaged in the writing of full-length Broadway plays. Her first was *I, Myself* (1934), and in 1933 she wrote *Glory,* which was chosen by Maude Adams as the vehicle for a return to the theater under John Golden. In 1938 Miss Bushnell was co-author of *Case History,* which she directed and staged at the Lyceum Theatre in New York.

She then turned to writing one-act radio plays for such programs as "The Magic Key," the Edgar Bergen show, and the RCA Victor hour. In 1942 her husband joined her as co-author of these radio plays. A long illness compelled Miss Bushnell to discontinue the writing of radio scripts, for she could no longer contend physically with the speed required in that medium. It was then that she turned to the work which she has found the most satisfying, the writing of novels.

"As to my theory and practice of fiction," she has said, "I feel that within everyone there is always the urge to express one's feelings toward life, toward people, and toward good and evil. I think a book should first arise from a desire to say something about a way of living or a trend of thought. The second stage is to work out the plot line of a story which can be interesting as a mere story and yet emphasize this idea or viewpoint. Then comes the blowing of the breath of life into the characters; and this part both permits and demands: it permits the author to express through the mouthpiece of his characters all that he would like to say, and it demands an observant mind that has studied other people and himself with an impartial curiosity. I thoroughly believe no one is originally good or bad; there are always circumstances which have created that good or that evil. Beginning with that attempt at understanding and using the double-lensed spectacles of humor and pity, the author should succeed in filling his books with human beings, not mere characters. A story without a purpose is valueless, but a purpose without a story is seldom heeded."

Tide-Rode (1947), her first novel, is set in a Maine seacoast town in the 1860's and 1870's. It is the melodramatic story of a sea captain, Caleb Dow, his wife Delight, and his aged grandmother who lives in France but manages to dominate her grandson. Caleb is a man endowed with grace, power, family, and wealth. In the old days seamen said a vessel was "tide-rode" when they meant she was anchored and helpless against the elements which battered her. This well describes Caleb, for he is bedeviled by his very gifts, and the book shows how he is eventually freed from his anchors.

Rock Haven (1948) concerns two brothers, Ulysses and Virgil Ulmer, the one good and the other evil, and their relationship in Maine in the early 1900's. Perhaps this book actually emphasizes the value of time more than any other theme. Ulysses knows that time is eternal, and so he accepts it as a friend by whose side he walks. Virgil considers time as a thing of short duration. He fears time, and consequently combats it and tries to outrun it. The Chinese and occidental philosophies are contrasted; the author evinces her belief that Ulysses' Chinese philosophy is to be preferred as the only one that brings peace.

Pay the Piper (1950) is laid in the Middle West, France, and Boston. It is the story of Keith James-Winter, a man who is gifted in voice, looks, intelligence, and all that should have made him one of the world's greatest singers. He lacks the two other essentials for success, the capacity for hard work and the strength to sacrifice worldly comforts. Keith becomes a "paid piper," a false teacher who sings the song of fame to others in order that he may rob them of their purse. With him is contrasted a young singer, Al Murphy, who possesses all the qualities that the failure lacked. Opposite Al is Jennifer, who typifies the young, talented singer who falls into the wrong hands and finds her voice ruined by poor teaching. Back of these three, and binding them together, is Rolf Gjerdrum, a Norwegian pianist, who represents all that is fine and honest in music.

CABELL *to* CUTHBERT

JAMES BRANCH CABELL

Artist: L'Engle

was born on April 14, 1879, in Richmond, Virginia. In 1898 he graduated with high honors from the College of William and Mary, where as an undergraduate he taught French and Greek. His first job was as copyholder on the Richmond *Times.* From 1899 to 1901 he worked for the New York *Herald,* and then he transferred to the Richmond *News.* His first stories appeared in magazines in 1902. During the next ten years, in addition to writing fiction, he did genealogical and other research work in America, France, Ireland, and England, and he also devoted some time to free-lance writing. From 1911 to 1913 he worked in coal mines in West Virginia. In 1919 he became genealogist of the Virginia chapter of the Sons of the Revolution, and later he held similar positions with other historical societies in Virginia. He was editor of the Virginia War History Commission from 1919 to 1926. On November 8, 1913, he married Priscilla Bradley; they had one son. Mrs. Cabell died in 1948; in 1950 Mr. Cabell married Margaret Waller Freeman.

In addition to novels Mr. Cabell has written short stories, poetry, drama, essays, history, autobiography, literary criticism, and genealogies. Two books answer critics who did not like the novel *Jurgen: The Judging of Jurgen* (1920), incorporated into the thirty-second chapter of *Jurgen,* and *Taboo* (1921). An acute study of a contemporary novelist, *Joseph Hergesheimer* (1921), sheds light also on Mr. Cabell's philosophy of life and art. *Some of Us* (1930) and *Preface to the Past* (1936) contain literary criticism. Three books give genealogical accounts of his or of his wife's family: *Branchiana* (1907), *Branch of Abingdon* (1911), and *The Majors and Their Marriages* (1915). *These Restless Heads* (1932) consists of short essays on life and writing. *Special Delivery* (1933) is a packet of replies to correspondents. *Ladies and Gentlemen* (1934) reassesses the reputations of twenty famous real or fictitious personalities. *Let Me Lie* (1947) is subtitled "An Ethnological Account of the Remarkable Commonwealth of Virginia."

As a novelist Mr. Cabell is a romanticist who tends to invert the usual materials of a romancer, and who, in turning them upside down, as it were, satirizes romantic illusions. Romance ordinarily approves love, courtesy, truth, gallantry, chivalry, heroism, justice, loyalty, purity, fidelity, and religious faith. Mr. Cabell views these abstract qualities with irony if not with hostility, for he ridicules romanticists and questions traditions, customs, and dogmas. Yet in one of his most popular books, *The Cream of the Jest,* he states that "it is only by preserving faith in human dreams that we may, after all, perhaps some day make them come true." He objects to realistic fiction, but his own writings portray many of the unpleasant aspects of life. *Jurgen* (1919) first brought popular attention to Mr. Cabell, ironically enough, through an attempted suppression of the book on charges of obscenity.

The greater portion of Mr. Cabell's writings up to 1929 have been woven together into a lengthy saga of adventure and commentary thereon called *The Biography of the Life of Manuel.* The action in most of these stories is laid in the mythical kingdom of Poictesme, which is indeterminately located somewhere in southern France. The ruler of this domain is Manuel, a swineherd who rises to be Count of Poictesme. After his death a legend grows about his name until he becomes known as the Redeemer. The characters in the *Biography* purport to engage in romantic adventures, but subtly by irony, anagram, symbol, and other devices the author often turns the incidents into analyses of unpleasant contemporaneous social life or unworthy personal conduct.

These novels show a profound knowledge of classical and medieval literature. Numerous parallels remind the reader of *The Iliad, The Odyssey, The Aeneid, The Faerie Queene, Paradise Lost,* and medieval metrical romances. In the dream life of the male characters there appear such famous ladies of romance as Eve, Helen of Troy, Ettarre, Mélusine, Melior, Anaïtis, and Guenevere. As a novelist Mr. Cabell's manner is urbane; his mood is skeptical and ironical; his tone is gently mocking. His highly mannered style contains archaic words and phrases, jeweled sentences with sparkling figures of speech and epigrams, sophisticated conversation, and philosophical meditation. Original lyric poems are inserted in the stories, and two books of poems form a part of the *Biography.*

Mr. Cabell's first book was *The Eagle's Shadow* (1904), a satire on money-grubbing. His second, *The Line of Love* (1905), contains short stories which are set in medieval times beginning in 1293 and which deal in a sophisticated manner with the romance of history. *Gallantry* (1907), set in the eighteenth century, and *Chivalry* (1909), set in England and on the continent in the fourteenth and fifteenth centuries, similarly are short stories with romantic motifs. *The Cords of Vanity* (1909) deals with contemporary Virginia. *The Soul of Melicent* (1913, revised as *Domnei,* 1920) pictures the medieval world. Thereafter Mr. Cabell's books were fitted together into the *Biography.* On the completion of that saga he wrote a book of serenely detached and philosophic essays with autobiographical overtones, *These Restless Heads* (1932), and changed his name to Branch Cabell. In 1942 he resumed his full name.

The sequence of events in the chronology of the *Biography* is to be followed only by reading the books in the order in which Mr. Cabell has arranged them. The intricate family relationships of Manuel and his descendants have been clarified in *The Lineage of Lichfield* (1922). *Beyond Life* (1919), a nonfiction prologue to the *Biography,* gives Mr. Cabell's "observations on the limitations of human nature," and elaborates his philosophy of life and art. The first novel in point of time is *Figures of Earth: A Comedy of Appearances* (1921), which introduces Manuel, the founder of Poictesme, and pictures his quest—at times ruthless—for the unattainable and his death, which he faces to save his daughter Melicent. Manuel's summation of his career shows how little respect he entertains for human virtues: "Yet, looking back, . . . I seem to see only the strivings of an ape reft of his tail, and grown rusty at climbing, who has reeled blunderingly from mystery to mystery, with pathetic makeshifts, not understanding anything, greedy in all desires, and always honeycombed with poltroonery." This man became a "Redeemer" who spent three days in a tomb before his resurrection. *The Silver Stallion* (1926) develops the theme of the influence of Manuel the Redeemer on the lives of his followers and shows how this adulterer and murderer emerges in legend, largely made up by the child Jurgen, as a man of high moral character worthy of worship.

The Music from Behind the Moon (1926) relates the adventures of a poet who seeks the ultimate of perfection in expression, only to discover that a distant ideal is a more effective inspiration than the same ideal intimately known. *The Way of Ecben* (1929) has as its theme the quest of the unattainable. *The White Robe* (1928) tells how a lad who made a pact with the Dark Master runs in the shape of a wolf, is committed to a monastery, grows in grace and ecclesiastical stature, and at his death goes to the heaven he has preached about but has not believed in. These three novels form a trilogy, *The Witch Woman* (1949).

Domnei (1920) has Perion of the Forest recognize that Melicent has a spiritual grace which transcends her physical beauty; thus is illustrated, in a sense, the reason for the medieval adoration of the Virgin Mary. Yet Mr. Cabell remarks in the "Afterword" that the worship of "the lady" was a malady of the times, and thus he prepares the way for the anti-romantic attitude which he demonstrates in later books.

Jurgen (1919) is the tale of a middle-aged pawnbroker whose wife, Lisa, vanishes at the bidding of the Devil. Jurgen seeks her; a magic shirt carries him to "the garden between dawn and sunrise." He meets his youthful sweetheart, who does not recognize him. Later he encounters the earth goddess who permits him to relive a day of his youth. The boyhood sweetheart again loves him, but he cannot capture his former illusion. Then Jurgen moves skeptically among famous ladies in mythology and fiction; he visits legendary lands, lives in Hell, and tarries a while in his grandmother's Heaven. At last, though offered any one of the beautiful women of legend, he returns to Lisa to resume his commonplace earthly life. Human weakness makes a mockery of romantic virtues.

The High Place (1923) follows the career of Florian de Puysange, who as a child had been promised a glimpse of "The High Place" where dwell the pagan gods and goddesses, including the beautiful sleeping princess Melior. When he grows to manhood, he possesses the princess for a few weeks and lives in complete happiness. But disenchantment comes quickly, as it does to others of Mr. Cabell's characters who seek the unattainable.

Something About Eve (1927) concerns Gerald Musgrave who, like Jurgen, eventually forgoes the romantic existence to pursue a life of respectability. Each of the ten short stories in *The Certain Hour* (1916) utilizes as its hero a poet whose test of character comes at "The Certain Hour." The poets include Shakespeare, Herrick, and Pope; their affairs with women invariably bring disillusionment. *The Cords of Vanity* (1909 and 1921), with Robert Townsend as the chief character and America as the setting, has the theme of romantic pursuit and the subsequent relapse into mediocre respectability. *From the Hidden Way* (1916 and 1924) contains poems supposedly written by Townsend. *The Jewel Merchant* (1921) is a dramatization of one of the short stories in *The Certain Hour.*

The Rivet in Grandfather's Neck (1915) satirizes romantic idealism in the southern United States; Colonel Rudolph Musgrave gallantly sacrifices his reputation in taking blame upon himself for an illicit affair of the writer, John Charteris. *The Eagle's Shadow* (1904 and 1923) satirizes American money-worship. *The Cream of the Jest* (1917 and 1922), a satire on pretense, pictures the quest for ideal beauty in a story of the experiences of Felix Kennaston, a writer, who escapes into a dream world of the past. *Sonnets from Antan* (1929) contains poems supposedly written by Gerald Musgrave.

The last volume in Mr. Cabell's arrangement of the *Biography* is *Straws and Prayer Books* (1924), an explanation of the saga. An escape from the pedestrian world and from crass Suburbia, he states, is sufficient reason to explain his efforts: "Man lived, for the most part of his conceded time, . . . a meager and monotonous existence: this he alleviated by endlessly concocting fictions which bedrugged and diverted him."

In 1934 Mr. Cabell returned to the writing of novels; these are not included in the

Biography, but have been grouped in trilogies. *The Nightmare Has Triplets* is a trilogy of novels which recount romantic adventures in the land of dreams and mythology. The first, *Smirt* (1934), begins the story of a professional writer living in Richmond, Virginia; the incidents are similar to those in the *Biography. Smith* (1935) concerns incidents in the Forest of Branlon, where this writer, now known as Mr. Smith, has become a local god. *Smire* (1937) converts the dreamer into a vagabond poet with an attractiveness that incessantly draws ladies to him, until his dream ends at the mouth of the Potomac River, on the Virginia side.

Heirs and Assigns, another trilogy, consists of *The King Was in His Counting House* (1938), a story of sixteenth-century Italy and of gallant courtiers and beautiful ladies at the court of Ferdinand, Duke of Melphé; *Hamlet Had an Uncle* (1940), which purportedly tells the true story of Shakespeare's Hamlet to demonstrate that the real hero is his uncle Wiglerus; and *The First Gentleman of Virginia* (1942), which concerns a Virginia Indian prince who follows the Spaniards to Florida and to Spain in colonial times and comes to dislike Spanish customs and ideas; he resents further encroachment upon his people.

A third trilogy, *It Happened in Florida,* contains *The St. Johns* (with A. J. Hanna, 1943), a social history of the area through which this Florida river flows; *There Were Two Pirates* (1947), which deals with José Gasparilla, Florida's most celebrated buccaneer; and *The Devil's Own Dear Son* (1949), the story of Diego de Arredondo Dodd, the manager of a tourist home in Florida, who turns out to be the son of the youngest and most virile of the seventy-two princes of Hell, a most peculiar and unusual place where a sinner-exclusion policy is adopted to ease the housing shortage and where each demon is provided with a shorter torture week.

HOLGER CAHILL

Arni

was born in St. Paul, Minnesota, on January 13, 1893. Though he went to a number of colleges and schools to study with teachers whom he admired, such as Thorstein Veblen in economics, Horace M. Kallen in esthetics and the history of ideas, and Stuart Davis and Arshile Gorky in painting, he considers himself self-educated. He has had to make his own living since he was twelve, and for that reason both his education and his apprenticeship as a writer and critic took a long time. Most of his writing has been done in his spare time, except for about a year in 1928–29 and the period since 1943 when he has devoted his full time to composition.

For the past thirty years, Mr. Cahill has been concerned with fostering American art. Since 1918 he has been a contributor to magazines on the subject of American art and life; his articles, short stories, and sketches have appeared in many publications. From 1921 to 1929 he was associated with the Newark Museum which, under its distinguished director, John Cotton Dana, was a pioneer in collecting and exhibiting American art and in relating art to the interests of the average man. Here Mr. Cahill had his basic experience in museum work, organizing exhibitions and purchasing collections of contemporary American art. Since 1929 he has been in charge of numerous exhibitions, and from 1935 to 1943 he was director of the Federal Art Project of The Works Progress Administration.

Mr. Cahill's non-fiction books include *Pop Hart* (1928) and *Max Weber* (1930), monographs on American artists; *A Yankee Adventurer* (1930), a biography of the American soldier of fortune who organized the first modern Chinese military force; *American*

Folk Art (1932); *American Painting and Sculpture* (1932); *American Sources of Modern Art* (1933); *Art In America in Modern Times* (1934); *Art in America: A Complete Survey* (1935); *New Horizons in American Art* (1936); and the extensive catalogue of the Newark Museum's thirty-fifth anniversary in 1943.

Profane Earth (1927), his first novel, is a counter-statement to the stock-market optimism and the expatriate tendencies of the 1920's. It tells the story of a second-generation American who moves from a small farming village to a manufacturing town and then goes to the University of Chicago. In the environment of the city with its chaos, its restlessness, its brutalities, its hungers, and its cultural barrenness, he feels that the answer is not to escape to Europe but to take his stand on the American earth, face its realities open-eyed, and work for the things he believes in.

Look South to the Polar Star (1947) is a novel that appears superficially to be a story of intrigue, adventure, and military action on the eve of Pearl Harbor. The main characters are an American scholar who has disappeared, his daughter who is wanted by the Japanese, and the daughter's lover. Beneath this tale of action is a novel of atmosphere and ideas which brings China and its teeming world of people, the land, the great Yangtze River, Chinese history, politics, poetry, art, Confucian wisdom, and Taoist brilliance and paradox close to the American reader. The title, which is taken from the Chinese classics, gives the clue to the fundamentally deeper elements of the novel: the transcendence and harmonizing of opposites.

JAMES M. CAIN

Blackstone Studios

son of a college professor and a singer, was born in Annapolis, Maryland, on July 1, 1892. At eighteen he graduated from Washington College at Chestertown, Maryland, of which his father was president. While an undergraduate James Cain exhibited complete indifference to campus affairs; he took no part in athletics or extra-curricular activities, held no jobs, and declined to edit the campus magazine. After graduation he was a reporter on the Baltimore *American* and the Baltimore *Sun*. There he met H. L. Mencken, who encouraged him to write and later published Cain's first short stories, "The Baby in the Icebox," "Pastorale," and others in *The American Mercury*. When the United States entered World War I, Mr. Cain enlisted as a private and served with the American Expeditionary Force in France. In 1919 he was editor-in-chief of *Lorraine Cross,* the official newspaper of the 79th Division. After the war he continued in newspaper work as a member of the staff of the Baltimore *Sun*. His next venture was in the academic world; he became professor of journalism at St. John's College at Annapolis. After a year there, he joined the staff of the New York *World* to write editorials under Walter Lippmann. In September, 1947, Mr. Cain married the widowed Florence Macbeth Whitwell, formerly prima donna of the Chicago Civic Opera Company.

It was while writing for *The World* that he published his first book, *Our Government* (1930), a candid if comic picture of American politics in a series of sketches and caricatures of the men and the machinery that govern us. Mr. Cain wrote a play which, although it closed on the road, brought him into contact with the late Vincent Lawrence, the Broadway playwright, whom he acknowledges as his "intellectual parent."

Often placed in the "hard-boiled" school of novelists, Mr. Cain has taken exception, in his preface to *Butterfly,* to the whole concept of classification, and in his preface to *Three of a Kind* has disclaimed any "conscious effort to be tough, or hard-boiled, or grim, or any of the things I am usually called. I merely try to write as the character would write, and I never forget that the average man . . . has acquired . . . a vividness of speech that goes beyond anything I could invent." His first book in this style of the "average man," *The Postman Always Rings Twice* (1934), is about Frank Chambers, a young poolroom hanger-on, who comes to a lonely gasoline station in California, falls in love with the Greek proprietor's wife, and murders the husband. This novel, a best seller, was banned in Canada.

Serenade (1937) is the tragic story of John Howard Sharp, an opera singer, who loses his voice, goes to Mexico City, and there meets Juana, an Indian prostitute, who brought back the vibrant quality of his singing. *Mildred Pierce* (1941), set in Glendale, a suburb of Los Angeles, describes the hasty marriage, separation, and subsequent rise of Mildred from the owner of a pie bakery to control of a restaurant chain. A triangle arises when she falls in love with her daughter's friend, a bankrupt playboy.

Love's Lovely Counterfeit (1942) is about racketeering in a midwestern city where Sol Caspar has control. Ben Grace, a former football star, is Sol's restless chauffeur. By supplying the reform party with information, Ben helps rid the town of Sol. Ben takes over and conditions are no better. *Three of a Kind* (1943) contains three novelettes: "Career in C Major," about a woman with an ambition to be a singer and her husband, an engineer, who has an operatic voice; "The Embezzler," about a young bank official and the wife of a dishonest teller; and "Double Indemnity," in which a woman plots the "insurance" murder of her husband.

In 1940, on a trip to Virginia City, Nevada, in connection with a picture, Mr. Cain conceived the idea for *Past All Dishonor* (1946), which has its setting in that city during Civil War days; frontier life provides the melodramatic background for the story of a Confederate spy and a prostitute. In *Butterfly* (1947) a Kentucky farmer and his grown and attractive daughter find their incestuous inclinations complicated by law and conscience, by his unfaithful wife, by her former lover and father of her illegitimate son, and by the man who has stolen the father's wife.

In the preface to *Three of a Kind* Mr. Cain expressed a desire "to tell tales of a wider implication than those which deal exclusively with one man's relationship to one woman." He has done this in *The Moth* (1948), the story of thirty years in the life of a man forced to leave home at twenty-two because of his love for a very young girl. The vicissitudes of his existence during the depression and through World War II are climaxed by his return home to the girl whose image never left him.

ERSKINE CALDWELL

was born near White Oak Church, Coweta County, Georgia, on December 17, 1903, the son of a Presbyterian minister whose duties as secretary of the denomination required him to visit and reside for several months at each parish. He attended primary school for one year in Virginia, grammar school in Tennessee for another year, and high school in Georgia for the same length of time. His mother taught him in the interim. His father owned one of the first automobiles in the South, and the boy had many memorable experiences; his father was arrested for frightening horses, and on another occasion the boy was held captive by moonshiners in the mountains of Virginia. At fourteen he felt the wanderlust, but his mother restrained him. In 1920 he entered Erskine College in Due West, South Carolina, but at the end of the year he went to sea on a boat carrying ammunition to the seaports and coasts of Central America.

In 1922 he tried college again at the University of Virginia, where he held a scholarship offered by the United Daughters of the Confederacy. He worked at nights in a poolroom to earn money for his room and board. At the end of the school year he engaged in a variety of occupations, but there always existed in his mind the thought that he would write professionally. In 1924 he studied at the University of Pennsylvania, where he earned his way by serving as bodyguard for a Chinese student. In 1925 he returned to the University of Virginia. In March, 1925, he married Helen Lannigan, by whom he had two sons and a daughter. He took a position as cub reporter on the Atlanta *Journal,* but soon migrated to Maine where he engaged in writing for five years. *Tobacco Road* (1932), a stark regional novel, took hold slowly. In 1933 *The Yale Review* published "Country Full of Swedes" and awarded it a one-thousand-dollar prize for fiction. Hollywood called him to write screen plays. In February, 1939, he married Margaret Bourke-White, the famous photographer, and together they did a book on their observations in Europe, where he was a correspondent. In 1941 he was a war correspondent in Russia for *Life* magazine. In December, 1942, he married June Johnson, by whom he has a son.

Year by year Mr. Caldwell's books, which picture the people caught at the bottom of the social and economic ladder, have captured ever-increasing public interest. He shows the disinherited in all their poverty, their lack of ambition, their strange mental states, their sexual perversions, their cruelties, and their humor. The stories are usually short, striking, and honest portrayals of some aspect of human conduct. The poor white people are nearly always preoccupied with sex, and there are many passages in which the humor and the action have been called bawdy. Several communities have attempted to ban one or more of Mr. Caldwell's books; in 1950 the Supreme Court of Massachusetts forbade the sale in that state of *God's Little Acre*. By 1949 his books had sold fifteen million copies in American editions, and some five million copies abroad in fourteen languages. The dramatization of *Tobacco Road* established a new record for continuous performance in New York and elsewhere.

Besides his stories and novels, Mr. Caldwell has written several non-fiction works. *Some American People* (1935) is fundamental reporting on the lives of persons in various parts of the country during the depths of the depression. *Tenant Farmer* (1935) describes the sharecropper's life and outlook. *You Have Seen Their Faces* (1935) contains text by Mr. Caldwell and pictures by Margaret Bourke-White descriptive of black and white sharecroppers in the cotton states. *North of the Danube* (1939) describes his travels in Czechoslovakia in 1938. *Say! Is This the U.S.A.?* (1941) gives the impression and feel of America. *All-Out on the Road to Smolensk* (1942) is an eye-witness account of six months of the Russian defense against Germany. Since 1940 he has been editor of *American Folkways,* a series of regional books, nineteen of which had been published by 1949. *American Earth* (1931) was his first collection of short stories. Other collections include *We Are the Living* (1933), *Kneel to the Rising Sun* (1935), *Southways* (1938), *Jackpot* (1940), and *Stories* (1944).

Tobacco Road (1932), his first novel, is the story of Jeeter Lester and his poor-white family in a remote corner of northern Georgia. The land was productive in his grandfather's time, but through laziness and poor management the family has lost its property and lives there by the courtesy of its owner. The theme is the deterioration of a once-strong family. *God's Little Acre* (1933) portrays with broadly humorous strokes the family of Ty Ty Walden, a greedy and lustful man, who for fifteen years has dug vainly for gold on his Georgia farm. Two pretty daughters provide a tragic ending to the story. *Journeyman* (1935) describes the activities of Semon Dye, a lecherous and dishonest evangelist, who swindles a farmer out of his property and shoots a Negro for objecting to the seduction of a colored girl.

Trouble in July (1940) is about three-hundred-pound Jeff McCurtain, sheriff of Julie County, Georgia, a political appointee whose laziness, evasiveness, and dilatoriness provide the basis for his refusal to remain on duty when a Negro is lynched by a drunken mob. *All Night Long* (1942) concerns the happily married manager of a collective farm when the Nazis pour over the border into Russia. He joins a guerrilla band and engages in exciting adventures. *Georgia Boy* (1943) is the life story of Morris Stroup as seen through the eyes of his twelve-year-old son, William, and of Handsome Brown, a feeble-minded Negro yard boy. *Tragic Ground* (1944) deals with Spence Douthit, an ambitionless man in a small town with a powder plant that has closed; not until social workers prod him does he take a job.

A House in the Uplands (1946) pictures Grady Dunbar, a plantation owner, who gambles away his estate and pays attention to Negro girls, but who opposes bad social and economic conditions. *The Sure Hand of God* (1947) concerns a woman without moral scruples who, at thirty-five, seeks a man to take care of her and another to marry her daughter. *This Very Earth* (1948) tells the tragic events that occur to the family when Chism Crockett, a farmer, moves to town. *Place Called Estherville* (1949) is a novel about a small town in the South, and deals with the social and economic relationships of Negroes and whites. *Episode in Palmetto* (1950) narrates events in the life of a young schoolteacher in a small southern town.

TAYLOR CALDWELL

was born in Preswich, Manchester, England, on September 7, 1900, in a family descended from the Scottish clan of MacTavish. Her father, a commercial artist, moved to the United States in 1907 and settled in Buffalo. There Miss Caldwell grew up, attended the University of Buffalo, from which she graduated in 1931, and became a stenographer. During World War I, from 1918 to 1919, she was a yeomanette in the United States Naval Reserve. In 1919 she married Fairfax Combs and in 1931 Marcus Reback; she has a daughter by each marriage. From 1924 to 1931 she served with the United States Immigration Service in Buffalo.

Miss Caldwell's immensely popular novels contain vivid action portraying scenes and personages of the past. Her insight into character gives depth to her rushing narratives.

Dynasty of Death (1938), her first novel, traces the fortunes of several generations of the Bouchard family which manufactured munitions in Pennsylvania from 1837 to 1917. *The Eagles Gather* (1940) continues the narrative of the Bouchard family from 1918 to 1928. *The Earth Is the Lord's: A Tale of Genghis Khan* (1941) is a novel describing the early years of the thirteenth-century Mongol chieftain who conquered much of Asia, the Near East, and Hungary.

Time No Longer (1941), published under the pseudonym "Max Reiner," is a story of the dangerous forces unleashed by Hitler in the 1930's in Nazi Germany. *The Strong City* (1942) pictures the steel industry in Nazareth, Pennsylvania, and the rise of Franz Stoessel, a harsh and self-seeking German foreman. *The Arm and the Darkness* (1943) portrays the emergence of the democratic spirit in the conflict between the Roman Catholics and the Huguenots in the France of Richelieu and Louis XIII in the 1570's.

The Turnbulls (1943) studies the poisonous nature of hatred. John Turnbull, forced into an early marriage, steals other men's patents and acquires a fortune in America. *The Final*

Hour (1944), third in the Bouchard series, shows a split between Antoine and Henri; the latter decides to fight Hitler to help democracy and save his fortune. *The Wide House* (1945) shows the rascally storekeeper, Stuart Coleman, developing a sympathy for refugee Jews in the 1850's in upper New York state.

This Side of Innocence (1946) is about a wastrel who makes a fortune but learns that money is not everything. *There Was a Time* (1947) pictures the career of a British boy, who migrates to Buffalo, New York, and becomes a writer. This book has some autobiographical elements. *Melissa* (1948) studies a society girl whose upbringing has made her innocence as dangerous to others as to herself. She becomes the wife of a publisher in 1860, and their problem is a serious one. *Let Love Come Last* (1949) is a family chronicle of William and Ursula Prescott beginning in the 1880's. Wealth pours in upon him, but his children are unhappy.

DOROTHY CANFIELD

Eliascheff

daughter of James Hulme Canfield, college president and educator, and of Flavia Camp Canfield, a woman of considerable artistic and literary talent, was born on February 17, 1879, in Lawrence, Kansas, where her father was a professor at the state university. Her formal education was conditioned to a great extent by her father's subsequent career; she received her bachelor's degree from Ohio State University while her father was president of that institution. Later, when her father was librarian at Columbia University, she pursued graduate courses there leading to a doctorate in romance languages in 1905. With her mother, who studied art abroad from time to time, she early became acquainted with several European countries, and France has been a second home to her.

Although Dorothy Canfield had prepared herself for an academic career, she served for only a short period as secretary of the Horace Mann School, a progressive institution connected with Columbia. Thereafter, in 1907, she married John Redwood Fisher, whom she had met at Columbia, and together they decided to take up residence in southern Vermont, which had been the home of the Canfields since 1764. There they have lived, except for short intervals, in the midst of the Green Mountains in a simple white farmhouse which they have adapted to their particular needs, often with their own hands. There they have raised their two children, written constantly, entertained their many friends and visitors, and carried on the impressive array of activities to which they have devoted themselves.

Early in World War I, the Fishers decided that they must do what they could to help their friends in France. So it was that Mr. Fisher volunteered for ambulance service, first with the French and later with the American army. His wife soon followed him abroad to devote herself to several relief projects. She played an important role in the establishment of a printing press to provide books and magazines for blinded French soldiers; when her husband was placed in charge of an American Ambulance Field Service training camp, she ran the camp commissary within earshot of artillery fire; she helped, also, to establish a convalescent home in southern France for children from the invaded areas. Out of these experiences came two of Mrs. Fisher's most interesting collections of short stories: *Home Fires in France* (1918) and *The Day of Glory* (1919). Although dealing immediately with aspects of French life during the war, today they still represent one of the best interpretations in American literature of the fundamental traits of French character.

In 1919 the Fishers returned to the United States to a life of many interests. Mrs. Fisher cannot be characterized merely as a novelist; she is a woman of letters in all that the name implies. The numerous undertakings to which she has turned her energies and her enthusiasm include the Book-of-the-Month Club, on whose board she has sat since the organization's inception in 1926. Another of her most constant interests has been education, of children as well as of adults. While living in Rome in the winter of 1912, Mrs. Fisher became acquainted with Madame Maria Montessori and on her return to the United States she wrote *A Montessori Mother* (1914) to explain to Americans this progressive system of child training. Her long connection with the American Association for Adult Education resulted in *Why Stop Learning?* (1927). *Our Young Folks* (1943), which studies the problems of youth in an industrialized society as well as the difficulties to be faced following World War II, grew out of her six years as a member of the American Youth Commission of the American Council on Education.

During World War II, Mrs. Fisher again devoted much thought and energy to many relief projects; her favorite, however, was the Children's Crusade for Children, for the success of which she was largely responsible. In addition to these specific interests, with Mr. Fisher's help she carried on a constant campaign for better human relations of every kind: family, social, and international.

In addition to the two volumes of short stories about French life, Mrs. Fisher is the author of *Hillsboro People* (1915), a series of sketches and stories of the Vermonters whom she knows so well. In reviewing another collection of stories, *Raw Material* (1923), *The Bookman* observed: "'Old Man Warner' is as perfect a picture of Vermont life as 'The Death of the Hired Man.' It is like Frost's poem in its completeness—this sketch is a work of art." The comparison is particularly apt when one considers that for many years the two writers have been friends and, part of that time, neighbors. *Basque People* (1931) contains stories based on true histories told to her while she was living in France during World War I and on subsequent visits. The short stories in *Fables for Parents* (1937) are concerned with the relationships between parents and child or among various members of a family group. A novella, *The Knot Hole* (1943), movingly describes the plight of French prisoners under the Germans. It received one of the O. Henry Memorial award prizes the year it appeared. Among her translations is Papini's *Life of Christ* (1923).

Her first novel, *Gunhild* (1907), contrasts a beautiful, self-centered American girl traveling through Norway with a peasant girl whose depth of soul shows up the superficiality of the society girl and captivates the suitor. *The Squirrel Cage* (1912) compares the life of a young woman who makes a "suitable" marriage in an ultra-materialistic society with that of her lover, who has the courage to live the simple life that his ideals dictate. *The Bent Twig* (1915) is the story of a midwestern university professor's daughter who, in spite of the temptations of a more worldly life, clings in the end to the traditions and ideals of her plain-living, high-thinking parents. *Understood Betsy* (1917), the story of the lonely little city girl who finds sympathetic relatives and a home in Vermont, has become a classic among children's stories.

The Brimming Cup (1921) recounts the marriage of Neale and Marise and in the end shows how a love triangle is happily solved by the husband's wisdom and the wife's ideals. *Rough Hewn* (1922) pictures Neale and Marise from childhood to the time of their engagement. In *The Homemaker* (1924) a discontented and talented housewife and a poet-dreamer husband who is a misfit in the business world successfully change places as the result of an accident. *Her Son's Wife* (1926) deals with the unusual course of action chosen by a grandmother to provide a proper home for a grandchild whose mother is totally unfit for the task.

The Deepening Stream (1930) tells the story of Priscilla, Francis, and Matey Gilbert, children of a French professor and his flighty wife, against the background of the differing cultural standards of American and French family life. In their formative period, Priscilla learns that the art of living consists in keeping busy and never thinking or feeling deeply; Francis learns to see his own advantage and to play his parents off against one another; only Matey tries to find something beautiful and enduring in life, and because of this she is able to make her own marriage gracious and permanent. *Seasoned Timber* (1939) draws the full-length, detailed portrait of a man of great character and distinction who refuses to take advantage of other people for his own personal gain. This study of a poor academy in rural Vermont symbolizes the present-day struggle between dictatorships and democracy.

LEGRAND CANNON, JR.

was born in New Haven, Connecticut, on December 1, 1899. After earning a degree of Bachelor of Philosophy at Yale in 1920, he went on to Harvard to receive the degree of Master of Business Administration in 1922. After ten years in business he decided to devote himself to writing. Since 1932 he has spent much time near Mount Chocorua, admiring the mountain and the New Hampshire countryside that it dominates. In 1922 he married Jeannette Peabody; they have four children and live in New Haven.

A Mighty Fortress (1937), his first novel, is about Zeke Peele, born in 1828 on a New Hampshire farm, who becomes a Boston pastor, marries a slave trader's niece, joins the abolition movement, loses his job, and becomes a better man and husband. *The Kents* (1938), a story of American business from 1860 to 1890, concerns a family on Wall Street that does well until Jim unwisely plunges and brings about his death. Years later young Jim drives hard to get wealth. *Look to the Mountain* (1942) is a long novel about pioneering in New Hampshire from 1769 to 1777. Before they were twenty, Whit Livingstone and Melissa Butler discover that they want each other, but they know, too, that there is no place for them in the snug, settled village of Kettleford. They set off together up the Merrimack River to the country of lakes and streams under the shadow of Mount Chocorua. The book is notable for its picture of courage, thrift, industry, and the belief in man's ability to achieve a place for himself on this earth.

TRUMAN CAPOTE

Florence Homolka

was born in 1925 in New Orleans. He has written speeches for a third-rate politician, danced on a river boat, painted flowers on glass, read scripts for a film company, studied fortunetelling, worked on *The New Yorker* magazine, and selected anecdotes for a digest magazine. The first of his stories to attract attention was written when he was seventeen, and in 1948 he won the O. Henry Memorial award for the best short story of the year. In 1948 he made extended visits to Haiti and to France. His work owes something to Proust and William Faulkner. *Tree of Night* (1949) contains eight short stories with psychic or supernatural backgrounds. *Local Color* (1950) includes notes and sketches of places he has visited and of people he has met.

Other Voices, Other Rooms (1948), his first novel, is the story of Joel, a thirteen-year-old New Orleans boy with homosexual tendencies, and his experiences in a desolate Louisiana rural community during one long summer as he moves painfully and at times terrifyingly into emotional maturity.

ROBERT SPENCER CARR

Glidden

was born on March 26, 1909, in Washington, D.C. At the age of fifteen he made front-page headlines in Columbus, Ohio, by selling his first stories to national periodicals. At seventeen his first novel, *The Rampant Age,* promised a brilliant career; Hollywood and leading magazines bid for his writing. At twenty, with more experience than many writers collect in a lifetime, Carr deliberately abandoned writing. For years he roamed the country, working on newspapers, in factories, as secretary to a psychoanalyst, in employment agencies and travel bureaus, and as a truck driver. Only an occasional short story revealed his maturing power and talent. Five years of foreign travel far off the beaten track produced his second novel. The war found him a private in the infantry. After the war he went to the mountains of New Mexico and worked three years upon *The Room Beyond,* the major book for which he prepared himself by twenty years of travel and study. He now lives near Fort Myers, Florida.

Rampant Age (1928), his first novel, tells the causes and cure of juvenile delinquency in the jazz age of 1920 in the story of Paul Benton, who moves from the country to a city, attends high school, and joins the fast set. Drinking, petting, and speeding reflect, the author indicates, the parents' extravagance. *The Bells of St. Ivan's* (1944) is a touching tale of an American engineer's return in 1943 to a small Ukrainian village and his talks with the peasants about the changes which have occurred. Particularly he learns the meaning of the reopening of the church and the improved situation of the priest. He is present at the dramatic ringing of the bells of Saint Ivan's. *The Room Beyond* (1948) is an unusual novel in plan and substance; it portrays the obsessive love which Dr. Daniel Bryce has during fifty years for Miss Christina, a saintlike person who continues to reappear in spite of conclusive evidence of her death. The materials of comparative religion and mystical experience are dramatized in the form of a romantic mystery story; three different solutions are given to the enigma of life and death in time: materialistic, psychological, and spiritual.

CONSOLATA CARROLL

is the pseudonym of Sister Mary Consolata of the Order of the Sisters of Mercy. She was born in 1892 in Rome, New York. She attended Rome public schools and was graduated from the Rome Free Academy. She says: "I spent the formative years of my life close to the convent of the Sisters of the Holy Names. In the groves and on the waters that adjoined the convent grounds I shared the play of the young boarders under the supervision of these good nuns. The lovely refining associations of that time left a lasting impression on my mind." She studied home economics at Pratt Institute and was recommended by the Institute for a teaching position at Mount Saint Mary's College in Plainfield, New Jersey. After five years of teaching she became a novice at the Motherhouse of the Sisters of Mercy who conducted the school.

Her subsequent teaching and study were in the field of English. She was graduated from Fordham University with a Master of Arts degree. She spent a summer at the Breadloaf School of English in Ripton, Vermont, and has studied at Columbia University. She is a member of the faculty of Georgian Court College in Lakewood, New Jersey.

She says, "I became interested in creative writing because my pupils were; in order to help them, I took courses in short-story writing. When I had finished a story that I thought would interest a student desiring to write, my friendly critic advised: 'You do not have to write about what your *students* know; they can do that. Write of the things *you* know.' I believe that *Pray Love, Remember* grew out of that remark."

Pray Love, Remember (1947) gives autobiographical reminiscences in fictional form of the author's early childhood and of the mores of a Catholic family of moderate means. There are kindly descriptions of family, neighbors, and friends, including a brother-in-law who belongs to the printers' union and a dear elder sister. *I Hear in My Heart* (1949), containing further reminiscences in the same vein, tells why and how an upper New York state girl, a graduate of Pratt Institute and a teacher, becomes a convent nun.

GLADYS HASTY CARROLL

Clara E. Sipprell

was born on June 26, 1904, in Rochester, New Hampshire, the daughter of Mr. and Mrs. Warren V. Hasty. Her parents had lived in South Berwick, Maine, and returned there when Gladys was less than a year old. Here she was educated in the district school and in Berwick Academy, an institution once attended by Sarah Orne Jewett, a lifelong resident of South Berwick. Later Gladys entered Bates College at Lewiston, Maine, and was graduated in 1925. A day after commencement she was married in the Bates chapel to Herbert A. Carroll of the Class of 1923. Their first home was in Fall River, Massachusetts, where Mr. Carroll taught English in Durfee High School and pursued graduate studies at Brown University. In the following summers both studied at Harvard and at the University of Chicago. In 1928 they moved to New York City, where Mr. Carroll took his doctorate at Columbia University and where Mrs. Carroll wrote two juvenile books, *Cockatoo* (1929) and *Land Spell* (1930). In 1930 Dr. Carroll became professor of educational psychology at the University of Minnesota. A son, Warren Hasty, was born in 1932. The Carrolls traveled widely in this country and abroad, and they built a home in South Berwick. Early in 1941 Dr. Carroll joined the faculty of the University of New Hampshire at Durham, about fifteen miles from their home. In the spring of 1941 their daughter Sarah was born. Mrs. Carroll received the degree of Doctor of Literature from the University of Maine in 1940 and from Bates College in 1945.

Her first novel, *As the Earth Turns* (1933), takes the family of Mark Shaw through the four seasons of the year in Maine to show the changes which affect the people, changes which bring love, marriage, birth, and death. Mark's love of the soil is shared by his daughter Jen, who marries a Polish boy. *A Few Foolish Ones* (1935) pictures four families of different temperaments in a Maine community in the sixty years after 1870. Kate Bragdon's love for Stephen Blaine withers when he shows signs of being a drifter; only those who love the soil prosper, she thinks. *Neighbor to the Sky* (1937) follows the fortunes of two young Maine people. Luke is satisfied to remain on the farm, but his ambitious wife, Margery, urges him to go to college. He becomes a teacher in Wisconsin, but in the depression they return to their Maine farm. *Head of the Line* (1942) contains short stories.

Dunnybrook (1943) is a fictional history and genealogy of Berwick, Maine, a community in which Mrs. Carroll hopes that homeless people of other lands will discover "a comforting picture of what free men can build in a free world, though freedom be their only wealth, and their own minds and hands their only tools or weapons." *While the Angels Sing* (1947) is a touching Christmas tale of small-town doubters and the manner in which Widow Selena Monroe brings happiness and faith to the home of her daughter, Julie. *West of the Hill* (1949) portrays the power of love in transforming the lives of Molly, a young, lonely, and unwanted girl, and of Brad, a country boy who proposes to her out of kindness. They run away, marry, and grow in grace during the first two years of their union. *Christmas without Johnny* (1950) is about a troubled nine-year-old boy misunderstood by adults guilty of the sins of blindness and omission.

(WILLIAM) HODDING CARTER (JR.)

was born at Hammond, Louisiana, on February 3, 1907. He grew up in Louisiana and spent his summers at his grandmother's home on the Mississippi River. In youth his anger was aroused by white boys who tormented Negro children. At fourteen he saw a lynch victim hanging from a tree. These unpleasant pictures left indelible impressions upon his mind. He attended Bowdoin College at Brunswick, Maine, and received his bachelor's degree in 1927; a year later he graduated from the Columbia University School of Journalism. The next school year was spent at Tulane University as a teaching fellow. In 1929 he became a reporter on the New Orleans *Item-Tribune,* and in 1930 the night manager of the New Orleans office of the United Press. Soon he transferred to the Associated Press at Jackson, Mississippi. In October, 1931, he married. When he was dismissed for insubordination, he and his wife founded a newspaper of their own at Hammond. In 1936 they moved to Greenville, Mississippi, where they established the *Delta Star* and crusaded against the evil prejudices that beset our democracy. In 1938 he took over the fifty-year-old Greenville *Democrat-Times,* consolidating the two papers as the *Delta Democrat-Times,* an afternoon daily. After a year in 1939–40 as a Nieman Fellow in journalism at Harvard University, he joined the staff of *PM,* a new experimental liberal newspaper in New York.

Carter had joined the National Guard in 1938, and with his unit he entered the army in November, 1940. An accident cost him the sight of his right eye, but he remained in the service in public-relations work in Washington and in editorial work on *The Stars and Stripes* and *Yank* in Cairo, Egypt. During these years he wrote *Lower Mississippi* (1942), a volume in the "Rivers of America" series, and was joint author of *The Civilian Defense of the United States* (1942). At the close of his army service he returned to his newspaper in Greenville; soon his vigorous editorials attracted national attention. In 1945 he held a Guggenheim fellowship; in 1946 he was awarded a Pulitzer prize for editorial writing and a War Department citation. *Southern Legacy* (1950) explains the attitudes and traditions of his home community in an anecdotal, autobiographical way. The reasons are given for the existence of the Ku Klux Klan, the poor whites, and other groups holding the idea of "white supremacy." The social and religious basis of life in the South is analyzed.

The Winds of Fear (1944), a powerful novel about the use of violence between races, describes the mounting racial tension in Carvell City and the naming of Cancy Dodd, a backcountry man, to put fear—fear of God, of the white man, and of the law—into every Negro's mind. Cancy's brutality sows the wind and reaps the whirlwind. "If you have not lived in Carvell City," wrote Mr. Carter, "it is too easy to denounce its masters, forgetting that they are also slaves of the fear which impels them." *Flood Crest* (1945) portrays Senator Pikestaff, a southern demagogue, seeking re-election with rabble-rousing arguments during the time that the Mississippi River is in flood.

MARIAN CASTLE

Jafay

was born on November 5, 1898, in Kendall County, Illinois. Her father, Oliver C. Johnson, was a Presbyterian minister; her mother, Anna French Johnson, was an author and lecturer. Her ancestors seem to have been highly dissatisfied and restless Britons who emigrated to this country in the seventeenth and eighteenth centuries to father an impressive progeny, and to establish numerous schools, churches, and towns.

Her early life was the usual unsettled one of a minister's family. Her education was acquired in a series of middle-western schools and colleges. She spent her summers doing "Chautauqua work," which meant booking, acting as advance agent, and superintending throughout western Canada and the United States for that now dead, but once potent, institution for uplift, entertainment, and "hokum." She majored in economics at the University of Chicago, from which she graduated in 1920. Ill-health then sent her to Albuquerque, New Mexico, where she did social work. She was married to Edward Carrick Castle in 1924, and they have made their home in Denver, Colorado, ever since.

She began to write soon after her marriage: at first, action stories under a pen name; then short articles and essays for a variety of magazines. Her chief interest in writing has been to present what seems to her a provocative or appealing portion of the American scene.

Deborah (1946), her first novel, pictures the compelling American urge toward education, that great, bootstrap-lifting dream of middle-class, middle-western America after the first pioneer tidal wave was spent. The story concerns a girl on the Dakota prairies, her two marriages, and the lives of her children and grandchildren. *The Golden Fury* (1949), a selection of the Dollar Book Club and an alternate selection of the Literary Guild, was written out of Mrs. Castle's affection for the Rocky Mountain West, with its majestic terrain and its brief, sometimes seamy, and occasionally heroic history. Based on rather extensive research and many personal interviews, it shows life in the boom mining camps of the young state of Colorado from 1878 to 1909.

ROY CHANSLOR

was born in Liberty, Missouri, on August 25, 1899. When he was six his family moved to Reno, then a frontier town, baffling to his churchgoing mother and delightful to the boy. One of his brightest memories is the spectacular fire which destroyed the huge Palace Gambling House; to enjoy that sight he "played hooky" for the first but by no means the last time. He was unsuccessfully exposed to education in schools in Floristan, Sacramento, Long Beach, and Berkeley, California, and was spectacularly expelled from the University of California in 1923 for publishing D. H. Lawrence and Upton Sinclair in a sophomorically iconoclastic magazine called *The Laughing Horse.*

His non-academic education began at sixteen with a job as lifeguard at a beach resort; he doubled at night as a barker on "The Race Through the Clouds." Later he became an ill-paid reporter doing amusing work; sports writer, book and movie reviewer and copyreader in New York and Washington; producer of a newspaper play called *Tabloid;* free-lance writer of magazine fiction; scenaist in Hollywood with more than fifty produced screenplays; and novelist. He lives with his wife, Majorie Torrey, the artist, illustrator, and author, on a hilltop in Encino, above the San Fernando Valley of California.

Of his novels he says: "If my work has a theme it is a simple one: Men and women must stand on their own feet and pay their way; there is no substitute for character, integrity, and courage. Or, as a character in my third novel says, 'no substitute for guts.' I try to make a few affirmative statements. I believe in people and in the American dream."

Lowdown (1931), his first novel, is a study in violence, the story of the influences motivating a racket overlord and of the two women from two different worlds who loved him. *Hazard* (1947) is a story of flight and return; of a woman obsessed with the need for risk, possessed by the fever that is gambling; and of the man who hunted her and helped her bring herself back, alive in every sense of the word. *There's A New Wind Blowing* (1950) is a tale of life against death: life personified by two men, one of them a Negro, who are fugitives from "justice," death by a girl with a suicide compulsion. Its climax describes a hard-won victory.

MARISTAN CHAPMAN

is the pseudonym of John Stanton Chapman and his wife, Mary Ilsley Chapman. They have written novels, juveniles, and mystery stories together. In 1948 they announced the forthcoming publication of six historical novels about Tennessee; this saga will cover the history of the region from de Soto's arrival in 1540 to the end of World War I in 1918.

Stanton Chapman was born in London, England, on May 21, 1891. He was educated privately and from 1910 to 1920 was an aeronautical engineer. During World War I he served with the British Air Service and then was assigned to the United States Army Signal Corps. In London he met and married Mary Ilsley on February 26, 1917. He came to the United States in the same year and was naturalized in 1926. He has contributed articles to engineering and scientific journals.

Mary Ilsley Chapman was born on September 10, 1895, in Chattanooga, Tennessee, the daughter of an Episcopal minister with parishes in Tennessee, Georgia, and West Virginia. She attended the Duval English-French School in Chattanooga and Kemper Hall Convent School in Kenosha, Wisconsin. She completed her education abroad. At the outbreak of World War I, she was in London, where she served as secretary to a member of Parliament and later in the British aircraft service.

The Chapmans do all their work in collaboration. They have written a series of some twenty-five "Glen Hazard" books for boys and girls. Their only collaborative work not located in the east Tennessee mountain locale is *Imperial Brother: A Life of the Duc de Morny* (1931). "We write about people we know and like," says Mrs. Chapman, "with the hope of giving pleasure to people who like to read. It is as simple as that."

The Happy Mountain (1928), their first novel, describes the mountain folk with a sympathy that gave this book a high place among new regional novels. It is the story of a mountain boy who goes into the "far'n beyond" where there are wide valleys and a sea; when he learns that another boy is wooing his sweetheart, he returns home to tell about his wanderings. *Home Place* (1929) contains some of the characters in *The Happy Mountain* and tells the story of a mountain boy who makes a home for himself and his beloved. *The Weather Tree* (1932) brings an "outlander" to a Tennessee village. He proposes to cut down a great white oak which has served as the weather prophet for the region. This and other mistakes force him to leave the community of Glen Hazard.

Rogue's March (1949) is about a Tennessee mountain man who, although loyal to the American cause, falls in love with the daughter of a notorious Tory and returns after the Battle of King's Mountain in 1780 to claim her as his bride. Margaret Brooke, the heroine, lives on the plantation "Rogue's March." Lantry Ward, the hero, is an express rider for the Colonists. Backwoods life and tradition are described fully.

JOAN CHARLES

was born in Cincinnati, Ohio, on March 5, 1914. She was educated in preparatory schools, Sarah Lawrence College, and the Columbia University School of Oral Hygiene. After her marriage in 1939 to Charles Underwood and her daughter's birth two years later, she began to write; her novels appeared under her own name, while she used the pen name of "Charlotte Underwood" for her magazine stories. In 1944 André Maurois persuaded her to try her hand at translation; this occupation has taken up a great deal of her time since. Among these translations are *Woman without Love* and *From My Journal* by Maurois, *Old Man Goriot* by Balzac, and *Madame Bovary* by Flaubert. She also teaches an advanced short-story-writing course at Queens College in Flushing, Long Island, New York.

The Dark Glass (1944), her first novel, tells about the return to sanity of a girl, Ann, who has become unbalanced through a series of threats to her security in marrying the wrong husband. Her innocence cannot withstand the cynicism of her environment, but the love of a good physician helps her recover. *Son and Stranger* (1945) portrays a son who is imprisoned in his mother's too greatly possessive love and his problem of breaking away. *And the Hunter Home* (1946) tells about a man's return from painful experiences in war and in a Japanese prison camp, and the help his sister and a friend give in his slow readjustment. *Wrong Turning* (1947) deals with an adolescent girl's efforts to find emotional security and a satisfactory compensation for the affection and understanding she does not receive from her parents.

BORDEN CHASE

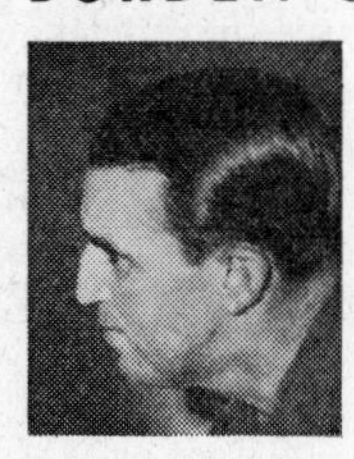

was born in Brooklyn, New York, where he spent his first sixteen years and grew up with an accent and with the firm conviction that the Dodgers were always "robbed." At seventeen he joined the navy. Subsequent to World War I he plied a large number of trades—shipyard worker, hack driver, carnival high diver, milk-wagon driver, construction worker on buildings and bridges, sandhogger, and commercial diver. He married Lee Keith, a concert pianist who was playing in Carnegie Hall, New York City, while he was working under the East River on the Eighth Avenue Subway tunnels. He has done numerous original plays for motion pictures.

East River (1935), his first novel, has a background of tunneling under New York City's East River, and tells the story of two workers and the two women they love. *Sandhog* (1938) gives further details of the process of building a viaduct under a river in this story of a man who gives up a boss's job to fight for better working conditions for men in this occupation. *Blazing Guns on the Chisholm Trail* (1948) is a melodramatic tale of the West and of the experiences and romance of a Texan heading home after the War between the States.

MARY ELLEN CHASE

Eric Stahlberg

was born at Blue Hill, Maine, on February 24, 1887. She studied at Blue Hill Academy and the University of Maine, from which she graduated in 1909. In college she wrote juvenile stories. For several years she taught history in western boarding schools, and then in 1918 she went to teach English in the University of Minnesota, where she earned her master's degree in 1918 and her doctorate in 1922. Smith College called her to a professorship of English literature in 1926. She teaches three days a week and devotes the remainder of her time to writing, lecturing, gardening, and bird study. She has traveled in many countries. Before World War II she spent most of her summers and the years 1935 and 1936 in England, where she enjoyed exploring on foot the tiny villages of the southern counties, Cornwall being her favorite. *This England* (1936) and *In England Now* (1937) are witty and understanding essays. Her other books include several texts and compilations of scholarly essays. *The Girl from the Big Horn Country* (1916), *Virginia of Elk Creek Valley* (1917), *Mary Christmas* (1926), and *The Silver Shell* (1930) are stories for children. *Jonathan Fisher* (1948) is a biography of a Maine preacher. Miss Chase has set down reminiscences in *A Goodly Heritage* (1932) and *A Goodly Fellowship* (1939).

Uplands (1927), her first novel, pictures the hilly farming land of Dorset, Maine, as a background for the story of the escape of Martha Crosby from an environment of poverty to a convent after the death of her sweetheart, Jarvis Crosby, who shared her views. *Mary Peters* (1934) is about a sea captain's daughter who returns to her Maine home after spending the early years of her life on board a sailing ship; she grows old and wise in simplicity while leading a full life.

Four generations of the Crocketts, a New England family, are pictured in *Silas Crockett* (1935). Silas is a clipper captain; Nicholas, the son, is lost at sea in a storm; Reuben, the grandson, captains a coastwise steamer and then a ferryboat; and Silas, the great-grandson, is compelled to leave college to work in a herring factory. *Dawn in Lyonesse* (1938) compresses into forty-eight hours the story of Ellen and Derek, modern dwellers in Cornwall, England, whose experiences parallel the ancient love affair of Tristram and Iseult.

Windswept (1941) is a chronicle of three generations of family life in an isolated spot on the blustery coast of Maine. *The Plum Tree* (1949) characterizes Emma Davis, a nurse who runs a home for aging women and who aspires to the inward grace symbolized by the blossoming plum tree outside her window. Her qualities as a human being are tested when three eccentric old ladies suddenly become dangerous.

ELIZABETH PICKETT CHEVALIER

Max Munn Autrey

was born in Chicago on March 25, 1896. She grew up in Oak Park, the west Chicago suburb. Her father, Montgomery Pickett, in 1908 won the Chicago *Tribune's* first play contest with his entry *The Fourth Physician*. In her senior year at Oak Park High School she wrote month by month a serial for the student paper. While at Wellesley College, from which she graduated in 1918, her verse was included in *The Poets of the Future* (1917), and her only short story, "The Return of Vach," appeared in O'Brien's collection of *The Best College Short Stories of 1918*. In June, 1918, she worked in a can factory for seventeen cents an hour. She had been offered a scholarship in the School of Civics and Philanthropy of the University of

Chicago, but her industrial experience convinced her that social uplift along these lines was not her forte. In August, 1918, she went to Washington as publicity representative for the American Red Cross Nursing Service, and stayed on until December, 1924, to write World War I section of the *Official History of the Red Cross Nursing Service* and *The American National Red Cross, Its Origin, Purposes and Services,* which local chapter secretaries today call their "Red Cross Bible."

In 1924 she took a job with the Fox Film Corporation, making movie shorts in New York. Transferred to Fox West Coast Studios in 1926, for two years she edited features, wrote titles and original dog and horse "operas," and continued to produce and direct scenic and short subjects. Her Indian story *Redskin* became the first all-color outdoor motion-picture epic. From 1929 to 1936 she lived on a Kentucky farm. In 1936 she married Stuart Chevalier and has since lived in California. One of the first governors-at-large of the American Red Cross, she has been active in streamlining its organization.

Her first novel, *Drivin' Woman* (1942), tells of fifty years in the experiences of Merry Moncure, another of that remarkable generation of post-war southern women who, with little left except their brains, character, and courage, succeeded in making distinguished careers. With Merry's love story is told the saga of the daring, picturesque, but long since vanished tobacco speculators on the hogshead markets of Cincinnati, Louisville, and St. Louis, who were put out of business by the rise of Tugger Blake, typical of the ruthless but able industrial pioneers of the period from 1870 to 1910. This novel was a selection of the Literary Guild. "One reason," says Mrs. Chevalier, "why this my first novel was translated into many languages is that the experience of women in Europe after V-E Day paralleled the experiences of American women whom my post-Civil War heroine portrayed."

ANN CHIDESTER

Lotte Jacobi

was born and raised in Stillwater, Minnesota, where her mother's people were pioneers and where she still resides. She is of Welsh and Irish descent. Her father's people, who were Hoosiers, came over from Wales and fought in the American Revolution. Ann Chidester was educated in parochial and public schools in Minnesota. Her stories have appeared in *The Atlantic, Collier's, Cosmopolitan,* and other leading magazines. "All that one is," she has stated, "is in one's work."

Young Pandora (1942), her first novel, is a story about Jody Barker, a midwestern girl born in 1921, and her experiences at the state university, her start as a writer, her first love affair, and her plans to tour the country in a jalopy. *No Longer Fugitive* (1943) has the theme of man's quest of self-knowledge in the story of Liam Moore, a youth of twenty, who wonders about his loneliness and refuses to be drafted into the army because he wants to be at peace with all people. *The Long Year* (1946) pictures the depression year of 1933 in High Falls, Minnesota, as it affects the employees of the Hasswell factory. Kay Hasswell, a world-traveled and thrice-married woman, returns to run the mill and becomes a symbol of the harshness and inhumanity of the intangible terror called "business recession." *Mama Maria's* (1947) brings together at a motel a tiny, elderly lady, the proprietress; a girl who wants to get away from home, and a mechanic who works for Mama Maria. Their triangle is played out against others visiting the motel. *Moon Gap* (1950) is about Cassie King, a Nevada girl, who is deserted by her husband and who comes to her father's home in the Mojave Desert ghost town of Moon Gap to secure the freedom she needs. The eerie atmosphere is well portrayed.

DONALD BARR CHIDSEY

Ben Pinchot

was born on May 14, 1902, at Elizabeth, New Jersey, where he attended the public schools and Bartin High School. In 1942 and 1943 he was an American Field Service ambulance driver in the Middle East and Africa. He now resides in Lyme, Connecticut. His non-fiction books include *Bonnie Prince Charlie: A Biography of the Young Pretender* (1928), *Marlborough: The Portrait of a Conqueror* (1929), *Sir Walter Raleigh: That Damned Upstart* (1931), *Sir Humphrey Gilbert: Elizabeth's Racketeer* (1932), and *The Gentleman from New York: A Life of Roscoe Conkling* (1935). *John the Great* (1942) recreates the fabulous period in which John L. Sullivan was America's champion heavyweight boxer. Mr. Chidsey has also written a vast amount for magazines, mostly adventure fiction and travel articles.

Mr. Chidsey's first novel was *Pistols in the Morning* (1930), a romantic adventure story of Mississippi River steamboating days and of Felix Blake, a gambler, whose daring deeds win a wealthy girl. *Weeping Is for Women* (1936) tells how George and Miriam Crawford hope to send their son and daughter to college and then to travel around the world. *Panama Passage* (1946) is an historical novel of the building of the Panama Canal and of the love affair of an engineer. The Jeffersonian Embargo provides background in *Stronghold* (1948) for the story of two Connecticut apprentices who outwit customs agents and who later fall in love with Deliverance Watts, their employer's daughter.

WALTER VAN TILBURG CLARK

was born at East Orland, Maine, on August 3, 1909. The family moved west in 1917, and he attended school in Reno, Nevada, and subsequently the University of Nevada, of which his father was president; thereafter he did two years of graduate work at the University of Vermont. For ten years he taught English and coached dramatics and sports in the public schools of Cazenovia, New York. After a brief sojourn in Taos, New Mexico, he moved to an old ranch in Washoe Valley, Nevada, where he lives at present, devoting his full time to writing. Although Mr. Clark is a lecturer at a number of writers' conferences, he is congenitally, philosophically, and violently opposed to any kind of platform lecturing. His first writing was almost entirely poetry, but he later contributed a number of articles and short stories to magazines. His stories have appeared several times in *The Best Short Stories* and the *O. Henry Memorial Collection*. "The Wind and the Snow of Winter" won the O. Henry award in 1945. He married Barbara Morse of Troy, Pennsylvania, in 1933; they have two children.

The Ox-Bow Incident (1940), his first novel, is a study of mob psychology, based upon the lynching of three supposed cattle rustlers in Nevada in 1885, but with contemporary implications concerning the difference between democratic and totalitarian concepts of justice. *The City of Trembling Leaves* (1945) combines a picture of the sensitive adolescence and slow maturing of Tim Hazard, revealed largely through the effects of a prolonged and hopeless high-school love affair in the Reno, Nevada, of the 1920's, with a representation of the difficulties of artistic growth (Tim is a musician) in the indifferent environment of modern, small-town America. The interdependence of the two themes, and their ultimate resolution into one, indicates a musical approach to the problem of form; the artist-in-America theme is reinforced by the secondary and finally almost contrapuntal theme of Tim's friendship with Lawrence Black, a painter.

The Tracks of the Cat (1949) tells the story of the pursuit of a marauding mountain lion by the three sons of an isolated ranching family during a three-day October blizzard in the Sierras. The tale of the actual hunt is reinforced and given symbolic implications by the parallel struggle, in the minds of all concerned, with a legendary black lion introduced to them years before by the very old and cryptic Indian, Joe Sam, who is their hired hand. *The Watchful Gods* (1950) contains a number of short stories and a novella.

DONALD HENDERSON CLARKE

was born on August 24, 1887, in South Hadley, Massachusetts. He attended public schools in Holyoke, worked for ten cents an hour in the public library in order to gratify a passion for reading, wrote a large part of the monthly high-school *Herald,* and was chosen its editor-in-chief in his senior year. He was voted worst-behaved, best-dressed, and most sarcastic of that class. He entered Harvard in 1904, forgot to take his fall hour examinations in 1905, traveled in the West Indies and South America in 1906, and went to work in the circulation department of the New York *World* in 1907; after a few months of posting advertisements with a magnetic tack hammer, he became a staff reporter. From vacation on Cape Cod in the summer of 1908, he telegraphed E. Lloyd Sheldon, then a "cub" on *The World,* "Let's resign and take a trip." Sheldon wired back, "Have resigned. Where are we going?" They then worked on newspapers in Memphis, Tennessee; Little Rock, Arkansas; New Orleans, Louisiana; Montgomery, Alabama; and Charleston, South Carolina. They sold stories by wire to newspapers throughout the country.

When he was not welcomed back on *The World,* young Clarke returned to Harvard, only to be suspended, although he was on the dean's list, during final examinations in his junior year in 1911. He returned to the newspaper business, first on the Jersey City *Hudson Observer,* and then once more on *The World,* where he was a staff reporter until 1920. He served two periods on the New York *American* and one on the New York *Times.* When no newspaper would pay him the salary he demanded, he wrote stock-market letters for a brokerage house. On learning that this firm was a "bucket shop," he went to work for Goldwyn Pictures. He remained with that company while it passed through mergers which resulted in the Metro-Goldwyn-Mayer combination. While with the latter company, he underwent full Freudian psychoanalysis in 1927 and 1928 and thereafter began to write novels. In 1931 he resigned from Metro-Goldwyn-Mayer and since then has written perhaps thirty books, some magazine stories, a few screenplays, and a dozen or more radio programs. In 1941 he was beset by illnesses, operations, and inertia, and did no writing, except one screenplay, until 1948. He married Miss Gladys Webber of New York City in 1929; they live in Santa Monica, California.

Millie (1930), his first novel, is the study of a red-haired woman with an inferiority complex, whose unconscious compulsion to love the forbidden man results in a headlong rush to moral destruction. *Impatient Virgin* (1931) concerns an ardent orphan brought up under the influence of a charming but rather eccentric uncle. *Young and Healthy* (1931) tells the story of the adolescence and young manhood of a New York newspaper reporter with an inferiority complex and few inhibitions. *The Chastity of Gloria Boyd* (1932) pictures a girl with a bad background and nondescript heredity, but so beautiful that most men wish to forgive her, help her—and make love to her.

John Bartel, Jr. (1932) is the story of a young man who is guided in love, marriage, and work by a burning desire to compensate in his own career for the errors of his divorced parents. *Regards to Broadway* (1935) takes a group of young persons in New York from 1915, when they were afire with radical ideas including free love and socialism, to money-making middle age and moral and physical deterioration. In *Alabam'* (1934) a lovely, not too intelligent southern girl hitchhikes to Hollywood, lives in a motor court, suffers deceptions and disappointments, including involvement with underworld denizens, and finally becomes a glamour girl of motion pictures—a story with its foundations in the real lives of living persons.

Kelly (1935) concerns an Italian girl who cherishes ideals despite the fact that she is a Broadway manicurist with a father who is sent to Sing Sing and a brother who is a gangster. She searches for and finds love and middle-class happiness against an authentic background of that Broadway where the upper and the underworld blend. Walter Winchell gave this book "orchids." *Millie's Daughter* (1939) is more the story of the mother than of the daughter; perhaps the author was more interested in the doctor than in either. *Murderer's Holiday* (1940) was written for fun. Lewis Barrett, father of Danny, about whom events revolve, is the retired, wealthy, and "respectable" Louis Beretti. *A Lady Named Lou* (1941) is a novel of the transformation of a New England cab driver's daughter into a glamour girl. *Joe and Jennie* (1949) is the story of a curious romance between an unusually tall young woman with her conflicts, and a Napoleon-sized older man with a conqueror's ambition. It describes amusingly the gayer life at Southern California beaches.

ROBERT MYRON COATES

Arni

was born on April 6, 1897, in New Haven, Connecticut. He entered Yale, where his studies were interrupted for a year and a half during World War I by service in naval aviation. Following his graduation in 1919, he worked for a time as a writer for a newspaper syndicate and for a rubber company. His heart was not in this work, and so in 1921 he went to Europe. For five years he wrote Sunday magazine stories for the New York *Times* and other publications. Soon after his return to this country, he began contributing to *The New Yorker* and later became associated in an editorial position with this magazine. *All the Year Round* (1943) contains twenty-eight short stories. All of Mr. Coates' books are clearly related to, and are an interpretation of, the times about which they are written.

His first novel, *The Eater of Darkness* (1929), which is a commentary on the rather Dadaist period which followed World War I, burlesques mystery novels which continually shift the scene, and also describes an ingenious scientist who, with the aid of a radio, murders twenty people. *The Outlaw Years* (1930) is a serious history of the land pirates who from 1800 to 1835 operated along the Natchez Trace, the overland trade route running through Kentucky, Tennessee, and Mississippi. *Yesterday's Burdens* (1933), a commentary on the boom-time era of the 1920's, is a novel about Henderson, a man who typifies a young man of New York in a series of half-hearted alcoholic passions and infidelities.

The Bitter Season (1946) portrays the confusion, disorder, and violence of war as experienced by the fearful people of New York in the days preceding the invasion of Europe in World War II. Its theme is that all people share the guilt as well as the pains of war. *Wisteria Cottage* (1948) is a reflection of the neuroses and uncertainties which troubled Americans at the end of the first half of the twentieth century. The story concerns Richard Baurie, a schizophrenic with a Messianic complex, who eventually murders two members of a family who befriend him.

ELIZABETH COATSWORTH

Hobbs Studio

was born on May 31, 1893, in Buffalo, New York. She was educated at Vassar and at Columbia, where she received her master's degree in 1916. The following years she traveled in the Orient and Europe and began publishing poetry. A little later she became interested in writing for children, a field in which she has published many books, including *The Cat Who Went to Heaven,* winner of the Newbery award for 1930. Still later she wrote several novels and books of short essays. Her short stories appear from time to time in magazines and in collections. Poetry remains her favorite medium, although she continues to work in all others. In 1929 she married Henry Beston, the naturalist and writer. They have two daughters and live in Maine above Damariscotta Pond on the land which Mr. Beston has described in *Northern Farm.* Elizabeth Coatsworth has also used this neighborhood as background for several books, including her first novel, *Here I Stay.*

In *Here I Stay* (1938) a Maine community is about to migrate to Ohio. Margaret Winslow alone withstands the group enthusiasm and remains; the story concerns the experiences of her solitary year, and the cycle of the seasons which threaten and shape her life until she ceases to be alone. It is primarily a study in fidelity. *A Toast to the King* (1940) concerns three loyalist sisters who during the Revolution outrage and then win the sympathies of the people of the small Massachusetts town in which they live; two of them, however, lose their lovers in the conflict.

The Trunk (1941) describes a modern crisis between a fastidious, conventional woman and her artist husband. The story is laid in a clearing at the edge of the jungle on the coast of Guatemala, and deals with a series of conflicts: between nature and the dwindled European population of the settlement, between a local girl and her mad father, between husband and wife, but above all between values. Only when the heroine is able to recognize that the new and savage realism in her husband's work is an advance and not a degeneration is peace possible between them.

JOHN COBB

Fabian Bachrach

is the pseudonym of John C. Cooper III, who was born in Atlantic City, New Jersey, on September 14, 1921. He lived in Jacksonville, Florida, until the age of twelve. Then his family moved to Princeton, New Jersey, which he has called home ever since. He attended Phillips Exeter Academy and studied at Princeton University, leaving in February, 1942, to join the army air forces. He served as a navigator in the Eighth Air Force, and on completion of his tour was assigned to the Air Transport Command, flying to Africa, India, and Okinawa. On returning to civilian life, he resumed his studies, graduating from Columbia in 1948. Thereupon he began the study of law. He has held the usual young writer's odd jobs while "bumming" around the country, and he worked briefly as a reporter on a paper in Princeton, New Jersey. He uses a pseudonym to avoid confusion with his father, the author of *The Right to Fly.*

The Gesture (1948), his first novel, attracted considerable attention for its picture of an air-force major who tries to express in words and in action the ideals for which he thought World War II was being fought. He is a failure because he cannot deal with people; he keeps his ideals but loses his life. Though the setting is wartime England, attention is concentrated on questions of administrative control and the moral problems it raises for a sensitive human being in an age in which value is largely a question of social efficiency.

HAMILTON COCHRAN

was born on September 9, 1898, in West Philadelphia, Pennsylvania, the son of a Presbyterian minister. When he was a boy of nine, his family moved to Swarthmore, Pennsylvania. Just before his graduation from Swarthmore Preparatory School, he enlisted in the United States Coast Guard and served eighteen months overseas aboard the cutter *Algonquin,* doing convoy duty between Gibraltar and English ports. Upon his discharge he served briefly in the merchant marine. In 1919 he entered the University of Michigan, majored in journalism, and graduated three years later. Then he engaged in advertising work in New York City, and he has remained in this field except for a two-year period of government service. In 1931 and 1932 he was Commissioner of Public Welfare for the Island of St. Thomas in the Virgin Islands. There he did research on the history of the Virgin Islands and learned about buried treasure and native superstitions from witch doctors and other natives. Since 1944 he has been in the advertising department of *The Saturday Evening Post.*

His first book was *These Are the Virgin Islands* (1937). His second was a juvenile, *Buccaneer Island* (1941). His subsequent books have been historical novels, beginning with *Windward Passage* (1942), based on the life of Sir Henry Morgan, the freebooter. *Captain Ebony* (1943) is a romantic tale of a Virginia gentleman who entered the slave trade in the 1840's in the Danish West Indies. *Silver Shoals* (1945) is a story of an English boy's treasure hunting off the Bahamas with Captain William Phips in the seventeenth century. *Rogue's Holiday* (1947) details the romantic adventures of an English lieutenant, Robert Maynard, who in 1718 is captured by the pirate Edward Teach, known as Bluebeard, talks his way out of immediate trouble, and then is marooned by a wreck on the Carolina coast.

MARIAN COCKRELL

was born in Birmingham, Alabama, on March 15, 1909. She has lived there the greater part of her life, with scattered visits to Warrensburg, Missouri; St. Augustine, Florida; Hollywood, California; and New York. She attended Sophie Newcomb College in New Orleans for three years and then spent a season at the Metropolitan Art School in New York. After living in Hollywood and in Salome, Arizona, she returned to Birmingham. She now resides in California. *Shadow Castle* (1945), a juvenile, is the story of a little girl who follows a dog through a mountain tunnel and emerges into an enchanted valley.

Yesterday's Madness (1943), her first novel, is about childhood friends who marry on a rebound: Phyllis because she expects a child and Ives because he has been jilted. They return from New York to their village home, where they overcome gossip and attain love at last. *Lillian Harley* (1943) is a pleasant tale about a small-town girl whose unhappy love affair sends her to New York, where she becomes a successful dress designer by the age of twenty-one and, in due season, wins a wealthy husband. *Something Between* (1946) pictures a meddling boy, Austin Towles, in the small town of Knowlton; he learns of the love affairs of his mother and two aunts, and he captures a murderer.

LESTER COHEN

Arni

was born in Chicago, Illinois, on August 17, 1901. His father is Dr. Hyman Cohen, the author of medical and other literature and a pioneer in the development of public-health service in the United States. His father's forebears wrote commentaries on the Talmud and other holy books. Lester Cohen went to public schools in Chicago but as a child truant was subject to the influence of the streets. Vaudeville theaters especially attracted him. He attended classes at the University of Chicago for a few weeks, but found them dull and boresome. He worked on various newspapers and in the advertising sections of several department stores.

He did the work in motion pictures in which most contemporary authors sooner or later engage, just as historically they once worked as journalists and pamphleteers. He wrote one of the notable pictures of the screen, "Of Human Bondage." But Hollywood and pictures seemed too constricting. He longed to see the great world and its countries, peoples, and cultures. He circled the globe and wrote his conclusions in a book called *Two Worlds* (1936). This was probably the first book to forecast the divided world of today. It also predicted that France, then very strong, would become a weak nation, and that China and Russia would grow in power. *Billy Mitchell* (with Emile Gauvreau, 1942) is a biography, and *Oscar Wilde* (1928) is a play.

Sweepings (1926), his first novel, is the story of American business enterprise and the building of the country from 1790 to 1917, from the time of the Revolution to World War I. In essence its theme is that the sons of the inheritors, like the sons of Peter Pardway, the ironmaster, cannot carry on the work of the fathers, but that the fruits of the founders' labors would be inherited by the managers in what has been referred to as "the managerial revolution." *The Great Bear* (1927) paints a picture of the ability, vanity, and ultimate annihilation of the stock-market speculator, Thane Pardway, who operated in the Chicago Pit in the 1880's. *Coming Home* (1945) is about a Marine who had fought on Guadalcanal, and was forced to battle, in the courts of Pittsburgh, the same social elements he had opposed abroad. Its theme is the justice due the soldier, his place in society once he returns, and his reward.

MERLE COLBY

Fabian Bachrach

was born on December 3, 1902, in Lodi, Wisconsin, the son and grandson of clergymen. The American branch of the Colby family, the founder of which came to Boston, Massachusetts, in 1640, has contributed numerous members to the service of the country. Mr. Colby was educated at the Evanston, Illinois, High School and at Harvard, winning the Harvard Club of Chicago scholarship in 1920. At Harvard in his freshman year he won the Emily C. Whitcomb medal for the best undergraduate poem, and became Pegasus (poetry and review editor) of *The Harvard Advocate* when Oliver LaFarge and Walter Edmonds were successively presidents of this undergraduate literary magazine.

For the six years following graduation in 1924, Mr. Colby managed the firm of importers and booksellers, N. J. Bartlett & Co., of Boston, resigning in 1930 to devote all his time to writing. He spent the next few years in Toulouse, Paris, and Palma de Mallorca. Returning to Boston in 1937, he became successively state editor of the Massachusetts Writers' Project and then principal editor of the Federal Project in Washington, in which capacity he traveled extensively throughout the United States, Alaska, Puerto Rico, and the Virgin Islands. He spent more than ten years in government service in Washington, working for the Office of War Information under Elmer Davis, the War Manpower Commission under Paul V. McNutt, and the Office of War Mobilization and Reconversion under John W. Snyder, and finally joined the White House staff of Dr. John R. Steelman, the assistant to the President.

Mr. Colby resigned from government service in December, 1947, to write his novel about Washington and atomic energy, *The Big Secret.* Since December, 1948, he has been a member of Arthur Newmyer & Associates, a Washington public-relations firm. He lives in Alexandria, Virginia, and has an "international family" of three children, born in Paris, Mallorca, and Boston. Mr. Colby has written numerous books of non-fiction, some of which are *A Guide to Alaska* ("American Guide" series, 1939); *Profiles* (picture books) of Alaska, Puerto Rico and the Virgin Islands (1940–41); and *Handbook for Youth* (1940). During the war, he wrote the Alaska volume in the army's series of world pocket guides for American soldiers, as well as several other pamphlets printed and distributed by the War Department for the use of servicemen's discussion groups.

As a writer, Mr. Colby has shown himself less interested in character delineation as such than in the interplay of ideas and the variety of the American scene.

All Ye People (1931), his first novel, is a broad panorama of social and economic life on the frontier in 1810 as seen by a young Vermonter joining the tide of people moving westward. *New Road* (1933) portrays the founding of a pioneer Ohio town in 1820 by Martin Ward, an aristocratic Marylander, and Hagor, the widow of one of the first settlers. They marry and share good and bad fortune during a period of eighteen years. *The Big Secret* (1949), a Literary Guild selection, is a satire on Washington bureaucracy, but has as a serious underlying theme the necessity for free interchange of scientific information.

LONNIE WILLIAM COLEMAN

was born on August 2, 1920, in Bartow, Georgia. He graduated from the University of Alabama in 1942; while there in 1941 he won the *Atlantic Monthly* story contest for college students, and in 1942 the *Mademoiselle* magazine short-story contest open to any American writer under the age of thirty. He became an ensign in the navy in October, 1942, and participated in the invasions of Sicily, Italy, France, and Okinawa, and in the occupation of Japan. After this tour of duty he taught for a short time at North Carolina State College, and then he lived in Guatemala for several months. He is at present an associate editor with the Curtis Publishing Company in New York City. At the University of Alabama he wrote a burlesque melodrama, "Hellcat Hattie and Kingdom Come" (1942), and several other plays which were produced by college groups and the Montgomery Little Theatre.

Escape The Thunder (1944), his first novel, is a story of violence, cruelty, and passion in the life of Negroes in Montgomery, Alabama. *Time Moving West* (1947) tells of the clash of wills and personality on a troop transport in the Mediterranean. *The Animals in the*

Zoo (1950) concerns the responsibilities of an individual to himself, to those he loves, and to his society; its characters are a small colony of Americans during the prelude to one of the traditional Central-American revolutions.

ALICE ROSS COLVER

was born on August 28, 1892, in Plainfield, New Jersey; she spent an uneventful girlhood in this small suburban town not far from New York City. She was much preoccupied with tennis, skating, and basketball. Although she professes not to be a good student, she studied at Wellesley College and there became convinced that she wanted to write. Her first book was a juvenile and was written during the first year of her marriage. In addition to writing several juvenile series and more than two dozen novels, she was co-author of *Dream Within Her Hand* (1940), a biography of Cornelia Chase Brant, and she has been responsible for a number of miscellaneous books. *If You Should Want to Write* (1938) is a textbook for teen-agers. Besides short stories and articles, she has described her extensive travels.

She began writing immediately after graduating from Wellesley; her first book was accepted immediately, and she was requested to write three more. This group was known as the "Babs" series. It was followed by the "Jeanne" series. Jeanne was a French refugee who came to America during World War I for adoption by an American woman. Following these eight books, her publisher persuaded her to try her hand at a novel. *The Dear Pretender* was the result, and it sold in England, on the continent, and to the movies.

"I have three grown children," Mrs. Colver has stated, "and consider my calling as a wife and mother far more important than my literary career. This theme more or less runs through most of my books—the thought that marriage is a career which is ennobling and challenging and requires the best that a woman can give."

In *The Dear Pretender* (1924) Nan advertises for a place as foster mother in a wealthy home, gets such a job, and marries the father of the children. More than a dozen novels preceded *Adventure for a Song* (1939), the story of a girl who spent her junior year in college abroad. This book was selected as one of the best of its age group in 1939. *Adventure on a Hilltop* (1940) concerns a girl who wants to write. *Joan Foster, Freshman* (1940) describes Joan's freshman year at college. *There's Only One* (1941) tells of the tangled love affairs of three girls and their boy companions. *Not Just to Remember* (1941) is the romance of a New York City stenographer.

Adventure in the West (1941) is a story based upon Mrs. Colver's son's experiences during a summer on a ranch. *Forever Is So Long* (1942) tells of Gae Marshall and her suitors. *The Merivales* (1943) is a picture of a wartime family and the effect of the mother's departure to become a Wac. *Fourways* (1944) presents the marriage problems of a New England farmer and his city-bred wife from 1923 to 1943. *Homecoming* (1945) describes the return of a young veteran from the South Pacific and the problems of readjustment in a New Jersey family. *Uncertain Heart* (1947) is the story of a girl who could not decide between a business career and her marriage and family.

Joan, Freelance Writer (1947) is a career book for girls in their teens. *Kingsridge* (1948) is a narrative of the struggle between family pride and prejudice on one side and the clear-eyed impatience and unfettered thinking of youth on the other. *Joan Foster, Sophomore* (1948) gives the story of Joan as a college undergraduate, and her third year is pictured in *Joan Foster, Junior* (1949). In *Joan Foster, Senior* (1950) Joan plans a career involving travel.

JACK CONROY

was born on December 5, 1899, in a coal camp near Moberly, Missouri. His father, a shot firer, was killed by a premature blast in the mines when Jack was ten. At the age of fourteen he went to work in the car shops of the Wabash Railway at Moberly. After taking a night course in high school, he entered the University of Missouri in 1920. He left a year later because he found the military training too onerous. A number of years were then spent as a migratory worker: in steel mills, coal mines, road gangs, rubber plants, and automobile factories. He began to write verse, and with Ralph Cheyney edited three annual anthologies of verse expressing spiritual or social discontent, *Unrest* (1929, 1930, 1931). H. L. Mencken became interested in his short stories about the depression and published a number of them when he was editor of *The American Mercury.*

Mr. Conroy was awarded a Guggenheim fellowship in 1935 to make a study of the migrations of workers from the South to the North. He used the material he gathered during the tenure of his Guggenheim fellowship to write, in collaboration with Arna Bontemps, *They Seek a City* (1945), a social study of Negro migration in the United States. A by-product of Mr. Conroy's travels as an industrial worker is a group of occupational "tall" tales, two of which were utilized in juvenile stories written in collaboration with Arna Bontemps, *The Fast Sooner Hound* (1942) and *Slappy Hooper* (1946). Mr. Conroy's interest in this subject is also reflected in *Midland Humor* (1947), a compilation of midwest folklore from pioneer days to the present. Since 1947 he has been associate editor of *The New Standard Encyclopedia.*

Mr. Conroy has said, "I want to demonstrate in my writing that the life of common workers and the stench of their sweat is as authentic literary material as the vicissitudes of society folks and others who appear, in fiction at least, to exist in an economic vacuum."

The Disinherited (1933), the story of Larry Donovan's odyssey from job to job, is a partly autobiographical first novel. It deals with the experiences of a number of people helpless in the grip of economic forces they cannot alter, influence, or even understand. *A World To Win* (1935) also outlines the economic problems of its characters. Most important among its people are two half brothers. The first is a down-to-earth worker who progresses from intolerance and narrow-mindedness to social comprehension; the second is a dilettante who first leads a pseudo-literary existence but at length arrives at an understanding with his half brother after experiencing great spiritual and physical suffering.

FANNIE COOK

Todd Studios

was born in St. Charles, Missouri, and was educated in the St. Louis public schools and at the University of Missouri. During the years in which she was bringing up young sons, she kept house, taught English part time at Washington University in St. Louis, edited the *Bulletin* of the Missouri League of Women Voters, and occasionally had a story or verse published. In 1935 she began to devote her major time to writing. She died on August 25, 1949.

The Hill Grows Steeper (1938), her first novel, pictures Harriet Andrews, who had begun in youth to hate male domination as exemplified in her grandfather, refuses the love of Raeburn Streator for a career, has an affair with a man who refuses to marry her, and then once again faces the problem of independence or marriage. *Boot-Heel Doctor* (1941) is the story of struggling sharecroppers in southeast Missouri and of the helpful services of a physician in times of illness, flood, and race troubles.

Mrs. Palmer's Honey (1946) traces the growth of a St. Louis Negro servant girl into a labor leader; it received the first George Washington Carver award. *Storm Against the Wall* (1948) is the story of an American-German-Jewish family from the St. Louis World's Fair in 1904 to the end of World War II. *The Long Bridge* (1949) concerns a painter, his trials, his love affair, and the impact of the world of money upon his artistry.

LOUISE FIELD COOPER

Theodore Haley

was born on March 8, 1905, and brought up in Hartford, Connecticut. After leaving boarding school, she held a society reporter's job on a Hartford newspaper. Then she worked in a bookshop, and later married a lawyer. They live in the country outside New Haven, Connecticut, with three children and a constantly shifting population of animals. For four years during World War II they cared for two English sisters who were nine and eleven when they arrived. "Our emotional life centers largely in the animals," Mrs. Cooper states; "indeed, it is no unusual thing to go into the kitchen and find a mallard duck begging for Boston lettuce in front of the icebox. We always travel back and forth to the seashore with a great Dane, several ducks, and the most docile of the bantams in the back of the car. All this complicates our life terribly; there is nothing that can be done."

The Lighted Box (1942), her first novel, pictures the happy Connecticut home of Walter and Amanda Robinson, the coming of Mrs. Celeste Gilman into Walter's life, and the solution of the triangle: Celeste is marooned at a dinner party in the Robinsons' house, and she shows her true, unpleasant quality. *The Deer on the Stairs* (1943) describes the indecision of Iris Crane, a young red-haired wife, who thinks that she is in love with a tax assessor's clerk in a New England village. For two days she asks her neighbors what to do, and Mrs. Ellin Lay tries to help her make up her mind.

A volume of short stories and sketches, *Love and Admiration* (1944), deals with Mrs. Findlay, and the quiet excitements of daily life in the southern Connecticut country. *Summer Stranger* (1947) is about Emily, a seventeen-year-old high-school girl, whose visit to a lower New England seacoast colony is enlivened by many unexpected experiences, including a murder. It pictures vividly the life of the seashore colony which remains intense for the brief time until it stops so completely at the end of the season.

ELIZABETH CORBETT

who has given the reading public a galaxy of characters which includes "young" Mrs. Meigs, Charley Manning, and Cassandra Blake, was born on September 13, 1887, in Aurora, Illinois, the part of the Middle West about which she so dearly loves to write. Twenty-five years of her early life were spent in a national soldiers' home, where her father was an officer. Her reminiscences of those years went into *Out at the Soldiers' Home* (1941), which is considered a real addition to Americana.

Miss Corbett graduated from the University of Wisconsin in 1910 with a Phi Beta Kappa key and a firm determination to become a novelist. Her greatest assets in achieving that ambition were her parents, who sympathized with her struggles, paid her bills, and took her early defeats more to heart than she herself did. Her father was of Irish descent; her mother's family came from New England. She has one brother and one sister. Long years of association with the devoted, if argumentative, Corbetts gave her that background of family life which she uses in so many of her books. Elizabeth Corbett is a very versatile writer. Through all her books, however, runs evidence of a deep sympathy with human nature. She believes that "the proper study of mankind is man," and she views humanity without fear and without cynicism.

Success came with tantalizing slowness. However, while she was still a resident of Wisconsin, she published three novels: *Cecily and the Wide World* (1916), the story of a young married couple who must undergo a separation and heartbreak in order to learn the meaning of the word "union"; *The Vanished Helga* (1918), which deals with a wealthy and beautiful woman who fancies herself above love and fails to meet the test when it finally comes to her; and *Puritan and Pagan* (1920), in which the Puritan is an artist, the Pagan an actress, and the painter hero is torn between them.

A year after her father's death Miss Corbett decided to move to New York "to try life on a shoestring." The shoestring held from the beginning, and grew stronger as readers began to recommend her books to one another. For some years now she has lived in an attractive studio apartment furnished with American antiques and housing some choice books and a small but interesting collection of flowing-blue Staffordshire. She is a sociable person, and is never happier than when entertaining, either at home or on her boat, a roomy and comfortable, if old-fashioned, cabin cruiser.

Her first two New York books were experiments with a new medium, biography written entirely in dialogue. *Walt: The Good Gray Poet Speaks for Himself* (1928) makes use so far as possible of Whitman's own words, and, except for the New Orleans episode, adheres closely to known facts. In similar fashion *If It Takes All Summer* (1930) tells the life story of Ulysses S. Grant.

The Young Mrs. Meigs (1931) introduces this lively and lighthearted octogenarian stubbornly determined to maintain her independence against the well-meant but meddlesome efforts of her children to break up her establishment and have her "make her home" with one of them. In *After Five O'clock* (1932) a young career woman who has sacrificed everything to her own success finds the price too high. In *A Nice Long Evening* (1933) Mrs. Meigs reappeared, by reader demand; this time she is threatened by something worse than her daughter Millicent, but has the pleasure of having a baby in her flat for companionship.

The House Across the River (1934) is inhabited by a mysterious Frenchman, M. Armande; and on the right side of the river, in the fashionable suburb of Hillport, lives a beautiful young Frenchwoman married to an American. Suspicion centers on her, at least in her husband's mind, when Armande is found dead under strange circumstances. For once, the author here depends principally on plot. In *Mr. Underhill's Progress* (1934) a man of fifty rebels against the necessity of continuing to do what is expected of him and, considerably to his own surprise, manages to make an entirely fresh start. *The Constant Sex* (1935) portrays Hilda Stanton, who for ten years has kept house for her father and six brothers; she breaks away, only to find her lot worsened.

Mount Royal (1936) contains four short novels, three of them tragic in their nature, the fourth the story of a wonderful friendship between two elderly widows. *Mrs. Meigs and Mr. Cunningham* (1936) aroused hope in a good many aged hearts; it tells how Mrs. Meigs, eighty-two by this time, acquires a new and very persistent suitor.

The Langworthy Family (1937), a more ambitious novel than any of its predecessors, tells of Colonel Sam Langworthy of Mount

Royal, who deserves and achieves happiness but cannot retain it. *Light of Other Days* (1938) is the somber story of a man who spends his life in perpetual self-sacrifice, and of the woman who must stand by and see it happen. *She Was Carrie Eaton* (1938) takes us back to Mrs. Meigs' girlhood in Ohio in the 1870's. *The Far Down* (1939) deals with a class now practically extinct, the old-fashioned servitor Irish.

Charley Manning (1939) tells of a cosmopolitan bachelor, again back in Mount Royal, who is generous to all, despite the fact that none are charitable to him. *The Queen's Holiday* (1940) is a story of exiled European royalty, and of a queen who tires of maintaining her position even in exile. *Mr. and Mrs. Meigs* (1940) shows our heroine as a married woman and the mother of young children.

Faye's Folly (1941) portrays the home front during the American Civil War; the bullet that killed Lincoln also killed Frederick Faye, and left a complicated destiny to his cherished only daughter. *The Kimball Collection* (1942) is perhaps the author's most amusing book. The collection proper is of ancient Greek art; but a second collection is the one portraying the beloved but often provoking Kimball relatives. *Early Summer* (1942) is the story of an idyllic but uneasy marriage. In *Excuse Me, Mrs. Meigs* (1943) the heroine finally becomes Mrs. Cunningham, but remains unsatisfied. *Golden Grain* (1943) deals with the strange situation which arises when, to the horror of the woman he really loves, Sam Martin marries for financial reasons a woman whom he cannot help addressing as "Aunt Sadie."

The Red-Haired Lady (1945) is about a writer, and the book is primarily concerned with her writing, although Cassandra Blake has many other activities. This work is to some extent autobiographical. *Lady With Parasol* (1946) is a highly sympathetic story of a warm-hearted if eccentric old maid and her beautiful but selfish niece. *Immortal Helen* (1948) deals with a small-town tycoon, Christopher "Duke" Hastings, who carries a lovely vision forever in his heart, but encounters considerable difficulty in his daily life. *Eve and Christopher* (1949) portrays a father and daughter who understand and appreciate each other: it takes old Christopher Hastings to manage the beautiful, tempestuous Eve. *The Duke's Daughter* (1950) tells about what happens to Eve Hastings, now a widow and restless and lonesome, when she meets Phil Dunham, a strange and peculiar personality.

PAUL (FREDERICK) COREY

the youngest in a family of seven, was born on a farm in Shelby County, Iowa, on July 8, 1903. He began his education in a one-room Iowa schoolhouse, graduated from Atlantic, Iowa, High School in 1921, and received his bachelor's degree from the University of Iowa in 1925. His scholastic work was unspectacular, but in 1947 he was cited as one of the outstanding living alumni of the University of Iowa. Between 1925 and 1931 he worked in Chicago and New York at various jobs. In 1928 he married Ruth Lechlitner, the poet, and they spent a year traveling and living in France, England, and Spain. In 1929 they bought an abandoned few acres in Putnam County, New York, and two years later retired there to live and write.

Since 1931 the Coreys have never lived in a home they did not build with their own hands. They built two in New York state and one in The Valley of the Moon, California. It is Mr. Corey's philosophy that true creativeness goes deeper than writing books, painting pictures, or composing symphonies. The genuine artist fashions everything within his control, and true effort begins with the family and the home. Mr. Corey feels that the soul of America is being strangled by the slick excellence and perfectionism of our economic system and that urban life is being reduced to streamlined potential slums. Meanwhile the land, the only stable part of any nation, is dying. To gain their own security, families must build their own homes away from the cities. On this theme Mr. Corey wrote *Buy an Acre* (1944) and *Build a Home* (1946). Two juveniles have similar content: *The Red Tractor* (1944) portrays the struggle of a boy and his family against a "chain" farm, and *Five Acre Hill* (1946) pictures a family who build their own home in the country.

Three Miles Square (1939), Mr. Corey's first novel, was the beginning of a trilogy covering the period from 1910 to 1930 in Iowa. *The Road Returns* (1940) and *County Seat* (1941) completed the story of the Mantz family and its struggle to break with the land. *Acres of Antaeus* (1946) describes vividly the battle of small farmers against giant corporation farms during the depression years. *Shad Haul* (1947) tells the story of a cooperative venture in shad fishing on the Hudson River and is the one deviation in all his books from emphasis on land. *Corn Gold Farm* (1948) is the story of a boy's and his father's reclamation of an old abandoned farm by modern soil-conservation methods.

THOMAS BERTRAM COSTAIN

Chidnoff

was born on May 8, 1885, in Brantford, Ontario, Canada. He left high school at seventeen to become a five-dollar-a-week reporter on the Brantford *Courier*. After seven years in newspaper work, which had carried him to the editorship of a small daily, the Guelph *Mercury*, he joined the staff of the Maclean Publishing Company in Toronto, Ontario, and became editor of a number of trade papers, finally becoming general managing editor of the company. After ten years as editor of *Maclean's Magazine*, during which time that publication grew from a very small periodical to one of considerable size and influence, he was invited by George Horace Lorimer to join the editorial forces of the Curtis Publishing Company. He became chief associate editor of *The Saturday Evening Post* under Lorimer and for fourteen years did most of the contact work. Leaving *The Post* to become a story editor, first with Twentieth Century-Fox and later with Samuel Goldwyn, he spent a little over two years in the motion-picture field. After launching a new magazine, *Cavalcade*, which did not survive the difficult days of the middle 1930's, he joined the staff of Doubleday Doran as advisory editor on a part-time basis. He married Ida Randolph Spragge of Guelph, Ontario, in 1912 and has two daughters. He lives in Lakeville, Connecticut.

With Rogers McVeagh he wrote *Joshua* (1943), a non-fiction study of the conquest of Canaan. Mr. Costain is engaged on what he considers the most important work of his life, a twelve-volume history designed for general reading and to be called *The Pageant of England*. The first volume is *The Conquerors* (1949).

At the age of fifty-five he began writing historical novels because of a lifetime interest in history. He had done a book of six sketches of forgotten characters in history who had played remarkable roles. His agent, Miss Bernice Baumgarten of Brandt and Brandt, advised him to use these sketches as a basis for fiction, and the first four novels he published were about men who had appeared in the book.

His first novel, *For My Great Folly* (1942), pictures the adventures of a romantic pirate, John Ward, who roamed the Mediterranean in the first years of the seventeenth century. This was selected by the Book League and so achieved a much wider circulation than most first novels. *Ride With Me* (1943), a story of the Napoleonic wars, takes a young crusading newspaper publisher into the midst of the English military and political campaign against the French. It was chosen by the People's Book Club. *The Black Rose* (1945), a selection of the Literary Guild, is about a young English nobleman who in the thirteenth century fights his way into the China of Kublai Khan. On his return he must choose between an English heiress and a girl of the East. *The Moneyman* (1947), a Book-of-the-Month-Club choice, is a story based on the career of the fabulous Jacques Coeur, the furrier, who was the "moneyman" in the reign of Charles VII of France in the fifteenth century. The background includes the siege of Orleans, the heroism of Joan of Arc, the war with England, and the end of the age of chivalry. *High Towers* (1949) is based on the exploits of the ten Le Moyne brothers in French Canada in the eighteenth century; the action is laid in Montreal and New Orleans, which was founded by the Sieur Bienville, one of the brothers. *Son of a Hundred Kings* (1950) is a family story set in Canada in the 1890's. The chief character is an English boy, shy and appealing, who steps off the boat at Halifax; on his coat is an oilcloth sign: "This is Ludar Prentice. He has no money. He is going to his father at Balfour, Ontario. Be kind to him." Called "the boy with a sign," Ludar makes his handicapped way in the New World. A family feud and love adventures provide the basis for a full account of life in Canada at the end of the nineteenth century. Ludar has some of the qualities of Dickens' David Copperfield.

JAMES GOULD COZZENS

Anthony J. Peters

was born in Chicago, Illinois, on August 19, 1903, but is a Chicagoan only by this accident and never lived there. His ancestors were natives of Rhode Island, where the unusual name is an old one. He grew up on Staten Island, New York, attended as a child the Staten Island Academy, graduated from the Kent School, and in 1922 entered Harvard. During his sophomore year, 1923–24, his first novel, written when he was 19, was published. In his junior year he took a leave of absence to write a second novel. In the fall of 1925 he embraced the opportunity to go to Cuba as a teacher of the children of American engineers at a sugar mill in Santa Clara province. After some time spent in Europe he returned to this country and has lived since 1933 on a farm in New Jersey. In 1938 he served for a year as a guest editor of *Fortune* magazine. From 1942 through 1945 he was a staff officer in the army air forces.

Confusion (1924), *Michael Scarlet* (1925), and *Cock Pit* (1928) were youthful novels. A certain advance is apparent in *The Son of Perdition* (1929) which, in the Cuban setting of Cock Pit, shows an all-powerful sugar-company boss reaching the limits of his power. *S.S. San Pedro* (1931) concerns the loss of a passenger liner off the Atlantic coast, and the reactions of those aboard to the approaching danger. *The Last Adam* (1933) is about a gusty, coarse, and inefficient physician who dominates a Connecticut village.

Castaway (1934) is an experimental fantasy, not always clear, about a man lost in a department store. *Men and Brethren* (1936) deals with the problems of an Episcopal parish. *Ask Me Tomorrow* (1940) develops the character of a young American in Europe who longs to be a writer but must earn his living as a tutor. *The Just and the Unjust* (1942) deals with the theory and practice of the law in an eastern county seat. *Guard of Honor* (1948), which won the Pulitzer prize, is a study of the interaction of human and military values at an army air force base in Florida in 1943.

ALFRED LELAND CRABB

was born on January 22, 1884, near Bowling Green, Kentucky. He numbers among his ancestors some good Indian fighters, some Revolutionary soldiers, some soldiers of the War of 1812 and others of the War between the States, some Baptist preachers, some teachers, and many farmers. He studied at Bethel College in McKenzie, Tennessee, at Western Kentucky Teachers College, at Columbia University, at the University of Chicago, and at George Peabody College for Teachers at Nashville, Tennessee, from which he received his doctorate in 1925. He was given the degree of Doctor of Literature by the University of Kentucky in 1942. In 1911 he married Bertha Gardner; they have one son.

Dr. Crabb taught in the rural schools of Kentucky, in the consolidated school at Saint Gabriel, Louisiana, and served as principal of the McKinley School in Paducah, Kentucky. He taught in the Western Kentucky State Teachers College for several years and was its dean for two years. He has been a professor at Peabody College since 1927 and editor of *The Peabody Journal of Education* since 1932. After publishing textbooks, biographies, and a brief history of Peabody College, he undertook to write a series of historical novels about the city of Nashville.

Dinner at Belmont (1942), his first novel, pictures five dinners from 1858 to 1865 as the background for an account of life during the War between the States. *Supper at the Maxwell House* (1943) is about Reconstruction days and the opening of the Maxwell House on September 22, 1869. *Breakfast at the Hermitage* (1945) tells of the rebuilding of Nashville and of a poor boy who realizes his ambition to grow up to be a builder of beautiful homes. *Lodging at the Saint Cloud* (1946) narrates further events of the Civil War period, centered mainly around the activities of three spies sent by General Nathan Bedford Forrest into beleaguered Nashville. *Home to the Hermitage* (1948) presents episodes in the lives of Andrew Jackson and his wife, from the time of their arrival at the Hermitage until her death, just before he became President. *A Mockingbird Sang at Chickamauga* (1949) is descriptive of the terrible conflict waged on September 19 and 20, 1863. *Reunion at Chattanooga* (1950) portrays events in the Tennessee city during the years of the Reconstruction after 1865.

CLARKSON CRANE

was born on September 20, 1894, in Chicago, Illinois, and lived there until he was sixteen. He finished school in California and graduated from the University of California at Berkeley in 1916. There followed a year of writing, and then he enlisted and drove an ambulance in World War I. After leaving the service he did more writing in Carmel, California; New York; and San Francisco. During this time several of his stories were published in *The Smart Set* and *The Dial*. He spent several years in Paris and there wrote his first novel. In the late 1920's he returned to San Francisco, lectured in the University of California Extension Division, and worked as reference librarian in the Mechanics Library.

The Western Shore (1925), his first novel, portrays "college life" at the University of California in twenty episodes. *Mother and Son* (1946) describes the unhappiness of a widow who refuses offers of marriage from a banker, a professor, and an artist to remain with her son. *Naomi Martin* (1947) is about a stenographer in San Francisco in the winter of 1914 who does not realize the instability in her character in her affairs with men.

HUBERT CREEKMORE

was born on January 16, 1907, in Water Valley, Mississippi. He attended Water Valley High School and the Marion, Alabama, Institute, graduated from the University of Mississippi in 1927, attended the Yale Drama School from 1927 to 1928, and earned a master's degree at Columbia University in 1940. For a time he worked in Washington, D.C., for the Veterans' Administration and for the Social Security Board. Shortly after he was transferred to Jackson, Mississippi, he became an editor on the Mississippi Writers' Project. During World War II he served in the navy from 1942 to 1945, rising from a yeoman to a lieutenant. Since the war he has been engaged in editorial work, free-lance writing, and lecturing. His writing career began in grammar school, and during his college years the example of William Faulkner, then postmaster of the University station, spurred him to write stories and two novels. His first books were poems: *Personal Sun* (1940), *The Stone Ants* (1943), *The Long Reprieve* (1946), *Formula* (1947), and *No Harm to Lovers* (1950). He has edited *A Little Treasury of World Poetry* (1950).

"My fiction, as well as my poetry," he has said, "is meant to express my concern with form and style as a medium for projecting an evaluation and a sympathetic interpretation of American life and its traditions."

His first published novel, *The Fingers of Night* (1946), with a background of Mississippi hill-farmer life, tells of a young girl's emergence from the bigotry of her father's domination over the family's religious, social, and emotional life. After a series of trials arising from her natural conflict, she achieves a sense of personal, moral liberation. Though she murders her new-born child out of delirium and terror, she frees her conscience for the future by refusing to let a Negro who had helped her suffer for her crime, for through her ordeals she has come to understand the nature of the strangling burden of hate and fear that oppresses them all. *The Welcome* (1948) is an attempt to define the modern basic necessity of marriage by questioning its usefulness and success in the light of modern neurotic life, modern woman, and divorce. The problem is posed mainly on the negative side—the alternative of *not* marrying, with emphasis on submerged homosexuality to dramatize the negative choice—with variously successful married couples to demonstrate the positive choice.

HOMER CROY

was born on March 11, 1883, near Maryville, Missouri, on a farm which he still owns and which has served as a background for much of his fiction, tall tales, and humorous writing. In his youth he worked at farm labor and wrote on the side. One day while still in high school he showed his father a check for eight dollars from *Puck* magazine, and from then on the ambition to become a writer was uppermost in his mind. Following his graduation from high school, he went to the University of Missouri and was the first student in the newly established School of Journalism. There his support came largely from his writings for newspapers. He did not get a degree because he failed senior English.

On leaving the university, Mr. Croy went to work on the St. Joseph, Missouri, *Gazette*, a newspaper which earlier had had on its staff such men as Eugene Field and Walter Hines Page. Soon he was off to New York, where he took employment with Theodore Dreiser, then editor of three Butterick magazines, and began turning out a vast quantity of humorous pieces. His fame as a humorist was so great that *West of the Water Tower* (1923), a down-to-earth novel about life in a Missouri town, was issued anonymously, but soon critical acclaim lifted the book into the best-seller class. Shortly thereafter Mr. Croy went to Hollywood to prepare the script for Will Rogers' first talking motion picture, *They Had to See Paris.* More of Will Rogers' pictures were based on stories by Mr. Croy than on those of any other writer.

In addition to his novels, Mr. Croy has written non-fiction works: *How Motion Pictures Are Made* (1918); *The Last Word* (1932), a collection of tombstone epitaphs; *Country Cured* (1943), an autobiography; *Wonderful Neighbor* (1945), a partly autobiographical account of American farm life; *Corn Country* (1947), a volume in the "American Folkways" series, which spins humorous yarns in the midst of excellent reporting on the social life and manners of the Middle West; *What Grandfather Laughed At* (1948), a collection of the humor of Grandpa Croy's day; and *Jesse James Was My Neighbor* (1949), a biography of the famous bank robber.

His first novel, *Boone Stop* (1918), tells the story of a Missouri family from the viewpoint of a boy; there are humor and pathos in the account of the father who is a religious fanatic and who believes that the world is coming to an end. Mr. Croy has said this is "the best book I ever wrote." *Turkey Bowman* (1920) is about a boy who runs away from home. *West of the Water Tower* (1923), set in a small Missouri town, tells what happens to a boy who wrongs a girl. This book reverses the usual emphasis by following the career of the boy who, after many misadventures, at last finds the opportunity to make good.

R. F. D. No. 3 (1924) is about Josie Decker, the young and beautiful daughter of hard-working parents who live on a farm on a rural route near Junction City, Missouri. Josie wins a beauty contest and dreams of Hollywood fame. She jilts Orville Vert, rebuffs prosperous Bush Higbee, and then runs away with a flamboyant salesman. She does not wed him during their few whirling days in the city, and she returns home and marries Higbee.

They Had to See Paris (1926) concerns Mr. and Mrs. Pike Peters of a small Oklahoma city. When oil is found on their place, Mrs. Peters takes the family to Paris to achieve culture and mend Pike's manners. They rent a chateau, hire a tutor in social graces, and meet a marquis who will marry daughter Opal for two hundred thousand dollars. Pike exposes their folly and orders them home. Opal finds happiness with a radio salesman. *Fancy Lady* (1927) pictures the unsettling effect of higher criticism upon the fundamentalist faith of the Missouri evangelist, Mrs. Zella Boone. Her son brings home from college new, upsetting ideas. At last she finds peace with a boyhood admirer, now a judge.

Caught (1928) portrays Mrs. Connie Webb, who goes to New York to study voice and philanders with Ed Floto; her confession brings no pardon from her husband. *Coney Island* (1929) shows Chic Cotton caught by the glamour of the big resort; he falls in love with a wire walker, but in the end changes his mind in favor of his patrician sweetheart. *River Girl* (1931) realistically pictures the clash in 1860 of two Mississippi River captains for Odette, a girl, and for supremacy. *Headed for Hollywood* (1932) is about Pearl Piper, an Iowa girl, who wins a beauty contest that sends her to the movie capital. Her father, a medicine-show man; Aunt Minnie; and an Indian go along to help her accept inevitable failure with good humor.

Sixteen Hands (1938) portrays Sweeney Bliss, his family, and his blue-ribbon-winning mule, which stands sixteen hands high. The French ambassador hires Sweeney to work in Washington, where the family has a variety of experiences in love and diplomacy. *Mr. Meek Marches On* (1941) satirizes the blind faith of a Missouri shoe-store owner in his notion that taxes can be reduced. *Family Honeymoon* (1942) tells how the marriage of Professor Jordan and Hetty Armstrong, a charming widow, is almost ended when her four children accompany them on the wedding trip.

DALE CURRAN

Skippy Adelman

was born in Poplar, Montana, on March 26, 1898. He grew up on a cattle ranch; as for his education after leaving the country schools, he calls it "mainly self-inflicted." At eighteen he was editor (and typesetter and pressman) of a small-town weekly newspaper, the Brockton *Bulletin*. After serving in the army from 1917 to 1919, he left Montana for Seattle, where he found his knowledge of the printing trade an excellent means of earning a living and of providing the necessary leisure time for avocational writing. In 1925 he moved to New York, where he has lived ever since. His interest in jazz of the purist or New Orleans type, which had started back in Montana with a small semi-professional dance band, was revived when he met Art Hodes, outstanding blues pianist; in partnership they founded and edited *The Jazz Record,* a monthly magazine, from 1943 to 1947.

A House on a Street (1934), his first novel, tells about a Dartmouth College man of 1926 who loses his job in the crash of 1929 and suffers in the depression. *Piano in the Band* (1940) gives the inside story of professional music and the troubles of a dance band caused by conflicting temperaments when some of the men want to play real jazz instead of commercial entertainment music. *Dupree Blues* (1948) also has the background of an orchestra, and tells the story of the simple, well-intentioned trombone player who falls in love with the scheming girl singer and finds himself living out the inescapable and tragic story of a blues ballad. He plays his music from the heart.

CLIFTON CUTHBERT

was born April 4, 1907. One of a globe-trotting actor clan, he spent the first five years of his life in Australia, Hawaii, California, and other Pacific areas. During the middle and late 1920's he contributed verse and criticism to *The Nation, Hound and Horn, Poetry,* and other magazines, and in 1931 was one of a trio of young writers at Chapel Hill, North Carolina, who edited *Contempo,* a little magazine. During World War II he was an army newsman with an armored division.

His first novel, *Joy Street* (1931), is a stylized and colloquial account of the tribulations of a young bootlegger. *Thunder Without Rain* (1933) concerns the then forbidden theme of incest; the Christian sense of sin and evil acts as a superhuman tragic force. *Art Colony* (1933) satirizes amorous and other posturings at a summer art colony. *Second Sight* (1934) examines the psychological implications of a young man's ardent love for an older woman. *Another Such Victory* (1937) describes the activities of various cliques and factions in a Connecticut town during the New England textile strike of 1934. *The Robbed Heart* (1945) is a novel of race relations set against the jazz-music background of New York's Harlem. Denis Sloane, the only son of a well-to-do New York family, falls in love with Judy Foster, a well-educated Negress reared by cultured and conservative parents.

D'AGOSTINO *to* DUNCAN

GUIDO D'AGOSTINO

Charles A. Bolger

was born in New York City in 1906, the son of Italian immigrant parents. Educated in the New York public schools, he began working and writing in advertising agencies, later turning to fiction and publishing his first short story in *Esquire* magazine in 1934. After having published a number of stories, he studied the technique of writing at Columbia University, mostly for the purpose of confirming what he had learned by the painstaking process of putting words on paper and receiving a great quantity of rejection slips.

During the war Guido D'Agostino served with the Office of War Information in Italy. At this time he wrote "The Dream of Angelo Zara," a propaganda piece broadcast many times to the enemy, prophesying the death of Mussolini. Rewritten into a short story, this tale appeared in many anthologies and was reprinted in Whit Burnett's *Story: The Fiction of the Forties* (1949). Guido D'Agostino is married to a French fashion designer and spends his time between New York and a farm in Pennsylvania where he pursues his love of animals and of the soil and the people who till it, as well as his passion for hunting and fishing.

Olives on the Apple Tree (1940), his first novel, is primarily concerned with the problem of Americanization. The fundamental worth of the immigrant appears in his contribution to our way of life in remaining himself and not in trying to shed his own background and culture in a quick attempt to make money, change his name, and become Americanized. Marco, the protagonist, says, "It is not for the olive to shout that it is an apple. It is to work, to grow and mature, that is the best way for the Italian to become an American." This is probably one of the very few novels written about Italians in America that attacks the problem of Americanization at its roots and offers some solution to the mass of first-generation Americans who can never seem to make up their minds about themselves and their place in our society. Marco's hobo experiences have given him an understanding of what newcomers to this country should do and be to meet the tests of good citizenship.

Hills Beyond Manhattan (1941) tells the story of a French architect suddenly thrown into bewildering contact with an American small-town social set—people who set themselves up as dictators of taste and culture and who pride themselves on their Anglo-Saxon heritage to the exclusion of all else. In trying to adjust himself to the American way of life, Chaurbord becomes interested in the problems of the workmen on a country estate where he is employed. He meets Sheila Stewart, and soon his Americanization is complete. *My Enemy the World* (1947), set in New York in 1910, shows the effect of an Old-World culture upon a boy who has been raised on the streets of Greenwich Village among criminal companions and is then sent to Italy to be educated, returning as a man to confront with his now-European mentality the raw problems of his youth.

MAUREEN DALY

was born in County Tyrone, Northern Ireland, on March 15, 1921, but grew up in Fond du Lac, Wisconsin. She first won literary distinction when she was fifteen with a short story entitled "Fifteen," which placed fourth in a national short-story contest sponsored by *Scholastic* magazine. The next year she won first place with a story called "Sixteen," which was included in the annual O. Henry Memorial award volume for 1938 and in thirty-five other anthologies. Since then she has never stopped writing.

When she was a student at Rosary College, she began to record that special summer when she was seventeen, and this reminiscence became the novel *Seventeenth Summer* (1943), which won the Dodd, Mead Intercollegiate Literary Fellowship contest. After graduating from college and completing her novel, she joined the staff of the Chicago *Tribune* as a reporter and as the author of "On the Solid Side," the first nationally syndicated newspaper column for teen-agers. She has written *Smarter and Smoother* (1944), a lively handbook for high-school boys and girls, and has edited *My Favorite Stories* (1948), an anthology. Miss Daly is now an associate editor of *The Ladies' Home Journal.*

Seventeenth Summer (1943) tells the story of the friendship and love of Jack Duluth, a boy of eighteen, and of Angie Morrow, a girl of seventeen, during three months. They go out together for the first time in June, have dates over "cokes" at the corner drugstore where the younger set congregates, take rides in Jack's "jalopy," and go to the movies. Jack's former girl friend interferes, and Angie's father gruffly disapproves. They learn the meaning of social customs, and when a misunderstanding separates them for a time, they endure mental torture. As Jack waves good-bye at the end of the season when a train carries Angie off to college, they both realize that they will never again experience anything quite so wonderful as that seventeenth summer.

MARCIA DAVENPORT

Halsman

was born on June 9, 1903, in New York City, the daughter of Alma Gluck, the famous singer. Her stepfather is Efrem Zimbalist, the violinist. As a small child she lived with her mother in Italy and Switzerland, and returned to this country in 1909. Her education included study in an Anglican convent, a Quaker school in Philadelphia, the Shipley School at Bryn Mawr, and finally Wellesley College, which she left in her sophomore year. Somewhat later she received a degree from the University of Grenoble in France, where she studied French history and literature. She spent several years in journalism, was on the staff of *The New Yorker,* and at present is a regular contributor on musical and operatic subjects to *Stage* magazine. Shortly after her marriage to Russell W. Davenport, she began work on *Mozart* (1932), a biography. She then turned to the writing of fiction. She lives in New York.

Mrs. Davenport's first novel, *Of Lena Geyer* (1936), gives the career of Lenska Gyruzkova, a famous opera singer who took the name of Lena Geyer. She was born in Bohemia to a scrub woman. She studied in America, made her début at the Metropolitan, and rejected all suitors, including a duke, to live only for her voice. In *The Valley of Decision* (1942) the Irish-born maid, Mary Rafferty, works for seventy years after 1870 for a Pittsburgh ironmaster and comes to represent the integrity and best quality of the Scott family. *East Side, West Side* (1947) gives a panoramic account of the contrasts in the varied life of New York City in the tenements, in café society, and in aristocratic circles, with the many nationalities represented. This is the background for the story of Jessie Bourne, a beautiful, wealthy, unhappily married woman nearing forty years of age, who shows the greatest disdain for her rich husband and his class, and who in the course of the seven days of the novel finds the right man, a former "Dead End kid" risen to a general's rank. Jessie hates the upstart, successful newcomers to New York because "they are the rootless, heartless, hard-boiled element which gives us our reputation for being what we are not. You have to be born here to live in it by your heart, not by your wits."

DAVID DAVIDSON

Vandamm

was born on May 11, 1908, in New York City. He was educated at Townsend Harris Hall, the College of the City of New York, and the Columbia University School of Journalism, where he earned the degrees of Bachelor of Arts and Bachelor of Literature. Although he determined in his teens that he wanted to become a novelist eventually, he took the long way around, and did not actually undertake the writing of long fiction until shortly after his thirty-eighth birthday. Meanwhile he worked ten years as a newspaperman, with the New York *World,* the Baltimore *News-Post,* and the New York *Post;* spent almost six years as a radio writer; and passed more than three years in government service. The latter period included press and radio work with the Office of Inter-American Affairs in Washington, Ecuador, and New York from 1942 to 1944. In 1945 and 1946 he served in Germany as a civilian specialist with the army in its information control division, being charged specifically with helping establish six democratic German newspapers in Bavaria.

A year in Europe on a Pulitzer traveling scholarship from Columbia University in 1931–32 was to serve as a determinant in the making of his first two novels. It evoked in him a special interest in the contrast of American mores and moral attitudes with those of other peoples. Each of his novels pictures an American in a foreign land.

The Steeper Cliff (1947), his first novel, is set in occupied Germany in the months immediately following V-E Day and deals specifically with the problem of courage, moral and physical. A young American officer, whose work requires him to pass judgment daily on the behavior of various Germans in the Hitler era, finds himself faced ultimately with the question of how well he himself would have stood up had he been born a German. He comes thus to identify himself with a missing Bavarian journalist, an outstanding anti-Nazi of his own age and general make-up. In the search for this counterpart of himself, Adam Lorenz, and the reconstruction of Lorenz's life under Hitler, Lieutenant Cooper finally finds his answer.

The Hour of Truth (1949) deals with the strivings of men for assurance of strength and adequacy, exploring the theme on a number of levels. The protagonist, William Harmon, finding himself hemmed in by the "sovereign" women of his household, seeks escape by joining a good-will mission to a run-down republic in South America. There he finds that most of his companions are similar "runaways," seeking an illusion of manhood by living among peoples even weaker and sicker than themselves. Ultimately he alone among them finds his "hour of truth" in a bold action that restores his feelings of adequacy. *In Another Country* (1950) pictures three students in London in 1932 and their outcome twenty years later in terms of national preconditioning.

VALENTINE DAVIES

was born in New York City on August 25, 1905. He was educated at the Horace Mann School and at the University of Michigan, where he completed his course in 1927. After two years in his father's real-estate business, he studied with Professor George Pierce Baker at the Yale Drama School. The following year his first play, "Three Times the Hour," was produced by Brock Pemberton. Subsequently he wrote "Keeper of the Keys," and "Blow Ye Winds" (1937). In 1941 he sold an original picture story, "Syncopation," and moved to the West Coast. A year later he entered the United States Coast Guard Reserve, in which he served for three and a half years as a lieutenant (senior grade), acting for most of the time as personnel officer at the Coast Guard operating base in Wilmington, California. After the war he returned to picture writing. In 1947 he wrote "Miracle on 34th Street," which won the Academy award for the best original motion-picture story of the year. Other pictures which he has written, either alone or in collaboration, are "Three Little Girls in Blue," "You Were Meant for Me," and "It Happens Every Spring." Since 1941 he has been working and writing primarily for motion pictures; both of his novels were first developed for the screen. Since *Miracle on 34th Street* was selected as a Book-of-the-Month-Club dividend and *It Happens Every Spring* has likewise sold well, it is interesting to point out that not only are many novels the basis for good screenplays, but original screen stories are also capable of successful development into novels.

Miracle on 34th Street (1947), his first novel, is the story of a man who believes himself to be Santa Claus and his influence upon a huge New York department store and ultimately upon a larger segment of the public, many of whom are surprised to find themselves sharing his simple faith and good will. *It Happens Every Spring* (1949) is the story of a young chemistry instructor, imbued with a secret passion for baseball, whose scientific experiments give him the opportunity to become the greatest pitcher in the big leagues.

CLYDE BRION DAVIS

Leja Gorska

was born in Unadilla, Nebraska, on May 22, 1894. He grew up in Missouri and attended schools in Chillicothe, Ohio, and Kansas City. After studying at the Kansas City Art Institute, he was an apprentice printer, an apprentice commercial artist, a traveling salesman for a law-book firm, a detective, an electrician, and a rancher. In 1916 he worked on the Albuquerque *Journal.* He served as an enlisted soldier in World War I. Following the armistice in 1918, he worked on the *Pontanezen Duckboard,* a soldier newspaper in Brest, France; when he returned to America he entered upon a newspaper career with the Denver *Post.* Later he was on the staffs of the Denver *Times,* the Denver *Rocky Mountain News,* the San Francisco *Examiner,* the Seattle *Post-Intelligencer,* and the Buffalo *Times.* In 1941 he was European correspondent for several United States newspapers. Other experiences include ten months in Hollywood, three months as motion-picture script writer in New York, a period as a journalism teacher at the University of Buffalo, and two years as assistant editor of a New York publishing firm. *The Age of Indiscretion* (1950), a non-fiction work, wittily shows that American culture, in the broad sense of the word, has not declined in the last fifty years but has advanced to a marked degree.

"I consider the novel an art form and not a medium for propaganda," Mr. Davis has said. "When one of my characters develops ideas on philosophy, politics, human behavior, art, or economics (which is frequently the case), they are the sort of ideas which I consider both plausible and interesting for one of his or her mentality and background to entertain. It seems to me that this should be one of the first principles of novel writing, but it is curious how often some critics observe: 'Davis obviously is using so-and-so as a mouthpiece to express his own convictions.' Well, when and if I ever become sufficiently Messianic to believe that God has given me, and me alone, the solution to the various and interlocking problems of mankind, I sincerely hope that He also will endow me with enough initiative to stand on my own feet and speak on my own behalf.

"None of my characters is a symbol. I have no St. Georges and I have no dragons. I have no Mr. Goods and no Mr. Bads, no solid whites nor solid blacks. Consequently, my novels may seem monochromatic for those who love only the theme of virtue rewarded and evil punished."

Davis' first novel, *The Anointed* (1937), is the story of a young American sailor who believes that God has elected him to solve the secret of the universe and who, in a mood of perverse innocence and worldly-wise naïveté, navigates his own mind. *"The Great American Novel—"* (1938) is the saga of Homer Zigler, a newspaper man, who hopes some day to write the great American novel; the book is a chronicle of his dreams and day dreams, his domestic life, and his workaday existence on newspapers in Cleveland, Kansas City, San Francisco, and Denver. *North-end Wildcats* (1938), a juvenile, relates the adventures of a group of boys in the Midwest in the early 1900's.

Nebraska Coast (1939) is a novel based in part upon the experiences of the author's grandfather in moving from the Erie Canal to Nebraska in the stirring 1860's and tells of the Macdougall family's pioneering life on the ill-fated Steam-Wagon Freight Road. *The Arkansas* (1940), one of the "Rivers of America" series, is the story of the history and folklore of the full length of the Arkansas River which rises in the Colorado mining country and crosses Kansas, Oklahoma, and Arkansas before emptying into the Mississippi.

Sullivan (1940) relates the earthy, amusing, and fantastic adventures of Gilbert Sullivan, an American newspaper artist hitchhiking to parts unknown; in a Mexican tavern he suddenly feels that he can and someday will float in the air. *Follow the Leader* (1942) is the story of Charles Martel, a puny, sickly boy who rose from his commonplace midwestern life to fame and fortune, told against a background of historical incidents which directly and indirectly shaped his life. *The Rebellion of Leo McGuire* (1944) is the first-person story of a self-styled "honest burglar" whose rebellion against the injustices of society is somewhat unorthodox.

The Stars Incline (1946) is the portrait of a newspaper man who, in the course of his work in Denver, New York, Spain, and Normandy at the time of the invasion, comes to realize how he wasted his affection on a beautiful but unworthy wife and how necessary to him is the love of a loyal woman. *Jeremy Bell* (1947) is the story of Jeremy and his friend, Sam Brock, two seventeen-year-old boys who set out, just before the Spanish-American War, to see the world and who see more than they expected both in Chicago and in an Arkansas slave lumber camp.

Temper the Wind (1948) is the story of Floyd "Cowboy" Shandy, a war veteran, prize fighter, and garage mechanic, who has returned after the war to his Wyoming home town. The novel gives a vivid portrayal of a boxer's moods, thoughts, and actions before, during, and after his big fight. *Playtime Is Over* (1949) is about Steve Lewis—soldier of fortune, lover of women, man of action—whose adventures have taken him into the Central American wilderness, the voodoo-ridden jungles of Haiti, and the pampas of the Argentine. After his discharge from the army, he tries philosophically to fit the pieces of his life together on an isolated, abandoned Arkansas farm.

H(AROLD) L(ENOIR) DAVIS

was born in Yoncalla, Douglas County, Oregon, on October 18, 1896. His mother's forebears were early settlers who crossed the plains from Tennessee in 1852, and five generations of them still live there. His father was a country schoolteacher, also a Tennessean, whose family went west in the 1870's to escape the devastation of the Civil War. The earliest years of his life were spent on a homestead adjoining a village of inbred mongrel Indians who stole whatever they could find and drank everything that could be swallowed. At the age of nine he went to work as a typesetter and printer's devil for a country newspaper at Oakland, Oregon. When he was ten, he herded sheep on a mountain ranch near Elkhead. His family moved to Antelope, a town located in the eastern Oregon sagebrush on the old freighting line into the desert. He was eleven at the time, and he says of this period: "I worked punching cattle, drove a derrick team for a haying crew, herded sheep and tied fleeces at shearing time, learned Spanish from the Mexican sheepshearers, and set type and printer's-deviled on the Antelope *Herald.*"

When he was twelve he lived in a steamboat town on the Columbia River and remained there until he graduated from high school. At seventeen he was a deputy county sheriff. When war came in 1917, he enlisted as a private. His spare time was devoted to reading, and soon he was composing poetry. Some of it, sent to Harriet Monroe's magazine *Poetry,* won a prize in 1919. Robinson Jeffers and H. L. Mencken suggested in 1928 that he write prose; except for brief intervals he has devoted himself to that medium ever since. In 1932 he received a Guggenheim fellowship to visit Mexico. His first novel won a Harper prize in 1935 and a Pulitzer prize in 1936. A collection of his poetry is entitled *Proud Riders* (1942).

Mr. Davis is an authority on western history and culture. "Creative writing," he has said, "should deal with all that part of life and of the world that has not yet been transformed into art, including, of course, the mind and soul of the writer himself. Its job is to transform some part of this raw material into a work of art. That can be done only with material that, in its relation to art, is new and untouched. It cannot be done with material that has already been transformed into a work of art of any kind."

His first novel, *Honey in the Horn* (1935), is a story of the homesteading period in Oregon from 1906 to 1908; the romance of Clay Calvert is set against the background provided by the restless, crude, and lusty people who crowded into the wide-open spaces of the Northwest. Told with gusto in the tall-tale fashion of Mark Twain, the story is rich in homely metaphors expressed in pungent conversation; a touch of Paul Bunyanism appears in the exaggerations, anecdotes, and poker-faced humor uttered in a western drawl. *Harp of a Thousand Strings* (1947), with a setting in the era of the French revolution, is a story contrasting the American way of life, which is man against nature, with the European order, which is man against humanity. Three American sailors meet in a warehouse in Tripoli during the Barbary War and remain until they can depart. Tallien, a local official, tells of his part in the French Revolution and in the government of post-revolutionary France. *Beulah Land* (1949) is a full presentation of the various kinds of love which are possible in a country in process of formation: love of family, of one's people, of humanity, of one's environment, of parents, of country—a complete catalogue. The story concerns the long, hazardous journey of two youngsters from the Cherokee country of western North Carolina to their Beulah Land in Indian Territory, now Oklahoma. Ruhama, an impulsive, half-Indian girl, accompanies Askwani, an Indian-bred foundling white boy.

KENNETH S. DAVIS

was born in Salina, Kansas, on September 29, 1912. He holds degrees from Kansas State University and the University of Wisconsin. He has been a reporter on the Topeka, Kansas, *Daily Capital*; an information specialist with the United States Soil Conservation Service; the editor of a war-plant newspaper; a war correspondent attached to SHAEF in England and France; and an instructor in journalism at New York University. In 1950 he was special assistant to Milton S. Eisenhower, President of Kansas State College. Mr. Davis was a member of the United States delegation to sessions of the international general conferences of UNESCO in Mexico City in 1947 and in Beirut, Lebanon, in 1948. He wrote *Soldier of Democracy* (1945), a biography of General Dwight D. Eisenhower. A simplified version, *General Eisenhower, Soldier of Democracy* (1949), was issued as a juvenile.

Mr. Davis' novels are concerned, on dissimilar levels and in radically different ways, with the conflict between the "will to death" and the "will to life" which he regards as central to the experience of our times.

In the Forests of the Night (1942), his first novel, has for its main character William Kendall, a United States forester of fine potentialities, whose death-drive, expressed in alcoholism, brings tragedy to himself and to all who are intimately involved with him. This stark, elemental story won the Friends of American Writers award. *The Years of the Pilgrimage* (1948) is much more complex, dealing with the central theme on levels ranging from the most violent physical action to the most abstract metaphysics. The main characters are Harcourt Stevens, a mystic and intellectual fascist whose "vitalism is essentially a deathism," and Ferris Morehead, Jr., a young minister whose rationalism, unhappily influenced by Kierkegaard and the subsequent "theologians of crisis," makes war on his neo-orthodox theology. He is finally driven in pain to reject both his theology and his ministry. Around the abstract opposition of these two men spreads an action of terror and unnatural passion which can find final and decisive adjustment only in violent death.

MICHAEL De CAPITE

Fayer

was born on April 13, 1915, in Cleveland, Ohio, of parents of Italian descent. He graduated from Lincoln High School in Cleveland in 1933 and from Ohio University at Athens in 1938. During his college years he had vague unformed ideas about a literary career. Joseph Conrad and Mark Twain were his favorite authors and he imitated them. When he discovered Sherwood Anderson, he awakened to the true possibilities of writing, and thereafter he began composing seriously. Following graduation, he spent some time dissolving the illusions gathered in college. He was a laborer, a reporter, and a traveler from east to west looking for something to do. In 1939 he went to Chicago and became a police reporter on *The Press*. During the academic year 1939–40, he studied architecture and fine arts on a scholarship at New York University. In the fall of 1940 he moved to Claremont, New Hampshire, where he wrote news, features, and sports on the town newspaper. In April, 1941, he took up residence in New York, where in the following January he became a press officer in the United Nations information office. Later, after a mission to England, he entered the army, served with the field artillery and the Office of Strategic Services, and ended his military career with *Yank* and the army news service in New York. Following his discharge he made an extended trip to England, France, Czechoslovakia, and other European countries. In 1949 he was in New Delhi, India, as a press officer with the United Nations Commission for India and Pakistan.

His first novel, *Maria* (1943), is the story of three generations of an Italian-American family in the United States, with emphasis upon the steadfastness and faith of the grandmother, Maria, and the grandson, Paul, who does not understand his background. It concerns two conflicting cultures and their slow adjustment to each other. *No Bright Banner* (1944) portrays the childhood and young manhood of Paul Barone, the son of an Italian immigrant. It is set in the period from 1920 to 1941, and the theme is related to the perplexities, confusions, and fears faced by the *interbellum* generation. *The Bennett Place* (1948) describes the character of Katharine Bennett, whose life in an old mansion becomes a focus for the thoughts and problems of a small midwestern university town. Katharine herself is a symbol of an America that has become a myth and is no longer real as the country moves into another stage of its history. This book won the award of the Friends of American Writers for the best novel written by a Midwesterner in 1948.

SYLVIA DEE

Elliott Erwitt

was born in Little Rock, Arkansas, on October 22, 1914. Her mother was and is a newspaperwoman, now on the editorial staff of the Rochester, New York, *Democrat and Chronicle,* and also the author of some four hundred published songs. Sylvia Dee's grandmother wrote such songs as "Put Away the Baby Clothes" in the 1890's. As a child, Sylvia Dee was tutored in a rather haphazard fashion while touring the country with her stepfather who was a concert violinist. She attended school so short a time in each city that no teacher ever learned her first name.

When she was eighteen she had her first popular song published. The years that followed served as a period of apprenticeship, during which she published many songs. In 1945 she wrote, with Sidney Lippman, the composer, "Chickery Chick," which sold a million records and stayed on the Hit Parade for fourteen weeks. Other popular lyrics by her include "It Couldn't Be True," "My Sugar Is So Refined," "After Graduation Day," and "Laroo Laroo Lilli Bolero," which is based on a Druid chant. With Mr. Lippman she wrote the lyrics for the George Abbott show, "Barefoot Boy With Cheek" (1947).

Sylvia Dee turned to prose and wrote her first novel because she felt that too much false humor has been written about teenagers in situations and plots which are unnecessary because "the normal everyday life of a teener is exciting enough in itself."

And Never Been Kissed (1949), her first novel, tells the story of Flory from the age of thirteen when she is mad about one boy until she is seventeen and in love with another boy. Of the novel the author has written: "Nothing sensational happens. Instead, I have tried to show how Flory's imagination creates an exciting life out of the everyday existence she leads." *Dear Guest and Ghost* (1950) pictures the Helmakobblers: Mrs. Helmakobbler, a kind and neighborly soul; Fred, her toothpaste-salesman husband; Thelma, their bookish daughter; and Stevy, their wolfish son; and, most of all, Leicester, a friendly ghostly veteran of the War of 1812 who occupies the house to which they move and who is seen only by Mrs. Helmakobbler of the simple heart and uncluttered subconscious. During the course of the story Leicester solves all the family problems and proves himself worthy of his permanent spot in the guest room.

DAVID CORNEL DeJONG

was born on June 9, 1905, in Blÿa, a small village in the province of Friesland in The Netherlands. When he was thirteen, his parents brought him to Grand Rapids, Michigan, where he continued his education. At fifteen he studied in a business school and then went to work. For three years he was in a bank, and then went to a preparatory school by earning his way as a clerk and soda jerker in drug stores. He took his bachelor's degree at Calvin College and his master's at Duke University, and did further graduate work in English at Brown University until 1934. He began writing poetry while in college and published several poems in *Poetry* and other magazines. From 1929 to 1930 he taught in the Edmore, Michigan, High School, and at this time he wrote his first short stories. Following the acceptance of his first novel, he chose Providence, Rhode Island, for his home, and he still resides there. For several months in 1938 he lived in New York City and at that time received a Houghton Mifflin fellowship for *Old Haven*. In 1939 he made his first visit to Holland. In 1945 he married Helen Elizabeth Moffitt. Eighteen of his short stories are collected in *Snow-on-the-Mountain* (1946). *Across the Board* (1943) and *Domination of June* (1944) are volumes of poetry. Mr. De Jong's autobiography of his first sixteen years is *With a Dutch Accent* (1944).

Asked about his motivations as a writer, Mr. DeJong replied: "If I should have to state why I write fiction, or write at all, or write about the things I do, I could say little more, I suppose, than that I seem to be able to write better than anything else, that I write fiction because it serves largely to keep my head above water economically, that only occasionally am I moved by indignation, nostalgia, or sentiment at picking the themes I do; most of the time I can keep convincing myself that all these have no abiding or integral part in art, that is, what I consider my art. My first books were mainly about my native Holland, but only because my publishers insisted on a Dutch theme. Personally I am much more interested in contemporary American life around me, psychologically and satirically."

Belly Fulla Straw (1934), his first novel, concerns a Dutch immigrant family which comes to America in 1913 and settles in Michigan. The head of the family, Harmen Idema, clings to his old-world traditions and customs despite the Americanization of the rest of the family. After the death of his wife, he returns to The Netherlands. *Old Haven* (1938), which is based on the author's memories of Holland, is a story of provincial Dutch life from 1901 to the outbreak of World War I in 1914. The central character is Tjerk Mellena who at eight is going to school, later enters the army, and finally marries. *Light Sons and Dark* (1940) pictures an American family living on a run-down midwestern farm. The father, a weak ne'er-do-well, favors his twin dark sons, while his wife favors those of lighter complexion. Joe, one of the latter, finds his way into a better life.

Day of the Trumpet (1941) portrays life in a small Dutch city just before and during the occupation by Nazi troops from August, 1939, to May, 1940. It is a story of submission to the invader's will. The main characters are a ten-year-old boy who maintains faith in God's goodness and his grandmother who has inspiring moral courage and resourcefulness. *Benefit Street* (1942) is about the fourteen tenants of an apartment house on Benefit Street in Providence, Rhode Island, during the hurricane in 1938. *Somewhat Angels* (1945) characterizes a mother with three sons in the army during World War II and the four women who are close to them. *The Desperate Children* (1949) is a psychological story of two boys, one eleven and one fifteen, living in the no-man's land between childhood and the complexity of the adult world; pictured are their relations with each other, and with teachers, parents, and others.

HENRY DENKER

was born in New York City on November 25, 1912. After attending New York City elementary schools, he completed the pre-law course at New York University and went on to graduate from the New York Law School. At the age of fifteen he began working to make a future education possible; his jobs included those of stock boy, office clerk after school hours, and shoe salesman. While attending law school at night, he worked in department stores. Besides being a lawyer, he has been a consultant on taxation and on labor relations, sales manager of a legal publishing company, and a radio writer. In 1949 he was writing and directing "The Greatest Story Ever Told," a program which won more awards in a single year than any other on the radio.

Of his writing Mr. Denker has said: "If there is anything unusual about my technique, it is that I write to a good degree in dialogue. This is done intentionally for what I believe is a good reason. Through dialogue both character and story are revealed in the most effective way. I have little time for authors who take endless pages in describing and building character. Essentially, to me, a character is what he does and says, and the author's opinion of him is of little value. I believe that reading a book should be living life through the eyes, ears, and experiences of the protagonist. And the less the author intrudes, the more realistic is the experience."

I'll Be Right Home, Ma (1949), his first novel, reveals what a destructive business prize fighting is and probes into the psychological factors that make a man earn his living by the destruction of other men. Danny Callahan, essentially a shy unaggressive boy in New York's Hell's Kitchen, becomes a fighter because his mother's unfaithfulness drives his father to suicide. The book has colorful and authentic descriptions of fight scenes.

My Son, The Lawyer (1950) describes the destructive effects of the compulsions of parents to live their lives and realize their ambitions through their children. It follows the career of David Brown from the time his mother insists he become an attorney until he is finally disbarred. Laid in an authentic New York Jewish background, it is the story of many first-generation immigrant families of all religions and origins.

PRUDENCIO de PEREDA

was born in Brooklyn, New York, of Spanish parents, on February 18, 1912. He started thinking and worrying for himself at the age of six months, when his mother neglected him to prepare for expected twins. For Prudencio that event might have been the start of being constantly lonely, for he was considered odd because of his early love of books and a youthful determination to be a writer. There had been no writers in his family. His schooling was of the common variety, terminated by graduation from the College of the City of New York, where he majored in Spanish and planned to teach, but his chief interest was literature and writing.

He began writing in Spain on a visit in 1933, and published his first story in 1935 and about fifty others since then. In 1937 he met Ernest Hemingway and worked with him on two films, "Spain in Flames" and "The Spanish Earth." Mr. de Pereda, who prepared a Spanish translation of the latter, has said, "I sometimes wonder if I ever would have made it without turning up the paths Ernest Hemingway pointed out." Mr. de Pereda's early subject matter revolved mostly about Spain and the Spanish Civil War, which moved him very much. His later material deals with the army and World War II. Some of his shorter tales have been printed in O'Brien's *Best Short Stories,* the *O'Henry Memorial Award* volume, and in each of the four *Cross Section* volumes.

"I am a propagandist," Mr. de Pereda has stated, "and I never invented a character in my life. I never had a protagonist I didn't admire and envy. I'm interested in recording the high-water marks of little people who are little only in the sense that they lack the recognition, the rewards, and fulfillments they richly and justly deserve. We are all in a process of evolution, and the goal is a kind of ideal being who will not be perfectionist or god-like, not ultra-scientific or superhuman, but will possess an unlimited capacity for living and humanity, unmolested by the inhibitions and fears that keep us down. John said it pretty well when he wrote that the Kingdom of God is in man himself.

"I like to write about the times when somebody I know or heard about shows some of those qualities here and now, especially in those cases where the man, woman, or child is not recognized or honored for those things by his neighbors and the world. He or she does not expect it. To be specific, in *All the Girls We Loved* I wrote a war novel in which none of the characters was a hero in the accepted sense, but was a hero in the truer sense."

All the Girls We Loved (1948), his first novel, pictures the violence and bitterness of emotions generated in the soldiers of World War II. One of these soldiers is Al Figueira, who serves as an observer and confidant of the GI's and whose remarks serve to tie together the many stories which comprise the book. *A Man on the Cross* (1950), with its scene in Spain, marks a return to two of the earliest and most forceful influences in Mr. de Pereda's life: Spain and Catholicism. "I think I have a new tolerance now," he has said, "and I have tried to make an objective picture of what it means for a Catholic to try to be a Christian in fascist Spain." The story deals with the Passion Play in a small pueblo, and how the "new order" has affected the simplicity and truth of what should be nothing more than a humble peasant offering.

AUGUST (WILLIAM) DERLETH

was born in Sauk City, Wisconsin, on February 24, 1909. After attending the local schools, he went to the University of Wisconsin, from which he graduated in 1930. His writing career began when he was thirteen, and since the age of fifteen his annual literary output has been large. He writes poetry, short stories, pastiches, serious novels and mystery stories, some plays, biography, history, and criticism. A rapid composer and one of the most versatile writers in America, he produces more than half a million words annually. By 1949 he had published fifty-six books and had twenty-one others ready for publication. Yet in spite of his busy pace as a writer, he participates fully in the life of Sauk City: he was director of the local board of education for six years; served in various capacities from secretary to president of the local men's club, akin to a chamber of commerce; was an organizer of the parent-teacher association in Sauk City; is a sponsor of boy scouting; and serves as member of a county commission on juvenile delinquency. His home is open to young people, who come to play his extensive collection of phonograph records or to examine his almost complete file of comic cartoons. He is one of the few authors who have never left their native *milieu* to live and write in New York or some other great city. Sauk City is a village of two thousand inhabitants and is located about twenty-five miles from Madison, the seat of the University of Wisconsin. He has been literary editor of the Madison *Capital Times* since 1941, and since 1939 he has conducted the affairs of Arkham House, a publishing firm in Sauk City.

Mr. Derleth has written the "Judge Peck" mystery stories; has edited eight collections of fantastic prose and poetry; and has written for the "Rivers of America" series *The Wisconsin: River of a Thousand Isles* (1942), and for the "Railroads of America" series *The Milwaukee Road: Its First 100 Years* (1948). He has produced biographies of Zona Gale and H. P. Lovecraft. *Beyond Time and Space* (1950) is a collection of short narratives in the field of science fiction arranged chronologically from Plato's account of Atlantis to outstanding modern writers.

Mr. Derleth's serious work has consistently portrayed life in Sac Prairie, the fictitious name of his home town. The Sac Prairie saga is an attempt to mirror life in a typical midwestern village from 1830 to 1950; about half of the contemplated fifty volumes have been published. Eight of these are collections of poems, three are of miscellaneous prose, three are collections of short stories, four are historical novels, and three are modern novels.

Wind over Wisconsin (1938) is chronologically the first novel in the series; its theme is that of materialism versus idealism, and it pictures Wisconsin in the 1830's, with the fur trade entering its decline, the Indians making their last stand against the white invaders, and the period of settlement about to begin. The central character is Chalfonte Pierneau, who lives through the change which transforms Wisconsin from a fur-trapping to a wheat-growing community. *Restless Is the River* (1939) tells the story of pioneer life in Sac Prairie from 1839 to 1850; the central character is an exiled Hungarian count who moves unflaggingly through good fortune and bad in his ambition to establish a wine industry. *Shadow of Night* (1943) is about a man with revenge in his heart who undergoes a change of feeling because of the influence of the kindly people in Sac Prairie. *Still Is the Summer Night* (1937) portrays the love of two brothers for one woman against the Sac Prairie of the 1880's. *Evening in Spring* (1941) is a patently autobiographical story of young love in Sac Prairie in the 1920's. Steve Brendon and his friend Margery are in high school. The parents object to their association because Steve is a Catholic and Margery is not. Teachers and townspeople also meddle in the youngsters' lives.

Sweet Genevieve (1942) is a "light" novel which tells of Jenny Breen's departure from Sac Prairie and of her return to her home and sweetheart. *The Shield of the Valiant* (1945) is the author's most ambitious novel to date; behind the foreground story of the banker's son who falls in love with a girl from across the tracks lies the author's thesis that in every American community there are a few "valiant" souls who, by example of word and deed, oppose social injustices. *Place of Hawks* (1935) contains four novelettes dealing with strange obsessions and madness. *Country Growth* (1940) and *Sac Prairie People* (1948) are collections of short stories of farm and village life in the Sac Prairie area. *Any Day Now* (1938) portrays the lifelong regret of a woman who refused to marry a young physician because of her mother's advice.

Mr. Derleth is the author of two additional historical novels: *Bright Journey* (1940), dealing with the northwest fur trade from 1812 to 1843, in a story which is largely the fictional biography of Hercules Dousman, a well-known American trader of the period; and *Westryn Wind* (1950), a novel of the 1840's concerning the famous lead-mining region of southwestern Wisconsin. Although these two books are not part of the saga series, they embody a few scenes laid in Sac Prairie.

BERNARD (AUGUSTINE) De VOTO

was born on January 11, 1897, in Ogden, Utah. His father was of Italian descent and his mother was the daughter of a pioneer Mormon family. From the local schools he went to the University of Utah for one year and then transferred to Harvard University. During World War I he was a lieutenant in the infantry. He graduated from Harvard in 1920, and from 1922 to 1927 taught English at Northwestern University. From 1929 to 1936 he taught literature and writing at Harvard. Since 1927 he has made his home in Cambridge, Massachusetts, although for periods of time he has carried on elsewhere his work as author and editor. In 1936 he succeeded Henry Seidel Canby as editor of *The Saturday Review of Literature* and while on this assignment lived in New York for two years. He has conducted the "Easy Chair" department in *Harper's Magazine* since 1935.

Mr. De Voto is profoundly interested in the history of the American frontier, the westward expansion of America, the religious sects of the Mormons, Shakers, and Millerites, and the utopian economic experiments at Oneida and Brook Farm. An outspoken and tough-minded critic of literature and life, Mr. De Voto has wielded immense influence in bringing clarity into discussions of current events as well as into interpretations of the lives and achievements of Americans of earlier times. Between 1939 and 1942 he wrote three novels and a short story under the pseudonym "John August."

Mark Twain's America (1932), one of several of Mr. De Voto's books devoted to this author, pictures the humorist's background and examines the roots of the mature writer's ideas in his boyhood life. *The Year of Decision* (1943) describes some of the people and events in the West of 1846. *Across the Wide Missouri* (1947), which won the Pulitzer and Bancroft prizes for history in 1948, chronicles the Rocky Mountain fur trade which flourished in the 1830's. *The World of Fiction* (1950) explores the relationships between writer and reader.

His first novel, *The Crooked Mile* (1924), has for its theme the failure of the industrialized people at the base of the Rocky Mountains to live up to the beauty and power symbolized in the towering peaks. Gordon Abbey realizes that his family in its third generation has deteriorated from the strength of the pioneer. *The Chariot of Fire* (1926) portrays Ohio Boggs, a religious fanatic, whose mystic visions cause him to gain amazing power over his followers in Illinois in the 1830's. *The House of the Sun-Goes-Down* (1928) pictures some of the cheating ways of the frontier town of Windsor in the late 1860's. James Abbott, a Confederate army officer, goes west to find freedom and gains it amid dishonest men. *We Accept with Pleasure* (1934) studies the inability of a group of young Harvard men to overcome the depressive effect of World War I.

The three novels written by Mr. DeVoto under the name of "John August" include the murder mystery, *Troubled Star* (1939), and two spy stories, *Rain before Seven* (1942), about two men accused of burning a factory, and *Advance Agent* (1942), about a millionaire in Massachusetts with Nazi sympathies. *The Woman in the Picture* (1944) concerns the way in which loyal Americans foil a plot of a fascist-minded man to destroy American democracy.

Mountain Time (1947) has Cy Kinsman, a surgeon home from World War I, realize that he ought to drop his profession. At the same time a woman, a boyhood friend of the doctor, decides to leave her mentally adolescent husband. Both go to a western town, and there work out their solution. The emphasis in the novel is on the discovery of the unconscious forces which make for self-destruction.

MARY FRANCES DONER

Phyfe

was born on July 29, 1893, at Port Huron, Michigan. She attended the Convent of the Immaculate Heart and high schools in Detroit and St. Clair, Michigan, and then went on to study at Columbia University. At this time she became a steady contributor to periodicals, and by 1934 some two hundred and fifty short stories, serials, and articles from her pen had appeared in magazines. She has covered music for the Boston *Traveler* and conducted classes in creative writing at the Boston Center for Adult Education. Although most of her adult life has been spent in New York and Boston, she now divides her time between New York and Michigan.

Eight of Miss Doner's romantic serials were published in book form in the early 1930's, and then she began to realize the value of her early Michigan background as a locale for her novels. It became her desire to present a picture of the Great Lakes country and the people who contributed to its growth. She spent part of the summers in her youth aboard her father's freighters and came to know and love the lakes and islands, the rivers and the ports. The recollections of these experiences qualified her actually to compose the stories conceived in those impressionable years.

Gallant Traitor (1938) is a love story with an immediate setting in one of lower Michigan's great cherry orchards, for which the state is famous. *Some Fell Among Thorns* (1939) finds its drama in the devotion of a self-made young Great Lakes captain for a girl whose sense of values was developed with difficulty. In *The Doctor's Party* (1940) a physician in a small Great Lakes town, aware that a crisis impends in the lives of certain local people whom he has brought into the world, gives a Christmas Eve party to which he invites them. His challenge, "What has each of you done with the life that was given you?" brings about a dramatic *dénouement*. Although the action moves from a little Great Lakes town to New York and back again, *Chalice* (1940) is essentially the story of a woman's mental and spiritual growth, of her childhood spent near the lakes and rivers she loved, of the freighters that ply the waterways, and of the men whose lives revolve about those ships.

Not By Bread Alone (1941) is the story of three generations of women of a single family, all of whom love weak but well-meaning men. It is the particular story of Maggie, who year after year sailed the lakes for the long eight-months' season in the galley of a freighter with Joe, her ineffectual husband; it describes a woman's loneliness in a world of men, her longing for her children, and her efforts to create a sound and happier future.

The Great Lakes and the Chautauqua circuit provide the background in *Glass Mountain* (1942) for the story of a brave woman and a man whose ambition nearly ruins both their lives. *O Distant Star!* (1944) introduces an ambitious little Boston Irish seamstress in the 1860's. When Boston capital is invested in the Michigan iron ore and copper mines, there is an exodus of Boston labor to Michigan's Upper Peninsula, and Delia Clune is taken as a bride to Marquette. Her life there among the miners, and her final reconciliation of dreams with reality provide the drama of this story.

Blue River (1946) is the saga of one man's dream of an auto empire along the shores somewhat north of Detroit, of his brief realization of that dream, and of the ultimate success of a marriage that almost failed because of a sister's jealousy. *Ravenswood* (1948), with a background of the chloride deposits for which Michigan is famous, tells of a salt industry, the family that controls it, and their impact on a Great Lakes town.

Cloud of Arrows (1950) concerns Beth Fairfield, who goes to New York in the 1930's to be an illustrator. She meets and loves a cynical editor, but marries another man, goes to Michigan to live, and, following the breakup of her marriage, returns to the editor.

JOHN RODERIGO DOS PASSOS

Artist: L'Engle

was born on January 14, 1896, in Chicago, Illinois. The greater part of his youth was spent in Washington, where he first went to day school, and on a farm in Westmoreland County, Virginia. His father was a lawyer from Philadelphia, the son of a Portuguese immigrant and of a lady of Quaker extraction. Dos Passos Senior, who wrote several books on the theory of law, told his son tales of his experiences with the Pennsylvania troops in reserve at Antietam. Mr. Dos Passos' mother was also involved in the Civil War. Her ancestors were Marylanders, and she was a small child in Petersburg during the siege. "The Mason-Dixon Line," says Mr. Dos Passos, "was the first fence I ever sat on."

He attended Choate School in Connecticut and Harvard College. After receiving his bachelor's degree in 1916, he went to Spain to study architecture. On the entrance of the United States into World War I in April, 1917, he enlisted in a French ambulance corps and later transferred as a private to the United States Medical Corps. His first two novels are based on his military experiences. After the war he stayed in Europe to travel and write. He read extensively in French, and though he was not a member of the expatriate café society, he was listed as another spiritual casualty of the "lost generation." When he returned to the United States, he settled in New York City. In the intervals of his apprenticeship as a novelist, he became a roving journalist. His reportorial trips took him to Europe, the Near East, and Mexico. At home he covered such political events as Presidential campaigns. *Journeys Between Wars* (1938) contains some of his work in this period.

In the later 1920's Mr. Dos Passos wrote plays and executed sets for a small theater in New York's Greenwich Village. In 1929 he spent a long summer in Soviet Russia, attending the theater, trying to learn the language, and walking and riding in the Caucasus. "There I found myself, as usual, on the fence," says the author. "It was already becoming evident that the radical movement which has so changed the minds of so many men of my generation was not to turn its fine hopes into realities. I began to think that what we Americans needed was a good solid fence of our own to sit on to lift us above the ruthless contests of political dogmas that were already beginning to tear Europe to pieces."

In 1930 Mr. Dos Passos moved to Cape Cod and has since used Provincetown as a base for explorations of his own country through field trips and extensive reading on the origins of the American way of thought and behavior. The immediate result of the trips, before and after the move to Provincetown, was the three parts of the long novel, *U.S.A.* One product of his reading was an examination of freedom as our leaders and people in the early days of the republic understood it. This was called *The Ground We Stand On* (1941).

In World War II Mr. Dos Passos returned to his role of roving journalist. In *State of the Nation* (1944) he recorded his impressions of the home front and the men and women who formed the first links of the supply chain. In 1945 he examined the extremities of this chain as a correspondent for *Life* magazine. His findings—the vital, constructive mood of men fighting in the Pacific; the dull defeatism of the men at peace in Europe; and the tragic loss of purpose somewhere in the two oceans and one continent between the two theaters of war—were fully documented in *Tour of Duty* (1946).

In 1946 he still found himself on the fence, this time a ramshackle structure which divides war from peace. He discovered that even the young men in the Pacific merely hoped that what they would find upon their return from the war would not be worse than what they had left. "This is not an age of illusions," he said. "We can only hope that it will become an age of clear thinking."

In 1949 Mr. Dos Passos found himself less and less interested in the struggle between capitalism and socialism, and more and more interested in trying to discover new paths toward freedom. His attitude toward the Kremlin—"I think the only sensible one"—is "my country right or wrong." With regard to the political opinions of a novelist, Mr. Dos Passos has said, "Opinions of this sort leave a pretty stale aftermath, and are not nearly so much to the point in discussing the work of a novelist (or journalist even) as the critics contend." *The Prospect before Us* (1950) diagnoses the state of the hemisphere.

Mr. Dos Passos' first novel, *One Man's Initiation: 1917* (1920), is the story of the grievances against war held by a disillusioned young man who joined the ambulance corps to serve in France in World War I. *Three Soldiers* (1921) vividly pictures typical Americans in World War I in their training, fighting, and leisure moments to show the unpleasant side of war and their grievances. *Manhattan Transfer* (1925) is written in a newsreel technique and is composed of a large number of descriptive and narrative scenes. As the characters develop and begin to interact upon each other, the staccato and syncopated quality of New York emerges.

42nd Parallel (1930) is the first of three novels forming the trilogy, *U.S.A.* In this work Dos Passos introduced three new features into the framework of the narrative: "The Camera Eye," "Biographies," and "Newsreels." "The Camera Eye" passages are impressionistic sketches of Dos Passos' personal experiences. Acting as the small self-portrait in a painting, they are the devices through which the narrative is integrated with the author's stream of consciousness. The "Biographies" are the figures of influential Americans, contemporary to the narrative, canonized by their fame. They are enlarged portraits which provide a framework of truth for the story. The "Newsreels," which were incorporated into the technical plan after the novels had been started, are headlines and news stories which typify American life and struggles. They add the new dimension of time to the framework. The title, *42nd Parallel,* is derived from the theory of climate which holds that storms in America travel from west to east on a path roughly corresponding to this line of latitude. The story deals with the lives and fortunes of young people who are blown toward New York City on this path of storm. *1919* (1932) carries the chronicle of life in America through the years of World War I and continues to record the adventures of the five young people who first appeared in *42nd Parallel. The Big Money* (1936) completes the description of life in America to 1929. The three books were published in one vollume as *U.S.A.* in 1937. With something of the power of a camera with a sound track, this novel pictures almost every aspect of American life. The good and the bad, the hopeful and the despairing, the pleasant and unpleasant aspects of American life flash and crackle like scenes in a technicolor movie.

With *Adventures of a Young Man* (1939) Mr. Dos Passos initiated the Spotswood series and in this novel begins an analysis of American life in the 1920's and 1930's. The story is about Glenn Spotswood and his adventures as he grows up, his worries about sex, his reaction to industrial and social problems, and his decision to join the Communist party, but his story is one of progressive disillusionment, and he dies on the battlefield in the Spanish revolution. In *Number One* (1943) Glenn's older brother, Tyler, is the main character. He is the intellectual force behind a demagogic politician whose life and career resemble Huey Long's. Tyler learns that it is necessary to give oneself for the good of society and, further, that it is indispensable for an individual first to create a self worthy of such a sacrifice. *The Grand Design* (1949) pictures the city of Washington from the inauguration of Franklin D. Roosevelt in 1933 through World War II. The father of Glenn and Tyler, Herb Spotswood, becomes the main character. He is a successful radio commentator who was at one time a pacifist and a worker in the League of Nations. His liberalism, as did his sons', reaches a dead end of frustration and disillusion.

LLOYD CASSEL DOUGLAS

Mina Turner

was born in Columbia City, Indiana, on August 27, 1877, the son of a Lutheran preacher. He attended country schools as a boy and was privately tutored by a father who wished to refresh his own college Greek by teaching it to his son on the long buggy rides through dust and mud and snow while attending to pastoral duties. At Wittenberg College in Springfield, Ohio, of which the elder Douglas was an early alumnus, the son took up residence in 1894 as a preparatory student, continued through the Bachelor of Arts course to a degree in 1900, and received a master's degree in 1903. He also attended the Hamma Theological Seminary, receiving the degree of Bachelor of Divinity in 1903, and thus spent nine years in all on one campus. He was not an outstanding student, took no prizes for scholarship, and made no records in athletics. He played an organ in church to help with his expenses but made no pretense of being a musician; he worked as a newspaper reporter in vacations, but without distinction. He had a private longing to be a writer but while in college showed no particular aptitude for writing.

He was ordained into the Lutheran ministry in 1903 and began preaching as pastor of Zion Lutheran Church at North Manchester, Indiana. A year later he married a former college friend, the daughter of a clergyman. Very soon Mr. Douglas began delivering occasional addresses at high-school commencements and club affairs for which he received small fees to supplement the beggarly wages then paid to ministers in little towns. His next pastorate was in Lancaster, Ohio, at a somewhat better salary. During this period two girl babies arrived, and the business of delivering addresses in neighboring towns for fifteen dollars and railroad fare became increasingly important. Those little journeys broadened the young preacher's experience, gave him access to many influential and stimulating friendships, and made him feel that his ministry was a bit wider than the square acre of his pastorate.

When he was thirty-one, Mr. Douglas was elected minister of the Lutheran Memorial Church at Washington, D.C., where he followed an eminent preacher who had occupied that pulpit for forty years. The old congregation's adjustment from the conservative ministry of the venerable prophet to the more lively and informal preaching of the young man from Ohio was polite but difficult. Three years proved the impossibility of reconciling divergent viewpoints. The young minister recognized his unsuitability for this task and was delighted when in 1911 he was called to the University of Illinois as director of religious work.

In 1915 Mr. Douglas became the minister of the First Congregational Church of Ann Arbor, Michigan. This was distinctly a "college church." Mr. Douglas says he had "more fun" in Ann Arbor than anywhere else, primarily because he liked to preach to students. Shortly after taking up his residence there, he announced that the doors of the church would be closed at 10:45 on Sunday mornings and that anybody who wanted to get in had better arrange his program with that regulation in mind. The students thought this was funny and came to church to see whether it was true. It was true; and it remained true for six years. One Sunday Mr. Douglas said he didn't want any more pennies in the collection baskets. The next Sunday there was such a weight of copper offered to the church that the deacons fairly staggered down the aisle with it. The students were hilarious. He omitted the usual prayer of thanksgiving.

There followed five years at First Church, Akron, Ohio, from 1921 to 1926 in the maddest period of the rubber industry, and then, from 1926 to 1929, a brief but sufficiently long ministry in Los Angeles. In 1929 Mr. Douglas accepted an invitation to become the minister of St. James United Church in Montreal. He has always entertained a great fondness for Canadians. His two daughters are married to Canadians; one to a surgeon, the other to a mining engineer. Mrs. Douglas died of a lingering illness in 1944. Her husband often said of her that it was doubtful whether he would ever have written any stories but for her earnest belief in his ability and her constant encouragement. At present, seventy-three and badly crippled with arthritis, Mr. Douglas lives quietly in the home of his elder daughter and her husband, the John Weldon Wilsons in Las Vegas, Nevada. When the weather becomes too hot in summer, he retreats to a hotel apartment in Los Angeles. With publication of *The Big Fisherman* in 1948 he announced that he would write no more novels.

Mr. Douglas' first venture in fiction made publishing history. In 1928, after having written two books of religious essays, he commenced another in an effort to show the practical results of secret philanthropy. It seemed too good an idea to be buried in a volume of essays, and he attempted to project it in novel form. This book, rejected by several publishing houses, was brought out timidly by a small denominational press and had the benefits of almost no promotion. It had been in circulation for two years before it reached the best-seller list. This book, *The Magnificent Obsession* (1929), has sold more than a million copies in this country. The story concerns a young man, Bobby Merrick, who puts Christian principles into practice, becomes a famous brain surgeon, and makes a surgical invention that saves the life of his sweetheart.

Forgive Us Our Trespasses (1932) tells of a young journalist, Dinny Brumm, whose life is filled with hatred and cynicism as a consequence of the bad treatment suffered by his mother at the hands of his materially successful father. Dinny loses his sweetheart because their ideals differ. Then he awakens and gains a new attitude. Like many of the Douglas novels, this is a story of redemption. *Precious Jeopardy* (1933) is a Christmas story which tells how a businessman caught in the depression and in jeopardy of his life learns to live more happily. *Green Light* (1935) tells how Dr. Harcourt, dean of a midwestern cathedral, gives comfort and assistance to all kinds of people who need help. A young surgeon is the main character, and he sacrifices his professional standing to save his superior. *White Banners* (1936) is the story of the imprint of Hannah Parmalee on the Ward household in which she works as a servant. She applies the rule of sincerity and achieves magical results in influencing the lives of many people. *Home For Christmas* (1937) tells of the return of the five adult Claytons to the little farmhouse where they had spent their childhood for an old-fashioned and very successful holiday.

Disputed Passage (1939) pictures in the background of medical school and hospital a bitter antagonism between an eminent neurologist and one of his students; they find that their obligation to science and their respect for each other are more important than a clash of temperament. In *Dr. Hudson's Secret Journal* (1939) there is an expansion of the ideas lying behind *The Magnificent Obsession,* but the book is not a sequel to the earlier novel. *Invitation to Live* (1940) has Dean Harcourt of *Green Light* send a giddy heiress on a strange and adventurous mission which influences affirmatively her life and the lives of her friends.

The Robe (1942), the author's first attempt at an historical novel, is the story of the Roman soldier who, while in charge of the crucifixion, gambles for Christ's mantle and wins it. Impressed by the dying man's courage and faith, Marcellus journeys into Galilee, *incognito,* to learn about the Divine Carpenter from those who had known Him intimately; the Roman is converted, espouses Christ's cause, and suffers martyrdom. This novel has sold more than two million copies in America and has been published in seventeen foreign languages. *The Big Fisherman* (1948) is an impressionistic biography of Simon Peter, and concerns itself primarily with his relation to his Master. This book had the largest advance sale of any novel ever published. Mr. Douglas said, "This will be a good one to quit on."

CLIFFORD DOWDEY

Henry Klatt

was born in Richmond, Virginia, on January 23, 1904, the descendant of families which had lived in Virginia since the early seventeenth century. He attended John Marshall High School in Richmond and studied from 1923 to 1925 at Columbia University. By 1923 he knew that he intended to be a professional writer. For a year he was a reporter and book reviewer on the Richmond *News-Leader,* and then he returned to New York to work on the editorial staff of various magazines, including *Munsey's* and *The Argosy*. In the late fall of 1935 he resigned his editorial position to devote his time to writing. Believing that the best way to obtain knowledge of one's country is to live in its various sections, he migrated to sample life in Florida, the mountains of North Carolina, the country of Connecticut, a city in Texas, a ranch in Arizona (not a dude ranch but one where he worked cattle), and in the Bay region of California. In 1938 he was awarded a Guggenheim fellowship. During World War II he engaged in confidential work for various government agencies, including the War Department. *Experiment in Rebellion* (1946) is a non-fiction, informal, personalized history of the Confederacy told from the viewpoint of the leaders in Richmond.

"I have tried to write," he has said, "not about the cloak-and-sword aspect of Virginia, but about the yeomanry, the ideal Jefferson class, the people who are carrying on in their own way the basic American tradition. It is this class which had the hardest struggle in making its readjustments after the Civil War." In his latest work Mr. Dowdey has dealt with sociological and psychological problems.

Bugles Blow No More (1937), his first novel, is a romantic tale of love leaping barriers in a picture of Richmond from the night of secession in 1861 to the end of the Civil War in 1865. *Gamble's Hundred* (1939) gives much economic and social history of tidewater Virginia and pictures young Chris Ballard coming to grips with the problem of ordinary men's rights endangered by aristocrats. *Sing for a Penny* (1941) portrays the freebooting industrial era from 1865 to 1900 in the story of Kirby Herron, a Virginian, whose shabby origins lead him to fight to control railroads and paper mills.

Tidewater (1943) takes a young Virginia aristocrat to the Tennessee wilderness just as the panic of 1837 occurs. *Where My Love Sleeps* (1945) is about Blount Mathis, who sees clearly the best future interests of the South while fighting in 1864 around Petersburg and Richmond. *Weep for My Brother* (1950) describes the troubles of Chris Mather who looks after his mentally ill brother Lacy, a young man whose "difference" leads to crime and a period of residence in a sanitarium. The emphasis is on the problem of maladjustment.

ANNE MILLER DOWNES

John Gass

was born in Utica, New York. Her family, mostly musicians and artists, were also interested in education. She graduated from Utica Academy and the New Paltz State Normal College. After studying at the Columbia University School of Journalism, she taught in the Knox and Laura Jacobi schools. Studying music from babyhood, she played at a public appearance when eight years old, later did concert work as a pianist, and taught music. Her writing career began with poetry. Her first short story was published by H. L. Mencken in *The Smart Set* in April, 1923. A professional writer in the newspaper and magazine fields for many years, Mrs. Downes reports on the positive side that her main interest in life is close observation of the struggles, escapes, tragedies, and hopes of her fellow men. In October, 1927, *The Atlantic Monthly* featured her article on "The High Cost of Illness," first bringing this subject into public debate. As a direct result, Congress authorized a five-year commission to study the question; hospital insurance was the eventual result of these studies. In 1917 she married Frank Harley Downes of New York City. They built a home in Scarsdale, New York, where they still live "unfashionably happily."

In her novels Mrs. Downes endeavors to picture the real American, a much misinterpreted individual. She feels that a false picture of America, a picture of synthetic movie stars, millionaire playboys, cowboys, Indians, Dead-End kids, sharecroppers, gunmen, and murderers—although we have them all—has been presented to the world, giving foreign dictators and demagogues the opportunity to stress our supposed decadence and impotence. She believes the real American of religious faith, industry, and inventive genius should receive more sympathetic treatment; that the homelover, the hard worker, who exists by the million from high executive down through all classes to the scrubwoman, should be better understood; that the multitude of workers who have fed half the world, fought and won six wars and built a free country with a type of civilization never before seen in the world should receive their due; and that the real American, humorous, homely, and likeable despite his faults and shortcomings, should be portrayed in strong novels. She believes realism lies somewhere between glamorous heroism and mud-wallowing brutality. She is striving to attain that realism.

Her first novel, *So Stands the Rock* (1939), is the story of Jessie Perkins, a beautiful, practical woman as firm as the granite foundation of her native Vermont. *Until the Shearing* (1940) tells how a sensitive, precocious boy, the son of a famous actress, grows up in northern New York under the guidance of the rich wisdom of his father's family and the companionship of a fascinating family of musical geniuses. *Angels Fell* (1941), with a unique setting in an old Greenwich Village bookshop, is the story of the tragedy of an American girl's overweening ambition for social and financial success. Irene Blyth tries to add wealth to the aristocratic position of her husband.

Heartwood (1945), a Vermont story, involves a mountain boy who typifies the wonderful quality of "expectancy" in American youth. His entire life is shaped by his knowledge of and love for woods and forests. His loyalty to the elfin mountain girl, Lin, and his love for the minister's daughter create a struggle that tests his character in a very unusual way. *Mary Donovan* (1948) tells of a Massachusetts woman's attitude toward divorce; it became a very controversial book. An emotionally immature husband whom she loves pulls her one way, and three fine children and her home exert a pull in the other direction; her solution of the problem provides the story.

The Eagle's Song (1949) has a Mohawk Valley setting. In the long life of Laommi Ayres from a charming boy to an old crippled soldier is depicted the beginning of a settlement at the time of the French and Indian Wars, the expansion of the community to a large city, and the growth of the country to the end of World War I. One sees the onset of decay despoiling the beautiful Green, the cheap labor, the commencement of Americanization, and their development into the problems America faces today.

ROBERT LUTHER DUFFUS

The New York Times Studio

was born in Waterbury, Vermont, on July 10, 1888. After a boyhood in New England, he worked his way through Stanford University in California where he received a bachelor's degree in 1910 and a master's in 1911. Thereafter he was a reporter for two years and then until 1918 an editorial writer on the San Francisco *Bulletin*. After another year of editorial writing on the San Francisco *Call,* he moved in 1919 to the New York *Globe,* with which newspaper he remained until its discontinuance in 1923. Then he became a free-lance writer and roving reporter. In 1937 he joined the editorial staff of the New York *Times,* where he had previously been a member of the Sunday staff. He lives in Westport, Connecticut.

His non-fiction books include *The American Renaissance* (1928), *Mastering the Metropolis* (1930), *Books—Their Place in a Democracy* (1930), *Santa Fé Trail* (1930), *Our Starving Libraries* (1933), *The Arts in American Life* (with F. Keppel, 1933), *Democracy Enters College* (1936), *Lillian Wald* (1938), *L. Emmett Holt* (with L. E. Holt, Jr., 1940), *The Valley and Its People: A Portrait of TVA* (1944), and *The Innocents at Cedro: A Memoir of Thorstein Veblen and Some Others* (1944).

Mr. Duffus' novels show a strong Vermont influence. The earlier ones are romantic and optimistic. "They have been written," he has said, "as diversions in the midst of a busy journalistic life, and are a kind of escape from the sometimes bleak realities of today's events."

Roads Going South (1921), his first novel, is an account of the growth into self-knowledge of Joe Chapin, a New England boy, who feels the need to harmonize in himself the conflicting inheritances from father and mother. In New York he gains perspective. This book has some autobiographical overtones. *The Coast of Eden* (1923) brings to New York a young California lawyer, Kenneth Ballantine, who marries the wrong girl and realizes that he loves his boyhood sweetheart. *Tomorrow Never Comes* (1929) is a humorous tale of the love of Rafael for Vitoria in a Central American country and satirizes the ease with which war is made, the manners of foreigners, and the exploitation of oil lands.

Jornada (1935) is a romance set against the background of the War with Mexico in 1846, when a wagon train carries arms to rebels against the Mexican governor at Santa Fé. *The Sky But Not the Heart* (1936) presents many of the political problems of the early 1930's in a tale of the exile of political dreamers to an island. *Night between the Rivers* (1937) suggests the quality of true liberalism and analyzes the Marxist basis of a general strike in New York during eighteen hours, as seen by a woman decorator and a discharged radical teacher.

Victory on West Hill (1942) is about a man ninety-one years old who wants to stay alive to teach his grandson the faith animating Washington. *Non-Scheduled Flight* (1950) is the story of the passengers and crew of an airplane bound from New Orleans to Guatemala, in which the life stories of the characters are interwoven; in essence it is a study of the clash between human fate and human desire.

DAVID DUNCAN

Monterey Studio

was born in Billings, Montana, on February 17, 1913. After graduating from Montana State University where he majored in psychology, his interest in working with people led him into the field of labor economics, and for ten years or so he acted as counsel for various labor unions, as manager for a housing project, and as a social worker. Although his travel has been limited to the North American continent, he has lived in Idaho, Nebraska, Nevada, California, New York, and Washington, D.C., as well as Montana. Much of the material for *The Bramble Bush* was drawn from a stay of six months in Mexico.

Remember the Shadow (1944), his first novel, deals with the complex psychological situation in the family of Howard Jones, an anthropologist, whose second wife is recovering from a mental illness in a lonely cottage on a mountain top. The attending physician dies in the fall of a bridge as he comes to examine her progress. *The Shade of Time* (1946) is a mystery novel concerning a group of scientists and near-scientists living on California's Monterey Peninsula who endeavor, through the interpretation of "the theory of atomic displacement," to discover the murderer of one of the group's members whose theory it was. *The Bramble Bush* (1948) is a story of Mike Finney, a modern "man without a country," who returns to the United States from Mexico and finds himself pursued as a murderer because he has taken the name of Philip Tremaine. The events portray how a decent, straightforward individual struggles against deceit, greed, and hostility.

The Madrone Tree (1949), a choice of the Book League of America, reveals the powerful undercurrents affecting the lives of the people in a small town, the intertwining of individual motives creating a widening mesh of dramatic incident. Mysterious happenings occur near the madrone tree, strange fears hover, and sinister and horrifying results follow. Not until the very end, when the madrone tree is stripped of its eerie significance, are the characters and plot proved all too human. *The Serpent's Egg* (1950) is set in wartime San Francisco but concerns only civilian affairs. The point of departure is a dispute between labor and management in the transportation industry, and the novel shows that the course of such disputes is determined by individual motivations, by the hopes, fears, and ambitions of the people involved rather than by any ideologies.

THOMAS WILLIAM DUNCAN

was born on August 15, 1905, in Casey, Iowa. He started his college work at Drake University in Des Moines, Iowa, but received his bachelor's degree *cum laude* in 1929 at Harvard, where he won the Lloyd McKim Garrison prize in poetry. After college he worked for a year as a reporter on the Des Moines *Tribune,* and then took his master's degree at Drake University in 1931. From 1934 to 1938 he taught English at the Des Moines College of Pharmacy. During this period he also served as a book reviewer on the Des Moines *Register*. From 1942 to 1944 he taught journalism at Grinnell College in Iowa, acting also as director of public relations for the college. Mr. and Mrs. Duncan make their home on the desert at Apple Valley, California, where they own a small ranch. They also own a house trailer and spend about half their time in travel. Mr. Duncan's books of poetry include *Hours from a Life* (1927), *From a Harvard Notebook* (1929), his Garrison prize poem, and *Elephants at War* (1935).

Mr. Duncan's first interest in his novels has

always been in people; his novels are especially notable for their excellent character delineation.

O, Chautauqua (1935), his first published novel (he had written and discarded two earlier stories), deals with four days in the life of a Chautauqua troupe, and presents a valuable picture of a vanished American institution. For this novel Mr. Duncan drew upon his own experiences: for two summers when he was eighteen and nineteen he traveled as an actor with a similar group. *We Pluck This Flower* (1937), a novel set in Iowa, recounts the search of Ella Corkhill for security and happiness. It covers the ten years from her college days to the time of her second marriage. *Ring Horse* (1940) is the story of Danny Gilpin, an old circus clown, and his best friend, Silver Fire, a performing ring horse. *Gus the Great* (1947) a selection of the Book-of-the-Month Club, is a long, robust novel about the rise and fall of A. H. Burgoyne, big-time promoter and showman extraordinary.

EASTMAN *to* EUNSON

ELIZABETH EASTMAN

was born on November 16, 1905, in South Carver, Massachusetts, and attended schools in Boston. She later taught in rural Vermont and subsequently worked in bookshops in New York and Philadelphia. Her first stories were published in a Boston newspaper while she was in high school. Since then she has published stories in several of the leading magazines. One of her short stories, "Like a Field Mouse over the Heart," has been printed in three anthologies.

Miss Eastman's first novel, *Sun on Their Shoulders* (1934), explores a new group of foreign-born Americans; it is the story of a Finnish family in the cranberry bogs of Cape Cod. *The Mouse with Red Eyes* (1948), set against a background of New York City and the Vermont countryside, is essentially a psychological novel which deals with heroine Alexandra Hubbell's subconscious terror of her fiancé and her discovery of his true identity.

EVELYN (SYBIL MARY) EATON

Erich Hartmann

was born in Montreux, Switzerland, on December 22, 1902, of Canadian parents. She was educated at Heathfield, a fashionable school in Ascot, England. She graduated in 1920, was presented at court, and made her début. She then took secretarial training and worked as a translator with the Lithuanian Legation in London. After holding several other positions, Miss Eaton left London to take up residence in Paris, where she worked in the Paramount studios at Joinville. Miss Eaton was married in 1928 and divorced in 1934. She has one daughter, Teresa Neyana Eaton. She came to the United States in 1937 and became a citizen. In 1945 she served as a war correspondent. She resides in Wingdale, New York.

Miss Eaton's books include two volumes of poetry, *Stolen Hours* (1925) and *Birds Before Dawn* (1943); a novel for boys, *John—Film Star* (1937); a book of autobiographical sketches, *Every Month Was May* (1947); and a biography of Mother Elizabeth Seton, the founder of the Order of the Sisters of Charity in the United States, *Heart In Pilgrimage* (with E. R. Moore, 1948). *The North Star is Nearer* (1949) contains further autobiography.

Her first novel, *Desire—Spanish Version* (1933), set against a Paris moving-picture studio, is the love story of Bibsou, a violinist, and Halina Domska, a Polish woman. *Pray to the Earth* (1938) portrays a French boy's harrowing experiences after he is alone in the world, following the Spanish civil war, and his desire to achieve a freedom like that found in "the large and sacred rhythm of the earth." *Quietly My Captain Waits* (1940) tells about the last eleven years of French rule in

Acadia before Madame de Freneuse is exiled. *Restless Are the Sails* (1941) is a romance of the siege of Louisburg in Nova Scotia in May to July, 1758. The hero marries an Indian girl and then falls in love with the governor's daughter. *The Sea Is So Wide* (1943) reveals the pitiless way the Acadians were transported from their Canadian home and sent into remote areas of the British empire. *In What Torn Ship* (1944) is the story of the Corsican patriot, Pascal Paoli, who commanded the forces which expelled the Genoese in 1755. *By Just Exchange* (1950) carries the bankrupt Michael Daigle from London to America in the 1770's. A Quaker girl must decide between him and her sect.

WALTER D(UMAUX) EDMONDS

was born on July 15, 1903, in Boonville, New York, where he grew up with the Erie Canal at his front door. He began his education at the Cutler School in New York City, and continued his preparatory education at St. Paul's School in Concord, New Hampshire, and at the Choate School in Wallingford, Connecticut. In 1926 he graduated from Harvard. While at college he was elected to Signet, the undergraduate literary society, and was a contributor of poems and articles to *The Harvard Advocate,* of which he became editor. While taking a course under Professor Charles Townsend Copeland, Mr. Edmonds wrote as a required theme his first story about the Erie Canal country, "The End of the Towpath," which was published in *Scribner's Magazine.* From that moment Mr. Edmonds decided to earn his living by writing.

Mr. Edmonds has chosen for his special province the region of upper New York state and its key periods in history. "I like independent people and their virtues," says Mr. Edmonds, "and I try to follow them, as I believe they have contributed to the growth of this country—both for good and (occasionally) for ill."

Rome Haul (1929), his first novel, is a story of canal-boat life on the Erie Canal in its heyday; a young farm boy goes to work as a driver and later becomes the owner of his own boat. Marc Connelly made a play of it, "The Farmer Takes a Wife." *The Big Barn* (1930) also deals with the Erie Canal country in the 1860's; Ralph Wilder, a farmer, wins leadership in Boonville through intense determination; he wants his sons, Bascom and Henry, to carry on the family tradition on the soil. *Erie Water* (1933) tells the story of the building of the Erie Canal from 1817 to 1825. Jerry Fowler, a young carpenter, falls in love with Mary, a girl from Albany, and their romance threads through this historically accurate tale.

Mostly Canallers (1934) is a collection of twenty-three short stories which recreate life on the Erie Canal. *Drums Along the Mohawk* (1936) vividly recreates scenes in the Revolutionary War in 1776–77 as it was fought in the Mohawk Valley of New York. The story of Gil Martin and his wife, Magdelana, illustrates the struggle of young pioneers to establish themselves in the midst of Indian cruelty and Tories. *Chad Hanna* (1940) relates the adventures of a runaway stable boy who joins a traveling circus and also portrays the struggle of small enterprise to compete with big business. The setting is the Mohawk Valley in the 1830's. Of *The Matchlock Gun* (1941) May Lamberton Becker said: "As literature, this story for ten-year-olds ranks with anything Mr. Edmonds has written for adults." This story was awarded the Newbery medal in 1942. *Young Ames* (1942) is the episodic story of a poor but ambitious young man of the 1830's who makes his fortune in business in New York City and marries his employer's niece.

Tom Whipple (1942), the story of a Yankee lad who decided to see something of the world and did so, illustrates the resourcefulness and the single-minded courage which are the heritage of the free-born. Another story for young boys is told in *Two Logs Crossing* (1943). *Wilderness Clearing* (1944) is a novel of young love set in the Mohawk Valley in 1777 pioneer days; young Dick Mount proves that danger has matured him and that he and sixteen-year-old Maggie Gordon can face the perils of life together safely on a farm. *In the Hands of the Senecas* (1947), set in the Finger Lakes district of New York in 1778, describes a Seneca Indian raid and the resourcefulness of two thirteen-year-old children, Ellen Mitchell and Peter Kelly, and of two adults, Caty Breen and Delia Borst, who patiently rebuild their broken lives. *The Wedding Journey* (1947) describes a honeymoon trip to Buffalo and Niagara on an Erie Canal packet boat in 1835.

PAUL ELDRIDGE

was born on May 5, 1888, in Philadelphia, Pennsylvania. He was educated both here and in Europe, chiefly in France. After taking his bachelor's degree at Temple University in Philadelphia, he attended the University of Pennsylvania, from which he received his master's degree in 1911. For the next two years he attended the University of Paris and in 1913 became lecturer on American literature at the Sorbonne. In 1914 he returned to the United States and accepted a position as teacher of romance languages in the New York City high schools.

Mr. Eldridge's books include four volumes of poetry, *Vanitas* (1920), *Our Dead Selves* (1921), *Cobwebs and Cosmos* (1930), and *I Bring a Sword* (1945). His collections of short stories are *And the Sphinx Spoke* (1921), *Irony and Pity* (1926), *One Man Show* (1933), *Virgins and Other Stories* (1945), *The Truth about Phyllis Warren* (1945), and *Men and Women* (1945). Books of maxims are *Horns of Glass* (1943), *Devil's Tree* (1946), and *Blue Flames* (1948). "The Intruder" (1928) and "The Bed Remains" (1948) are plays.

The effect of Mr. Eldridge's European education has been to give his work a continental air. The keystone to his philosophy of life and letters—irony for man's folly and cruelty and pity for man himself—has remained intact through the storm and stress of the years, a philosophy, he thinks, somewhat out of keeping with a generation infatuated with horror and imbued with sentimentalism.

My First Two Thousand Years (1928), the first novel in a trilogy, is the story of Isaac Laquedem, who is "cursed" with perennial life and youth. *Salome, The Wandering Jewess* (1930) follows the sex adventures of Salome over two thousand years of her varied life. *Invincible Adam* (1932), a pseudo-philosophical novel, retails the erotic and humanizing adventures of Adam through thousands of years from ancient Africa to modern New York.

If after Every Tempest (1941) recounts the experiences of a French couple, a playwright and the wife of an actor-manager, who flee to Paris. She returns to her husband and comic adventures follow. *Madonna with a Cat* (1942) pictures the strange consequences when Puss-in-Boots becomes a man in ancient Spain. *Two Lessons in Love* (1946) contains two short novels: "Master of Hearts," about a man who, once deaf, regains his sense of hearing and by hiding this fact learns remarkable things; and "Mr. Lowell and the Goddess," a tale of an artist's love for a beautiful woman whom he worships as a goddess and thereby kills as a woman.

And Thou Shalt Teach Them (1947) is a novel in diary form about a New York City high school, and reflects the current crisis in public education, the demoralization of the faculty and student body, and their idealism. *Misadventure in Chastity* (1948), a novel dealing with prohibition days, is the gay adventure of a Don Juan who loves only married women and who finally meets his doom.

EDWARD ELLSBERG

Blackstone Studios

was born in New Haven, Connecticut, on November 21, 1891; shortly thereafter his family moved to Denver, Colorado. He attended the University of Colorado for one year, 1909–10, and then was appointed to the Naval Academy, where he graduated with honors in 1914. While at the Academy he twice won the Navy League medal for essays on naval topics. Upon graduation he was attached to the *Texas* and served on her at Vera Cruz, Mexico, in 1914 during the American occupation. In 1916 he returned to Annapolis for post-graduate work and then was sent to Massachusetts Institute of Technology for further study in naval architecture. During World War I Mr. Ellsberg was stationed at the Brooklyn Navy Yard, where he refitted German passenger ships for transport duty. He was later assigned to supervise the building of the battleship *Tennessee.* At the end of the war he returned to the Massachusetts Institute which awarded him the degree of Master of Science in 1920. In 1926 he was detailed as salvage officer of the submarine *S-51.* As a result of that operation he was awarded the Distinguished Service Medal by the navy and was recommended for promotion to the rank of commander.

He resigned from the service on completion of the *S-51* salvage work, and became chief engineer of the Tide Water Associated Oil Company in New York. On the sinking of the *S-4* off Provincetown in December, 1927, he volunteered for service during rescue work. The court of inquiry which investigated the *S-4* disaster characterized Commander Ellsberg as "the foremost expert in the United States and probably in the world on deep-sea rescue work." On December 8, 1941, the day after Pearl Harbor, Commander Ellsberg rushed to Washington to volunteer for active service in the navy; he was sent "Somewhere East of Suez" to conduct salvage operations. In recognition of his work he was raised to the rank of captain.

His first book, *On the Bottom* (1929), is the story of the salvage of a submarine that was rammed and sunk off Block Island. *Thirty Fathoms Deep* (1930) is an adventure story in which the technique and perils of deep-sea diving are entwined with pirates and Spanish gold. *Pigboats* (1931) dramatizes the exciting role which the submarine plays in modern warfare. *S-54* (1932) is a collection of five stories about modern seafaring and the loyalties and sacrifices of sailors.

Ocean Gold (1935) is the fast-moving story of the salvage of sunken treasure off the coast of Peru. *Spanish Ingots* (1936), its sequel, relates the adventures experienced by the salvage crew on the trip home from Peruvian waters. *Hell on Ice* (1938) is a graphic retelling of the navy-sponsored expedition of the *Jeannette,* which set out in 1879 to find the North Pole via the ice-packed, arctic waters north of Bering Strait. This dramatic and tragic story is told in the words of Chief Engineer George Melville, one of the few survivors of the expedition. *Men Under the Sea* (1939) narrates the salvaging of the *S-51,* the work on the *S-4,* and the rescue of thirty-three men from the *Squalus. Treasure Below* (1940) contains further treasure-salvaging adventures.

Captain Paul (1941) is an historical novel telling the story of John Paul Jones, America's first naval hero. *I Have Just Begun to Fight* (1942) is an adaptation for younger readers of *Captain Paul.* Captain Ellsberg's experiences as commander of salvage operations in Eritrea during the early days of World War II are told in *Under the Red Sea Sun* (1946). *No Banners, No Bugles* (1949) recounts the adventures of the salvage forces, afloat and ashore, in the Mediterranean during the North African invasion in 1942 and 1943, when Captain Ellsberg was principal salvage officer for General Eisenhower and the army in that theater of operations.

GUY ENDORE

was born Sam Guy Endore in Brooklyn, New York, on July 4, 1900. His father was born in Austria and his mother in Russia. His upbringing varied according to the fluctuations of the family finances, from an orphan asylum in Ohio to a private secondary school in Vienna. He graduated from Columbia College in 1923, took a master's degree in romance languages in 1924, and worked for a while for a doctorate, receiving a fellowship to France in 1926. He discontinued his studies when he married Henrietta Portugal; they have two daughters. Having chosen to engage in a literary career, Mr. Endore translated books from French and German and did other odd jobs to earn a living. "In spite of travel, education, and a 'literary career'," he has said, "my life up to nearly the age of forty is best expressed by two words: poverty and insecurity." Hollywood found Mr. Endore, and in 1949 he was with Warner Brothers finishing a screenplay. His non-fiction books include *Casanova* (1929), a comprehensive biography, and *The Sword of God: Jeanne d'Arc* (1931).

"My urge to write," Mr. Endore has said, "is fundamentally an attempt to clarify for myself the person I am and the world I live in. I am not sure that I have gotten much further than the discovery that I am the product of a world-wide conspiracy of each against everyone. I dare say that my work does not express me, as yet. I am at work on a *magnum opus,* a book about myself. I think I begin to understand at least certain phases of myself, and thereby can understand, appreciate, and sympathize with others."

The Man from Limbo (1930), his first novel, describes Harry Kling's poverty-stricken origins in New York's East Side and his dreams of wealth which lead to harrowing experiences. *The Werewolf* (1933), set in the time of the siege of Paris and the Commune, is about a man who is born with hair on his hands, the sign of the werewolf and of his predestination to evil. He murders lambs and then human beings. *Babouk* (1934) portrays the evils of capitalism in a story of the slave trade in Haiti when Toussaint L'Ouverture led the rebellion. *Methinks the Lady* (1945) is a terror story about a psychoanalyst's wife who thinks she has a dual personality and her arrest for murder.

STUART DAVID ENGSTRAND

was born on March 13, 1905, in Chicago, Illinois. He received his education at State Teachers College at De Kalb, Illinois, which he attended from 1925 to 1928. On May 18, 1935, he married Sophia Belzer, by whom he has two children. The Engstrands make their home in Van Nuys, California.

Mr. Engstrand's first novel, *The Invaders* (1937), tells how a man devotes himself to his debt-burdened farm in the Southwest and the effect of his marriage to a city girl who shows instability when she falls in love with an expelled teacher. *They Sought for Paradise* (1939) relates the story of the Bishop Hill Colony, a utopian community of Swedish Lutherans founded in Illinois in the 1840's. *Spring* (1941) is a story of the betrayal of Norway by a young Quisling who returns home a Nazi after ten years in Germany and joins the attack on his town. His mother kills him and heroically takes the family to the hills for safety. *The Sling and the Arrow* (1947) studies the plight of the homosexual, Herbert Dawes, a dress designer, who goes to pieces when his wife threatens to have a child by another man. *Beyond the Forest* (1948) portrays the effect on a husband of a dissatisfied wife who tries to escape from a Wisconsin settlement located in the backwoods. *Son of the Giant* (1950) is about a father and son who develop hatred for each other. The father is virile. The son is weak; he is haunted by the memory of his dead mother.

LOULA GRACE ERDMAN

was born in Missouri near Alma, "a town about the size of a postage stamp," on a farm on which her father, grandfather, and great-grandfather had lived. After attending country school, she went to Higginsville, Missouri, High School. She received her bachelor's degree in 1931 at Central Missouri State Teachers College at Warrensburg and her master's degree in 1941 at Teachers College, Columbia University. She started teaching in the country school of her childhood, and then moved to Texas to teach in a junior high school. In 1945 she began teaching creative writing at West Texas State College at Canyon, Texas.

The special problems of teachers and of children in country schools form the major theme of Miss Erdman's short stories, novels, and articles. Her first book was a juvenile, *Separate Star* (1944), which tells the story of Gail Warren, who goes to a small town, Clayton, to teach in her first school. With courage and common sense she meets a great many problems, some of them traditional for a young teacher, some of them not so usual. *Fair Is the Morning* (1945) concerns a friend of Gail Warren, Connie Thurman, who goes into a country school and successfully solves many problems.

The Years of the Locust (1947), Miss Erdman's first novel for adults, compresses the history of a middle-western community, the flavor of the period, and a forward and backward view embracing three generations within the brief three-day interval between a death and a funeral. This book won the ninth Dodd, Mead–Redbook novel award. *Lonely Passage* (1948), with its scene in Missouri, is primarily concerned with the drama of human loneliness as it especially concerns one young girl, Thurley Renfro. *The Edge of Time* (1950) portrays the homesteaders in 1885 settling the Texas Panhandle.

DOROTHY ERSKINE

was born in Steubenville, Ohio, on September 11, 1906, the daughter of Inez Matlack and De Witt Erskine. Her formal education ended with her marriage when she was nineteen and a junior at Ohio State University. This marriage concluded in divorce thirteen years later. Reading, writing, and, of necessity, breadwinning are her only real interests. Writing and medicine remain the two pursuits which, from her viewpoint, merit serious consideration: a good hospital or a fine bridge of words, the only rational construction. Her interest in people is clinical but consuming. The food they eat, the clothes they wear, their loves, their thoughts, and the motives behind their actions—these are important. Miss Erskine has been described as "a serious comedienne—mannered and masterful, witty and wise—who observes her fellow man with an X-ray eye."

The Crystal Boat (1946), her first book, is an historical novel about the sure faith, the dirt, the poetry, and the pageantry of thirteenth-century Scotland. The harsh plot of a lovely girl who becomes the king's mistress, much to her sorrow, is borrowed from the old ballad, "The Queen's Marie." *Miss Pettinger's Niece* (1949) is a picture of the small Pennsylvania town of Lafayetteville, where the whole of small-town America comes into focus. Miss Erskine does not think that any of her characterizations are overdrawn, because she does not think that it is possible to exaggerate human stupidity and folly. Through the character of Miss Therese Mellinet, a woman who speaks her mind, Miss Erskine reflects some of her own convictions and opinions, which seem to be that American small towns may be consistently dull and occasionally unpleasant, but that the people enjoy their life and laugh a lot at each other's foibles.

JOHN ERSKINE

James Abresch

was born October 5, 1879, in New York City. He graduated from Columbia College in 1900, received his master's degree there in 1901 and his doctorate in 1903. From 1903 to 1909 he taught English at Amherst College in Massachusetts, and then returned to Columbia College, where from 1916 to 1937 he was professor of English. He took occasional leaves of absence to lecture and to write, and in 1919 to serve as educational director of the American University at Beaune, France. Since 1937 he has been professor emeritus at Columbia.

Throughout his life, music has been Dr. Erskine's second career, in the course of which he has toured as piano soloist with the New York Symphony Orchestra under Walter Damrosch, played with the symphony orchestras of Detroit, Minneapolis, and Chicago, and served from 1928 to 1938 as president of the Juilliard School of Music, of which he has been a trustee since 1927.

During his career as a writer Dr. Erskine has published more than fifty books. His early writing was devoted to educational and scholarly work. He produced a number of anthologies and collaborated in editing the four-volume *Cambridge History of American Literature* (1917–21). Since then he has written several volumes of poetry, collections of essays, opera librettos, short stories, informative books on music, biographies, and his autobiography.

The Memory of Certain Persons (1947), the first of four volumes of autobiography, pictures with nostalgic flavor his childhood and youth in the 1880's and 1890's. *My Life as a Teacher* (1948), the second, describes his experiences and educational adventures at Amherst College, at Columbia University, and at the American University at Beaune. *My Life in Music* (1950) portrays the personalities he has known and his work at the Juilliard School of Music. *My Life as a Writer* will complete the series.

Dr. Erskine has applied to fiction some of the techniques of poetry. Especially has he focused upon single moments in history to present contemporaneous problems "under forms which have been somewhat timeless in the race memory." His books are notable for their re-creation in modern terms of myths and fables and for allusions to great literature. His brilliant conversational technique is never dulled by pedantry.

His first novel, *The Private Life of Helen of Troy* (1925), tells what happens to Helen after her return to Sparta following the fall of Troy. It is a novel of ideas scintillating with wit and skepticism. *Galahad* (1926) pictures the famous knight as something of a prig in his relations with the strong-minded Guenevere. *Adam and Eve* (1927) portrays Eve, who wants a home, struggling against Lilith, the bachelor-type girl. Eve reforms Adam, puts him into clothes, and leads him to say ironically, "It's a man's world." *Penelope's Man* (1928) retells the story of Odysseus to show that he has been unfaithful for the same reason as other men with a philandering tendency. *Sincerity* (1929) raises the question of frankness between married couples in a tale of Isabel Beaunel, who writes an essay on "Sincerity" but fails to be sincere and straightforward with her husband.

Uncle Sam in the Eyes of His Family (1930) is an allegorical satire on the foreign relations of the United States, educational policies, marriage customs, and other matters. *Cinderella's Daughter* (1930) is a group of tales reworking several myths. *Unfinished Business* (1931) takes Richard Ormer, a wealthy manufacturer, to the gates of Heaven, where he learns that he never completed his good or evil intentions, and, having recovered his health, he sets out to correct his defect of incompleted action. *Tristan and Isolde* (1932) is a thoughtful commentary upon chivalric and Christian ideals as seen by Palamede, the Arab who was Isolde's unsuccessful lover.

Bachelor of Arts (1934) describes the younger generation as a cynical yet courageous lot. *Forget If You Can* (1935) deals with the theme that a man cannot forget any past indiscretion of his wife. *Solomon, My Son* (1935) is a character study of the young son of David, and his efforts to grow into the wisdom of his father and to complete the temple. *The Brief Hour of François Villon* (1937) concerns that climactic moment when the Frenchman was a famous poet and a hunted criminal. *The Start of the Road* (1938) portrays Walt Whitman in New Orleans in 1848 and his love for a Paris-educated quadroon girl who becomes the mother of his son. His love for the South and his unwillingness to fight in the Civil War are thus explained. *Give Me Liberty* (1940), a tale of the early days of the Revolutionary War in Virginia, tells the life history of David Darrill from the age of ten in 1759 until the clash of arms. He is slow to understand Jefferson and Patrick Henry. *Casanova's Women* (1941) pokes fun at Casanova and all he represents.

Mrs. Doratt (1941), the story of a mysterious woman, is a novel in which the author is the main character. At the insistence of a strong-minded aunt, in *The Voyage of Captain Bart* (1943), a New England boatbuilder goes to sea and finds the one woman in his life, the beautiful wife of a South American revolutionist. *Venus, The Lonely Goddess* (1949) is a departure from Dr. Erskine's earlier fiction and strikes a deeper note. The idealistic Venus marries into the higher group of Greek gods, idealistically takes a hand in the Trojan War, and learns something about love as mortals practice it.

ELEANOR (ROSENFELDT) ESTES

Soichi Sunami

was born on May 9, 1906, in West Haven, Connecticut, the child of parents who lived much in the world of books. Her early education was received at Union Grammar School and West Haven High School. In 1923 she entered the New Haven Free Library training class for a six-months' course, and thereafter she was a children's librarian until 1931. Following a year of study at the Pratt Institute Library School, she joined the staff of the New York Public Library. In 1932 she married Rice Estes, a fellow-student at Pratt; they have a daughter. Her early writing was in the field of children's books: *The Moffats* (1941), *The Middle Moffat* (1942), *Rufus M.* (1943), *The Sun and the Wind and Mr. Todd* (1943), *The Hundred Dresses* (1944), and *The Sleeping Giant* (1948).

The Echoing Green (1947), her first novel, portrays the development of Jemmie Hand, a New England girl, who fights for her dreams and convictions. It recreates a young girl's intense emotional life with all its strange ecstasies, poignant humiliations, and great hopes. Her father dies a drunkard, and the mother and children endure poverty.

DALE EUNSON

was born in Neillsville, Wisconsin, on August 15, 1904. In 1910 his family moved to Montana, and he attended schools in Acton, Billings, Moore, and Lewistown. Moving to California in 1922, he attended the University of Southern California at Los Angeles for a year, and then began writing publicity for Metro-Goldwyn-Mayer. Later he became secretary to Rupert Hughes, the novelist, and in 1930 went to New York as secretary to Ray Long, editor of *Cosmopolitan.* Mr. Eunson became associate editor of the magazine in 1933, but left after two years to devote more of his time to writing; however, between 1943 and 1948 he was fiction editor of *Cosmopolitan.* He is the co-author of two plays: "Guest in the House," written with Hagar Wilde, and "Loco," composed with his wife, Katherine Albert. In 1949 he was engaged in writing plays and scripts in Hollywood. He is the father of Joan Evans, the motion-picture actress.

Homestead (1935), his first novel, describes the difficulties of pioneers in the story of a young homesteading couple in the early part of the twentieth century when the government opened the Montana lands to public settlement. They dream of a successful crop, but annually for ten years hail, drought, rain, and blizzards bring disappointment. *The Day They Gave Babies Away* (1947), a Christmas story, tells how Mr. Eunson's father when only twelve years old assumed authority over his four orphaned brothers and sisters and doled them out to willing foster parents among the neighbors in their community.

FARALLA *to* FURNAS

DANA FARALLA

was born Dorothy Wein on August 4, 1909, in Renville, Minnesota. Her ancestry is Danish, French, and Austrian. She is a graduate of the Ithaca Conservatory of Music where she majored in dramatic art and won the Walter Hampden and the Frederick Warde scholarships in dramatics. She has been a professional actress, a writer of publicity for an art gallery in New York City, a screen-story analyst, and a scenario writer. She was married to the late Dario Faralla, a motion-picture executive and producer. She has traveled extensively in Europe and the West Indies, and has lived for long periods of time in France, Denmark, Switzerland, Italy, and Bermuda.

The Magnificent Barb (1947), her first novel, is set in the hunting country of Georgia. Kevin Fitzgerald's love of horses is inherited from a reprobate old Irish grandfather who has been a jockey in the old country, and his dream is of a superior horse, a Barb with a legendary white foot. In the boy's faith there is the essence of magic, for he finds a sore, ill-conditioned beast in a gipsy caravan, nurses him to strength and vigor on the run-down plantation, and develops a steeplechase winner. Tragedy is coincident with the victory, but the book ends on a note of hope.

Dream in the Stone (1948) is a story about a young boy and girl among the fisherfolk of Jutland, and tells how they occasionally see a splendid, wicked, heroic baron, a figure of three centuries before, and the beautiful mistress who had left the court for love of him. It is not quite a ghost story, nor yet quite a story of a shift in time; but it is a tale in which everything, the Danish land and sea, the baron's magnificent golden stallion, even a huge lump of sea amber, all have a strong and profoundly haunting and arresting quality.

JAMES THOMAS FARRELL

was born in Chicago, Illinois, on February 27, 1907. He was brought up in a lower-middle-class, Irish-American, Catholic environment. His preparatory education was received at St. Anselm Grammar School and St. Cyril High School in Chicago. During these early years his dominating interest was baseball; in high school he also won letters in football and basketball. After finishing high school Mr. Farrell went to work in an office of the American Railway Express Company. Deciding to become a lawyer, he entered the University of Chicago. He was there but a short time when he left to become a writer. He "bummed" his way to New York and slept the first night in Union Square. For a short time he was a clerk in a United Cigar Store. Drifting from one job to another he peddled advertising, worked as a salesman, and became a filling-station attendant. Finally he returned to the University of Chicago on borrowed money. He accumulated three years of university education by 1929, but thereafter he devoted his full time to writing. Mr. Farrell has written much literary criticism. He has attacked the misapplication of Marxism, and has stressed his belief that there is no real Marxian basis for the evaluation of books. *The League of Frightened Philistines* (1945) and *Literature and Morality* (1947) contain interpretive essays which expound the principle that good books are the most civilizing of agencies.

Mr. Farrell's short stories have been collected in *Calico Shoes* (1934); *Guillotine Party* (1935), which includes "Studs," the original sketch of Studs Lonigan; *Can All This Grandeur Perish?* (1937); *The Short Stories of James T. Farrell* (1937), which unites in one volume the three earlier books; *$1000 a Week* (1942); *Fifteen Selected Short Stories* (1943); *To Whom It May Concern* (1944); *When Boyhood Dreams Come True* (1946); *The Life Adventurous* (1947); and *An American Dream Girl* (1950).

His first novel, *Young Lonigan* (1932), is a story of boyhood in South Side Chicago. It is a stream-of-consciousness novel about Studs Lonigan, a young Irish boy, from the time he graduates from grade school until he enters high school. *Gas-House McGinty* (1933) follows the career of a dispatcher in an express company, a shallow, ignorant, proud, yet dream-haunted young man. *The Young Manhood of Studs Lonigan* (1934) carries the young Irish boy of Mr. Farrell's first novel from his high-school days in 1917 to 1929 as he slowly goes to pieces morally through his weakness. *Judgment Day* (1935) completes the trilogy which brings the life story of Studs Lonigan, tough boy of the streets, to its conclusion. *Studs Lonigan* (1935) collects the trilogy in one volume.

Life among the poverty-stricken Irish of Chicago is portrayed in *A World I Never Made* (1936), the story of Danny O'Neill. Some of the characters from the Studs Lonigan trilogy reappear in this novel. *No Star Is Lost* (1938), the sequel to *A World I Never Made,* continues the story of Danny O'Neill and his family. *Tommy Gallagher's Crusade* (1939) gives the character and background of a young man who stands on street corners selling anti-Semitic literature. *Father and Son* (1940) takes Danny O'Neill through adolescence.

Ellen Rogers (1941) is the story of a girl in a good Chicago Catholic family who has promiscuous relations with boys for the sake of the thrill. Ed Lanson, a tough and shallow cheat, outplays and leaves her. She commits suicide. *My Days of Anger* (1943), the fourth in the Danny O'Neill series, covers the years from 1924 to 1927 when he is in college and is trying to learn to write. *Bernard Clare* (1946) is about a young man who leaves Chicago in 1927 to write in New York a story on the meaninglessness of life. *The Road Between* (1949), a sequel with the boy's name changed to Carr, shows his pathetic rootlessness as he indulges in almost fruitless introspection. He has turned his back on his past, and his former associates disown him.

HOWARD FAST

was born November 11, 1914, in New York City. He received his education in its public schools. After attending George Washington High School, he had no desire to go to college; he tried to enlist in the navy, but was rejected because of his youth. Leaving home, he worked his way south, later returning penniless to New York. An interest in art led him to enter the National Academy of Design, a free art school. To stay there, he worked part time at the New York Public Library. While at the academy, he began writing and sold his first story. A career in art seemed unattainable, and so he left the academy to see the country. By hitchhiking from one place to another and by working at odd jobs—everything from delivery boy to construction worker on a dam—he saw a good part of the United States and at the same time experienced in the depression years the vicissitudes of life which supply the raw material for fiction. In 1935 he received a fellowship to the Bread Loaf School of English, and the following year, on the publication of his third novel, he decided to devote himself completely to writing. During World War II from December, 1942, to November, 1943, he was a member of the overseas staff of the Office of War Information. In 1944 he did work on a special army film project; he then went overseas as a war correspondent. He has written, in addition to his novels and biographies, numerous short stories. His juveniles include *Haym Solomon* (1941) and *Goethals and the Panama Canal* (1942). *Patrick Henry and the Frigate's Keel* (1945) and *Departure* (1949) contain short stories.

Mr. Fast has been associated with liberal and left-wing political organizations in the United States, and he has been invited abroad to represent this sector of American opinion. It is as a writer of historical novels that Mr. Fast is best known.

Mr. Fast's first novel, *Two Valleys* (1933), recounts episodes in the Revolutionary War on the frontier in western Pennsylvania and Kentucky. *Strange Yesterday* (1934) is a chronicle of five generations in the Preswick family from the end of the Revolution to 1930. *Place in the City* (1937), set in Apple Place, a tenement in New York City, has a poet fall in love with a music teacher's wife and three daughters rebel against their father. *Conceived in Liberty* (1939) pictures Allen Hale, a Mohawk Valley boy, during the desperate winter of 1777–78 at Valley Forge, where he was a soldier with Washington.

In 1939 Mr. Fast went to live on an Indian reservation in Oklahoma in order to collect material for his next book, *The Last Frontier* (1941). This novel is about the three-hundred-mile trek in 1878 of the Cheyenne Indians from Oklahoma to Wyoming, which they considered their rightful land. *The Unvanquished* (1942) is the story of the "times that try men's souls"—the four months of the American Revolution from the disaster in Brooklyn on August 27 to Christmas night in 1776.

The life story of the fiery propagandist of the Revolutionary War is told in *Citizen Tom Paine* (1943). The rise and fall of the Negro during the Reconstruction period in the South is depicted in *Freedom Road* (1944). *The American* (1946) is a biographical novel based on the life of John Peter Altgeld, midwestern politician and governor of Illinois during Cleveland's administration. *Clarkton* (1947) is a novel about a strike in a Massachusetts mill town and the brutal methods used to combat it. The story of children living in a New York City slum is told in *The Children* (1947). *My Glorious Brothers* (1948) describes the freeing of Israel from the Syrian-Greek overlords a hundred years before the birth of Christ. *The Proud and the Free* (1950) pictures a Pennsylvania regiment in the Revolutionary War in 1781.

WILLIAM FAULKNER

was born on September 25, 1897, in New Albany, Mississippi, the descendant of a grandfather who was the author of a popular southern romance. William Faulkner grew up in Oxford, Mississippi, and there attended public school. In 1918 he enlisted in the British Royal Air Force. After World War I he studied at the University of Mississippi in Oxford, where for a time he served as postmaster of the University station and where he now resides. In New Orleans he made the acquaintance of the novelist Sherwood Anderson, who made possible the publication of Mr. Faulkner's first novel, *Soldier's Pay* (1926). As early as 1922 Mr. Faulkner had printed a poem in *The Double Dealer* magazine; collections of his verse include *The*

Marble Faun (1924), *Salmagundi* (1932), which also contains essays, and *The Green Bough* (1933). Fame and notoriety came with the publication of the deliberately startling *Sanctuary* (1931). Some of his short stories have been printed in popular magazines, such as *The Saturday Evening Post,* as well as in reviews and little magazines, and they have been collected in *These Thirteen* (1931), *Idyll in the Desert* (1931), *Miss Zilpha Gant* (1932), *Doctor Martino* (1934), *The Unvanquished* (1936), *Knight's Gambit* (1949), and *Collected Stories* (1950).

In 1950 Mr. Faulkner was awarded the 1949 Nobel prize for literature "for his forceful and independently artistic contribution to modern American fiction."

Somewhat like Edgar Allan Poe, Mr. Faulkner pictures men and women whose minds have become unbalanced, and he emphasizes incidents which arouse terror, horror, and grotesque humor. However, where Poe dealt with minds eroded by strange diseases, Mr. Faulkner deals with degeneracy and idiocy traceable to heredity, social diseases, environment, and poverty. His characters are usually inhabitants of the imaginary Mississippi town of Jefferson, which is not unlike Oxford; members of three families —Sartoris, Compson, and Snopes—wind their soiled way through a century. The romantic glamour of the pre-Civil War South has altered into ugliness, cruelty, and lust, because an aristocratic society has deteriorated through miscegenation, alcohol, greed, and ignorance. The novels and short stories of Mr. Faulkner comprise a saga not unlike the Rougon-Macquart series of Émile Zola or the *Comédie Humaine* of Honoré de Balzac, in that the downfall of the aristocratic Sutpens and the rise of the Snopeses typify the degeneration of southern culture. Mr. Faulkner's narrative method is often difficult to follow, and his style, at times one of the most beautiful and poetic in modern fiction, is ornate and involved. His philosophy, especially as his work emphasizes the abnormal and subnormal in human behavior, has seemed pessimistic and nihilistic, but in *Intruder in the Dust* (1948) an affirmative attitude appears in the suggestion that the white people have a responsibility to improve the conditions of the Negro in the deep South.

Soldier's Pay (1926), his first novel, pictures the return of a wounded aviator, Donald Mahon, to his Georgia home and to his shallow fiancée, a southern belle who fails to help him recapture the will to live. Margaret Powers, a war widow, does fill his need; self-sacrificially she marries Donald. The novel describes the inability of the "Lost Generation" in the post-World War I era to adjust itself to the ways of civilian life, and the themes of futility and disenchantment are stressed. Yet something of the transcendentalism of Mr. Faulkner finds its first expression in Margaret's character. *Mosquitoes* (1927) relates the conversations and adventures during five days of a group of New Orleans aesthetes aboard a luxurious yacht which is disabled in a swamp among the gnats. The talk ranges from sophisticated gossip to wisdom, most of it in the tradition of Bohemianism.

Sartoris (1929) chronicles the life of an aristocratic family of that name in the imaginary town of Jefferson, Mississippi, during the era before the Civil War. The Snopes family begins to elbow its way into leadership as the older families show marks of deterioration; the theme of the decadence of southern aristocracy now overshadows in Mr. Faulkner's fiction the theme of futility. The characters in this novel reappear in other books, and many of the incidents now treated briefly are developed more fully in later short stories and novels.

The Sound and the Fury (1929) employs the technique of stream-of-consciousness—interior monologue, free association, and shifting sequence of time and place—to reproduce the private worlds of degenerate members of the Compson family. Benjy is a congenital idiot. Quentin's mind has become deranged by brooding upon his sister's wanton conduct and by his own sense of having been guilty of incest. The store clerk Jason labors under a sense of wrong; vengefully he drives a niece, Miss Quentin, to run away.

As I Lay Dying (1930) is a tragic story of the Bundrens, a family of Mississippi mountaineers, who become degraded and sordid through poverty and ignorance. The main episode concerns a thirty-mile march of the family with the corpse of the mother; strange and horrifying events occur along the way. Degeneration and deterioration of the human being seem to have reached a nether limit, not so much because these people are wilfully perverse as because they lack almost every dignifying thought and action prescribed by normal social custom.

Sanctuary (1931) was written to shock the American public into buying this book; to achieve that purpose Mr. Faulkner invented "the most horrific tale he could imagine." The main incident concerns a college girl, Temple Drake, who goes to a bootlegger's hideout with her companion of the moment when their automobile breaks down. The gangster Popeye drives away the boy and victimizes Temple. For a time she willingly consorts with this evil man, and then her mind becomes deranged. Murder, rape, lynching, and other forms of violence emphasize the degeneracy of which mankind is capable.

Light in August (1932) deals with the problem of mixed white and Negro blood, and with the southern and northern attitudes toward miscegenation. The central character is Joe Christmas, a Negro who is almost white and who in mature life tries to overcome a sense of racial inferiority by having relations with white women. He murders Miss Burden, one of these white women, when she preaches repentance; he is shot down by a lynching party.

Pylon (1935) has as its protagonist a newspaper reporter who becomes entangled in the lives of airplane pilots, mechanics, and their dependents in New Orleans at the Mardi Gras air races. Chief among the characters are a woman, two men who live with her, and a little boy who does not know which man is his father. The numerous incidents include the death of the husband in an airplane crash. The carnival spirit in the city provides an ironic background for tragic and sordid episodes.

Absalom, Absalom! (1936) tells the story of a West Virginia mountaineer, Thomas Sutpen, and his ill-fated attempt to found an aristocratic family and home in Yoknapatawpha County, Mississippi, in the years before the Civil War. Mixed blood and mixed castes create problems which cause the murder of the only white son and of Sutpen himself. In the end, in 1910, the mansion burns, and only a half-breed moron, Jim Bond, survives as an ironic memorial to Sutpen's dream. The story is told through the midnight conversations of two young men, Quentin Compson of Jefferson and Shreve Cannon of Canada. Through their eyes are seen romance and tragedy, their social implications, and the reasons for each cruel and horrifying event.

The Wild Palms (1939) tells two stories alternately. One concerns a New Orleans medical student, Harry Welbourne, who takes a woman artist from her husband. They share extreme hardships, and when she is about to have a child, Welbourne performs an illegal operation with fatal results to the woman. His memory of his love prevents suicide, and so he goes to jail where he can nourish his grief. The second story takes a young convict through a series of events on the flooded Mississippi River. He saves a woman's life, but because he thinks of women as destroyers, he avoids any relationship with her and gladly returns to prison.

The Hamlet (1940) pictures the Snopes family who achieve riches by trickery in a country store. Their rascalities include giving worthless IOU's, accepting money from their neighbors for useless Texas horses, and selling valueless land supposedly rich in treasure. One comic episode portrays an idiot in love with a cow; the events of this story precede those in *Sanctuary*.

Intruder in the Dust (1948) is about the arrest of Lucas Beauchamp, a Negro, for murdering a white man. While a mob assembles, two sixteen-year-old boys, one white and one black, and an elderly spinster of excellent family gather evidence to prove the innocence of the imprisoned man. The theme of race relations and the duty of the white man to promote the interests of the Negro emerges in this novel.

RAOUL C. FAURE

Emmett E. Smith

was born on September 10, 1909, in Cairo, Egypt. He was educated at the University of Paris, where he received the degree of Doctor of Law and diplomas in political science and economics and in commercial science. Following graduation he trained for business and stockbroking in London. Then he went to Egypt, where he worked in an import-export firm as a stockbroker and as cotton-plantation supervisor for six years. Eventually he decided to give up business and write. He traveled in the United States, Mexico, and Central America and was in the United States on his way to Tahiti at the outbreak of World War II. He remained near San Francisco, writing and working in the shipyards. His first book was prepared, he says, "as a reaction to rush and din."

Mr. Faure has stated his theory of fiction thus: "Many recent novels are too lifelike (not life-size), too realistic, too social, too photographic, too much an enlarged or fictionalized report; they compete too directly with the newspaper and the magazine story in technique, even in the case of the superabundant historical novels; and they fight a losing battle. The novel should plough new ground more often. Painting, after the advent of photography and then of motion pictures, was forced to give up literal representation and struck a gold mine in its various deviations: impressionism, expressionism, and surrealism. If painting, in the face of the threat of photography and motion pictures, had stubbornly refused to change its course, it promptly would have slipped to second or third rank. The average present novel courts this danger. The remedy obviously lies in meaningful deviations from our too literal realism, in a certain deliberate variation from true focus.

"My central themes have been drawn from the great Greek and Near Eastern myths and not from the transitory though pressing present social and economic problems and their no less evanescent though so very arresting solutions."

The Spear in the Sand (1946), his first novel, describes the danger of ultimate perfection. The hero, who is marooned for thirty years on a Pacific island, senses the problem and defends himself with the ordinary weapons of intellectual resource and contrived pastimes. He perceives the fact that ultimate perfection would mean the complete annihilation of his humanity. *Mister St. John* (1947) is the story of a surgeon who wonders whether he has lost anything during the thirty years he has ruled love out of his life. The doctor achieves the ultimate excellence, the summit of the mountain that symbolizes the perfection of his love, only by losing his life.

Lady Godiva and Master Tom (1948) retells the legend with psychological interpretations and with Peeping Tom altered from an old man to a handsome, romantic young tailor. The heroine's passionate nature, her lust for power, her consequent hatred for her husband, her pathetic ride as a result of boredom, and her affair with the tailor are only blind, awkward, incomplete gestures by a woman straining toward perfection. She fails and the book is the chronicle of her failure. The author reveals a secondary purpose in his deliberate attempt to remove the glamour from a rather incomprehensible feat of exhibitionism by a lady whom legend has strangely turned almost into a saint.

KENNETH FLEXNER FEARING

Arni

was born in Oak Park, Illinois, on July 28, 1902. He attended the public schools of Oak Park and received his bachelor's degree from the University of Wisconsin in 1924. Upon graduation he began his writing career as a newspaper reporter in Chicago, but soon thereafter removed to New York City to engage in free-lance writing. Since 1924 he has held several publicity and editorial positions. He received Guggenheim fellowships in 1936 and 1939. Mr. Fearing is married, has one son, and lives and works in New York City.

His first book, *Angel Arms* (1929), is a volume of poems in a conversational idiom which discards the usual conventions of poetry but which reproduces, often with startling irony, the harsh and painful truth of daily experience. Five more collections of poetry followed: *Poems* (1935), *Dead Reckoning* (1938), *Collected Poems* (1940), *Afternoon of a Pawnbroker* (1943), and *Stranger at Coney Island* (1949). In the introduction to *Collected Poems,* Mr. Fearing has said, "The idea underlying my poetry, as well as anything I write, is that it must be exciting."

The Hospital (1939), his first novel, is an X-ray catching a single, elastic moment in the lives of the people in a large metropolitan institution: doctors, nurses, patients, outpatients, relatives and friends, and maintenance men. Throughout the book it is always three o'clock in the afternoon, with a young woman in the hospital's clinic, fearing a diagnosis of tuberculosis, as the focal point of the story. *Dagger of the Mind* (1941) is a psychological murder mystery. *Clark Gifford's Body* (1942), although laid in a mythical country, describes in modern terms the life, death, and apotheosis of the revolutionary zealot John Brown. The action, covering sixty years, centers in the seizure of a radio station, a contemporary equivalent to the attack at Harper's Ferry. Many of the central character's words and actions are a literal transcription of John Brown's, and the protagonist is seen through the eyes of friends, enemies, and neutrals. *The Big Clock* (1946) is a novel of pursuit, of a man in search of himself. The hero, an unconscious rebel against organized society, is forced against his will into this hunt for himself, which becomes both self-examination and an effort to escape. The action takes place within the machinery of a large magazine combine.

FEIKE (FREDERICK) FEIKEMA

Sifford Studio

was born January 6, 1912, in Rock Rapids, Iowa, just a few miles from the Minnesota and South Dakota borders, in the territory he calls Siouxland in his novels. His parents are of Frisian descent. Feike is the oldest of six brothers, the shortest of whom is six feet three. He himself stands six feet nine and weighs 270 pounds. He attended Calvinistic parochial schools in Iowa and lived on the farm until he was eighteen. After receiving his degree from Calvin College in Grand Rapids, Michigan, in 1934, he wandered for three years over the United States from coast to coast, doing odd jobs as factory hand, filling-station attendant, weekly-newspaper editor, salesman, bus boy, hired man, poet, carpenter, painter, and harvest hand. Following study in 1937 at Nettleton Commercial College in Sioux City, South Dakota, he got a job as reporter on the Minneapolis *Journal* and began writing a novel in his spare time. His health broke down from overwork in April, 1940, and from then until March, 1942, he was a patient in a tuberculosis sanitarium. He gained back 104 pounds, left the hospital, and took a job on the staff of the magazine *Modern*

Medicine. He quit in January, 1943, to become assistant campaign manager for Hubert H. Humphrey in his race for mayor of Minneapolis, but in June he decided to enter upon a full-time writing career.

In discussing his plans for future writing Mr. Feikema has said: "I want to keep my mind open as long as I can and, in the meantime, record as Chaucer did. My point of view is this. Suppose we have a rosebush before us. Some writers will describe only the lovely petals. Others will describe only the manure and dirt in which the bush grows. Others, the rare ones like Chaucer and Shakespeare, will describe the entire process—soil, roots, stalk, leaves, petals, rain, sunlight. That too is my goal. Truth is beauty, the full truth."

The Golden Bowl (1944) concerns Maury Grant, a young Oklahoma farmer, whose trail after work carries him and his guitar to the farm of Iver Thor in the golden bowl of South Dakota, where Thor's daughter stirs the two men into a conflict of ideas. This conflict is between the solipsist impulse and the gregarious instinct. *Boy Almighty* (1945) is a partly autobiographical novel describing two years spent by a sensitive young writer as a patient in a midwestern tuberculosis sanitarium. Here the theme is the conflict of vitality as opposed to the rules of life and society. Out of that conflict comes understanding, the first beginnings of Eric's maturity, and the realization that there are three stages in his concept of God: at first an enlarged "strict father," then "a vindictive fate," and third "the way things are."

This Is the Year (1947) describes the conflict between ignorant vitality and nature's blind power, through the picture of the annual hope of an ignorant but headstrong Frisian farmer for a bumper crop; in the end he realizes that his land will produce nothing. The book was intended as a Greek tragedy in which Pier, who is Everyman, finds that ignorance is his undoing. *The Chokecherry Tree* (1948) concerns a boy who has "flunked out" of theological seminary and the state university and who comes to the Iowa village of Chokecherry Corner. Here he tries to adjust himself to the customs of the local people and ultimately, with the aid of his childhood sweetheart, achieves contentment. The theme concerns the conflict between the aspiring average ego and the soaring strong or above-average ego. It is the story of the little man taught to have the hunger of the big.

A projected trilogy, *World's Wanderer,* will describe the conflict between vitality and controls, and will be concerned with the history of the good and evil produced by the modern creative or inventive mind. "Love" in the large sense must reconcile and create a working pair of the opposing forces. *The Primitive* (1949), the first volume in the series, is about a youthful giant's awakening to his powers of good and evil. *The Brother* (1950) continues the story of Thurs Wraldson, his farm and college youth behind him, who invades New York City, where his searching mind and tremendous size create excitement.

EDNA FERBER

was born in Kalamazoo, Michigan, the daughter of a merchant born in Hungary and a mother born in Milwaukee, Wisconsin. For a time the family lived in Iowa and then in Appleton, Wisconsin, where Miss Ferber completed high school. Her father had become blind, and she was forced to relinquish plans to study for the stage. Her graduation essay described the life of women workers in a local mill. The editor of the Appleton *Daily Crescent* recognized her ability to report observations clearly and gave her a job as a reporter at three dollars a week. She covered the courthouse, city hall, fire department, and police department—places where the lively detail of human experience filled her mind with unforgettable incidents for later use. Her writing attracted the attention of the Milwaukee *Journal*, which engaged her as a reporter and feature writer.

Meantime she was trying her hand at short stories and a novel, *Dawn O'Hara* (1911), which became her first book. Short stories about Emma McChesney, a traveling saleswoman who sells Featherbloom petticoats through the Middle West, brought national fame to Miss Ferber. The freshness of these stories was due in part to their style and in part to their original subject matter: they were the first stories dealing with women in business. On them was based her first play, "Our Mrs. McChesney" (1916).

After years of success with shorter fiction, Miss Ferber gave up the writing of popular-magazine stories to produce plays and novels. Her first published comedy, written with Newman Levy, was *$1200 a Year* (1920). Her novel, *So Big* (1924), because a popular favorite and won a Pulitzer prize in 1924. *Show Boat* (1926), a novel which was turned into an operetta, a motion picture, and a radio program, established her fame as a romantic novelist equally adept with contemporary and with historical materials. Other plays, written in collaboration with George S. Kaufman, became Broadway hits: "Minick" (1924), "The Royal Family" (1928), "Dinner at Eight" (1932), "Stage Door" (1938), and "The Land Is Bright" (1941). *A Peculiar Treasure* (1933) is autobiographical.

The short stories written in her early career deal with people who do things, not romanticized persons of consequence, but the common city folk who fill their jobs well, or make happy homes, or show a knack for building a durable happiness in ordinary, homely, commonplace, and wholesome patterns of work and duty. Her characters reflect the moods and attitudes of average humanity: shrewd observations make her people seem as recognizable as the family next door. Their talk is crisp, slangy, and often amusing, faithfully reflecting the nature of each person: it has the quality of the authentic spoken word of both the period of time and the character. Humor and skillful technique give a rapid pace to her stories. Without intruding a thesis into her writings, she weaves each story around a worth-while idea. The failure of men and women to find happiness arouses her deepest sympathy; possibly her warmest appreciation goes out to women like Emma McChesney who beat down the barriers of useless restrictive custom.

Although the settings of her early stories are in the Middle West of her youth, Miss Ferber has gone for materials for her novels to the Mississippi River, Oklahoma, Connecticut, Texas, California, New Orleans, and other areas. Her stories, whether contemporary or historical, stress people rather than places, with the result that background, though adequately presented, is subordinate to action and character. Plots have never interested her, so that her books are almost plotless. Character and dialogue are the outstanding characteristics, with vivid background as a third strength.

Her first short-story collection was *Buttered Side Down* (1912). Three books—*Roast Beef Medium: The Business Adventures of Emma McChesney* (1913), *Personality Plus: Some Experiences of Emma McChesney and Her Son Jock* (1914), and *Cheerful—By Request* (1918)—contain related stories about the vital and charming Emma, her marriage and graceful acceptance of age, and her son's career as an advertising man. Miss Ferber's other books of short stories are *Half Portions* (1920), *Gigolo* (1922), *Mother Knows Best* (1927), *They Brought Their Women* (1933), and *One Basket* (1947).

"All my novels with the exception of *Show Boat*," Miss Ferber has said, "have an inner theme and meaning which are not apparent to the casual eye. *Show Boat* was pure romance. The others have not only been American in characterization and theme and background; they have commented on a phase of life or criticized a way of life which seemed to me to be deeply imperfect. It is, perhaps, this meaning below the surface which has kept them alive these past twenty-five or thirty years, and which causes them to be included in the classroom lists of most colleges, universities, and high schools."

Miss Ferber's first novel, *Dawn O'Hara* (1911), is about a sprightly Irish-American girl from Milwaukee who goes to New York to write human-interest stories "with a punch in them" for a newspaper. She marries Lester Orme, a reporter, whose expensive habits and drunkenness bring him to ruin. She finds happiness at last, after a breakdown, with a German physician. *Fanny Herself* (1917) is the story of Fanny Brandeis, a business woman, who is faced with the choice between greater business success and marriage with the man who has loved her for years. *The Girls* (1921) concerns three sisters in the Thrift family, each of whom represents her own generation in rebellion against the preceding one: great-aunt Charlotte surrenders in the Civil War period; her niece, Lottie, rebels late and somewhat apologetically in the 1890's; and Charley, a grandniece, is continuously rebellious in the years beginning in 1910.

So Big (1924) is ostensibly about Dirk DeJong, who in childhood was nicknamed "So Big" and who grows up to be a financially successful plodder. His mother, Selina DeJong, is the memorable character in the book; she is the daughter of a gambler and the wife of a truck farmer, and she dreams of having a son with a big spirit and not a cramped soul lacking beauty and strength. Material success leaves him unimpressed. *Show Boat* (1926) treats episodically three generations of a Mississippi River showboat family. Captain Andy Hawks takes his prim New England bride into the business, and she runs it well after his death. Magnolia, the daughter and major character, is the leading lady on the showboat until she leaves to follow Gaylord Ravenal, her gambler husband, to Chicago. Kim, Magnolia's daughter born in 1889, becomes a famous actress in New York.

Cimarron (1930) is a romantic historical novel about Oklahoma following the land rush of 1889. The story of Yancey Cravat and his gentle-bred southern wife, Sabra, who is able to do a man's work when necessary, is told against a background of frontier problems, Osage Indians, and the discovery of oil. *American Beauty* (1931) traces the decay of the Oakes family in Connecticut. Founded in 1700 by an aristocrat, Captain Orrange Oakes, who built a fine house on a thousand-acre tract, the family by 1870 sees its direct descendant marry a peddler, and by 1890 the child of that union marries a Polish farm hand. In 1930 the Chicago millionaire, True Baldwin, originally of lower-class stock, returns to the community of his forefathers and buys the house and remaining three hundred acres from Orrange Oakes Olszak, the last of the family.

Come and Get It (1935) is the history of a Wisconsin family from 1850 to 1929; Barney Glasgow, a lusty swashbuckler, fights his way from choreboy in a lumber camp to become Wisconsin's lumber king, and his son, Bernie, becomes a freebooter in another but no less gaudy age. *Nobody's in Town* (1938) contains two short novels on the theme of the pampered softness of the modern generation. The title story is about a successful Wall Street man and the five people who make his life comfortable: a Central Park employee and his daughter, a maid, a fruit retailer, and a garbage collector. "Trees Die at the Top" has Mrs. Jared Content III and her family cross the continent complainingly in a luxury train to be at the deathbed of her father, a pioneer, whose difficult trip to the West in a prairie schooner in 1849 resulted in the establishment of the family fortune.

Saratoga Trunk (1941), set in New Orleans and Saratoga, New York, in the 1880's, is the story of Clint Maroon, a former Texas cowboy, and of Clio, a beautiful young adventuress, daughter of a New Orleans aristocrat and his mistress. Now at eighty-nine and very wealthy, he is famous for the benefactions that have brought him national prominence. He tries to tell unbelieving reporters how he stole his fortune, but they will not listen.

The facts are that the young couple set out to attain riches and got them. At the races in Saratoga, where they had planned to gamble, they met the Morgans and Vanderbilts and decided to play with railroads and not with race horses. *Great Son* (1945) is a story about Seattle, Washington, and its romantic history as seen through the experiences of four generations of the Melendy family from 1851 to 1941. The twin themes are faith in American courage and the importance of a genuine working democracy.

HARVEY FERGUSSON

Artist: D. C. Parrot

was born on January 28, 1890, in Albuquerque, New Mexico. During his boyhood this city still retained something of the atmosphere of a wide-open frontier town with public gambling and crowded saloons. The surrounding country was wild, and he spent much of his youth afield with horse and gun. He was educated in the public schools of Albuquerque, at the New Mexico Military Institute, and the University of New Mexico, finally taking his bachelor's degree at Washington and Lee University in Lexington, Virginia, where his father had graduated shortly after the Civil War when General Robert E. Lee was its president. During and after his college years, Harvey Fergusson spent several summers working for the United States Forest Service as a timber cruiser and map maker. In 1912 he began the study of law in Washington, where his father was a representative in Congress. He soon abandoned school for a job as a reporter on the Washington *Herald.* Subsequently he worked for short periods on the Savannah *Morning News* and the Richmond *Times Dispatch.* Returning to Washington, he sat in the press gallery at the Capitol for a couple of years as a correspondent and for seven years was editor for the Frederick J. Haskin Syndicate. In 1923 he went to New York, where he spent about eight years as a free-lance writer, and made frequent trips to the Southwest. In 1932 he moved to California, where he has lived ever since, mostly in Berkeley, but part of the time in Hollywood.

Mr. Fergusson has published four works of non-fiction. *Rio Grande* (1933) is a history of the Rio Grande Valley in New Mexico from prehistoric times to modern, treating this small scene as a paradigm of the history of western civilization from the stone age, through a feudal epoch, to the coming of the machine. *Modern Man* (1936), which was written partly on a Guggenheim fellowship, is a study of ethics in the modern world and embodies a philosophy which is implicit in much of the author's work. *Home in the West: An Inquiry into My Origins* (1945) is a study of the author's background and early years, including portraits of his grandfather, who was a freighter over the old Santa Fé trail, and his father, who went west with the railroad as a pioneer lawyer and politician. *People and Power* (1948) is a study of political life as human behavior.

The Blood of the Conquerors (1921), his first novel, is a study of the relations between the Spanish and the Anglo-American racial strains in the New Mexico of his boyhood. It is a story of young love defeated by racial and social prejudice. *Capitol Hill* (1923) is laid in the Washington of the years leading to World War I. It is a satirical picture of political life in Washington, done from the viewpoint of a humorous bounder with a flair for the ladies, who exploits the pretentiousness and intrigue of his environment with great success. *Women and Wives* (1924) is a study of marriage laid in the same city.

Hot Saturday (1926) is a short novel portraying the events of a single day in a small western town. Its central figure is a naïve and romantic young girl in pursuit of a husband to fulfill a typically American dream of wealth and social splendor. *Wolf Song* (1927) is laid in the Southwest of the 1840's when the mountain men rode the beaver trail, and is a lyrical expression of the heroic tradition of pioneer life. *In Those Days* (1929) also deals with the pioneer past, but in very different terms. It covers fifty years in the life of a man who goes west shortly after the Civil War, and records the impact upon his personality of a period of swift and incalculable change. *Footloose McGarnigal* (1930) is a light satire upon the idea of romantic escape. It is the story of a young man who goes west, inspired by the tall tales of a pioneering uncle, and encounters a good many adventures but also considerable disillusion.

Followers of the Sun (1936) is an omnibus volume with an introduction, containing the three southwestern novels, *Wolf Song, In Those Days,* and *The Blood of the Conquerors.* Taken together, they record a fairly complete social history of the region for three generations. *The Life of Riley* (1937) is the story of a man born in a small western town who has a triumphant youth as an athlete and sportsman, is a hero in World War I, and can never thereafter adjust himself to the routine and chicanery of small-town business. *Grant of Kingdom* (1950) is based on the history of one of the old Spanish land grants in the Southwest, and describes how Jean Ballard, a former mountain man and trader, transforms two thousand square miles of wilderness into an organized community. The descriptions of the countryside are excellent.

MICHAEL FESSIER

was born on November 6, 1905, in Angel's Camp, California. He served first as a printer's apprentice on the Bakersfield, California, *Morning Echo.* Later he was a reporter on the San Francisco *Chronicle,* the *Examiner,* and the Long Beach *Press-Telegram.* Subsequently he edited papers in Burlingame and San Rafael. After writing stories for *Esquire, Story,* and *Harper's,* he entered a period of motion-picture work. In 1949 he was devoting himself completely to fiction.

"The only philosophy I have achieved so far," he has said, "is that a fiction writer should not depart for too long from his medium; the name one carves in celluloid is as perishable as that which one carves on a wave."

Fully Dressed and in His Right Mind (1935), his first book, is an allegorical novel with a modern setting in which the author deals with the problem of good and evil. John Price meets a girl who symbolizes unattainable goodness. She saves him from an evil old man, but she eludes him. *Clovis* (1948) is a witty satire upon the unreadiness of society for intelligent rulers. Clovis, a speaking and thinking parrot, learns this sad truth in the jungle and in American homes. He asks to be an ordinary parrot.

BEN FIELD

Elizabeth Timberman

was raised and educated in New York City. During World War I, as a schoolboy, he gained experience at farming when he was hired by a dairyman in upstate New York. He quit teaching school in 1940 to work in a machine shop. He also was a logger in the woods in the Upper Delaware River Valley in Pennsylvania and New York.

The Cock's Funeral (1937), his first book, contains thirteen short stories which give various aspects of the struggle of impoverished farmers to retain their land. Mingled with the hard fight are flashes of cockfighting, baseball, and the excitement of boys on their way to a sheep dip. *The Outside Leaf* (1943) is about twenty-year-old Moe Miller, who takes over his unsuccessful Jewish father's broadleaf tobacco farm in Connecticut, and by hard work and with modern machinery gets a good crop. He marries red-haired Mary Foley, a Polish-Irish girl. Here portrayed are the influences at work in a rural community when the hero marries a Catholic girl and when the engrafted Yankee qualities of the boy are relaxed for a deeper understanding of the father from whom he revolts.

Piper Tompkins (1946) is the story of a Connecticut farm boy who breaks away from his family and goes to work in a defense plant. At first he disagrees with the union, just as he did with his family, but in the end he sees the value of developing a more sociable attitude. Piper is a tough, of the same type as Moe Miller, and is subjected to more rapid and sweeping changes than those of the farm. He grasps the idea of human brotherhood. *The Last Freshet* (1948) set in the logging country of the upper Delaware River valley, pictures Virge Doggity, a widower at forty-nine, who looks after the widows, Frances and Ellen, of his two sons who were killed in the war. This novel probes the question whether a man terribly hurt by life can sidestep the duties of our times without doing himself irreparable harm.

IRVING FINEMAN

Simon Moselsio

was born on April 9, 1893, in New York City. He attended public schools there until his interest in science took him to the Massachusetts Institute of Technology, from which he graduated as a civil engineer in 1917; he also earned a degree at Harvard. He was engaged in graduate research when World War I took him as an engineer officer into the navy, where he remained for five years. Then he practiced civil engineering in this country and in Canada. While he was on the engineering faculty of the University of Illinois from 1925 to 1928, his observation of the dilemmas of modern youth moved him to write his first novel, *This Pure Young Man* (1930), which won the Longmans, Green prize and launched him on a literary career. He taught literature at Bennington College from 1932 to 1938. Between books, Mr. Fineman has written for motion pictures. He married Helene Hughes in 1935; they have two sons.

He believes that his writing has benefited from his scientific training and experience, which served to enlarge his powers of observation and analysis, while his omnivorous reading of good literature since childhood helped develop his style. He contends that the functions of the writer and the scientist are related: while the scientist reveals the order in physical nature, the writer reveals the order in human nature. His scientific background proved useful especially in writing the novel *Doctor Addams,* which Clifton Fadiman called "the best medical novel since *Arrowsmith.*"

Irving Fineman, though a lover of fine prose who labors to achieve works of beauty and distinction, is not a believer in art for art's sake. The substance and significance of a work of art are of primary importance to him; its form and style should serve to stir and move the reader to both enjoyment and understanding. This he learned from the Bible and from Shakespeare.

His first novel, *This Pure Young Man* (1930), dealt with the losing struggle of a young architect to put his ideals into practice. Mr. Fineman has observed that a writer's first book, like the first utterance of a newborn child, is apt to be a cry of distress. As he matures, the writer, like the child, is likely to find in life, however troubled, more optimistic and satisfying things to express. *Lovers Must Learn* (1932) is a love story told alternately from the viewpoint of the man and the woman. *Hear, Ye Sons* (1933), the story of the European background of an American Jewish family, expresses the author's belief in the importance of tradition to modern man; the book has become something of a classic in its field and has been published in The Modern Library.

Doctor Addams (1939) is a study of the dilemma of the modern man of science who wields tremendous and godlike powers in the laboratory, but is as fumbling in his social and personal life as any ignorant peasant on the land. *Jacob* (1941), written in the form of an autobiography of the Biblical patriarch, epitomizes in the conflict of Jacob and Esau the age-old conflict of the man of delicate sensibility and the man of violence. *Ruth* (1949) also deals with a Biblical figure in order to pose the still moot problem of the treatment of the alien in a land surrounded by enemies, as well as the timeless question of the place of woman in a man-made world.

ANNE BENSON FISHER

was born on February 1, 1898, in Denver, Colorado. She attended the University of Denver and the University of Colorado Medical School and graduated as a nurse from Park Avenue Hospital in Denver. Before her marriage to Professor Walter Kenrick Fisher of Stanford University, she was a bacteriologist and worked for the United States Bureau of Animal Industry at Denver to save livestock during World War I. Later she established her own clinical laboratory at Salinas, California. During her career, Mrs. Fisher has experimented with many fields of writing to elicit the best results from her talent.

Her first published book, *Look What Brains Can Do* (1932), is a satire. *Career for Constance* (1936) is a light romance. *Live with a Man and Love It* (1937) and *Brides Are Like New Shoes* (1938) give advice on marriage. *Wide Road Ahead* (1939) is a biographical adventure. *Cathedral in the Sun* (1940) is the story of three generations of Indians and their relationship with the mission at Carmel, California. *The Salinas* (1945) is a history in the "Rivers of America" series. *Bears, Pirates and Silver Lace* (1946) is a juvenile historical tale.

No More a Stranger (1946) tells the story of Robert Louis Stevenson's life in Monterey, California. *Oh, Glittering Promise* (1949) concerns Charles Morgan, a pick-and-shovel miner in the Gold Rush of 1849, his hopes and disappointments, and the choice he must make between a greedy wife and her generous, warm-hearted rival. *It's a Wise Child* (1949) is a roguish account of the saints and rascals of old Monterey, California, in the late 1870's and tells how they all, down to the last Chinese laundryman, befriended a motherless child.

VARDIS FISHER

Hans George Block

was born March 31, 1895, in Annis, Idaho, in a shack which he has said resembled Lincoln's birthplace. His grandfather, Joseph Oliver Fisher, was among the first settlers in the upper Snake River Valley, sent there by the Mormon Church to found a colony. His mother was Temperance Thornton, descendant of an old English family; two of her uncles crossed the plains with Brigham Young on his first trip.

Mr. Fisher received his early education in the frontier schools of Idaho. During World War I he was invited into the air corps, but finding the life of a penniless cadet not to his liking, he withdrew and waited for the draft. He became a corporal in the artillery at Fort Rosecrans in San Diego, California, but the war ended before he sailed for France. After the war he returned to his education, receiving his baccalaureate from the University of Utah, and his master's and doctor's degrees *magna cum laude* from the University of Chicago. He taught English at the University of Utah from 1925 to 1928 and at New York University from 1928 to 1931, and then abandoned the teaching profession to devote all his time to writing.

From 1935 to 1939 Mr. Fisher was director of the Federal Writers' Project in Idaho and in the latter period regional editor for the Rocky Mountain states. The *Idaho Guide,* the first state guide to appear, was written almost entirely by him, as were also *The Idaho Encyclopedia* and *Idaho Lore.* He has no religious affiliations; he belongs to no organizations or clubs, except the local chapter of the Idaho Grange. He serves or has served on a few committees interested in preserving freedom. Since 1936 he has been outspokenly anti-communist. He lives at Hagerman, Idaho, where his avocations are horticulture and politics. He has published a book of verse, *Sonnets to an Imaginary Madonna* (1927); a book of essays, *The Neurotic Nightingale* (1935); and a history, *The Caxton Printers in Idaho* (1944).

Toilers of the Hills (1928), his first published novel, is a story of Dock Hunter and his desperate wife Opal on the Antelope Hills of eastern Idaho. *Dark Bridwell* (1931) is the tale of a whimsical and philosophic brute and drunkard who took his beautiful wife and his children to a lonely mountain spot which almost destroyed all of them.

In Tragic Life (1932) is the first novel in a tetralogy portraying the life of Vridar Hunter, generally assumed to be Mr. Fisher himself. This story tells of the boyhood and adolescence of an abnormally sensitive child who is virtually driven insane by the rigors of a frontier outpost and the Calvinism of his mother. *Passions Spin the Plot* (1934) continues the story of Vridar, dwelling chiefly on his first years in college and his wild love affair with a part-Indian girl, Neloa, his childhood sweetheart. In the conclusion of that story he marries her, and *We Are Betrayed* (1935) chronicles the course of their unfortunate marriage and her suicide. In this novel Vridar pursues his academic training in Chicago. *No Villain Need Be* (1936) finds the modern pilgrim striving for understanding of and mastery over himself.

In April: A Fable of Love (1937) chronicles the dream fantasies of a very homely, introverted, and lonely girl and her achievement of happiness. In the delicate whimsy of this book Mr. Fisher departed completely from the stark realism of his earlier novels. *Forgive Us Our Virtues* (1938) is a psychological novel about marriage, feuds in a university faculty, and neuroses in a small town.

Children of God (1939), which won the Harper prize, is the story of the Mormons from the sect's beginnings to the end of the first sixty years, with the persecutions, heroism, and the great migration across the plains. Joseph Smith and Brigham Young are the principal characters. This novel has been officially repudiated by the conservative faction of the church. *City of Illusion* (1941) is a story of the Comstock Lode in Virginia City, Nevada. The chief character is the incredible Eilley Orum Cowan, who made a huge fortune, set up as the social arbiter of Nevada, and went down to defeat in bankruptcy and insanity. *The Mothers: An American Saga of Courage* (1943) is the story of the tragic journey to California in 1846 of the Donner party, with its cannibalism, unbelievable sufferings, and heroism. The story is told from the viewpoint of the mothers.

After twenty years of studying anthropology and religion, Mr. Fisher began a series of twelve novels under the over-all title of *The Testament of Man.* His project is "an adventure in self-discovery which the intelligence of man owes to his spirit"; but he regards his efforts as no more than an "attempt to pioneer in a most exciting and very difficult field." The thesis is that man must free himself from the vast burden of superstitions, attitudes, and cults inherited from his primitive past, most of which frustrate rather than serve his development, before he can proceed to that "great stage of civilization not too far ahead of us in which freedom from fear will be achieved, not with social securities and economic guarantees, but by liberating the spirit of man from its ancient bondage."

The first five volumes, now published, are laid in prehistoric times. The sixth will deal with King Solomon and his age; the seventh, with the Maccabean period, in which Hellenism and Judaism engaged in what scholars generally agree in calling the most important historical conflict for the Western world; the eighth about Jesus; the ninth about the Christian church in its beginnings; the tenth in the fourth century; the eleventh in the thirteenth century; and the twelfth and concluding volume in our time.

Darkness and the Deep (1943), the first in this series, deals with primitive ape-man when he is struggling to formulate language and establish simple social relationships. *The Golden Rooms* (1944), the second, is the story of Harg, one of the first men to make fire; of the first primitively organized war; but, above all, of the emergence of the concepts of the ghost and of the supernatural world. The third, chronicling man's slow climb from darkness and the deep, is *Intimations of Eve* (1946), concerned chiefly with the evolving place of woman in primitive society and the beginnings of the matriarchal age. By this time human beings are worshiping the Moon-woman, later to be, scholars believe, the goddess of Semitic nomadic tribes. In *Adam and the Serpent* (1947) phallic symbolisms are evolving, and man is disputing the supremacy of woman; here begin some of the concepts which are so integral a part of masculine psychology today. *The Divine Passion* (1948) pictures the dawn of recorded history, and adumbrates, in its sun- and sex-worship and its sacrificial rites, some of the basic materials of the Old Testament. Man has conquered woman, the patriarchal age is in full flower, one of the first of the ascetic prophets has risen, and the stage is almost set for the most ancient of the civilizations of the Mediterranean basin.

MARTIN FLAVIN

was born on November 2, 1883, in San Francisco, California. His roots are deep in the American soil and in the state of California, for his maternal grandfather, a distinguished jurist, migrated to California from his native state of North Carolina. Mr. Flavin's father died while the son was young, and later his mother remarried. He grew up in Chicago, attended public schools there, and was a student at the University of Chicago from 1903 to 1905. His chief interest was the theater, particularly the comic opera. After leaving college, he wrote short stories with some measure of success, but feeling that he was too young to write the things he desired, he deliberately put writing aside. For a dozen years, during a successful business career, he did not write a line. One day there occurred an incident which demanded dramatization, and he wrote it into a play. He was now thirty-four years old and still active in business, but he began to write during his leisure time. Five years later he produced a play on Broadway, and thus in 1923 with the production of "Children of the Moon," he ceased to be a businessman and became a playwright. In 1929 he was the toast of Broadway when three of his plays were running simultaneously; they were "The Criminal Code," "Broken Dishes," and "Cross Roads." When he was fifty-seven, he wrote his first novel. He has traveled widely in Europe, and has visited Africa, Russia, China, and Japan. His first nonfiction book, *Black and White* (1950), is a record of his African experiences, chiefly in the Congo.

Mr. Flavin has said, "I am primarily a writer, not in the sense of writers who have a passion for words, but in the sense of setting forth ideas—ideas of all sorts and dimensions, without qualification beyond the one that they be interesting to me."

Mr. Littlejohn (1940), his first novel, which superficially recounts a bored businessman's escape from a humdrum life, is in reality a quest for an answer to the problems posed by his own life and by mankind in general. *Corporal Cat* (1941) dramatically exploits the motif of fear in the story of a German parachutist who is separated from his companions. *Journey in the Dark* (1943), which won the Harper award and the Pulitzer prize, is a study of values in the modern world, and in effect is a denunciation of the moral indirection that results from the possession of extreme wealth. *The Enchanted* (1947) describes the adventures of a group of Spanish refugee children who finally find a haven on a Caribbean island. The parable of the tale is succinctly stated in the Biblical quotation, "Suffer the little children to come unto me, for of such is the Kingdom of Heaven."

BERRY FLEMING

was born on March 19, 1899, in Augusta, Georgia. He graduated from Harvard College in 1922, and from that year until 1938, when he returned to Augusta, he lived in New York City, with the exception of two years spent in England and western Europe. His writings include poetry, many short articles, and a history, *199 Years of Augusta's Library* (1949). He has collected much other historical data on colonial Augusta from which he expects to compile a chronology of his native city. A prominent participant in civic affairs, he was a leading force in the local political reforms of 1946.

The Conqueror's Stone (1927), his first novel, an adventure story laid in the Carolinas in 1766, tells of the return of long-lost Nicholas Waine to his father's plantation on Hilton Head Island; he brings with him a pirate captain and a ship of pirate gold. *Visa to France* (1930) is the story of Clement Train, an American novelist, during a summer at a French seaside resort, where he becomes involved in the near-tragedy of a young American pair and numerous European visitors.

The Square Root of Valentine (1932) tells of the struggles of a young man to bring peace out of the conflict within himself between the poetry of his spirit and the materialism of his employment; on a summer morning he plays truant from Wall Street and, pursuing many half-suspected truths of religion, science, art, and love, he moves finally to the solution of his conflict. *Siesta* (1935) draws a portrait of an Alabama city in the stifling heat of a summer drought; the stories of numerous southerners interlock with those of several northern visitors. The intense realism shows impartially how the Deep South lives and thinks.

To the Market Place (1938) recounts the fate of a group of young people from New England, Kentucky, and the deep South who have come to New York to sell their wares in the market place in the glamorous days of the late 1920's. *Colonel Effingham's Raid* (1943) brings home to his native town in Georgia a retired army colonel who, unused to civilian ways, is scandalized by political corruption and enters into battle against it armed with little more than the sometimes embarrassing weapon of integrity.

The Lightwood Tree (1947) is the story of George Cliatt, a middle-aged teacher, who dares champion an unpopular civic cause in a southern city of today; the courage of his action and the cause for which he sacrifices himself are shown in their historical development through other critical moments in 1863, 1783, and 1742 in the city's two-hundred-year-long history. These flashbacks portray courageous Americans of earlier days serving the cause of justice and liberty with sacrificial ardor.

INGLIS (CLARK) FLETCHER

Artist: Elizabeth Dodd

was born in 1888 in Alton, Illinois, and grew up on Illinois soil, although her ancestral roots were in North Carolina. She attended the public schools of Alton and the Washington University School of Fine Arts in St. Louis. After completing her education, she journeyed to the West Coast, spending years in California, Washington, and Alaska. Out of her Alaskan experiences came a book which was thrown away during a fit of housecleaning. She went to Africa to study native customs and witchcraft. The entire trip involved some forty thousand miles of travel by train, boat, bushcar, dugout canoe, and motor lorry; she was carried in a machila, a hammock slung over the shoulders of the native bearers, and sometimes she sailed in primitive Arab dhows. Back in the United States, Mrs. Fletcher turned to writing and to lecturing widely on her African experience. One day in San Marino, California, she went to the Henry E. Huntington Library to see what she could discover about her Carolina ancestors. Her casual interest in her forebears led her imagination to the Carolina tidewater, and she spent the next six years in writing and research for her first novel on colonial Carolina. The Fletchers then moved to North Carolina, living at Clarendon Plantation, lent them by the owner. During their stay they found a place of their own in Chowan County, Bandon Plantation on the Chowan River near Edenton. They moved into their home in December, 1944, and there they live and work.

Mrs. Fletcher combines with all the necessary qualities of romantic drama a close and correct attention to historical detail. Her thorough study of original documents—old manuscripts, court records, letters, diaries, and wills—lends accuracy to her historical novels.

Out of Mrs. Fletcher's African experience came her first two books: *The White Leopard* (1931), an adventure story of Stephen Murdoch in the steaming tropic heat of the African bush; and *Red Jasmine* (1932), in which a British couple go on an important diplomatic mission to Aziziland, where the natives invade the English community.

Raleigh's Eden (1940), Mrs. Fletcher's first historical novel, deals with the rising tide of revolt against King George III and against taxation without representation. The story concerns plantation life in the fertile land in the Albemarle Sound region of North Carolina from 1765 to the end of the Revolutionary War. Adam Rutledge and Mary Warden, representatives of two aristocratic families, are the principal characters. *Men of Albemarle* (1942), a study of morals and manners in colonial America, has for its setting North Carolina in the years from 1710 to 1712. The theme is the fight for "liberty under law" and the establishment of the English common law in America.

Lusty Wind for Carolina (1944), an historical novel of the Huguenot settlers on the Cape Fear River, depicts the struggle to rid the sea of its pirates and open the trade routes from the plantations to world markets. *Toil of the Brave* (1946) also has as its background the southern campaign of the Revolution; it opens shortly after the terrible winter at Valley Forge and closes with the Battle of King's Mountain on October 7, 1780. Captain Huntley, a liaison officer for George Washington, is the hero. *Roanoke Hundred* (1948) is an account of the first settlement of Englishmen in America; it is the story of a group of 108 men led by Sir Richard Grenville in 1585 to Roanoke Island. Besides describing the colonizing venture, it tells the story of Grenville and his family in Cornwall. *Bennett's Landing* (1950) concerns the strife between Roundhead and Cavalier in England and the successful colonization of the New World by opponents of Cromwell.

ESTHER FORBES

was born in Westborough, near Worcester, Massachusetts, into a solid New England family whose interests were focused on literature, law, and education, and whose hobbies ranged about the history and quaint antiquities of an earlier and more exciting New England. One of her ancestors, Rebecca Chamberlain, died in jail in Cambridge, Massachusetts, while imprisoned as a "witch." Miss Forbes' father was a judge; gardening and study of the Near East were two of his hobbies. When she went west in 1916 to study for two years at the University of Wisconsin, where she gained perspective to view her background with detachment, she already had in the family attic a trunk literally stuffed with manuscripts of the stories she had composed during her school days. At the university she wrote "Breakneck Hill," a short story which was selected as one of the best of the year by the O. Henry Memorial award committee.

In 1920, when she joined the editorial staff of the Houghton Mifflin Company, book publishers, her associates immediately recognized not only a stern and uncompromizing critic, but also a writer with a strong and creative imagination. Always a rapid and concentrated worker, she completed her first novel during this period, the result, she says, of "Wednesday afternoons and Saturday mornings at home." Yet she rewrites carefully and discards so much that she has the feeling she is a slow writer. She spent seven years on *Paradise* and five years on *The Running of the Tide*. Her biography, *Paul Revere and the World He Lived In* (1942), was awarded the Pulitzer prize in history and was a Book-of-the-Month-Club selection. On the completion of that book she took a long vacation in New Mexico. For young readers she has written *America's Paul Revere* (with Lynd Ward, 1942) and *Johnny Tremain* (1943), the story of an apprentice during the Revolutionary War, which brought her the Newbery medal in 1944. In 1946 she wrote the text for *The Boston Book,* a volume of pictures and documentation with photographs by Arthur Griffin. She is a fellow of the American Academy of Arts and Letters, and five colleges have honored her with the degree of Doctor of Literature. For many years she has lived in Worcester and there does her writing.

With the zest and zealous passion of the scholar and historian, she investigates every detail of the period about which she plans to write, and then invests the stolid facts of history with an imaginative glow that imbues them with a living reality. In an essay on the historical novel she has stated that the historical romance, the type she writes so admirably, is first, foremost, and always a novel; that it should be judged by no other standard; and that it must avoid the danger of being swallowed up in any pattern, especially the pattern of the hero as master of the forces operating in his generation. Most of her books have a leading character who is a victim of circumstances and not their master. Honesty and freshness must mark an author's presentation of the most enduring of human qualities, dynamic aspiration and integrity in the midst of changing conditions. Romantic decoration and gaily colored storytelling cannot be entirely dispensed with, but these trappings must not overshadow the lifelike qualities of characters who reflect the eternal basic problems of man's relation to God, to nature, and to his fellow men. The era in which the story is located, therefore, is almost entirely secondary. What is important is the degree of truth, of art, and of illumination which a writer can bring to it.

O, Genteel Lady (1926), her first novel, tells about Lanice Bardeen, a fashionable young lady of Boston in the days of Holmes, Longfellow, and Emerson; she travels to Europe, meets the Robert Brownings in Italy and George Eliot and Tennyson in England. This novel was the third book distributed by the newly established Book-of-the-Month Club. *A Mirror for Witches* (1928) is about Doll Bilby, the small daughter of parents burned on the charge of witchcraft at Mont Hoël in Brittany about 1650. She is brought to Massachusetts, and soon she is accused of being under demonic control.

Miss Marvel (1935) concerns two sisters, Gwendolyne and Angelica Marvel, who in a male-scarce Massachusetts town build a protective wall around them and live in a dream world. *Paradise* (1937) is an historical novel about the Parre family in the town of Canaan in the Massachusetts Bay Colony in the years after 1639. Jude Parre builds "Paradise," his home, and rises to eminence. His son brings an English wife who creates trouble. The Indians nearly destroy them in King Philip's War. *The General's Lady* (1938), set in the Revolutionary War, concerns a Tory girl who marries an American general to save the family fortune. Later she loves a British officer, and matters grow complex when the general is murdered.

Johnny Tremaine (1943) is a story of Boston at the beginning of the Revolutionary War and concerns a boy who burns his hand when a crucible of silver breaks. He helps Paul Revere start on his ride. *The Running of the Tide* (1948) pictures Salem, Massachusetts, from 1790 to 1815 in the heyday of its glory as the home port of famous sailing vessels, when the Inman and Crowninshield families sent clipper ships to the four quarters of the globe. This work was awarded the Metro-Goldwyn-Mayer novel prize, which carries a minimum award of one hundred and fifty thousand dollars. It was also a Book-of-the-Month-Club selection.

KATHRYN FORBES

Max Yavno

was born in San Francisco on March 10, 1909, the daughter of Della Jesser Anderson, whose mother was a Norwegian immigrant, and Leon Ellis Anderson, whose mother was a Forbes of Forbestown. She attended San Francisco schools, and in 1926 married Robert McLean. They have two sons, Robert, Jr., and Richard, and have lived in Burlingame, California, since 1929. Miss Forbes has done publicity work for clubs, and has also written scripts for radio.

Her first book, *Mama's Bank Account* (1943), contains a number of sketches about a Norwegian couple that come to San Francisco, have three children, and grow into good Americans. The mother ingeniously triumphs over obstacles and molds a beautiful spirit into the family. *Transfer Point* (1947) is about Alice Barton, a ten-year-old San Francisco girl, who in 1919 tries to get aboard a trolley car without paying and who in 1921 pays her fare as a symbol of her growing up.

FELIX C. FORREST

Artist: Albert Lake

was born on July 11, 1913, in Milwaukee, Wisconsin. He has spent much of his life abroad, but he has also lived in a wide variety of places in the United States. By profession he is a government scientist. During World War II, he spent three and a half years in the army. Apart from professional activities, his interests include writing novels, collecting out-of-the-way phonograph records, sampling foreign cookery, and pursuing a keen, though non-professional, interest in psychiatry.

Ria (1947), his first novel, is about an American woman's search, with the aid of a psychiatrist, for the cause of a numbing pain in her right hand; she traces it to an incident in her sixteenth year when she became involved in the fate of a German officer of World War I. There is allegorical significance in the events. *Carola* (1948) is about Carola Lainger, an American girl married to a Chinese man, and her attempt to adapt herself to Oriental customs, especially the rigid family rule. The story, told in flashbacks, includes much melodramatic incident about revolution, murder, and sickness.

PAT FRANK

was born in Chicago, Illinois, on May 5, 1907. After attending Peddie School in Hightstown, New Jersey, from 1920 to 1925, he spent one year at the University of Florida. From 1926 to 1928 he was a reporter on the Jacksonville, Florida, *Journal,* and then moved to New York to work for the *World* and the *Evening Journal.* From 1932 to 1940 he covered the State and War departments and the White House for the Washington *Herald.* In 1940 he revealed the Nazi penetration into the Western Hemisphere. Joining Robert Sherwood in what became the Office of War Information, Mr. Frank shortly was despatched to Australia, where he served from 1942 to 1944 as a special assistant to the American Minister and to the Allied Political Warfare Council. After a period of service in Turkey, he became a war correspondent on the Italian front and remained with the Fifth Army until the victory on the Po River. He reached Milan in time to see Mussolini hanging by his heels. After that he saw the war in France, attended the Potsdam conference, went into Austria and Hungary, resigned, and came home in 1945 to write fiction. He married June Mickel in 1928; they have three children.

Mr. Adam (1946), his first novel, is part satire and part fantasy. The story concerns an atomic explosion that has been set off accidentally in Mississippi and has had the amazing effect of rendering all human beings sterile. The end of the human race seems imminent until Homer Adam, a geologist, appears. He was safely protected by being in a Colorado lead mine at the time of the explosion and was unaffected by the atomic rays. He becomes immediately valuable as parent of a new race; the Army wishes to declare him its secret property. *An Affair of State* (1948) satirizes the United States Department of State and bureaucracy in Washington in a story of Jeff Baker, a young official in the American Embassy in Budapest, who discovers a Russian plot to overthrow Stalin, but who is under suspicion because of his friendships.

WALDO FRANK

Lotte Jacobi

was born on August 25, 1889, in Long Branch, New Jersey. At Yale his excellent scholarship won him membership in Phi Beta Kappa and his bachelor's and master's degrees in 1911. After a summer spent on a ranch in Wyoming, he returned to New York to work on the *Evening Post.* Later he transferred to the *Times.* In 1916 he founded and was editor for one year of *Seven Arts* magazine. He has traveled widely in Europe and in Latin America. Generally recognized as an authority on the culture of South America, he was invited in 1948 by the government of Venezuela to come to that country to prepare a new biography of the great liberator, Simón Bolívar. He has contributed many stories and essays to magazines and has written a number of books dealing with art, literature, and cultural history. His interpretations of American civilization, *Our America* (1919), *The Re-discovery of America* (1929), and of the Hispanic world, *Virgin Spain* (1926) and *America Hispana* (1931), are accepted as authoritative. Two volumes of his lectures delivered in the universities of Latin America exist only in Spanish editions; but most of his books, both the fiction and the cultural criticism, have been translated into the leading European languages, including Russian.

Mr. Frank has been identified with left-wing social and political groups, and for many years was a contributing editor of *The New Republic.* His wide acquaintance with members of the liberal parties in foreign countries has given him, at times, the position of a spokesman. His lecture tours through South America have brought him considerable attention. In April, 1935, he participated in a three-day congress of American revolutionary writers in New York City. Mr. Frank was unanimously elected chairman of a new League of American Writers, which became affiliated with the International Union of Revolutionary Writers. He believes that "Socialism must come, and must be fought for," but he has his own definition of socialism.

Although he tried in those days to work with the communists, whom he considered the vanguard of the revolutionary movement, he always disagreed with the ideology of Marxism. At the time of the first Moscow trials, he broke finally with the orthodox communists, and his book, *Chart for Rough Waters* (1940), contains a severe attack on Stalinism. Earlier he had predicted the failure of the entire socialist movement unless it achieved what he calls "the dimension of depth," by which he means religious and mystical values. Mr. Frank's novels are based on an aesthetic vision of life which embodies these values. He regards the novel as essentially "the poem," and has always been hostile to the realistic schools which limit the world to "the empirical reports of the five senses." "Realism," he says, "is not real."

Many studies of Waldo Frank's aesthetic conception of the novel have been published, most of them in Europe, Russia, and Latin America; but it is difficult to compress in a few words its essential and distinguishing features, since what is involved is a basic and original vision of reality. The traditional novelist (and this includes such moderns as Joyce, Lawrence, and Proust) presents the individual to the reader as a separate integer combined more or less complexly with other individual entities. Mr. Frank's view is different. The individual for him scarcely exists, except in the barely emergent, contingent phase of a life organism that includes the time, the place, the society in which the individual is immersed. All this vaguely discloses the cosmic; and only as the cosmic becomes explicit and conscious does the individual become a real person. The best of Mr. Frank's fictions, particularly the three major "symphonic novels" beginning with *The Death and Birth of David Markand,* are stories of this emergence.

It must not be inferred, however, from the quality of vision and of attitude toward life which these novels all reveal, that they are didactic. They are primarily stories—dramatic, lyrical, and epic; but the aesthetic form in which they are molded depends on the author's philosophy, one might say on his religious vision.

The Unwelcome Man (1917), his first novel, deals with the stunting of an individual's life by outmoded precedent. Quincy Burt, an unwanted child in a large Long Island family, finds his idealism out of place at home, in college, and in business. He drifts into mediocrity. *The Dark Mother* (1920) describes the spiritual problems and adventures of two young men who come to New York, one from the West, one from New England. *City Block* (1922) has been called a collective novel. It is a design of related short stories dealing with the lives of men and women dwelling in a single poor street of New York City. Each story reveals the characters at some climax, where their separate lives become spiritually joined. *Rahab* (1922) tells the story of a romantic southern woman who wanders to New York after her life is wrecked. She sinks in the social scale, becoming finally the keeper of a house of assignation; but she never loses her sense of spiritual purity or her need to seek truth and God. In *Holiday* (1923) the dramatic conflict between blacks and whites in the deep South is depicted: the attraction between races as well as their hostilities is described. It is the story of a lynching. In *Chalk Face* (1924), a mystery story, Dr. John Mark tries to relate his spirit to the rhythm of the universe. He makes his will so strong that in his second self, his "chalk face," he commits murder. With this book the phase of what Mr. Frank calls his "lyrical novels" ended.

After a long interval devoted to works of cultural criticism and history, he published the first of what he entitles his "symphonic novels." *The Death and Birth of David Markand* (1934) is about a wealthy businessman whose desire for higher values brings him into touch with every liberal idea in 1913; he finds in Marxism a valid answer and orients his life by this revolutionary doctrine. At the close, having "died," he is spiritually born. *The Bridegroom Cometh* (1938) concerns the economic and spiritual factors which keep the individual from achieving fulfillment. It is the story of two New England sisters who eventually come to New York. One ends tragically after becoming involved with the gangster world of the prohibition period; the other, after an unhappy marriage to a wealthy and sensitive young business man, identifies herself with the working class. For a time she joins the communist movement, but breaks with this when she comes to understand its want of respect for personal values. Her adventures are an odyssey of her struggles for spiritual birth and parallel those of David Markand.

Summer Never Ends (1944) shows how a lawyer in love with a working girl finds in the social demand for success his tragic undoing. *Island in the Atlantic* (1946) covers three generations of life in New York City from the Civil War to World War I. The city is the real hero—or heroine—of the story. The epic is developed through the relationship of two boys who meet for the first time in the draft riots of 1863. One is the son of a wealthy and powerful Knickerbocker family; the other is a Jew whose parents have emigrated from Europe. They meet again later and become law partners. Their lives and those of their families involve all the conspicuous elements of the New York world, including politics, business, culture, and revolution.

The Invaders (1948) technically marks a return to the more lyrical form of the early novels, but with a new directness and maturity of vision. It concerns a man with a deep world consciousness whose home in New England, where he is quietly at work, is invaded by individuals who represent the greatest world problems in intimate form. The ensuing tragedy reveals the hopelessness of the efforts to solve the troubles of the international world so long as the identical causes of conflict and destruction remain rooted in the individuals who compose it.

ROSE FRANKEN

was born in Texas in 1898, the daughter of Michael and Hannah Lewin. At an early age she was brought to New York, where she has made her home ever since. She received her education at the Ethical Culture School and from private tutors. In 1917 she was married to Dr. S. W. A. Franken. They had three children, Paul, John, and Peter. Some years after Dr. Franken's death she married her present husband, William Brown Meloney V. Mrs. Franken began her writing career with short stories, and later she turned to novels and plays. The play "Claudia" (1941) has been immensely popular, as has been the Claudia saga, of which some two million copies have been sold.

Mrs. Franken's first novel, *Pattern,* was

published in 1925 and met with great critical acclaim. Then she turned to plays and wrote "Another Language" (1932). The novel *Twice Born* (1935) was later dramatized into the play "Outrageous Fortune" (1944); some critics consider it her best play. Then came the Claudia novels, interspersed with the plays "Doctors Disagree" (1940) and "Soldier's Wife" (1945). In addition, there appeared several novels written in collaboration with Mr. Meloney.

It is interesting to note that Mrs. Franken possesses an equal facility in writing novels, short stories, plays, movies, and radio sketches. It is her belief that a basic sense of form and composition permits one to function in all types of literary creation.

Pattern (1925), her first novel, is the story of Virginia Lee, whose youthful marriage causes her to depend too much upon her mother. She must grow up and adjust herself to mature responsibilities. *Twice Born* (1935) is about an orphan son of a Russian violinist, Darry Kavinki, who lives in a tenement in a constant state of friction with his brother. *Of Great Riches* (1937) tells about the marriage of Denny Peters, age twenty-four, and Theodora, age eighteen, and their early years together in a modest New York apartment house. Her success as a novelist lifts these comparatively shallow people into a wholly different society.

Claudia (1939) is the first volume in a saga of the married life of David Naughton, an architect, and of Claudia Brown, an inexperienced girl, two wholesome youngsters whose love for each other is greater than their differences of opinion. The Claudia stories have an earthy lustiness seasoned with the basic salt of comedy which makes their appeal universal. This book covers four years in the life of these wholesome young people who are anxious to retain their happiness. *Claudia and David* (1940) pictures their removal to an apartment, a visit to Hollywood, and the help given by the maid, Bertha, in the birth of a second child. *Another Claudia* (1943) shows Claudia growing up and having a third baby. David enlists after Pearl Harbor, and Claudia suffers a breakdown. *Young Claudia* (1946) pictures David's return from the war, Claudia's experiences as an actress, and her befriending a teen-age girl. *The Marriage of Claudia* (1948) pictures the family on a farm, where a third boy is born. David learns that he has tuberculosis and that he must take a rest cure. *From Claudia to David* (1950) depicts the time the family spends in the Adirondacks during the convalescence of David. He makes a good recovery, but he is unwilling to resume his profession until the accidental death of their oldest child stirs him to new energy.

BENEDICT FREEDMAN

was born in New York City on December 19, 1919, the son of David Freedman, who was one of the earliest and most successful comedy writers for radio. David Freedman invented the "Baby Snooks" character for Fanny Brice and wrote the original Eddie Cantor show and many other works. Mr. Freedman attended Public School 87 and Townsend Harris High School in New York City. He left Columbia University after three years, but with a prize in logic, to study at Curtiss-Wright Technical Institute, where he received a degree in aeronautical engineering. Until his marriage he did editorial work on a mathematics magazine, was clerk for a consulting actuary, and performed miscellaneous tasks in radio and motion pictures. In 1939 he went to Russia in an attempt to collect royalties on his father's novel, *Mendel,* which had been a best seller; on the way he visited Japan and China. When Germany attacked Poland, he returned to the United States. During the war years he taught mathematics and worked for an aircraft company. He has been a comedy writer for the Red Skelton radio program since its beginning.

Benedict Freedman collaborates with his wife, Nancy, and a list of their joint works is given in her biography, which follows.

NANCY FREEDMAN

was born on July 4, 1920, in Evanston, Illinois, the daughter of an eminent Chicago surgeon, Dr. Hartley F. Mars. After attending grade school in Evanston and Los Angeles, she completed her high-school work at Hollywood Professional School. For two years she attended Los Angeles City College; for one year she studied art at the University of Southern California, and for one year at the Art Institute of Chicago. Until her marriage to Benedict Freedman on June 29, 1941, she appeared on stage and radio as Nancy Mars, and took leading roles in Max Reinhardt's productions of "Faust" and "The Miracle." She played in a stock company for several seasons, worked as a dramatic actress on the Texaco Star Theater and on radio Station KNX.

Mr. and Mrs. Freedman work together in writing plays, short stories, and novels. They begin by preparing a complete and detailed outline. There follows a period of research in which every unfamiliar subject in a proposed book is thoroughly studied. For example, for *Mrs. Mike* they needed to learn about bears, wolves, and Irishmen. Each writes the scenes in which he feels the most interest and then the two review every sentence of the final version. Their literary criteria are simplicity, freshness, and drama.

Back to the Sea (1942), published under the pen name of "David N. Benedict," is a novelette of the Norwegian resistance. *Mrs. Mike* (1947) is the story of the struggle of a young Irish girl from Boston in the pioneer country of her husband, Royal Canadian Mounted Police Sergeant Mike Flannigan. *This and No More* (1950) is a novel of struggle and acceptance leading to a happy marriage in New York City in the period from 1915 to 1930.

JOSEPH FREEMAN

was born on October 7, 1897, in the Ukraine, Russia, and was brought to the United States in 1904. He became naturalized in 1920, a year after he received his bachelor's degree from Columbia College, where he specialized in literature, history, and philosophy, captained the varsity debating team, wrote for campus publications, and won membership in Phi Beta Kappa. During World War I he was in the Students' Army Training Corps. Following graduation he became a newspaperman, covering the United States, France, England, Italy, Russia, Germany, Cuba, and Mexico. He has been public-relations counsel for civic groups, and has edited literary and political magazines. He was a co-founder and editor of *The New Masses* from 1926 to 1937, and of *The Partisan Review* from 1934 to 1936. He has lectured extensively, been active in the theater, "ghosted" speeches for leading political figures, and worked in Hollywood and for the radio. In the summer of 1945 he toured with USO in France, Germany, and Austria.

He began publishing verse and fiction as a fifteen-year-old high-school student in Brooklyn. Since then hundreds of poems, critical essays, articles, book reviews, and stories have come from his pen. He has published books on American foreign policy and Russia. His autobiography, *An American Testament* (1936), has been compared with that of Henry Adams. The central theme of his novels is man's struggle with the forces of history and of his own nature: a struggle for love, justice, freedom, and salvation.

His first novel, *Never Call Retreat* (1943), is the story of one man's adventures, physical and spiritual, through the perilous jungle of the twentieth century. The adventures include love, marriage, two world wars, communism, fascism, university life, a concentration camp, dreams about the French Revolution, visions about early Christianity, flight to America, and readjustment to the world. Because the hero is a history professor, his life is a long search for historical analogies that will illuminate the present, for truths and virtues that will lead man beyond his primeval heritage of pride, corruption, and cruelty to mastery of himself and his future.

The Long Pursuit (1947) is a comedy about a Hollywood show which tours Germany five weeks after V-E Day. It is a picaresque story of a producer who pursues an army nurse across Europe while battling with members of his cast as to "who shall dominate whom." The rapid action is set against bombed cities, hilarious GI's, American, French, and German women, and the moral holiday which followed the war. Through the comedy there surges the conflict between tyranny and freedom, and between evil and the moral law. The book is in the hard-boiled tradition.

PHILIP FREUND

was born in Vancouver, British Columbia, on February 5, 1909. He graduated from Cornell in 1929 and subsequently received his master's degree there in 1932. He has been on the faculties of Cornell University, the College of the City of New York, Hunter College in New York, and the University of British Columbia. For four years during World War II he was with the army pictorial service in the motion-picture division. Immediately afterward he was consulting editor for Young America Films and motion-picture consultant for the Anti-Defamation League. For some years he lived in Europe. His first book, *The Merry Communist* (1934), is anti-Marxist, frivolous in tone but serious in intent. *How to Become a Literary Critic* (1947) contains essays on Henry James, Melville, Conrad, and others. His poetry is collected in *Private Speech* (1949). His short stories are in *The Show* (1935), *The Young Greek and The Creole* (1944), *Three Exotic Tales* (1945), and *A Man of Taste* (1949). Several of his shorter plays have been published, and two of his full-length plays have won prizes. He has written extensively in the field of the drama and has experimented with narrative techniques in presenting speculations about contemporary art, science, and religion. His characters also debate politics.

The Evening Heron (1937), his first published novel, is a study of the continuing influence of medievalism in modern life. The action shifts from Paris during Léon Daudet's Royalist uprising to an island wilderness in Michigan. The central character is a successful actress who leaves the Paris stage in 1927 for a more contemplative life after experiencing a tragic occurrence. *Dreams of Youth* (1938), on the theme of futility, portrays a disillusioned, weary, French novelist, whose tenaciously held opinions influence a number of students at an American university where he lectures.

Book of Kings (1938) begins a trilogy of novels about the Lauer and Zoltan families in the East Seventies and Eighties of New York City. Mike Lauer is a Hungarian who wants to be a German like his neighbors. His brother, Louis, a minor politician who calls himself King of Yorkville, looks down upon his in-laws, the Zoltans. A nephew, Jacob, feels superior to his father's dairy business and adopts a similar haughty manner. *The Dark*

Shore (1941) pictures a disillusioned, Texas-born Jewish boy who, after a visit to Spain, finds peace in Morocco. *Edward Zoltan* (1946), a sequel to *Book of Kings,* describes the experiences of a wealthy young member of the Zoltan family who interests himself in the world of art and the ballet with disillusioning results. *Stephanie's Son* (1947) completes the Zoltan trilogy and concerns Michael Lauer, Edward Zoltan's seventeen-year-old cousin, who is mystical by nature and is converted by the woman leader of an unorthodox religious cult, one of many that flourish in New York City. The trilogy has been published as *The Zoltans* (1948).

Easter Island (1947) is the tale of three men of different temperaments and interests, one of them an anthropologist, who are thrown together in 1914 on a desolate island of ill repute. It is a novel concerned primarily with the problem of good and evil. The anthropologist and a rancher fight against the spiritual contamination of the island. A half-mad Peruvian does not; he spends himself in lunatic sadism, the unpleasant results of which form the basis of the action.

ELIZABETH HOLLISTER FROST

was born in Rochester, New York, the daughter of Emily Weed Barnes and George Cooper Hollister. Her great-grandfather was Thurlow Weed, friend of Lincoln and Ambassador to England during the Civil War. She was educated at St. Timothy's School at Catonsville, Maryland, and in youth lived between Rochester and Nantucket Island, where the family has spent part of each year for four generations. She married Eliott Frost, psychologist and writer, who died in 1926. To him are dedicated three books of verse: *The Lost Lyrist* (1928), *Hovering Shadow* (1929), and *The Closed Gentian* (1931). Through her second marriage to Walter Dabney Blair she has come into a family of painters and architects, some of whom live in the romantic village of St. Cirq-la-Popie, in the old Kingdom of Navarre, where they paint and write in this Gothic fastness as though they were living in the twelfth century.

"A novel is really a dream and arises from the same source," Mrs. Frost has said; "it is through the marriage of dream and reason, of fantasy and reality that art forms take shape. We all dream half our life. asleep; the artist dreams the rest of his life, awake. As André Gide says, 'The most beautiful things are those that madness prompts and reason writes. It is essential to remain between the two, close to madness when you dream, and close to reason when you write.' I write because I believe the marriage of fantasy and reason, and the art forms it produces offer a natural and a needed expression of the conscience and grandeur of the race."

The Wedding Ring (1940), her first novel, depicts with simplicity the strange lives of a group of peasants in St. Cirq-la-Popie in France. It points out the nobilities and savagery of an isolated people motivated by the basic passions of life. *This Side of Land* (1942) is the story of the early English settlers on the Island of Nantucket and has for its *leitmotif* the elements of birth, mating, death, and the harvest. It is not a historical novel in the usual sense of the phrase, but achieves the paradox of touching the universal while the human story remains so individual as to be unique. It is laid in Mrs. Frost's own house, built in 1722, on the moor at Nantucket. *Mary and the Spinner* (1946) is a novel about the Virgin Mary, and tells the greatest of all stories obliquely. The occurrences of the night Christ was born are innocently recounted by five of Mary's friends. It has been hailed as a Christmas classic for Jew, Catholic, and Protestant alike and was a choice of the Catholic Book-of-the-Month Club in January, 1947.

FRANCES FROST

was born in St. Albans, Vermont, on August 3, 1905, the daughter of Amos and Susan Frost. She attended Middlebury College from 1923 to 1926 and then was a newspaper reporter before completing her college education at the University of Vermont in 1931. For a time she taught the writing of poetry at the latter institution. By her first husband, W. Gordon Blackburn, whom she wed in 1926, she has a son and daughter. Her books of poetry include *Hemlock Wall* (1929), *Blue Harvest* (1931), *Woman of the Earth* (1934), and *Little Whistler* (1949). *Windy Foot at the County Fair* (1947) is a juvenile novel.

Her writings describe the beauty of New England scenery. Her prose has a lyric quality and a homely robustness of humor. Her best characterizations are of elderly people who live on farms or in small villages.

Innocent Summer (1936), her first novel, captures the spirit of childhood in this story of six boys and girls in a Vermont village from June to September. One dies of tuberculosis, others feel the beginning of love, and one learns that he is an illegitimate child. *Yoke of Stars* (1939) tells the life story of Judith York from childhood in Vermont through college to an unfortunate marriage and her return home at the age of twenty-eight to raise her children alone and to achieve fulfillment at last. *Kate Trimingham* (1940) tells about a Vermont music teacher in her seventies who gives her pupils goodies. One day a child's ambiguous suicide note turns the town against her. *Village of Glass* (1942) has a young poet cry out against the senselessness of war, and yet he goes out as an airplane pilot.

IOLA FULLER

was born on January 25, 1906, at Marcellus, Michigan. She won Phi Beta Kappa honors at the University of Michigan, and while doing graduate work there in creative writing in 1939 she received the Avery Hopwood award. She is married to R. A. McCoy and resides in New Mexico.

The Loon Feather (1940), her first novel, is a story of the fur-trading days on Mackinac Island in Lake Huron, and of the conflict between the whites and Indians on that frontier. This novel was praised by S. V. Benét for "the author's genuine and imaginative feeling" and for her ability "to show history as something lived out through the daily lives of people rather than as a hair-raising succession of escapes and adventure." The story is told by Oneta, who is a daughter of Tecumseh, and who lives for a time in the home of her mother's second husband, a French trader, and then in the tents of the Indians. Although the life of Mackinac is portrayed in all its variety, interest centers in Oneta's unfolding character as an old civilization is replaced by a new one.

The Shining Trail (1943) is a story, told from the Indian viewpoint, of Black Hawk, the famous Indian chief, and of the Black Hawk War in the summer of 1832. The warrior is pictured as a man who lived nobly and fought valiantly, and the Sauk Indians, whom he led, are shown to be a people struggling to survive. Howard Fast, who praised this historical novel about Indians as one of the best he had ever read, stated: "The book is the forest, the campfires, the sparks trailing toward the sky, the complete and wonderful identification of a people with their surroundings. In a sense, she has merged both her style and the rhythm of her prose into one with the subject matter of her writing. . . . This is a really beautiful book." The portrayal of Indian customs is admirable.

MARGARET FULLER

was born in Brooklyn, New York, on January 23, 1872, but since childhood has made her home in Norwich, Connecticut. Because she was too delicate to attend school, her father directed her education. She had one year at Norwich Free Academy and began the study of Greek and Latin. On several occasions she made long winter visits to an uncle's home in South Carolina, and resided a year in England with an aunt. Her first visit to Paris occurred at this time. The poet Edmund Clarence Stedman was a neighbor in Norwich, and for five years she was his literary secretary; about him she wrote a biography, *A New England Childhood* (1917). A humorous story in verse about Noah's Ark is in *The Complete History of the Deluge* (1936). *It Is All So Simple* (1947) is a small book about words.

One World at a Time (1922), her first novel, tells her own experiences as a child in visiting her uncle's home on the Bellefount plantation in South Carolina. He is pictured as a trustful yet absent-minded person who dominated the household. *Alma* (1927), the first volume in a trilogy on mother love, portrays a Danish cook of forty who immigrates to the "free country" to find a husband. The quest of this woman symbolizes the search of all who seek fulfillment. *Her Son* (1929), based in part upon the life of Miss Fuller's father, describes Laura Wolcott's life from the time she persuaded her mother to put lace on her petticoats to the proud moment she leaves the White House where her son is President. In her heart has burned the ambition to create a boy in the image of greatness.

The Golden Roof (1930), which completes the trilogy, portrays Nikole Hansen, a woman who devotes her life to the care of her grandmother, her husband, wounded soldiers in World War I, and her young son. Finally in America there comes a prospcct of lasting happiness. *This Awakening* (1948) tells a family legend of Miss Fuller's aunt's devotion to the sweetheart of her youth. The setting is in London in 1850. The style is notable for its simplicity and power.

MARTHEDITH FURNAS

Underwood & Underwood

was born on March 18, 1904, in Indianapolis, Indiana, where she went to public school and Tudor Hall, a school for girls. In her sophomore year she left Vassar College because she no longer wanted to study required courses in mathematics. After a year at Columbia University, she stayed in New York and worked as a dress model in a Fifth Avenue shop and in wholesale dress houses. She was also a fashion reporter for *Women's Wear*. In 1927 she went to Ceylon, India, where she was married to an employee of a large importing house; it was here that their daughter was born. The family returned to St. Louis for a year and then went back to India again. In 1931 they moved to Charleston, South Carolina. After her husband's death in 1940, she moved to Connecticut and eventually New York.

Her first novel, *The Night is Coming* (1939), tells the story of Stella Buchanan who takes over, at his death, her father's Illinois store and in the next forty years proves herself a shrewd business woman. *A Serpent's Tooth* (1946) is a chronicle of four generations of a midwestern family, with emphasis upon the childhood, growth, and rebellion of a girl against her unfriendly mother. *The Far Country* (1947) tells the story of the transcontinental migration to California in 1846 as set down in the diary of Unwin Shaw, an invalid, who as a youth was a storekeeper in Kentucky.

GABRIEL *to* GUTHRIE

GILBERT WOLF GABRIEL

Margaret Bourke-White

was born on January 18, 1890, in Brooklyn, New York. He graduated from Williams College in 1912. His writing career began in the same year as a cub reporter on the New York *Sun;* later he was its literary editor from 1915 to 1917 and music critic from 1917 to 1924. Within six years he had taken two leaves of absence: one to study music in Rome with Respighi, and the other to serve in World War I as a second lieutenant of infantry. The postwar period found him back on the *Sun* covering concerts and operas. In 1924 he transferred to the *Telegram,* returned to the *Sun* a year later, and from 1925 to 1929 worked for the *American.* He was also dramatic critic for several magazines. In World War II Mr. Gabriel was a public-relations officer in the Office of War Information in Alaska; he prepared the first propaganda leaflets to be dropped over Kiska and Attu. From May to September, 1944, he was stationed in London as deputy chief in charge of publications for the Psychological Warfare Division. He does his writing in his home near Brewster, New York, where he lives with his wife Ada Gabriel, the painter and lithographer.

His non-fiction books include *The Seven-Branched Candlestick: The Schooldays of a Young American Jew* (1917) and *Great Pianists and Composers* (1927). *The Adventures of Peterkin* (1916) is a children's story.

Jiminy (1922), his first novel, tells how the poetess, Jiminy, and the artist, Benvenuto Renni, try to solve the mystery of the lost sonnets of Raphael and achieve a love for each other. *Brownstone Front* (1924) portrays the burden of respectability and tradition, as symbolized by a house on East Eightieth Street in New York City, weighing down the younger members of a family. *I, John Lewis* (1932) tells the story of a clerk in John Jacob Astor's expedition to establish a fur-trading post at the mouth of the Columbia River in Oregon in 1811.

Great Fortune (1933) ostensibly concerns a playwright who wants a commission to write a drama about a group of acquaintances, but the core of the novel concerns those people who live beyond their means and come to grief in the stock-market collapse in 1929. The playwright learns that his backer has committed suicide, and so his plan to expose the extravagance of wealth-seekers ironically rebounds to affect him. *I Got a Country* (1944) presents much information about Alaska as background for the story of three American soldiers and what the cold northland does to them: a Floridian takes to love and drink; an Illinois man cracks up; and a Brooklyn boy becomes a weather expert.

Love from London (1946) is about three American soldiers rooming in Adelaide Square in London in World War II. Dria, a waitress, falls in love with John Howe Wells, a Boston snob. *I Thee Wed* (1948) tells of the attempt to bring Marie Antoinette from prison in France after the French Revolution to a small community at Azilum in northeastern Pennsylvania near Towanda. The hero is Alan Ruff, a young American surveyor.

FRANCES GAITHER

Lotte Jacobi

was born in Somerville, Tennessee, on May 21, 1889, the daughter of Paul and Annie Jones. Three grandparents were southern-born, but the fourth, her mother's father, was a native of Maine and a graduate of Bowdoin College, where he formed the friendship with a young man from Tennessee which led him into law practice and marriage in that state. When Frances was two years old, her family moved to Corinth, Mississippi, where she grew up and attended public school. She received her college education at the Mississippi State College for Women at Columbus, Mississippi, from which she graduated in 1909. In 1912 she married Rice Gaither, a newspaperman then on the staff of the Mobile, Alabama, *Register*. Later he became editor of the Meridian, Mississippi, *Despatch*. During the early 1920's they lived and wrote at Fairhope, Alabama. Since 1928 they have made their home in New York, where Mr. Gaither is a member of the Sunday staff of the *Times*. She has written all her books in New York.

She did her earlier work in shorter form: some thirty-odd short stories and four masques and pageants, one of which was produced by the University of Virginia at its centennial in 1921. Her first book, *The Painted Arrow* (1931), a Junior Literary Guild selection, is the story of a French boy whom Bienville placed with the Gulf Coast Indians to learn their language and customs. *The Fatal River* (1931) is a biography of the explorer La Salle. *The Scarlet Coat* (1934) and *Little Miss Cappo* (1937) are books for children. All of these except the last grew out of research in southern history in the period of French exploration. A vision of a new world was probably the inspiration of this group of books which, however true to original facts and sources, are essentially romantic in intention and execution.

Little Miss Cappo, which set out to tell the story of a little girl's education by the Moravians at Salem, North Carolina, necessarily began on an Alabama plantation in the early nineteenth century. Research for it brought to the author's eyes a whole body of unexploited, documentary material on daily plantation life and gave her the idea for doing three novels on slavery, which she considers her most important work to date. These are in intention and execution the very opposite of romantic.

Follow the Drinking Gourd (1940) creates the grim, small world of a remote, absentee-owned plantation with its succession of hard-driving overseers and the slaves who have no recourse but to run away. The story of these slaves, the novel does not concern itself with white people except as they touch the fate of the Negroes. *The Red Cock Crows* (1944) describes an abortive slave rebellion, its discovery, and tragic aftermath. The most important character is Scofield, the trusted head man on a rich plantation and a powerful preacher, mystically led to rouse his people against the whites and at last to fall a martyr to the violence he has himself instigated. *Double Muscadine* (1949), a Book-of-the-Month-Club choice, studies the effect of slavery on white people themselves in their most secret hearts and dearest relations. A quadroon woman is being tried on the charge of poisoning her master's family; her lawyer drags into the light the owner's weakness for his light-colored wenches, and there is grief and suffering throughout his household. Syke Berry, the lawyer, the son of a poor farmer, has a lucky hunch and thus frees Aimee, the light-skinned and attractive slave girl who stands wrongfully accused. These three books, each complete in itself and unrelated in persons and story, are chronologically consecutive and, taken together, present a rounded picture of slavery from the underside, examining one by one the forces of destruction at work from within.

PAUL GALLICO

Arne Glantz

was born in New York City on July 26, 1897, the son of parents who had recently immigrated to the United States from Trieste, then a part of Italy but since 1947 a free territory under the jurisdiction of the United Nations. The father had come to America at the age of fourteen as a concert pianist. Ten years later he returned as a solo pianist with American symphony orchestras, and then he decided to remain in New York City as a teacher of piano and composition.

Paul Gallico attended public schools and Columbia College, where he distinguished himself as a cheerleader and a member of the eight-oared crew, which he captained in his senior year. He dropped out of college to serve in the navy as a seaman gunner during World War I, but he finished his course in 1921. A year later Mr. Gallico began working on the New York *Daily News* as a motion-picture reviewer, but soon transferred to the sports department. Becoming sports editor in 1924, he remained with the newspaper a dozen years.

In 1936 he left the *Daily News* to become a free-lance writer. For several summers he was in England, where he wrote his first book, *Farewell to Sport* (1938). His short stories and articles appeared in the major magazines, and his biography, *Lou Gehrig, Pride of the Yankees* (1942), became the basis of a motion picture. Several original stories were also filmed in Hollywood. In 1944 he went to France as a war correspondent of *Cosmopolitan* magazine to report on the Maquis and the American soldiers' activities. He has published two books of short stories, *Golf Is a Friendly Game* (1942) and *Confessions of a Story Writer* (1946). His most successful and best known story is "The Snow Goose," a tale of frustration, love, and sacrifice at the time of the Dunkerque débacle.

Adventures of Hiram Holliday (1939), his first novel, tells of a bespectacled proofreader on a vacation in Europe some months before the outbreak of World War II. His six strange experiences include the kidnaping in London of a dauphin, the capture of a Russian spy in Paris, and equally amazing moments in four other cities. *Secret Front* (1940) continues the exploits of Hiram Holliday, who becomes Warsaw correspondent of a New York newspaper. When the Germans invade Poland, he suffers injuries in a bomb explosion, escapes to Rumania and thence to England for more adventures. *The Lonely* (1949) pictures during Christmas week in 1944 an American lieutenant falling in love with an English girl although he is already engaged to a young Long Island society lady. He comes home to look over the situation and decides on the new love. *The Abandoned* (1950) is about Peter, a boy who cannot resist collecting stray kittens, and his adventures on land and sea.

ERNEST KELLOGG GANN

Harold Mack, Jr.

was born on October 13, 1910, at Lincoln, Nebraska. He graduated from Culver Military Academy and spent two years at Yale. For seventeen years he was a commercial airlines pilot, and during World War II he received a distinguished service award for his record in the Air Transport Command. He resides with his wife and three children in California, where he is the owner of a fleet of tuna boats. "A Nice New Pair of Wings," a story, won the *Collier's* Star Award in 1948. He is also the author of several children's books on aviation.

Island in the Sky (1944), his first novel, is a story of a world inhabited by individuals who have a kinship amounting to a religious vocation. It is concerned with the flight of the *Corsair,* an army transport plane, and its crew of five when they are forced down in the uncharted wastelands of Northern Canada. *Blaze of Noon* (1946) tells about four barnstorming brothers, the Flying MacDonalds, a happy and reckless lot who fly because they like it better than anything else in the world, and about the men who blazed the trail for commercial aviation, flying the mail through days and nights of ice and storm without the aid of modern flight instruments or radio. *Benjamin Lawless* (1948) spans two decades and four continents to describe the life of a man torn between two dreams: the life of adventure and the life of home and security. *Fiddler's Green* (1950) has as its background the West Coast fishing industry and concerns the men who make this industry the dangerous and exciting job that it is.

MARTHA GELLHORN

Lejka Gorska

was born in St. Louis, Missouri. After study at John Burroughs School in St. Louis, she attended Bryn Mawr College in Pennsylvania. During the great depression in 1935 she made a survey of the living conditions of people in the industrial and rural areas of the United States. Much of her time since then has been devoted to international journalism as a correspondent for American magazines. She was in Czechoslovakia at the time of the Munich pact on September 30, 1938, and the subsequent absorption of Czechoslovakia into Hitlerite Germany. She reported the civil war in Spain, the war of Russia upon Finland in 1939, and the Sino-Japanese war in 1940–41. From 1943 until the end of World War II she was a war correspondent for *Collier's* magazine in England, Italy, France, Holland, and Germany. During the fall and early winter of 1945–46 she was with the American occupation troops in Berlin, and then from March to May, 1946, she reported the war in Java. For a year she lived in London working on her novel, *The Wine of Astonishment,* and on short stories. Upon her return to the United States in April, 1947, she finished her novel and then moved to Cuernavaca, Mexico, where she now has her residence. For six months in 1949 she was in Europe to prepare special feature articles for *The Saturday Evening Post.*

Much of Miss Gellhorn's fiction is based upon the events and people she has observed as a reporter. Her novels deal with justice and injustice, and show how people react, grow, or resign themselves when confronted with the specific injustices they see in their own lives and times. Thus *The Wine of Astonishment* is the story of two men growing in war, the greatest kind of mass injustice, and recounts the final and specific reaction of one of them. The women also grow in this culture of injustice; all love in war thus seems to be accidental and incidental, and it is only a part of the inhuman grinding together of human beings which is their wartime lot.

What Mad Pursuit (1934), her first novel, is about three girls of nineteen who leave college to experience life. *The Trouble I've Seen* (1936) presents sympathetically the problems of people living in bewilderment, misery, and humiliation as recipients of relief in the depression in the 1930's. Joe's optimism gives the theme: "We can't be ashamed; we may as well go ahead and die if we are ashamed." *A Stricken Field* (1940) pictures the terrified citizens of Prague in Czechoslovakia at the time of the Munich pact when Hitler got the signal to appropriate by *anschlusz* the small neighbor state. An American reporter, Mary Douglas, pleads for humane treatment of refugees.

The Heart of Another (1941) is a collection of short stories ranging in place from Corsica to Finland via Cuba, and concerning human beings in conflict or compromise with their times. *Liana* (1944) is about the beautiful, illiterate, mulatto wife of a rich landowner on a Caribbean island, where she remains virtually a prisoner until her husband goes to war in 1942. *The Wine of Astonishment* (1948), set against the Bulge operation of World War II, concerns two pairs of lovers who are drawn together as a result of their loneliness and disillusionment.

ROBERT GIBBONS

Lawrence Kahn

and his twin brother, Michael, were born on May 1, 1915, at Tuscaloosa, Alabama, sons of an Alabama father and an Irish mother. The family eventually numbered ten. They lived in a dozen Alabama small towns, a composite of which is reflected in Pineboro, the scene of the author's second and third novels. Robert Gibbons attended public schools in these towns and studied at the University of Alabama and at Alabama Polytechnic Institute, receiving the degree of Bachelor of Science from the latter. He has delivered newspapers, farmed, dug ditches on an RFC project, administered a county agricultural conservation program, taught college freshmen, and served aboard an LST naval craft. In 1937 he married Janie Moore of Tuscaloosa; they have two children.

Robert Gibbons says that he cannot recall when he first contemplated becoming a writer: "It seems that I have been writing something or other all my life." His first published story was "A Loaf of Bread," which was later reprinted in *The Best Short Stories of 1942*. In 1942 he was awarded an Alfred A. Knopf fellowship and in 1943 a Julius Rosenwald grant for writing fiction.

Robert Gibbons' short stories and novels are all laid in the South, not because he thinks the South is more worthy of representation or more interesting than other sections of the country, but because it is the region which he knows best. He feels that the problems and conflicts of the actors in his novels and stories are fundamentally human and not characteristic of the South alone.

Bright Is the Morning (1943), his first novel, tells the story of a crisis in the relationships of a landowning Alabama farm family and of the way a father's understanding resolves the conflict between his two sons. *The Patchwork Time* (1948) is a study of conflicts, fundamentally sexual, stirring below the surface of Pineboro, a small deep South town, and describes the struggle of Johnny Somers, a young teacher of history in the high school, who after a delayed adolesence achieves maturity and understanding.

WILLA GIBBS

was born in Hanna, Alberta, Canada, on September 25, 1917, the daughter of American citizens who had gone "adventuring" in the Northwest shortly after their marriage. Both were natives of Yolo County, an agricultural community in northern California. Her father was an attorney and her mother was a schoolteacher. During World War I her father abandoned the legal profession to raise wheat in Canada, and became a victim of the "black" influenza then prevalent. The family returned to Yolo County after his death and Mrs. Gibbs was forced to give up teaching, which was then even less remunerative than it is now, in order to rear her two children. She achieved success as an insurance salesman and became an executive. Willa, though not a Catholic, spent her grammar-school years in Holy Rosary Academy, a convent in Woodland, the seat of Yolo County. While in Woodland High School, she became a "reporter" for the local newspaper at no salary, but with a warning from the managing editor not to be a nuisance. He later relented to the extent of five dollars a week. She worked for several years on various newspapers as a reporter and in 1948 resigned from the courthouse and police beat of the Red Bluff, California, *Daily News* to marry Floyd Charles Millsap of Woodland. They now live on a farm just outside the town of Yolo.

Miss Gibbs' first book, *Tell Your Sons* (1946), is an historical novel of the Napoleonic era showing the personal hold which the Little Corporal had over the people associated with him. The inception of this novel dates back to 1930 when, as a thirteen-year-old graduate of grammar school, Miss Gibbs wrote a story about the Consulate. Fascinated by the era, she read everything about the period she could find and took copious notes on no fewer than fifteen hundred books. In her senior year at high school, she began another Napoleonic novel and worked at it steadily, but laid aside the manuscript after three years. In the next five years she completed four modern novels in the process of mastering dialogue and scene structure. Finally, while living in San Francisco, she began work on *Tell Your Sons.* She wrote and rewrote for four years, and subjected the book to forty-two revisions.

The Tender Men (1948) deals with the problems of young people during the depression of the 1930's. The point of the book is that communism in the abstract has a great deal to recommend it, but that it is an inappropriate form of government for the people of the United States. A secondary point is that the true and good way of combatting its growth here is by self-reform. Young Ed Wicks comes from Dakota to San Francisco to be a newspaperman. He falls into the ugly cycle of no-job-no-experience, no-experience-no-job that felled so many young people. Embittered, lonely, and hungry, he listens to the communists and comes under their influence. Too late they discover they have made him into a better American and have failed entirely to convert him. The finale dramatizes the idea that, while the adoption of some features of Marxism could improve us, accepted as a whole it could only destroy us.

SUSAN GLASPELL

John Gregory

was born on July 1, 1882, in Davenport, Iowa. Her mother was of Irish parentage and her father of English descent. After studying in the Davenport public schools, Susan Glaspell went on to take the degree of Bachelor of Philosophy at Drake University in Des Moines, Iowa. She had begun to write in childhood, and during her college days she sent stories to magazines and also wrote news items for local newspapers. On the day following her graduation she became a reporter of legislative news for the Des Moines *News* and later a general reporter for the Des Moines *Capital.* After two years she returned to Davenport to devote her time to writing fiction. In 1909 she began a year's stay in Paris.

Upon returning to the United States she lived for a time in Idaho and then went to Provincetown, Massachusetts. In 1913 she married George Cram Cook, also of Iowa, a writer and dramatist. In association with other writers they founded the Provincetown Players and changed a shed on the wharf into a theater. She served as actor, dramatist, and producer. Later she and Mr. Cook assisted in converting a stable in Greenwich Village, New York City, into the Playwrights' Theatre, and here continued during the winter season the work started in the summer in Provincetown. They settled down, and Provincetown was Miss Glaspell's home until her death on July 27, 1948. In 1922

Mr. and Mrs. Cook went to Greece to study the ancient culture of that land. For nearly two years they lived at Delphi on Mount Parnassus. Mr. Cook died there on January 14, 1924. Upon her return to America she wrote *The Road to the Temple* (1926), a biography of Mr. Cook, which contains much of the story of her own life.

She wrote a number of very successful one-act plays, including "Trifles" (1917), about an incident in Iowa, and "Suppressed Desires" (with G. C. Cook, 1917), a satire upon the new Freudian psychology. Full-length plays then followed: "Bernice" (1920), "Inheritors" (1921), "The Verge" (1922), "The Comic Artist" (with N. Matson, 1927), and "Alison's House" (1930), a play based on the life of Emily Dickinson and a winner of the Pulitzer prize. *Lifted Masks* (1912) contains short stories.

Miss Glaspell's novels delve into the inner core of being of women whose problems, arising from the ordinary vicissitudes of life, bring them unhappiness and sometimes carry them to the brink of mental instability. Quietly and with keen psychological insight, Miss Glaspell probes into these minds with a physician's care to cure rather than to wound. Her facts are stated directly and somewhat austerely, and her characterizations have something of this forthrightness. The stories contain very striking incidents which, though seemingly melodramatic, have a basis in fact. Her original manner of treating her themes develops tension and subtle excitement.

The Glory of the Conquered (1909), her first novel, is a psychological study of a university professor of biology, Karl Hubers, who goes blind as a result of his carelessness just before his research is to bring a new discovery, and about his wife, Ernestine, who gives up her career as a painter to carry forward her husband's work and to prevent him from yielding to despair. When he dies, she must again adjust her life. *The Visioning* (1911) portrays in the setting of an army post the attempt of Kate Jones to reveal the double standard of judging men and women, as well as the narrowness of some people. She befriends a chorus girl who had relations with Major Darrett, an admirer of Kate. *Fidelity* (1915) describes the effect on her family of a young woman's elopement with a married man and her difficulties in attempting to achieve a normal home life in the midst of frowning neighbors. Yet Ruth Holland does not marry Stuart Williams when he is divorced, for she maintains her independence of spirit.

Brook Evans (1928) contrasts two idealists, Naomi and Brook Evans, who are mother and daughter, and portrays the decline of the Puritan standards in New England. Naomi represents the ascetic ideal of the 1880's, and Brook in the 1920's wants fullness of life and beauty. *Fugitive's Return* (1929) concerns the marriage of Irma Lee and Dan Shraeder. Dan decides to seek a freer life. Irma plans to commit suicide, but a friend takes her to Greece where she gains new courage and a compelling task. *Ambrose Holt and Family* (1931) tells the effect on a well-to-do son and daughter-in-law of the return of Ambrose Holt, who had deserted his family many years earlier. His bedraggled condition horrifies Blossom and Lincoln, and the story relates their response to this situation. The theme is the need to escape an imprisoning environment.

The Morning Is Near Us (1940) is a psychological novel about Lydia Chippman, who returns to her home place after an absence of twenty years. Vague hints suggest that she is unwanted; she looks into matters and discovers startling facts about her family. *Norma Ashe* (1942) is about a woman who fails in life because she has given up her dream. As a girl in South Dakota, she imbibed a zeal to do good. Now at fifty, alone and penniless, she sets out to recapture the lost vision. *Judd Rankin's Daughter* (1945) concerns the difficulties of a young returned soldier, Judson Rankin, who must adjust his thinking to the liberalism of his father and mother and to the conservatism of his employer. His mother recalls her youth in Iowa as she tells the story of her son.

ARTHÉMISE GOERTZ

was born on November 9, 1905, in New Orleans, Louisiana, where she attended Newcomb College of Tulane University. After graduating in 1925, she married Hector Alfonso, a member of an old Creole family, who stirred her interest in Spanish, French, Creole, and Latin-American cultures. She also took a position with a steamship company which acted as agent for a Japanese line. In 1934 she spent a year traveling on foot from town to town in Mexico. The flavor of the countryside around Orizaba is in her first book, *South of the Border* (1940).

Her interest in Japanese culture won her a scholarship in 1939 for study in Tokyo. The only American at the school, she donned native clothes and lived in Japanese style, with the intention of writing another travel book. With the attack on Pearl Harbor on December 7, 1941, she was confined to her dwelling but was not put in a concentration camp; nevertheless she burned all her notes, diaries, and the manuscript of a book. Housed with non-interned missionaries, she became ill with beriberi because of a diet of wormy rice boiled without salt.

In December, 1943, she was repatriated after a three-months' trip on the mercy ship *Gripsholm.* On arriving in New York she learned that her husband had been killed in action on November 6, 1943. Too ill to return to the South, she remained in the city. By 1946 she had recovered sufficiently to study her surroundings in Flushing, New York, where she lived with her mother. A novel about suburban New Yorkers was taking shape in her mind, and so she rode the buses and subways in the hope of writing books with warm human appeal brightened with humor. In 1948 she took up residence in Mandeville, Louisiana.

"During my wartime experiences," she has said, "I observed human nature in the raw, under most difficult, indeed desperate conditions. For all the greed, hate, and smallness of soul I saw, I saw twice as much generosity, love, and grandeur of spirit. When I was hungry, friends among the enemy brought me food, and when I was cold, my countrymen gave me clothes through the American Red Cross. With all I have seen, my faith in human nature is strengthened rather than shaken. And I'd like to tell everybody that no matter how bad things are, they'll be good again. Just hold on and hope!"

Her first novel, *Give Us Our Dream* (1947), pictures the suburban life of New York City in an account of the people who reside in a large apartment house. The central character is Mrs. Marston, a woman with field glasses, who peers out the window and tries to be helpful. *The Moon Is Mine* (1948) is about Pat Egan, a white-collar girl, and her dreams of getting a rich husband. She charms a millionaire and then walks out on him.

PEGGY GOODIN

was born May 18, 1923, in Kansas City, Missouri. Her early life was spent in Bluffton, Indiana, a small town on the banks of the Wabash River. She worked during high school and college days in a library, a factory, and a department store. After graduating from the University of Michigan, with time out for a semester at the Leland Powers School of the Theater and Radio in Boston, she worked in New York City as an editorial assistant for *The Woman's Home Companion.* Her graduate study at McGill University in Canada was interrupted by a brief stay in a tuberculosis sanitarium. Upon her recovery she received a master's degree from McGill University in 1949, and then went to Europe where she spent the summer in Paris and in Collioure, a French fishing village in the Pyrénées. Now, back in the United States, she has this to say about her writing: "In the past I have liked to write prose with humorous intent, but I think that, if I have any consistent purpose, it is simply to interest my readers."

Clementine (1946), which won the Avery Hopwood award at the University of Michigan, is the humorous account of a tomboy growing up in a small town in Indiana. It is filled with small-town details: the colorful county fair, a grammar-school oratory contest, Clementine's first trip to New York, and her recognition of first love. *Take Care of My Little Girl* (1950) is a satirical novel about college sororities. Liz, a freshman, enters the university convinced that she must be a "Queen," like her mother. The novel takes her through the maze of rushing, pledging, and "Hell Week," but Liz decides that she cannot opportunistically make friends solely on racial, religious, and financial grounds.

DAVID GOODIS

was born in Philadelphia. At the age of eleven he decided on aviation as a career, made a parachute out of an old tablecloth, and began an experimental jump from a second-story window. A maid caught him just in time; thereupon the frustrated youth began writing a blood-and-thunder story about one "Pilot Crackstone, the Flier of the World War." Later, after he had graduated from Temple University, Mr. Goodis made a second start with a novel called *The Ignited*. The title was accurate; he threw the manuscript into the furnace. A second novel also was written and discarded. Then old Crackstone came back to mind and in modern dress proceeded to shoot down Axis airmen in a series of aviation stories extending over five years; he had a third incarnation in a radio serial. Meanwhile Mr. Goodis had been a shipping clerk, day laborer, and dock worker. His first published novel led him to Hollywood as a writer for motion-picture firms. *Dark Passage* (1946) and *Nightfall* (1947) are mystery stories.

Retreat from Oblivion (1939), his first novel, is the story of two couples whose infidelities occur against the background of war in Spain and China. *Behold This Woman* (1947) portrays the evil Clara Ervin, second wife of an elderly Philadelphia clerk, as she bosses him and her stepdaughter, Evelyn.

PAUL GOODMAN

was born on September 9, 1911, in New York City. He has said: "I know the schools of this place and time and the streets of the Empire City and the wild rocks along the Hudson River. I am concerned with naturalizing the family, primary education, and community layouts. I should like to destroy the rationalizations by which we protect ourselves from our primary anxiety, our fear of giving way to joy and creation. I would awaken people to the fact that the vast social machine to which they adjust is really themselves—we are society—it is the system of the resignations that we have made." Mr. Goodman has taught at the University of Chicago, the Manumit School of Progressive Education, and New York University. His books include *Communitas* (1947), about community planning; *Kafka's Prayer* (1947); *Art and Social Nature* (1947), essays on anarchist theory; *Stop Light* (1941), a volume of dance plays; and several books of poetry. *Faustina* (1949) is a tragedy. *The*

Facts of Life (1945) and *The Break-up of Our Camp* (1950) contain short stories.

The Grand Piano; or, The Almanac of Alienation (1942), his first novel, is plotless and without a setting, although the events have New York City as a background. In a sense it is a surrealist allegory in the fashion of the medieval play, *Everyman,* and the action consists of discussions and arguments by the characters. One represents the declining Marxian viewpoint, and others represent order, disorder, adolescence, and tradition. *The State of Nature* (1946) is a story of the social and psychological relations which make people desire war in order to regain their basic nature; the end shows the feverish and explosive joy required to wage peace, if peace, indeed, is to be achieved. *The Dead of Spring* (1950) forms, with the preceding two novels, a trilogy.

CAROLINE GORDON

Hans Namuth

was born on October 6, 1895, on her grandmother's farm, "Merry Mont." Since this was located on the line between Kentucky and Tennessee, she is uncertain which state claims her allegiance. Her mother's family, the Meriwethers, came from Albemarle County in Virginia in the early part of the nineteenth century and settled in that part of Tennessee which is known as "The Black Patch" because dark-fired tobacco is raised there. They had been tobacco planters in Virginia, and they continued as such in "the West."

Her father came from Virginia as a tutor in her mother's family and later married her mother. During Caroline's childhood he conducted an old-fashioned classical school for boys in Clarksville, Tennessee. He believed that Latin, Greek, and mathematics were the foundations of knowledge; Caroline and her brothers received their early education from him. She did not attend school regularly until she was fourteen, when her family had moved to another town where she entered public high school. She graduated from Bethany College in 1916, and thirty years later received from it the degree of Doctor of Literature.

In 1924 she married Allen Tate, the poet; they have one daughter, Mrs. Percy Wood, Jr. In 1928 Mr. Tate received a Guggenheim award for creative writing, and the family spent the next two years in France. On their return to the United States, they bought a farm on the Cumberland River, near Clarksville, Tennessee, and lived here until 1932. when they went abroad once more. Since 1946 Mr. and Mrs. Tate have divided their time between New York and Princeton. She teaches a class in the short story at the Columbia University School of General Studies. Caroline Gordon has done newspaper work in the South and in New York City, but her major concern all her life has been the writing of fiction. Her short stories have been collected in *The Forest of the South* (1946). She received a Guggenheim award in 1934 and won second prize in the O. Henry collection in 1936. With her husband she edited *The House of Fiction* (1950).

Of her writings Miss Gordon has said: "My stories, I think, are all one story, and as yet I hardly know what the plot is. Like most fiction writers, I seem to spend my life contemplating the same set of events. Each novel is what I make of these events."

Penhally (1931), her first novel, tells the story of four generations in a Kentucky mansion, "Penhally," beginning in 1826 with a quarrel between brothers over the custom of primogeniture. *Aleck Maury, Sportsman* (1934) is the life story of a scholar who loves hunting and fishing but who subsides into teaching for a living and sport for his real vocation. *None Shall Look Back* (1937) is about the proud Allard family of Kentucky whose tobacco lands border on the Tennessee state line. After the battle of Chickamaugua, the South collapses, and the losing fight of bluff, courageous General Bradford Forrest becomes a central motif. *The Garden of Adonis* (1937) portrays three southern groups in conflict: Ote Mortimer, a sharecropper, kills Ben Allard, a plantation owner, and Jim Carter marries a manufacturer's daughter. *Green Centuries* (1941) pictures on the southern frontier of 1769 Rion Outlaw's establishment of a home and his brother Archy's decision to remain with the Cherokee Indians. *The Women on the Porch* (1944) presents the problem of Catherine Chapman, whose husband is unfaithful. She returns to her home in Tennessee and there with relatives reviews her thoughts and feelings. A modified stream-of-consciousness technique is employed.

CHARLES O. GORHAM

William Teftwich

was born on September 25, 1911, in Philadelphia. He was educated at Clark School and Columbia College. For a time he was a reporter on the New York *Herald Tribune,* and later was an editor for publishing firms. During World War II he served with the British and United States air forces as navigator. He has traveled in Scandinavia, England, France, Belgium, Spain, Portugal, and the Canary Islands. He now devotes his full time to writing. He is married and is the father of three children.

The Gilded Hearse (1948), his first novel, is the story of one day in the life of a publicity man for a successful New York publishing firm, with acidly etched portraits of young co-workers engaged in deceiving the public and cutting each other's throats. *The Future Mr. Dolan* (1948) is a study of juvenile delinquency in the Yorkville district of New York City, where the streets are sunless, smelly, and garbage-littered; here Mattie Dolan begins life in a tenement and grows up into a warped man as the result of his cruel childhood. Only his Uncle Fred is not considered a fool; all other people are "suckers" waiting to be cheated.

HERBERT GORMAN

was born on January 1, 1893, in Springfield, Massachusetts. Through his maternal grandmother he is a descendant of the well-known Griswold family of New England. He attended public schools, including Technical High School in Springfield, but his education came chiefly through omnivorous reading: for eight or ten years he spent many hours a day in the public library. He worked as a cobbler, mail-room helper in a newspaper office, rubber-stamp maker, clerk in a bank, and minor assistant for a lumber company. At the age of nineteen he played in vaudeville and several theatrical productions. His poetry in 1915 led to book reviewing for the Springfield *Republican* and later to a position as general reporter on the Springfield *Union.* In 1918 he moved to New York City to work on the Liberty Loan and later returned to newspaper work in New York, serving successively on the *Sun* (1918–21), *Post* (1921), *Times* (1921–27), and *Herald-Tribune* (1927–28). For a time he was assistant editor of the weekly, *The Freeman.* During his newspaper days he held such varied positions as reporter, suburban editor, motion-picture editor, dramatic editor, city editor, and literary editor. For three years he lectured on journalism at New York University, and for two years he wrote scripts and handbooks for the National Broadcasting Company's University of the Air. Since 1928 he has devoted himself mainly to writing his books, living for extended periods in France, England, and Mexico. He has also visited

Switzerland, Ireland, and Scotland, where he did research for his biographies and novels.

Besides being a novelist, biographer, and poet, Mr. Gorman is a discerning critic. His biographies include *A Victorian American: Henry Wadsworth Longfellow* (1926), *Hawthorne: A Study in Solitude* (1927), *The Incredible Marquis: Alexandre Dumas, pére* (1929), *The Scottish Queen* (1932), and *James Joyce: A Biography* (1940). In 1923 he edited *The Peterborough Anthology*. His critical works include *James Joyce: His First Forty Years* (1924), *The Procession of Masks* (1923), and *The World's Great Novels* (two series, 1944–45). His books of poetry are *The Fool of Love* (1920), *The Barcarolle of James Smith* (1922), and *Notations for a Chimaera* (1926).

Mr. Gorman's objective in writing historical novels is to capture a reality and make great past events as vivid as the contemporary scene. He says: "I don't believe in romanticizing or putting famous people up on pedestals. I want flesh and blood in my novels. Let's see the mole on Lincoln's cheek and the wart on Cromwell's nose. But let's have sympathy, too. Practically all historical personages have had a hard time of it; otherwise they wouldn't be historical personages. And the Time-Spirit must be caught with the character, as well. A rounded picture that radiates truth and carries some philosophical meaning for our time, that is what I aim for."

Mr. Gorman's early novels grew out of his newpaper experience and pictured life as he saw it around him. His first work of fiction, *Gold by Gold* (1925), is about a poor widow's son, Karl Nevins, whose poetic temperament leads him to escape from a New England manufacturing town to Greenwich Village, where his lack of ability shows up in his descent into a life of frustration and futility. An experimental technique, similar to that in James Joyce's *Ulysses*, is used in this story, possibly for the first time in America. *The Virginities* (1926) portrays the decay of Puritan morality in New England in the eventual union of John Gaul and Lalage Trent, who have broken from the ancient code and who try to rise above their bespattered pasts. *The Place Called Dagon* (1927) pictures a Massachusetts community that retains the superstitious darkness of witchcraft days. Jeffery Westcott comes to stir in them again the old beliefs. A young physician saves his sweetheart from this environment. Mr. Gorman is on record as fervently hoping that these three apprentice works may be forgotten.

Jonathan Bishop (1933) deals with the collapse of the French empire in 1870–71 under Napoleon III and the Prussian victory in a story of the romantic adventures of an inquisitive, thoughtful American youth who seeks an answer to the fundamental problem of the place of intellect and spirit in a world of action. He falls in love with a woman spy, fights in the battle of Sedan, and dies in the last days of the Commune. *Suzy* (1934) is an adventure story about Susan Dillworthy, an American girl, who is with an unsuccessful variety act in London and who then goes to Paris, where, during World War I, she marries a lover of Mata Hari, the famous spy. Suzy's life parallels the fortunes of France.

The Mountain and the Plain (1936) pictures events in the French Revolution as they are seen by a young American, David Livingston, who has gone to France to sell tobacco and pork. He meets Thomas Paine and other leaders, and he gets caught up in the political maelstrom. *Brave General* (1942) is about Georges Boulanger, the general and Minister of War whose intrigues almost overturned the French republic in 1888. In the background are portrayed the flaws which made possible the idealization of a weakling and blunderer. *The Wine of San Lorenzo* (1945) is set in the time of the war between Mexico and the United States in 1846 and vividly pictures the fight at the Alamo and other battles and the surrender of Mexico City to General Scott. The story is about Charley Livingston, a Massachusetts boy, who is reared by General Santa Anna under the name of Juan Diego. *The Cry of Dolores* (1948) concerns Mexico's ill-fated revolution of 1810, the first struggle for freedom from Spain, and the leadership of Miguel Hildalgo y Castilla, a parish priest and reformer. The story concerns Luz, a simple Indian girl who escapes from a Spanish soldier, and Ciriaco, her mestizo son, who turns back to Indian ways.

CHRISTINE NOBLE GOVAN

George Hull

was born in New York City on December 12, 1898. Her family moved to the South when she was four and a half, and she has lived in Sewanee, Nashville, Franklin, and Chattanooga, which has been her home for the past thirty years. She has taught school, been a librarian, peddled bread and milk from door to door, worked in a photographic shop and in bookstores, and has given lectures on books and reading. For over twenty years she has been a book reviewer, first as literary editor on the old Chattanooga *News* and currently on the Chattanooga *Times* and the Atlanta *Journal*. Her husband is librarian of the University of Chattanooga; they have three children. Mrs. Govan has written ten children's books and three mysteries. Her first short story, "Miss Winters and the Wind," was printed in the O. Henry prize collection of 1947. The first of her children's books was *Those Plummer Children* (1934). This and two other Plummer books, *Judy and Chris* (1936) and *Narcissus and de Chillun* (1938), have a mellow regional flavor.

When asked about her experiences as a writer, Mrs. Govan stated that there seems to be a prejudice in the minds of northern publishers and librarians toward books about southern children. "A book about a bound-girl in New England is hailed as an historical find, while a book about southern colored children as free as the air and as happy as crickets is frowned upon as putting the Negro into an inferior position." She feels that all children know far more about northern books and their people than about southern books and their characters, and also that northern children have been given fewer books about the South than is necessary if they are to acquire a fair picture of the entire country.

Her first novel, *The Shadow and the Web* (1940), is a psychological study of a well-known family in middle Tennessee. It is the story of the brilliant Miss Wardlaw, a teacher in charge of a respected girls' finishing school at Murfreesboro and of the greed and weaknesses of several members of her family who destroyed the school and the headmistress. *Jennifer's House* (1945) is the story of a large and well-to-do family living on the outskirts of Nashville at the beginning of this century. The story involves the love stories of three generations and the romance and glamour of marriages and of ambitious financial manipulations.

DOROTHY GRAHAM

Artist: Dudley Carpenter

was born on December 13, 1893, in New Rochelle, New York. She was educated in Lausanne, Switzerland, and Florence, Italy, where she gained an insight into the culture and psychology of Europe. On July 23, 1924, she married James W. Bennett, formerly a consular officer in China. Her first book, *Through the Moon Door* (1926), described Peking and many aspects of their life there. Later she spent three years collecting material for *Chinese Gardens* (1938), an historical record which interpreted important phases of Chinese art, religion, and philosophy. This is a definitive work, since the subject had never before been attempted and, owing to the destruction by the Japanese in the war, cannot be done again. Besides having lived seven years in China, Dorothy Graham has traveled three times around the world and spent much time in Hawaii, Italy, and France.

The purpose of all her novels is to show the effect of time-honored traditions on the American character and the impact of the dynamic American on the older civilizations.

Her first novel, *Lotus of the Dust* (1927), is a story of the international set in Peking. *The French Wife* (1928) describes Americans in France. *Candles in the Sun* (1930) is a satirical study of Americans set against an Italian background. *The China Venture* (1929) deals with three generations of an American family in the China trade, depicting the early Canton merchants and the Opium War, the Boxer Rebellion, and the revolution of 1927. *Wind Across the World* (1947) is concerned with the construction of the Shanghai-Nanking railroad. The characters progress from the time of the tyrannical dowager empress through the first phases of the student revolution which effected such drastic changes in modern China.

DOROTHY FREMONT GRANT

was born on October 8, 1900, in New York City, the daughter of Francis Murray and Henrietta Addison Fremont. Mrs. Grant is a collateral descendant of Joseph Addison, the English essayist, and a direct descendant of Rev. Samuel Langdon, rector of Harvard College at the time of the American Revolution and earlier the cartographer, following the French and Indian Wars, of the present boundary of the United States and Canada. She has had ink in her blood since high-school days when for compositions she used to submit "wild-west thrillers or sob stories of the New York slums." Her first practical experience came during World War I when she interrupted her education to volunteer for the navy and was assistant to the editor of *The Naval Medical Bulletin*.

She has traveled extensively in the United States and in France. In 1931 she founded, edited, published, wrote, and circulated a bi-weekly newspaper on Long Island. After she sold the paper in 1938, she began contributing to national Catholic magazines. She has always been a deep student of American history. After several years of "neither-hot-nor-cold" religious convictions, she entered the Roman Catholic Church on September 4, 1934. She is married to Douglas Grant, the artist; they have one daughter. Her non-fiction books include *What Other Answer?* (1943); *War Is My Parish* (1944), the story of Catholic chaplains in World War II; *So! You Want to Get Married!* (1947); *John England: American Christopher* (1949), and *Born Again* (1950).

The central theme in all her work is Christian dogma. Her purpose is to show the practicality of Christian dogma over the so-called practical and also dogmatic systems of philosophy devised by men, and to reaffirm historical truth where it has been deliberately or accidentally distorted by historians. Her special interest is in American history and the contemporary ideological threat to the "American way," and she has a genuine interest in all history since the year A.D. 1.

Margaret Brent, Adventurer (1944) is an historical novel of the dauntless woman friend of the Calverts who established Maryland. The setting is St. Mary's, and the events concern the early settlement in the years from 1638 to 1649. *Night of Decision* (1946) pictures colonial New York between 1683 and 1690, when a Catholic, Thomas Dongan, was governor. The story concerns a Protestant heroine who marries a Catholic follower of Dongan. *Devil's Food* (1949) presents a contrast between Christian dogma, principles, and moral ethics and the loose, lax expediences of pragmatism. It is the story of a young modern who rebels against the authority of her parents and her church. It is vividly demonstrated that without the safe anchorage of an authoritative rule of life young people who are "free" of such safeguards become devil's food: one goes either to God or to the devil.

JAMES GRAY

was born on June 30, 1899, in Minneapolis, Minnesota, the son of James Gray, one-time mayor of Minneapolis and long an editor of the Minneapolis *Journal*. He was graduated from Western High School in Washington, D.C., and from the University of Minnesota in 1920. Immediately thereafter he joined the staff of the St. Paul *Pioneer Press* and *Dispatch*, which papers he served for twenty-five years in various capacities as editorial writer, columnist, dramatic critic, and book editor. In 1946 he became the literary editor of the Chicago *Daily News* and professorial lecturer in creative writing at the University of Chicago. He resigned in 1948 to become professor of English at the University of Minnesota. His first interest as a creative writer was in the theater. A play written while he was still an undergraduate at the University of Minnesota was produced in 1921 by a Minneapolis stock company, and other plays of his authorship have been presented by professional and amateur groups in Minnesota communities. His non-fiction books include *The Illinois* (1940), a volume in the "Rivers of America" series; *Pine, Stream and Prairie: Wisconsin and Minnesota in Profile* (1945); and *On Second Thought* (1945), a collection of critical essays dealing with leading contemporary novelists, chiefly of America and England.

Mr. Gray's novels have a Minnesota background. It is his theory of regionalism that, since human intelligence is spread in a thin veneer over the surface of the earth and human emotions are everywhere directed toward the achievement of the same ends, the best place for the individual writer to examine the plight of man is the locale he knows best through daily association.

His first novel, *The Penciled Frown* (1925), is a satiric study of the bright young man taking his first steps in journalism and the arts, self-consciously assuming the mask of the most austere of arbiters. *Shoulder the Sky* (1935) is the story of a young man's simultaneous adjustment to marriage and to the problems of practicing medicine in a small Minnesota community. The underlying theme is that "Tobacco Road," like "Main Street," is a path that crosses America from east to west and north to south. To walk it with eyes open is to witness shocking scenes that may contribute much to a man's education as a social being.

Wake and Remember (1936) is a study of grief, of a young widower's growing awareness of the needs of his two small sons and of his special responsibility toward them. Rankin, a sensitive man of great intelligence, has attempted to care for his sons during the year since their mother died. Yet her radiant memory has served to blur the harsh realities of life. Slowly he gains clarity of perception and sees his duty.

Wings of Great Desire (1938) is a family chronicle describing the experiences of a man and wife in the political world of the late 1890's and in trying to pass on to their four children a sometimes confused but always conscientious view of the "good life." *Vagabond Path* (1941) portrays the failure of a man of genius whose lack of a sustaining philosophy undermines a distinguished literary gift. Michael Fontaine actually is a successful writer, but a sense of futility depresses him. He is able, however, to supply strength and courage to the son of the one woman he truly loved.

ANNE GREEN

Yvonne Adam

was born on November 11, 1891, in Savannah, Georgia. Her parents moved to France when she was a few months old. She is some eight years older than her novelist brother Julian, who was born in France and who writes his fiction in French. The children grew up in Paris, spoke both French and English, and attended French schools. However, the family always considered itself American. An account of her first twenty-one years has been given by Miss Green in *With Much Love* (1948). As soon as she could be admitted into service after World War I began, she became a nurse in military hospitals and devoted four years to this work. She then toured Europe and visited her relatives in America. On the advice of John Macrae, a cousin who headed an American publishing firm, she began to write fiction. She spent most of World War II, from November, 1940, to September, 1945, with a relative in Baltimore. She now resides in Paris with her brother. "I lead a quiet life," she has said; "my main interests are reading and writing. My novels more or less write themselves. That is, I begin with one character in mind; others seem to shape themselves and the plot without any conscious plan of mine."

Her first novel, *The Selbys* (1930), is largely autobiographical; it is the story of Barbara Winship, the Selbys' niece, who comes from Georgia to live with them in Paris. Miss Green's other novels, generally light and whimsical in character, are based upon imagined characters. *Reader, I Married Him* (1931) pictures the Douglass family, charming southerners, who live in Paris without funds and without a desire to work, but who seem to get what they want. *Marietta* (1932) portrays a professional charmer, daughter of a Virginia scholar in Paris, and her attempt to snare the man her sister, Lucille, marries.

A Marriage of Convenience (1933) concerns Claire and Antoine, French youngsters who are designed for each other but who resist their relatives' urgings. After many serious and amusing turns, they marry. *Fools Rush In* (1934) describes the career of Eleanor Rockwell, whose amazing experiences since her birth in Baltimore arise from persecution by Jim Donohue. *That Fellow Percival* (1935) is about the North family in Paris and the effect of the arrival of an efficiency expert, Percival. *Winchester House* (1936) tells of the many amusing and exciting adventures of Agnes Winchester, who leaves a large mansion in New York City to breathe freedom.

16 Rue Cortambert (1937) portrays expatriate Americans in Paris who are involved in a philanthropist's plan to persuade a rich widow to adopt twenty orphans. *Paris* (1938) describes a working family in Paris in the story of Helen Martin, the youngest daughter of a poor carpenter, a lame girl who rises in twenty years to become at twenty-three a famous hat designer. *The Silent Duchess* (1939) is an historical novel about noble and court life in France on the eve of the French Revolution, as related by an elderly and fastidious duchess. *The Delamer Curse* (1940) tells how Isabelle Hart, an American girl, solves the mystery of the curse that for two hundred years has killed each member of the Delamer family, including her mother, before the age of thirty.

The Lady in the Mask (1942) is set in the court of Ludovico Sforza in the Milan of 1494 in the late Italian Renaissance, when Leonardo da Vinci was the favorite painter. *Just before Dawn* (1943) portrays the "gay, laborious, and serious race" of French artisans in a story of three generations of the Elliott family in France between 1865 and 1940. *The Old Lady* (1947) has Madame Delatour visit her widowed daughter in America and strike up a friendship with a young girl next door. They go to France together.

ELEANOR GREEN

was born on February 8, 1911, in Milwaukee, Wisconsin, where she attended Milwaukee Downer Seminary from 1925 to 1928. She then went to Sarah Lawrence College in Bronxville, New York, from 1928 to 1930, and the following year studied at the Neighborhood Playhouse in New York. She acted in a stock company for a summer and, more because of circumstances than deliberate choice, then turned to writing. Now, although her interest in the theater remains, her creative interest and effort are unreservedly in the field of fiction. In 1949 she was awarded a Guggenheim fellowship. One of her short stories was included in the *O. Henry Memorial Prize Stories*. When asked to describe her work, she said it is easier to describe her interests: they are "people, and what they do to one another."

Her first book, *The Hill* (1936), pivots on a young girl through whose eyes the reader comes to know her family and their individual histories, although the story itself covers only one afternoon. *Pastoral* (1937), about two people living for a year together in the country, resembles the armature on which a plastic figure is molded into shape, for this is less a "story" than an evocation to compassion. *Ariadne Spinning* (1941) portrays a small-town minister's wife and the confusion and crises she must undergo before she is capable of courage. *Dora* (1948) describes a woman from the age of ten to the end of World War II. A character with at least the normal number of conceits, she has perhaps more than her share of sensitivity and self-doubt, so that when her husband returns safely at the end of the war to tell her he loves someone else, her suffering is almost unbearably acute. However, she emerges from this ordeal with faith, scarcely triumphant but reasonably strong and, at last, unafraid.

JOSIAH E. GREENE

Blackstone Studios

was born on March 22, 1911, in Duluth, Minnesota, where his grandfather was a pioneer settler and jurist, his father a lawyer and county attorney. He was educated at Duluth Central High School and at Brown University in Providence, Rhode Island, where he was elected to Phi Beta Kappa and received his bachelor's degree in 1933. He worked in the office of a New Jersey dairy from 1934 to 1937, and then devoted his full time to writing. He had already published some short stories for boys; now he wrote two mystery novels, *Madmen Die Alone* (1938) and *The Laughing Loon* (1939). He also did a column of mystery-story reviews for the Providence *Sunday Journal*. He was married in 1942 to Miss Elizabeth deCourcy of Darien, Connecticut. His first serious novel was completed under difficulties after he had entered the army, where he spent three and a half years in the air corps, engaged largely in Link trainer work at Chanute Field, Illinois, at Truax Field, Madison, and at Lowry Field, Denver, with an interval in Italy touring heavy-bombardment bases with a mobile training unit instructing combat crews in the operation of the automatic pilot and bombsight. Since the war he has been living and writing in the little town of Washington, Connecticut.

Not In Our Stars (1945), his first novel and winner of its publisher's centenary award, is a case history of bad labor-management relationship. The scene is a large eastern dairy farm, and its sixty-odd characters range from top executive to barn hand. It traces the growth of ill-feeling, aggravated by human weaknesses, on both sides from the birth of misunderstanding to disastrous climax. *A Bridge at Branfield* (1948) deals with the social problems of a small western Connecticut town which loses its young people to the cities because of the stifling of local opportunity. An election brings about fumbling attempts by the town's leaders to diagnose a difficulty they sense but resent, and a sex murder finally spotlights the frustrations of the town's youth.

WARD GREENE

was born in Asheville, North Carolina, on December 23, 1892. He was educated in the public schools of Atlanta and also studied at the Atlanta Art School. From 1912 to 1913 he was a student at the University of the South at Sewanee, Tennessee, and in the latter year he became a reporter on the Atlanta *Journal*. He served this newspaper as a war correspondent in France and Germany in 1918 and 1919. In 1921 he became an executive of the King Features Syndicate.

Cora Potts (1929), his first novel, is the story of a woman who uses fair means and foul to achieve her ends in the South between 1900 and 1920. She leaves home at fourteen, has affairs with men, develops a product to bleach Negroes' skin, and when wealthy marries a good man. *Ride the Nightmare* (1930) follows the roguish career of Jake Perry, a preacher's son, who leaves home at sixteen with a sense of his superiority. He becomes a flamboyant publicity man, nearly drinks himself to death, and at last decides to behave. *Weep No More* (1932) portrays the decline in manners in Corinth, where the tradition of southern chivalry has become a parody of its pre-Civil War standard.

Death in the Deep South (1936) is a grimly realistic tale of the trial for murder and the lynching of a young northerner in a southern community; it is based on the Leo Frank case. *King Cobra* (1940) pictures, in the era of President Harding, the rise of a masked order which sought to keep the South safe for white Protestants. *Route 28* (1940) is a comic tale set on a highway in central New Jersey on a Fourth of July. *What They Don't Know* (1944) sketches life on the home front on Long Island during World War II.

ELGIN GROSECLOSE

Harris & Ewing

was born on November 25, 1899, at Waukomis, Oklahoma, in what is known as the Cherokee Strip, where his father had staked out a claim during the famous Run of 1893. Pioneer American stock, the first Groseclose settled in Virginia about 1750 and founded the town which now bears their name. Following his graduation from the University of Oklahoma in 1920, Elgin Groseclose taught for two years from 1920 to 1922 in the high school conducted by the Presbyterian missionaries at Tabriz, Iran, and served also as secretary of the Persian Committee of the Near East Relief. While he was living the quiet life of a teacher in the mission school, a revolt broke out and the city was under siege for a week, during the course of which the school compound was riddled with machine-gun bullets.

Mr. Groseclose's work with the relief organization took him to the Caucasus, where he spent some time at the notable City of Children, the Alexandropol orphanage, a converted army post sheltering some twenty-five thousand war orphans under the care of the Near East Relief. The independent republics which had been formed in this mountain region following the Russian Revolution had just been overthrown by the Red armies, and the Soviets were in the course of liquidating all opposition by the now-familiar process of mass arrests and executions. The Soviets were extremely suspicious of relief work, which they regarded as some nefarious American imperialism, and the most innocent-looking American was regarded as a possible foreign agent. While passing through the Batum customs en route home, Mr. Groseclose was searched and a suspicious-looking document was found on his person: a memorandum of a life insurance policy with the serial number printed on it. This was translated as "life police, number, etc." He was arrested, charged with espionage, and spent a month in a Soviet prison.

On returning to America in 1923, Mr. Groseclose completed his education with the master's and doctor's degrees from American University at Washington, D.C., and began his professional life as an economist. He entered government service as special agent and financial specialist in the Department of Commerce, subsequently spent several years in Wall Street, was financial editor of *Fortune* magazine during its early days, and later taught economics and finance at The College of the City of New York and business English at the University of Oklahoma. In 1935 he returned to Washington as a financial economist.

While teaching at the University of Oklahoma he published his first book, *Money: The Human Conflict* (1934), a history of monetary experience. In 1943 he was appointed Treasurer-General of Iran and helped solve some of that country's fiscal problems. In 1944 he opened offices as an economic counsel in Washington, and has since been serving as consultant to a number of leading American corporations, as well as to foreign governments. He has also written *Introduction to Iran* (1947); *The Scimitar of Saladin* (1950), an adventure story for young people; and numerous monographs and articles on financial subjects. He married Louise Williams on June 25, 1927; they have four daughters.

His experiences abroad, and particularly the devoted, selfless work of the missionaries, made a deep impression and became the theme of his literary work in fiction. All his novels have a strongly moral and religious quality.

The Persian Journey of the Reverend Ashley Wishard (1937), his first novel, is the story of a young evangelist who discovers his true mission in an adventure with the nomads. *Ararat* (1939), which won the American Booksellers award in 1939 and the Foundation for Literature award for 1940, is a story of faith, laid in the environs of the great mountain of that name on the borders of Turkey, Russia, and Iran. *The Firedrake* (1942), which deals with the tragedy of separation, is the story of a young wife and mother who returns from the missionary field for the education of her children, achieves sudden fame as a novelist, and becomes involved in the interesting and tumultuous life of Boston during the clipper-ship era of the 1850's.

ALBERT JOSEPH GUÉRARD

was born on November 2, 1914, in Houston, Texas. He was educated in the elementary schools of Houston, in the École Pascal and Lycée Montaigne of Paris, in the Palo Alto, California, High School, and in the American High School at Paris. He was only twenty when he graduated from Leland Stanford University where his father, Albert Léon Guérard, has been Professor of General Literature for many years. The young novelist received his master's degree from Harvard in 1936 and his doctorate in English from Stanford in 1938. From 1936 to 1937 he studied at King's College in London. He taught at Amherst College from 1935 to 1936 and since 1938 he has been on the Harvard faculty. During

World War II, from 1943 to 1945, he was attached to the psychological warfare intelligence division of the army. He is the author of *Thomas Hardy* (1950).

Of himself and his writing Mr. Guérard has said: "At fifteen I began writing short stories strongly influenced by Hemingway. Other living novelists I admire greatly are Thomas Mann, Elizabeth Bowen, and Dorothy Baker. They are all psychological novelists, bent on exploring and clarifying little-understood aspects of human experience."

His first novel, *The Past Must Alter* (1938), is a psychological study of a sensitive boy of ten in 1915 who recoils from the conduct of his father and who hesitates to permit his mother to remarry. *The Hunted* (1944) portrays a college professor who marries a waitress and fails to comprehend her excellence. When they pursue an escaped convict, she realizes that she, too, is a "hunted" one, an ununderstood and hated person. *Maquisard* (1945) is a Christmas tale about a French guerrilla fighter who in December, 1944, feels a moment of salvation.

Night Journey (1950) deals with the self-doubts and introspection of an intelligence agent in a European country who suspects himself of betrayal and desertion, although he is not guilty of these crimes.

JOHN GUNTHER

Marcus Blechman

was born in Chicago, Illinois, on August 30, 1901. He attended public schools and then the University of Chicago, from which he graduated in 1922. He worked at all sorts of jobs before becoming a cub reporter. From 1924 to 1936 he served in Europe as a correspondent of the Chicago *Daily News*. During that time he was successively in charge of this newspaper's bureaus in every important European capital, and in addition he traveled widely through the whole length and breadth of the continent; he covered everything from wars in Syria to revolutions in Spain, from conferences at Geneva to *coups d'état* in the Balkans.

Just before the outbreak of war in 1939 he revisited Europe, as a correspondent for the National Broadcasting Company, and saw seventeen countries on the eve of war. He circled Germany's perimeter, and secretly visited the Reich itself. He was in Moscow when von Ribbentrop flew in to sign the celebrated Russo-German pact; he was in the House of Commons when Great Britain declared war. He then covered the outbreak of the war both for the North American Newspaper Alliance and for *The Reader's Digest*.

Similarly, Mr. Gunther returned to London in 1941, again as a correspondent, to get a glimpse of Britain under its greatest ordeal. In 1943 he set out in the field once more, this time as a war correspondent accredited to General Eisenhower's headquarters; he represented the combined American press at the invasion of Sicily, and was the only correspondent present when General Eisenhower first landed on European soil. Mr. Gunther was then attached for a time to the British Eighth Army, and saw its operations at close range with Lord Gort, Field Marshal Montgomery, and General Alexander as his hosts.

John Gunther has worked in nearly every country in the world, watching history unfold year by year. His four "Inside" books have brought most of the world, including the United States itself, to the American reader's doorstep in a uniquely successful manner. *Inside Europe* (1936), *Inside Asia* (1939), *Inside Latin America* (1941), and *Inside USA* (1949) have all performed the same kind of service: that of bridging the gap between history and contemporary events, and of making the leading problems and personalities of world politics human and familiar to the average reader, without ever vulgarizing them or making them sensational.

His other non-fiction books include *Behind the Curtain* (1949); *Death Be Not Proud* (1949), a memoir of and tribute to his son; and *Roosevelt in Retrospect* (1950). He has conducted radio-network programs for the National Broadcasting Company, and he has made extensive lecture tours. Between trips he lives in midtown Manhattan in New York City.

"I have always been interested in fiction—indeed, I started my literary life that way," Mr. Gunther has stated, "but in recent years all my energies seem, in some perplexing way, to have gone in the other direction. I suppose it was hard to be interested in stories about imaginary people when the impact of brutal fact was so tremendous in real life. Hitler and Stalin had more reality to me than anything I could invent."

The Red Pavilion (1927), his first novel, tells the life stories of a group at a dinner party in Chicago, with emphasis upon the effort of Richard and Shirley Northaway to find a basis for reuniting and compromising their individualistic desires. *Eden for One* (1927) is a fantasy in which John Lancelot dreams that, although he has the power of having his wishes come true, he never achieves happiness. The book is an allegory of the restlessness of mankind and its need to feel contented. *Bright Nemesis* (1932) deals with political intrigue in a Balkan state in a tale of an American newspaper correspondent's search for the murderer of two boys from the United States. *The Troubled Midnight* (1945) is set in Istanbul, Turkey, in the Spring of 1944 just before the allied invasion of France; the tale is of an American woman's love for a German and a Britisher.

ALFRED BERTRAM GUTHRIE, JR.

Erich Hartmann

was born January 13, 1901, at Bedford, Indiana. He grew up in Choteau, Montana, where his father was high-school principal and, later, newspaper owner and editor. He graduated from the University of Montana in 1923 and three years later moved to Lexington, Kentucky, where he spent twenty-one years in the editorial department of the *Leader*. While at Harvard University on a Nieman fellowship in 1944, he first seriously undertook the writing of fiction. He resigned his newspaper position in 1947, and now lectures on writing at the University of Kentucky. A student of western history and a collector of western Americana, he plans to do a series of four novels on the westward movement.

The Big Sky (1947), his first novel, is a story of the fur trade and the mountain man and covers the period from 1830 to 1843, when the great migration to Oregon took place. The central character is a young Kentuckian who runs away from home, joins a keelboat expedition up the Missouri River, and in succeeding years learns to love the mountains and to live like an Indian. An impulsive and headlong character, he spoils the only life to him worth living by killing his best friend.

The Way West (1950) describes the hardships and aspirations of the company of men and women who journeyed by wagon train to Oregon from Independence, Missouri, in 1846. Each person goes for different reasons: Dick Summers, the guide, is homesick for the wilderness country of his youth; Lije Evans and his wife patriotically want America to own the Northwest; and shiftless Hank McBee is running away from debts. Their experiences represent in a microcosm the working of the American democratic process. This novel was awarded the Pulitzer prize in fiction in 1950.

HALE *to* HURSTON

GARTH HALE

is the pseudonym of Albert Benjamin Cunningham, who was born in Linden, West Virginia, on June 22, 1888. He graduated in 1913 from Muskingum College at New Concord, Ohio, and from Drew University in Madison, New Jersey, in 1915. He received his doctorate from New York University in 1926. He has taught English at Lebanon University in Ohio, at the College of Puget Sound in Washington, at Washington State College, at the Shippensburg, Pennsylvania, State Teachers College, and since 1929 at Texas Technological College at Lubbock. He has written a number of mystery novels, among which are *Death Rides a Sorrel Horse* and *The Strange Death of Manny Square*. Dr. Hale's chief literary interests are the novel and literary criticism.

The Manse at Barren Rocks (1918), his first novel, describes from the viewpoint of a young boy the experiences of a Baptist preacher's family accepting primitive conditions in West Virginia. *Singing Mountains* (1919), a sequel, shows Ben growing up and in love. These two novels are notable for their local color. *The Chronicle of an Old Town* (1919) pictures a dismissed preacher from the East receiving a cordial welcome in an Ohio town. *Strait Is the Gate* (1946) shows Lena overcoming the handicap of an imprudence. *The Pounding Wheel* (1947), a railroad romance, has an engineer's wife signal to the superintendent her husband's whereabouts by the color of the ribbon in her hair. *The Victory of Paul Kent* (1948) is the tale of a young, incorruptible Methodist preacher who risks his future by telling what he knows about a murder. *After the Storm* (1949) is a narrative, with a college background, of a young woman who tries to live down a fatal mistake. *One Big Family* (1950) presents with sympathetic understanding the problem of three generations of a family living under one roof.

JAMES NORMAN HALL

Loomis Studios

was born on April 22, 1887, at Colfax, Iowa. After attending the public schools in the town of his birth, he entered Grinnell College in 1906. From his graduation in 1910 to 1914 he was a social worker with the Boston, Massachusetts, Society for the Prevention of Cruelty to Children. At the beginning of World War I in 1914, he enlisted as a private in Lord Kitchener's Volunteer Army and saw action as a machine gunner in the battle of Loos with the 9th Battalion of the Royal Fusiliers. Released from duty with the British army in October of 1916, he immediately joined the Lafayette Flying Corps of the French Foreign Legion. After this unit was incorporated into the American air service, he was commissioned a captain in the 94th Pursuit Squadron. Six months before the end of the war, he was shot down behind enemy lines and was captured. *Flying with Chaucer* is an account of his six months in a German prison. Following honorable discharge in March, 1919, he remained in the United States until January, 1920, while he and Charles Nordhoff wrote a history of the Lafayette Flying Corps. In January, 1920, the two friends went to the Island of Tahiti in the South Seas. There Mr. Hall married Sara Winchester, the half-Tahitian daughter of a British sea captain; they have a son and a daughter.

In his own right Mr. Hall is the author of *Kitchener's Mob* (1916), an account of his adventures in the British army; *High Adventure* (1918), a narrative of his flying experience; *On the Stream of Travel* (1926); *Mid-Pacific* (1928); *Flying with Chaucer* (1930); *Mother Goose Land* (1930), a children's book; *The Tale of a Shipwreck* (1935), his adventures on a trip to Pitcairn's Island in search of material to complete the *Bounty Trilogy; The Friends* (1934), a poem about the poetry of Edwin Arlington Robinson; *Dr. Dogbody's Leg* (1940), a series of taproom tales; *Lost Island* (1944), about the natives of a Polynesian island; and *A Word for His Sponsor* (1949), a narrative poem. The novel, *The Far Lands* (1950), a Literary Guild choice, portrays the early Polynesian migrations across the Pacific.

Mr. Hall's other books were prepared in collaboration with Charles Nordhoff. *The Lafayette Flying Corps* (1920) is a history of this famous flying unit. *Faery Lands of the South Seas* (1921) is a narrative of travel in the South Pacific. *Falcons of France* (1924) is a story about the heroic fliers of World War I.

Mutiny on the Bounty (1932), the first volume of the famous trilogy, tells the story of the revolt under Fletcher Christian on an English ship returning from the South Seas in 1789, as told by Roger Byam, a young midshipman. *Men Against the Sea* (1934) describes Captain Bligh's amazing feat of navigating a twenty-three-foot, unarmed, open boat, containing eighteen men, through thirty-six hundred miles of uncharted ocean to the Dutch colony of Timor. *Pitcairn's Island* (1934) portrays the wanderings of Christian and his fellow mutineers until they arrive at Pitcairn's Island, where they burn the *Bounty*. Only one man survives their strange adventures. The trilogy was published in one volume in 1937.

The Hurricane (1936) is a tragic romance and a character study set against the background of a violent storm on the island of Manukura in the Low Archipelago. *The Dark River* (1938) is a romantic tragedy of an Englishman and a native girl on Tahiti. *Botany Bay* (1941) deals with a young American Loyalist who is sent from Newgate prison to a penal colony in Australia in 1788. *Men without Country* (1942) concerns five convicts who escape in 1940 from Cayenne in French Guiana and find haven on a tramp steamer that takes them to England. *The High Barbaree* (1945) is a fantasy of an Iowa aviator who dreams of landing on a beautiful Pacific island with his uncle and sweetheart.

ALBERT HALPER

was born on August 3, 1904, in Chicago, Illinois, the son of Lithuanian immigrants. His father operated a grocery store on the West Side. After attending grammar school and high school, Albert Halper went to work, drifting from job to job. In the course of seven years he was employed in a mail-order business, in a factory making loose-leaf binders, in a firm distributing beauty-parlor supplies, in a jewelry store, in an electrotype foundry, and in the central post office in Chicago.

He studied accounting in night classes at Northwestern University, and he also attended evening law school, but completed none of these courses. He first aspired to be a songwriter, and he composed songs that were performed in night clubs in and near Chicago. After fourteen months as a mail clerk and just as he received a promotion, he resigned in the latter part of 1928 to go to New York City and devote himself to the task of putting his experiences on paper. His first published novel, *Union Square,* was a Literary Guild selection. In 1934 he held a Guggenheim fellowship. *On the Shore* (1934) contains short stories.

Mr. Halper has been called a proletarian writer because he reflects the hopes, aspirations, dreams, and defects of the common people. Yet he considers himself a commentator on or historian of present-day society. The subject matter of his novels and short stories derives largely from personal experience in the jobs he has held and in the places he has lived.

"I haven't much to say about writing," Mr. Halper has said. "I'm a writer. I try hard. It's become a way of life now. The payoff is a man's work. It's either good or not so good. My early work, especially the picnic scenes in *The Foundry,* was influenced by the painter Breughel. Maybe I should have been a painter instead of a writer. I'll never know. We're all children stumbling in the dark. I try to say a few words about it, the clearest way I know how."

Union Square (1933) shows the social tensions, frustrations, and unhappiness of people living in the tenements in New York City near communist headquarters. Grievances aired by speakers in the public square lead to a riot, and unemployed Hank Austin is crippled by a kick of a policeman's horse. *The Foundry* (1934) details the lives of workers and employers in a Chicago electrotype foundry in the year preceding the crash of 1929. *The Chute* (1929) pictures the assembling of merchandise by roller-skating workers who make a game of their high-speed job in a Chicago mail-order house and who develop a class-conscious spirit. These three books can be classed as proletarian novels.

Sons of the Fathers (1940) portrays the reactions of Saul Bergman, a Russian immigrant who is a small grocer in Chicago, and his great distaste for World War I. He had come to the United States to gain freedom in the hope that his children might not have to wage war. His intellectual son dies on the battlefield in France, another son is a slacker, and four younger children await the storm. *The Little People* (1942) deals with an exclusive Chicago department store, where clerks, floorwalkers, a hatter, and the elevator boy are helpless in the grip of their bosses and their routine jobs. Each dreams of a lucky break that never comes. *Only an Inch from Glory* (1943) is the tragic story of four closely interknit, ambitious yet uncertain people in New York City. Sam Gluckman wants to be a playwright and an aviator, partly to impress Dorothy Lynch, an art student from Indiana, who tries to cover her failure by knowing famous people. She in turn has a number of affairs with men while Frank Keenan, a Boston accountant, waits to marry her. Anne, Sam's wife, hopefully dreams of having a baby.

ALBERTA PIERSON HANNUM

Kossuth

was born on August 3, 1906, at Condit, Ohio, the daughter of Adelle Evans Pierson and James Ellsworth Pierson. Educators were to be found on both sides of the family, the Piersons descending from Abraham Pierson, first president of Yale, with Dr. Jarvis Evans more recently president of Northwestern University. Her own schooling began in the country schoolhouse at Condit, named for that pioneering branch of the Pierson-Condit family who numbered among their predecessors professors at Princeton, Rutgers, and Amherst, and a cofounder of Mt. Holyoke. From Condit her education proceeded through the public schools of Columbus. In 1927 she graduated from Ohio State University, where she was president of the Women's Self-Government Association, president of Delta Gamma Sorority, and a member of Mortar Board. Miss Pierson pursued postgraduate work at Columbia University. Her first love of the mountains, about which she wrote subsequently, came from early vacations spent in the vast beauty of western North Carolina. In 1929 she married Robert Fulton Hannum. The Hannums live in the country outside Moundsville, West Virginia; they have two daughters.

Having no knowledge of novel technique but with a feeling for music, she composed her first book, *Thursday April,* in the form of a tone poem. From novel writing she went to short stories with the same southern mountain locale; one of them was reprinted in an O'Brien collection. During the confusions of World War II she broke completely away from regional material to write about the humorous but enduring ways of family life, centering in the zestful adventures of its children. In 1943 she prepared the section on the mountain people in the symposium, *The Great Smokies and the Blue Ridge.* Just before the outbreak of World War II Mrs. Hannum became acquainted with the Navajo Indians, through friends who owned an Indian trading post high in the Arizona desert, and thus she became interested in the water colors of a little Indian boy, Beatien Yazz, the son of the traders' handyman.

Mrs. Hannum's books have a "combination of ordinariness and fantasy, of ease and intensity." Her themes are the pity and the beauty and the humor of all human things; she does not overlook danger and sordidness, but neither does she overlook nobility and greatness in the flow of life that makes design. She suffuses her stories with a warm poetic glow which illuminates the elemental depth of these feelings in all peoples, whatever their surface and environmental differences. Her style is like homespun which has the bright colors of the slow, strong, regional speech of her mountain people. The flavor of the folk idiom reflects the passion and sadness of the traditional folk ballad.

Thursday April (1931), written with appealing and poetic simplicity, is about a North Carolina mountain woman who yearns for some return for her own love for her husband, Joe. When this seems not to be, she channels her devotion to her last two children that they may have the fullness of life which she has always wanted for herself. Ironically, when the children are gone, she finds she still yearns for some word from Joe. This first book, with its tendency to pungent underwriting, was hailed as a novel of distinction. *The Hills Step Lightly* (1934) is the story of the love of Deborah Deane for a man she sees only four times, but which in its restraint deepens to the fire and motivating center of her life.

The Gods and One (1941) is the maturing experience of a lonely, sensitive mountain girl whose brief time of ecstatic happiness leaves her desolate with the thoughts of bearing an illegitimate child. She flees for a period to the offered refuge of a lusty and polygamous moonshiner to gain food and shelter for her boy. In her return to face her own community, she achieves an understanding of truth. *Spin A Silver Dollar* (1946) is the account of two moderns who blithely buy a Navajo trading post and discover the ancestral genius of a child painter. *Roseanna McCoy* (1947) concerns the Hatfield-McCoy feud in the West Virginia mountains as a background for two of its young people, who could have been two people anywhere, whose right to love and happiness is threatened by prejudices and war. Mrs. Hannum departed as much as possible from her former use of idiom and local color, using only enough to keep valid the Americana angle of the incident. Although not an historical novel, it is based upon what actually happened in August, 1880, to Roseanna and Jonse Hatfield. Their love cannot halt the black hatred of their families, nor could that blight deter them. A universal quality emerges in this strong plot narrated with poetic beauty.

JOHN HARRIMAN

Chester T. Holbrook

was born at Purchase, New York, on September 29, 1904. After studying at St. Mark's School at Southboro, Massachusetts, he went in 1920 to Europe where his education was continued under tutors. From 1924 to 1930 he was a reporter on the New York *Evening World,* and from 1933 to 1937 he was an investment manager. Since 1930 he has been a free-lance writer.

Winter Term (1940), his first novel, is an indictment of the small, exclusive preparatory school which seeks to perpetuate the aristocratic tradition. *The Career of Philip Hazen* (1941) portrays the changes in Wall Street after the crash of 1929 in a story of the conservative, aristocratic Hazen and a cynical, unsentimental go-getter, Gerard Swade. *The Magnate* (1946) describes the operations of high finance in the years from 1922 to 1929 in the story of a man who organizes a vast utilities empire.

BERNICE KELLY HARRIS

was born in October, 1894, in Wake County, North Carolina, the daughter of down-to-earth farmers. She attended Mt. Moriah Academy in Clayton and Cary High School, and then went on to Meredith College in Raleigh, from which she graduated in 1913. In 1917 she began teaching high-school English in Seaboard, North Carolina, and has made her home in that city ever since. During several summers she studied playwriting at the University of North Carolina, and she has written a number of one-act plays based upon regional material. Seven of these plays are in her *Folk Plays of Eastern Carolina* (1940). In 1926 she married Herbert Kavanaugh Harris, a farmer and cotton ginner.

Mrs. Harris has stated that her philosophy can be summed up tersely in the phrase, "People will do." Of her novels she has said: "It is always people in my writing; the focal point is what people are in spite of circumstances and sometimes, of course, because of them. But the emphasis is on integrity, beyond circumstances of living or color or creed. I have come to admire tremendously the spirit in human beings. My visits with sharecroppers have left me admiring as often as pitying. The sum total of joy and misery, I truly believe, has very little to do with color and very much to do with their human relationships. It is important to deserve as well as to demand, to emphasize integrity and not just pigmentation. Crusaders might work on that angle as well as on anti-segregation."

Purslane (1939), her first novel, is about daily life in the family of John Fuller, a North Carolina cotton farmer, in the early years of the twentieth century. Many of the events are drawn from experiences in Mrs. Harris' home community, and some of the most dramatic ones, like incidents in Greek tragedy, reflect the universal experience found in country neighborhoods. *Portulaca* (1941) presents facets of human behavior in a small, non-industrial, southern town, with the unpleasing side highlighted but with the pleasant side not neglected. The story is a framework to present a variety of characters. The young wife who is the chief protagonist learns that the town, which she once thought mean and petty, is a worthy community.

Sweet Beulah Land (1943) deals with the big farms in North Carolina under the sharecropping system, but the book makes clear that it is not so much a system as a set of circumstances that make some people sharecroppers and some plantation owners. The story concerns a poor young man who falls in love with the daughter of an aristocratic family. *Sage Quarter* (1945), a nostalgic picture of childhood in the early twentieth century, portrays the large Ardley family in the countryside of North Carolina as seen through the eyes of a little girl.

Janey Jeens (1946), the story of the long and happy marriage of a Negro couple, treats with dignity the theme that "Negroes are human beings." Never once in the book is Janey's color mentioned, and many readers do not recognize that the novel is about a colored family. Janey's integrity is more eloquent than her pigmentation. *Hearthstones* (1948), set in the Roanoke River country of North Carolina, tells about two deserters: one leaves Lee's army in the 1860's and the other the United States army in 1941. The four elderly Day sisters, whose brother had deserted Lee, adopt the second one and lead him to return to fight for his country. These four sisters, with nothing but a breath and a few acres of land, make a life for themselves on an isolated island and illustrate the invincible toughness of the human spirit.

CHARLES YALE HARRISON

Blackstone Studios

was born on June 16, 1898, in Philadelphia, Pennsylvania. He was educated in the public schools of New York City and Montreal. His formal education ended in the fourth grade; after that his father's extensive library, in which he read widely, became his school. He served as a machine gunner in France and Belgium and fell wounded at Amiens on August 8, 1918, while a noncommissioned officer of the 14th Battalion, Royal Montreal Regiment. After World War I he worked at various occupations: he managed a motion-picture theater in Montreal, sold real estate, and was a reporter on Canadian and United States papers. He has also written the first book-length biography of Clarence Darrow, several brochures on public housing, and *Thank God for My Heart Attack* (1949), a book dealing with the cardiac seizure which he suffered in 1947. He resides in New York City.

Generals Die in Bed (1930) is an autobiographical war novel, anti-militaristic in tone, which tells the story of a group of privates in the Canadian Expeditionary Force in World War I. The title of this novel has been adopted into the language as an ironical expression. *A Child Is Born* (1931) is an account of social injustice as shown in the tragic lives of a family living in a poverty-stricken section of Brooklyn; the central theme is based on the effect of adverse social circumstances in creating a juvenile criminal. *There Are Victories* (1933) is a psychological novel which pictures the tragedy of a young woman who forsakes her church and who can find no adequate compensation in modern materialistic society. Ruth Courtney struggles unsuccessfully through thirty-seven years of her life to achieve some measure of love and beauty. The New York *Times* stated that the portrayal of Ruth is "wholly convincing" and that "Mr. Harrison's realism, both of words and action, is at times blisteringly terrible, but it is invariably justified."

Meet Me on the Barricades (1938) is a satire which pokes fun at fascism and communism. Its central character is a mild, henpecked, little man with a weak heart who compensates for his lack of real adventure by heroic daydreams in an imaginary revolutionary world. *Nobody's Fool* (1948), also a satire, is the story of a New York public-relations firm which sets out to create the so-called common man for purely commercial purposes. In essence, the novel exposes the cynicism, the ruthlessness, and the corruption which motivate certain high-pressure manipulators of American public opinion. Jack Sherrod, the chief character, wonders whether "all this shoving, shouting, and showmanship" is necessary.

ERIC HATCH

was born on October 31, 1901, in New York City. At nineteen he left St. Paul's School to enter his father's investment banking business. During World War I he was in the service with a national guard unit. In 1928 he left business to devote full time to writing stories, novels, and motion-picture scripts. He married Gertrude Thomas in 1929; they live in Hollywood.

He writes entertaining popular novels which are enlivened by a pleasant vein of humor and by light, satirical characterizations.

A Couple of Quick Ones (1928), his first novel, is about Martin Jones, a playboy who wakes up in Greenwich, Connecticut, married to an actress. He goes to work as a floorwalker, recoups his lost fortune, gladly loses his wife, and regains the girl who had jilted him. *Romance Prescribed* (1930) pictures a novelist undergoing a useful remodeling of manners at the hands of a nice girl and a wise fisherman on a houseboat. *Lover's Loot* (1931) describes the effect of a girl's mistaking a young lawyer for a physician. *Five Days* (1933) is a merry tale about the adventures of Beadleston Preece, a sportsman, who loses his fortune and steals a yacht.

Road Show (1934) concerns a man unfortunate in Wall Street and a colonel who escape from a private sanitarium where they are recuperating. *Fly by Night* (1935) tells what happens to Brett Dixon when his father sends him away from home to test the loyalty of the boy's fiancée. Brett meets some chorus girls and marries one of them. *My Man Godfrey* (1935) portrays high life in New York City in a story of an ex-forgotten man and a beautiful but dumb member of the "Four Hundred." *Good Old Jack* (1937) recounts the experiences of John Holcombe after he loses his money in Hollywood; two astute girls help him achieve success. *The Captain Needs a Mate* (1938) describes the adventures of a man who buys a palatial yacht and takes his friends on a cruise.

Unexpected Uncle (1941) tells how Seton Mansley, who wants to be helpful when he finds beauty in distress, helps to straighten out the love affair of a girl found weeping in an exclusive shop in Palm Beach, Florida. *Words and Music* (1943) describes two country girls who go to New York to aspire to careers, one as a singer and the other as an actress. *Unexpected Warrior* (1947) shows what happens when the meek husband of a very successful actress becomes a soldier. *Beautiful Bequest* (1950) details the adventures of a veteran who is visited by the ghost of an Irish wartime friend and who becomes more closely acquainted with the beautiful girl bequeathed to him by the Irishman.

WALTER HAVIGHURST

was born on November 28, 1901, in Appleton, Wisconsin. He grew up there and in Decatur, Illinois. From 1919 to 1921 he was a student at Ohio Wesleyan University. He graduated in 1924 from the University of Denver, did graduate work at King's College, London, and received a master's degree from Columbia University. Since 1928 he has taught English at Miami University in Oxford, Ohio. He learned to splice a rope on Great Lakes ore boats and sailed in a dozen steam and sailing vessels in the Atlantic and in the Pacific before graduating from college. He has written three non-fiction books: *Upper Mississippi* (1937), a volume in the "Rivers of America" series; *The Long Ships Passing* (1942), the history of transportation on the Great Lakes; and *Land of Promise* (1946), an account of the settlement of the Northwest Territory. With his wife he has written two juveniles about Norwegian pioneers, *High Prairie* (1941) and *Song of the Pines* (1949). A general theme in Mr. Havighurst's books is the growth of regional character and culture in the Middle West. The moods and ideas of his characters reveal the spirit of that area.

Mr. Havighurst's first novel, *Pier 17* (1935), deals with the crew of the *S.S. Pamona* and a seaman's strike on a West Coast dock as Adrian Scarf betrays his union comrades. *The Quiet Shore* (1937) portrays the antagonism and class distrust of the farm and city branches of the Bradley family on a Lake Erie homestead from the Civil War swamp era to the industrial age. *The Winds of Spring* (1940) describes pioneer Wisconsin in the years from 1840 to 1870 and brings into that community a learned ornithologist. *No Homeward Course* (1941) concerns three men and a woman who have been picked up by a German raider in the Caribbean Sea in World War II. *The Signature of Time* (1949) traces the changing fortunes of the Hazard family on a Lake Erie island from the time of Jason Hazard, woodsman and trapper, to the return of Mawry Hazard, war correspondent, from a German prison camp at the end of World War II.

EDWARD HAVILL

was born in Rochester, New York, on November 29, 1907. After graduation from high school, he left Rochester and its schools to learn about life while doing merry-go-round operating, newspaper and advertising work, caretaking, landscaping, house painting, and paper hanging. He lived chiefly in small communities before returning north, and now lives with his wife and three children in the Finger Lakes country. The first story he published in America appeared in *Story* magazine and then there were other stories in *Harper's Bazaar*. One of these was reprinted in the O'Henry Memorial collection for 1940.

Tell It to the Laughing Stars (1942), his first novel, has Steve Lanely, a gifted commercial artist, resign his job in Rochester, New York, and move to Keuka Lake to escape the falsities of society and to straighten out the emotional life of his wife and himself. *The Low Road* (1944) has autobiographical overtones in the story of a writer and his wife who await the birth of their first child in a cabin on the wooded shores of Keuka Lake. *Big Ember* (1947) pictures a Norwegian immigrant family establishing itself on a Minnesota farm in 1862. An attack by Sioux Indians, who are resentful of the encroachment of whites on their lands, brings tragedy and destruction, but these hardy pioneers rebuild their homes and their lives on their isolated farms.

HIRAM HAYDN

was born on November 3, 1907, in Cleveland, Ohio, the son of a college professor and the grandson of a president of Western Reserve University who was also a noted Presbyterian minister. A graduate of Amherst, he received his doctorate in comparative literature at Columbia University in 1942. He taught from 1928 to 1944, at first in a private school for boys and later at Western Reserve University, the Woman's College of the University of North Carolina, and in the summer session of the Columbia University Graduate School. He now conducts a novel workshop at the New School for Social Research, and is editor of the general quarterly, *The American Scholar,* as well as editor of a book-publishing firm. He wrote a non-fiction book, *The Counter-Renaissance* (1950), a history of the revolt against reason and moralism led by Montaigne and Machiavelli. Mr. Haydn's other books include *The Portable Elizabethan Reader* (1946), *A World of Great Stories* (with John Cournos, 1947), and *Thesaurus of Book Digests* (1949).

Mr. Haydn is preoccupied in his novels with the general theme of the discrepancy between the dream or the ideal and the actuality. The terms in which this general proposition has been stated differ, however, from book to book. In the first one, the central character comes to a realization that only those dreams or ideals which are firmly rooted in reality have positive meaning. The struggle to achieve reality is also emphasized in the second book, but here the philosophical solution is replaced by a psychological one. This trend is carried further in *The Time Is Noon,* but considerably broadened in scope through an appeal for an "ethic of health" which suggests that there will be no resolution of the problems of "making democracy work" until individuals attain complete integration.

His first novel, *By Nature Free* (1943), portrays the conflict between Philip Blair, an idealistic writer, and his brother, Harry, who has been associating with Nazis in Colombia, South America. Philip clings to ideas of social freedom and almost loses his wife to Harry. *Manhattan Furlough* (1945) tells about Sergeant Andrew Carver's visit to New York to explain his part in the death of a young soldier. He lacks courage to state the situation frankly to the boy's parents. *The Time Is Noon* (1948) is the story of six young people and their blind search for happiness in the world of false security in 1929; the book raises the serious question whether Americans are willing to make democracy work as a way of life. Lloyd Morris stated that "few recent novels have achieved as comprehensive a portrait of our national life in geographic scope, social diversity, and economic contrast."

ALFRED HAYES

Rose Wolfe

was born in London, England, in 1911. He grew up in New York and attended school in that city. There, too, he worked for a time as a newspaperman and writer for magazines and radio. In 1943 he entered the army and served in Italy. While in Rome he met Roberto Rossellini and Luigi Zampa, and assisted the former on the motion picture, "Paisan." Mr. Hayes returned to America in 1945 and went to Hollywood to work for Warner Brothers. His poetry won the Eunice Tietjens prize. He is married and has a daughter. He has written *The Big Time* (1944) and *Welcome to the Castle* (1950), volumes of poems. He was co-author of "Journeyman" (1938), a dramatization of a novel by Erskine Caldwell, and " 'Tis of Thee" (1940), a musical comedy.

Mr. Hayes' poetry and fiction are written in short, staccato style, similar to that of Ernest Hemingway. Emphasis is on sharp pictorial effect through the unexpected thrust of a startling detail. His vivid dialogue is appropriate to his fully visualized characters. Yet his realistic manner, though hard-boiled in tone, never altogether hides a nostalgia for something softer and kinder in life than the harshness he portrays.

All Thy Conquests (1946), his first novel, tells the story of the liberation of Rome in September, 1944, by American troops and portrays the attitudes of both groups: the confused uncertainty and the hopeful dreaming of the defeated Italians, and the somewhat hard-hearted firmness of the conquerors who see new dangers of fascism arising. *Shadow of Heaven* (1947) pictures Harry Oberon, a union organizer, who feels old at forty and wonders about the validity of labor organizations, love, and life. *The Girl on the Via Flaminia* (1949) depicts the relationship between a lonely American soldier and a hungry, respectable Italian girl in the Rome of World War II. They take an apartment on the Via Flaminia during Christmas week in 1944. Lisa agrees to the arrangement solely to get food and trinkets, while Robert needs companionship. There is no love and little understanding between them, and in the end she is arrested for immoral conduct. The background portrays the dismal misery, confusion, and disorder of the distressed and demoralized populace.

DORSHA HAYES

Leja Gorska

was born in Galesburg, Illinois, a descendant of Gen. Henry Knox, commander of artillery in the American Revolution and Secretary of War in Washington's cabinet. She attended the elementary school of the University of Chicago and Mrs. Finch's School in New York City. She studied ballet dancing with Pavlowa and Fokine, and then, after considerable theatrical experience which included being a dance soloist in Shubert revues, she entered the concert field and gave dance recitals. She also founded a small art theater of the dance, which gave weekly performances over a period of seven or eight years. For many years she was interested in the labor movement and served as educational director for a New York union. Tired of hearing what is wrong with America, she took up the question, "What have we Americans to be thankful for?" in her first book, *The American Primer* (1941). A second non-fiction book, *Chicago: Crossroads of American Enterprise* (1944), is an anecdotal history of Chicago from the early days to the 1930's.

Miss Hayes' deep interest as a novelist lies with human beings in their psychological conflicts. "Characters in life are not static," she has stated; "they are ascending or descending. This movement is portrayed in *Mrs. Heaton's Daughter,* the girl slowly battling her way up, the mother sinking lower and lower."

In stating her opinion about current fiction, Miss Hayes has said: "It seems to me that too much writing is done from the thinking viewpoint to the exclusion of that of feeling-perception. I am not speaking only of the 'hard-boiled,' journalistic type of fiction, but of the attitude to be found in much current writing in which what a character thinks is described, but what he *feels* is left to guess work. It is not, I think, either sentimental or romantic to say that the crucial decisions for good or ill in the lives of most people are made as much on a basis of feeling-perception as on rational thinking. Americans are apt to be immature where it comes to feeling; they tend to be sentimental. Thus there is an inclination to be 'tough' about it, denying the feeling values."

Mrs. Heaton's Daughter (1943), her first novel, with a background of Broadway and the theatrical district, is a psychological study of a mother, whose career as a singer had been frustrated by her father, and the way she goads her daughter to be a dancer. Mrs. Heaton's decay is that of any human being who fastens upon another through failure to live out an individual destiny, seeking instead to live vicariously. A life-urge toward growth, more than her love for a fine man, helps Diana make something of herself. *Who Walk with the Earth* (1945), a social novel which sounds a warning against the lack of democracy in unions, gives the arguments on both sides in the labor-management conflict. The story, which reflects Miss Hayes' first-hand experiences as a union employee, concerns a wealthy young Harvard graduate whose ideals lead him to participate in the labor movement in New York.

WORTH TUTTLE HEDDEN

was born on January 10, 1896, in Raleigh, North Carolina, the daughter of a minister long prominent in the Southern Methodist Episcopal Church. By her own admission she hated school, but spent two intensive years at Martha Washington College in Abingdon, Virginia, received her bachelor's degree from Trinity College (now Duke University), and spent a year at the School of Journalism of Columbia University. She then worked for a women's vocational bureau in Richmond, Virginia, and married a northerner who is now director of port development for the Port of New York Authority. Having achieved a perspective of the South and wishing to write about colored people, she went to Louisiana, where she taught for a year at Straight College, a Negro institution.

Her first novel, *Wives of High Pasture* (1944), is based on the Oneida Community in 1857 and tells how Mark Winstanley, a man from England on a walking tour, meets Pilgrim Sawyer and causes her to refuse to marry the leader of the colony. *The Other Room* (1947) concerns Nina Latham, a southern girl reared to believe in white supremacy, who in the early 1920's teaches in a college for Negroes in New Orleans.

ERNEST HEMINGWAY

was born in Oak Park, Illinois, just outside of Chicago, on July 21, 1898. He was the son of a well-known physician, and on trips with his father into northern Michigan he evinced an interest in those sports which, outside of his writing, have been his chief preoccupation: big-game hunting and fishing. At grade school in Oak Park and at the Oak Park High School, he was outstanding in boxing and on the football field; while still in his teens he began to earn his own living doing odd jobs, working as a day laborer and farm hand, and for a short time acting as a fighter's sparring partner.

Instead of going to college, he obtained a place as a reporter on the Kansas City *Star*. A few months later he volunteered as an ambulance driver and went to France with an American unit before our entry into World War I. He enlisted in the Italian Arditi and fell wounded; these experiences furnished the material for the great war scenes in *A Farewell to Arms*. The Italian government honored him with two of its highest medals, the Medaglio d'Argento al Valore Militare and the Croce di Guerra.

Back in the United States after the war, he married Hadley Richardson in September, 1921, and took a job as reporter on the Toronto *Star*, which in December sent him abroad as European correspondent. He reported the post-war disturbances in the Near East and the revolution in Greece, and then went to Lausanne in November, 1922, to report the peace conference. At this time a suitcase containing all his manuscripts—a novel, eighteen stories, and thirty poems—was stolen. When he returned to Paris to write for the Hearst newspapers, he began anew, receiving much encouragement in his work from Gertrude Stein and Ezra Pound.

In *Poetry* magazine for January, 1923, appeared his first signed literary piece. With the publication of *The Sun Also Rises* (1926), a novel, and *Men Without Women* (1927), a collection of short stories, Ernest Hemingway's originality of style and forcefulness of presentation were generally recognized. His name became symbolic of a staccato, short-sentence style and of a subject matter which included violence, athletic prowess, toughness, sex, frank language, the drinking of alcoholic beverages to excess, and an obsession with death. He was praised for giving a new direction to fictional prose style and was imitated by many established and many more beginning writers.

In the latter part of 1927 he married Pauline Pfeiffer, a writer in the Paris office of *Vogue* magazine, and they moved to the United States where they established residence in Key West, Florida, for the ten years from 1928 to 1938. During these years his reputation grew as a sportsman, fisherman, boxer, and big-game hunter; he exercised regularly and energetically to overcome the troublesome weaknesses which hung on as a result of war wounds. He brought back in 1934 from a big-game hunt in Africa a collection of mounted heads and other trophies. At this time, too, he designed a fishing boat, the *Pilar,* which he piloted on fishing cruises to the Bahamas. It was in 1935 at Bimini that he showed his prowess as a boxer by more than holding his own with Tom Heeney, the British Empire heavyweight champion.

Hemingway loved Spain best after the United States, and when the army revolt led by General Francisco Franco burst into civil war on July 18, 1936, the novelist became greatly aroused, raised forty thousand dollars on personal notes to purchase ambulances for the Loyalist forces, and made several trips to Spain to report the events for the North American Newspaper Alliance. From these experiences and interest came *For Whom the Bell Tolls* (1940), his own favorite among his novels. On November 21, 1940, he married Martha Gellhorn, the novelist, in Cheyenne, Wyoming. Their honeymoon carried them to China as war correspondents to cover the Japanese systematic campaign to seize northern China. On their return the Hemingways settled down in Havana, Cuba.

Immediately after the attack on Pearl Harbor by the Japanese on December 7, 1941, Mr. Hemingway offered the services of himself and his yacht to the navy. For the two years from 1942 to 1944 as a Q-boat in Naval Intelligence it cruised in various disguises off the north coast of Cuba in search of German submarines, an exceedingly dangerous mission. When the submarine menace ended in the spring of 1944, he flew to England to join the Royal Air Force as an accredited correspondent. He was on many operational missions. On July 20 he joined the United States army ground forces as a correspondent for *Collier's* magazine. With the troops of the 4th Infantry Division of the First Army he shared hardships during an eighteen-day battle in November. Generally he roved about with his jeep to make contact with French irregulars, and from these guerrilla soldiers he often gained valuable information. For his services he was decorated with a Bronze Star. On his return in 1946 he married Mary Welsh in Havana. She is from Minnesota and worked on newspapers and in the London bureau of *Time* magazine when Mr. Hemingway met her in 1944.

In February, 1949, while shooting wild fowl in Italy, Mr. Hemingway was the victim of a strange accident. A tiny fragment of shotgun wadding fell into his eye, and its presence was not discovered for several days; by this time blood poisoning had set in, and it spread so rapidly and so virulently that his doctors despaired of his recovery. He was given only a short time to live, but he confounded his physicians and threw off his illness.

For some years prior to the accident, Mr. Hemingway had been at work on a war novel of large proportions, which he knew he could not finish in a short time. He therefore set aside this work and began immediately to write a novel which had been taking form in his mind. Many of his works had been written under such pressure: *The Sun Also Rises* was written in Valencia, Madrid, and Paris in six weeks; on a single day in Madrid when the bullfights had been snowed out in May, he had written three memorable short stories: "The Killers" before breakfast, "Ten Indians" after lunch, and "Today Is Friday" that night.

Ernest Hemingway is physically large and robust, six feet tall, carrying a weight of about two hundred pounds. He is the father of three sons, one by his first wife and two by his second. His home in Cuba is named "Finca Vigia" ("Lookout Farm"), and the house is of Spanish style. On the fifteen-acre estate are gardens and a swimming pool.

Mr. Hemingway's non-fiction books include *Today Is Friday* (1926), a play; *Death in the Afternoon* (1932), about bullfighting; and *Green Hills of Africa* (1935), an account of a big-game hunting trip. His short stories have been collected in *In Our Time* (1925), *Men Without Women* (1927), *Winner Take Nothing* (1933), and *The Fifth Column and the First Forty-Nine* (1938).

The Sun Also Rises (1926), his first novel, describes the Americans who in the 1920's were given the name of the "Lost Generation" because they lived in Europe rather than at home and because they felt that World War I had doomed their lives. The young men and women in the novel spend their days in liquor, love, and fights, seeking in alcohol and physical sensations relief from their gloomy thoughts. *The Torrents of Spring* (1926) is a parody that satirizes and burlesques the style of Sherwood Anderson.

A Farewell to Arms (1929) is the love story of an American, Lieutenant Henry, attached to the Italian army, and of Catharine Barkley, an English nurse. The fighting in Italy in World War I supplies the background; one of the most memorable episodes is the retreat from Caporetto. This work immediately achieved best-seller status and confirmed Mr. Hemingway's position as a stylist whose short, pungent sentences vividly recreate scenes, people, conversation, and the mood of the times.

To Have and Have Not (1937) is about Harry Morgan, a strong, tough, individualistic fisherman with a fast motor boat in Key West, Florida. He engages in smuggling and rum-running for support, and he dies from an escaping bank robber's bullet. Contrasted with Morgan and other "have nots" are rich yacht owners, writers, and artists, the "haves." The theme as stated by Morgan is: "One man alone ain't got," meaning that an individual cannot win in life by himself.

For Whom the Bell Tolls (1940) concerns Robert Jordan, an American on the Loyalist side in the Spanish civil war in 1936, who is deep behind the fascist lines with orders to blow up a bridge. During four days he guides guerrillas and sleeps in caves, meets and loves a Spanish girl, Maria, destroys the bridge, and dies by a fascist bullet. The thesis of the book is that the death of a man like Jordan who is fighting in a cause cannot be viewed with indifference by lovers of freedom.

Across the River and into the Trees (1950) is a love story of a war-scarred colonel, Richard Cantwell, aged fifty-one, and an eighteen-year-old countess in postwar Venice during the three days before he dies of a heart attack. He talks about love, death, happiness, sorrow, hunting, food, and war. He berates the highest officers in World War II and praises infantrymen's courage.

JOSEPHINE HERBST

was born on March 5, 1897, in Sioux City, Iowa. Her parents had moved to Iowa from Pennsylvania in the 1880's. The families of both of her parents had come to this country from Germany and Switzerland shortly after 1700. She attended high school in her native city and studied at Morningside College, the University of Iowa, and the University of California, from which she graduated in 1918. In college she earned part of her way by typing, teaching, and working in a print shop. She went to New York in 1920 and worked in a department store and in a charity organization as a case worker; later she was a publicity writer and an editorial reader for H. L. Mencken. From 1922 to 1925 she lived in Germany, France, and Italy. Her interest in writing began in childhood; her first published story appeared in *The Smart Set* in 1923. On October 21, 1925, she married John Herrmann, who was a member of the staff of the magazine *transition.* She returned to Europe in 1930 and visited the Soviet Union and Austria. In 1932 she spent a year in Mexico and in 1935 went to Germany for the New York *Post.* In 1937 she was a correspondent in Spain during the bombardment of Madrid; in 1939 she traveled in South America. A Guggenheim fellowship was awarded her in 1936.

Her first novel, *Nothing Is Sacred* (1928), is the story of a small-town family, betrayed to disaster by a weak son-in-law, but held together by strong family affection and an old-fashioned code of honor. *Money for Love* (1929) tells of a young actress who loses her pride of life through the defeat of her first love and, humbled, seeks to regain her lost world through mistaken and mercenary means.

Pity Is Not Enough (1933), *The Executioner Waits* (1934), and *Rope of Gold* (1939) compose a trilogy narrating the rise, the fall, and the continuing adaptations of an American family, the Trexlers, during three critical periods of our national life. *Pity Is Not Enough* deals with the crisis in the decades following the Civil War. A Trexler son, deeply imbued with faith in the American dream, goes forth as a youth of nineteen to seek the family fortune. He first loses his sense of moral values as a carpetbagger in the South; then he loses his health and his hopes in his search for gold in the Black Hills. Finally he loses his reason and his life. *The Executioner Waits* carries the story to the years between 1918 and 1929 For second-generation Trexlers the American dream in terms of cash success has faded. The young people, disillusioned by World War I and family misfortunes, turn to other goals for satisfactions greater than material success and family ties can give. *Rope of Gold* follows the younger Trexlers into the depression from 1933 to 1937. The chaotic era is still interpreted in terms of the family but it is no longer a solid entity. The members are so scattered that their story is told through the lives of other people—a farm organizer, an automobile manufacturer, and a union organizer—who hear the sounds from Europe that foretell the second World War.

Satan's Sergeants (1941) describes the envy and disruption that fall upon a rural community in Bucks County, Pennsylvania, when farming fails the natives and wealthy newcomers from the city rush in to turn the land from production to purposes of pleasure. *Somewhere the Tempest Fell* (1947) presents Adam Snow, a mystery writer and former youthful soldier in World War I, who is challenged by the events of 1939 and by the fate of his young daughter to create significance out of a meaningless past in which he achieved success without gratification.

VIRGINIA HERSCH

was born Helen Virginia Davis in San Francisco, California, on May 31, 1896. She graduated from the University of California with the degrees of Bachelor of Arts and Doctor of Jurisprudence. She contributed to the university magazines, both legal and literary, and was awarded the Emily Chamberlain Cook poetry prize. She went to France and in Paris married the artist, Lee Hersch. Her first attempt at professional writing was a magazine article in French explaining modern American literature. In her books her aim has been to combine the truth of non-fiction with the imaginative insight and interest of a novel.

Bird of God (1929), her first book, is a fictionalized biography of the mysterious sixteenth-century painter, El Greco. *Woman Under Glass* (1930) is the story of St. Teresa of Avila, who was at once a great mystic and a great organizer and feminist, and who experienced within the confines of her religious vows the full life of a woman. *Storm Beach* (1933) is a story of several generations of a proud Jewish family living in Charleston, South Carolina, during the first part of the nineteenth century. Centering on the story of Judith and her love for a Gentile, it traces an unadmitted and often indefinable boundary of discrimination.

The Seven Cities of Gold (1946), based on the Coronado expedition, describes the first planned entry of Europeans into what is now the United States, and their weird relationship with the Indians of the Southwest and the Spanish colonists of Mexico. Though the expedition was a futile search for gold, the young soldier hero of the novel drew full compensation from the adventure and its results. *To Seize a Dream* (1948) is set against a background of France in the first half of the nineteenth century, in which Napoleon and Talleyrand, Stendhal, Balzac, Dumas, Ingres, George Sand, Chopin, and the young Cézanne played their successive parts. It tells the story of Eugene Delacroix, one of the great geniuses of French painting.

JOHN HERSEY

Hulburd

was born in Tientsin, China, on June 17, 1914, the son of American parents. He first attended schools in Tientsin; later he studied at the Hotchkiss School in Connecticut, at Yale, and at Clare College of Cambridge University in England. He was private secretary to Sinclair Lewis in the summer of 1937, and then became an editor of *Time*. As a correspondent in the Orient for that magazine, he interviewed such leaders as Chiang Kai-shek, Matsuoka, and General Homma. Something of that first-hand knowledge of fighting men went into Mr. Hersey's first book, *Men on Bataan* (1942). *Into the Valley* (1943) describes an episode in a battle on Guadalcanal. The book attempts to recapture the feelings of the author and of several Marines who went down into the jungle valley of the Matanikau River. He returned to the Far East in 1945 for *The New Yorker* and *Life,* and there gathered material for *Hiroshima* (1946), an account of the atomic bomb-explosion over that city.

Mr. Hersey's first novel, *A Bell for Adano* (1944), portrays an Italian-American major who employs his authority to reconstruct a Sicilian village and to infuse in the people the principles of democratic idealism. This book received the Pulitzer prize. *The Wall* (1950) pictures the extermination of the Jews in the Warsaw ghetto during the war years from 1939 to 1943; at first they have trouble with their papers, their rations, and their working conditions, and then they perceive that the Germans plan a total annihilation of those who live inside the wall. The story is told from the viewpoint of an archivist.

HARRY HERVEY

was born on November 5, 1900, in Beaumont, Texas. He has lived in New York, Pennsylvania, South Carolina, Georgia, Florida, Alabama, and California. He has traveled extensively in the Far East and Africa. In 1925 he went on an expedition up the Mekong River in Indo-China and reconstructed the history of several ruined Khmer cities built by the same mysterious race that created Angkor in Cambodia. He attended Georgia Military Academy at Atlanta, and Sewanee Military Academy in Tennessee, but did not go to college. At sixteen he sold his first story to *The Smart Set*. One of his early tales is included in O'Brien's *Best Short Stories of 1924*. He spent considerable time in Hollywood writing motion pictures;

among his most successful films are "Shanghai Express" and "The Road to Singapore." *Where Strange Gods Call* (1924) and *King Cobra* (1928) are accounts of his travels.

He is loath to discuss the technique or trends of writing and is content to leave talk about these matters to those who cannot create: a writer's voice is more eloquent, he feels, when it is muted and contained within the limits of his own work. He has definite ideas about craftsmanship: he desires to achieve a fusion of style and material, and to realize a balance between unreality and reality.

Caravans by Night (1922), his first novel, is a romantic tale set in India and Tibet that discloses, through a plot of intrigue and adventure, much of the color, the manners, and the customs of these two countries. *The Black Parrot, A Tale of the Golden Chersonese* (1923) concerns an American girl traveling in Asia who becomes involved in a series of dangerous situations which culminate in the solution of the mystery of the Society of the Black Parrot. *Ethan Quest, His Saga* (1925) is a novel of frustration and disillusion, taking a young man from his dreams of the East into its reality—and his disintegration.

Congai (1927) exposes the decadence and corruption of colonial rule in France's far-eastern possession of Indo-China, using as its principal protagonist a beautiful and tragic half-caste girl who rises from a child of the jungle to become the mistress of the governor. *Red Ending* (1929) is the tragedy of a selfish mother who absorbs and destroys her two sons and who goes on in bitter triumph; the setting is Charleston, South Carolina. *The Iron Widow* (1931) is a narrative of brutal life and death in a French African prison in Senegal where the malice of two continents accumulates in the shadow of Madame Guillotine, "the iron widow." *The Damned Don't Cry* (1939), a hard-hitting, uncompromising novel of poverty and violence in a southern town, tells the story of Zelda O'Brien, born in the shadow of the gas-house, who aspires to a dream of beauty only to see it become sordid reality in her hands.

School for Eternity (1941) explores the lives of a group of people brought together for a week-end party in the fabulous castle of the equally astonishing Count Girghiz on a West Indian Island; an earthquake climaxes the gathering, but the reader is left to draw his own moral as to the value and the disposition of these lives. *The Veiled Fountain* (1947) is a psychological and somewhat mystical novel about a young English composer whose life and career are influenced by a three-faceted woman who symbolically represents the trinity of love and who reveals herself in these guises—as creator, preserver, and destroyer—to the young musician. The novel works out their destinies against the background of Kashmir and the Himalayas. *Barracoon* (1950) concerns slave trading on the west coast of Africa in the nineteenth century. This powerful and sensitive story pictures a rich Lisbon merchant's daughter who hates barracoons (slave pens).

EDWARD HARRIS HETH

was born in Milwaukee, Wisconsin, on September 13, 1909. After attending the University of Wisconsin and spending several summers in Maine, Paris, and Germany, he ran a flower shop in Milwaukee for four years and then went to New York to write, leaving the shop in his sister's charge. Usually he lives in Wales, Wisconsin, where he built a country place with some fairly spectacular gardens: a terraced garden (four terraces encircle the house), a hill garden, and large wild plantings of lilies, hyacinths, and daffodils. Gardening comes naturally to him, but he has no time for farming his forty-one acres of land. He has done radio work, edited a Federal Writers' Project in Milwaukee, and written a newspaper column. His forty short stories have appeared in publications here and in England. Three of these have attracted wide attention: "Big Days Beginning" is in the *O. Henry Memorial Award Stories of 1936,* "Homecoming" appears in O'Brien's *Best Short Stories of 1936,* and "Under the Gingko Trees" is reprinted in *Best Short Stories of 1947.*

Mr. Heth has said: "I am still concerned chiefly in writing the best novel I know how —one that will reflect through character and mood, rather than the artifices of plot (though I have respect for plot), life as it presents itself to me. A good book should be a kind of globe in which all facets of life are reflected. The writer's hand, holding that globe, is important and yet should remain invisible. What should be visible, however, is how that hand turns and fondles and shifts that globe to catch the refractions of light— or, if you will, of life."

Some We Loved (1935), his first novel, describes the love Paul Bingham, a teacher of English, has for Laurie Matthias, the daughter of a music composer. Her mother's affair with an artist forces her to choose between love and the self-sacrifice entailed in caring for her abandoned father. *Told with a Drum* (1937) portrays a German-American family divided by conflicting national loyalties in World War I. *Light over Ruby Street* (1940), a story of Negroes in St. Louis, pictures a half-white mother's ambition for her daughter, who prefers simple and elemental love to social success or wealth. *Any Number Can Play* (1945) has Charley King, a gambler, review his career one September evening after he learns that a fatal illness will soon close his life. He recalls his wife's lonely years and his son's sense of shame.

We Are the Robbers (1947) deals with the theme of man's responsibilities toward himself—that he alone is ultimately responsible for his own life. The central character is a woman who destroys herself through her refusal to face this fact. *If You Lived Here* (1949) has a teacher review the fifty years of her life during a two-day celebration honoring her services. She meditates on the conduct of a wayward pupil and on the love affair of a fellow teacher with a bartender. More specifically, during these two days she asks herself the question whether she has been able to teach her pupils anything or, for that matter, whether any of them has ever wanted to learn what she might teach them of love and honesty and man's dignity. The question is never answered directly in the book, but the reader is allowed to draw his own conclusion from the contemporary action as well as various flashbacks, each of which shows the teacher, Miss Lizzie, at a moment of crisis.

JOHN HEWLETT

was born on May 30, 1905, in Conyers, Georgia. After graduating from Riverside Military Academy, he attended Emory University in nearby Atlanta for a single week. A year's wandering over the country ended in a Georgia town where he bought a small newspaper. A pioneer exposer of the Ku Klux Klan, he quickly lost the paper's few readers. With only fifteen dollars left in his pocket, he set out to make a career in New York. The succeeding years found him working for the United Press, the New York *Daily Mirror,* and many other papers. Later, in France, he worked on the Paris edition of the New York *Herald.* After the blood purge in Germany, he was accused by the Nazis of prying into state affairs and was unceremoniously expelled from the country. Since 1938 he has contributed to the major magazines, syndicates, and newspapers. His short story, "The Russian Gesture," is in Whit and Hallie Burnett's anthology of the best fiction of the 1940's published in *Story* magazine.

He has written a medical history, *Surgery*

Through the Ages (1944), and a book of adventure, travel, and romance in South America, *Thunder Beats the Drum* (1944), which describes a one-man search in Matto Grosso in Brazil and the Beni country of Bolivia for the lost British explorer, Colonel Fawcett. *Like Moonlight on Snow* (1946) is a biography of Simon Patino, the tin king of Bolivia.

Cross on the Moon (1946), his first novel, is a realistic picture of a Georgia village. *Wild Grape* (1947) is the story of a Georgia girl whose mother's skin is darker than the soil but whose own is as white as that of her half sister who lives with their father. As she grows up, she faces the problems of a woman with some black blood and with a beauty desired by white men. *Harlem Story* (1948) concerns a yellow-haired girl with Negro blood who passes for white in New York's Harlem in order to marry a white man. These three novels form a trilogy on various aspects of race relations in the North and South. *Devil's Thumb* (1950) is an historical novel of the period of reconstruction in Georgia and deals with the area devastated by General Sherman on his march to the sea.

STEFAN HEYM

Gabriel D. Hacket

was born on April 10, 1913, in Chemnitz, Germany. After attending schools in Chemnitz and Berlin, he studied at the University of Berlin. In 1935 he came to the United States and entered the University of Chicago, where he achieved his master's degree in 1936. His active opposition to Hitlerism was reflected in *Deutsche Volksecho,* an anti-Nazi German-language weekly, which he edited from 1937 to 1939. He joined the United States army in March, 1943, and participated in the fighting in the European theater of operations.

Hostages (1942), his first novel, tells of the conflict between Nazi Germany and Czechoslovakia in a story of the invader's decision to execute a group of twenty hostages because a German officer's suicide is made to look like a murder. *Of Smiling Peace* (1944) pictures all that is evil in men and in the mechanics of war as the Nazi Germans and French collaborationists in North Africa become desperate losers in World War II.

The Crusaders (1948) follows an American army division from the Normandy invasion through the liberation of Paris, across to Germany into the Battle of the Bulge, and during the occupation of a Ruhr industrial town. Some of the action relates to the corruption of occupation, but most of the novel is a portrayal of men under the stress of war. "I wrote this novel," said Mr. Heym, "because of the terrible finality of the silence of the dead, and because I want peace. I tried to show not only the immediate impressions of the war but also its complexities. It was a necessary and holy crusade."

GRANVILLE HICKS

Lotte Jacobi

was born in Exeter, New Hampshire, on September 9, 1901. He attended the public schools of Framingham, Massachusetts, and graduated from Harvard in 1923. For two years he studied at the Harvard University Theological School and then, giving up his plan to enter the ministry, began to teach Biblical literature and English at Smith College. From 1924 to 1927 he was literary editor of *The Universalist Leader* and while in that position wrote his first book, *Eight Ways of Looking at Christianity* (1926). For six years thereafter he taught at Rensselaer Polytechnic Institute. His magazine articles in *The American Mercury* and *The Forum* indicated that he had adopted liberal sociological and political views. The depression, together with a reading of the writings of Karl Marx and his followers, confirmed his interest in communist ideas. On the establishment of the weekly *The New Masses* in 1934, he became its literary editor and remained a member of the staff for five years; he resigned from the magazine and from the Communist party in the fall of 1939. His liberal views were included in *The Great Tradition* (1933), a history of American literature from 1865 to 1930. He became a center of controversy, both literary and political, and as a consequence was dismissed from his position at Rensselaer in the spring of 1935. A Guggenheim fellowship was awarded to him in 1936 for the study of recent British literature. In 1938–39 he served as counselor in American civilization at Harvard University. Since 1942 he has been director of Yaddo, a community of creative artists, musicians, and writers at Saratoga Springs, New York. *Small Town* (1946) is a book of essays.

Mr. Hicks' first novel, *The First to Awaken* (with Richard M. Bennett, 1940), concerns a New England bank teller who awakens in the year 2040 after a hundred-year sleep to find the world systematized into a co-operative society where a four-hour workday prevails. Money, the root of all evil, has lost its stranglehold on people. *Only the Storm* (1942) brings Canby Kittredge home to Massachusetts from New York City, where he has been a successful advertising man, to think over the faults of big business and his own error in becoming attracted to communism. *Behold Trouble* (1944) portrays the tormented thoughts of a conscientious objector, a youth who has been victimized by his environment.

CHESTER BOMAR HIMES

M. Smith

was born in Jefferson City, Missouri, on July 29, 1909. Both his parents were teachers, and as his father accepted a succession of college posts, the family moved from Missouri to Ohio, from Mississippi to Arkansas, and again to Ohio. Chester Himes completed high school in Cleveland and from 1926 to 1929 attended Ohio State University. After a variety of jobs, he worked for two years on the Ohio State Writers' Project, and for a short time as a feature writer for the Cleveland *Daily News*. In 1941 with his wife, a social worker, he moved to Los Angeles and during the war was employed as shipfitter, sheet-metal mechanic, and riveter in shipyards and aircraft plants in Los Angeles and San Francisco. In 1944 he was awarded a Julius Rosenwald fellowship.

In his novels Chester Himes portrays the problems of Negroes as a minority group. His objective is not to present merely the injustice of prejudice. He attempts to go further and show its destruction of human personality and its wanton dissipation of man's God-given nobility.

His first novel, *If He Hollers Let Him Go* (1945), is a first-person narrative about a young Negro war worker who tells of the frustrations inherent in an industrial job of minor supervisory capacity, the racial conflict arising therefrom, and the resultant compulsive behavior which drives him into a position of desperate insecurity. *Lonely Crusade* (1947) is a thoughtful, subjective novel depicting the fears, distortions, and anxieties to which Negroes are heir in their attempts to push beyond the confines of segregation and to seek integration into the community at large. It analyzes the psychological effects of this endeavor on members of both races, many of whom are persons of good will. It differs from most novels based on this theme in that it does not derive its motivation from the effects of racial injustice, but from its characters' intellectual limitations and traditional preconceptions which confine them to habit and withhold from them the nobler instruments of reason and conscience.

MAURICE GERSHON HINDUS

was born in Bolshoye Bikovo, Russia, on February 27, 1891. His father was a hard-working peasant farmer, a kulak. After his father's death in 1905, the boy and his mother came to America. At first he earned his living by working in a shop in New York City; then he attended Stuyvesant High School for two years. He went to work on a farm in North Brookfield, New York, where he completed his high-school education. He applied for admission to the Cornell State Agricultural School but was rejected. Colgate University, however, accepted him, and in 1915 he received his bachelor's degree, and the next year his master's. The following year he spent at Harvard, and then he began work as a free-lance writer. In 1931 Colgate awarded him the degree of Doctor of Literature. From 1942 to 1944 he was a war correspondent in Russia for the New York *Herald Tribune*. At present he resides in New York City.

Mr. Hindus originally intended to be a scientific farmer. "My experience in farming in Russia as a boy and in this country as a youth," he has said, "is the intellectual key I have used in nearly all my writing on Russia and other countries, including our own. Without my agricultural experience I never should have thought of writing, and I can think of no more helpful preparation for a person who wants to write on foreign affairs than a few seasons spent on a good farm anywhere in this country. Since the most troubled areas in the world are the backward nations, a knowledge of farming gives a writer new eyes with which to appraise the fierce struggles that are now shaking backward countries."

His informative books on history and politics include *The Russian Peasant and the Revolution* (1920), *Red Bread* (1931), *Broken Earth* (1931), *The Great Offensive* (1932), *Mother Russia* (1943), and *The Cossacks* (1946). *Humanity Uprooted* (1931) is important as a summation of the original aims and attitudes of the Russian Revolution as conceived by Lenin and subsequently subverted by Stalin. Two works gave an accurate prophecy of future events: *Hitler Cannot Conquer Russia* (1941) forecast the failure of the German invasion, and *Russia and Japan* (1942) predicted the inevitability of a conflict between those two great powers. *Bright Passage* (1947) was an argument for a Czechoslovakian Catholic-Communist coalition which would be practicable provided East and West would not interfere; Russia interfered in 1948. *In Search of a Future* (1949) is an interpretation of the Middle East. *Green Worlds* (1938) is an autobiographical account of the author's early years in the United States.

Asked about the relationship between a writer's historico-political works and his novels on these same subjects, Mr. Hindus stated: "I have always been more interested in the impact of ideas on the human personality than in the ideas themselves. The drama of history has fascinated me infinitely more than the religious, political, intellectual, or economic movements that have shaped its course. I have always viewed it from the bottom up rather than from the top down."

Under Moscow Skies (1936), his first novel, is a panoramic view of domestic life in Russia under the first five-year plan in the story of an American correspondent's love for a leading Bolshevik's wife. *Sons and Fathers* (1940) is about the Russian revolution and shows the conflict between a father, ruthlessly eager to destroy the Tsarist order, and his son, a physician, whose humanitarian ideas bring on tragedy. *To Sing with the Angels* (1941) dramatically portrays the ruthless subjugation of Czechoslovakia to the Nazis. An idealist, a convert to Hitlerism, helps to introduce into his country the new order of cruelty, murder, and Gestapo control.

JOSEPH GEORGE HITREC

Conrad Eiger

was born at Zagreb, Yugoslavia, on February 28, 1912, where he received a humanistic education and later studied literature and languages at the University of Zagreb. His writing career began at the age of seventeen with a prize-winning essay in a magazine contest in his native city. At nineteen he published a collection of short stories and poems. He went to India on a vacation in 1932 and decided to remain; he learned English, joined a British advertising agency in Calcutta, and then in 1935 transferred to Bombay, eventually becoming manager. He met Mahatma Gandhi and other Indian leaders and became deeply interested in the Indian struggle for freedom. During World War II he worked on government information and advertising; ill health forced his resignation in 1944. An intense curiosity about the lives and struggles of Indian peoples, sharpened to compassion by a continued exploration of the country, resulted during the war years in a series of short stories, a play, and the first draft of *Son of the Moon.* On his arrival in the United States in May, 1946, he married Miss Leyla Saygin, whom he had met in India. They are now settled permanently in this country and are becoming American citizens. *Rulers' Morning* (1946) is a collection of seventeen stories about India and the problems she encounters on the road to freedom.

His first novel, *Son of the Moon* (1948), winner of the Harper prize, concerns Vijay, a young high-caste Hindu, who returns from England with plans to modernize and industrialize India and to free the people from ignorance and superstition. He learns that he must merge the old with the new.

ALICE TISDALE HOBART

was born on January 28, 1882, in Lockport, New York, the descendant of a long line of New Englanders stemming from Rebecca Nourse, who courageously protested against the hysteria of witchcraft which spread over Salem, Massachusetts, in 1690. Her refusal at seventy-two to believe in witches brought down upon her the charge of witchcraft for which she was hanged. Her spirit of independent thinking is much admired by her descendants. When Alice Nourse was only two, the family moved to Chicago, where her father carried on his career as a musician. Soon after the family's arrival in the city, Alice became a victim of spinal meningitis, from which she has never entirely recovered. After seven years' residence in the city, her mother fell ill, and in the hope of bringing her back to health, the family moved to Downers Grove, on the edge of the prairie west of the city. When Alice was ten, her mother died. During her freshman year at Northwestern University her father died. Later she attended the University of Chicago, but illness prevented her from graduating. In 1949 Mills College in California awarded her the degree of Doctor of Laws.

In 1908 she visited her sister Mary, a teacher in a girls' school in Hangchow, China. The Oriental world stimulated her imagination. In the months that followed, she began to write. Physically fragile, she could work only part of the time. From her letters home she developed travel essays which were first published in *The Atlantic Monthly.* Much expanded, they were made into three books: *Pioneering Where the World Is Old* (1917), *By the City of the Long Sand* (1926), and *Within the Walls of Nanking* (1928). They cover the experiences of her sixteen years in China.

She met Earle Tisdale Hobart in Hangchow while she was visiting her sister. They were married in Tientsin on June 29, 1914, and spent their honeymoon in Peking, China's ancient capital, and in a temple near the Great Wall. Mr. Hobart worked for an American oil company, and during the next thirteen years they lived in many parts of China and traveled extensively in the line of duty. In 1927, while he was manager for the company in Nanking, the Chinese Nationalists, during the social revolution which swept them into power, demanded the expulsion of all foreigners. In an attack by soldiers on their home, Mr. Hobart was injured, and most of the Hobarts' possessions were swept away. The manuscript of her first novel was rescued by their Chinese houseboy. At that time Mr. Hobart resigned from the oil company and returned to the United States. Later they went to France and Germany, where Mr. Hobart had accepted a position with an export company. In 1929 they returned to America and settled in the city of Washington, where Mrs. Hobart wrote *Oil for the Lamps of China.* In 1933 Mrs. Hobart went back to China alone to see what had taken place in the social revolution which occurred after her departure. On her return to Washington, she wrote *Yang and Yin,* which she considers her most philosophical novel. In 1935 she and her husband settled in California, where she wrote two of her American novels, *Their Own Country* and *The Cup and the Sword.* When the Japanese struck at Pearl Harbor on December 7, 1941, Mr. Hobart offered his knowledge of the Orient to the army and was sent to India. Mrs. Hobart was not permitted to accompany her husband and so she went to Mexico to live and to study the aftermath of the Mexican social revolution which had started a year before the beginning of the Chinese upheaval. This experience was the basis of her novel, *The Peacock Sheds his Tail.*

The dominating theme of Mrs. Hobart's novels is the problem of man's responsibility to society. A secondary theme is the relationship between alien races both here and abroad. She has embraced the theory that the good, the earnest, and the ordinary people can be portrayed and made interesting. She believes our middle class, both through neglect by writers and by critical oversight of such fiction in this field as does appear, has steadily lost interest for the reader in favor of the poor, the abnormal, and the bizarrely rich characters. Thus inadvertently our literature has played into the hands of communist propaganda and has permitted the untrammeled march of the communist belief that the middle class, on which we build our democracy, is both uninteresting and ineffectual. She believes that to portray the "medium" people in our society takes more effort and more skill than to picture the more startling extremes in society and that that class should engage the attention of more of our novelists in surveying the contemporary scene.

Mrs. Hobart's first novel, *Pidgin Cargo* (1929), later entitled *River Supreme* (1934), is the story of the forty-year struggle of an American to put steamboats on the upper Yangtze River. It portrays the beginning of the long drawn-out industrial revolution in China and the conflict between West and East as the steam-driven ships took away the livelihood of the native boatmen. *Oil for the Lamps of China* (1933) depicts a young American businessman in China and his wife caught in the impersonal machine of American big business as it slows down during one of the violent phases of the Chinese social revolution. It contrasts American efficiency with China's age-old idea of responsibility to the individual.

Yang and Yin (1936) pictures the strife between East and West exemplified in the ancient and beautiful Chinese concept that all life is divided into the opposing forces, male and female, which seek harmony and finally attain it. The philosophies of East and West are contrasted through their attitudes toward sickness and pain. The harmony between the two opposite races is found in the friendship of an American doctor and a Chinese scholar. The story is laid against a background of social revolution extending from the time of the Boxer Rebellion in 1900 to 1932 when Chiang Kai-shek was the great hope of China.

Their Own Country (1940) continues the story of Hester and Stephen Chase, the leading characters in *Oil for the Lamps of China,* on their return to the United States. Here they encounter in the search for employment during the grim years of the depression many of the same patterns and portents, problems and challenges that they had thought were unique to China, a country of hungry, unsheltered millions. *The Cup and the Sword* (1942) is a chronicle of three generations of the Rambeau family and the history of the wine-growing industry in California, with special attention to the effect of Prohibition upon the people and the business. It deals with the problem, an integral part of all Mrs. Hobart's novels, of man's responsibility for integrity in our democratic, free-enterprise system.

The Peacock Sheds His Tail (1945) pictures the effect of the social and industrial revolution on three generations of an aristocratic Spanish-Mexican family. One of its members marries an American man. This story surveys the difficulty races encounter in learning to exist side by side, probes the age-old problem faced by a man and woman learning to live together, and explores the dilemma arising from a man's conflicting obligations in his business relationships. *The Cleft Rock* (1948) is the story of a powerful California family and of California's Central Valley, where water means the difference between poverty and plenty. It pictures the way in which large operators are driving from the valley the small farmers who are less able to establish their right to water for irrigation purposes; it also shows that these large owners are exhausting the underground supply of water by overuse, thus returning large sections to unproductive desert. Again there is presented the problem of man's responsibility to society, the predominant theme of all Mrs. Hobart's novels.

LAURA Z. HOBSON

Halsman

was born Laura Keane Zametkin in New York City, and grew up on adjacent Long Island. After graduating from Cornell University, she went to work as a copywriter in an advertising agency. Then came a brief interlude as a reporter on the old New York *Evening Post* and later as fashion copywriter with a Fifth Avenue department store. In December, 1934, she began to write promotion for *Time, Life,* and *Fortune* magazines; she resigned in 1940 when she had become promotion director of *Time.* The following year, in deciding to undertake creative writing, she thought only of short stories, a few of which she had written as a hobby. In addition to short stories, she had completed a juvenile and a novel by 1943. Taking time only to write four short narratives and one original story for the movies, she devoted the next three years to the writing of *Gentleman's Agreement.* Many of her friends and advisers counseled her against doing a novel about anti-Semitism on the ground that it would be handicapped by people's unwillingness to face so difficult and controversial a subject. When the manuscript was half-completed, the editor of *Cosmopolitan* magazine bought it for serialization. While the novel was still in galley proof, Darryl F. Zanuck purchased the film rights for Twentieth Century–Fox for his only personal production in 1947. Mrs. Hobson lives in New York City with her two small sons.

The Trespassers (1943), her first novel, has for its theme the rejection of refugees in a story of a scientist and his American benefactress. *Gentlemen's Agreement* (1947), on the theme of anti-Semitism, details the experiences of a reporter who poses as a Jew. His sister, fellow office workers, hotel managers, and others reveal that barriers prevent complete participation in American life. *The Other Father* (1950) is a story of a "normal" family, dealing particularly with the relationship between a father and his daughter. Andrew Dynes, while having a love affair with a young woman, discovers that his daughter is in love with a married man older than she. The father reviews his own unhappiness and his conduct as a parent.

CLAUDIA HOLLAND

Wendell B. Powell

was born Claudia Mildred Emmerson on December 8, 1903, in Portsmouth, Virginia. Her forebears, both maternal and paternal, settled in Virginia in early colonial times. After attending the public schools and Woodrow Wilson High School in Portsmouth, she spent two years at Stuart Hall, a school for girls, in Staunton, Virginia. She studied in France and Switzerland. In 1928 she married Bernard P. Holland, Jr., an attorney; they have two children. With the exception of ten years in Washington, D.C., they have lived in Virginia.

"My central interest in writing," Mrs. Holland has stated, "is humanity in many of its phases. Excluding actual personalities, I write of people as I know them to be and do not wander from the field of my own intimate knowledge of the types that appear in my books."

Primrose Path (1947), her first novel, was written primarily for laughs (in a time when laughter was needed) about a group of people in Virginia who prove that they can lead the good life in conjunction with their own chosen brand of fun. *Center Aisle* (1949), a satiric story set on a wedding day in a small Virginia town, good-naturedly pricks the bubble of ancestor worship in Virginia and protests against the adulation, amounting to worship, that is sometimes bestowed upon a man for the sole reason that he lived a long time ago and was able through divers means to bequeath to his heirs a wealth of material possessions. Through the experiences of the Lathrop family it appears that false values can create tragedy and distort the course of human lives throughout succeeding generations.

MARJORIE HOLMES

G. Provenzano

was born September 22, 1910, in Storm Lake, Iowa. Her talent for writing was manifested at an early age; in fact, she claims to have written her first novel, a saga of the local grocery boy, at the age of twelve. An understanding English teacher, Miss Dewey Deal, observed her early efforts with real interest and encouraged her. "You must make the most of your talent," she once wrote on an English paper; "you can write beautiful things for people who crave beauty —there is a duty." Miss Holmes kept those words always, and often found them a spur when she later became discouraged. She was graduated from high school at the age of sixteen, and from Cornell College in Mount Vernon, Iowa, at twenty. The following year, while working as a secretary at the State University of Iowa, she met and married Lynn Mighell, an engineering graduate. They moved to Texas, where their first child, a daughter, was born. At first she wrote steadily for the "pulps," gradually working her way into the first-class magazines with articles and stories. Due to her husband's many professional transfers in engineering, they have lived in eight states and are now residents of Washington, D.C. The Mighells are the parents of three children, a daughter and two sons. Marjorie Holmes is well-known as a lecturer, radio personality, and teacher of writing.

Her first novel, *World by the Tail* (1943), is an intense, colorful, somewhat stylized chronicle of the depression's effect upon an Iowa family. *Ten O'clock Scholar* (1948) deals with the career of a young school superintendent with a passion to improve the public schools. It throws a glaring spotlight on some of our educational problems and offers constructive remedies. The novel's gayer side deals with the young educator's marriage to a warm-hearted and seemingly frivolous wife. "This brilliantly conceived book," said the Philadelphia *Inquirer,* "covers virtually every method, every conflict, every larger dream of the teaching profession and does more for the men and women who follow its star than any other contemporary work of fiction." The New York *Times* called it "a lively satire."

MRS. KENNETH HORAN

was born Kenneth O'Donnell in Jackson, Michigan, in 1890. After attending the University School for Girls in Chicago, she studied at Vassar College from 1904 to 1907. In 1908 she married Dr. Francis Horan, now deceased. She wrote literary articles for the Chicago *Evening Post,* was literary editor in 1915 of the Chicago *Journal of Commerce,* and contributed to the literary pages of the Chicago *Daily Tribune.* In 1947 she married John William Rogers, and they reside in Dallas, Texas. She is a contributing literary editor of the Dallas *Times-Herald.*

Remember the Day (1937), her first book, tells a story about the author's childhood in Michigan. Her father owned several newspapers and to his home came Jane Addams, Theodore Roosevelt, and Sarah Bernhardt, each of whom created humorous situations. *It's Not My Problem* (1938), a choice of the Literary Guild, presents in diary form a year in the author's life when she refused to go to Hollywood, where her children would be in an atmosphere of sham and falseness. Nor would her surgeon husband go. *Oh, Promise Me* (1938), a sequel to *Remember the Day,* deals further with the manners and customs of the time, and tells of her father's election to Congress and her Aunt Melony's fourth marriage. *Night Bell* (1940) is about Rose Morgan who, during a period of convalescence, becomes acquainted with the problems of a hospital and the personalities of some of the doctors, nurses, and patients.

I Give Thee Back (1942) treats of the unstinting way in which Nora Osborne pours out her life for an adopted boy, the orphan son of the only man she loved. When the boy grows up and becomes a famous physician, he falls in love with a worthless woman. Then Nora needs a friend to help untangle her emotions. *A Bashful Woman* (1944) is a family novel of Michigan from the 1890's to 1940 with Sally Evans as the central character. Her childhood is darkened by unpleasant comments about "those Welsh," and she is nearly an old woman before the light of understanding begins to shine. *Papa Went to Congress* (1946), is a humorous account of a Republican in Congress, and of his efforts to achieve rural free delivery by legislation during Cleveland's administration. Mama, the two girls, Mama's sister Sophie, and Mama's sister Melony accompany the family to Washington, as does the cook, Mrs. Flynn, and the yard man who is a trusty from the Michigan penitentiary. Their adventures are hilarious. *Mama Took Up Travel* (1948) is the story of how the whole family went to Europe, making the "Grand Tour" mostly on passes procured by Papa's newspaper. Both these family chronicles are continuations of *Remember the Day.*

PAUL HORGAN

Catharine Mechem

was born on August 1, 1903, in Buffalo, New York. He attended a private school in Buffalo until his eleventh year when, because of his father's health, the family moved to Albuquerque, New Mexico. During his high-school years Paul was a cadet in the New Mexico Military Institute. On the death of his father in 1922, the family returned to Buffalo. He attended the Eastman School of Music in Rochester, New York, to study singing. For three years from 1923 to 1926 he participated in production work on the stage, acting, singing, writing, dancing, and constructing scenery. In 1926 he returned as librarian to the New Mexico Military Institute and to devote part of his time to writing. Six short stories about Mexico are in *The Return of the Weed* (1936). *Figures in a Landscape* (1940) contains stories and essays.

His first novel, *The Fault of Angels* (1933), winner of the Harper prize, is a comedy of manners about musicians. A youth looks after the welfare of a new conductor of an opera company. The latter's wife palpitates to do good and manages chiefly to create minor disturbances. *No Quarter Given* (1935) is a character study of a music composer who is dying of tuberculosis, his wife who supports him in her Santa Fé home, and an actress who is his mistress. The story is told in flashbacks during the last three weeks of his life. *Main Line West* (1936) is about the early years of Danny Milford and his mother, who is deserted by her traveling-salesman husband. She turns to evangelism and pacifism and loses her life at the hands of a mob. *A Lamp on the Plains* (1937), a sequel, shows Danny starting out for himself at thirteen by riding a freight train to Vrain, New Mexico, where kindly persons shelter and educate him.

Far from Cibola (1938) describes a New Mexico crowd listening to a government reply to a local request for poor relief. Contrasted are the harsh, demanding quality of the group and the private sentiment of each person. *The Habit of Empire* (1939) deals with the colonization of New Mexico in 1598 and culminates in the tremendous Battle of Acoma. *The Common Heart* (1942) is about a physician who brings his bride to New Mexico and their difficulties. After the birth of a son they drift apart but are reunited.

HENRY BEETLE HOUGH

Sylvia Salmi

was born in New Bedford, Massachusetts, on November 8, 1896. His unusual middle name derives from that of his grandfather, Henry W. Beetle, who was a whaling captain. Mr. Hough graduated in 1918 from the Columbia School of Journalism, and even as an undergraduate wrote for several newspapers, among them the Boston *Transcript*, the *Christian Science Monitor*, and the New York *American*. In his senior year he was co-author of a study of the press which won a Pulitzer prize. Mrs. Hough, the former Elizabeth Wilson Bowie, is also a graduate of the Columbia School of Journalism. After leaving college, Mr. Hough spent several years in public-relations work in New York and Chicago. In 1920 he and Mrs. Hough bought a country newspaper and began to send their roots into the earth. The paper was the famous *Vineyard Gazette*, which they have managed ever since and brought to a position of national prominence. Mr. Hough has told the full story in *Country Editor* (1940) and *Once More the Thunderer* (1950). He is also the author of *Martha's Vineyard* (1936) and *Wamsutta of New Bedford, 1846–1946* (1946).

That Lofty Sky (1941), his first novel, concerns a German cadet on a battleship who goes ashore at Port Quentin in South Africa, misses his connection back, gets listed as a deserter, and now as a lone man against the pack comes to understand his warped nature as a Nazi; with the aid of an English girl he learns the meaning and responsibilities of freedom. Mr. Hough gathered material for this book on a trip to South Africa in 1937. *All Things Are Yours* (1942) tells about Carlotta Badoni, a New England girl, who rises to fame in the 1860's as an opera singer and gives up love for a career. The "success" story of the singer and the parallel story of Joe Van Deveren, a ruthless, self-made man who helped her, form a characterization of the times. *Roosters Crow in Town* (1945) pictures the wartime activity of a small New England town. A farm boy works on a local newspaper, looks into the mystery of his father's suicide and gains help from a schoolteacher before joining the army. *Long Anchorage* (1947) is a romantic story about New Bedford, beginning in 1847, and of Russell Ashmead who wishes to go to sea but whose responsibility to manage the family cotton mill keeps him at home. The novel is particularly notable for its authentic picture of the transition of New Bedford from a shipping center to a manufacturing community, and for its accounts of long monotonous days and sudden moments of excitement aboard whalers.

ELIZABETH METZGER HOWARD

was born in Wilkes-Barre, Pennsylvania, but her home was in Bedford, the Bedford Village that Hervey Allen has made famous. She attended numerous schools, and then studied at Columbia University, mostly under Professor Walter B. Pitkin. Before very long she was selling stories and doing editorial work for Condé Nast, Dell, and other publishers. In 1928 she married Frank Liddon-Howard, a mining engineer from Rhodesia. They lived in Africa for two years and then moved to Florida. They have one son. Mr. Howard is now a consulting horticulturist, his hobby being orchids. In 1946 Mrs. Howard won the Doubleday prize of twenty thousand dollars and the Metro-Goldwyn-Mayer prize of one hundred and twenty-five thousand dollars with her only novel.

Before the Sun Goes Down (1946) describes the rich and poor sides of the town of Willow Spring, Pennsylvania, in the 1880's by having well-to-do children visit the Negro shacks of Mudtown and become acquainted with unpleasant social facts. Dr. Dan Field watches after the children in the hope that they will help usher in a better world.

FLORENCE RUTH HOWARD

was born in Wolford, North Dakota. She spent her childhood in Saskatchewan, Canada, where her father owned a large ranch. She does not remember when she learned to ride, but by the time she was five she had her own pony. She always rode to and from school on her own horse. Originally she planned to make music a career, and for several years she studied at the Toronto Conservatory of Music. She writes, as few authors can, of horses and the people who own and love them. Her writings reflect the poetry and wonder that a great race horse evokes. She is married to Philip MacDonald, a writer of detective fiction. For the past twenty-one years she has resided in California. Since childhood, it has been Mrs. Howard's ambition to be a poet. She is at work upon a book-length poem in honor of her son, Howard Miller, whose death in an accident at twenty-two closed a promising career in music.

Green Entry (1940), her first novel, deals with the triangle of a mother, son, and stepfather and tells how the son and stepfather become friends through a mutual love of horses. There are autobiographical elements in this story. *View from a Window* (1942) concerns a too superior human being who regards the rest of humanity coldly and from a great distance, as if it were an ant hill. Through being instrumental in causing the death of a much-loved horse, he discovers that he is, after all, only one of the ants—not a bad thing to be. *Sailmaker* (1948) has a triangle composed of the horse Sailmaker; Alex, the female owner of the horse; and Locarno, the horse's jockey, who loves the horse with a love greater than that which he could give to any woman. The drama is seen entirely through the eyes of Guy and Lynne Stanton, a couple that had been separated during the war. Their love is the contrasting background for the struggle between Alex Dunhill, a beautiful and unscrupulous woman with green eyes, and the dark, imperious jockey. Her harsh conduct includes whipping Locarno and poisoning the horse. The ranch background is fully described.

GEORGE HOWE

Dimitri Wolkonsky

was born at Bristol, Rhode Island, on April 19, 1898. After attending local schools and St. George's at Newport, Rhode Island, he studied at Harvard College, from which he graduated in 1918, and at Harvard Architectural School, where he earned the degree of Master of Architecture in 1925. Since that time he has been a practicing architect. He married Elisabeth Parker in 1928 and they have four children. In 1944–45 he served with a detachment of the Office of Strategic Services with the Seventh Army in Algiers and France. He now practices architecture in Washington and operates a farm in Fulton, Maryland.

Slaves Cottage (1935), his first novel, is a study of the New England seacoast village of Hope and the Vandeleur family from its beginnings in the eighteenth century to the present. Henry and his wife Rosalind, the younger generation, move to end the aloofness which separates their father from the workers in the family mill. The theme is the age-old conflict between new ideas and old, and the need to make adjustments to fit new conditions.

Call It Treason (1949) became a national best seller even before publication. It won a prize of fifteen thousand dollars in a contest sponsored by the Christophers for a book "written in accordance with Christian principles and not against them." Although the background of the Christophers is Roman Catholic, the author is a Protestant. An unusual story lies behind the writing of the book. During five months that he was hospitalized for leg and jaw injuries following an automobile accident, he composed the novel by dictating into a recording machine through his wired jaw. These notes later were fashioned into a finished tale. The details of the story were checked in person by Mr. Howe, still on crutches from his accident, when he returned to Europe and went over the hero's entire itinerary by jeep.

Call It Treason is a fictionalized account of the adventures of young Germans who volunteered to spy for the Americans behind the German line. The episodes are based upon real events, and the author makes use of the actual techniques employed by the army's secret service. Behind the three protagonists are the three motives of espionage: riches and risk and faith. The book is a spy thriller with a moral. The sensitive idealist searches his heart with unsparing honesty and arrives privately at the Way of the Cross.

RICHARD GIBSON HUBLER

Martin Harris

was born on August 20, 1912, in Scranton, Pennsylvania. He attended Dunmore High School, Wyoming Seminary at Kingston, and Swarthmore College at Swarthmore, all in Pennsylvania. Upon graduation in 1934, he joined the army air corps as a cadet but resigned six months later with the belief that flying was merely an excellent hobby. After a short period of work as an insurance investigator in Boston, he went to New York to work on *Newsweek* magazine and served as editor of various departments from 1935 to 1939. On leaves of absence he visited northern and eastern European countries, including Russia. He also wrote radio news programs and was chief feature writer for *Cavalcade* magazine. He won a prize for the best work in *Harper's* magazine. In 1940 he became a departmental editor of the experimental newspaper, *PM*. In December, 1942, he was commissioned in the Marine Corps as a first lieutenant and served in the Pacific and at home until November, 1945. Subsequently he was under contract to Hollywood studios but soon resigned to be at liberty to write a series of novels dealing with the spiritual dilemmas of our time. He has done almost every kind of writing from librettos and plays to novels and poetry. His non-fiction books include *Lou Gehrig* (1941), *I Flew for China* (with Royal Leonard, 1942), and *Flying Leathernecks* (1944).

His first novel, *I've Got Mine* (1946), is the story of a party of Marines who make a secret landing on a Pacific island during World War II. The locale of *The Quiet Kingdom* (1948) is the islands of the West Indies where a group of eccentric strangers make their attempt to escape from the world.

In 1949 Mr. Hubler was engaged in the first of a series of nearly forty novels, the basic plan of which deals with the various aspects and reactions of the soul within the framework of events, both past and modern. Three have been completed, but the author plans not to offer any for publication until several more are finished. The first is *The Pass,* a study of the psychological attitudes of a mining town in the West in 1866; the second is *One Kind of Flesh,* a story of the state of mind of a country village in 1948 brought about by a contemplation of the moral aspects of the atom bomb; and the third, *True Love, True Love,* is the exposition of the effect of first love upon a boy of ten. The fourth, now being composed, is *The Cave,* a story of Hollywood and its effect upon its audience; the fifth will be *Markwell,* a satire on the Civil War.

ETHEL HUESTON

was born in Cincinnati, Ohio, on December 3, 1887, the daughter of the Reverend Charles Wesley Powelson, who became known as the horse-racing preacher of Iowa. She attended public schools and high school in Mt. Pleasant and Burlington, Iowa. Her writing career began in her sophomore year in Iowa Wesleyan College. After graduating in 1909, she worked for a publisher in Chicago until in 1910 she married John William Hueston, a Presbyterian minister. They settled in St. Louis. After he became ill, they moved to Albuquerque, New Mexico, where their daughter, Buell, now Mrs. N. A. Baird, was born. It was in Trinidad, Colorado, that she wrote her first book, *Prudence of the Parsonage* (1915). For a time they lived on a homestead ranch in Idaho, where Mr. Hueston died in 1915. She then moved to Chicago. She married Edward J. Best; he died soon after from an illness contracted overseas in World War I. After traveling a good deal, she spent her winters in New York and her summers in Maine. She married Randolph Blinn, an editor and columnist and for a time an assistant to the director of the Bureau of Foreign and Domestic Commerce in Washington, D.C. Following his death, she moved to New York. Her non-fiction books include *Coasting Down East* (1924), an account of a motor tour along the Maine coast to Calais, and *Preacher's Wife* (1941), a biography of her mother, who raised a family of eleven children on a minister's salary of four hundred dollars a year.

Mrs. Hueston is the author of forty books. Her early novels concern the romances of ministers' daughters. Others deal with the family life and professional difficulties of preachers. She has also written historical romances and studies of the effect of the depression on middle-class families.

After writing eight romances, she published *The People of This Town* (1929), an account of a minister's wife who leaves her husband after twenty years and earns her own way by teaching music. *Rowena Rides the Rumble* (1931) is about two lighthearted young people who tour the country with a chaperone to advertise an automobile. *Good Times* (1932) pictures four young people, victims of the depression, who seek to better themselves by hitchhiking from New York to South Dakota and who become communists. *That Hastings Girl* (1933) describes life on a South Dakota ranch in the story of a girl from a wealthy home in the East who cares for her two young half sisters.

Blithe Baldwin (1933) has a girl achieve independence on a Wyoming ranch despite her father's insistence that she finish college. *Beauty for Sale* (1934) pictures the four Strand sisters, daughters of a poor minister; Mary breaks her back in a sledding accident, and the others earn money to pay for operations. *Star of the West* (1935) is an historical novel portraying the Lewis and Clark expedition from 1804 to 1806; the Shoshoni Indian girl, Sacagawea, guides the group.

The Man of the Storm (1936) is an account of the Spanish and French in early St. Louis in a story of Tempête, who claimed to be an Indian but talked like an educated Englishman. *Calamity Jane* (1937) traces the career of the famous markswoman from Laramie, Wyoming, in 1875, to her death in Deadwood, South Dakota, in 1903, and gives an account of Sioux Indians and frontier life in the Black Hills. *A Roof over Their Heads* (1937) portrays the Merediths, a family in an Iowa town, who go to pieces in the depression. *High Bridge* (1938) shows four people ready to end their lives achieving a solution to their problems. *The Honorable Uncle Lancy* (1939) burlesques the publicity stunts of politicians in the tale of a senator up for re-election and a minister.

Uncle Lancy for President (1940) is the story of a political campaign in which an infant and an adolescent niece play a part. *This One Kindness* (1942) concerns a dying woman's request to her daughter that she not make the mistake of taking things as they come. *Drink to Me Only* (1943) is about a woman married to a dipsomaniac and her efforts to cure him. *Mother Went Mad on Monday* (1944) shows how a mother knits a closer family web in wartime and how this unity helps them bear the news that son Larry is missing in action. *No Shortage of Men* (1945) deals with hasty marriages and divorces in wartime. *Heaven and Vice Versa* (1946) pictures the complications in a home when a woman's twin sister brings a prospective fourth husband and three GI's as guests. *Please, No Paregoric* (1946) tells how a returned, wounded veteran and his emotionally upset neighbor regain stability on a trip across the country. *The Reverend Mister "Red"* (1949) describes the unorthodox but effective methods used by a minister and his wife to further the cause of their community center. They build a happier marriage in the process. *The Family Takes a Wife* (1950) deals with the amazement of a returned veteran's family when he announces his marriage to a refugee girl.

HELEN HULL

was born in Albion, Michigan. She was educated at Michigan State College, the University of Michigan, and the University of Chicago, where she received her bachelor's degree in 1912, later doing graduate work there. Upon graduation she taught English at Wellesley College and proceeded to combine a teaching and writing career. Her first short stories appeared in 1915. In 1930 she was awarded a Guggenheim fellowship for creative writing, upon which she spent six months in England. She has also traveled in southern Europe and the Near East. Miss Hull lives in New York City, where she teaches writing at Columbia University. She edited *The Writer's Book* (1950). *Uncommon People* (1936) and *Octave* (1947) contain short stories.

Miss Hull's novels depict American family life; her plots are concerned with what people think and feel in the course of everyday events. Her gift is one of penetration into character. She has dealt with the problems of compatibility in marriage, motherhood, and divorce with courage and a rounded wholeness.

Quest (1922), her first novel, traces a girl's search for an understanding of life because of a broken home. *Labyrinth* (1923) deals with the problem of a wife-mother who turns her home over to servants while she goes out to work. *The Surry Family* (1925) portrays smalltown and rural life in the story of the nagging monotony of a couple; the children reject the parents' conservative ideas. *Islanders* (1927) chronicles three generations of the Darcey family who move from Michigan to California to seek gold, with emphasis on the self-reliant women alone on their domestic islands. *The Asking Price* (1930) describes the family life of a woman who represses her professor husband's poetic inclinations and insists on reorganizing his life.

Heat Lightning (1932) concerns the petty disagreements arising during a week in a crowded midwestern home when Amy returns from the East to escape her worries over the apparent disintegration of her marriage. *Hardy Perennial* (1933) is a comedy of manners set in the New York home of Horace Prescott, a lecturer and writer, whose poses almost destroy him during the depression. His wife, believing that love is a hardy perennial, tolerates his vagaries. *Morning Shows the Day* (1934) pictures the life from youth to middle age of seven people who comprised the editorial board of a high-school annual.

Candle Indoors (1936) deals with a father's efforts to guide the lives of his three children whose affection centers in their dead mother. *Frost Flower* (1939) recounts four climactic days in the life of Andrew Fulton and his second wife when their happiness is threatened by the vindictive widow of a former lover. *Experiment* (1940) contains four novelettes about close family relationships. The first three, "Experiment," "Food for Thought," and "Snow in Summer," portray happiness and success. The fourth, "With the One Coin for Fee," is an intricate tale of disaster about two sixty-year-old spinsters who meet after a separation of many years and are trapped in a house during a New England hurricane. Opposite in character and temperament, they achieve an understanding of each other during the storm.

Through the House Door (1940) portrays a mother, Agatha Townsend, and her married daughter, Beatrice Downing, who become breadwinners in their homes. Agatha writes fiction because her husband is irresponsible. Beatrice's husband, a scientist, loses his eyesight. *Hawk's Flight* (1946), set in contemporary Connecticut, brings Carey Moore back to her country home to recover from a breakdown suffered after the death of her husband, a psychiatrist. There she retraces her past and makes a retrospective study of four marriages and their quality.

HOWARD HUNT

Erich Hartmann

was born in suburban Buffalo, New York, on October 9, 1918. His youth from 1925 to 1932 was spent in Ft. Lauderdale, Miami Beach, and Hollywood, Florida. He graduated from Brown University in 1940. During World War II he was a gunnery officer on the North Atlantic patrol in the navy. He wrote his first novel in 1942 while he was hospitalized. Honorably discharged, he became an editor of *The March of Time,* a monthly documentary film, and later joined *Life* magazine as a war correspondent in the South Pacific. From 1945 to 1946 he worked with the Office of Strategic Services in China. In 1946 he received a Guggenheim fellowship in creative writing. As a diplomatic attaché, Mr. Hunt served on the staff of Ambassador W. Averell Harriman during 1948 at European Recovery Program headquarters in Paris.

His first novel, *East of Farewell* (1942), describes the experiences of the officers and men on a destroyer convoying merchant vessels to England in World War II. *Limit of Darkness* (1944) presents the life stories and philosophies of five navy fliers in the South Pacific during a twenty-four-hour period. *Stranger in Town* (1947) concerns a veteran's readjustment after World War II. Major Anthony Fleming, a prominent sculptor, has had an unhappy love affair and on his return struggles to find the right girl. *Maelstrom* (1948) portrays the search of a rich girl for happiness after her marriage has failed. After experiencing the brutality of a gangster, she finds her true lover. *Bimini Run* (1949) details the cross-tensions arising among the people aboard a chartered fishing cruiser in the Bahamas.

FANNIE HURST

Lotte Neustein

was born on October 18, 1889, in Hamilton, Ohio, in the same room where her mother first saw the light of day. The Hursts were residents of St. Louis, Missouri, but it was the mother's desire that the child be born in Ohio. Originally both her mother's and her father's families emigrated from Bavaria, Germany, about the time of the Civil War. On her father's side the stock goes back two generations into Mississippi and Tennessee soil. After receiving her bachelor's degree at Washington University in St. Louis, Fannie Hurst did graduate work at Columbia University. At an early age she desired to write, and this activity has remained paramount, although her interests reach out actively in many directions. During her undergraduate years she wrote a great deal, and she exhibited qualities of leadership that early identified her with journalism, the theater, and academic life. Her first printed story appeared during her college years in *The Saturday Evening Post.*

The transition from her protected environment in the Middle West to the strangeness of New York City was sharp and difficult for this only child. Once in the city, she wrote with unflagging zeal despite the failure of her early work to reach print. For years on end she knocked in vain on editorial doors. Her success, when it came after a long period of disappointments, was startling and instantaneous. Almost overnight it seemed that the magazines of America began to clamor for her work; quickly her name was on the lips of American and overseas readers.

In the midst of her busy literary career, Fannie Hurst has devoted much time and energy to social problems. She has been chairman of committees on national housing, workmen's compensation, and the national advisory committee to the Works Progress Administration in 1940 and 1941. She is married to Jacques S. Danielson; they reside in New York City.

Fannie Hurst has interpreted every phase of life and every kind of human being. Her first novel, *Star Dust* (1921), demonstrated her ability as a novelist after a long career as a short-story writer, and *Lummox* (1923) placed her in the front rank. Her stories vary in form and technique, and she has launched fearlessly into new and untried fields. *Appassionata,* for example, employs successfully the method of telling a story in the "you" style, a novelty and variation from the traditional method of employing either the first or the third person.

Asked about her interest in social problems, Fannie Hurst replied: "My interest is the outgrowth of my pen's itch to interpret the social scene. I am alert to, and want to be alerted to, people at first hand—their problems, dilemmas, doldrums, hopes, frustrations, and realizations. I am primarily interested in their behaviorisms as they live and breathe outside the pleasant confines of my workshop or 'Ivory Tower.'"

On the subject of fictional technique Fannie Hurst has said: "The terms 'technique' and 'style' are too often loosely interchangeable and create confusion. 'Technique' involves the mechanical processes of packaging the theme or idea. 'Style' and 'fashion' are likewise frequently confused. For instance, Ernest Hemingway has established a fashion for the Jason, picaresque school of writing with a highly emotional background. His literary style, his balanced sentence, and his lyrical smoothness are, however, part and parcel of the texture of the man, as much so as the color of his eyes, the manner of his speech and gait. Hemingway disciples (may their number decrease!) follow a fashion, not a style. Therein lies their weakness, the weakness of most imitators. Fortunate the author who early recognizes that imitation is a weak crutch! The carbon-copy school of literature has one virtue—it rubs out easily and never occupies precious space on the five-foot bookshelf of classics."

Her non-fiction books include *No Food with My Meals* (1936) and *White Christmas* (1942). In 1949 she was at work on an autobiography, *Self Portrait.* Her short-story collections include *Just Around the Corner* (1914), *Every Soul Hath Its Song* (1916), *Gaslight Sonatas* (1918), *Humoresque* (1919), *The Vertical City* (1922), *Song of Life* (1927), *Procession* (1929), and *We Are Ten* (1937).

Her first novel, *Star Dust: The Story of an American Girl* (1921), describes the life of Lilly Becker from her childhood in a boarding house to her success at the age of forty, when she finds a richer fulfillment in her daughter's beautiful singing voice. *Lummox* (1923) is the story of Bertha, a large, inarticulate woman, who almost mutely lives a life that is supremely eloquent. *Mannequin* (1926) pictures a girl stolen from a good home and reared amid poverty; her innate fastidiousness leads her upward to wealth and high position. *Appassionata* (1926) studies the conscience of an Irish Catholic girl, Laura Regan, who renounces the world to become a nun.

Five and Ten (1929) portrays the rise of a clerk to wealth and his discovery of a very old truth about happiness and the eventual gift of his fortune for advancing science. *Back Street* (1931) is about Ray Schmidt from the age of thirteen in Cincinnati in 1894 to 1930 and her life on the back street of men's affections. *Imitation of Life* (1933) has Bea Pullman learn that business success brings hollow fame by comparison with a life of goodness and service. Friends desert her, and love passes her by.

Anitra's Dance (1934) presents the life of a musical composer whose noisy family delays the completion of a symphony. Only his daughter Anitra has his artistic genius. *Great Laughter* (1936) studies a rich grandmother shaping the lives of the Campbell children and grandchildren. *Lonely Parade* (1942) shows that the rewards of marriage outweigh the success a single woman can have. *Halle-*

lujah (1944) concerns Lilly Brown, a small-town Missouri girl, who sacrifices herself for her mother who commits a murder and her drunken husband. *The Hands of Veronica* (1947) is a study of a girl with a gift for healing; the theme concerns the problem of reconciling science and religion. *Anywoman* (1950) describes the transformation of Rose Cologne, a small-town girl who is contented with her station in life until she meets Frank Caesar, who represents everything that is different in the world.

ZORA NEALE HURSTON

was born on January 7, 1903, at Eatonville, Florida, the first incorporated Negro town in America. Her father was a Baptist preacher and carpenter; her mother sewed for the community. She attended the village grammar school and early gained a reputation for being difficult both at home and at school; there was talk about the need to break her spirit. Nearby was a community of white people from the Middle West and upper New York, some of whom discovered Miss Hurston's talent and gave her books to read. She visited the estates of these people and enjoyed warm friendships with them; for this reason, she has said, "I have never been able to achieve race prejudice." She graduated in 1921 from the high school of Morgan College in Baltimore. She studied at Howard University in Washington, D.C., from 1921 to 1924. In 1928 she received her bachelor's degree at Barnard College of Columbia University, where Professor Franz Boas secured for her a fellowship in anthropology to do research in folklore. For four years she was engaged in this work, and it was during this time that she became interested seriously in writing. She wished to give a picture different from that usually presented by authors who emphasize race consciousness. She wanted to write about her people as they are and not to repeat stereotyped characters and sentiments. From 1936 to 1938 she visited Haiti and the British West Indies on a Guggenheim fellowship; her experiences are given in *Tell My Horse* (1938). *Men and Mules* (1935), a collection of Negro folk stories, describes the voodoo practices of colored people in the South. *Dust Tracks on a Road* (1943), her autobiography, received the Annisfield award for promoting better race relations. She is head of the dramatic department of the North Carolina College for Negroes at Durham, North Carolina.

"When professional 'race champions' demand of me why I am not more race conscious," Miss Hurston has stated with respect to her novels, "I ask them: what on earth is the good of it? Why should I be proud that I was born a Negro? For that matter, why should you boast of the accident of being white? My color in no way adds to nor detracts from my integrity or my talents. If you argue that it gives me a handicap, all right! I accept it and go right ahead. I am an American, and we are the nation of folks that play the odds to win. That puts me right in company with the rest. Besides, how can I honestly denounce you for racial bias if I am playing the same game?"

Her first novel, *Jonah's Gourd Vine* (1934), is about a yellow Negro preacher and his tiny brown wife and his other love affairs. *Their Eyes Were Watching God* (1937) describes a Negro girl's unhappiness as the wife of a mayor and her return at the age of forty to the sunny farm country to enjoy the beauty of growing things and the uninhibited naturalness of her people. *Moses: Man of the Mountain* (1939) gives a Negro folk interpretation of the Hebrew leader and the cruelties endured by the Israelites at the hands of Pharaoh. *Seraph on the Suwannee* (1948) relates the affairs of a beautiful Negress and the white son of a plantation owner.

JACK IAMS

Myron Ehrenburg

was born Samuel H. Iams, Jr., in Baltimore, Maryland, on November 15, 1910, but he never learned to answer to anything but "Jack" and saw no purpose in writing under a name that he hardly recognized. He attended public school in Waynesburg, Pennsylvania, then took a rather long jump to St. Paul's School at Concord, New Hampshire, and graduated from Princeton in 1932. He went directly into newspaper work, landing a job, to his astonishment, with the London *Daily Mail.* After two years there, during which he married, he joined the Baltimore *News-Post* and, in 1937, the Pittsburgh *Press;* in 1938, on the strength of two accepted novels, he attempted again to retire, this time to the Virgin Islands. Once more he returned home without funds and went to work for the New York *Daily News,* remaining there until 1942 when he joined the Office of War Information as an overseas bureau head in Brazzaville, Africa, in Lisbon, and in Brussels. He returned to this country at the end of 1945 and has since resided in Bay Head, New Jersey, devoting himself, in spite of earlier lessons, completely to writing. His mystery novels include *The Body Missed the Boat* (1947), *Girl Meets Body* (1947), *Death Draws the Line* (1949), *Do Not Murder before Christmas* (1949), *What Rhymes with Murder?* (1950), and *A Shot of Murder* (1950). He married Dorothy Aveling on January 4, 1934; they have three children.

Nowhere With Music (1938) was light in vein but suffered from that semi-autobiographical intensity that is often found in first novels. *Table for Four* (1939) deals with two young married couples, one sedately provincial, the other rather wildly cosmopolitan, who go to Paris together. Its purpose, if any, was to suggest that either of these extremes is more palatable when diluted with the other. A frolicsome humor enlivens the narrative.

Mr. Iams' next three novels had some similarity of theme—impatience with the humbug that surrounds so much of American advertising, journalism, and public relations, in that order. *The Countess to Boot* (1941) is the story of an idealistic artist who, as an employee of an advertising agency, is obliged to depict, for instance, the tragedies of using the wrong toothpaste and who attempts unsuccessfully to escape to tropic isles. A countess, who is from Minneapolis, acts as a sort of ribald Greek chorus. *Prophet by Experience* (1943) describes the efforts of various magazines and newspapers to exploit a hermit whom they bring back to civilization; civilization comes out second best. *Prematurely Gay* (1948) pictures a brash young press agent who saves a hair-dye company's falling sales on the principle of "If you can't lick 'em, join 'em"; he foists on the country a preparation designed to achieve that distinguished silvery lock. The sardonic Greek chorus, in this case, is the heroine, whom the press agent does not quite win at the end, although it is implied that he will if he reforms.

ALBERT E. IDELL

Frank Turgeon

was born on June 21, 1901, in Philadelphia, Pennsylvania. While attending Germantown High School, he worked as a grocery clerk, typist, and truck helper. From 1919 to 1921 he was a student in the School of Industrial Art, was secretary to its director, studied accounting at night school, and boxed in amateur and semi-professional prize fights. In 1921 he worked at accounting during the winters and variously as harvest hand, railroad-car repairman, laborer in a packing plant, and short-order cook in restaurants during the summers. After spending six months in Europe with a group of artists, he hitchhiked through Germany and worked passage home on the *America*. He spent the years 1926 and 1927 in Sicily and in the latter year began specializing in building-and-loan and bank accounting; in 1929 he became a partner in the manufacture of fibre specialties. During 1931–32 he audited banks in western North Carolina and at about the same time began the study of restaurant accounting; he also promoted prize fights in Asheville. He started a lending library in 1930 and still has an interest in the business; he was consultant to the Philadelphia school district on school lunchrooms during 1932, and became supervisor in 1933. He has been engaged in writing since 1941.

His first novel, *Pug* (1941), attacks the exploitation by newspapers of amateur athletes through Golden Gloves tournaments and similar circulation-building activities, and pictures the effect these enterprises have on the participants. This partly autobiographical book won the Bookman's prize of one thousand dollars for the best novel by anyone connected with the book trade. *Cross in the Caribbean* (1941) is an allegorical novel, the subject matter of which is the necessity for restating Christianity in terms to suit a modern world and the fate of those reformers who attempt it. The story concerns a group of priests, natives, and various other inhabitants of a Caribbean island who watch a sculptor engaged in chiseling a figure of Christ on the cross on one of the island's mountain tops.

Centennial Summer (1943) describes the life of the Rogers family in Philadelphia during the centennial celebration in 1875 and 1876. *Bridge to Brooklyn* (1944) chronicles the Rogers family's move to Brooklyn; the climax of the story is reached with the opening of the Brooklyn Bridge in 1883. *Stag Night* (1946), published under the pseudonym of "Phillips Rogers," is a satire on the inability of the modern businessman really to relax and enjoy himself, told through the story of a stag dinner given once a year by the male members of a country club. *The Sea Is a Woman* (1947) is an attempt to consider certain problems arising after World War II in terms of life aboard a converted troop transport on its way from San Pedro, California, to New York, in 1921.

The Great Blizzard (1948) concerns further adventures of the Rogers family during such events of the 1880's as the election of Cleveland, the Ryan-Sullivan fight, the unveiling of the Statue of Liberty, and finally the great blizzard of 1888. The Rogers family trilogy attempts to furnish a complete picture of American life—its manners, thoughts, and political and social history—during the period following Reconstruction and prior to the "Gay Nineties."

JACKSON *to* JOSEPH

CHARLES JACKSON

was born on April 6, 1903, in Summit, New Jersey. He grew up in Newark, Wayne County, New York, where his youngest brother and oldest sister—there were five children—were killed in an automobile accident in 1916. At school, Charles invariably stood at the head of his class. He was musical, artistic, literary, and he acted in school plays. During his high-school days he clerked in a grocery store afternoons and Saturdays. Upon his graduation he went to work for the weekly *Courier* and soon was appointed local editor. In 1924 he went to Chicago to be a book salesman and for eighteen months he worked in Krock's bookstore. When he felt that he had learned enough about Chicago, he moved to New York and obtained a job with the Doubleday bookstores. During this period he wrote a novel which he has not published. His excessive work brought on a case of tuberculosis which directly and indirectly blighted his life for the next ten years. For a year he concealed his illness in order to avoid returning home. In the spring of 1928 he suffered a severe hemorrhage and was taken to a hospital and then to a sanitarium established by Dr. William Devitt at Allenwood, Pennsylvania. His right lung was collapsed permanently and his weight declined from 135 pounds to 101 pounds. Attracted to Davos, Switzerland, by Thomas Mann's *The Magic Mountain,* he remained two years. His improvement was so rapid that he skated, went bob-sledding, and took long walks over mountain trails. Since that time his health has been excellent. He left Switzerland in 1931, took an excursion to the Riviera, and then sailed for America. He had begun to write at Davos, and on reaching New York he wrote steadily. In 1937 he began preparing radio scripts. On March 4, 1938, he married Rhoda Booth. They have two children. Now he devotes full time to writing. *Sunnier Side* (1950) contains twelve short stories giving reminiscent pictures of his youthful days in an upstate New York village.

Mr. Jackson belongs to the group of writers who deal with themes drawn from morbid psychology: he handles them with insight into the principles of psychiatry.

The Lost Weekend (1944), his first novel, one of the year's most discussed books that was made into an equally popular moving picture, portrays the painful thoughts of a serious alcoholic, Don Birnam, a sensitive, charming, and educated man. During five days when he is alone he has a great desire for strong drink to which he yields, and then he reviews the events of his life and the cause of his strange malady. *The Fall of Valor* (1946) tells of the disintegration and destruction of a marriage because of homosexual tendencies on the part of the husband. *The Outer Edges* (1948) recounts the effect of a news story of a youthful sex maniac's murder of two children on a number of persons at crises in their lives, frightening and causing anxiety in parents, producing feelings of guilt in a sensitive man, and merely amusing others.

SHIRLEY JACKSON

was born on December 14, 1919, in San Francisco. She left California when she was sixteen and has lived in the East—New England and New York—ever since. At Syracuse University she founded and edited the college literary magazine, and at graduation in 1940 she married Stanley Edgar Hyman, folklorist, critic, and author of *The Armed Vision;* they have three children, and live throughout the year in Westport, Connecticut.

Her principal interest is English fiction, which she has read exhaustively, particularly the eighteenth-century novel. Her ambition is to write as well, she says, and suspects it is a good deal harder to superimpose order and pattern on the modern world. Although her study of witchcraft and black magic has been extensively publicized, she insists that it represents no more than a field of interest and a hobby, like drawing and teaching fiction writing, which she did briefly at Bennington College.

The Road Through the Wall (1948), her first novel, is the story of one summer in a California suburban town; it is focused on the children of Pepper Street and shows the precariousness of the middle-class "good life" when it is cruelly exposed to the world by the tearing down of a protecting wall. *The Lottery* (1949) is a selection of short stories united thematically by the recurrent figure of James Harris, the daemon lover. The title story, when it appeared in *The New Yorker* in 1948, created a literary sensation, and it has since been included in numerous anthologies.

ELIZABETH JANEWAY

Hal Phyfe

was born on Pineapple Street in Brooklyn, New York, in 1913. She attended the Shore Road Academy in Brooklyn, Swarthmore College, and Barnard College of Columbia University, from which she graduated in 1935. From her earliest years she was interested in writing, and her first national recognition came while she still was at Barnard when she won the *Story* magazine intercollegiate short-story contest in 1935. She is married to Eliot Janeway, the well-known economist-commentator; they have two sons and live in Bethel, Connecticut.

Her advice to young writers is to study poetry and anthropology: poetry because it is concentrated, and anthropology because writing is a form of control over one's environment.

The Walsh Girls (1943), her first novel, is a psychological novel telling the story of two sisters, daughters of a pompous minister, and their loves and their hates. Helen marries a German professor who dies in the Dachau concentration camp; she then returns home to marry the boy next door, and Lydia, a spinster, moves in with Helen when the bank forecloses on her house. The theme concerns "the failure in human relationship of two highly individual women and the final adjustment of their lives in relation to each other and to two very different pasts." *Daisy Kenyon* (1945) is an historical novel of the confused world of 1940–42, with a Washington, D.C., background. Daisy, Dan O'Mara, and Peter Lapham are seeking happiness and the meaning of life. *The Question of Gregory* (1948) is the story of men and women forced by moral crisis and emotional shock into re-appraisal of themselves and their world. Their only son's death so affects John and Ellen Gregory that John wanders for a time and Ellen returns to her wealthy family in Connecticut. The setting is Washington, New England, and Detroit.

RUSSELL JANNEY

was born on April 14, 1884, in Wilmington, Ohio, where his father was principal of the high school. His family moved shortly thereafter to Chillicothe, Ohio, and then to Keene, New Hampshire. His interest in the theater developed in Keene, then a one-night stand for all road shows going from Boston to Canada; at the age of twelve he posted bills for the theater. He also wrote lyrics for popular songs, some of which he sold for what he then considered the excellent price of ten dollars. After graduating from Yale in 1906, he went to London, where he established himself as a writer for magazines and as a theatrical press agent. In this latter capacity he was associated with Beerbohm Tree, George Edwardes, and other leading British managers. He returned to the United States and continued his theatrical work, simultaneously writing short stories for *The Smart Set* and producing material for the first "Ziegfeld Follies." As a press agent he worked for some time for Theda Bara, first "glamour girl" of the motion pictures. His own theatrical productions have included "White Eagle, "Marjolaine," "June Love," "The O'Flynn," and "Sancho Panza," which featured Otis Skinner as its star. "The Vagabond King" (1925), of which he is co-author, has been played to audiences all over the world and is still being performed. In 1949 he was a member of the jury which convicted eleven Communist party leaders of advocating overthrow of the United States Government by force. His interest in life, he says, is Tolerance, the theme of *The Vision of Red O'Shea* (1949), a ballad. Mr. Janney has a son, William, who was an actor and is now in radio work.

The Miracle of the Bells (1946), his first novel, is the story of a Broadway press agent whose publicity stunt for a motion-picture actress snowballs into a "miracle" that affects the lives of the people of the town in which it occurs. It is based on many characters Janney had known in real life, and the author believes that it contains a message of tolerance and brotherhood. A Quaker himself, Janney did considerable research in Catholic matters in writing this book, which deals with a small Pennsylvania mining town whose inhabitants are predominantly Polish Catholics.

CLARE JAYNES

is a pen name employed by Mrs. Jane Rothschild Mayer and Mrs. Clara Gatzert Spiegel.

Maurice Seymour

Mrs. Mayer was born in Kansas City, Missouri, on December 30, 1903. She graduated from Vassar College in 1925. In 1927 she married David Mayer, Jr., and moved to Glencoe, Illinois, where she and her husband live with their three children: David III, Mary Jane, and Phillip.

The central purpose of "Clare Jaynes" is to portray men and women who are meeting the basic emotional problems, particularly those of marriage and family life confronting most people today.

Maurice Seymour

Mrs. Spiegel was born in Chicago, Illinois, on December 6, 1904. She was a student at Vassar College from 1922 to 1923. On December 1, 1923, she married Frederick W. Spiegel. This union ended in divorce in 1950. They have two sons. She lives in Highland Park, Illinois.

Mrs. Mayer and Mrs. Spiegel have never written separately. Their first published works were short stories.

Instruct My Sorrows (1942), their first novel, tells how a wealthy Chicago woman of thirty-three finds peace after the death of her husband. *These Are the Times* (1944) portrays the possessive wife of a famous orthopedic surgeon and her unwillingness to allow him to join an overseas medical unit. *This Eager Heart* (1947) is a story of the MacFarlans on a Montana ranch, who after twelve years of completely harmonious marriage come near to splitting up because of the man's self-accusations.

JOHN EDWARD JENNINGS, JR.

Fabian Bachrach

was born on December 30, 1906, in Brooklyn, New York. His father was a surgeon, and his mother was the founder and long-time head of New York Interpreted, an organization engaged in explaining New York City's cultural values to strangers. John Jennings received his early education in several preparatory schools, and he attended the Columbia University School of Mines and New York University. He has been writing since 1932. During World War II he was officer in charge of the naval aviation history unit. He married Virginia Lee Storey in 1931; they have one son. His non-fiction books include *Our American Tropics* (1938) and *Boston, Cradle of Liberty, 1630–1776* (1947).

Next to Valour (1939), his first novel, deals with life in the New Hampshire settlements between 1746 and 1759 in the story of James Ferguson, who came from Scotland to the Indian-infested wilds and joined Rogers Rangers. *Call the New World* (1941) tells of Peter Brooke's part in the War of 1812 and in the wars of liberation under Símon Bolívar in South America. *Gentleman Ranker* (1942), about General Braddock's defeat in 1755, shows Stephen Trent, an English gentleman, serving as a private in the army.

The Shadow and the Glory (1943) portrays the organization of the American Continental army in a tale of Davy Ferguson, son of the immigrant James Ferguson, from June, 1755, to the Battle of Bennington. *The Salem Frigate* (1946) details the adventures of the *Essex* in 1779 in a story of Tom Tisdale, a young physician, and Ben Price, a carpenter, who marries Tom's sweetheart. *River of the West* (1948) pictures the founding of Astoria at the mouth of the Columbia River in 1811 by the expedition sent out by John Jacob Astor to establish a fur-trading post in the Northwest. The central figure is Rory O'Rourke, Astor's confidential agent. *Sea Eagles* (1950) concerns the adventures of two romantic members of the American navy during the Revolution; the climax comes with the famous battle of John Paul Jones' *Bon Homme Richard* against the *Serapis*. *The Pepper Tree* (1950) is a tale of romance and adventure in the East Indies.

CORNELIA JESSEY

was born on February 9, 1910, in Jeannette, Pennsylvania. She grew up and went to school in Prescott, Arizona. She received a bachelor's and a master's degree at the University of California in Berkeley, where she majored in English and psychology but took degrees in English only. She holds a general secondary teaching credential in California. For two years she engaged in social work, and for seven years she taught English and citizenship to adults. Her chief occupation other than writing has been puppetry. She and her husband, Irving Sussman, have their own traveling puppet theater, the Don Quixote Marionette Theatre, which travels throughout California and the Southwest, giving shows for children's theaters, schools, colleges, recreation centers, and veterans' hospitals. They make all their marionettes, write all their shows, and act all the parts.

Her primary interest in writing is psychological and philosophical rather than sociological, although she uses a sociological framework. Above all, she is interested in man's search for meaning, his groping for ethical concepts and religious values—the implications and responsibilities of being human.

The Growing Roots (1947), her first novel, portrays a handful of people seeking meaning and recognition as human beings rather than as racial entities in the "new world," the great dream of democracy. It also depicts the second generation in one of the children whose sense of keen individualism is the fruit of the effort made by her forebears; this in itself brings forth an entirely different kind of problem, that of retaining one's individuality and yet being integrated with one's past and one's present and the lives of one's fellow men. *Teach the Angry Spirit* (1949) deals with the same situation, using a different racial background. The first was Jewish, the second Mexican. It is the story of the efforts of a handful of young people to find some meaning and integration of their lives in the democratic dream, of their endeavor to feel like human beings and to establish themselves as part of this brave concept. Especially is it the story of a young boy who accepts the entire "burden of his duress": all that is involved in his existence, all the responsibilities of being human.

JOSEPHINE W. JOHNSON

Herbert Matter

was born on June 20, 1910, in Kirkwood, Missouri. Her family moved in 1912 to a hundred-acre farm, and there she gained an abiding love of the countryside. She attended Washington University and the St. Louis Art School, but left without taking a degree. She painted murals for two elementary schools in St. Louis and has exhibited water colors. She has taught at Iowa University and at the Peoples Art Center in St. Louis. She has also been on the staff at the Breadloaf School of English of Middlebury College in Vermont. She has been actively interested in the co-operative movement and in social and political reform. She is married to Grant Cannon, managing editor of the *Farm Quarterly*, and lives in Newtown, Ohio; they have two children. Miss Johnson's short stories have appeared in *Winter Orchard* (1935) and in the O. Henry and O'Brien story collections. She was awarded the special O. Henry prize in 1935. *Year's End* (1937) is a book of poems. *Paulina: The Story of the Apple-Butter Pot* (1939) is a children's book.

Now in November (1934), her first novel and winner of the Pulitzer prize, is a realistic story in poetic prose of farm life in the Middle West, where the Haldemarne family has struggled for ten years against drought and debt. After a year of failure and tragedy, Marget looks back into the past and tells the meaning of events that occurred "in November." *Jordanstown* (1937) is the story of the struggle between rich and poor people in a small midwestern industrial town during the depression in an account of Allen Craig, whose family fortune has been lost. He moves to the poor side of town, organizes a newspaper, the *Voice*, and is arrested in a Labor Day parade. *Wildwood* (1946) is a study of a young girl's loneliness and suffering. Edith Pierre gains all the comforts of life but little understanding treatment when she is adopted into the home of a well-to-do pedantic ornithologist and his rather bloodless wife. Edith is unhappy in her surroundings and dreams of love and fulfillment.

IDWAL JONES

was born in the north of Wales on December 8, 1891, and came to the United States as a child. His moorland background was later incorporated into his published works, especially his juvenile novel of the Welsh gipsies, *Whistler's Van* (1936). He has lived in upper New York state, where he attended public schools, in Pennsylvania, and in California. One of his first ventures in his early days in California was the attempt to operate a gold mine close to the Poker Flat of which Bret Harte wrote; Mr. Jones' interest in metals and the early history of the state helped in the writing of *Vermilion*. He entered newspaper work and became a book reviewer on the San Francisco *Chronicle* and later was dramatic editor and columnist of the San Francisco *Examiner*. Meanwhile he married Miss Olive Vere Wolf, who had been a teacher in Hawaii and San Francisco. They have one daughter, Dilys, who in 1949 was a journalist in Paris. From 1927 to 1929 Idwal Jones lived in France and Italy. Returning to America in 1930, he joined the staff of the New York *American* as an editorial writer, columnist, and editor of the Sunday book page. He also became book critic for the old *Life* magazine. He has lectured on writing at Claremont College and at Stanford University.

In 1933 he returned to San Francisco, where he wrote a series of special foreign articles for the *Chronicle* and for various magazines. He has written hundreds of articles on history, anthropology, customs, mining, viticulture, folklore, and travel. He has translated several books from French, Spanish, and Italian. However, it is as a writer of California history, scenes, and episodes that he is most widely known. *Vines in the Sun* (1949), a non-fiction book, is a history of grape growing in California. *China Boy* (1936) contains six short stories about Japanese and Chinese in California. *Gold-Dust Empire* (1950) deals with San Francisco in the Civil War period.

Gorham Munson has stated that the two words which summarize Idwal Jones are integrity and magic: "Again and again it is a character outstanding for integrity that he depicts best. He stands for principle as a ruling force, for inflexible loyalty to a man's sense of his inner grain, for the kind of self-respect that is a mainspring of action. His best-drawn characters are men and women the reader can look up to. The magic of his style is in the tradition of Cicero. He has an earthy mysticism and presents a fusion of downright earthiness and rich suggestiveness of a strangeness in our planetary life."

The Splendid Shilling (1926), his first novel, is the story of a gipsy boy who leaves his Welsh village to cross the Atlantic and find in California during the gold-rush days of 1850 the fulfillment of his dreams. *Steel Chips* (1929), a study of the impact of the machine philosophy on the mind and soul of men engaged in routine work, pictures in detail a machine shop and the hopes of the men who work there. The story is of Bram Dartwell, who serves his apprenticeship under his father and rises to be a foreman at forty. *Black Bayou* (1941) is a romance of Cajun muskrat trappers who object to a plantation owner's draining of the swamp to grow sugar cane. The real protagonist of this profound tale is "the active-contemplative philosophy of St. Theresa de Avila, with the thesis of the superiority of the balanced faculties as the true key to the life of the spirit in a world of turmoil and evil." *The Vineyard* (1942) is a history of the wine industry in California from 1910 to 1940, with the focus on the Regola family and the search for the White Pendle grape, a strain that disappeared during Prohibition. *High Bonnet* (1945) is an autobiography of a French chef, and describes his apprenticeship and education, arduous toil, aesthetics, and discipline. *Vermilion* (1947) has the theme of the continuity of life in a story of several generations of a family controlling cinnabar mines in California for a century.

NARD (MAYNARD BENEDICT) JONES

was born in Seattle, Washington, on April 12, 1904. He graduated from Whitman College at Walla Walla, Washington, in 1926; in his junior year he sold his first story, and since then has had more than three hundred published. During World War II he was a public-relations officer for the Thirteenth Naval District and the Northwest Sea Frontier. Thereafter he was manager of the New York office of Miller Freeman publications. He married Elizabeth Dunphy in 1928; she died in 1940. He married Anne Marie Mynar in 1942. He has a son by the first marriage and a daughter by the second. His books include *West, Young Man* (with J. G. Gose, 1937), a juvenile; *The Case of the Hanging Lady* (1937), a mystery story; and *Evergreen Land* (1941), a book about the state of Washington.

Mr. Jones' novels are among the first serious realistic treatments of life in the Pacific Northwest. His major theme concerns the gradual demoralization of the people of the United States as the frontier disappears. This hypothesis holds that when the American people reach the end of their period of migration, they will change their type of government to match that of Europe. Mr. Jones' novels portray the steady alteration of the pioneers' concept of individualism and the rise of a theory of collectivism.

Oregon Detour (1930), his first novel, portrays life in Creston, a small wheat-farming community of the Northwest, through the eyes and experiences of Etta Dant from her days in high school until she is married to Charlie Fraser. *The Petlands* (1931) chronicles events in the lives of three generations of the Petland family against the background of the growth and development of Seattle. This was the first full-length novel to employ Seattle as a setting. *Wheat Women* (1933), set in the farm country around Walla Walla, Washington, traces three generations in the family founded by Jackson Lynch. The son Todd sacrifices his wife Cora on an altar of wheat, and then harsh and calculating Julie, his second wife, leads them into tragic circumstances. This realistic novel is the first to include a description of cannibalism, a theme hitherto not admitted to pioneer stories. *All Six Were Lovers* (1934) concerns a group of men who are the lovers of Leah, a woman in the western ranch country. She has died before the story opens, and the life account of each man is told in flashbacks as the men serve as pallbearers at the funeral of Leah.

Swift Flows the River (1940) portrays pioneer days on the Columbia River as a background for the story of Caleb Paige, whose parents are killed in an Indian raid in 1856. Caleb takes his first steps toward fulfilling his ambition to be a river pilot when his foster father takes him on a gold-hunting expedition. *Scarlet Petticoat* (1941) pictures early nineteenth-century fur-trading days on the lower Columbia River. The principal character and narrator is the historical figure, Alexander Henry, who was an assistant to the factor at Fort George. *Still to the West* (1946) is about the building of the Grand Coulee Dam on the Columbia River. The central character is Ellen O'Malley, the granddaughter of a pioneer. *The Island* (1948) deals with the period before and during World War II in the Puget Sound area. Lou Benedict tells the story of Jack Madcliff's life from college to his suicide in Atlantic City. Lou also expresses many opinions about contemporary persons and events.

MILDRED JORDAN

was born on March 18, 1901, in Chicago, Illinois. After attending Northwestern University for two years, she transferred to Wellesley College, from which she graduated in 1922. She then taught basketball to a boys' club at Hull House in Chicago and also sold a one-volume encyclopedia. She is married to J. Lee Bausher, a hosiery manufacturer, and makes her home in Reading, Pennsylvania. She is the mother of three daughters and a son, but her domestic duties have not prevented her from traveling extensively in Europe, Canada, and the West Indies, nor have they interfered with such strenuous hobbies as tennis, skating, and skiing. She performs ably on both harp and piano. *The Shoo-Fly Pie* (1944) and *"I Won't," Said the King* (1945) are juveniles.

One Red Rose Forever (1941) is an historical novel based on the life of "Baron" Stiegel, the German immigrant whose glassware is famous for its fine quality and delicate workmanship. *Apple in the Attic* (1942) describes a Pennsylvania Dutch farmer who vowed during a quarrel with his wife that he would never speak to her again, and kept his promise. *Asylum for the Queen* (1948) portrays the plans of French aristocrats to rescue the royal family during the Revolution of 1789 and to take Marie Antoinette and the Dauphin to the little village of Asylum, near Towanda, Pennsylvania, where a safe retreat was being prepared for the exiles. The action centers in Pierre de Michelait, an engaging young man. *Miracle in Brittany* (1950) is a tale of peasants' faith. A mysterious stranger looks for the Saviour in a little village. There is warmth, understanding, and artistry in the telling.

DONALD JOSEPH

Studio Clements

was born in Cuero, Texas, on April 22, 1898. He received his education at the University of Texas, earning a bachelor's and a master's degree, and at the University of Toulouse, France, where he attained the degree of Doctor of Literature with honors in the shortest time that any foreigner, up to that date, had ever received it. After working in a bank at San Antonio, he taught French at the University of Texas. He resigned in January, 1945, to devote full time to writing. He has traveled extensively in Europe, and especially in France and England; and he has also been in Mexico, Cuba, and many parts of the United States. Since 1921 he has made his home in Austin, Texas. He has edited two books by Hewitt L. Ballowe: *The Lawd Sayin' the Same* (1946), stories of the lower Mississippi, and *Creole Folk Tales* (1947).

October's Child (1929), his first novel, studies the adolescence of Lucius Deering from the moment he finds a dead canary in the attic until he becomes ready, through the help of a college roommate, to start forth on his own. *Long Bondage* (1930) portrays in the life of Louise Bannerton the long servitude of a woman to her father, her husband, and her son. She gains freedom at last with the man she ought to have married earlier. *Four Blind Mice* (1932) continues the story of Lucius Deering from college days into middle age. His wife leaves him after the birth of a son, and the last part of the novel, an account of the father-son relationship, shows the boy drawing away from his possessive parent. *Straw in the Wind* (1946) has the theme of race hatred and violence in the South in the early nineteenth century. A Negress accused of murder is ostracized by whites and blacks and has no one to befriend her until the wife of a judge steps forward.

KAFKA *to* KUHN

JOHN KAFKA

was born in Vienna, Austria, on December 26, 1905. After taking his doctorate at the University of Vienna, he began his literary career with a volume of half-symbolic short stories, *Das Grenzenlose* (*No Limits,* 1925). In 1925 he went to Berlin to become a critic of drama, music, and art, and an editor for the newspapers and magazines of the Ullstein syndicate. In 1930 he was appointed traveling reporter with the special assignment of covering the most notorious crime cases in Italy, France, and Scandinavia. After Hitler's ascendance in 1933, Mr. Kafka returned to his native Vienna where he wrote his first novel, *Geschichte einer grossen Liebe* (*The Story of a Great Love,* 1935). Having moved to Paris in 1936, he became a writer of screenplays in the French language; one of his creations, "Carrefour," won a French state award. In 1938 he moved to London to write his first English-language picture, "Dead Man's Shoes." On the outbreak of World War II he emigrated to the United States, where he subsequently wrote a great number of screenplays and original motion-picture stories for Hollywood companies. In 1945 he became an American citizen. He is married to Trudy Burr, a stage actress.

A disciple of Dr. Sigmund Freud during the brief period when the master of psychoanalysis held classes at Vienna University, Mr. Kafka still occasionally dabbles in that psychiatric doctrine. In 1945 he invented a new test which is now being tried out in psychoanalytic clinics in New York and Los Angeles. Such "excursions into the inside world" are deemed by Mr. Kafka as vital exercises for fiction writing.

John Kafka is not related to the late Franz Kafka, nor does he think he has any literary affinity to the Czech writer. But once as a child he happened to meet his great namesake, and the brief conversation exchanged at this meeting is remembered by John as one of the unique and indestructible spiritual experiences of his life.

The Apple Orchard (1947), John Kafka's first American novel, is the "biography" of an apple orchard in Idaho in the 1860's. It begins life as the center and means of subsistence for a truly Christian community; then it goes down as the victim of stupid, ruthless exploitation during the gold-rush days; its remnants linger on through the deadly stillness of a ghost town until its final resurrection, on a co-operative basis, as one of the biggest apple orchards in the world. It is also the story of the whole American West which, in the last century, lived through exactly the same cycle.

Sicilian Street (1949) is also a "pioneer story" but in a quite different sense. It tells of the insurmountable obstacles encountered by a young couple who want to Americanize a street in the heart of Manhattan. This street harbors an old Sicilian puppet show that represents traditions with origins dating back to earliest times of history, and a populace transplanted almost intact from a small town in ancient Sicily to this overcrowded New York slum. It is Peri, the puppeteer's granddaughter, who together with her American sweetheart rebels against that background and tries to do her modernizing pioneer work by replacing the puppet theater with a streamlined up-to-date American drugstore. The novel is a "blow-by-blow" account of that clash between two worlds; it is also the story of modern man suddenly facing the sunken world of the past and having a chance to discuss, with people belonging to bygone ages, the question whether humanity, in its progress, is achieving anything.

HARNETT THOMAS KANE

was born on November 8, 1910, in New Orleans, Louisiana. While a sophomore at Tulane University, from which he graduated in 1931, he began working on New Orleans newspapers, serving in all editorial capacities, including that of city editor and copy editor, political correspondent, and feature writer. During the Louisiana scandals of 1939 he headed the staff in gathering information and writing interpretive stories on this national sensation; this experience led to his first book, *Louisiana Hayride, American Rehearsal for Dictatorship* (1941). In 1943 he resigned from newspaper work to devote full time to writing. He has held two Rosenwald fellowships for research in southern history. In 1943 he taught at Loyola University of the South. His other non-fiction books include *The Bayous of Louisiana* (1943), *Deep Delta Country* (1944), *Plantation Parade* (1945), *Natchez on the Mississippi* (1947), and *Queen New Orleans* (1949).

"In my books," says Mr. Kane, "I have tried to give a fair and true picture of the southern people and their scene, past and present, recognizing but not overstressing some of the South's unique cultural heritage. I have sought to bring to life some of the highly colored personalities who are often more vivid than any fictional characters, past and present."

New Orleans Woman (1946), his first novel, is a fictionalized biography of Myra Clark Gaines, a red-haired beauty who was the storm center of the most remarkable case in the history of the American courts; she sought to regain the name and fortune of which she had been robbed. *Bride of Fortune* (1948) is a biographical novel based on the life of Mrs. Jefferson Davis, telling the role played by a remarkable southern woman in the shaping of her husband's life and in the events leading up to and through the Civil War. *Pathway to the Stars* (1950) recounts events in the life of John McDonogh, prominent merchant and philanthropist, who left his fortune to establish schools in Louisiana.

MACKINLAY KANTOR

was born at Webster City, Iowa, on February 4, 1904. His mother was a daughter of pioneer parents with an inheritance of Scotch, Irish, and Pennsylvania Dutch ancestry. His father, who was born in Sweden, was of Portuguese-Russian stock. The boy's parents were divorced during his infancy. He was reared by his mother, a newspaperwoman who influenced and encouraged him to write. His youth was spent in Iowa, with brief interludes in Chicago. At the age of seventeen he began work with his mother on a small daily paper, the Webster City *News,* which suspended publication four years later. Mr. Kantor then went to Chicago, where he supported himself for the next few years by working at various jobs in stores and factories. In 1922 he won a statewide short-story contest conducted by the Des Moines *Register;* this experience crystallized his intention to become an author.

While in Chicago Mr. Kantor met Irene Layne, a young commercial artist, and they were married on July 2, 1926; they have two children. The novelist and his wife spent the earlier years of their marriage in Chicago and Iowa and moved to the East in the depths of the depression. In Westfield, New Jersey, and in the nearby mountain community of Free Acres, Mr. Kantor labored through 1933 on his Gettysburg novel, *Long Remember.* He first went to Hollywood in 1934, and has returned at intervals ever since. He wrote the original story of the motion picture "The Best Years of Our Lives." During World War II Mr. Kantor was a war correspondent in England with the Royal Air Force. His designation as a non-combatant irked him; he completed a combat preparation course and flew many missions as a gunner with the American fliers of the 8th and 9th Air Forces. On November 26, 1947, he received the Medal of Freedom; he was the only American war correspondent to be personally decorated by General Carl A. Spaatz. The citation said in part: "Through his personal experience and his participation in actual combat operations with American airmen, he became familiar with the problems and characteristics of the air force and skillfully carried the soldier's story to the people. Through his courage and initiative and the heartening interest reflected in his writings, Mr. Kantor contributed immeasurably to the morale of the armed forces and to the enlightenment of the American people at home."

Mr. Kantor's books include *Turkey in the Straw* (1935), a collection of ballads and other verse; *Angleworms on Toast* (1942), a book for children; *Author's Choice* (1944), a selection of forty of his short stories; and *But Look, the Morn* (1947), an autobiography of his childhood.

Diversey (1928), his first novel, was the earliest of the Chicago gangster tales, and created a pattern later followed by other novelists. It is an exciting portrait of machine guns operating in political and bootleg feuds. *El Goes South* (1930) is a realistic story of a Chicago suburban family when a father of four children finds his second wife and the husband of his eldest daughter in love. *The Jaybird* (1932) is about Abner Feather, a fifer in the Civil War, and his grandson, Kenny, who go west when the boy's mother runs away with a traveling salesman. The old man's favorite tune is "Jaybird," and he gives that name to himself.

Long Remember (1934), the book that brought fame to the author for his successful application to the historical novel of the realistic method, pictures the Battle of Gettysburg so graphically that the reader seems to be a shuddering eyewitness. *The Voice of Bugle Ann* (1935), perhaps the most widely read of Mr. Kantor's works, is the story of a fox hunter in Missouri and his hound with a peculiarly clear bark; the master shoots a man suspected of killing her. *Arouse and Beware* (1936) is another historical novel of the Civil War, although not conceived on the grand scale of the Gettysburg book. It concerns two Yankee soldiers who escape from a Confederate prison and meet a murderess; together they escape to the northern lines.

The Romance of Rosy Ridge (1937) has its setting in Missouri just after the Civil War and concerns the courtship of a wandering musician and the daughter of an embittered Confederate veteran. *The Noise of Their Wings* (1938) deals with the plans of a rich tomato canner to restock the country with carrier pigeons that had been extinct since 1914. A Florida "cracker" is enriched by finding a pair of the birds. *Valedictory* (1939) pictures a high-school janitor watching the Class of 1922 receiving diplomas; it is his last night of work, and he reviews the many times he helped these boys and girls. *Cuba Libre* (1940) is about a Cuban orphan boy who is smuggled to Iowa by members of a regiment of soldiers in the Spanish-American War. Years later two of them find him in Cuba helping his country.

Gentle Annie (1942), a tale of Oklahoma in 1901, relates the story of a pretty girl who complicates the lives of a railroad detective and two young Oklahoma farmers who have become train robbers. *Happy Land* (1943) tells the story of a pharmacist whose son is killed in the war. The father wonders what in the boy's short life was worth dying for. The grandfather's ghost appears to review the youth's life. *Midnight Lace* (1948) is about a milliner from Chicago who in 1911 arrives in Lexington, Iowa, and helps Ben Steele to social and political heights, only to face disaster from Senator Newgate's lust. *Wicked Water* (1949) depicts the life and love of a professional killer employed by cattle barons during the range wars in the West. *The Good Family* (1949) portrays a young married couple, struggling in poverty, who try to shun the responsibilities of approaching parenthood, but who eventually build a rewarding existence for themselves and their children.

Signal Thirty-Two (1950) spiritedly and compassionately pictures the life of policemen of the 23rd Police Precinct in New York City as they deal with people in trouble.

WALTER KARIG

was born on November 13, 1898, in New York City, but his father, an embosser and engraver by trade, soon moved his family to Glen Ridge, New Jersey, where Walter grew up as a country boy. He attended public school in Glen Ridge and edited the high-school paper and yearbook. Upon finishing high school, he began commuting to the New York School of Fine and Applied Arts; his study there was interrupted by World War I. He volunteered but was rejected by all American military services because of astigmatism. In Quebec he joined the Foreign Legion and served ten months overseas with the French. After the armistice he joined General Haller's Free Polish Army, rising in rank during eight months of service from second lieutenant to captain.

Returning to America in 1919, Mr. Karig married and went to work as a sports writer on the Norfolk *Virginian Pilot.* Shortly after becoming editor of the Elizabeth City, North Carolina, *Herald* in 1920, he decided to move to New York. There he got a part-time job on the *Herald* as its district reporter for northern New Jersey, and a regular job as police-court reporter on the Newark *Evening News.* Mixing a roving and adventurous career with his regular duties, he worked for twenty-one years on the *News;* he was chief of its Washington Bureau from 1934 to 1942. In 1937 he became United States correspondent for a group of British newspapers, including the London *Star* and the Manchester *Guardian;* from 1938 to 1942 he was on the editorial board of *Liberty* magazine.

He attempted to join the navy in 1941 before the attack on Pearl Harbor; in a civilian capacity he worked intimately with Secretaries Edison and Knox. The Magazine and Book Section of Navy Public Relations was his creation, and he was its first commander, recruiting professional writers to fill the staff. He was made a captain and assistant director of public relations in 1945, and was easily persuaded to remain after demobilization. He is now special assistant to the Chief of Naval Operations.

In 1929 Mr. Karig discovered the "pulps," and in his spare time he wrote, under one name or another, juvenile and adult adventure stories. One of this series was published as his first book, *Hungry Crawford, Legionnaire* (1929). As "Carolyn Keene" he wrote most of the Nancy Drew books, a popular series for girls; as "James Cody

Ferris" he wrote many of the X-Bar-X Boys series; and as "Julia K. Duncan" he was the author of the Doris Force series for boys and girls. Under the pen name of "Keats Patrick" he turned out *Death Is a Tory* (1935), an adult mystery novel. Mr. Karig has published under his own name several non-fiction books; the first was *Asia's Good Neighbor* (1937). *Battle Report* (1944) is a five-volume narrative of the navy at war. His wife, the artist Eleanor Freye Karig, and his two daughters are joint authors and illustrators of *The Pig in the Parlor* (1949), a book about pets.

"If there is any theme common to my books," says Captain Karig, "it is a desire to report things as they are, either with historical accuracy as in the *Battle Report* series; realistically as in the novel *Lower Than Angels,* which sought to tell the story of the little people without romancing; or satirically as in *Zotz,* which was essentially a good-humored report on little minds in big places."

Mr. Karig's first novel to be published under his own name was *Lower Than Angels* (1945), a case history of a common man, Marvin Long, from his birth in Brooklyn to his death on Staten Island, where he raised his family and ran a delicatessen store. *War in the Atomic Age* (1946) is a thinly disguised fiction relating to the possibilities of warfare under new conditions. *Zotz* (1947) concerns an etymologist, Dr. John Jones, whose specialty is Asiatic languages, who visits Washington, D.C., to offer a secret to the government with which to win the war. Red tape gets in his way.

NORMAN KATKOV

Lotte Jacobi

was born on July 26, 1918, in a Russian village some fifty miles northwest of Odessa, the first of four sons of Hyman and Melia Katkov. His parents brought him to America in 1921 and settled in St. Paul, Minnesota. At the University of Minnesota, from which he graduated in 1940, he wrote short stories which achieved no commercial or critical success. There followed two years of professional inactivity; he worked daily in his father's grocery store in St. Paul. He went into the army in 1942, serving until disability forced him out late in 1943. During this period he edited the Fort Snelling *Bulletin,* and wrote for it a weekly short story with an army theme. Some of these were reprinted in *Yank,* the army newspaper. At this time his short stories found a sympathetic reception in the hands of Allen Marple, then fiction editor for *Collier's.*

Immediately after his discharge, Mr. Katkov went to work as a police reporter for the St. Paul *Pioneer Press.* Haunting police headquarters and writing nightly, he sold his first story to *Collier's* in the early spring of 1944. There followed a long association with that magazine and with Allen Marple. In the fall of 1944 Mr. Katkov left St. Paul and found a job on the New York *World-Telegram.* Here he worked for four years as rewriteman, reporter, and feature writer. For some two years, 1946–48, he had a roving assignment in New York, roaming the city nightly afoot and appearing in the city room of the newspaper sometime before dawn to write his daily human-interest feature. In July, 1948, he left the newspaper business to devote himself entirely to fiction. He resides in New York City.

"What you have to learn first," he says, "what you must know from the start is that you're not the best writer who ever lived. Weigh yourself, and then if you want to write, do the best you can. It's no sin to write books if you go with the best you have in you; and it's no sin either to try and get better. There is a mark you set for yourself as a writer, how you'd like to write, and how good you'd like to be, and you're not a failure if you don't come close. You're a failure if you throw away the pen and leave the typewriter and don't even try."

Eagle At My Eyes (1948), which caused a minor sensation, is the often brutal story of a Jewish-Gentile marriage told from the viewpoint of the young Jewish husband and stressing the anti-Gentile feeling of his family. Joe Goodman, a St. Paul newspaper reporter, falls in love with and marries Mary Simpson despite the protests of his hysterical mother and his gentle, big-hearted father. The family had passed through the pogroms in Russia and thus achieved its bitterness.

A Little Sleep, A Little Slumber (1949) is the fictionalized story of Mr. Katkov's father's life in America. "What he was (he died in March, 1948) is all in there," Mr. Katkov says. "He was an extraordinary man, the most devoted to his children I've ever seen. He had the most humility, the most generosity, the most fear, and the most bravery of any human being I ever knew."

STANLEY KAUFFMANN

Lucas & Monroe, Inc.

was born in New York City on April 24, 1916. He attended public schools and New York University, from which he received the degree of Bachelor of Fine Arts in 1935; his major study was dramatic art. While still an undergraduate he began to write and publish plays; his first, "The Red Handkerchief Man," was accepted when he was seventeen, and by 1945 he had published more than forty, most of them in one act. His children's play in rhyme, "Bobino," was produced at the Adelphi Theater in New York in 1944. For ten years he was a member of the Washington Square Players, a repertory company, with whom he worked as actor, playwright, and stage manager.

Mr. Kauffmann's theater training shows in his novels, at least to the extent that they attempt to reveal character more through action than analysis; he is impatient with novels which plod and digress and in which authors feel that lengthy exploration of character or background is an excuse for poor storytelling. He would like to divide his time, in the future, fairly evenly between novels and plays. His principal theme, up to *The Hidden Hero,* has been the conflict between ideals and harsh realities; his chief interest is shifting to morality, in the largest sense: an inquiry into what moral and spiritual standards are available to reasonable men in a world where the established standards of two thousand years are, in his opinion, crumbling.

The King of Proxy Street (1941), his first novel, probes the conflicting doctrines of predestination and free will. A novelist with one year to live discovers that his last novel, which he is currently writing, is absolutely charting and predetermining the life of a neighbor of his who is desperate for a faith; the effect of this odd relationship on these two men is pursued to its conclusion. *This Time Forever* (1945) is described by the author as a romance in Hawthorne's sense; that is, it presents the truth "under circumstances . . . of the author's own choosing or creation." Novels generally present a cross-section of many moods and emotional colors; in a romance one may select a single emotional strand and expand it beyond its size in actual life. In this tale a harassed young composer spends a few summer weeks in idyllic surroundings with a sympathetic and lovely girl, an experience which alters his career. *The Hidden Hero* (1949) deals with the subject of moral cowardice. Through catastrophe, a girl is brought face to face with the fact that she is a moral coward; the book deals, in suspenseful terms, with her search for strength to meet the effects of that tragedy. She was unwilling to tell the truth about her father, a Nobel prize-winner.

LENARD KAUFMAN

John Glidden

was born in New York City on August 20, 1913. He received his education in the public schools and at Columbia University. When he was twenty he sold his first short story to *Prairie Schooner,* and later he sold a series of short narratives to *This Week;* simultaneously he was doing night-club publicity in New York. It was while he was engaged in radio work that he wrote his first novel at night and during weekends. On the publication of his second novel, he was invited to come to Hollywood to help prepare the motion-picture version of "Tender Mercy."

"The most important thing a writer learns," Mr. Kaufman has said, "is discipline. Books and courses in writing are not much help because each writer has a different set of problems to work out for himself. The discipline is in teaching oneself what to retain and what to reject in stories and books. Writing is the result of personal experience, creative ability, and integrity. The minute a writer stops reaching out and is content to prepare what he thinks the public will like, he ceases to be a writer."

The Lower Part of the Sky (1948) is a modern allegory. It is a novel of the irony of belief, and concerns three slum children and their search for God. *Tender Mercy* (1949) concerns a good man who finds himself on the horns of an unhappy dilemma when the husband of the nurse of his idiot son engages in blackmail. It poses the problem: How far can a good man go in surrendering to evil? *Jubel's Children* (1950), with its setting in a Pennsylvania town, tells about an antique dealer and his experiences in living with his married children.

ELIZABETH DEWING KAUP

was born on Washington Square in New York City on November 26, 1885. Her parents were the artists, Thomas W. Dewing and Maria Oakey Dewing. She started to write even before she began to attend school at the age of eleven. She grew up in New York; Cornish, New Hampshire; London; and Paris. She has traveled extensively and has lived in many parts of the United States. She has known intimately a cross section of human society: ranch hands, stagehands, professional and business people, millionaires, and the inner circle of the Four Hundred. She married Carl Bender in 1923 and became the mother of two daughters. In 1930 she married William C. Kaup. Until 1929 she wrote under her maiden name, Elizabeth B. Dewing. She now resides in New York City.

Other People's Houses (1909), her first novel, deals with a New England spinster who writes, a very handsome young man with whom she is in love, and an older and somewhat disreputable woman of the international set. *A Big Horse to Ride* (1911) is about a girl who becomes a famous dancer, and deals with her professional and private life; it includes a cast of many rather spectacular characters. *My Son John* (1926) is the story of a genius, told through letters and from the differing viewpoints of many people.

Eagles Fly High (1929) is a retelling with overtones of the story of Nellie, the beautiful cloak model. *Not for the Meek* (1941) concerns a Danish immigrant who makes a fortune in the steel industry in Pittsburgh in the era between the two Roosevelts. *Seed of the Puritan* (1943) portrays a hardheaded Yankee who becomes successful in machine politics; the political background is sketched in considerable detail. *Repeat with Laughter* (1948) has the theater as its background; it is about an actress who never grows old, her two daughters, one son-in-law, and a magician who retires to the contemplative life.

CLARENCE BUDINGTON KELLAND

Chase-Statler

was born on July 11, 1881, in Portland, Michigan. He was educated in the public and private schools of Detroit. In 1902 he graduated from the Detroit College of Law. From 1903 to 1907 he was a reporter and political editor on the Sunday edition of the Detroit *News*. His start as a writer came in the field of juvenile fiction, and he was editor of *The American Boy* from 1907 to 1915. He was also a lecturer at the University of Michigan on juvenile literature during the last two years of his editorship. During World War I he was overseas publicity director of the YMCA. In 1942 he was publicity director for the Republican National Committee during the presidential campaign of Thomas E. Dewey.

Mr. Kelland has been a voluminous writer of novels for over thirty years, and most of them have been serialized in magazines. His first novel after World War I was *High Flyers* (1919), a tale of love and intrigue at the beginning of airplane manufacturing in the United States. *The Little Moment of Happiness* (1919) contrasts French and American sexual morality. Between 1920 and 1922 he produced five books on the life of Catty Atkins. *Conflict* (1923) describes the conquest of cruelty and hardness by kindness and goodness. *Contraband* (1923) is the exciting story of a young girl's attempts to reform a town through her liberal newspaper. In *The Steadfast Heart* (1924) a sense of duty provides an escape from all pitfalls for the chief character.

Miracle (1925) treats of the spiritual redemption that comes to a cruel and ruthless man after he goes blind. *Rhoda Fair* (1926) is the story of a clever confidence woman who is forced to choose between respectability and a precarious social prestige; for the sake of her daughter she allies herself with the honest elements of society. *Dance Magic* (1927) is a critical examination of the values that await the professional performer on the stage. *Knuckles* (1928) is a tribute to rural life as opposed to life in metropolitan New York; neither gangsters nor their machinations diminish the charm of a lumbering camp in Vermont. *Dynasty* (1929) traces the evolution of a successful business house through three generations.

Hard Money (1930) recounts the trip of a Dutch peddler to America in the early nineteenth century; what he learns about finance enables him to become a successful banker. *Gold* (1931), a sequel to *Hard Money*, relates how the daughter of the Dutchman, Van Horn, carries on his enterprises in a manner befitting her father's reputation. *Speak Easily* (1932) catapults a young college instructor into the world after he has inherited a fortune; he becomes a wiser teacher as a result of his experiences. *Great Crooner* (1933) is the waggish tale of a country lad who rises to opulence and fame as a crooner because of a trick tenor voice. *Cat's-Paw* (1934) portrays the son of a missionary, who has just returned from China, in a battle against the corrupt politics of a boss-ridden city. *Jealous House* (1934) continues the history of the Van Horn banking family originated in *Hard Money*.

Dreamland (1935) is the humorous yarn of a young man who develops his character by studying a manual on character-building. *Roxanna* (1936) has as its heroine a young lady who forsakes school to become a cook; she succeeds in making her uncle's run-down restaurant a thriving business enterprise. *Spotlight* (1937) is focused on a society girl who makes a successful career of singing in a night club. *Star Rising* (1938) traces the history of a foundling who is deserted in a theater but who rises to become a famous star on the stage. *Skin Deep* (1938) describes the farcical adventures of an earnest young astronomer who inherits a beauty salon. *Arizona* (1939) is a tale of adventure in that state during Civil War days.

Scattergood Baines (1940) has the titular character involved in love, murder, and high finance; he solves every problem presented to him. Baines, one of America's most familiar fictional characters, is a fat Yankee promoter with endless resourcefulness. *Valley of the Sun* (1940) concerns Arizona in the period following the Civil War. *Scattergood Baines Pulls Strings* (1941) finds the chief character as versatile in getting out of difficulties as before. In *Silver Spoon* (1941) the loss of a fortune leads to a young man's finding himself. *Sugar Foot* (1942) continues the swashbuckling history of Arizona. *Archibald the Great* (1943) is an entertaining mixture of gangsters in Hollywood and on a ranch in Arizona.

Heart on his Sleeve (1944) provides the opportunity for a young lady, allegedly beautiful but dumb, to show her father that she can run his factory profitably when he is ill. *Alias Jane Smith* (1945) recounts the complications that ensue when a refugee meets a Grand Duchess in the United States. *Land of the Torreones* (1946) is an adventure story, set in Arizona, involving a group of escaped Nazi prisoners. *Double Treasure* (1947) pictures a modern treasure hunt on Long Island. *Merchant of Valor* (1948) is a romance set in sixteenth-century Italy. *Stolen Goods* (1950) is set in a department store.

JOHN KELLY

was born in Jersey City, New Jersey, in 1913. He graduated from Yale in 1934, and then studied at King's College of Cambridge University, where he took a bachelor's degree in 1937 and a master's in 1941. During 1938–39 he attended Harvard University. In World War II he was an economist with the Board of Economic Warfare and the Foreign Economic Administration. He has traveled extensively in Europe, North Africa, Turkey, and throughout the Balkans.

All Soul's Night (1947), his first novel, pictures the psychological difficulties of three people in a New England town in 1939. Mac Gregor, a scholar-athlete, heads toward suicide; Crosby is a brooding hedonist; and Ida Brinner is a frustrated Englishwoman. *Alexander's Feast* (1949) is a psychological novel about Alexander Orville, a state senator, and his second wife, Norma. She has a lover, Paul Carewe, with whom Alexander's daughter, Adele, falls in love. She has returned from a period of study in Europe.

JUDITH KELLY

Reddy Stevenson

was born on January 4, 1908, in Toronto, Canada. Her childhood was spent in Boston, and she was educated at Vassar College, from which she received her bachelor's degree in 1931. After graduation she worked until her marriage to William D. English, a lawyer; they have three children.

It Won't Be Flowers (1936), her first novel, is the story of political currents and their effect on Bridget Smith. Young and cultured, she comes under the influence of a communist and goes through a period of doubt and intellectual growth. *Marriage Is a Private Affair* (1941), which was awarded the Harper prize, is a study of a wife's discontentment because her young husband keeps busy as an architect. In her late twenties, fearing she is becoming middle-aged and unwilling to be stifled, she takes a lover as a means of solving her problem. She recovers her balance and saves her marriage. *A Diplomatic Incident* (1949) describes an imaginary diplomatic negotiation between Americans and Russians in the Department of State in Washington. John Wilson rejects a Russian proposal, but his son is sympathetic.

BAYNARD (HARDWICK) KENDRICK

Glidden

was born on April 8, 1894, in Philadelphia, Pennsylvania. His childhood was spent traveling over the southeastern part of the United States with his father. He was educated at the Tome School in Port Deposit, Maryland, and the Episcopal Academy in Philadelphia, where he graduated in 1912. Less than an hour after hearing of the declaration of World War I in 1914, he enlisted in the Canadian army, the first American to volunteer. After four and one-half years' service with the Canadian Expeditionary Forces, he returned to New York to begin a career in the business world. In 1921 he became secretary of a company in Florida, and during his six years with that firm he read law in his spare time. Other enterprises occupied him from 1929 to 1931.

The great depression following the stock-market collapse of 1929 turned Mr. Kendrick from the world of business to that of letters. He began by writing short stories and novelettes. He also made a thorough study of the ways of the blind in order to write a series of detective stories. During World War II, he was an instructor in special courses for blinded veterans. In 1946 he was presented with a plaque by General Omar Bradley for this work. Mr. Kendrick's first book, *Blood on Lake Louisa* (1934), is a detective novel with a Florida background. For the following ten years his output consisted of detective novels and short stories of other types. In *The Last Express* (1937) he created a new sleuth, the blind Captain Duncan Maclain, who solves crimes in six stories.

His experiences enabled him to write his first serious novel, *Lights Out* (1945), the story of the rehabilitation of a blinded soldier at an army hospital. The young man learns new social values in discovering among his friends a Jew and a Negro. *The Flames of Time* (1948), a Literary Guild selection, is an historical novel of eastern Florida in the period from 1787 to 1813, with its culmination in the rebellion of 1812 in which Artillery Armes operates as a secret agent for the United States in its attempted conquest of Spanish Florida. Artillery, who grew up under the tutelage of a freebooter and as a blood brother to a Seminole Indian, is torn between conflicting loyalties and two great loves.

LOUISE ANDREWS KENT

was born in Brookline, Massachusetts, on May 25, 1886. She went to Miss Haskell's School and Simmons College, where in 1909 she received a bachelor's degree in the School of Library Science. Equipped for the librarian's profession, she did not practice it, but instead wrote a Boston *Traveler* column over the signature of "Theresa Tempest"—a forerunner of her editorials published from 1928 to 1931 in the Boston *Herald* with considerable success. A visit to some friends at the age of seventeen started her writing by a kind of dramatic shock. Her hosts owned "Naulahka," Rudyard Kipling's former house in Brattleboro, Vermont. The first night there the young Miss Andrews could not sleep.

She roamed about the house and as the dawn broke found herself in Mr. Kipling's study. Animated by his spirit, she feels sure, she sat down at his desk, fingered the great master's pencils, and began to write. She has never really stopped since. In 1912 she married Ira Rich Kent, the editor and publisher, who died in 1945; they had two daughters and a son. She spends part of each year at Kents' Corner, Calais, Vermont, which has been the background for much of her writing. Mrs. Kent's first book was a juvenile, *Douglas of Porcupine* (1931). She has written many other books, including an historical-geographical series, and *Village Greens of New England* (1950).

The Terrace (1934), her first novel, is a chronicle of the leisurely life of the well-to-do Meredith family somewhere north of Boston, as recorded in the diary of Sally Austin, an orphan who moves from family to family. *Paul Revere Square* (1939) portrays the aristocratic manners and aloofness of a Boston family and the experiences of a Vermont girl cousin who inherits a fortune. *Mrs. Appleyard's Year* (1941) pictures a happy family atmosphere with its private jokes and easy humor, its quarrelings and quibblings. *Country Mouse* (1945) presents Mrs. Appleyard as the sponsor of the Roland Hill, Vermont, Institute of Arts and Letters, which flourishes amid difficulties.

THEDA KENYON

was born in Brooklyn, New York, the daughter of the late Rev. Ralph Wood Kenyon, the founder of the Order of the Daughters of the King. Among her ancestors were five Colonial governors. In England her family traces back to two lines of royal descent and to two signers of the Magna Carta. She was graduated from Packer Collegiate Institute, and while still in school was publishing in accredited magazines. Her books include a volume of poetry, *Certain Ladies* (1930), and *Witches Still Live* (1929), an anthropological study. *Scarlet Anne* (1939), a book-length poem, took her in recital to eleven states from Maine to Florida. For several years she also gave historical costume recitals throughout the East. She has taught at Hunter College; at the Blowing Rock, North Carolina, Graduate School of English; and at New York University. Her books since 1939 are concerned with controversial periods of American history, with backgrounds taken from original sources. Her characters, minor as well as major, are products of their time and their environments; they reflect contemporary moods.

Jeanne (1928), her first novel, is the story of Jeanne d'Arc, daughter of Doyen d'Arc of Domrémy, who becomes the Maid of Orleans. *Pendulum* (1942) pictures three generations of American women from the 1890's to the start of World War I. *The Golden Feather* (1943) concerns events leading to the settlement of Virginia and Massachusetts Bay. The events deal with the times of Charles I, Bishop Laud, and Anne Hutchinson. The story concerns brothers, Ajax and Gerald Stacy, whose activities lead to exile. *Black Dawn* (1944) pictures the Stacy descendants in the Reconstruction period. A New Englander goes to Virginia to teach Negroes; because she is misunderstood, she does not reveal her relationship to the southern branch of the family. *That Skipper from Stonington* (1947) tells the life story of Captain Richard Fanning Loper of Connecticut, the first man to build ships with iron frames and the inventor of the screw propeller. At ten he was a stowaway on a whaler, at sixteen master of his own vessel, and soon the owner of a fleet. *Something Gleamed* (1948), a story of the American Revolution, stresses the yearning for freedom on both sides of the Atlantic in a tale of a girl shanghaied in London to be a hostess to British troops in America.

SOPHIE KERR

was born in Denton, Maryland, on August 23, 1880. After graduating from Hood College in 1898, she did graduate work at the University of Vermont, where she received a master's degree in 1901. She entered upon newspaper work in Pittsburgh, Pennsylvania, and edited the women's page of the *Chronicle-Telegraph* and later the women's Sunday supplement of the *Gazette-Times.* Her stories for *The Woman's Home Companion* led to her appointment to the staff; she rose to be managing editor. In 1904 she married John D. Underwood and for a number of years wrote as Sophie Kerr Underwood. Her short stories are published in *Love at Large* (1916), *Confetti* (1927), and *Sound of Petticoats* (1948). *Big-Hearted Herbert* (with A. S. Richardson, 1934) is a play. She resides in New York City.

Miss Kerr writes stories and novels which detail the adventures, romance, and marital problems of men and women in ordinary walks of life. A pleasant vein of humor adds sparkle to her writing. Most of her stories are set on the Eastern Shore of Maryland, a neighborhood whose rural charm and large estates she pictures sympathetically.

Blue Envelope (1917), her first novel, concerns a girl who carries a chemical formula to Washington, unwillingly gets mixed up with a spy ring, and finds romance. *The Golden Block* (1918) is a story of career versus love as experienced by a girl who manages a manufacturing company. *The See-Saw* (1919) studies the married life of a husband who loves pleasure and a wife who stops making concessions. *Painted Meadows* (1920) is about a woman who almost destroys her second marriage by remaining faithful to the memory of her first husband.

One Thing Is Certain (1922) has a preacher's daughter marry sensibly to her regret; she helps her daughter avoid a similar loveless marriage. *Mareea-Maria* (1929) traces the conflict between a woman and her son's Italian wife. *Tigers Is Only Cats* (1929) humorously details the adventures of Aunt Katie Plummer with Sissie, a man-eating tiger. *In for a Penny* (1931) portrays the problems in early marriage of a southern girl with a horror of debt and a spendthrift husband who threatens to leave her when she places an inheritance in a trust fund.

Girl into Woman (1932) is about a gently reared girl whose shrewd, seemingly emotionless father gives her the impression that all pleasure is forbidden. She runs away with a chauffeur, finds herself and baby abandoned, and at last returns home a wiser woman. *Stay Out of My Life* (1934) pictures a clever, haughty businesswoman who traps a man into an engagement and a warmly human friend to whom he is attracted. *Miss J. Looks On* (1935) narrates the extravagances and failure of the wealthy Birrole family when caught by the crash in 1929, as seen by the wife's secretary, Miss Johanson. The consequent disintegration of each member of the family is traced.

There's Only One (1936) is about a girl, reared by another woman, who works as a maid in her mother's Park Avenue home to satisfy her yearning to learn about her background. *Fine to Look At* (1937) tells about a smooth-talking senator whose wife quietly sticks to her home tasks while he pays attention to a girl employee. When the latter sees that she has been used in shady political deals, she accepts the love of a classmate. *Adventure with Women* (1938) portrays the conflict between a possessive grandmother and a young wife for dominance over the latter's husband, who solves the problem by a show of strength. *Curtain Going Up* (1940) is about Nora Croft, the author of a Broadway hit, who is cheated by the agent who sold the play. *The Beautiful Woman* (1940) shows that Eve, in spite of clothes and masculine attention, really gets less than Jenny, her plain and sensible sister. *Jenny Devlin* (1943) brings home to America a girl, reared in France, who must make the adjustment to her new surroundings. *Love Story Incidental* (1946) tells of Ann Linton's disillusioning experience in Hollywood when she visits her divorced actor-father. David Blake helps her understand many things. *Wife's Eye View* (1947) anatomizes the book and magazine publishing world in a story of a writer who wins a big prize but lacks stability. *As Tall as Pride* (1949) concerns Rome Whitten, whose lack of height embitters his life and impels him to commit murder.

FRANCES PARKINSON KEYES

was born on July 21, 1885, at the University of Virginia, the daughter of Dr. John Henry Wheeler, then head of the university's Greek department. She spent most of her childhood in Boston and attended a fashionable private school there. She traveled to Europe and studied at Geneva and Berlin, journeying extensively on the continent and in England. Two other years were spent largely in Vermont, where she was taught by a German governess. Her attainments as a linguist—she speaks four languages—thus have a firm foundation. At the age of eighteen Miss Wheeler married Henry Wilder Keyes, whose home was near Haverhill, New Hampshire. He had already made a name for himself in state politics; he had banking and manufacturing interests. He became Governor of New Hampshire in 1917, and in 1919 was elected to the United States Senate and served three terms, declining in 1937 to run for a fourth.

By the time Mrs. Keyes was twenty-one she had two sons, and a few years later a third was born. Yet almost every day she managed to write a little, for her determination to be an author dated back to early childhood. As she became more and more familiar with life at the national capital, it occurred to her that many women throughout the country would be interested in reading about it, and she felt that her background of thirteen years on a New Hampshire farm should enable her to write in a way to please them. These essays were published in *Letters from a Senator's Wife* (1924) and *Capital Kaleidoscope* (1937). Her other non-fiction books include *Silver Seas and Golden Cities* (1931), the record of a journey through the Latin lands; three biographies of saints: *Written in Heaven: The Life on Earth of the Little Flower* (1937), *The Sublime Shepherdess* (1940), about Saint Bernadette of Lourdes, and *The Grace of Guadalupe* (1941); *Crescent Carnival* (1942), about New Orleans; *Along a Little Way* (1940), an account of how and why she became a Roman Catholic; and *All This Is Louisiana* (1950). *The Cost of a Best Seller* (1950) is about her experiences as an author.

Mrs. Keyes' first novel, *The Old Gray Homestead* (1919), tells about the poor Gray family, with whom a young widow boards. She bestows benefactions on all and her love on the eldest son. *The Career of David Noble* (1921) traces the rise of a Vermont boy to fame as a surgeon and his discovery that his love for Jacqueline Huntington is as important as professional success. *Queen Anne's Lace* (1930), about a woman's part in her husband's success, tells how a country girl assists a rural lawyer to work up to the Presidency of the United States. *Lady Blanche Farm* (1931) describes a Vermont homestead whose blighting curse is removed by a young architect.

Senator Marlowe's Daughter (1933) records the career of Faith Marlowe from the age of eight. She marries a Prussian nobleman, lives in the royal circles of Europe, and then returns to win the seat in Congress once held by her father. *The Safe Bridge* (1934), set in Vermont in the early nineteenth century, is about a banished Scottish girl who must decide between her husband and her former lover, a British soldier. *Honor Bright* (1936) chronicles the record of three generations of the family of Senator Reeves Stone of Massachusetts; he married the wrong girl and set a precedent for unhappy marriages.

Parts Unknown (1938), a story of the American diplomatic service, shows a wife leaving her husband because he resigns. Later, after he becomes rich, she helps him be an ambassador. *The Great Tradition* (1939) shows a boy with an American mother and a German father adopting Hitler's views and then realizing that the true way of life is in the United States. *Fielding's Folly* (1940) has a Vermont girl refuse to surrender her independence when she marries a Virginian who expects her to be a subservient wife. *All That Glitters* (1941) is a long novel about Washington, D.C., in 1925–40, the time of fat profits, the stock-market crash, and the New Deal, when two young newspaper reporters are subjected to the test of old-fashioned morality. *Crescent Carnival* (1942) is a panoramic novel of manners about the great plantation houses in Louisiana in a story of the Breckenridge family from 1890 to 1940.

Also the Hills (1943) deals with the Farman family in New Hampshire and the three children who desert the farming tradition during the war years, 1940–43. Jerome becomes a banker; Jenness has an affair with a congressman; and Judith becomes a nurse. *River Road* (1945) portrays three generations on a Louisiana sugar plantation from 1918 to 1942. *Came a Cavalier* (1947) pictures a New England girl, a Red Cross worker in World War I, who marries a Frenchman and takes pride in her children. *Dinner at Antoine's* (1948) exhibits carnival celebrations and society life in New Orleans; beautiful Odille St. Amant is murdered in the famous restaurant. *Joy Street* (1950) is about a Boston girl in a fashionable family who marries against her father's wishes.

EDWARD KIMBROUGH

was born on August 15, 1918, in Meridian, Mississippi, but at the age of six moved with his family to Tampa, Florida, where "land was booming and hurricanes brooding in the wings." The hurricane burst, and the Kimbroughs went to New Orleans, arriving just in time for the great flood of 1927. The stock-market collapse of 1929 found them back in Meridian, where Edward graduated from high school. He attended George Washington University in Washington, D.C., for one year and then enrolled in the University of Alabama, where he received his bachelor's and master's degrees, was elected to Phi Beta Kappa, and taught on a fellowship. He was appointed to the faculty there in 1941 and at present is an assistant professor of English, specializing in the teaching of creative writing. In 1943 he won a Julius Rosenwald fellowship and in 1944 was awarded a Houghton Mifflin literary fellowship.

"Politically," says Mr. Kimbrough, "I am a liberal who refuses to be 'organized.' And I am dead sick of fiction in which economics is the heroine and politics the hero. The basic stuff of fiction, to me, is character conflict, man in his individual relation to man, and man in his relation to his God. Politics and economics and sociology are only surface aspects of more basic human motivations which I am interested in discovering and exploring and dramatizing in my novels."

From Hell to Breakfast (1941), his first novel, traces the rise of the Mississippi demagogue, Gus Roberts, to United States Senator on a platform of race hatred and labor-baiting. *Nightfire* (1946) treats of a young Mississippian in a planter's family getting a better understanding of a Negro. *The Secret Pilgrim* (1949) is the story of the lifelong conflict between two men and two attitudes toward life as it exists in a small southern town.

RONALD KIRKBRIDE

was born on February 1, 1912, in Victoria, British Columbia, Canada, of American parents. He is a direct descendant of the Joseph Kirkbride who sailed with William Penn in the *Welcome* in 1682. Although the Kirkbride family settled in Philadelphia, a good deal of Ronald's childhood was spent in the deep South. He wrote four books before he was twenty-one, and at twenty-two was an editor of *Story* magazine. Later he went abroad to the little village of Kirkbride in Cumberland, England, to write a novel about his ancestral home, and then to London where he remained for several years, with time out for newspaper work in France, Italy, Sweden, and other countries. Returning to the United States after World War II was declared, Ronald Kirkbride, who for some years had held a pilot's license, became editor of technical handbooks for the Douglas Aircraft Company. In Los Angeles two of his plays were produced. He has also written several screen scenarios and many short stories. His nonfiction books are *Letters of an Unknown* (1931), a collection of missives dealing with the hopes and doubts of lovers on a trip through Europe, and *The Private Life of Guy de Maupassant* (1932). *River of Souls* (1934) is a book of poems.

"An author's purpose in all his works," Mr. Kirkbride has said, "is to reveal and capture the vision and the possibility of a deeper, wider, broader, saner way of life, to rediscover the spirit inherent in human personality, and to explore that ocean of deeper reality over which the mind can sail, but upon which the vessel of thought has not yet been fully launched. The creative magic of our feeling—this he attempts to capture and bring before the mind even as the emotional and feeling life of man has been rendered coherent through the medium of music. He seeks to stab the reader's spirit wide-awake, so that he will be able to grasp and realize the infinite mystery and the possibilities which lie deep within us."

Dark Surrender (1933), his first novel, is an idyllic portrait of a southern plantation and a Negro poet who goes to Harvard, becomes a lawyer in a white firm in New York, and then returns to the South self-assured that the future of the Negro lies in living with his own people. *Armerdale* (1940) pictures an American who returns to his ancestral home in Cumberland, England, expecting to find his cousins living on a grand scale; he learns, instead, that his relatives are existing in poverty in the depressed area in the country. The American stands by his British cousins and helps them to win a success and a decent future. *Broken Melody* (1942) concerns a young American composer of symphonic music and the three women who helped him achieve success in Los Angeles.

Winds Blow Gently (1945), the first book in a saga of Quaker life to be called *David Jordan, Quaker,* deals with the Jordan family, who leave the Blue Hills of Pennsylvania and move to a run-down plantation in South Carolina. Joseph Jordan, the father, fights for the rights of the Negro and is killed by the Ku Klux Klan. David meets his young Nina, and his sister Faith is married to the Quaker doctor. *Still the Heart Sings* (1946) tells of Karin Frazer's visit to his cousin, Zekel Rossie, in the great mountains of New Hampshire. Zekel is a sculptor who, in refusing to bow to convention, produces a work for the town bank of Colton. The greatness of this statue is beyond the comprehension of the populace. It instills in the people an accumulating terror which finds outlet in ostracism of the Rossies and the burning of their farm buildings. Simultaneously with this tragic culmination occurs the death of Leda, the child of earth and air, whom Karin has come to love so deeply. *Spring Is Not Gentle* (1949) continues the

Quaker saga. David Jordan marries Nina, and the family start a co-operative farm. Nina finds this work not to her liking, and this, along with David's creed of nonviolence in wartime, causes a misunderstanding and separation.

JOHN KLEMPNER

Glidden

was born on August 4, 1898, in New York City. Brought up and educated there, he studied at Columbia University in the School of Journalism until World War I took him into the navy. When he returned, he entered the School of Business Administration. He followed a business career for many years, rising in position to treasurer of a large chemical company. The urge to write, long dormant, returned in the mid-1930's. All spare moments after business hours and Sundays, holidays, and even lunch hours were devoted to writing; in a year and a half he completed his first novel. In recent years he has devoted all of his time to writing. He now lives in Los Angeles.

He belongs to the realistic school of writers; his characters are warm and believable, and his dialogue mirrors everyday conversation. Because of his background, his novels have a New York setting and a distinct New York flavor.

No Stork at Nine (1938), his first novel, is the story of a man plagued by uncertainties, chief of which is the suspicion that his wife has a lover. In her absence over a weekend he relives the story of his marriage, and when she returns her explanations lead to the basis for a more solid future. *Once Around the Block* (1939) pictures office workers in a story of a white-collar Brooklyn family living by dint of hard work on the edge of insecurity, of their trials and their gallantry, and of their camaraderie and their never-failing humor.

In *Another Night Another Day* (1941) the problem concerns a forthright working wife. Her unstable husband becomes unbearable, and she leaves him. *Letter to Five Wives* (1946) is the story of a charming divorcée who sends a letter to five of her women friends, stating that she is about to elope with one of their husbands, but not revealing which one. Each of the wives goes back into her past, discovering reasons for suspecting that she is the one. *Hurry Hurry Home* (1948) shows the relationship of two sisters, one struggling to keep her large family together, the other living the glamorous life of a nightclub singer.

MANUEL KOMROFF

was born on September 7, 1890, in New York City. He studied engineering, music, and art at Yale, and served as a correspondent in World War I in Russia, China, and Japan. After the war, he reviewed motion pictures for the professional paper *Film Daily*. He entered publishing in 1921, and for five years served as the first editor of the Modern Library. Later he founded the Black and Gold Library and the Library of Living Classics. Since 1919 he has written one hundred and thirty short stories; one of them is included in Edward O'Brien's collection of the world's finest short stories. It is as a novelist, of course, that Mr. Komroff made his reputation; most of his novels have been historical. Thorough research enables him to recreate vividly the periods about which he writes. *The Grace of Lambs* (1925) and *All in One Day* (1932) are collections of short stories. *How to Write a Novel* (1950) is a practical manual on the craft of creating long fiction.

In speaking of his fiction Mr. Komroff has said: "I feel that neither plot nor characterization is as important as the 'compelling emotion.' The world of ideas must be larger than any single group of characters. The theme must carry philosophy, or a story falls apart."

Juggler's Kiss (1927), his first novel, chronicles the life of a lad who receives advice from a stranger at each crisis in his life. *Coronet* (1929) traces the decline of blooded aristocracy and the rise of wealth to power in this panoramic romance covering the years from 1600 to 1919. A crown that brings evil is handed down through the generations. *Two Thieves* (1931) traces the careers of the two men who were hanged with Jesus, who is never mentioned by name but referred to by Pilate as a "wild mountain prophet." *New York Tempest* (1932) contrasts the haves and have nots in a reconstruction of a rich man's murder of a prostitute in New York City in 1836. *I, the Tiger* (1933) is a commentary by a circus animal on mankind's ways as compared with jungle life. *Waterloo* (1936) describes the hundred days in Napoleon's life after his escape from Elba to the Battle of Waterloo, with realistic pictures of soldier and civilian suffering.

The March of the Hundred (1939) is an allegorical story of the twenty-year wandering after World War I of a group of men who are always the last detachment in a lost war. *The Magic Bow* (1940) is a romance of Paganini and the story of his rise to fame. *In the Year of Our Lord* (1942) gives twenty-four dramatic incidents in the life of Christ. *Feast of the Jesters* (1947) shows that great power corrupts both the ruler and society in a tale about a troupe of French actors who go to Vienna at the time of the Congress in 1815. *Echo of Evil* (1948) portrays in a present-day setting the way a crime committed twenty-two years earlier, when Aunt Anna killed her husband, haunts an ordinary middle-class family.

FERENC KÖRMENDI

was born on February 12, 1900, in Budapest, Hungary. His father was a leading lawyer and one of the founders of the Hungarian Democratic Party, a political and social organization of the liberal urban citizenry. Ferenc was educated at Lutheran College in Budapest and at Budapest University, where he majored in law and history. He published his first poems and short stories in 1917 in Hungarian newspapers and magazines. From 1919 to 1922 he was associate editor of the literary weekly *A Hét*. His first novel, *Escape to Life* (1932), won the International Novel Prize. From 1933 to 1938 he was literary correspondent of the Budapest daily *Pesti Napló* and contributor to many leading European newspapers and magazines; he wrote short stories and articles on literature and other cultural subjects. He traveled extensively all over Europe, lecturing on literature in several European capitals.

Under the pressure of growing Nazism, he and his wife left Hungary early in 1938, and after a brief stay in Italy and Switzerland they went to England in January, 1939. During World War II he lived in London, broadcasting over the BBC as a Hungarian political commentator. He was one of the founders, and from 1941 to 1945 acting president, of the Free Hungarian P.E.N. Group in London. He came with his wife to the United States early in 1946, and they expect to become American citizens. His books include *Martyr* (1921) and *Serenade* (1935), collections of short stories, and *Adversary of Men* (1941), a drama about the impact of Hitler and Nazism on Western civilization.

The center of his literary interest and activities is the psychological novel with the political and social background of the times.

Escape to Life (1932), a picture of conflict between success and failure, concerns a happy and successful man who becomes the target of a parasitic group of former friends, but is saved by his firmness and integrity from becoming a victim of foul schemes or emotional temptations. *Via Bodenbach* (1933), a story of the revolt of illusion against reality, describes a brief encounter between a young woman and a young man which seems to change their lives. *The Happy Generation* (1934) portrays the dissolution of a way of life in a family chronicle covering the first three decades of the twentieth century, the era of the splendor and decay of the Hungarian middle classes.

Sinners (1936) tells about a murder that is committed unintentionally; another murder was intended but not actually committed. Who is guilty and who is innocent; who is to be punished and who should be forgiven? Human law may have a formal answer, but a final solution can be found only deep in our minds and hearts. *The Island* (1937), a novel of passion versus love, pictures a small island in the Mediterranean as the magic scene of the unending search for happiness of lonely people who, driven by dark instincts and emotions, stumble into the realm of the irrational, inevitably missing the real values of their lives. *That One Mistake* (1938), with the theme of pity mistaken for love, describes a marriage ruined by differing outlooks, emotions, and social backgrounds of husband and wife who do not realize their mistake before it is too late.

Dream at Dawn (1938), which contrasts dull order with happy chaos, is about a young woman trying to escape from her humble life into a world of dreams, for which she sacrifices her family. The awakening is frustration and loneliness. *Weekday in June* (1943) depicts a day in the lives of two men, one of whom is a political mass murderer and the other a victim of the former's bomb outrage. The story is set against the background of rising Nazism during the restless summer of 1939, and has the theme of "hatred victorious." *Years of Eclipse* (1949) deals with the little man in great times. The setting is wartime London from 1939 to 1946. Against the background of gigantic historical forces fighting their life-or-death battle, a small group of young Continental emigrés struggle hard, some of them with and some without success, to readjust themselves to an alien world and to build new homes and new lives.

HERBERT KRAUSE

was born on May 25, 1905, in Fergus Falls, Minnesota. After a rather informal grade-school education, he worked on his father's farm for four years to earn his way through the Park Region Academy in his home town. He received his bachelor's degree, *magna cum laude,* at St. Olaf College at Northfield, Minnesota. While there, he worked in newspaper offices and as a hired hand shocking and threshing grain on a farm near the Red River Valley. He earned his master's degree in 1935 at the University of Iowa with a volume of verse and in the same year went to the Bread Loaf School of English at Middlebury, Vermont. During the year 1936 he taught at the University of Iowa and won the midwest Folk Drama Tournament with his one-act play, "Bondsmen in the Hills." Since 1938 he has been head of the Department of English in Augustana College at Sioux Falls, South Dakota.

His first novel, *Wind Without Rain* (1939), which won the Friends of American Writers award, portrays two boys' fear of their harshly violent father on a poverty-stricken farm in Minnesota. They are afraid of eternal punishment, debt, and popular opinion. *The Thresher* (1946) tells the story of Johnny Swartz, son of an intensely and narrowly religious father and husband of a wife obsessed with a fear of divine punishment. Johnny craves power, which the wife symbolizes as a threshing machine.

HARRY HARRISON KROLL

was born on February 18, 1888, in Hartford City, Indiana. He grew up among small farmers and sharecroppers. From 1911 to 1921 he was a rural-school teacher and high-school principal in Alabama. He then spent four years at Peabody College for Teachers in Nashville, Tennessee, where he earned his baccalaureate in 1923 and his master's degree in 1925. After teaching in Lincoln Memorial University and Iowa Wesleyan University, he moved to the University of Tennessee Junior College at Martin. *I Was a Share-Cropper* (1937) is his autobiography.

Mr. Kroll's novels are straightforward, unsentimentalized, and realistic accounts of life in the South. They deal with the social problems inherent in the plantation system. The pictures of sharecroppers and mountain people, as well as of their mode of life, contain strong scenes of poverty and discontentment. Emotions of pity and anger are relieved by humor, but the author's prevailing mood is deeply serious.

The Mountainy Singer (1928), his first novel, pictures the customs and social life of the people in the Tennessee mountains in the story of a sensitive boy and his romance in young manhood. *The Cabin in the Cotton* (1931) concerns the conflict between a rich planter and his poor tenant farmers on a plantation in Mississippi. An overseer exposes the owner's dishonest practices. *The Ghosts of Slave Driver's Bend* (1937) is a thrilling tale of a physician's rehabilitation of an abandoned plantation that was once a prison farm. *The Keepers of the House* (1940) tells about an overseer whose anger at his Mississippi plantation master in pre-Civil War days leads him to join the Union Army and to assist in the capture of Vicksburg to prove that he is not "poor white trash."

The Usurper (1941) portrays Stan Butterworth's successful efforts to supplant the aristocratic plantation owners. He becomes a banker and powerful man in the changing economy of a southern cotton community. *The Rider on the Bronze Horse* (1942) pictures Mississippi plantation life in a story of Eli Arn, an ambitious farmer, who marries the daughter of a rich planter-politician and rises to power, only to be betrayed by his evangelist brother for again meeting the poor girl whom he had victimized in youth. *Rogue's Company* (1943) is a fictionalized life story of the Tennessee desperado, John Murrell, who throve on crime in the 1820's. His downfall in 1834 is brought about by a tenacious investigator who proves that he was stealing and selling slaves.

Perilous Journey (1943), which was begun by Clifford M. Sublette and concluded by Mr. Kroll, tells about Jim Dalrymple, who in 1821 started on a flatboat from the Upper Ohio Valley to sell his stock and find his father in New Orleans. *Waters over the Dam* (1944) tells the story of an eighteen-year-old boy on an Alabama farm in the 1920's. *Fury on the Earth* (1945) describes the frontier river town of New Madrid in the southeastern part of the Missouri Territory in 1811, when earthquakes destroyed the community. *Their Ancient Grudge* (1946) is the story of the Hatfield-McCoy feud told from the viewpoint of six women, five Hatfields and one McCoy, whose lives it seared.

Darker Grows the Valley (1947) is a panoramic narrative covering one hundred and fifty years after 1778, when Josiah Clinch, a North Carolina farmer, packed his family and belongings off to the West. A brother, David, filed a rival land claim, and five generations thereafter continue the conflict. *Lost Homecoming* (1950) is about a successful novelist who grew up in the cotton country and returns to his home community. He is greeted with mixed reactions because of his portrayal of sharecroppers, and he reviews his life in long flashbacks.

RENE LEILANI KUHN

Halsman

was born on March 2, 1923, in Honolulu, Hawaii, where her father was telegraph editor of the Honolulu *Star-Bulletin*, and her mother was an International News Service correspondent. When Rene was but a few months old the family returned to Shanghai, where she spent her early childhood. She was educated at private schools in California, Pennsylvania, and Connecticut. She attended Swarthmore College from 1940 to 1942, and received her bachelor's degree from the University of Michigan in 1944. She has also been a student at the University of Mexico. In her junior year at the University of Michigan, she won an Avery Hopwood award for short-story writing, and her first novel won the major Avery Hopwood prize for fiction in 1944. During 1947 and 1948 she wrote and appeared with her mother on a regular weekly quarter-hour period for the National Broadcasting Company. In February, 1949, she went to London as assistant press officer in the United States Information Service.

34 Charlton (1945), her first novel, is the story of Katherine Conant, a modern girl living with her grandparents, her mother, and her two aunts in the stifling atmosphere of an old house in Greenwich Village in New York City. Katherine leaves to escape from the grandmother's selfish pettiness. *Cornelia* (1948) depicts a selfish woman whose eye is on the main chance. She leaves her devoted husband for gay friends and a career as a fashion designer. The two bewildered children appeal to their father for relief, and Cornelia comes to her senses.

La FARGE to LYTLE

CHRISTOPHER La FARGE

Artist: Albert Sterner

was born on December 10, 1897, in New York City, the son of the noted architect, Christopher Grant La Farge. He attended St. Bernard's Preparatory School in New York City and the Groton School in Massachusetts before going to Harvard, where he received his bachelor's degree in 1919. He also studied at the Harvard Graduate School of Architecture and the Pennsylvania Architectural School, from which he graduated in 1923. In World War I he served as a second lieutenant of infantry. On his discharge he resumed architectural work.

Christopher La Farge began his literary career in 1911 and wrote intermittently throughout his college days and his years as a practicing architect. He was editor of *The Grotonian* in 1916, *The Harvard Monthly* in 1917, and *The Harvard Advocate* during 1918 and 1919. He is also a painter and has exhibited watercolors at the Ferargil and Wildenstein Galleries. In 1941 he received a Carnegie grant-in-aid to study opera at the Metropolitan; as a result of that work, he has written a libretto in verse. In 1943 he was a war correspondent in the Southwest Pacific. Mr. La Farge is married and is the father of three children. His books include *Poems and Portraits* (1940); *The Wilsons* (1941), short stories about a newly rich family; *East by South-West* (1944), ten short stories about the war; *Mesa Verde* (1945), a dramatic poem; and *All Sorts and Kinds* (1949), short stories

Hoxsie Sells His Acres (1934) is a novel in verse which concerns itself with the impact of land development on the lives of a Rhode Island community. *Each to the Other* (1939) is also a novel in verse concerned with the problems of creating a happy and successful marriage. This was a Book-of-the-Month-Club selection and was awarded the A. C. Benson medal of the Royal Society of Literature after its publication in England. *The Sudden Guest* (1946) is the story of the impact of the hurricanes of 1938 and 1940 on an autocratic and completely selfish woman.

OLIVER La FARGE

Margaret Mc. K. Burge

was born on December 19, 1901, in New York City, the son of Christopher Grant La Farge, the noted architect. Among his ancestors he numbers Benjamin Franklin and Commodore Oliver Hazard Perry. He was educated at St. Bernard's School, Groton, and Harvard, from which he received his baccalaureate in 1924 and his master's degree in 1929. During the years 1924 and 1926 he was a Hemenway Fellow. At Harvard he was president of *The Advocate* and edited *The Lampoon.* He elected anthropology as his major study, did research for two years at Tulane University, and pursued his field work in Arizona, New Mexico, and Guatemala. He was research associate in anthropology from 1931 to 1933 at Columbia

University and has been president of the Association of American Indian Affairs since 1932. For three months in 1936 he assisted the Hopi Indians in drawing up a written constitution and forming a tribal organization. Mr. La Farge's special fields of interest are the cultural anthropology of the Highland Maya, and the problem of acculturation, that is, the imparting of a culture by one people to another, with special reference to the American Indians; his important books on this subject include *The Year Bearer's People* (1931), *The Changing Indian, A Symposium* (1941), and *Santa Eulalia* (1947). *All the Young Men* (1935) contains short stories, the majority of them about Indian life. During World War II, from 1943 to 1946, he was an officer in the army's Air Transport Command, and as such was responsible for assembling a complete history of all its activities. *The Eagle in the Egg* (1949) tells the story of this organization.

As a writer Mr. La Farge considers his central interest to be in the art of writing and not in any specific subject. "I write," he has said, "about those subjects with which I have had intimate contact." His first stories were about Indians, but since 1940 he has broken away from the entire subject in his fiction. This shift in interest is set forth in the last chapter of his autobiography, *Raw Material* (1945).

Laughing Boy (1929), his first novel and winner of a Pulitzer prize, is a prose lyric of love in the Navajo country. Laughing Boy, a skilled workman in silver jewelry and a maker of songs, loves Slim Girl, who is trying to achieve true spiritual kinship with her people after having been alienated and embittered by American schooling. The novel is particularly rich in its description of Indian arts and crafts. *Sparks Fly Upward* (1931) describes the turbulent life of a half-breed who is adopted by an aristocratic Spaniard in a Central American country. Although he is liked by the Spaniards, he prefers his mother's people, the Indians, and returns to them as leader of a revolution. *Long Pennant* (1933) is a sea story of the War of 1812; the brig *Glimpse,* sailing out of Rhode Island, spends three years harrying British shipping in the Caribbean. The central theme is homesickness, and Mr. La Farge had originally named the book *Hoi Nostoi,* for the story was derived as is the term from the Greek.

The Enemy Gods (1937) sets forth the problem of the Indian who today must attend a white man's school and make the choice between the culture of his tribe and that of his teachers. This story, concerning the Navajo Indians, describes the Indian way of life with great beauty and sincerity. *The Copper Pot* (1942) describes the spiritual maturing of a New England-born painter during a few months' stay in New Orleans.

MILLARD LAMPELL

was born in Paterson, New Jersey, on January 10, 1919. He attended the University of West Virginia, and later worked as a mechanic in a shipyard, fruit picker, checkweighman in a coal mine, newspaper reporter, and union organizer. He then joined a group of folk singers, the Almanac Singers, and toured the country with guitar and banjo, performing at union meetings and on picket lines, singing for steel workers in Pittsburgh, packing-house workers in Chicago, lumberjacks outside Duluth, railroaders in Denver, and longshoremen in San Francisco. During this period, Mr. Lampell composed many ballads, usually putting new words to traditional American tunes and taking his themes from the lives of the people for whom he sang. This led to his first major work, *The Lonesome Train* (1943), a cantata with music by Earl Robinson. This poem for voices tells of the journey of the funeral train carrying Lincoln's body home to Springfield. The central theme is Lincoln's identification with the struggles of the people, and his survival beyond death in their continuing lives. It was first produced in a nationwide broadcast by Norman Corwin. In 1946 another of his cantatas, *Morning Star,* was read by Robert Montgomery at the New York *Herald-Tribune* Forum.

During World War II, from 1943 to 1946, Mr. Lampell was a sergeant in the army air force and was responsible for writing and directing most of the official air force radio programs. On army assignment, he toured the hospitals, living among the wounded as a patient; out of his experiences he wrote a radio series dealing with rehabilitation which was published in book form, *The Long Way Home* (1946).

He also wrote a series of ballads for the motion picture "A Walk in the Sun," dealing with an infantry squad in Italy. He has written radio dramas for most of the major programs, including a special series for the United Nations. His radio plays have appeared in various anthologies, among them *Radio's Best Plays* and *Radio Drama in Action.* In 1947 Mr. Lampell abandoned motion pictures and radio to devote himself to full-time work as a novelist.

His first novel, *The Hero* (1948), describes the life of a Polish boy from a New Jersey mill town who calculatingly tries to use his football talent to escape his immigrant background by way of attending a wealthy "gentleman's university" in Virginia. The central theme of the book is the impact of American middle-class success myths on a working-class adolescent, a study of the false goals and subtle snobberies which infect Steve Novak, causing his destruction as an athlete, and finally the beginning of his maturity as a human being. The book also presents a portrait of the industrial aspects of college football, and the implications of hero-fixation in America.

BRUCE LANCASTER

was born in Worcester, Massachusetts, on August 22, 1896. He entered Harvard in the fall of 1914 and concentrated on the field of history and literature. The continuity of his study was broken when, as a member of Battery A, First Massachusetts Field Artillery, he was sent to the Mexican border during the Villa troubles of 1916. He returned to Harvard in the late fall of 1916 in time to see service as a varsity tackle. The respite from military life was short, however, and in the spring of 1917 he was in service again, his regiment being incorporated into the famous Yankee Division, the first complete United States army unit to reach France. Continually in action, his division did not return to the United States until the spring of 1919. That same summer Mr. Lancaster completed his college work and graduated from Harvard.

There followed some seven years of business in Worcester, varied by coaching football, as an avocation, at Harvard and at Worcester Polytechnic Institute. Passing the competitive examinations for the foreign service of the State Department, he was assigned to Kobe, Japan. In 1938 he published his first book, its choice of locale being dictated by his years in the Far East and his interest in and knowledge of that area. Since that time he has produced a steady flow of historical novels, most of them dealing with American history. His thorough knowledge of military matters, of the temper of the times, and of the people who lived in them imparts a vivid quality to his meticulously accurate historical reconstructions. It is obvious that he writes without preconceived ideas; he interprets history as it unfolds.

The Wide Sleeve of Kwannon (1938) is laid in 1691 at the station of the Dutch East India Company in the harbor of Nagasaki, the only window to the outside world which

Japan then allowed. The story deals with a Dutch soldier of fortune, attached to the company, and his adventures during that little known part of the "closed period." *Guns of Burgoyne* (1939) deals with Burgoyne's ill-fated expedition of 1777 down the Hudson Valley as seen through the eyes of a Hessian gunner; it shows the emergence of the American freeman from the viewpoint of an intelligent man from the depths of feudal Europe. *Bride of a Thousand Cedars* (with Lowell Brentano, 1939) is a vivid picture of life in Bermuda during the days of the 1861–65 blockade of the southern ports, and describes the impact of the blockade-runners on the island.

For Us, the Living (1940), outwardly a story of pioneer life in Indiana and Illinois, is actually a Lincoln book without being a "story about Lincoln," since "Tom Lincoln's boy," from late teens to maturity, is the dominating background figure but not the technical hero. *Bright to the Wanderer* (1942) deals with William Lyon Mackenzie's Canadian rebellion of 1837, which eventually led to the establishment of Canada's status as a virtually independent country. The close parallel between Mackenzie's rebellion and our own Revolution, the part played by the descendants of the Tory refugees, and the participation of Americans make this a North American rather than a Canadian story.

Trumpet to Arms (1944), a novel of our own Revolution, shows the war from Concord to Trenton and stresses the almost imperceptible growth of an American army as a unit in contrast to levies from the separate colonies. The action is centered on John Glover's amphibious regiment of Marbleheaders and other Massachusetts units. *The Scarlet Patch* (1947) pictures the War between the States, underscoring the important part played by the foreign-born in the Union army. The great bulk of these men, as the book brings out, were refugees from the liberal rebellions of 1848 in Europe; by 1861 they thought of themselves as Americans rather than as transplanted Europeans. The story, based very generally on the life of Baron de Trobriand, deals with a young French officer serving with a New York regiment composed largely of Frenchmen.

No Bugles Tonight (1948) is a story of the Union sympathizers in the South, with a young Ohio sergeant of artillery as the chief figure. Through his participation in the famous Andrews Raid he is drawn into secret service and makes contact with the southern Unionists. *Phantom Fortress* (1950) deals with the Revolution in South Carolina in 1781, focusing on Nathanael Greene and Francis Marion in their seemingly hopeless campaign to save the South from the Crown forces. Seen through the eyes of a Rhode Island cavalryman, the story stresses the equal importance of regular operations such as Greene's and the partisan work of such men as Marion, Sumter, and Pickens.

DOROTHY LANGLEY

is the pseudonym of Dorothy Richardson, who was born on February 14, 1904, of army parents at Fort Brown, Brownsville, Texas. Orphaned in her second year, she was brought up by grandparents in southeastern Missouri. On October 26, 1923, she married Robert C. Kissling; they have two children. Except for a period of three years in Hollywood, she has never earned or attempted to earn her living by writing alone; she prefers to do editorial work and write as she pleases. At present she is assistant editor of the *Journal* of the International College of Surgeons in Chicago. Her major interest is in poetry, and her poems have appeared in national periodicals. *The Hoogles and Alexander* (1948) is a book-length fairy tale for children.

Miss Langley is an implacable enemy of

the "formula" type of writing, and she deplores the current deterioration of style resulting from successful assaults upon the English language. She regards the propaganda novel with particular aversion, believing that, although a novel may carry a message, a message cannot carry a novel, and that non-fiction is the place for propaganda.

Wait for Mrs. Willard (1944), her first novel, describes the determined effort of a woman, married eighteen years to a dominating husband, to achieve happiness. After a bus accident she recuperates in a resort and finds a way to escape. *Dark Medallion* (1945), which won the Friends of American Writers award for the best novel by a midwestern author, portrays a ruined aristocratic family in southern Missouri and a little girl who thinks that her poetry will be better for their poverty and suffering in the years before World War I. *Mr. Bremble's Buttons* (1947) is about a man who takes refuge from his domineering wife and mother-in-law in a collection of buttons and in his conversations with God.

EDWIN LANHAM

Gorska-Hill

was born on October 11, 1904, in Weatherford, Texas. He was educated at Williams College and studied painting in New York and France, where he lived for four years. From 1930 until 1944 he worked in the newspaper business in New York, but he took frequent trips to the Southwest to gather material for his short stories and novels. In 1940 he held a Guggenheim fellowship, and in 1942 he was given the annual award of the Texas Institute of Letters. With Mrs. Lanham and their daughter, he lives in Clinton, Connecticut. *Slug It Slay* (1946) and *Politics Is Murder* (1947) are detective stories.

The Wind Blew West (1935), his first book, portrays a frontier Texas town to which a railroad entices settlers; after a disillusioned start they develop a substantial community. *Banner at Daybreak* (1937) deals with a Texan's readjustment after his failure as an artist in Paris and New York. *Another Ophelia* (1938) is a psychological novel of a Vermont girl's mental troubles after being drugged by a stranger and her father's efforts to help her. *The Sticklands* (1939) relates the attempt of a family to organize tenant farmers in Oklahoma to overcome the poverty that is debasing and oppressing them. *Thunder in the Earth* (1941) is a realistic, solid history of the oil boom in Texas in the 1930's in the story of Cobb Walters, a farm boy, who strikes oil, but whose reckless follies and personal excesses destroy him.

LIDA LARRIMORE

was born on June 27, 1898, in Girdletree, Maryland, the daughter of a clergyman. Her father moved from one parish to another in the course of his duties and gave his children the advantage, and sometimes the disadvantage, of attending a variety of schools. Where the schools did not maintain the standard he demanded for his children, he taught them himself. She graduated from Coburn Classical Institute at Waterville, Maine, spent three years at Colby College in the same city, and received her bachelor's degree from Dickinson College at Carlisle, Pennsylvania. Her writing career can be said to have begun when she was nine years old, and she admits that she never entertained the idea of following any other calling. Her first published work was a play, and she won several drama contests. She has also collaborated on amateur operettas and has managed a highly successful group of little-theater players. One entire summer she spent in Cambridge, Massachusetts, writing short stories for a Boston newspaper. She also taught English in the high school at Chester, Pennsylvania, until she resigned in 1928 to write her first novel. Miss Larrimore used to spend her summers near the sea in New England, but in recent years she has not roamed far from "Robin Hill," her home near Wayne, Pennsylvania, which she shares with her husband, Charles E. Thomas, and their two daughters.

Miss Larrimore's popular novels deal with typical romantic situations which face the average young girl who is perplexed when the time comes to choose a husband. The background often sets forth a family problem which affects the girl's happiness.

The Tarpaper Palace (1928), her first novel, pictures Mary Ellen longing for a charming garden with hollyhocks and butterflies, but all she ever has is a tarpaper palace. *The Wagon and the Star* (1929) portrays the successful rebellion of Elizabeth Lloyd against her rich, autocratic grandmother and her marriage to David Warren. *Mulberry Square* (1930) is a romance of two daughters of a physician and the young doctor who assists their father; the plain one wins over the proud, beautiful Celia. *The Silver Flute* (1931) tells how Barbara Thorne, aged eighteen, takes care of her three brothers and sisters when their father dies.

Robin Hill (1932) has Shirley Penfield learn that in choosing a husband something more dependable than attractiveness is necessary. Her cousin, Ricky, falls short of her standards, and she marries the quite substantial John. *Jonathan's Daughter* (1933) is about Ann Lowell, daughter of a writer, who has lived in fashionable boarding schools and drab boarding houses. *True by the Sun* (1934) has Jim Fielding turn to a gardener for advice and get a job and a sweetheart. *No Lovelier Spring* (1935) portrays a young girl's love when she meets the man her mother, a star actress, is engaged to marry. *Two Keys to a Cabin* (1936) has the theme of the need for comfortable comradeship and sincere love in creating a successful marriage.

Tuesday Never Comes (1937) is a story of a typical American family in the difficult days of war and depression. *Uncle Caleb's Niece* (1939) pictures Faith Merrill, a southern girl, as opening a boarding house on Cape Ann to help her family keep together after her father's death. *Stars Still Shine* (1940) poses the problem whether Kathleen should take Joe or Don. *Bugles in Her Heart* (1944) requires a girl to choose between a bachelor of forty and a young navy doctor. *Each Shining Hour* (1948) has a young girl brought up in wealthy and stuffy seclusion fall in love with the right man at the wrong time. *Faraway Haven* (1950) concerns a girl who is born and bred in the deep South, but who is unable to accept the prejudices and limitations of her environment; she goes North in the hope of either becoming reconciled to southern attitudes which are in many ways pleasing to her or of finding satisfaction in alien surroundings.

JESSE L. LASKY, JR.

Dorothy Gunn

was born on September 19, 1910, in New York City, the son of one of the pioneer founders of the motion-picture industry. His mother was a graduate of the Boston Conservatory of Music who exchanged piano for paint brush and became a well-known and internationally exhibited oil painter. The roots of the family were in California, for his father and grandfather were natives of that state. His grandfather was born in Sacramento, to which city the great-grandfather had come by ox team in the days before the gold rush.

Jesse, Jr., was educated, "but never taught to spell," in America and France. He emerged from the University of Dijon in 1931 with a fairly good French accent that was ruined in Spain when he went there to work for an American company. He left Spain in 1932 and traveled as a student, journalist, and guide through Palestine, Syria, Egypt, and Morocco. He wrote three volumes of poetry and became a fellow of the British Poetry Society. He turned to picture writing and has had more than twenty-five original screen plays produced: they run from "westerns" featuring Gene Autry to five of the biggest Cecil B. de Mille pictures, including "Samson and Delilah." He wrote a play that was produced in Los Angeles.

During World War II he served four years, from 1942 to 1946, in the army and became a captain in the Signal Corps. Two of these years were spent in the Southwest Pacific with combat photographic troops. He took part in assault-wave landings and participated in three campaigns. He wrote the narration for the army's documentary film, "Attack: The Battle of New Britain," which won a New York Critics' Award.

"My ambition," he says, "is to learn how to write well enough to convey the complex machinery of contemporary human feelings in simple and understandable terms by which I may achieve a personal peace of self-understanding more important than success itself."

No Angels in Heaven (1938), his first novel, portrays monotony as the number-one enemy of American marriage. *Spindrift* (1948) is a study of emotionally displaced persons who came out of World War II with restlessness and indecision about their own domestic patterns. The theme of the novel is found in this quotation: "After the storm had left the sea, the cold face of the beach blossomed with spindrift, the foam that blew restlessly to nowhere on the whim of the wind."

MARY LASSWELL

Shanabarger

was born in Glasgow, Scotland, on February 8, 1905, the daughter of Texas-born William Robinson Lubbock and great-granddaughter of Colonel Thomas Saltus Lubbock, founder of the Texas Rangers. Her formative years were spent in Brownsville, Texas. In childhood she learned about the barterings of Mexican generals, the intrigues of Mexican politicians and aristocrats, the industry of Mexican women who support their families by making laces and candies, and the stories of romance and banditry retailed by matriarchs from their rocking chairs. These refugees taught Mrs. Lasswell her Spanish songs and poems and introduced her to paper-bound novels from Spain. As a result she is bilingual and writes about Mexicans with the authority of one who knows them well and respects them. She graduated from the University of Texas in 1930, and then studied music in New York with Katherine Bellamann and later with Pasquale Amato. In 1936 she began teaching in San Diego, California. Two years later she married Clyde Lasswell, an officer in the United States navy.

The central theme of Mary Lasswell's books, serious or gay, is the need for accepting life as it is and recognizing that security and serenity come from inside oneself and do not depend on worldly possessions. She believes that charity, the tolerant recognition of mankind's inherent imperfection, is the supreme virtue. The immediate enjoyment of the small pleasures of life is part and parcel of her philosophy. The outstanding characteristic of her books is a love of the genuine. She wages unceasing warfare on the false, the pseudo-artistic, and the counterfeit.

Suds in Your Eye (1942), her first novel, is about Mrs. Feeley, who inherits a junk yard in Southern California and takes into her home two other poor ladies: Mrs. Rasmussen, a good cook, and Miss Tinkham, a pianist. They raise money to pay back taxes and drink a good deal of beer. In San Diego this book was classified on the best-seller lists as non-fiction. *High Time* (1944) shows how the three old ladies take care of orphans during the war and continue to drink beer. *One on the House* (1949) contains further adventures of the three old ladies, who leave their junkyard home to visit New York. They win a fortune on horses, lose it, take over a beer joint in Newark, New Jersey, and acquire an old car for the trip home. The three novels were issued in one volume as *Three for the Road* (1950).

LILIAN LAUFERTY

Lotte Jacobi

was born in Fort Wayne, Indiana. Her French ancestors came to that town when it was little more than an Indian village and their name was just undergoing a change from de la Ferté. She is a graduate of the Fort Wayne High School and of Smith College. A former newspaperwoman, she received her training from the late Arthur Brisbane, noted editor of the Hearst papers. She began as "The Girl Reporter," was in charge of the famous "Advice to the Lovelorn" for seven years, and has written many stories for the popular magazines, as well as programs for the radio networks for which she originated "Big Sister." Through her husband, James Wolfe, for eighteen years a basso with the Metropolitan Opera, she was plunged into the maze of intrigues, heartbreaks, jealousies, and loyalties of backstage life. Out of this experience she derived the material for *Baritone*. *The Crimson Thread* (1942) and *The Hungry House* (1943) are mystery novels.

Her first novel, *A Pair of Sixes* (1914), is a novelization of a Broadway play. *The Street of Chains* (1929) aroused a great deal of controversy since it was among the first of the books to discuss the now well-established theme of anti-Semitism. In Lilian Lauferty's book the conflict grows out of the disparate elements of Jewish and Gentile blood in the descendants of two ancient houses, one Jewish and great bankers, the other improvident French nobles.

Baritone (1948) concerns Anthony Carlos, who comes to New York from Italy and defies tradition to achieve a dramatic and smashing success at the Metropolitan Opera. The novel is not only the story of an egocentric artist who sacrifices everyone and everything on the way to his goal; it is also the study of those around Carlos and how his wife, his son, and his best friend manage to survive in the whirlpool of the artist's interests.

JOSEPHINE LAWRENCE

Phyfe

was born in Newark, New Jersey, and received her education in its public schools and through special courses at New York University. On leaving school in 1915 she joined the staff of the Newark *Sunday Call* as women's and children's editor. In 1946 she began doing a weekly book column for the Newark *Sunday News*. On October 19, 1940, she married Artur Platz. In 1921 she wrote for biweekly radio broadcasting the "Man in the Moon" stories; her early writing consisted exclusively of children's stories. She wrote the *Man in the Moon Story Book* (1922), the "Brother and Sister" series, the "Elizabeth Ann" series, the "Linda Lane" books, and the "Little Fellows" books.

Miss Lawrence's novels have their settings in Newark, and her characters are middle-class people engaged in the normal activities of love-making, homemaking, childbearing, and job holding. "My philosophic viewpoint," says Miss Lawrence, "is confined to the contemporary scene: the present holds me spellbound, and my novels are thematic because the problems of life at the ordinary, daily level seem to me to be vastly more important than anything already experienced."

Her first novel is *Head of the Family* (1932), a story of a modern marriage in which the wife and husband share finances on a fifty-fifty basis. *Years Are So Long* deals with the responsibility of children to care for their aged parents. *If I Have Four Apples* (1935) portrays the unhappy effects of installment buying during the depression years in the Penter family. *The Sound of Running Feet* (1937) raises the question of small pay versus none in a story about clerks who are paid though the business loses money. *Bow Down to Wood and Stone* (1938) studies the true meaning of sacrifice in a story of three sisters whose self-sacrifice is really selfishness. *A Good Home with Nice People* (1939) describes the difficulties of maidservants employed by harsh, dishonest, ill-tempered, and domineering women.

But You Are Young (1940) dramatizes the problem of supporting an unemployed family not eligible for relief in the depression. Kelsie, a high-school graduate, works as a manicurist to support her grandmother and her parents. *No Stone Unturned* (1941) is a character study of a father who possesses all the moral virtues and devotedly cares for his wife and children but who does not understand them. *There Is Today* (1942) answers affirmatively the question: Should a young couple marry if the boy knows he will be drafted in the army? *A Tower of Steel* (1943) probes the minds and aspirations of four young women working in a law office.

Let Us Consider One Another (1945) deals with the theme of racial intolerance in the marriage of a girl of Catholic and Protestant background to a Jewish army sergeant. *Double Wedding Ring* (1946) raises the question of when a mother's responsibility to her children ends. Four grown children do not want her to share in their lives. *The Pleasant Morning Light* (1948) deals with three girls in their twenties who are urged to marry on the theory that a woman without a husband has an incomplete life.

My Heart Shall Not Fear (1949) examines the questions asked by a young woman who has brought her first child into a fear-ridden world. The main setting is in a hospital. *The Way Things Are* (1950) has a simple, old-fashioned girl try to escape living with relatives by marrying an elderly man; then she falls in love with a boy of her own age.

MARGARET REBECCA LAY

Dolph Zubick

began life in a sharecropper house in the shadow of the Cohutta Mountains near Sugar Valley, Georgia; she was the last of eight children. She was born with the whole outdoors in her mouth, so to speak, and was the product of barefoot trails, grassy meadows, warm dim woods, and corn and cotton patches. She left Georgia for Washington state while still in high school, finished college there, and received a teacher's degree, although she wanted to become a newspaperwoman writing a little homey column. She realizes now that it is just as well that that dream failed to materialize, for she finds meeting deadlines a killing procedure. She lives in Seattle, Washington, in a studio-attic apartment, the upkeep of which is always sacrificed to her writing. Unless she can shut out school children and schoolwork at the day's end, take fresh heart from her view of Lake Union, the Olympic Mountains, and Puget Sound, and write for at least a half hour, that day is a failure.

Ceylun (1947), her first novel, pictures Brev Shore who had loved Ceylun Lithoway since she was a child; he felt she was as far above him as the moon, since she was an aristocrat and he was only a middle-class farmer who had managed to amass a little wealth. Ceylun's family become impoverished and marry her to Brev in name only to save their mortgaged estate. Separated more widely than united by wedlock, their life becomes a turbulent affair. Georgia is the setting, and the time is 1906.

Thornblossoms (1948) concerns a family poor in worldly goods in the Georgia of 1904; their family pride is a dominating characteristic affecting all their lives. Jon Thornblossom, the son, victim of too many love affairs, muddles his life by wavering between his old devotion to a girl of good family and his new love for the unconventional daughter of a tenant farmer, and by worrying over his mother's pride in the family name. He loses practically everything that makes life worth while before the various characters acquire a realization of true values.

MADELEINE L'ENGLE

was born on November 28, 1918, in New York City, daughter of the writer, Wadsworth Camp, and the pianist, Madeleine Barnett Camp. She was educated in New York, Europe, and the South, and was graduated from Smith College with honors. She has worked in the theater, in stock and on Broadway, with such actors as Ethel Barrymore, Eva LeGallienne, and Joseph Schildkraut. It was at her father's suggestion that she dropped her last name when she went on the stage. Despite her interest in the theater, she says, "There has never been a time that I can remember when writing wasn't the most important thing in the world to me." Since her marriage to the actor Hugh Franklin in 1946, Miss L'Engle has left the stage as an actress, though not as a playwright. At present she and her husband and daughter live in New York City and in Connecticut, where they rebuilt an old farm house. "18 Washington Square, South" (1944) is a play about two girls just out of college.

She believes that the whole purpose of art is communication, to reach as many people as possible, and to give them at all costs a glimpse of the infinite potentialities of man. In her view, our great possibilities are something we are apt to overlook; and books, plays, and music can remind us of them.

Her first novel, *The Small Rain* (1945), is the story of a young girl's growth into maturity and her realization that the career of a pianist (or a serious artist of any kind) is not glamour but hard work. *Ilsa* (1946) is a character study of a beautiful woman whose deep understanding and compassion and fortitude are always stronger than any outward adversity that would overcome a lesser woman. *And Both Were Young* (1949) presents the problems that arise when girls of many nations are thrown together in a boarding school in present-day Switzerland.

MEYER LEVIN

was born in Chicago, Illinois, on October 8, 1905. He grew up on the West Side and saw it change during his boyhood from a Jewish to an Italian community; the family did not move away until long after the neighborhood had gained an unsavory reputation as the bloody Nineteenth Ward of gangsterdom. In school and college he wrote for and edited student newspapers, and while at the University of Chicago he began part-time work as photographer on the Chicago *Daily News*. Following graduation in 1924 he became a reporter, feature writer, and eventually a columnist. His early short stories in *The Menorah Journal* dealt with Chicago's West Side and indicated his intention to use the Jewish neighborhood material with which he was best acquainted.

On a visit to Paris he considered becoming a painter, but disliked the idea of a ten-year apprenticeship. Until 1930 he worked for newspapers sporadically and then went to Palestine to live in a new-settlers' farm community. He was regarded as the first American to take part in this movement. Here he found what he considered to be an indication of his future cultural development, just as in Europe he found in the Jewish folklore of mystical Chassidism his spiritual sources in the past. He returned to the United States, and worked as actor, producer of marionette shows, assistant editor of *Esquire* and *Ken,* and movie reviewer. During World War II he became absorbed in reporting the travail of the Jews in Europe, sometimes as a newspaperman and sometimes as a film documentarist; in the latter activity he felt that he was writing with a camera. A by-product of this work is the picture book, *If I Forget Thee* (1947), with modern Palestine as its subject. In 1934 he married Mabel Schamp Foy, and in 1948, Tereska Szwarc. One son has been born to each union. In 1949 the Levins were living in France. *In Search* (1950) is a frank, outspoken autobiography portraying his pursuit of self-discovery.

"In my view," Mr. Levin has stated, "the function of the writer in modern times is somewhat akin to that of the ancient Hebrew prophet, except that the modern writer more consciously is engaged in the interpretation of material that will help humanity toward self-understanding. My own tendency in fiction is to write from the organic point of view: that is, the view of all society. My particular orientation is Jewish, but my work is conditioned through my upbringing in this country; my formation is American as well as Jewish in cultural environment. I believe that more than any other writer of my generation, I have consciously sought to define my work as that of an American Jewish writer. I do not, however, consider that I am limited to Jewish material as an author. I write in the tradition of the realists, having been most impressed by Dreiser and Dos Passos. I hope to develop my talent as a novelist performing his share, however small, in the total human search for truth."

His first novel, *Reporter* (1929), was designed as a typical American story based upon the author's newspaper experiences. A threat of libel action caused the withdrawal of the book from circulation. *Frankie and Johnny* (1930) describes the manners and customs of youth in the 1920's in a story of a poor boy, who has a routine job in a big mail-order house, and his girl. *Yehuda* (1931) grew out of the author's experiences in Palestine on a farm commune; this was the first novel about modern Palestine to be published in any language.

The Golden Mountain (1932) is a retelling of the tales of the wonder-rabbis, known as the Chassidim. This material was new to America, though many books on the subject have since been published. The rabbis' creed emphasizes universal immanence and a joyous celebration of life. "It is at once mystic and earthy," Mr. Levin has said, "and this outlook represented to me the east-European Jewishness that was the world of my direct forebears." This book contains the spiritual source material linking Mr. Levin to the past. *The New Bridge* (1933) is the story of the depression and its effect on an unemployed Polish immigrant who is about to be evicted from his apartment.

The Old Bunch (1937), which states the place of Mr. Levin's generation in the present American Jewish scene, is a long, panoramic novel describing the lives of eleven boys and eight girls who graduate from high school in 1921 and through further education become business and professional leaders by the time of the Century of Progress Fair in 1934. It is a study of the children of poor immigrants who have achieved middle-class comfort. *Citizens* (1940) concerns ten steel-mill strikers who were slain in an attempt to establish a picket line before a Chicago plant; the novel is a fictionalized account of an actual event which occurred on Memorial Day in 1937.

My Father's House (1947) is an attempt to tell the typical story of a Jewish survivor. In this case it is a child who, like all survivors, is obsessed with the idea that his family is alive somewhere. The story, a symbolic one expressed in terms of modern psychology, shows the child's reversion to infancy in order to achieve a wish to be reborn. The reincarnation myths of Chassidism, as well as the psychological orientation for which modern writers owe so much to Freud, served in the development of this story: there is also some influence of Franz Kafka apparent in it.

JANET LEWIS

was born in Chicago, Illinois, on August 17, 1899. After studying at Lewis Institute in Chicago, she attended the University of Chicago, from which she graduated in 1920. In 1926 she married Yvor Winters, the poet, critic, and professor of English at Stanford University; they have two children, a daughter and a son. Her books include a juvenile, *The Friendly Adventures of Ollie Ostrich* (1923); three books of poems, *The Indians in the Woods* (1922), *Wheel in Midsummer* (1927), and *The Earth-Bound* (1946); and *Good-Bye, Son* (1946), a collection of short stories. "The Wife of Martin Guerre," a story of sixteenth-century France, based on a famous case of circumstantial evidence, has been republished in an anthology called *Anchor in the Sea* (1946).

The Invasion (1932), her first novel, tells the story of the Johnston family along the St. Mary's River in northern Michigan. John Johnston, an Irish gentleman, came to America shortly after the Revolution and settled down with an Ojibway Indian wife. As a background to the story of the Johnstons is an account of the Indians who see their lands slowly passing from their hands into those of the white newcomers. *Against a Darkening Sky* (1943) characterizes Mary Perrault, a Scot by birth, who marries a Swiss gardener; through kindness and understanding she helps her four children. The setting is Encina, a town near San Francisco, in the 1930's. *The Trial of Sören Qvist* (1947) has a seventeenth-century background in Denmark and tells the story of the return of Niels Bruns to his home twenty years after his supposed body had been found in the garden of Pastor Sören Qvist, a saintly man who had been executed for the alleged murder. It appears that Niels' brother, Morton, had wreaked a brutal and terrible revenge for the pastor's refusal to allow his marriage to the cleric's daughter.

OSCAR LEWIS

was born on May 5, 1893, in San Francisco; except for a year spent overseas during World War I he has lived there most of his life. He has written much about his native city, and his work accurately depicts the qualities that have long made San Francisco unique among American cities. Although the bulk of his writing has been on historical or biographical subjects, he has frequently turned to fiction, most of which has a California locale. In addition he has edited and written introductions to numerous volumes on western historical or literary subjects, and has contributed to a variety of magazines.

I Remember Christine (1942) is a satirical, retrospective novel dealing with the life of James Horton, a San Francisco millionaire whose career had just been treated in a pretentious, authorized biography financed by his son. Reading this, a friend of the family undertakes to set down his own memories of the capitalist, of his family and mistress, and of the period in which they lived. This gives the narrator an opportunity for an extended play of irony in contrasting the real Horton with the figure presented in the "official" biography, and in bringing to light certain episodes in his life which were suppressed by the earlier writer. As it turns out, the central figure of the novel is not Horton himself but his mistress, patient, understanding, amoral Christine Winton. It is a leisurely novel of life and changing social mores covering six intensely active and interesting decades of San Francisco history.

The Uncertain Journey (1945) is on a quite different theme, being a study of how a sensitive and idealistic young man, caught in the depression of the early 1930's, meets the problems of adjusting himself to the world in which he finds himself. It revolves mainly about his romance with a girl he meets while he is a student at Berkeley, a girl who with the best of intentions exerts a continuously disruptive influence on his career. It is a story of the generation that came to maturity during the years between the two world wars, told with sympathy and candor and with a depth of understanding of the problems it faced.

SINCLAIR LEWIS

Pach Bros.

was born February 7, 1885, in Sauk Centre, Minnesota, the son of a country doctor. He attended public schools in Sauk Centre, and upon graduation from high school went to Yale. In college he began his writing career as an editor of the literary magazine. Having become interested in socialism, he interrupted his studies to become a janitor at Helicon Hall, Upton Sinclair's co-operative colony at Englewood, New Jersey. Before it burnt down, he drifted to New York to try his hand at free-lance writing, and he took a job as assistant on *Transatlantic Tales,* a magazine of translations. From there he went to Panama; after trying in vain to get a job on the canal, he returned to Yale and finished his education.

After graduation in 1908 he worked on a newspaper in Waterloo, Iowa. There followed a number of jobs, including work for a charity organization in New York and reporting for the Associated Press and the San Francisco *Bulletin;* for a time he served in Washington, D.C., as assistant editor of the *Volta Review,* a magazine for teachers of the deaf. He moved to New York and did editorial work until 1916, when he devoted his full time to writing. In 1920 *Main Street* was acclaimed as one of the first great realistic novels in the United States. Later books made an equally strong impression upon readers, and names like Main Street, Carol Kennicott, Babbitt, Arrowsmith, and others are likely to remain among those given universal currency by fiction. In 1925 *Arrowsmith* won the Pulitzer prize, but Mr. Lewis refused to accept it in protest against the restrictive terms of the award. In 1930 he received in Sweden the Nobel prize, and in his address of acceptance he commented unfavorably upon the conservative quality of the American Academy of Arts and Letters. He wrote essays, plays, and short stories; for a time he was an actor and a teacher of creative writing. Mr. Lewis first married Grace Hegger and subsequently columnist Dorothy Thompson. Mr. Lewis had two sons, Wells and Michael, one by each marriage; Wells was killed in World War II.

Mr. Lewis died on January 10, 1951.

Mr. Lewis' novels are concerned especially with those aspects of American social, business, and professional life in which are found shoddy thinking, loose ethical standards, and charlatanry. His satiric method involves the use of carefully reproduced colloquial speech, cartoon-like sharpness of outline in character portraiture, three-dimensional characterization, and a fullness of descriptive detail. Often one incongruous detail, like a preacher glancing at his watch while praying, imparts that special touch which marks Mr. Lewis' descriptions of places and people.

His first book was *Hike and the Aeroplane* (1912), a boy's story written under the pseudonym of "Tom Graham." *Our Mr. Wrenn* (1914), his first novel, is a story of a New York clerk who travels to England, where his shortcomings and loneliness provide a perspective with which to return to his job. *The Trail of the Hawk* (1915), a "comedy of the seriousness of life," portrays Carl Ericson, whose love of adventure leads him into aviation. *The Job* (1917) concerns a sheltered Pennsylvania girl who rises in New York to be a capable business executive. *The Innocents* (1917) is the charming love story of Mr. and Mrs. Seth Appleby, a New York City couple, who find a new home in Indiana. *Free Air* (1919) raises the question of freedom or conventionality in a story of a sheltered Brooklyn girl and an ambitious Minnesota garageman, who learn about America on a cross-country tour.

Main Street (1920), which is set in Gopher Prairie, Minnesota, is a satiric commentary on the mediocrity and dull mentality of middle-class life in small towns. The story revolves around Carol Kennicott's ambition to introduce new ideas. *Babbitt* (1922) is the story of the home life, business associations, and avocations of an American businessman. H. L. Mencken wrote in 1925: "I believe that *Babbitt* is one of the best novels written in America—solid and beautiful in design, and superb in detail." *Arrowsmith* (1925) is the story of the education and ideals of a true physician and man of science who resists the temptation to devote himself to money-making rather than truth. *Mantrap* (1926) pictures the experiences in Canada of a New York lawyer and another man's wife, whom the husband pursues. *Elmer Gantry* (1927) satirizes an immoral clergyman whose hypocrisy begins in college days. *The Man Who Knew Coolidge* (1928) ridicules self-satisfied Americans in Lowell Schmaltz, a fat, cigar-smoking man. *Dodsworth* (1929) portrays the retirement of an automobile manufacturer and his visit to Europe with his wife. Her snobbish discontentment and infidelity increase his sense of practical idealism.

Ann Vickers (1933) traces the life story of a social worker from her introverted college days to her career as a criminologist with a distaste for harsh prison methods. *Work of Art* (1934) has the theme that anything done honestly, sincerely, and well is a work of art. A hotel keeper does better than his brother, a writer. *It Can't Happen Here* (1935) pictures the threat of fascist dictatorship to America and what this country would become if Senator Windrip should be elected President. *The Prodigal Parents* (1938) is about middle-class Fred Cornplow of Sachem Falls, New York, who revolts against the extravagances of his children and the routine into which his life has fallen. He and his wife must return from Europe to help a son who is in trouble.

Bethel Merriday (1940) gives the life story of a girl whose ambition to be an actress begins in childhood and attains fulfillment in college, in a summer theater, and with a road company. *Gideon Planish* (1943) satirizes a former college dean who uses oratorical double talk to gain money for himself and his extravagant wife and to advance the presidential aspirations of Colonel Charles B. Marduc, founder of the Dynamos of Democratic Direction. At the end Gideon tries to "sell" a peace plan in Washington. *Cass Timberlane* (1945), an analysis of many types of women, pictures the intense love which a forty-one-year-old judge has for his young and unstable wife. *Kingsblood Royal* (1947) has a successful young banker learn that Negro blood is in his veins; by living among Negroes he discovers harsh facts about race relations. *The God-Seeker* (1949), Mr. Lewis' first historical novel, deals with a New England carpenter, Aaron Gadd, who goes to Minnesota in the 1840's as a missionary to the Indians and ends as a contractor.

LUDWIG LEWISOHN

Erich Hartmann

was born in Berlin, Germany, on May 30, 1883. Brought to America at the age of seven, he grew up in Charleston, South Carolina. He received his bachelor's and master's degrees in 1901 and the degree of Doctor of Literature in 1914 from the College of Charleston, and in 1913 was awarded a master's degree by Columbia University. His early career was in free-lance writing, literary criticism, and translation from the French and German. From 1911 to 1919 he was a professor of German language and literature at Ohio State University. In 1919 he became dramatic editor of *The Nation* magazine and was its associate editor from 1920 to 1924. A trip to Palestine in 1925 grew out of his active interest in the Zionist movement. Since 1948 he has been a member of the faculty of Brandeis University in Waltham, Massachusetts.

Mr. Lewisohn is a profound student of European belles-lettres and an acute critic of American literature; his works of criticism include *The Modern Drama* (1915), *The Spirit of Modern German Literature* (1916), *The Poets of Modern France* (1918), *Modern Book of Criticism* (1919), *The Drama and the State* (1922), *The Creative Life* (1924), *Expression in America* (1932), and *The Magic Word* (1950). *Upstream* (1922) and *Mid-Channel: An American Chronicle* (1929) are autobiographical. Three books—*Israel* (1925), *Rebirth* (1935), and *The Answer* (1939)—deal with the plight of the Jewish people in the modern world. Other books are *Cities and Men* (1927), *The Permanent Horizon* (1934), and *Goethe: The Story of a Man* (1949). *The American Jew: Character and Destiny* (1950) is an essay.

In his novels Mr. Lewisohn has been concerned with two major themes. The problems of marriage have been analyzed with candor and with sympathy for those people who have found themselves caught in the meshes of tradition or law through union with incompatible mates. The second theme, and the one which has engrossed much of his creative effort since 1925, is the age-old struggle of the Jewish people to secure freedom from oppression through the establishment of a nation of their own.

The Broken Snare (1908), his first novel, raises the question whether happiness is destroyed by the marriage bond in a story of a woman who, having lived out of wedlock for a time, persuades her lover to marry her. *Don Juan* (1923) portrays divorce laws as outmoded in a story of Lucien Curtin, who leaves his independent wife to be with an instinctively feminine woman and then finds himself ensnared by a seductive female. *The Case of Mr. Crump* (1926) deals with the problem of a young man who has been seduced into marrying a woman much older than himself. *Roman Summer* (1927) analyzes the debilitating effect of the genteel tradition on a young poet whose mother dominates his life. A trip to Rome teaches him the need for participating in everyday life.

The Island Within (1928) has the theme of the necessity for Jews to cling to their racial background and culture in a story about a Polish family that migrates to America and rises to wealth. The key narrative is about a boy who marries a Gentile girl. *Stephen Escott* (1930) studies the part that sex plays in American life in a Freudian commentary on New England puritanism and the dangers of inhibition. *The Golden Vase* (1931) examines the rôle of the literary artist in America in a story of a middle-aged novelist and an understanding woman. *The Last Days of Shylock* (1931) pictures Shakespeare's character in the years after the events of the play and makes him into a Zionist who finds peace in the sacred books of the Hebrews. *This People* (1933) contains five stories calling upon Jews to remain firm in the age-old and honored faith of Zion.

An Altar in the Fields (1934) pictures two sophisticates who marry in the 1920's and separate. A psychiatrist sends them to the African desert, where they gain a sense of balance and then return to America to live on a farm with their child. *Trumpet of Jubilee* (1937) narrates the terrifying experiences of Jews in Hitler's Germany and the escape of a murdered man's wife and son to America, where they face new problems. *Forever Wilt Thou Love* (1939) tells how Mark Clement, a talented architect, announces to his wife and four friends that he is resigning his position to recapture the lost verve in his work and to seek fulfillment in love with a more sympathetic woman. This novel contains a new blending of narrative and dramatic techniques. *Renegade* (1942) is an historical novel of France in the years preceding the French Revolution. A Jewish boy posing as a Gentile shows that a person is unable to hide his heritage or change his destiny. *Breathe upon These* (1944) is a story of Hitler's cruel treatment of the Jews and British conduct toward Palestine in 1942.

Anniversary (1948) concerns a twice-divorced young New England woman who wishes to marry a divorced man and must contend with public and family opinion. The story is told, in the manner of Robert Browning's *The Ring and the Book,* through the confessions or dramatic monologues of six characters.

VICTORIA LINCOLN

was born on October 23, 1904, in the mill town of Fall River, Massachusetts, where her father's family had for many generations been manufacturers of textile machinery. Her father wrote on economics and textile history and lectured at the Tuck School of Business in Dartmouth College. She was a bred-in-the-bone Yankee who was told often with pride that she was a lineal descendant of our Colonial governors. In 1926, just as she graduated from Radcliffe, the New England textile industries collapsed and "the shop" went into bankruptcy. She married Isaac Watkins, an Alabaman, and lived in the South, the West, Germany, and England; it was the period of prohibition and the depression. For her it was a time of intense individualism which found its expression in the romantic-satirical fantasy, *February Hill.*

In 1932 she separated from her husband and returned from England, where they were then living, to obtain an American divorce; during the following year she met her present husband, Victor Lowe, then an assistant in philosophy at Harvard, and in 1934 they were married. She had one child by her first marriage and two by her second. Her second marriage has been an unusually happy one; for a little while the couple lived in Cambridge, then for five years in Columbus where her husband was connected with the Ohio State University, and now in Maryland, where he is on the faculty of The Johns Hopkins University.

Suspecting that a long period of ill-health which followed the birth of her second child was largely of psychosomatic origin, she began, in 1937, a period of psychoanalysis lasting nearly three years. To its successful outcome she attributes not only the continual good health and vigorous working habits of the last ten years, but a vastly increased respect for people as people and a deepened insight, particularly into the realm of childhood.

After 1934 she turned her attention for a number of years exclusively to the short story. *Grandmother and the Comet* (1946) is a collection of her own favorite stories and poems of that period. *The Wind at My Back* (1948) is a group of three short novels including the lightly veiled autobiographical story of her own girlhood, "Before the Swallow Dares."

All Miss Lincoln's work since 1934 has been in a vein of conscious realism; although she deals by choice with highly emotional and imaginative characters, with people of an unusual degree of awareness, she writes with the expressed purpose of interpreting the common life that we share from the cradle to the grave, not from the social, political, or economic viewpoint, but from that of our interior symbolisms and mythologies. D. H. Lawrence's writings have influenced her fiction.

February Hill (1934), her first novel, describes in kindly and humorous fashion the Harris family which lives outside Fall River, Massachusetts. The mother supports the family on income gained from illicit weekends; the father, though a Harvard graduate, is a drunkard; Joel, a sensitive lad, is something of a scholar; and two daughters have tendencies similar to those of father and mother. Humorous, bawdy, and tender, it is the expression of the dream, common to all who are very young, of a utopian anarchy in which there shall be no soul "that lacks a sweet crystalline cry."

Celia Amberley (1949) is a full study of the emotional development of a personality from early childhood to maturity, a novel in which the emphasis lies not so much upon the outer differences of the period as upon the response of the individual in any era to the social structure and the climate of opinion in which he is born; the book stresses the interweaving of those influences with the fundamental, dateless impulses of individual life as they work together to develop a personality.

EMILIE LORING

was born in Boston, Massachusetts, where she grew up in an atmosphere of writing, publishing, and dramatics. Her father, George M. Baker, wrote plays for amateur production, and her brother, Robert, and her sister, Rachel Baker Gale, have written for the amateur and professional stage. "Our house was a theatrical workshop," Mrs. Loring has said; "it is small wonder that I developed a dramatic sense that will burst forth in my novels." She took up writing seriously after her two sons went away to school. At first she wrote under the pseudonym of "Josephine Story." She has written one play, many articles for leading magazines, and twenty-nine novels. Her first book was *The Trail of Conflict* (1922).

Mrs. Loring's novels concern the normal way of life of normal people whose lives are touched by romance, mystery, excitement, and human interest.

Hilltops Clear (1933) tells about Prudence Schuyler who has to clear away the prejudices she formed about rich suitors before she and Rodney Gerard can understand each other. *We Ride the Gale* (1934) concerns Sonia Carson who for a time turns against Michael Farr because of Guy Farr's desertion of her sister. *It's a Great World* (1935) employs the nation's capital as a background for the story of Eve Travis, who realizes that she loves Jeff Kilburn after she leaves him.

Give Me One Summer (1936) portrays the romance of Melissa Barclay and Lex Carson during a summer in Maine where he has come to settle his aunt's estate. His secrecy, arising from a confidential government job, causes Melissa to put him in probatim. *As Long As I Live* (1937) concerns a commercial artist in Boston when the heads of two rival advertising agencies vie for her services and love. *Today Is Yours* (1938) tells of Brian Romney's difficulties with his employees and wife when he returns home from the West to run the family factory. *High of Heart* (1938) is about an English heiress, reared in America, who is nearly kidnapped by gangsters on her American estate. *Across the Years* (1939) describes the complications when the plans for an American bombing plane disappear from a Senator's office in Washington. *There Is Always Love* (1940) brings a New England girl exciting adventures in a real estate office in New York when a castle is to be sold. *Where Beauty Dwells* (1941) deals with a New Englander who helps two girls from being evicted from their home in the West. *When Hearts Are Light Again* (1943) describes sabotage in a war plant. *Beyond the Sound of Guns* (1945) portrays the aftermath of war on a Western ranch. *Bright Skies* (1946) deals with a Red Cross worker in post-war Honolulu and her success in discovering Nazi intrigue and also the way to the Colonel's heart. *Beckoning Trails* (1947) pictures a New England college town and a mysteriously dangerous situation. *I Hear Adventure Calling* (1948) is set in a Maine summer resort with an art-colony atmosphere. *Love Came Laughing By* (1949) deals with secret documents that are trailed to Washington, D.C.

ERNST LOTHAR

was born in Bruenn, Austria, on October 25, 1890. He graduated from the University of Vienna in 1914 as a Doctor of Philosophy and in 1915 earned the degree of Doctor of Laws. He wrote his first book of verse at eighteen, and in the year 1918 was awarded the Bauernfeld prize for his first novel, *The Warlord.* During World War I he created quite a stir in his country with a book of essays in which he advocated Austria's alliance with England and the United States. For a time he was an assistant district attorney and later he became court councillor in the Ministry of Education. He abandoned public service in 1925 to devote himself to writing. He was drama critic of the Vienna daily *Neue Freie Presse* for twelve years and was Max Reinhardt's successor in the Theater Josefstadt in Vienna; he was ousted from this position by Hitler in 1938. Mr. Lothar arrived in New York in 1939; he lectured at Bard College and Colorado College. Mrs. Lothar, under the stage name of Adrienne Gessner, started her career on Broadway in "Claudia" and "I Remember Mama" with outstanding success. Mr. Lothar became a citizen in 1944 and from 1946 to 1948 was in the service of the American Military Government in Austria, where he was an adviser on cultural matters.

The Clairvoyant (1931) deals with the effect of knowing one's future before it happens. *Little Friend* (1933) is the psychological study, through the mind of a girl of twelve, of the antagonism existing between her Jewish father and aristocratic mother; when the child fails to reconcile them, she attempts suicide. *The Loom of Justice* (1935) portrays, against the inflexible legal code of Austria, the life story of a judge whose mercy-killing of his wife brings the knowledge that justice and law are not identical. *A Woman Is Witness* (1941) tells the story of the defeat of France from 1938 to 1940 in the diary of an Austrian journalist's widow who must die for shooting at a German officer.

Beneath Another Sun (1943) is a story of the South Tyrol at the time of the German-Italian agreement and refutes Hitler's theory of protecting the German minorities. *The Angel with the Trumpet* (1944) deals with the history of Austria from 1899 to the merger with Germany in telling the story of a house in Vienna and its inhabitants, the Alt family. *The Prisoner* (1945) is the story of a young Viennese prisoner of war who is brought to America and who recognizes the evil and deceit in Nazism. *Return to Vienna* (1949) pictures the return to the city of his birth of a man who had spent eight years in exile in the United States and describes the conflict between his loyalty to his new country and his love for his homeland.

ROBERT LOWRY

Helen Heyman

was born on March 28, 1919, in Cincinnati, Ohio, of English and German ancestry. His father, a West Virginian by birth, is a conductor on the Pennsylvania Railroad. Robert started to write in childhood; by the time he had finished high school, he had long since been thinking of himself as a writer. After six months at the University of Cincinnati, where he organized a literary magazine, he quit in 1938 to roam around the United States. He returned to Cincinnati the same year and bought a treadle-type printing press, which he installed in the basement of a house in Cincinnati's East End. For the next three and a half years he was an odd-job printer, typographer, and small-time publisher of "Little Man Books," in which many of his early stories appeared. He married in 1941, was drafted into the army a year later, and served thirty-nine months in Africa and Italy as a photo-reconnaissance enlisted man in the air corps. He continued to write as a soldier, completing most of the stories in *The Wolf That Fed Us* and the first draft of *The Big Cage*. Released from the army in September, 1945, he worked as production manager and book designer for New Directions while writing *Casualty*, his first novel; he quit in 1946 to write full time. He spent part of 1947 in Michigan completing *Find Me in Fire* and then went to Italy for a year in 1948. Divorced shortly after the war, he has remarried and has one child. In 1949 he became a book critic on *Time*. Mr. Lowry's stories have appeared in *The Best American Short Stories* of 1947 and 1948. *The Wolf That Fed Us* (1949) contains short stories.

"Good writing should hurt like life, smell like life, be as generous and as cutting and inconsistent as life," Mr. Lowry has said. "People are the important thing, either in or out of books. The single, central theme in my books is myself and the people I have known, loved, neglected, despised, laughed at or with, run to or from or at. I have always tried to take a close, hard look at everything in this whole stumbling, unsatisfactory, impossible, and undeniable world. Everything else I have to say about the subject is right there in the books, easy to get at and as stripped of poses, rhetoric, and convention as I can make it."

Casualty (1946), his first novel, describes moral rottenness in a wartime army camp in Italy. It is the story of the obscene army system's victory over individual decency. The central character is Joe Hammond, who dies after being run over by a truck. *Find Me in Fire* (1948) brings together two versions of the war's effect. One is direct: on a crippled soldier. The other is indirect: on the people of a small Ohio town who saw their war only at the movie, but were nevertheless touched, warped, or driven half crazy by it. The war is not only the fighting war, but also the even nastier elements that brought the war about, saw it through for five years, and are still present. Jim Miller works his way back to the wide world that hurt him but to which he belongs. All he has left is his stripped-down, savage self, but that may not be the least thing after all.

The Big Cage (1949) has been described by Mr. Lowry thus: "If a man isn't willing to put down the truth even to the point of humiliating himself, he ought to quit calling himself a writer If this book does anything, it shoves a reader's face hard into the sad, ridiculous, humiliating facts of the first eighteen years of one man's life. Nobody has failed to say that it is an autobiographical novel. How could it be anything else? I wrote the first draft in Italy during the lowest year of my life, 1944; I went back to Italy in 1948 and rewrote it. I think it is a true book; I also think that anyone who doesn't find it a funny book as well ought to get himself another book."

ANDREW NELSON LYTLE

was born on December 26, 1902, in Murfreesboro, Tennessee. He graduated from Vanderbilt University, where he was one of the writers, historians, and poets who called themselves the Fugitives. After study in France and as a member of the "47 Workshop" in playwriting under George Pierce Baker at Yale University, he acted on Broadway and on Long Island as one of the founders of the Hampton Players. In 1940 he held a Guggenheim fellowship. He has taught at Southwestern University, the University of the South, and the University of Iowa. He was editor of *The Sewanee Review* from 1941 to 1942. In 1948 he began teaching creative writing at the University of Florida in Gainesville. He was one of the "Twelve Southerners" who prepared *I'll Take My Stand* (1930), a manifesto of agrarians who believed some restraint must be put upon the monopolistic finance capitalism which they thought then was paving the way for the totalitarian state. Later in *Who Owns America* (1936) this group reexamined their position in a new declaration of independence. *Bedford Forrest and His Critter Company* (1931) is a biography of a Civil War cavalry general, often called the wizard of the saddle, the first head of the Ku Klux Klan and the last ruler of the Old South.

Mr. Lytle's novels present experience at several levels of interest. Asked to explain his method, he stated: "The novelist must try to render what happens in a given situation, not what seems to happen. If he is successful, he will turn out work with depth as well as surface; that is, the different levels will fuse as the skin to the flesh beneath, and the flesh to the bone, with the veins and arteries giving the movement of life. What results, then, will be organic and not mechanical.

"The performance of a novelist depends upon his private vision and his private discipline. The exhausting nature of creative work requires the artist to maintain a balance between his will and his physical, moral, and imaginative energy. Here lies part of the hazard and some of the mystery of the art of fiction."

The Long Night (1936), his first novel, is laid in the South of 1860. Ostensibly the story of a young man who avenges the death of his father at the hands of a wilderness gang, actually it is the story of the destruction of a young man's obsession by the greater violence of war, wherein he recovers his humanity but loses his purpose through the death of a friend. *At The Moon's Inn* (1941) deals with De Soto's entry into this country in 1539; the novel is an experiment in relating the historic image to fiction. *A Name For Evil* (1947) is a ghost story which embodies an underlying historic symbol of the plight of western civilization. A couple sets out to restore a southern mansion.

MACKAY *to* MYERS

MARGARET MACKAY

Bradford Bachrach

was born on November 19, 1907, in Oxford, Nebraska, the daughter of Thomas and Meta Mackprang. She graduated from the University of California at Berkeley in 1928. Four years later she married Alexander H. Mackay, who was killed in action with the British army in 1942. She lived in Peiping, China, from 1931 to 1935; in Tientsin, China, from 1935 to 1939; and again in Peiping from 1939 to 1941. From 1941 to 1945 she was a resident of Hawaii, and since 1947 she has traveled in ten European countries.

Mrs. Mackay has written through long periods of tragedy, illness, danger, and turmoil. She thinks that any writer who is born to it cannot help producing work with professional discipline, however difficult and inconvenient it may be. She writes every morning wherever she goes and despite all difficulties: *Give Him My Love* was produced at thirty-odd desks in ten different countries. This, she believes, illustrates the point that in order to write fiction one must have a great desire to do so. She is fascinated by international life, and all her novels have been about Americans and Britons in cosmopolitan settings. She likes best to live in the rural region near a capital to enjoy a mixture of quiet serenity and worldly stimulus.

Like Water Flowing (1938), her first novel, portrays a sensitive, cultured Chinese-American girl, Linda Heywood, her love for a young British officer, and the dilemma posed by her struggle against race prejudice; it is set in the charming Willow Pattern countryside outside Peiping. *Lady With Jade* (1939) concerns a cool, daring American woman who builds up a fabulous antique shop in Peiping despite the obstructions of civil wars, war lords, rivals, and cheats. Her passion for collecting imperial jade, and its symbolic role in her life, which gradually separates her from those who love her, is the unfolding drama of the book.

Valiant Dust (1941) is about a Scotch commercial pioneer family in Tientsin, China, between 1880 and the Boxer siege in 1900, and tells of Elspeth Maclaren, the staunch little heroine; of Philip, the sensitive young man in whose company she is shipwrecked on her way to China to marry Angus Maclaren; of her children and their eventual maturity. It describes authentically the struggles of the early foreign colonies, with their races and balls, their loneliness and gossip, pitted against the hard pioneer life of massacres and disease and international intrigue.

For All Men Born (1943) has Katherine Lathrop, a China-born American girl, forced to leave her home because of the Japanese invasion in August, 1941. She stops at Honolulu, falls in love, and has her wedding on December 7, 1941, interrupted by the attack on Pearl Harbor. *Homeward the Heart* (1944) discusses the wartime problem of separated couples in the love which arises when a married soldier with two children falls in love in Hawaii. *Great Lady* (1946) portrays China as a land of leisure and contemplation and of social upheaval. The events cover the Boxer uprising through the Japanese invasion to the revolution. The widow of an English diplomat, Felicia Dale, becomes a symbol of China's difficulties. *Sharon* (1948) deals with Hawaii in 1885 during the reign of King Kalakua when missionaries and gamblers and others were causing changes in the social and moral standards of the island people. Sharon, the beautiful daughter of an Irish sea captain and a Spanish mother, is the heroine. *Give Him My Love* (1949) is a novel set in London, Paris, and Rome after World War II. The theme is drawn from the Chinese proverb, "It is better to light one candle than to curse the darkness." The story concerns the brave, gay Mary Allistair, supposedly the widow of Brett Allistair, a brilliant and bitter man who was reported missing on an intelligence mission in France in 1942. Her problem is to build a rich and full life, following years of suspense and tragedy, after she finds that she has been cruelly disappointed.

WILLIAM MAIER

Murl Ogden

was born on November 3, 1901, in Schenectady, New York, the son of a Congregational minister, but has lived most of his life in New England. He attended public high schools and the Phillips Exeter Academy, and spent one year at Hamilton College and three at Princeton University, from which he graduated in 1924. After college he went into business and became vice-president and director of a manufacturing company. In 1930 he left business in order to write, and moved to his parents' home in an old house on Cape Cod. With the exception of one year of newspaper work and several shorter interruptions, he devoted the next ten years to writing short stories and magazine articles about wild life, conservation, and outdoor life. He went on active duty as an officer in the Marine Corps in 1942, and saw service in the Southwest Pacific; he was discharged as a major in the fall of 1945. He was married soon afterwards to Miss Helen Hamilton, whom he had met when they were on active duty. Since the war they have divided their time between Cape Cod and Carmel, California. Mr. Maier is now devoting full time to writing novels.

Mr. Maier believes that the novelist must work within the framework of his medium, that he must produce a structurally unified story, and that his major function is to broaden and deepen understanding and tolerance by revealing the true significance of misunderstood lives and attitudes and viewpoints. By a process of selection, organization, and unification, he tries to bring to light a fresh perception of the real meaning of the accepted and the ordinary.

Spring Flight (1943), his first novel, pictures life on Cape Cod as it is lived today by the poorer country people, without the romantic historical trappings of popular Cape Cod fiction. The confusing and frequently disastrous effect of summer residents and the wealthier all-year-round residents on the natives is depicted in the experiences of Debby, a girl who was brought up to a life of duck hunting, bird shooting, and fishing on an isolated farm. She rejects her natural heritage of love for knowledge of the outdoors in the search for a false sophistication.

Pleasure Island (1949) is a humorous satire on the manners and attitudes of American troops as seen through the eyes of a gentlemanly English planter on a Pacific island. Roger Halyard's bewildered effort to guard his daughters and to preserve the beauty and simplicity of the lives of his native tribesmen brings into satirical focus the absurdity of the souvenir-hunting, amorousness, inquisitiveness, and ebullience of American Marines. The theme concerns the meaning of war to civilians and soldiers.

NORMAN MAILER

John Popper

was born on January 31, 1923, in Long Branch, New Jersey. His boyhood was spent in Brooklyn, New York, from 1929 until his graduation in 1939 from Boys' High School. In his freshman year at Harvard College he made his first serious attempts to write; in his sophomore year he wrote about twenty short stories and a novel, and thus served a not indifferent apprenticeship. Shortly after his graduation in 1943 with a degree in engineering, he joined the army; before going overseas he married Beatrice Silverman. He was in the Philippines and Japan from 1944 to 1946. After his discharge in 1946 he wrote *The Naked and the Dead* in a year and a half. From October, 1947, to July, 1948, he lived in Paris and studied at the Sorbonne; he also made visits to England, Spain, Switzerland, and Italy. In the anthology *Cross Section* (1944) was published his short novel, "A Calculus at Heaven," which is about five men who are trapped by a Japanese platoon in the early days of the war; primarily it is the story of each up to the time he is killed. It contains in embryo many of the forms and themes which were later expanded into *The Naked and the Dead.*

Of his plans, he has said: "I have no concerted program. I would like to experiment and to grow, but I pursue this aim through no particular standards. Technique must always be secondary to the world one constructs in a novel. Writing does not occur in a vacuum; it moves people and affects them. These reactions, however, are so nebulous, so indiscernible, that to construct a book in terms of a message, of an effect upon people, is disastrous. Books may accompany social movements, but the relationship is always haphazard and unforeseen. I believe that any attempt to formulate social programs for writers is defeated in its conception."

The Naked and the Dead (1948) concerns the experiences of the thirteen men of a platoon in the 460th Infantry Regiment surviving the invasion of a Japanese-held island in the South Pacific. Very frank, nervous speech reveals their weariness and bitterness as they escape from the brink of disaster. Their talk is about the democratic process which has placed all types of men in the same undesirable situation far from their native land. They have grown skeptical and hold doubts concerning their loved ones at home. In the course of their duty on a reconnaissance patrol, they pass through a nightmare of experience as one after another is killed. The novel is written with a technique that is similar to that used by John Dos Passos in *U.S.A.*, but Mr. Mailer has imparted his own original touch to his presentation.

GEORGE MALCOLM-SMITH

was born on December 8, 1901, at Poultney, Vermont. He was educated in public and private schools in New England and at Trinity College in Hartford, Connecticut. He is assistant publicity manager of the Travelers Insurance Company at Hartford, and has many varied outside interests. They include American jazz music (he has conducted a radio program on the subject from radio station WTIC for more than six years); cartooning (he has contributed a weekly cartoon to *The Spectator* for almost twenty years); and the writing of articles, novels, and plays. He has written a number of children's stories, including the "Professor Peckam" series. His home is in Hartford, Connecticut.

Slightly Perfect (1941), his first novel, concerns an insurance actuary who commits an error in calculation and in humiliation disappears from his office. He becomes associated with a traveling carnival, in which his many talents win him the opportunity to become a successful showman. Ultimately, however, he returns to his beloved slide rule and statistical tables in the insurance office. The book was made into a musical comedy, "Are You with It?", which ran ten months on Broadway. *The Grass Is Always Greener* (1947) is the humorous story of a breezy West Coast newspaperman who, in a case of accidental "metapersonasis," exchanges bodies with a prosaic New England banker and attempts to live the latter's life as though nothing had happened.

ALBERT MALTZ

Bert Six

was born on October 8, 1908, in Brooklyn, New York, the son of a father who had migrated to this country from Lithuania. He attended public schools and then went on to take his bachelor's degree in 1930 at Columbia College. He graduated with honors in philosophy and as a member of Phi Beta Kappa. While at college he began to write plays and subsequently attended the Yale School of the Drama where he studied under George Pierce Baker. With George Sklar, a fellow student, he wrote "Merry-Go-Round," which was accepted for production on Broadway while they were still at Yale. The play, dealing with political corruption, opened in the Spring of 1932 in a New York that was already rocked by the famous Seabury investigation of the city's Tammany administration. It was immediately subjected to censorship attempts by the administration, but widespread public and newspaper protests brought about its reopening after a week's shutdown. "Peace on Earth" (with George Sklar, 1933) is an anti-war play, and "Black Pit" (1935) is a psychological study of an informer, set in the background of a mining community and played out against efforts at unionization.

In 1936 Mr. Maltz renounced the theater for fiction and began writing short stories. One of these, "The Happiest Man on Earth," won the O. Henry Memorial award in 1938. *The Way Things Are* (1938) contains short stories. Since 1941 Mr. Maltz has given part of his writing time to films; he collaborated on the screen play for "Destination Tokyo" (1943). He wrote "Pride of the Marines" (1945) and "The House I Live In" (1945); the latter, a short film, received an award for its contribution to racial tolerance.

Mr. Maltz's work as a whole is based upon a search for moral and social values in a world that, to him, is bitterly torn by personal, class, and national conflicts.

His first novel, *The Underground Stream* (1940), is a study of opposing moral and social principles as represented by two men, the personnel manager of an automobile plant and a communist industrial worker; the story is told in an atmosphere of violence in Detroit before the unions became dominant. *The Cross and the Arrow* (1944) is a study of character seen through the prism of Germany under the Nazis. It tells why Willi Wegler, a German drop-forge operator and holder of a war-service cross, shoots a lighted arrow into the sky to attract the attention of British bombers. *The Journey of Simon McKeever* (1949) is a tribute to the dignity and courage of the human spirit; the central character is an unconquerable old man of seventy-three who takes a strange and symbolic journey in search of a cure for his "arthureetis." He leaves the Thomas Finney Rest Home, where he has been a state-supported guest, to visit a famous woman physician in Los Angeles. Part of the journey is made by bus and by hitchhiking; an octogenarian couple take him to his destination and provide him with ambition, hope, and an outlook for the future.

JERRE MANGIONE

was born on March 20, 1909, in Rochester, New York, and for the first eighteen years of his life lived among his Sicilian-born relatives. He received his bachelor's degree from the University of Syracuse and after graduating joined the editorial staff of *Time* magazine. He later went to Washington to work for the Federal government as a writer and public-relations man; six of his ten years were devoted to the duties of special assistant to the United States Commissioner of Immigration and Naturalization. In this capacity Mr. Mangione also edited the Service's magazine. In 1947 he held a Guggenheim fellowship, which enabled him to spend several months in Sicily to gather material for *Island of My Fathers* (1950), a non-fiction account of the island after the war. He was book editor for the Robert M. McBride Company for three years. In April, 1948, he joined the copy department of N. W. Ayer & Son, an advertising agency. He is married and lives in Philadelphia.

Mount Allegro (1943), his first novel, embodies the author's recollections of his childhood in a Rochester neighborhood where most of his Sicilian-born relatives lived. The story of how these immigrant citizens try to fit themselves into the general American pattern is essentially the story of every minority group in this country. *The Ship and the Flame* (1948) is the story of the voyage of a ship and its passengers who are fleeing from the war. Each of the dozen or so passengers represents a different aspect of mankind's belief or despair in the face of uncertainty. It is a tense and exciting narrative as well as a political allegory.

WILLIAM MARCH

Mario Rosel

was born William Edward March Campbell at the northeast corner of Broad and Conti streets in Mobile, Alabama, on September 18, 1893, in a family with Scotch and English heritage. He lived in various small towns in the South until 1913, when he attended Valparaiso University in Indiana for one year. Later he studied law at the University of Alabama. He enlisted in the Marine Corps in 1917 and served overseas in World War I with distinction. Wounded and gassed, he was decorated with the Distinguished Service Cross, the Navy Cross, and the Croix de Guerre. On his return he worked for a steamship company in Mobile and rose to be traffic manager and vice-president. From 1932 to 1937 he lived and worked in Germany and England, and then until 1947 he resided in New York City. His home is now in Mobile. He began writing short stories in 1928; these are collected in *The Little Wife* (1935), *Some Like Them Short* (1939), and *Trial Balance* (1945).

Mr. March's writings belong to the school of fiction called naturalism, for he presents the harsh facts of life concerning the demoralization resulting from poverty, deceit, and oppression. His objective method emphasizes the presentation of many characters whose emotions are often projected into their environment of scenery and animals, so that these people possess unusual depths beneath their laconic exteriors. His originality of method is striking in portraying psychological responses through simple and natural speech.

Company K (1933), his first novel, portrays 113 members of a military unit by having each man tell his experiences in training camp, in active fighting, and back home again. From these sketches, some of which are shorter than a page, there emerges the rise and fall of emotional intensity as the soldiers react to events and personalities. It is a book about the men and not primarily about war. *Come In at the Door* (1934) reports the effect on a man of a childhood experience. As a small boy he had betrayed a Negro friend and had been present at the hanging. On his return to attend the funeral of his father, the man reviews his life in terms of the meaning of this dark stain on his subconscious mind.

The Tallons (1936), Mr. March's most original and possibly his best book, describes the love which Jim and Andrew Tallon, brothers in a poor Alabama family, have for Myrtle. She marries Jim because Andrew has a hare lip. Their love cools, and Jim threatens Andrew for betraying him. Andrew keeps off as long as he can and then kills his brother. The gallows and not Myrtle is his reward. *The Looking-Glass* (1943) is a psychoanalytic novel about an Alabaman who returns to the small town of Reddyville, which he had left because of a notion that he was part Negro. Now a physician, he is called upon to perform an abortion on the banker's daughter, a girl whose love had brought him back.

ELIZABETH MARION

Francis James

was born on January 31, 1916, on a farm in a neighborhood midway between the towns of Spangle and Fairfield, in southern Spokane County, Washington. Her mother's people were pioneers in Oregon and Washington; her father's family came west in style on the railroad before the turn of the century. Among them they provided her with half a dozen melting-pot racial strains. She is the oldest of seven children and was educated in one of the last of the one-room schools in the county. She attended Fairfield High School and graduated in 1933. In the next few years she learned the hard way to be a competent stenographer and a less efficient urban dweller; she was accidentally introduced to politics and to social work as practiced by WPA offices. The total of this fascinating and irrational knowledge seemed to her to be a proper burden to take back to the farm for consideration and possible future use. There, and more recently in the family's new home in Fairfield, she has been learning about writing and reading, music and cats, farms and small towns, and—always—people.

"I believe, with more passion than originality," she has stated, "that writers should and must have a profound respect for life, for their native tongue, and for the discipline of their craft, and that learning about these things can never be finished. They can be learned about anywhere and everywhere, including my own world which, I have been told by those who don't know, is no bigger or more eventful than Emily Dickinson's garden. What honest novelist could be ashamed to use a world less small than the one which a poet once made into a universe? A world, of whatever size or shape, shows its crowded wealth of life only to those who can, or will, look for it, and that wealth is the novelist's, to spend as he must. My own world is the shape and size of that part of the state which is called The Palouse, and I feel that in three books I have not begun to spend its wealth. All my work, past, present, and future, published, unpublished, and unwritten, is concerned with that same small world which has wealth enough for a hundred novelists."

Her first novel, *The Day Will Come* (1939), is a story of farm and family life, a variation on the silver-cord theme, and, says Miss Marion, "it is an exercise in unbridled lyricism, displaying my love of the English language and of native geography at the expense of the characters in the story." *Ellen Spring* (1941) is a study of marriage founded on corruption, using the same farm environment and a somewhat different handling of family-life background. It contains Miss Marion's first attempt to use her fondness for the abandoned old houses which still stand about everywhere in the region, like wry critics of an agricultural economy grown intensely mechanized and wildly financed. *The Keys to the House* (1944) was based on a rural murder, one incident taken from the vast storehouse of silent human drama which in rural communities seems always to be either discussed in practical understatement or put out of sight and out of speech by a kind of consent of the majority.

FRANCES MARION

was born on November 18, 1900, in San Francisco, California. She was educated at St. Margaret's Hall at San Mateo, the University of California at Berkeley, and the Sorbonne in Paris. During World War I she was a war correspondent. In private life she is the widow of Fred C. Thomson, the world's champion all-around athlete who became famous in the 1920's as a star in Western pictures. She is the mother of two sons. Frances Marion has written over three hundred scenarios for the screen, most of them original stories, and she prepared *How to Write and Sell Moving Picture Scenarios* (1937), a textbook. *Valley People* (1935) is a collection of short stories about a group of people in a northern California valley.

Minnie Flynn (1925), her first novel, is a story of an eighteen-year-old shop girl in New York who achieves her ambition to become a movie star under the expert guidance of Hal Deane, only to return to obscurity. *Molly, Bless Her* (1937) tells how the fifty-year-old Molly Drexel, a comedienne whose act is out of date, runs a home for indigent actors and then returns to the stage with great success. *Westward the Dream* (1948), the first volume of a trilogy, describes the building of a ranching empire in Southern California during the period from 1874 to 1914. John Markham takes his gently bred young wife over the mountains from Iowa and after her death stays on to build a new life for himself.

PERCY MARKS

was born on September 9, 1891, in Covelo, California. He received the degree of Bachelor of Literature from the University of California at Berkeley in 1912 and his master's degree from Harvard University in 1914. After terminating his formal education, he became supervisor of education at the State Infirmary in Tewksbury, Massachusetts. There followed a four-year period as instructor in English at the Massachusetts Institute of Technology; later he held teaching positions at Dartmouth College and Brown University. He stated his objections to the doctorate in *Which Way Parnassus?* (1926), and he never took that degree. Though Mr. Marks has devoted himself to the novel, he has never quite forgotten his connection with the teaching profession. *The Craft of Writing* (1932), *Better Themes* (1933), and *The College Writer* (1946) are textbooks for undergraduates.

His first novel, *The Plastic Age* (1924), is a realistic story of college life, describing sports, studies, sex, and other extracurricular activities in the years following World War I. *Martha* (1925) is a study of an Indian girl's struggle against her social environment, a struggle motivated by the knowledge that her father is a white man. *Lord of Himself* (1925) treats the theme of conflict with environment in another milieu; this time a rich young man masters the evil influences of an idle life. In *A Dead Man Dies* (1929) a pretty widow attempts to solace the loss of her first husband with two marriages; when she finally succeeds in finding a man who suits her, her children oppose the marriage. She fixes her true course in life only when the influence of her dead husband no longer controls her.

The Unwilling God (1929) pictures an intelligent college athlete who finally succumbs to the old school spirit in his senior year. *A Tree Grown Straight* (1936) is the story of a young man who happens to be in perfect equilibrium with life and describes his achievement of that balance. *And Points Beyond* (1937) is a character study of a young lawyer swayed by the conflicting desires of love, success, and humanitarianism. *What's Heaven For?* (1938) illustrates the theme that contentment demands an adjustment to earthly demands and individual capacities.

The Days Are Fled (1939) has a musician find happiness in recognizing his shortcomings as an artist; he compensates for his failure by attempting to teach others how to reach the heights. *No Steeper Wall* (1940) narrates the story of a young man who, after a disgraceful expulsion from Harvard, rehabilitates himself among the common folk of California. *Between Two Autumns* (1941) is the psychological study of a man who, although he has no bad intentions, creates evil through lack of understanding and imagination. *Full Flood* (1942) contains a psychological character analysis of a hunchback.

Knave of Diamonds (1943), in a departure from the norm of Mr. Marks' writings, is the story of a modern Robin Hood who turns jewel thief to supply the wants of the poor. *Shade of Sycamore* (1944) retails the wish of a young wife to leave her unfaithful husband in order to raise her son properly; after her husband is killed in the war, she discovers the inevitability of heredity. *Blair Marriman* (1949) is the study of a woman of great charm, both physical and mental, who can inspire love but not return it. In the end she suffers the tragedy of seeing herself clearly.

MELBA (GRIMES) MARLETT

was born on September 9, 1909, at Alliance, Ohio. On the distaff side her family consists of French and German people who have held strongly to their own cultures, making a knowledge of three languages advisable and lending a cosmopolitan flavor to family gatherings. Her mother was a musician and a teacher of harmony and composition; despite the fact that Melba learned to read at the age of three and showed a tremendous leaning toward books, the child was given fourteen years of the finest musical education available in piano, violin, and voice, with classical dancing and dramatics thrown in for good measure. When she was nineteen, she graduated from the University of Michigan, declared herself no musician, and began to write short stories which brought her encouraging letters from editors but remained unsold.

From 1930 to 1941 she taught English and dramatics at Mackenzie High School in Detroit, Michigan. She took her master's degree at Wayne University in 1939 and became a critic teacher before her resignation. In 1937 she married Norval W. Marlett, Jr.; they have one son. During her spare time in these years she continued writing, but it was not until she abandoned the short story for the novel form that she achieved publication. *Death Has A Thousand Doors* (1941) was brought out by the Crime Club and was followed by three other mysteries: *The Devil Builds a Chapel* (1942), *Another Day Toward Dying* (1943), and *Escape While I Can* (1944).

In 1947 Mrs. Marlett's life-long interest in the theater led her to write in collaboration with Schuyler Watts "The Garden Path," a three-act comedy; the capable protagonist is a handsome woman scientist and Nobel prize winner; she discovers that her very virtues make her an outcast from society. Mrs. Marlett followed this with a three-act play for a children's theater, "Runaway Clown," which won first prize in the Seattle Junior Play Contest for 1948.

More and more, Mrs. Marlett devotes herself to the careful delineation of character. Since weak people prove nothing, she prefers to picture the strong—good or bad, but potently so—for in the play of such characters against each other comes the conflict that makes a story, or life itself, interesting and revelatory.

Her first non-mystery novel, *Tomorrow Will Be Monday* (1946), deals with the problem of twentieth-century women who are held back by social conventions and yet see the door open to economic and personal freedom. General Franco promptly banned a proposed translation as containing ideas unsuitable for Spanish women. The story concerns three sisters who grow up with relatives after the mother dies. The oldest follows the pattern of becoming a perfect lady; the second makes a career for herself and marries happily; and the third, the prettiest, has a number of adventures in marriage. Mrs. Marlett presented the same premise in a novelette "In Name Only" (1947) in *The Woman's Home Companion;* the editor-in-chief reported that it brought one of the greatest barrages of mail ever to cross his desk; a subsequent reader-poll showed that the story had attracted more attention than anything the magazine had published in six years.

JACLAND MARMUR

was born in Sosnowiece, Poland, on February 14, 1901, and was brought to this country at the age of two by his parents, who settled in Brooklyn, New York. He was educated in the public schools of New York City and in 1918, after his graduation from Brooklyn Boys' High School, he left home for San Francisco with the intention of becoming a West Coast newspaperman. Instead, he shipped to sea. Following several voyages to Central American and Caribbean ports, he tramped across a large portion of Canada. After a brief time in New York he returned to the West Coast, where he worked in the northern California lumber camps, finally returning to the sea which he followed professionally for nine years. Much of Mr. Marmur's early work was actually written at sea, including his first book, *Ecola!* (1928). His first published work, a short story, "Copra," was written in a West Coast lumber port in long hand by the light of a kerosene bulkhead lamp. For several months during World War II he did special work for the Office of War Information; later he was at sea in various combat units of the Pacific fleet. *Sea Duty* (1944), a collection of stories of naval action in the Pacific, grew out of these experiences.

While the major portion of Mr. Marmur's work is set against the background of the sea, he does not at all consider himself a "sea writer." His interest is solely and constantly with people and the nature of man. His recurring theme is always the long, historical struggle—now once again, he thinks, in a cycle of steep retrogression—toward the freedom and the dignity and the integrity of the individual person.

Wind Driven (1932), his first novel, is a psychological story of Halvor Nettilson, a shipmaster in the latter days of sail, and the impact upon him and his daughter of a long, unfortunate voyage from Singapore to their final involvement in a South American revolution. *Three Went Armed* (1933) is an adventure novel in the romantic tradition and concerns itself with the human quest for the Ideal. The protagonists are an aristocratic Spaniard, a lusty sea pirate, and a priest.

The Sea and the Shore (1941) spans the decades between the two great wars, and its settings include the Brooklyn waterfront, the city of Buenos Aires, and the China coast on the morning the Japanese attacked the native quarter of the city of Shanghai. Its theme is the collapse in our time of all the old gods and the old integrities, and the search for some new and more valid ethic which shall once again sustain the race with honor.

Andromeda (1947) has its entire action on board a tramp steamer sailing from Singapore just ahead of the Japanese entry into the surrendered city. Outwardly the book is the story of her race for survival and her attempt to escape through Sunda Strait before the Japanese bottle up the passage. But the ship *Andromeda,* her two passengers (one of them an attractive woman), and her officers and crew serve as a microcosm of the world with human potential for good or for evil. Isolated from all ordinary communication, the ship becomes in fact a small world of her own, an earth afloat in space and time. And her population, under the strain and impact of constantly imminent destruction, plays out the theme of human choice between good and evil, slavery and freedom.

JOHN PHILLIPS MARQUAND

Dorothy Wilding

was born on November 10, 1893, in Wilmington, Delaware, of New England ancestry. His family had settled in Newburyport, a village thirty-two miles north of Boston, and it is in that Massachusetts community that Mr. Marquand now resides. His grandfather had done well in Wall Street, and the family had returned to the old home. In 1907 the financial depression took much of his father's inheritance, and the boy came to feel the pinch of hard times. With the help of friends and a scholarship he attended Harvard, where he helped edit *The Lampoon,* the undergraduate comic. A good student, he finished in three years, graduating in 1914. His major study had been chemistry, but he preferred to work with words, and so he took a place as a cub reporter on the Boston *Transcript.* When the National Guard was ordered to the Mexican border in 1916, he went off with Battery A. From that experience he proceeded immediately into World War I and saw action as a first lieutenant of artillery. Home from France, he took a reporter's job on the New York *Tribune,* and then shifted to the J. Walter Thompson agency. Finding no zest in preparing soap advertising, he tossed up his job and returned to Newburyport to write. His first fiction, an historical novel entitled *The Unspeakable Gentleman,* was purchased by *The Ladies' Home Journal.* His next went to *The Saturday Evening Post,* and thereafter for twenty years he received high prices for his stories; his name became synonymous with excellence in the periodical field. In 1921 he went to Europe, and met and married Christina Sedgwick, niece of the editor of *The Atlantic Monthly.* In 1937 he married Adelaide Ferry Hooker. There are two children by the first marriage and three by the second.

Among Mr. Marquand's earliest successes were a number of serial stories dealing with a Japanese secret agent named Mr. Moto; these achieved considerable popularity, and were so deftly woven that each tale seemed to lead directly into the next. The idea for his first serious novel, *The Late George Apley,* came at the moment when his success was greatest as a magazine writer. For the new book he drew upon the Boston life with which he was familiar; to the portrayal of the faded aristocrats whose meaning in life had eluded their grasp he brought the highest technical skill in developing setting, incident, conversation, and character. Since 1944 he has been a member of the panel of judges of the Book-of-the-Month Club.

Mr. Marquand's early work contains familiar romantic motifs. His first appearance in book form was in *Prince and Boatswain* (1915), a collection of sketches. *The Unspeakable Gentleman* (1922) is a novel about treason against Napoleon by a group of French plotters who have come to an American seaport. *Four of a Kind* (1923) contains four short stories. *The Black Cargo* (1925) pictures the heyday of traffic in spice and silks with the Orient in 1833 and New England shipowners' illegal traffic in slaves. *Warning Hill* (1930) is the story of a young man whose wastrel father has lost the family fortune. His love for a girl in a newly rich family wanes when she proves not up to his standard. *Haven's End* (1933) pictures two families, the aristocratic Scarlets and the ordinary Swales, from the time of King Philip's War to the present in the town of Haven's End in New England. *No Hero* (1935) is about an American flier who is stranded in Tokyo and accepts a job from Mr. Moto to find a secret formula in Manchoukuo. *Ming Yellow* (1935) pictures the sinister quality of interior China in an account of an American's visit to examine a collection of priceless porcelains. Bandits delay temporarily the success of the expedition.

Mr. Marquand's serious novels are concerned with the themes of the decay of families and the almost useless waste of human power in individuals who live according to the standards laid down by an earlier generation. In developing these themes he pictures with a fondness for detail the houses, furniture, art, social activities, and family relationships of Boston and New England. Environment, especially an environment of wealth, puts pressure upon individuals to make them conform. The Apleys and Charley Grays are not captains of their own fate, and the tragedy of their lives lies in their dim perception of a freedom lying beyond their reach. Calling Mr. Marquand the best satirist of our generation, James Hilton stated: "No writer can extract a wryer humor from the irritants of daily existence, or can play a wintrier sunlight over the destinies of his characters."

The Late George Apley (1937), which won the Pulitzer prize, is a novel in the form of a memoir or biography that seemingly is written to praise the subject; however, through its picture of a rich Boston family it actually serves as a satire upon the genteel age and the petrified social class in which Apley lived from 1870 to 1933. *Wickford Point* (1939) concerns the decadent Brill family which lives one hour north of Boston; these people have degenerated so that they have the power neither to act nor think. *H. M. Pulham, Esq.* (1941) is the memoir of a man's life as he writes it for the twenty-fifth reunion of his college class. The story makes it clear that his acts and his thoughts were shaped by the Boston environment in which he lived.

So Little Time (1943) builds up around the character of Jeffrey Wilson, a Broadway play doctor, a picture of the time from the autumn of 1940 to the end of 1941 when the Americans who had fought World War I to end all wars found themselves unable to stop the drift toward a new conflict. Wilson's technical skill lacks the true creative artist's ability, and his cleverness symbolizes the superficiality of his whole generation. *Repent in Haste* (1945) is the story of a war marriage that failed. *B. F.'s Daughter* (1946) concerns Polly Fulton, the daughter of Burton Fulton, a self-made industrial tycoon who dominates his daughter to such an extent that she in turn seeks to rule the men who enter her life. *Point of No Return* (1949) is the story of Charley Gray, who is midway in his career as a banker and whose wife prods him to seek a vice-presidency. He wonders whether intangible spiritual values are not of supreme importance, but concludes that he has passed the "point of no return" in his journey toward material success and high social position.

ELLEN MARSH

Larry Colwell

was born on February 19, 1922, in Coblenz, Germany, the daughter of an American officer of the Army of Occupation of World War I and a German girl, herself the daughter of a Rhenish mayor. Miss Marsh came to her father's country, specifically to New England, at the age of five months, and this began her intensive childhood of traveling back and forth across the Atlantic and of learning and unlearning languages, until at the age of nine she had mastered English, German, and French. She attended a large number of American and European schools, among them the Städtisches Lyzeum in Bonn and the École Internationale in Geneva, and spent many summers in her grandparents' home in the Rhineland. Her last visit to them ended during the war in 1940, when she managed to leave Germany via Italy before the frontiers were closed. Back in the United States, she went to college and, during her studies and the jobs that followed later, began planning her first novel, the central theme of which was the coming of National Socialism and its effect upon the Germans. She started writing it at twenty-one. She has published poetry and factual writings on the state of Nazi Germany.

Miss Marsh attributes her writing propensity to a state of mind inherited from her father, Fred T. Marsh, writer, critic, and editor. He started reading to her before she could walk, and she does not remember a time when it did not seem perfectly natural to write, beginning with a book she produced in the second grade at the expense of arithmetic lessons. This informality has persisted, and she writes, she thinks, more according to instinct than brain. She writes in order to write and not for any market—not from choice but out of an inability to do otherwise. The main thing, she believes, is to recognize the particular thing one can do and to do it with integrity. She found it easier to work in a fish cannery, on one occasion, than to earn a living by writing alone.

Drink to the Hunted (1945), her first novel, is the story of the German side of her family, taking them through the twenty years between world wars, with the rise of Nazism as a kaleidoscopic background for the inner life of a child torn between two cultures. The personal story of the child and her tempestuous mother and troubled grandparents runs its course against the bigger political and social story of Europe in those years, and the two are inextricably tied up. *Dull the Sharp Edge* (1947), less wide of scope and interior in its approach, describes the growth to womanhood and maturity of a young girl in America during the World War II, and the resolution of her conflicts.

EDISON MARSHALL

Jack Wood

was born on August 28, 1894, in Indiana, but much of his boyhood was spent in Oregon, where he attended the state university. During World War I he served as a lieutenant in the army; upon his return he married a southern girl, and for several years made his home in Medford, Oregon, eventually moving to Georgia. From 1920, when he wrote his first novel, until 1938 he was primarily a writer of magazine stories; with the exception of *Dian of the Lost Land* and one or two of the early novels, his books were typical short serials. In 1939 he began to write *Benjamin Blake,* which in length and structure is a real novel. Exclusive of his big-game memoirs, *Shikar and Safari* (1946), all his books since that time have been full-length novels. The flavor of authenticity in his adventure stories is the product of his hunting experiences in such places as Alaska, Africa, India, Burma, Indo-China, and China. His volumes of short stories include *The Heart of Little Shikara* (1922) and *Love Stories of India* (1950).

Mr. Marshall's stories of adventure are rich in accurate nature descriptions and the lore of wild animals. His tales are of the breathless, thriller type, and usually are set in places distant from civilization, in "the land of forgotten men."

The Voice of the Pack (1920) narrates the adventures of Dan Failing, who recovers from tuberculosis in the Oregon woods. *The Strength of the Pines* (1921) pictures the feud of two families in a remote part of the Oregon mountains; the climax is a fight with a bear in a raging blizzard. *The Snowshoe Trail* (1921) depicts the rescue of a man lost in the north woods; his sweetheart and a guide cross an icy torrent to save him. *Shepherds of the Wild* (1922) is a tale of a weak, country-club boy who turns into a strong, contented man of the open air while tending sheep in Colorado.

The Skyline of Spruce (1922) concerns the change of Ben Darby from a convict to a man of the open spaces in the north country. *The Isle of Retribution* (1923) takes a coddled and spoiled wealthy Seattle son of a fur merchant on a perilous trip to the Far North, where he realizes the importance of self-control. *The Land of Forgotten Men* (1923) portrays the flight of a southerner, Peter Newhall, to Alaska, where he is stranded when his vessel is blown to sea. *Seward's Folly* (1924) turns on the alleged refusal of the Secretary of State in 1867 to permit the purchase of Alaska from Russia and shows the strategic importance of the territory to the United States. *Ocean Gold* (1925) is about four boys' search for treasure hidden along the Alaska coast.

The Sleeper of the Moonlit Ranges (1925) has Breed Bert and an Alaskan guide in conflict for the love of Grace Crowell. *Child of the Wild* (1926) describes the shipwreck of a vessel on an uncharted reef on the coast of Alaska and the experiences of a seven-year-old boy who survives and grows up to be a game warden. *The Deadfall* (1927) shows an Alaskan woodsman overcoming great handicaps. *The Far Call* (1929) has Pal Loring set out with a group of men on a seal-hunting expedition to St. Paul, one of the Pribiloff Islands. *The Fish Hawk* (1929) pictures Soviet Russia as a "red terror" ready to use the Aleutian Islands for military bases against the United States. *The Missionary* (1930) concerns the trip of a preacher's son to right the injustice done by his father to a half-breed son in Alaska.

Forlorn Island (1932) describes the treachery of a gorilla-like mate on a yacht which is wrecked on an island in the Bering Sea. *The Deputy at Snow Mountain* (1932) concerns the rehabilitation of a man wrongly accused of murder; a judge's daughter has faith in him. *The Light in the Jungle* (1935) is about an American gambler, David Steele, who goes to the jungle in French Indo-China to avenge the murder of his father and to find a fortune in jade long hidden in a ruined temple. *Ogden's Story* (1934) describes the crash of a rich man's airplane on an Alaskan mountain top; he loses his memory and for several months lives like a primitive man among Indians who protect him.

Dian of the Lost Land (1935) concerns an American physician and a Slavic anthropologist who find in Antarctica a tribe of blond giants, the descendants of the Cro-Magnon race, in conflict with a generation of the Neanderthals. *The Stolen God* (1936) describes the hunt in Indo-China for a stolen jeweled Buddha. *Darzee, Girl of India* (1937) is about the adventurous hunt for a spy, Drummond, by an American civil engineer and a native dancer, Darzee, in India. *The White Brigand* (1937) is set in a remote province of western China, where the emperor desires to gain possession of a fabulous mine of jade. An American geologist and his niece assist the ruler, and the girl has a romance with the emperor's foster son, who turns out to be a missionary's child. *The Jewel of Mahaba* (1938) tells of four young men searching for a hidden treasure in India.

At this point in his career Mr. Marshall began to write historical novels. *Benjamin Blake* (1941), a Literary Guild selection, concerns an eighteenth-century, hot-blooded English boy of illegitimate birth who overcomes many obstacles, including an uncle's ill will, to become rich after adventures in the South Pacific. *Great Smith* (1943) is the fictionalized story of Captain John Smith from the age of seventeen, through a series of glittering adventures and love affairs, to the time he set sail for the New World and, finally, to the moment he is saved by Pocahontas and the Virginia Colony is spared from Powhatan's tomahawk.

The Upstart (1947) details the adventures of Jason Starbuck, beginning in Salem in 1795, after he has killed three Indians who murdered his parents. He loves Roxana, a refugee from the French Revolution, joins the Barbary pirates, and becomes a Moslem. *Castle in the Swamp* (1948) is a mystery story set in a sinister plantation swamp in South Carolina in pre-Civil War days. *Gypsy Sixpence* (1949) is about a British lieutenant betrayed to the Emir in northwest India in 1845. *The Infinite Woman* (1950) is the turbulent story of the life of Lola Montero, defiant child and beautiful woman, exotic dancer and mistress of a king. The action sweeps from England across all Europe to India. The events parallel those in the career of Lola Montez, the Irish-born actress who died in 1861.

ROSAMOND MARSHALL

was born on October 17, 1900, in New York City, the daughter of Charles Hull and Florence Hudson Botsford. She attended schools in the United States until she became twelve, when she was taken to Europe and was entered in the Lycée de Jeunes Filles in Dijon, France. Private tutors continued her English-language education at home. She attended high school in Vienna and matriculated at the University of Munich, where she studied languages, history, philology, and literature. During her student years she became interested in mountaineering and holds an unbroken record of opening twenty-two new routes with amateur guides in the Swiss, French, and Italian Alps. She has also climbed in the Polish Tatra. In 1950 she lived on Vancouver Island.

She began to "write" at the age of three when her first poem appeared in the New York *World*. Stories, playlets, poems, and a "western" novel were followed by her first historical novel in a setting of the French Revolution, written at the age of fourteen. She also wrote many popular novels in French which were published in France, and she acted as special correspondent for Italian, German, and French newspapers. Her first published novel in the English language, *None But the Brave* (1942), for young people, won the New York *Herald-Tribune* Spring book award; it is the story of the Netherlands' revolt against Spain.

Her first major novel, *Kitty* (1943), tells the story of a child of the London slums who becomes a great lady. *Duchess Hotspur* (1945) is the romance of an eighteenth-century duchess and an aspiring young Fleet Street journalist. *The Treasure of Shafto* (1946), also for young people, retails the adventures of an English and a Russian lad in their attempt to escape from a Prussian military academy in the eighteenth century. *Celeste* (1949) is a romantic novel in the setting of Southern California in 1905 and recounts the story of the love of a young girl of unconventional background for a millionaire oil promoter. *Laird's Choice* (1950) has its setting in nineteenth-century Scotland.

GEORGE VICTOR MARTIN

G. Nelidoff

was born in Chicago, Illinois, on December 16, 1900. In the course of an active and varied life he has been a housepainter, shipping clerk, printer, stevedore, and advertising manager. As an amateur boxer in and about his native city, he rolled up a string of eighteen successive knockouts in the ring. He studied music for concert appearance and also played the piano professionally at night clubs and cafés from Chicago to Miami Beach. Later, for two years, he was on the editorial staff of *Compton's Pictured Encyclopedia.*

An interesting fact in the career of Mr. Martin is that his formal education extended through only six months of high school, when he failed in English "because I stuttered so badly I couldn't stand up and parse a verb"; now he speaks before university faculty groups and over the radio. The speech defect was directly responsible for his various occupations; since oral expression was denied him, he could work only with his hands. He considers his ability and desire to write also attributable to this early repression.

His first novel, *Our Vines Have Tender Grapes* (1940), pictures the wholesome life of the Norwegian family of the Jacobsons on a fine Wisconsin farm in the 1920's. The governor of Wisconsin issued an official proclamation making this book required reading for all 4-H Club members and teachers in that state. *The Bells of St. Mary's* (1946) is a novelization of the motion picture which featured Bing Crosby and Ingrid Bergman. *Mark It with a Stone* (1947) is the first-person story of Joe Starck, an orphan who has been discharged from the army as a psychoneurotic. He settles on a Montana ranch near his dead buddy's parents, who take the place of the family he never had. A sister of his wife is bent on having him and causes tragedy.

F. VAN WYCK MASON

Conrad Eiger

was born on November 11, 1901, in Boston, Massachusetts, the descendant of a family which came to this country in 1623 and has had participants in all its various wars. He spent much of his boyhood in European capitals, living with his grandfather who was an American consul at various times in both Paris and Berlin. Mr. Mason participated in World War I at the age of sixteen as an ambulance driver in the Verdun area, ending the war as a second lieutenant of interpreters. On his return to civilian life he studied at the Berkshire School in Sheffield, Massachusetts, from 1919 to 1920, and then went on to Harvard where he received his degree in 1924. He entered business, founded and operated his own importing firm of Van Wyck Mason and Company, and in 1929 began his writing career. On vacations he traveled widely throughout the world and engaged in big-game hunting. At home he has engaged in many community activities, including active service in the National Guard. During World War II he served overseas with SHAEF as an historical officer; he rose from the rank of major to that of full colonel. His wartime decorations include the French Legion of Honor, the Croix de Guerre with palm, and three battle stars. He lives with his wife and two sons in the Green Spring Valley near Baltimore, Maryland.

Mr. Mason's first book was a mystery story, *Seeds of Murder* (1930). Since then he has published sixteen volumes about the central character of Major Hugh North of the United States army intelligence service. Almost without exception laid against foreign backgrounds, these stories are of international flavor and generally predict events of global importance.

His serious novels are based upon historical themes. The basic incidents are striking moments of major significance which have not received adequate attention hitherto from historians. The characters are drawn to conform to both biographical and historical fact, although a few of the personages are invented. There is a good deal of turbulence, of rough-and-tumble action, of military maneuver, of precise description of details of food, lodging, travel, weapons, and dress, and of the day-to-day duties of sea captains, buccaneers, soldiers, sailors, physicians, tavern keepers, and others.

"I have written," he has said, "both the historical books and the 'North' series with the intention of informing as well as entertaining people. The historical books are designed to remedy the deplorable lack of imagination with which history is taught in most of our schools. The 'North' books are intended to keep reminding the public that security is obtainable only at the price of eternal vigilance."

Captain Nemesis (1931) is about Nathan Andrews, a Carolinian who served in the British navy until he was court-martialed in 1772. With undying hatred in his heart against this injustice, which was occasioned by his colonial origin, he turned a band of convicts into a pirate-hunting crew until 1776. *Three Harbours* (1938), the first of a series of four novels covering the American Revolution as seen through the eyes of the maritime people of the colonies, is set in 1774–75 and tells of Rob Ashton, a young Virginia shipping merchant, struggling to recoup the family fortune. The action shifts from Norfolk to Bunker Hill and then to Bermuda. *Stars on the Sea* (1940) portrays the colonists as defying British authority in 1776–77 and shows the rise of the navy in privateering activity in Rhode Island, Charleston, and the Bahamas. The new flag with thirteen stars and thirteen stripes is flaunted in the face of the foe. *Hang My Wreath* (1941), published under the pseudonym of "Ward Weaver," is an historical romance of the Civil War just before the Battle of Antietam. Captain Hubert Cary proves his love for an English lady.

Rivers of Glory (1942) portrays the early growth and glory of American armed might in the years 1778 and 1779, in the period following the evacuation of Boston and ending with the siege of Savannah. *Eagle in the Sky* (1948) is the tale of the events in 1780 and 1781 leading to Cornwallis' surrender at Yorktown and of three young doctors in Boston, their careers, their love-making, and their adventures on land and sea. *Cutlass Empire* (1949) is based on the career of Sir Henry Morgan, the half-demon, half-genius seventeenth-century buccaneer whose first exploit was the seizure of a small ship from the Spaniards and whose last adventure was the looting and sacking of a Spanish city in America.

WILLIAM MAXWELL

Consuelo Kanaya

was born on August 16, 1908, in Lincoln, Illinois. He finished high school in Chicago and in 1930 graduated from the University of Illinois, at the same time winning a scholarship offered by the Harvard Club of Chicago. After receiving his master's degree at Harvard, he returned to the University of Illinois, where for the next two years he taught freshman composition, tutored an entire fraternity house, and did further graduate work in medieval French and English literature. In 1933 he gave up teaching in order to write novels, and wandered from pillar to post: from a beautiful old farm in Wisconsin to the railroad Y.M.C.A. in New York; to the West Indies; to the MacDowell Colony at Peterborough, New Hampshire; to Urbana, Illinois; and back to the Wisconsin farm. For ten years he was an editor of *The New Yorker*. He was married in 1945 to Emily Gilman Noyes, and they now live in Yorktown Heights, New York.

"Each of my novels," Mr. Maxwell has said, "is an indication of how the world appeared to me at the time I wrote. They are modest in subject matter, and I have hoped, through style, humor, and ideas of order and disorder, that it might be possible to arrive at some degree of universality." His novels possess a quiet realism of time and place, so that his scenes come alive and remain naturally vibrant. His incidents of everyday life—housework, dinner parties, gossips, unexpected guests, noisy children—are described in a prose that is rich in poetic phrases.

Bright Center of Heaven (1934), his first novel, is concerned with a day in the lives of the family and paying guests on a Wisconsin farm, and with the serio-comic social catastrophe that occurs when a Negro lecturer, a friend of the hostess, comes for a visit. *They Came Like Swallows* (1937) is a story of a woman who, by her presence and warmth, holds a group of conflicting personalities together until she dies in the influenza epidemic of 1918 and leaves them faced with the problem of how to manage, each for himself, without her. *The Folded Leaf* (1945) is a psychological study of two boys, one studious and one athletic, who are drawn together, at a time when neither one is happy, by the mutual and disastrous attraction of gentleness and violence. *The Heavenly Tenants* (1946), a story for children, tells how the archer, the water carrier, and other signs of the Zodiac come down to earth to look after a farm during the absence of its owners. *Time Will Darken It* (1948) concerns a morally ambitious man who very nearly destroys his marriage and himself by his effort to live up to the abnormally high standard he has set for himself. The background is a small town in Illinois in 1912. Austin King, a lawyer, invites foster relatives from Mississippi to visit his home. Martha, his wife, objects and then grows bitter when the family comes and the youthful Nora falls in love with Austin.

ELEANOR R. MAYO

was born on December 27, 1920, in Everett, Massachusetts. She spent her early childhood in Southwest Harbor, Maine. After graduating from the local high school, she studied at a commercial school in Boston, and her first job was with a Maine boat yard. While attending the University of California at Berkeley she helped manage a small ranch in the Reliez Valley. She moved to New York and worked for a printing house, the British Purchasing Commission, and *The Reader's Digest*. In 1946 she left New York and settled in Maine on Bass Harbor.

She has stated: "I would like to discard the words 'regional novel'—particularly when the novel concerns Maine. Fiction writers have ridden the Maine mare pretty thoroughly in the last few years. Local color and salty old characters have been handled with gusto. Maine is more than that—it's a place where a man has to work hard for a living and a lot of people live in small houses, too."

Turn Home (1945), her first novel, portrays the homecoming of a former bad boy in his small Maine town after fighting in Guadalcanal in World War II. He makes a place for himself through his own merits and not on his war record. *Loom of the Land* (1946) deals with Russ Walls' domination of his children and their eventual rebellion. Gene defies his father and suffers vengeance; Jake turns to drink and suicide; Mary is a frustrated painter; and Stanny wins his father's affection and gets what he wants. The mother tries to keep all in harmony.

JAY McCORMICK

F. Peter Weil

was born October 1, 1919, in Harbor Beach, Michigan, but grew up and attended public schools in Detroit, home port of the Great Lakes freighter of which his father is captain. Jay spent much of his youth on the lakes. At the University of Michigan, from which he graduated in 1942, he received Hopwood awards for creative writing in 1938, 1940, 1941, and 1942. He was editor-in-chief of *Perspectives,* undergraduate literary magazine, and senior editor of *The Michigan Daily,* the campus newspaper. During most of 1943 Mr. McCormick was a reporter on the staff of the Detroit *News.* He married Elizabeth McNeill and they are the parents of twin girls. In 1944 he began teaching creative writing at Wayne University in Detroit.

November Storm (1943), his first novel, deals with the growth of a sensitive boy who works as a deckhand aboard a Great Lakes freighter after the death of his parents in an accident, and with the related stories of several older men, most of them also members of the freighter's crew. The story reaches its climax during a violent storm which wrecks the ship. *Nightshade* (1948) is set mostly in a small midwestern town, and deals with the moral and psychological problems of two young men: one who tries to fight off a frustrating domination by his grandmother, and the other, his friend, who finds himself compelled to make a choice between two women exerting strong and conflicting influences upon his life.

HORACE McCOY

Patricia O'Meara Robbins

was born on April 14, 1897, in Pegram, Tennessee, and was educated in Nashville. He served in the air force in World War I, and from 1919 to 1930 was sports editor of the Dallas, Texas, *Journal.* He was one of the founders of the celebrated Dallas Little Theatre. During these years, in which he made periodic pilgrimages to Paris, he became acquainted with F. Scott Fitzgerald and other expatriates associated with *transition* magazine, and he began writing short stories, some of which attracted the attention of Edward J. O'Brien and other anthology editors. All these short stories were printed in obscure and "literary" magazines because of their realistic and experimental content. He went to Hollywood in 1931 as a screenwriter, and it was here that he wrote *They Shoot Horses, Don't They?* and *No Pockets in a Shroud,* which resulted in his establishment on the continent as one of the pioneers of the Existentialist school. All Mr. McCoy's novels have as their chief subjects anarchy, violence, sex, and frustration.

They Shoot Horses, Don't They? (1935), his first novel which has become a minor American classic, is the story of a young man whose goodness is destroyed by a partner in a marathon dance. He kills her. He tells his story while awaiting execution. *No Pockets in a Shroud* (1937) pictures a small-city newspaperman's crusade against crime, corruption, and the Ku Klux Klan and the trouble he suffers from the town's important people. *I Should Have Stayed Home* (1938) is a realistic exposé of Hollywood's lower levels in a tale of two decent, poor youngsters working as extras. *Kiss Tomorrow Good-Bye* (1948) is the story of a Phi Beta Kappa scholar who succeeds in turning himself into a vicious and completely unmoral criminal—a man whose contempt for law, order, and human life drives him relentlessly into a career of unrelieved evil. It is a story, punctuated here and there with brutal sexuality, of a ruthless drive for power guided by a mind of strange and terrifying dexterity.

CARSON SMITH McCULLERS

Louise Dahl Wolfe

was born on February 11, 1917, in Columbus, Georgia. During her years in Columbus High School she wrote stories and plays and at the age of eighteen became seriously interested in literary composition, although music vied with writing as her choice of career. In 1935 she went to New York to study at Columbia University and at the Juilliard School of Music. She had the misfortune to lose her tuition money on the subway and soon was working her way through school. On September 20, 1937, she married Reeves McCullers. In 1940 *Story* magazine bought one of her stories, and, thus encouraged, she settled down to a career of writing. In 1943 she received a literary award from the American Academy of Arts and Letters. In 1942 and in 1946 she was awarded Guggenheim fellowships. In 1946 she sailed for Europe and for a year lived in Paris, where she rediscovered in their setting those French writers who have left their imprint on her own sensibility: Baudelaire, Rimbaud, and Stendhal. She lives in Nyack, New York.

The Heart Is a Lonely Hunter (1940), her first novel, is a study of John Singer, a deaf-mute who has lost his only friend, another mute. Since he can only listen and not talk, he becomes the confidant of several people in the southern town in which he lives. *Reflections in a Golden Eye* (1941) is the story of a murder and its implications in a southern army camp in peacetime. Louis Untermeyer has said of this novel: "The story proceeds from some inner compulsion which is as unplanned and as inevitable as life itself. It is a story which flows in every paragraph, flows with strange and sinister twists and sudden humorous flashes, but flows always to its certain and incalculable end. . . . It is one of the compelling, one of the most uncanny stories ever written in America."

The Member of the Wedding (1946), a study of child psychology, has the theme of identity and the will to belong. A lonely, motherless, twelve-year-old Georgia girl, Frankie, has the obsessive notion that, when her brother marries, she will be incorporated into the marriage and will go off into the world with him and his wife. Frankie illustrates the universal desire of children for an answer to the questions, "Who am I? Where do I belong? Where can I belong?" The excitement of the wedding is pictured through her reactions, with her six-year-old cousin and the Negro cook as chorus. Mrs. McCullers' dramatic version of this novel was produced in New York in January, 1950.

WILLIAM McFEE

Pirie MacDonald

was born on June 15, 1881, on the sailing ship *Erin's Isle* of Belfast, Ireland. This vessel was built in his father's shipyard at Courtney Bay, St. John, New Brunswick, Canada; it was designed as a semi-clipper with a displacement of sixteen hundred tons. After William's birth, his father retired in London as what is called an "overlooker," or marine superintendent of sailing ships. He died when William was seven. William attended public schools in London until he was thirteen, and then went to what is now Culford School in Suffolk, England. Later he was a pupil apprentice.

His first position was as a draftsman and salesman in a London engineering firm. In 1906 he was employed by his uncle, the marine superintendent of another shipping firm, and sailed on its tramp steamers until 1911. In his bunk on the first of these vessels, the *Rotherfield,* Mr. McFee wrote *Let-*

ters from an Ocean Tramp (1908). The three other tramp steamers on which he sailed were the *Framfield,* the *Burrsfield,* and the *Fernfield,* all named after Sussex villages; he was chief engineer of the *Fernfield* until he left for the United States. Leaving ship at Wilmington, North Carolina, he took a train to Nutley, New Jersey, where he completed *Casuals of the Sea* and offered it to publishers without success. He then wrote the first version of *Aliens* in a month; that book, too, failed to find a publisher. He wrote another book, *The Scrap Log of a Privateer,* but after its rejection he withdrew it, and it has never been published. As he could not sell his books, he got a job with the United Fruit Company, which sent him to New Orleans, where he remained until 1914.

When World War I started in 1914, he returned to Liverpool, England, for service on transports; he was commissioned a sub-lieutenant in the Royal Naval Reserve. He became an engineer on a liner which had been converted to an aircraft carrier, and joined her in Port Said. She was one of the first vessels to carry planes. Later he was engineer-lieutenant, chief of one of the first naval fuel-oil carriers. He left this ship in Smyrna and returned to England, where he was demobilized. In 1919 he returned to this country and served United Fruit as chief engineer of various ships. In 1922 he came ashore "on leave of absence" to see if he could earn a living with his pen. In 1949 he was still on leave of absence, but apparently his success as a novelist had led the company to suggest in that year that he turn in his resignation! He settled in Connecticut, where he still lives. He became a citizen of the United States in 1925. In 1926 he wrote *The Life of Sir Frobisher,* the Elizabethan seaman, for Harper's "Golden Hind" series. *Sailors of Fortune* (1929) contains short stories. *In the First Watch* (1946) is an autobiography covering his years at sea.

"I have always resented the title of sea writer," says Mr. McFee. "I am a writer. It so happened that my family were seafaring, and it was as easy for me to go to sea as for Kipling to go to India. I doubt whether those who go to sea now would derive the satisfaction I got from tramp steamers. There is no longer any 'sea life' in the old sense. Radio killed it, and trade unions have exterminated the seaman, one of the few individualists who escaped the industrial revolution of the nineteenth century."

The major interest in his writings is not incident or adventure but character and his philosophical commentaries upon life and human conduct. Most of his stories are told ostensibly by Chief Engineer Spenlove, a man who translates the moods of people into literary experience. Spenlove is a raconteur whose chief interest is in the behavior of his contemporaries. A retiring and modest man, he meets in his voyaging many unusual men and women whose life histories attract his attention and cause him to meditate on the effect of love and other inner compulsions.

Casuals of the Sea (1916) depicts the life of the poor Gooderich family in a North London suburb who drift apart: Bert dies as a soldier; Minnie is an unrepentant Magdalen; and Hannibal, a dreamer, goes to sea. *Captain Macedoine's Daughter* (1920) contrasts eastern and western philosophies in an account of a rascal whose actions cause the death of his daughter. The setting is in the Aegean Sea. *Command* (1922) portrays a sailor's bravery at Saloniki when a submarine torpedoes a freighter in World War I. *Race* (1924) is about a young Frenchman, Louis Chaillu, who learns the ambitions of the seven Heath daughters when he comes to live with the family in London.

Pilgrims of Adversity (1928) describes the events which occur to the officers and men of the *Candleshoe,* a tramp steamer plying between Scotland and Central America. Their participation in a revolution determines their destinies. *The Harbourmaster* (1931) is the story of a man who made the mistake of living on land when he should have been at sea and who commits suicide. *No Castle in Spain* (1933) is about a New

York girl with modern ideas who falls in love with a member of the nobility in Colombo and finds life with his feudal family unbearable. *The Beachcomber* (1935) concerns Captain Neville, who can handle a ship under all circumstances, but who is helpless in the presence of women.

Derelicts (1938) tells the strange story of Captain Remson, who disappears in the Guiana jungle, a man whose upbringing in class-conscious, upper-level English society is his undoing. He deserts his wife and finally settles down on a hacienda in Central America. *Spenlove in Arcady* (1941) tells of the engineer's retirement at the age of fifty-eight in a home in the Connecticut hills, where he meets a writer's wife and young daughter, Perdita, and becomes interested in them. *Ship to Shore* (1944) takes Rosita Ross on a luxury cruise to forget her sweetheart's decision to marry his employer's daughter. She falls in love with the ship's captain. There is an excellent description of a fire at sea. *Family Trouble* (1949), with Spenlove now living in England with his new family, tells the story of a former shipmate, Jack Bannister, who rescues and then marries Roxane, and who has other disastrous love affairs.

RUTH ELEANOR McKEE

was born in Bardsdale, California, on August 6, 1903. After teaching in the Utah Street School in Los Angeles from 1923 to 1924, she completed her college program at the University of California at Los Angeles in 1926. From 1928 to 1936 she was a librarian in Honolulu, and in 1934 she received the Commonwealth Club of California's gold medal for creative work in literature. From 1942 to 1946 she was librarian for the War Relocation Authority in Washington, D.C., and since October, 1947, she has been in the signal section of the army's historical division. In 1927 she married Darr H. Alkire, from whom she is divorced. They have one son. Her non-fiction books include *California and Her Less Favored Minorities* (1944) and *Wartime Handling of Evacuee Property and Wartime Exile* (1946).

The Lord's Anointed (1934), her first novel, chronicles the history of New England missionaries in Hawaii from 1820 to 1900 in the story of Constancy Williams, the wife of a preacher, who helped the natives to become interested in the religion and politics of the mainland. She endures a life of hardship because her love overcomes the feelings of revulsion against her husband's ideas. *After a Hundred Years* (1935), a sequel, portrays Hawaii from 1920 to 1934 as seen through the eyes of Hale Carrington, Constancy's great-grandson, whose marital troubles with his satirically-minded wife form the narrative thread. He is a romantic writer who finds pleasure in the green island and its primitive people.

Under One Roof (1936) pictures on a Thanksgiving Day the history of each member of the McKelvey family of four daughters and three sons. The father, a tyrant with high blood pressure, serves to unite the family because of his heart attack. *Three Sisters* (with Alice Fleenor Sturgis, 1938) deals with women's war efforts in 1917 when a Pennsylvania manufacturer's daughters go to France. Elizabeth enters a hospital; Camilla works for the Red Cross; and Candy is a telephone operator with the Signal Corps near the front.

Christopher Strange (1941) takes in 1854 a dynamic, idealistic lawyer from Harvard to California, where he participates in almost every notable historical event until 1901. He introduces the culture of the East into the West, for he knows Emerson, Thoreau, and other famous men. *Storm Point* (1942) concerns Sheila Storm, the only child of a crippled mother and of an irritable, drunken father. The mother wants Sheila to be a dancer; the father urges her to be a pianist.

ROBERT McLAUGHLIN

was born in 1908 in Chicago, Illinois. After one year at the University of Illinois and two at the University of Colorado, he joined the staff of the *Rocky Mountain News.* Shortly thereafter he began free-lance writing and sold his first story to *Esquire* in 1930. Since that time he has had his short stories and articles published in many magazines. He was on the staff of *Time* and has been managing editor of *McCall's.* During World War II he served as a lieutenant and edited the *Chemical Warfare Bulletin* in Baltimore. Since 1947 he has been an editor of *Time* magazine. With his wife he wrote "Gayden" (1949), a play which starred Fay Bainter. Although he is working steadily on the writing of novels, the theater holds a compelling interest for him. *A Short Wait Between Trains* (1945) is a collection of eighteen short stories about army life and civilians in wartime.

His first novel, *The Axe Fell* (1939), deals with Beatrice Cenci, the daughter of a cruel and vicious father, whom she conspired to murder. She was executed for that crime in 1599. *The Side of the Angels* (1947) is a study of the entrapment of two brothers by forces they are unable to control. Each brother adopts a compromise belief; one follows the teachings of the non-communist Left, the other those of the not-quite-fascist Right; but both fail to achieve the goal they seek.

CLARK McMEEKIN

is the pseudonym under which Dorothy Park Clark and Isabel McLennan McMeekin write in collaboration. Each also writes under her own name.

Mrs. Clark was born on September 14, 1899, in Osceola, Iowa, the daughter of William and Eugenia Dowden Park. She attended Randolph-Macon Woman's College at Lynchburg, Virginia, and Columbia University. She is the wife of Edward Reep Clark, whom she married on September 1, 1923; they have two children and live in Louisville, Kentucky. She has written two mystery novels: *Roll Jordan Roll* (1947) with a saddle-horse stock farm in the Kentucky bluegrass country as a background, and *Poison Speaks Softly* (1947) with a racing-stable stock farm in the same region for a locale. Mrs. Clark has also written children's operettas and puppet plays. She has a deep interest in the children's theater.

Mrs. McMeekin was born on November 19, 1895, in Louisville, Kentucky. She was educated in private schools and graduated from the Westover School at Middlebury, Connecticut, in 1914. She attended the University of Chicago from 1915 to 1916. She is the wife of Samuel H. McMeekin and the mother of three children. Her home is in Louisville, Kentucky, and she has written its history in *Louisville, The Gateway City* (1946). Her novels for children include *Journey Cake* (1942), which won the Julia Ellsworth Ford prize award, and *Juba's New Moon* (1944). These books have their setting in Kentucky in pioneer days. *Kentucky Derby Winner* (1949), a Junior Literary Guild selection, is a factual and romantic recreation of the first Kentucky Derby of 1875. She has also written children's plays, poems, and a non-fiction book, *First Book of Horses* (1949).

The following novels were written by

"Clark McMeekin." *Show Me a Land* (1940) pictures the romantic life of Dana Terraine from the time of the Aintree Fair in England in 1816 to the first Kentucky Derby in 1875. *Reckon with the River* (1941) is an historical novel of 1805. Ma'am Cambrun, aged eighty, sets out from Redstone on the Monongahela River to find a treasure island on the Ohio. Her dauntlessness derives from her childhood captivity among the Indians. *Welcome Soldier* (1942) provides contrasting pictures of a rich Louisville girl in 1918 and 1942 as she appears at Camp Taylor, where in World War I she met a man whose love she pretends to have gained. *Red Raskall* (1943) is about a girl shipwrecked on the Virginia coast in 1816; she finds happiness with the aid of a stallion, Red Raskall. *Black Moon* (1945) concerns a young balloonist hiding with a riverboat circus on the Ohio and his love for a tightrope walker. *Gaudy's Ladies* (1948) describes the exploits of a Louisville gambler-actor on the Ohio River in the 1830's. *City of the Flags* (1950) is an historical novel of Louisville in the first year of the Civil War when the flags of the North and South were flown at almost every house. It is a story of the attempt to maintain neutrality in spite of circumstances leading to conflict.

MILDRED MASTERSON McNEILLY

Grady

was born on May 28, 1910, and brought up on her family's ranch in Kittitas County, Washington. She graduated in 1927 from Central Washington State College of Education at Ellenburg, attended Washington State College School of Journalism, and took advanced work in fiction technique at the University of Washington and the University of California at Berkeley. For years Mrs. McNeilly engaged in miscellaneous writing: publicity releases, magazine articles, radio scripts, and speeches for political candidates. Before 1944 she wrote a score of "who-done-it" mysteries for "pulp" magazines under the names of "Glenn Kelly" and "James Dewey." Her years of newspaper experience included work on *Western Features,* the Seattle *Star,* the Seattle *Post-Intelligencer,* and the Yakima *Daily Republic.* Assignments to meet ships coming from the northeast Pacific led to a consuming interest in Alaska. She voyaged up the Inside Passage, visited the territory, collected material, and studied Russian. Out of her long research came her first novel. She is married to Glenn McNeilly, a Los Angeles insurance executive; they have one daughter.

Mrs. McNeilly has said: "I attempt in my books to give a true and accurate historical background. My aim is to entertain, to present the historical background fairly, to write adventure-historical-romance novels in the old tradition, and to bring back the past in a way that will be interesting to readers and that will take them away, for a little while, from their everyday worries."

Heaven Is Too High (1944) is an historical novel about the Russian-American Company's efforts to establish a fur-trading post and to conquer the coast of Alaska in the years from 1790 to 1810. The story concerns Alexander Baranov and Count Danilo Chernov, who had earned the wrath of Empress Catherine the Great. *Praise at Morning* (1947) pictures Matthew Steel, who had risen from poverty to ownership of three fast sailing vessels prior to the Civil War. For a time neutral, he was instrumental in procuring a visit of the Russian fleet to American waters at a time when this show of friendship helped the North. *Each Bright River* (1950) describes occurrences in the Oregon country during the turbulent formative years from the first great westward migration in 1845 to 1853. It covers the "54–40 or fight" boundary controversy, the Gold Rush, and the Cayuse wars.

EDWARD McSORLEY

was born in Providence, Rhode Island, on July 6, 1902. His earliest writings were published in very obscure publications, and in one year he earned exactly ten dollars and the rent of a house. He wrote for newspapers and did publicity work for motion pictures, vaudeville, Tammany Hall, Negro labor committees, and African dancers. He also went to sea, fished, and farmed. He has lived in the country in Connecticut, on Cape Cod, and on a farm near Augusta, Maine.

Our Own Kind (1946), his first novel, tells of the kind and hopeful Ned McDermott, an Irish-American, who guides his grandson, Willie, into dreams of an education which the older man could not have. The other members of the family, who live in Providence, Rhode Island, strike at Ned by being unkind to Willie. When the old man dies, the young man is at a loss to know what to do. *The Young McDermott* (1949) follows Willie's career from the age of eighteen when he works as a copy boy on a newspaper through his days as a reporter to his service in the army and his return home.

ARTHUR MEEKER

Maurice Seymour

was born on Prairie Avenue in Chicago, Illinois, on November 3, 1902. His family has been in America for three hundred years and in Chicago for a century. After studying at the Chicago Latin School from 1916 to 1920, he went to Princeton for two years and then to Harvard for a year. After leaving college he worked as a reporter in Chicago. In 1926 he went abroad to gather material for his first novel, but he continued his journalistic career until World War II. He divides his time between Chicago, which he loves dearly, and Switzerland, where he writes faster than at home.

Arthur Meeker is a novelist of manners in the old tradition, his chief purpose being to mirror a social group and background faithfully. His two main fields are Chicago, where he was born, and seventeenth-century France, for which he has a warm feeling because of study and travel and an innate taste for the French language and literature. His novels group themselves in pairs: two light satires, two with musical themes, two with seventeenth-century background (one of these about the times of Louis XIII is in progress in 1950), and two about family life in Chicago.

American Beauty (1929), his first novel, with light satire pictures expatriate Americans in a European setting and shows Angelica Vane with the help of her mother, who rose from a cigar counter to wealth, trying to find a rich or titled husband. *Strange Capers* (1931) concerns Agatha Varney, an American girl living in Europe on an income from her rich uncle. When her love affair proves humiliating, she tries to get part of her uncle's fortune from his mistress to whom he left it.

Vestal Virgin (1934) pictures three generations of singers in pre-war Germany. Marie Langer develops a small voice into greatness; her able daughter finds everything so easy that she becomes bored; and her granddaughter sings equally well in Hollywood and in opera. *Sacrifice to the Graces* (1937), which shows the strength of New England moral standards, has an opera singer from Maine, Mary Louise Randall, become distressed when her European lover becomes infatuated with Tino Verona, another singer. Mary cannot accept the European attitude toward love.

The Ivory Mischief (1941), a Book-of-the-Month-Club selection, pictures the mixture of cruelty, poverty, and luxury in the France of Louis XIV in the late seventeenth century in a brilliant story of two sisters' love affairs and intrigues.

The Far Away Music (1945) portrays Chicago family life in the 1850's. Jonathan Trigg hears faraway music and goes to California. A sweetheart returns with him and causes a rift between him and his prosaic family. *Prairie Avenue* (1949), a Literary Guild choice, portrays the heyday and the decline of Chicago's Prairie Avenue, where the wealthiest citizens built homes. The time is 1885 to 1896, with an epilogue about 1918.

CHARLES (HENRY) MERGENDAHL

Stephen E. Merrill

was born on February 23, 1919, in Lynn, Massachusetts. He was educated at the Phillips Exeter Academy in New Hampshire and Bowdoin College in Maine. During the summers of his college years he studied the theater at the Harvard Summer School and joined summer stock companies as a "bit" actor. During this time he wrote a play, which was produced in Provincetown and New York. After graduation from college, he worked as a writer and assistant radio director for a New York advertising agency until he joined the navy in 1942. While serving as a lieutenant, he started writing fiction. He participated in many of the major actions in both the Atlantic and Pacific; but major actions take place in seconds and minutes, and he had ample time for his typewriter. While on active duty he wrote two novels and some thirty-five short stories. Eventually he was transferred to New York to write radio plays for the navy and then to Washington to write speeches and articles. After his discharge from the service, he moved to Damariscotta, Maine, with his wife and small daughter, where he wrote more short stories and his third novel. In 1949 he moved to New York City.

Nearly all of Mr. Mergendahl's work is concerned with the behavior of the young, wartime generation and with the motives that underlie the actions of both men and women caught in the greatest war in all history.

Don't Wait Up for Spring (1944), his first novel, concerns an unsuccessful playwright, Harry Trexler, his service in the navy, and his return to his unhappy southern wife. *His Days Are As Grass* (1946) tells of the life of Gordon Taylor and his death in the Pacific in World War II. *This Spring of Love* (1948) is a love story of Steve Ahlers, an American lieutenant, and Leslie Ross, whose husband has been missing in World War II for two years. They meet in New Zealand, where he is on leave.

ELLIOTT MERRICK

was born on May 11, 1905, in Montclair, New Jersey. He graduated from the Phillips Exeter Academy in 1923 and from Yale University in 1927. His first job was with the Passaic, New Jersey, *Daily News,* where he worked as a cub reporter. During 1928 and 1929 he did publicity and advertising writing in New York City, and from 1929 to 1931 he worked for the Grenfell Mission in Labrador, traveling with the trappers on the rivers and lakes of the interior. He drove a truck in Newark, New Jersey, for six months in 1932, and went from there to farming and writing in Vermont. From 1938 to 1939 he taught school in Vermont. Beginning in 1939 he taught English for three years at the University of Vermont. During World War II he edited and wrote for the Office of War Information. In 1945–

46 he was associate professor of English at Black Mountain College in North Carolina. He now lives in Asheville, North Carolina.

True North (1933) is a non-fiction tale of Mr. and Mrs. Merrick's travels in the Labrador wilderness. *From This Hill Look Down* (1934) is a collection of sketches and stories of Vermont. *Northern Nurse* (1942) describes the experiences of his wife, prior to her marriage, in a Grenfell hospital in Labrador. *Green Mountain Farm* (1948) recounts eight years in the life of the Merrick family in carving out their own way of life on a Vermont farm.

Ever the Winds Blow (1936), his first novel, portrays Henry Frain's rebellious days at Yale, his unhappy city experiences, and his contentment on a Vermont farm. *Frost and Fire* (1939) concerns a young trapper and trader, half Scot and Eskimo, and his struggles, joys, adventures, and loves in Labrador. *Passing By* (1947) is a novel about the crews of merchant ships during World War II and the love story of one able seaman.

GIL MEYNIER

was born in Pau in the Lower Pyrenees, France, on December 31, 1902. When he was six he had lived two years in England, spoke English with a Northumberland burr, and had forgotten French. By 1914 he had spent six years in Paris schools and no longer spoke English; he relearned it in 1918, this time with an American accent. Two foreign languages were required for a French baccalaureate, and so he learned Spanish in three months from a Castilian refugee; in his examinations he did better in Spanish than in English. Then he promptly forgot Spanish to make room for German, which he learned while he was in the French army of occupation following World War I. Upon his return to civilian life he went to work for an American travel agency in Paris. He forgot German, but picked up Italian as manager of the Naples and Rome offices of his firm. He first came to the United States in 1927 on a twelve-day business trip; he returned the same year as a tourist. After half a dozen round trips as a visitor, he applied for an immigration visa in 1931 and settled here permanently. He became a citizen in Tucson, Arizona.

Conducted Tour (1931), his first book, pictures a group of Americans being guided around Europe by a debonair French courier. *Stranger at the Door* (1948) is a study of a group of people and the various adjustments they must make to a society they do not understand. These adaptations range from complete, unthinking acceptance to equally complete, unthinking rebellion. One of the men has as his single ambition the desire to get even with a world which, he feels, has mistreated him.

JAMES A. MICHENER

Blackstone Studios

was born on February 3, 1907, in New York City. He worked his way through Swarthmore College as a hotel clerk and handyman. After graduating with highest honors in 1929, he went on to take his master's degree at Colorado State College. He was awarded scholarships to study in Europe and spent two and a half years there. For a time he held papers as an able-bodied seaman in the British merchant navy and sailed in the Mediterranean. He has traveled in Russia and Mexico. In this country he has lived in sixteen states and has traveled extensively in all forty-eight. "I've always had an itching foot," he has said, "which has taken me to a fair portion of the world. As a kid of fourteen I bummed across the country on nickels and dimes. Before I was twenty I had seen all the states except Washington, Oregon, and Florida. I had an insatiable love of hearing people tell stories, and what they didn't tell I made up. On my various bumming trips I was entertained by not less than fifty families who made me stay with them and share their food and friendship. This made me an incurable optimist."

When World War II broke out, he waived his Quaker principles and volunteered for service with the navy. Although he was trained for carrier duty in the Mediterranean, he was transferred to Washington because he could write. Insisting upon assignment to active duty, he was sent to the South Pacific. For several months he was concerned with aviation-maintenance problems in the Solomon Islands; he visited all the islands on which the Americans were then fighting. During a slack spell when he was stranded on a small island with nothing to do, he blocked out the outlines of some stories. These became the basis of his first book and won for him a Pulitzer prize in 1948. At the end of the war, his rank was that of lieutenant-commander in the naval reserve. On his release from duty, he returned to The Macmillan Company, New York book publishers, by whom he had been employed before enlisting as an apprentice seaman.

Mr. Michener is primarily concerned with American men and women and their relation to American society. In dealing with this subject he believes it is his responsibility as a novelist to tell a well-rounded story.

Tales of the South Pacific (1948), his first book, is a collection of stories set against the background of the southern islands. They are told by a young naval officer and concern the many people, both servicemen and the original inhabitants of the islands, whom he meets. These tales have been used by Rodgers and Hammerstein as the basis for the successful musical play named "South Pacific." *The Fires of Spring* (1949) pictures the early years of a sensitive Pennsylvania boy and contrasts the harsh experiences of adolescence with the dreams of young manhood. David Harper grows up in a poorhouse under his aunt's direction and then sees the secrets behind the scenes as a worker in amusement parks, chautauqua tents, and pulp magazines. He also attends college and marries his childhood sweetheart. Through his many friendships he gains courage to write a novel about his experiences.

KENNETH MILLAR

Olga Cotton

was born in Los Gatos, California, on December 13, 1915, of mixed Scotch-Canadian and Pennsylvania Dutch ancestry. After growing up in western Canada, he attended the University of Western Ontario, from which he graduated in 1938. On the day after receiving his diploma he married Margaret Sturm, who now writes novels under the name of Margaret Millar. After a period in which he taught in high school and later held a fellowship at the University of Michigan, in 1944 he entered the navy and became a commissioned officer on an escort carrier. Following his discharge in the Spring of 1946, he and his wife and daughter moved to California. Two years later he returned to the University of Michigan to complete his work for a doctorate. He has written three detective novels: *The Dark Tunnel* (1944), *Trouble Follows Me* (1946), and *Blue City* (1947).

The Three Roads (1948), his first serious novel, is a psychological story of a young lieutenant who has lost his memory and who tries to recall the incidents connected with the murder of his wife. His sweetheart somewhat half-heartedly tries to help him break through the mental difficulties which beset him.

MARGARET (STURM) MILLAR

Cotton Studio

was born in Kitchener, Ontario, Canada, on February 5, 1915. She studied at the University of Toronto and there began to specialize in psychiatry, an interest that is reflected in her novels. She left college at the end of three years in 1936, and two years later married Kenneth Millar, the novelist and teacher. She is the author of seven mystery novels: *Invisible Worm* (1941), *The Weak-Eyed Bat* (1942), *Wall of Eyes* (1943), *Fire Will Freeze* (1944), *Iron Gates* (1945), *The Devil Loves Me* (1947), and *Do Evil in Return* (1950).

Mrs. Millar disclaims any desire to compete with psychiatrists or write case histories instead of novels. She insists that fiction must aim at imaginative rather than scientific truth, and the kind of truth she is interested in is the truth of what makes people engage in such strange actions. She believes that professional writers can keep their writing fresh and vigorous only by continually experimenting with new forms and new techniques.

Experiment in Springtime (1947), her first serious novel, is a grimly satiric story of a young wife who is unsympathetic with the illness of her neurotic older husband. She realizes her true potentialities when a man she had once loved returns from the war. *It's All in the Family* (1948) is a warm, humorous account of a week in the life of a precocious eleven-year-old girl and the people in her small world. The mother's love for a neighbor causes complications.

ARTHUR MILLER

Peggy Plimmer—Black Star

was born in the Harlem section of New York City on October 17, 1915, but he grew up in Brooklyn where he still resides. He attended public schools and the Abraham Lincoln High School. Injuries to knees suffered on the gridiron later caused his rejection for military service. In 1934 he enrolled at the University of Michigan and wrote plays which won prize money sufficient to keep him in funds. After receiving his degree in 1938, he returned to New York, traveled along the Gulf of Mexico, married, and continued writing. His many jobs brought him close to the mass of men whose tensions and aspirations are the thematic material of his work; he has held jobs as dishwasher, stock clerk in a big auto-parts warehouse, truck driver, waiter, seaman, and shipfitter. He continues to take periodic turns as a factory worker, explaining: "Anyone who doesn't know what it means to stand in one place eight hours a day doesn't know what it's all about." His first Broadway play was "The Man Who Had All the Luck" (1944). "All My Sons" (1947) won the Drama Critics' award, and "Death of a Salesman" (1949) also won that award and a Pulitzer prize. In addition, he is the author of many dramatic pieces for radio's more serious programs. *Situation Normal* (1944) is about army life in World War II.

Mr. Miller has been greatly interested in the need for an affirmative philosophy in social thinking. People, he says, want to give of themselves, but too often they are trained to take. A condition of humaneness is necessary: "We are beginning to ask of the great man, not what has he got, but what has he done for the world. We ought to be struggling for a world in which it will be possible to lay blame. Only then will great tragedies be written, for where no order is believed in, no order can be breached, and thus all disasters of man will strive vainly for moral meaning."

Focus (1945), his first novel, is on the theme of anti-Semitism; it is "an artistic, dramatic, and uncompromising portrayal of the social and personal irony of racial intolerance." Mr. Newman is employed by a large corporation to see that only Aryans are hired. He becomes suspected of being Jewish, loses his job, and fights back.

CAROLINE MILLER

Wide World

was born on August 26, 1903, in Waycross, Georgia, a few miles from where the Suwannee River rises, the daughter of Elias and Levy Zan Pafford. Her mother's grandfather came to that community as a New Light preacher. Her grandfather built with his own hands a little church which still stands. All her relatives live in the same neighborhood. She graduated from Waycross High School in June and was married in August to the English teacher, William D. Miller, who taught her composition and literature. She is the mother of three children, including twin sons. Her hobbies of reading, music, and gardening are objectified in her writing. She now lives in Waynesville, North Carolina, with her husband, Clyde H. Ray.

Lamb in His Bosom (1933), her first novel, describes life on a Georgia farm in the days before the Civil War, and tells the story of Cean Carver, who marries Lonzo Smith and bears twelve children, some of them born under dramatic circumstances. When Lonzo dies of blood poisoning, she marries a wandering preacher who comes to the community. He goes off to the war, and the novel closes as Cean welcomes him home. The novel gives a warm and sympathetic account of backwoodsmen in the pine country and shows the quiet dignity inherent in simple lives. In 1934 it won the Pulitzer prize and the French Prix Femina America award.

Lebanon (1944) is the story of Lebanon Fairgale, a young girl living in the Georgia lowlands in the early nineteenth century. Rebounding from an early disastrous love affair, she persuades a barkeeper to marry her and go west, where the lonely frontier life is his ruination. She accidentally causes the death of a friend, and so gossip about her flourishes. At last a preacher, Jairus Mountjoy, twenty-three years her senior, marries her and gives her protection and guidance. "The words of the book are lovely words," stated *The Atlantic Monthly*.

HELEN TOPPING MILLER

was born on December 8, 1884, in Fenton, Michigan, the daughter of Isaac W. Topping. She attended Michigan State College in the class of 1905. The eldest of eight children of a literary mother, she began writing at a very early age, and contributed to the children's pages of *Saint Nicholas Magazine* at the age of fifteen. Her first short story was published in a "pulp" magazine in 1909. Following this, she wrote and published more than three hundred short stories, eleven serials, nine novelettes, and in 1949 completed her thirty-third novel. The family removed to Tennessee in 1908 and she was married to Roger Miller on June 16, 1910; they have one living child.

Sharon (1931), her first novel, takes a southern girl home to the Great Smoky Mountains after college with a determination not to be a weak, self-imprisoned failure like her father. *The Flaming Gahagans* (1933) tells how red-haired Abby is prepared to give up love to care for her financially embarrassed southern family. *Blue Marigolds* (1934) has a Georgia girl move to Washington, D.C., in the depression and become an interior decorator. *Splendor of Eagles* (1935) has a rich Virginia girl, Mikell Hare, in love with a mountain man. *Whispering River* (1936) is a romantic tale of Linda Rhett and Wayland Gannet in a North Carolina coastal town. *Love Comes Last* (1936) shows Thorne Tavenner facing adversity courageously; she helps to rehabilitate her family.

Let Me Die Tuesday (1937), set in a Florida coastal town, concerns Nancy Phipps' worries over her mother's romantic intrigues and her father's health. *Storm over Eden* (1937) portrays two Alabama sisters, one of whom nearly runs away with a man she is forbidden to know and the other marries a Texan. *Hawk in the Wind* (1938) has a Carolina widow carry on her husband's pulp mill with a young man from outside the mountain country. *Never Another Moon* (1938) has a girl in a booming oil town vow never again to fall in love under the moon; she finds her man under the noonday sun. *Next to My Heart* (1939) tells of Kathie O'Hara, a waif with a circus, who is adopted by the wealthy Towne family and who is loved by the father and two sons. *Song after Midnight* (1939) describes a Texas girl's hasty marriage to her art teacher in New York City and their many problems. They go to Louisiana, where he has inherited a large house. Her growing common sense straightens out their tangles.

The Mulberry Bush (1940) has a girl choose a newspaperman over a man from an old Maryland family. *Dark Lightning* (1940) is the romance of Adelaide and Garry on a Texas ranch where oil is found. *Who Is This Girl?* (1941) concerns Storm, a girl living with a supposed uncle in Texas; at his death her right to his property is contested. *When a Girl's in Love* (1941) is about Rosemary Mallard, whose life is spent in Washington hotels, fashionable Virginia estates, and coastal Florida because her parents are divorced. *Desperate Angel* (1942) deals with the four Sands sisters, especially Mardee, who looks like an angel, a "desperate angel."

Sheridan Road (1942) tells of Eden Faraday's unexpected acquaintance with Chicago gangsters connected with Nazis. *Hunter's Moon* (1943) has Burke Ryerson run away to a lodge in the Virginia hills to avoid marrying a rich man. *Last Lover* (1944) deals with a Tennessee farm family worrying over the wartime romances of a son and daughter. *Wicked Sister* (1945) is about family life in wartime and two sisters who love the same man. *Dark Sails* (1945) is an historical novel dealing with the eighteenth-century struggle of the English settlers in Georgia with the Spaniards. *Spotlight* (1946) pictures Alix Dempster's dream of happiness being spoiled by her sister. *Shod with Flame* (1946), set in the Civil War in 1863, portrays four Tennessee women divided in their loyalties between North and South.

Candle in the Morning (1947) brings home from World War II a WAC lieutenant to a grandfather, a deserted mother, a neurotic aunt, and two lovers. *The Sound of Chariots* (1947), with a background of John Sevier and the State of Franklin, has a Tory girl in 1780 fall in love with a Continental soldier. *Flame Vine* (1948) has a wealthy girl leave her family to become a dancer. *Trumpet in the City* (1948) is an historical novel about the interrupted wedding of a Georgia girl as the Revolutionary War breaks out. *Mirage* (1949) deals with the land-lease wars in Texas in 1885, and with the problems of a proud Alabama family, uprooted by the reconstruction in the South, who make new homes for themselves in the then turbulent Southwest. *Born Strangers: A Chronicle of Two Families* (1949) is a story of three generations in the nineteenth-century Middle West. The incidents are based on events in the lives of the author's family. *The Horns of Capricorn* (1950) brings a widow and her two marriageable daughters home among hereditary enemies in a North Carolina town. *We Have Given Our Hearts Away* (1950) portrays an unhappily married man worried over his growing children and his ex-sister-in-law with whom he is linked in gossip. They find happiness independently.

HENRY MILLER

K. Chester

was born on December 26, 1891, in New York City. His grandfathers came to America from Germany to escape military service. The family spoke both German and English at home. He spent much time on the streets of Brooklyn's Fourteenth Ward in the Williamsburg section, and there strengthened his native spirit of independence. He withdrew from the College of the City of New York because he did not wish to go through the required curriculum. For four years he worked for the Atlas Portland Cement Company in New York, and then his father gave him the funds to go to Cornell University. When he was twenty-one, in San Diego, he met Emma Goldman, the anarchist, and she opened up for him a new vista by introducing him to the European masters of literature, particularly Nietzsche. The I.W.W. movement and other political and religious ideas fascinated him, yet he never joined any clubs or organizations. During World War I he worked for a few weeks as a mail clerk in the War Department at Washington. For five years he was the employment manager of the Western Union Telegraph Company in New York City. During a vacation in 1922, he wrote his first book, *Clipped Wings*. He resigned his position in order to write, but from 1924 to 1934 he published only two short items; his first composition appeared in *The Crisis*, a magazine for colored people. He spent the years from 1930 to 1940 in Europe.

Henry Miller is not a novelist in the usual sense of the term; his books are all autobiographical and purposely lack the form of the novel. "I decided to write about myself, and in the first person, and as truthfully as I could," he has said. "When my work is examined *in toto*, I think it will be seen that I have written about as much non-fiction as fiction. I have tried to discover myself, and in so doing have found the world." He is engaged on a twenty-five-hundred-page book, *The Rosy Crucifixion*. His work has been criticized for its frankness.

His first published novel, *Tropic of Cancer* (1934), is a story of Mr. Miller's days in Paris. *The Smile at the Foot of the Ladder* (1948) is a story in the form of a fantasy of a clown who gives up his career to find happiness in being himself. The book is designed to be moral, allegorical, and symbolical.

MERLE MILLER

Erich Hartmann

was born in Toma County, Iowa, on May 17, 1919. He attended the University of Iowa from 1936 to 1940, interrupting his course to spend the year 1938–39 at the London School of Economics. After graduation he became Washington correspondent for the Philadelphia *Record*. During World War II he organized the Pacific and the continental editions of *Yank* and later was its executive editor in Paris. He has been an editor of *Time* and of *Harper's Magazine*. *We Dropped the A-Bomb* (1946) is an eyewitness account of the bombings of Hiroshima and Nagasaki as told to Mr. Miller by the radio operator of the plane which carried the bomb to the latter city. His fiction is concerned with his own generation and with the ways in which it differs from the previous period of Hemingway, Fitzgerald, and Dos Passos.

Island 49 (1945), his first novel, describes the invasion of an island in the Pacific in World War II and the reactions of a group of soldiers during a three-day period. *That Winter* (1948) is a story of the readjustment to civilian life of three returned soldiers. A wealthy man drinks himself to suicide; the others take up old tasks. *The Sure Thing* (1949) concerns a young State Department employee who becomes involved in the loyalty investigation in the Spring of 1947.

NOLAN MILLER

Axel Bahnsen

was born on May 4, 1915, in the village of Kalida, on the Augalaize River in northwestern Ohio. As a child he wrote plays which were produced in the barn of the local banker's son. The Millers moved to Detroit when the son was eleven. He attended Northwestern High School and from there went to Wayne University; he became literary editor of *The Collegian*. He subsequently did undergraduate and graduate work at the University of Wisconsin and the University of Michigan. After teaching at Mackenzie High School in Detroit and at Wayne University, he became writer-in-residence and a professor at Antioch College at Yellow Springs, Ohio. His first short stories won a Hopwood prize in fiction in 1943. In 1944 he entered the army and was discharged because of allergies which caused deafness.

Mr. Miller's chief concern in fiction is "what people are really like underneath their inarticulate exteriors: the emotions, the frustrations, the partially understood and never communicated 'ideas' which make each one 'tick'." These people move with naturalness in everyday situations.

Moth of Time (1946), his first novel, is the story of a family deserted by the father; it concentrates on the youngest son. The scene is Detroit during the first twenty years of this century. *The Merry Innocents* (1947) deals primarily with a midwestern college professor. The action takes place during Christmas vacation, and the book attempts to reproduce the magic spirit of the holiday season and its effect on the various characters.

RONALD ELWY MITCHELL

was born in England on June 1, 1905, of Welsh-speaking parents. He went to school in London and, following a brief term with a London publisher, studied at King's College of London University, where he received his bachelor's degree with First Class Honors in 1928 and his master's in 1930. He then traveled to America and for three years attended Yale on a Commonwealth fellowship. It was there that he took up playwriting, and within a few years eighteen of his one-act plays were published. His full-length plays have been awarded eight first places in national contests with some twenty-five productions. *Design for November* is based in part on Mr. Mitchell's play "The Kindest People," which won the Vagabond Theatre award. *Dan Owen and the Angel Joe* is based on his play "Alfred." Mr. Mitchell, professor of speech and theater director at the University of Wisconsin, became an American citizen in 1946. He is married and has two sons and one daughter.

Design for November (1947), his first novel, is set in an American university town. A poorly paid graduate assistant is not promoted because a talented refugee with a well-known name is a scoop for the institution. The assistant's wife, infuriated by the injustice, takes matters into her own hands. *Dan Owen and the Angel Joe* (1948) is a fantasy on two levels. On one level, Dan Owen, having endured his wife's nagging for years, beats her to death and shoots himself. On the other level he spends the afternoon fishing with his friend Joe. Both murderer and murdered come to judgment before an angelic court of friends and neighbors, and both their crimes are expiated at the end of the afternoon's fishing. The setting is a village in Wales.

MERRIAM MODELL

Halsman

was born in New York City and received her early education in its public schools. After receiving her bachelor's degree from Cornell University, she held a number of short-lived jobs, the only importance of which was their possible future use as literary material. She was a dress model, a scout for a fashionable fur house, and a salesclerk at Macy's. More in line with her desire to become a writer was her service as editor of two magazines, now defunct. Since then, Mrs. Modell has traveled on the continent and has become a wife and mother.

The Sound of Years (1946), her first novel, is the story of a seventeen-year-old daughter, born out of wedlock when her mother was part of a low social stratum; the girl later comes to her mother for refuge when the years have elevated her to another social level. *My Sister, My Bride* (1948) is the story of a woman's frigidity, and represents a serious attempt to show the far-reaching causes and effects of this condition and to make it better understood. This theme is treated with humor and irony.

ROBERT MOLLOY

Larry Colwell

was born in Charleston, South Carolina, on January 9, 1906. He was educated in private and public schools in Charleston and New York, and in parochial schools in Philadelphia. He worked at a variety of jobs, such as concert-hall usher, printing salesman, advertising salesman, and bank clerk. In 1936 he joined the New York *Sun* as assistant to the literary editor and in 1943 he succeeded to this position. In August, 1945, he resigned from the *Sun* to devote all his time to writing.

His novels have been generally characterized as partaking of the comedy of manners. "In many ways," he has said, "the truly comic novel is the equal of the most profoundly tragic. I do not feel inclined to make fiction a substitute for the teaching of history or the dissemination of theories; I feel that the novelist ought to report the facts that arise in his imagination and let the interpretation take care of itself. If I have a major theme it is that most people are frustrated. It is the attempt to adjust one's self to the unsatisfactory world that makes fiction and the drama."

His first novel, *Pride's Way* (1945), is a mildly satirical picture of old age and its crotchets, delusion, and southern pride. The story concerns two old ladies, widows and sisters, who had not spoken in six years but who in their Charleston, South Carolina, church in 1910 hear a sermon which leads them to a reconciliation. *Uneasy Spring* (1946) is a rather light treatment of a somber theme, second marriage, and of the years of restlessness that come with middle age. The story concerns a forty-six-year-old widower with two children who falls in love with a young and charming woman; he realizes his mistake in time and marries a woman of his own age. *The Best of Intentions* (1949) is a study of what might be called the subneurotic personality, here embodied in an unimportant little man who worries about things that will probably never happen and who has been led by the circumstances of his life and by his temperament to take the course of least resistance.

BUCKLIN MOON

was born in Eau Claire, Wisconsin, on May 13, 1911. He lived most of his life in Florida until he moved to New York after his graduation from Rollins College. His short stories have appeared in *Harper's, Esquire,* and other magazines, and in 1946 he was awarded a Julius Rosenwald Fellowship. He is the editor of *Primer for White Folks* (1945), an anthology of prose writings by and about the American Negro from slavery days to the present. *The High Cost of Prejudice* (1947) is a study of the cost in dollars and cents and cultural values of America's intolerance of Negroes. He has been an associate editor of Doubleday and Company since 1941.

The Darker Brother (1943), his first novel, presents the problems of a Florida Negro family that has moved north to Harlem in New York City. Ben, the main character, joins the army and discovers that the conditions for the Negro are the same everywhere. *Without Magnolias* (1949) portrays the difficulties of a Florida family in moving from the lower class to the middle class. The mother clings to the ways of the past; Luther joins the labor movement; Alberta goes to Harlem as a social worker and becomes frustrated; Bessie works for a college president. All discover that they owe their jobs to the whims of white people.

RUTH MOORE

was born in Maine, where her ancestors lived for five generations on an island a mile and a half off the coast and seventeen miles from Bar Harbor. Her family thought college would ruin her as a wife, but she went, nevertheless, and then moved to New York. She has taught school, written publicity, operated a farm in Maine and a ranch in California, and crossed the continent ten times.

Miss Moore is a regional writer who portrays with fidelity the everyday incidents in the life of small communities in Maine. She stresses the importance of work, integrity, kindness, and independence.

Her first novel, *The Weir* (1943), is a tale of the Turner and Comey families on a small island off the coast of Maine. Leonard Turner falls in love with a girl on the mainland, and she turns him down. *Spoonhandle* (1946) depicts Pete Stillwell and his sister, Agnes, whose need for money leads them to side with the summer people against their neighbors. *The Fire Balloon* (1948) details events in the summer of 1947 as Gram Sewell, of Scratch Corner, Maine, looks after the children and grandchildren. *Candlemas Bay* (1951) is about the wise and salty Grampa Ellis as he shoulders responsibility for his three daughters and son and their many children.

WARD MOORE

was born in Madison, New Jersey on August 10, 1903. His family soon moved to Montreal, where he lived until 1913; he then moved to New York to grow up in typical middle-class surroundings. Convinced that he had a literary vocation, he left high school to become a writer. His adolescent optimism unjustified, he worked at various unskilled jobs, as a bookseller, sheet-metal worker, and pattern clerk in a steel foundry. At intervals he opened his own bookstores, which invariably failed. He moved to Los Angeles in 1929, continuing in a more equable climate the routine hitherto practiced in New York, Milwaukee, and Chicago. He gravitated to rural life and has practiced farming more or less assiduously for some years.

Breathe the Air Again (1942), planned as a first volume of a loosely conceived trilogy, is a picaresque novel of the 1920's in which Simon Epstein experiences the depression sequence of looking for jobs, getting and losing them, and feeling the pinch of poverty.

Greener Than You Think (1947) is a satire in the form of *improbabilia.* A discovery which promises good for all mankind is utilized for personal profit with disastrous results which science, divorced from morality, is helpless to obviate.

MURRAY MORGAN

Virna Haffer

was born in Tacoma, Washington, on February 16, 1916. He was educated in the Tacoma public schools and graduated from the University of Washington in 1937 with a bachelor's degree in journalism. He held several newspaper jobs in the Pacific Northwest before entering the Columbia School of Journalism. While in New York he worked for CBS World News, *Time* magazine, and the New York *Herald Tribune.* Awarded a Pulitzer traveling scholarship in 1942, he and his wife spent a year in Mexico. During World War II he served as an enlisted man in the Alaska Communication System. He is now a member of the faculty of the College of Puget Sound at Tacoma, Washington.

While stationed in the Aleutians he wrote his first two books, *Day of the Dead* (1947), a mystery with a Mexican setting, published under the pseudonym of "Cromwell Murray," and *Bridge to Russia: Those Amazing Aleutians* (1947), the first comprehensive history and description of the chain of islands between the Pacific Ocean and the Bering Sea. Later, while stationed at the Pentagon, he did research work for his next book, *Dixie Raider* (1948), which describes the strange and dramatic career of the *Shenandoah,* a Confederate raider. *The Columbia: Powerhouse of the West* (1949) is an informal history of the Columbia River, with emphasis on the Grand Coulee Dam and the Hanford atomic project.

The Viewless Winds (1949), his first novel, is a story of class conflict in a small lumber town. In it, Mr. Morgan says, he tried to show "that both the mill owners and the union men are prisoners of their prejudices, and that their preconceived notions about each other lead them toward violence and destruction." The setting is in the town of Cove, Oregon.

CHRISTOPHER MORLEY

Lotte Jacobi

was born in Haverford, Pennsylvania, on May 5, 1890. His father was a distinguished professor of mathematics at Haverford College and later at The Johns Hopkins University in Baltimore. His mother was a musician. Both parents were English by birth, and in his youth Christopher Morley made several visits to England. He received membership in Phi Beta Kappa and graduated from Haverford College in 1910. He was a Rhodes scholar at New College in Oxford University from 1910 to 1913. Haverford College awarded him the degree of Doctor of Literature in 1933. He married Helen Booth Fairchild in 1914; they have four children. He did editorial work successively for Doubleday, Page & Co., *The Ladies' Home Journal,* the Philadelphia *Evening Public Ledger,* and the New York *Evening Post;* he was a columnist and contributing editor to *The Saturday Review of Literature* from its beginning in 1924 to 1940. He was one of the founders of the Hoboken Theatrical Company, which from 1928 to 1930 specialized in the revival of old-time melodramas. After ten years of success as an essayist and poet, *Where the Blue Begins* in 1922 brought him fame as a novelist. His home is on Long Island. *John Mistletoe* (1931) is an autobiography to the age of forty.

A poet, dramatist, essayist, and novelist, he is inclined to believe that his early writing was received with too much praise, whereas his later work of a more serious quality, like *Kitty Foyle* or *The Man Who Made Friends with Himself*, has been the cause of raised eyebrows and even dismay. The informal essay has been especially congenial to his lyrical temperament, and his fiction reflects his artistry in this genre. He is a witty commentator on the foibles, follies, and idiosyncrasies of human nature, as well as a writer of attractive nature descriptions. His satire and originality in phrasing are always delightful. His verse parodies are among the best in the English language.

Mr. Morley's books of essays include *Shandygaff* (1918), *Travels in Philadelphia* (1920), *Pipefuls* (1920), *Plum Pudding* (1921), *Inward Ho* (1923), *Powder of Sympathy* (1923), *Religio Journalistici* (1924), *The Romany Stain* (1926), *Off the Deep End* (1929), *Seacoast of Bohemia* (1929), *Born in a Beer Garden* (1930), *Ex Libris Carissimis* (1932), *Shakespeare and Hawaii* (1933), *Internal Revenue* (1933), *Old Loopy* (1935), *Streamlines* (1936), *Letters of Askance* (1939), and *The Ironing Board* (1949).

The volumes of poetry by Mr. Morley include *Songs for a Little House* (1917), *The Rocking Horse* (1919), *Chimneysmoke* (1921), *Translations from the Chinese* (1922, 1927), *Toulemonde* (1928), *Mandarin in Manhattan* (1933), *The Middle Kingdom* (1944), *Spirit Level* (1946), *The Old Mandarin* (1946), and *The Ballad of New York* (1950), "a constabulary roundup among verses" written in the years from 1930 to 1950.

His plays are "Three's a Crowd" (with Earl Derr Biggers, 1920), "One Act Plays" (1924), "Soft Shoulders" (1933), and "The Trojan Horse" (1939). He is the author of the following collections of short stories: *Tales from a Rolltop Desk* (1921), *The Arrow* (1927), and *I Know a Secret* (1927). *Two Fables* (1925) contains translations from the French of de Musset and from the German of Hauff. He is editor of *Bartlett's Quotations* (with L. D. Everett, 1937, 1948), *Modern Essays* (1921, 1924), *Two Prefaces by Walt Whitman* (1925), *Sherlock Holmes and Dr. Watson* (1944), and *Murder with a Difference* (1946).

Mr. Morley's first novel, *Parnassus on Wheels* (1917), recounts the adventures of two itinerant booksellers. Roger Mifflin, a professor, sells books to farmers from a van. He disposes of his business to Helen McGill, a New England woman, and their adventures together constitute the story. Roger's mood, and Mr. Morley's, is found in statements like this one: "It's no good writing down lists of books for farmers and compiling five-foot shelves; you've got to go out and visit the people yourself—take the books to them, talk to the teachers and bully the editors of country newspapers and farm magazines and tell the children stories—and then little by little get good books circulating in the veins of the nation. It's a great work, mind you! It's like carrying the Holy Grail to some of these way-back farmhouses."

The Haunted Bookshop (1919) has Roger Mifflin conduct a bookstore in Brooklyn. His fascinating talk about books charms, among others, a young couple who promptly fall in love. In contrast to their idyllic love affair is a German bomb plot which kills only the perpetrator. *Kathleen* (1920) is the amusing tale of Oxford students who find a letter signed "Kathleen" and who develop a romantic interest in her. An American Rhodes scholar tells about the boys' prank and wins her.

Where the Blue Begins (1922) is a fantasy, an allegory, and a satire in which all the characters are dogs. Gissing, something of a philosopher, wonders about God and freedom, and so he leaves his comfortable home in Canine Estates to try life in the city. He works as a floorwalker in a large department store, devotes time to the Church, and tries life as a mariner, but in none of these enterprises exists the contentment which appears in the blue flame of his own furnace fire. Happiness, the author indicates, begins at home with one's own thoughts and thrives apart from religious dogmatism. *Pandora Lifts the Lid* (with Don Marquis, 1924), a travesty on pirate and kidnapping yarns, is a story of the disappearance of seven young girls from an exclusive Long Island finishing school in company with a poetic and radical English teacher. A bootlegger's gang, a wealthy seventy-year-old businessman, and an aviator help to complicate and untangle matters.

Thunder on the Left (1925), a novel of great stylistic beauty, pictures a group of children at the birthday party of Martin, aged ten; they ask each other whether grown-ups are happy, and the children blow out the candles. The next scene shows the same children twenty-one years later at a picnic and reveals the effect of time upon them. The answers to the question appear in their actions and physical make-up. *Pleased to Meet You* (1927) reports on the life of the president of the new republic of Illyria and of his daughter when a suave visiting dignitary adds excitement to their daily routine. *Human Being* (1932), a study of the buried treasure in the heart of an average man, presents episodes in the life of Richard Roe over a period of thirty years. He is a traveling salesman for a publishing house, marries a shallow and jealous girl, goes into the stationery business, and opportunely drops dead.

Swiss Family Manhattan (1932) is about a Swiss family which takes a vacation journey by airplane. A storm wrecks the plane, but the family escapes in a balloon-raft and lands on the top of the Empire State Building. The main part of the story mildly satirizes New York City and its inhabitants whose strange goings on in traffic snarls and elsewhere seem quite barbaric. *The Trojan Horse* (1937) is a reworking of the story of the fall of Troy, with the tale of Troilus and Cressida as central to the action which ends on the evening of the surrender.

Kitty Foyle (1939) is the portrait of an American white-collar business girl in the 1930's, the daughter of an Irish-American night watchman. She grows up in Philadelphia around 1918, moves to the Middle West, and is in New York City with the depression and a serious love affair behind her and with a thriving cosmetic business to support her and give her pause before embarking upon further romantic adventures. Mr. Morley thought of calling the novel *Nation Wide*—a title designed to show the universal basis of the theme of the struggling "woman of the covered typewriter" whose trials and tribulations are comparable with those of the "woman of the covered wagon." The story is told through her reminiscences in a stream-of-consciousness technique.

Thorofare (1942), written in wartime to show the close spiritual kinship of Americans and Britishers, takes its title from the Atlantic Ocean, which is the thoroughfare or bridge between England and America at the same time that it is a barrier separating the two nations. The story recounts the adjustments that an English family makes in becoming part of the American way of life. The central characters are college teachers, and their thoughtful, witty remarks underline the theme of the book.

The Man Who Made Friends with Himself (1949) is a narrative of man's mistakes in the world and of his inability to distinguish between reality and illusion. The central character—the "I" who narrates the story—is Richard Tolman, a literary agent, who is dead before the story opens. An alter ego, known as That Man, appears when needed and as easily disappears. The theme is that man's happiness comes from his own imagination, his own soul. There is also a tragic political parable in the conclusion, where the fire in the night club is plainly a forecast of another and final world explosion.

EDITA MORRIS

was born in Orebro, Sweden, on March 5, 1903. After graduating from Brumerska Skolan, a private school in Stockholm, she began to write for magazines. In 1925 she married Ira V. Morris, the novelist. She spent three years in England, studied at Heidelberg University in Germany, and spent ten years in France, Mexico, and North Africa. On the outbreak of World War II she came to the United States and made broadcasts to Sweden for the Office of War Information. Her short stories have been represented six times in O'Brien's *Best American Short Stories* and also in other collections. *Birth of an Old Lady* (1938) is a group of realistic short stories with a fantastic, allegorical, and mystical quality. *Three Who Loved* (1945) contains three stories on the transforming power of love.

My Darling from the Lions (1943), her first novel, pictures two sisters, beautiful Anna and restless Jessa, and their uncle-in-law, Rolf, who grow up on the remote estate of "Berg" in northern Sweden. Anna seduces Rolf, and Jessa goes off to be a newspaperwoman. *Charade* (1948) portrays the lives of innocent people who suffer in Germany under Nazi ruthlessness and then escape to Poland. The young daughter, who tells the story, joins the children who march off to freedom in Switzerland.

IRA V. MORRIS

was born in Chicago, Illinois, on November 11, 1903. Educated in Europe, he returned to America to attend Milton Academy and Harvard University. He graduated in three years and then spent a year at Heidelberg University, Germany, where he took advanced philosophy courses. There followed a period of newspaper work in Washington and New York and then jobs in publishing firms in England and America. He had always wanted to write since he first published stories in school magazines. As early as 1925 the anthologist Edward J. O'Brien took an interest in his work, and *Best Short Stories of 1934* was dedicated to him and his wife, Edita Morris, the short-story writer and novelist. Together they have been represented eleven times in this annual collection.

Mr. Morris is interested in the psychological motives of his characters, and his novels usually are woven around psychological themes.

Covering Two Years (1933), his first novel, is a study of the morbid psychological traits of Judith Mahon, who has the fatalistic notion arising from a tragic occurrence that the past is her proper dwelling place. She resides in her uncle's house on Beacon Street in Boston, and only for a time does a New York lawyer draw her forth. *Marching Orders* (1938) tells about a Greek-born tailor living in Paris, who accepts an airplane from a client in settlement of a bad debt. Driven by an inner compulsion inexplicable to himself, Costas learns to pilot, while living a double life, with one phase centering around the worldly people at the flying club in Orly, the other around his own Greek family in his heavily furnished Paris apartment. Not until the book's last page does Costas understand that it is a death urge that drives him up into the clouds, so far from the familiar and safe world he has known.

Liberty Street (1944), a Literary Guild selection, pictures a group of refugees stranded in a Central American country, where the ambassador allows red tape to halt them. This swiftly moving story ends with the murder of the diplomat by an Armenian who has striven in vain for twenty-five years to join his brother in the United States. *The Tree Within* (1948) is a study of a normal Frenchman's reactions to national defeat and humiliation during World War II. A bank manager, he becomes aware of the futile materialism of French life, joins the Resistance, and suffers imprisonment in a concentration camp.

WRIGHT MORRIS

Glidden

was born in Central City, Nebraska, on January 6, 1910. As a boy he lived in the small towns and "whistle stops" up and down the Platte Valley, and later as a young man he spent several years seeing America. He went to college in Chicago and Southern California, spent a *wanderjahr* abroad in the early 1930's, and on his return married Mary Ellen Finfrock of Cleveland, Ohio. He received Guggenheim fellowships in 1942 and 1946.

Mr. Morris has united the art of photography with the art of fiction, and several of his books contain both pictures and text. One of these, *The Inhabitants* (1946), has been termed a sermon on the meaning of democracy. The photographs are not of people but of the things which people have made. Mr. Morris is interested in the effect that wood and stone in the form of houses have on human beings and in the influence that people have on these basic materials. This book forms a key to an understanding of his conception of the photo-text. Wherever things will speak for themselves, he uses photographs as a means of expression. Most of his work, however, has the form of the traditional novel.

As a novelist Mr. Morris is concerned with the tension existing between the small town and the big, the rural and the urban, the yokel and the sophisticate. He believes that this conflict is creative and represents a basic element in American life. When the tension slackens, some kind of provincialism results: the rural man becomes not a self-reliant farmer but a yokel, and the city man attains not masterfulness but the attitude of a bored sophisticate. Mr. Morris believes that an important American myth is found in the proverb, "Scratch a big man and you often find a small town." This tension, somewhat like an umbilical cord, maintains the connection between the small and the large, the root and the flower of the American dream.

My Uncle Dudley (1942), his first book, is a grass-roots odyssey of the footloose 1920's, with Uncle Dudley as the wily Ulysses of the open road. The old man gives a boy an insight into the fundamental American process. In *The Man Who Was There* (1945) Agee Ward, who is missing in action, turns up in the lives of all those people who knew him —and some who did not—as an active force. Absent things, the author seems to be saying, are those that are really with us, and in their absence they make their presence felt the more. *The Home Place* (1948) concerns Clyde Muncy, a former small-town boy, who brings his wife and two children from New York back to his home, a run-down Nebraska farm. In words and pictures, Muncy rediscovers the world he left behind, or thought he had abandoned, nearly thirty years before; he comes to the conclusion that he left more behind than he took away. His family discover this for themselves. *The World in the Attic* (1949) is about Clyde Muncy and his family who are on their way back to New York; they stop for a look at "the home town," and find themselves involved with Miss Caddy and her attic world. Miss Caddy's death and the drama of her life become a symbol of the tension and the promise which Muncy feels in his own life and which, the author feels, lies at the heart of the American dream.

FREDERIC MORTON

was born on October 5, 1924, in Vienna, Austria. His father, a manufacturer of metal goods, was arrested shortly after the annexation of Austria to Germany by Hitler in 1939 and placed in the Dachau concentration camp. After his release by bribery, the family fled to England. Frederic had planned to be a physician, but because the family was penniless he took work as an apprentice in a bakery in London. In 1940, at the onset of the blitzbombing, the family moved to New York City. Frederick attended a trade school with the idea that he would become a baker.

But a special entrance examination admitted him to the College of the City of New York, where he majored first in food chemistry and then in psychology. He received a bachelor's degree in 1947. Following graduate study at Cornell University and the New School for Social Research, where he earned a master's degree in 1949, he went on for a doctorate at Columbia University. Meantime his literary career began to take shape. In 1947 he won the Dodd, Mead intercollegiate literary fellowship prize and a fellowship to the Bread Loaf Writers' Conference at Middlebury, Vermont. In the summer of 1949 he taught creative writing at the University of Utah, and in the fall of that year began teaching at New York University.

His writings are concerned chiefly with the conflict between man and morals. He is influenced most by the ideas of Schopenhauer and Nietzsche.

The Hound (1947), his first novel, portrays the life of a young Viennese aristocrat who furthers his exterior well-being by a series of moral compromises. He does not commit infractions against the prevailing mores, but on the contrary he meticulously observes those which he knows to be wrong. When Nazism and World War II destroy the world of convention on which he has based his life, he too must founder. *The Darkness Below* (1949) describes the de-civilization of an Austrian intellectual in a slum bakery. He discovers in the primitive fullness of his surroundings the emptiness of his previous life, with its sterile restrictions and refinements. André Gide's *Immoralist* presents a parallel situation.

EDWA MOSER

was born in St. Louis, Missouri, on August 9, 1899. She graduated from Mary Institute and was majoring in English at Washington University in St. Louis when she married. After becoming the mother of two daughters and two sons, she attended the University of Colorado and the University of Mexico. Under her maiden name, Edwa Robert, she contributed stories and essays to *The Atlantic Monthly* during the early 1930's. For three years she conducted a class in creative writing at the Adult Education Center of Washington University. A frequent speaker at clubs and over the radio, she has lectured for the betterment of understanding between the peoples of the Americas. She is an ardent believer in peace through world federalization. *The Mexican Touch* (1940) is a travel book and also the chronicle of how, for a year, a woman and three children engaged in the adventure of seeing how "other people could be different and still be right." She resides in Tucson, Arizona.

Her first novel, *Wedding Day* (1944), is a problem in counterpoint, of love throughout the stages of contemporary life when "war, however distant, is nonetheless an invader into every home, and man, come thus far

. . . how far? . . . from ancestral savagery, can only dream of a perfection he cannot yet endure." *Roundelay* (1948) is the story of a woman only too keenly aware of the kind of world in which she would like to have her children live and of "this wayward planet" on which, and despite which, she hopes she can help them become such men and a woman that they may receive "joy, not sorrow, as the great inheritance."

WILLARD MOTLEY

Lee

was born on July 14, 1912, in Chicago, Illinois. He has made four transcontinental trips—by bicycle, "jalopy," thumb, and brake rods. During his days of wandering he was a student, football player, ranch hand, migratory laborer, cook, dishwasher, salesman, waiter, janitor, chauffeur, laboratory technician, and radio-script writer. He has also worked as a housing authority interviewer and as a writer for the Office of Civilian Defense.

His first novel, *Knock on Any Door* (1947), is about a boy, Nick Romans, who grows up on the streets of Chicago. He passes from juvenile mischief to crime. Reform school corrupts and hardens him; he eventually turns killer and dies in the electric chair. This story was made into a powerful motion picture, starring Humphrey Bogart, which became propaganda in the fight against juvenile delinquency.

EDWARD F. MURPHY

was born in Salem, Massachusetts, on July 21, 1892, a descendant of western pioneers. He received his early education in Saint Mary's Parochial School, situated directly opposite Nathaniel Hawthorne's birthplace; and some of his earliest impressions were the House of the Seven Gables and the abode of Doctor Grimshawe's secret. At fourteen he entered Epiphany College in Baltimore to study for missionary work among the Negroes of the South. He received the degrees of Master of Arts *summa cum laude* and Bachelor of Sacred Theology at Saint Mary's Seminary, and his doctorate at the Catholic University. He traveled extensively through Europe five times and tarried one summer at the Sorbonne in Paris. Father Murphy is dean of the department of philosophy and religion at Xavier University, an institution in New Orleans devoted to the enlightenment of the Negro.

His first writing consisted of stories for boys. As his interest in philosophy deepened, he contributed to periodicals many articles embodying Thomistic principles as a key to the solution of modern problems. His books include two juveniles, *Tale of Two Brothers* (1918) and *Just Jack* (1919); *St. Thomas' Political Theories and Democracy* (1921), in which are traced American liberties to a possible medieval source; *New Psychology and Old Religion* (1933); *The Tenth Man* (1936), a humanized narrative dealing with the American Negro; and *Handclasps with the Holy* (1938), a series of intimate introductions to the Saints.

The Scarlet Lily (1944), his first novel, is a Magdalene story, a fictional presentation of Mary of Magdala fallen from grace, groping in darkness, and at last finding the light. It won the Bruce-Extension literary award. *The Road from Olivet* (1946), a sequel, tells of Mary's activities in Italy before she went to France as a missionary. *Père Antoine* (1947), a fictionalized treatment of the relation of Church and State, is an historical novel about a Spanish priest whose attempt to transplant the Spanish inquisitorial methods into late eighteenth-century New Orleans arouses popular ill will. After a visit to Spain he returns with more charitable plans and at his death in 1829 is beloved by all. *Mademoiselle Lavalliere* (1948) is a novelized account of a contemporary of Sarah Bernhardt, who attained great laurels on the Parisian stage but played her greatest role apart from it. Eugénie Pascaline Feneglio began life in the slums of Toulon, where a nun befriended her. When the nun died, she turned away from God. After years of suffering as an orphan and as a seamstress, she went to Paris, and achieved spectacular success as an actress. Late in 1914 a priest told her "to come home," and, though refused admittance to an order of nuns, she dedicated her life to the Church. *The Song of the Cave* (1950), a selection of the Catholic Literary Foundation, tells the Biblical story of Ruth, the Moabite woman whom Boaz married. She possessed a strange capacity for loving against all odds.

PAUL MURRAY

Erich Hartmann

was born on August 12, 1920, in Kennewick, Washington. After living in Seattle, the family moved to New York; thereafter he lived and attended school in New York, Washington, and Philadelphia. His first ambition was to be an artist, and for several years he studied with the painter Victoria Hutson Huntley. He graduated from Swarthmore College in 1941. While there he did a great deal of little-theater work and wrote three one-act plays. His early interest in art, and his continued study of it, led to a scholarship at the Art Students League in New York in the winter of 1941–42. However, he did not pursue the life of a painter, going to work instead for Reuters, the British newsgathering agency, in New York, where he served as editor on the foreign news desk.

In December, 1942, he entered the army. For several months he attended a school for cryptanalysts, and in April, 1943, he was sent to North Africa and assigned to the code room of General Clark's Fifth Army headquarters. He remained in this post for two and a half years, moving with the Fifth Army from Africa into Italy; he proceeded successively to Salerno, Naples, Anzio, Rome, and so on up the Boot. During the winter of 1944–45 the army was held up by the Germans in the Apennines, but in consequence he came to know Florence, a city which has made a great impression on him. In the summer of 1945 his group went into the occupation of Austria, in Vienna, and it was from there that he was returned to the United States and was discharged in December, 1945. Since that time he has devoted himself to writing. In 1947 he returned to Florence to visit the people he had come to know so well there. He came home, via Paris, at the end of that year. Recently he has had a job with Pan-American Airways, flying across the Atlantic.

Once There Was a Waltz (1947), his first novel, gives a picture of Vienna in the immediate post-war period, telling the story of an American who, in trying to clear up the mystery surrounding the death of a friend, becomes involved with dangerous neo-Nazi forces. Elizabeth Bowen wrote: "Anybody who loves this beautiful, unhappily-fated city will appreciate Mr. Murray's unobtrusively good descriptions, and, in particular, relish his diagnosis of Viennese character. And anybody who has been in Vienna during these last years will see how true is this picture of occupation."

The Heart Is a Stranger (1949), a story of international marriage in Europe in the 1880's, concerns the intrigue into which a Viennese woman is catapulted when she marries an Italian count from Florence who is working for an Italian-French alliance in opposition to Austria and Germany.

JOHN MYERS MYERS

was born January 11, 1906, in Northport, Long Island, New York, the son of parents born in Tennessee. He studied at St. Stephens College, Middlebury College, and the University of New Mexico. He was a newspaper man, principally in Texas and New York, and did free-lance work in this country and abroad. For a time he wrote advertising copy in New York City and farmed in South Carolina. For five years he served in the army as enlisted man and officer. He married Charlotte Shanahan of Louisville, Kentucky, in 1943; they have two daughters. *The Alamo* (1948) is a history of that fortress, beginning with the founding of Spanish missions in Texas and leading up to the famous siege. *The Last Chance: Tombstone's Early Years* (1950) portrays the mining town in southeastern Arizona in the 1880's and 1890's.

Mr. Myers' first three books of fiction have been usually catalogued as historical novels, but they belong to an entirely different genre, that of literary evocation. The effort in each case was to build a story on the literary spirit rather than the historical sources of the periods in question. Of this persistent aim, *Silverlock,* dealing with the embodied land of literature, is the logical conclusion.

His first novel, *The Harp and the Blade* (1941), pictures tenth-century France in a story of Finnian, an Irish fighter-bard, who could write poems in four languages and recite them in seven. *Out on Any Limb* (1942) portrays the irrepressible spirit of youth in narrating incidents in the life of Ingram Applegarth, a young man in the England of Queen Elizabeth and Shakespeare. He hunts the murderer of his sweetheart's father. The background is well pictured. *The Wild Yazoo* (1947) tells of a young Virginia jack-of-all-trades, Mordaunt Fitzmaurice Godolphin, who leaves his parents' plantation and moves to the Mississippi in the 1830's and settles along the Yazoo River and rises to be a militia colonel. *Silverlock* (1949) is the story of the composite realm of international literature, visualized as a physical continent and visited by A. C. Shandon, an unread if not strictly illiterate and skeptical modern American.

NABOKOV *to* NORTH

VLADIMIR NABOKOV

was born in St. Petersburg, Russia, in 1899, in a family of old Russian nobility. His grandfather was State Minister of Justice under two czars; his father, a newspaper editor, participated in the liberal revolution of February-March, 1917, but opposed the Bolsheviks whose revolution was successful in October of the same year.

Vladimir Nabokov studied at Cambridge University, England, and from 1922 to 1940 lived in Germany and France. In 1940 he came to the United States with his wife and son, and in 1945 he was naturalized. In 1943 he held a Guggenheim fellowship. He has taught at Stanford University, Wellesley College, and Cornell University, where he is now chairman of the department of Russian literature. He has written monographs on the morphology and taxonomy of lepidoptera.

Under the pen name of "V. Siren" he wrote in Russian and enjoyed considerable celebrity outside his native land, where his writings were banned. Since coming to the United States he has written in English; his accomplishment is unique in turning in middle life from a highly individual style in one language to a new medium and achieving a new style equally original and rich. His books include *Nikolai Gogol* (1944), a biography, and *Nine Stories* (1947). Passages from his forthcoming autobiography appeared in *The New Yorker* magazine in 1950.

Laughter in the Dark (1938) presents a psychological story about a rich Berlin man whose mistress saps his vitality and takes his money for an artist. Blinded in an auto accident, he discovers what is happening. *The Real Life of Sebastian Knight* (1941) portrays the life of a Russian novelist by his secretary. *Bend Sinister* (1947) is a dramatic fantasy of a university professor who is menaced by the rise of totalitarianism and who goes down to defeat, madness, and death in the conflict between individual moral judgment and a tyrant State.

ELEANOR ARNETT NASH

James Abresch

was born on January 23, 1892, in Louisville, Kentucky. Her early life was spent chiefly in Savannah, Georgia, and in the south of France. She is the sister of Ogden Nash. After her marriage in 1916 she lived on Long Island where her interests were tennis, golf, and horses. She is a former president of the Women's Metropolitan Golf Association and the winner of a large number of tennis cups. For ten years she was clothes consultant and fashion lecturer for the Bonwit Teller women's store in New York. She resigned from this organization in January, 1949, to devote her full time to writing and to nation-wide lecturing.

Eleanor Nash did not take up writing seriously until she had also taken a full-time job; she discovered that the more she did, the more she could do. Working eight hours in the daytime, she wrote at night. She had a number of short stories published in American, and British and other foreign magazines. Although she enjoys writing short stories, her real interest is in novels, as she finds them a better medium for her type of writing, which stresses the development of character rather than plot.

As her husband was in Wall Street, she was able to write with authority on the conditions which prevailed there before and during 1929; she used this era as the background of her first novel, *Footnote to Life* (1944). The story concerns a man whose aim is the acquisition of power, but who comes to realize that real power can be achieved only through vast wealth. In his ruthless attainment of this end he kicks from behind him each rung of the ladder upon which he has risen. He dies, still trying to make his wife understand him.

Bachelors Are Made (1946) is the story of a man whose biased opinion of women was formed early in life by a selfish and possessive mother, causing him to shy away from all women, and one in particular, to remain a bachelor. *It Was Mary* (1947) chronicles the career of a "shanty Irish" girl who marries a man of considerable wealth and position. During her husband's lifetime she lives simply and quietly. But with the scandalous nature of his death, her deep love for him impels her to rebuild his name and erase the circumstances of his dying from public memory. This she achieves, thus making herself a moving force in society, not as herself but as his wife. This book was the selection of the Catholic Book Club and the Thomas More Club in September, 1947, although Eleanor Nash herself is an Episcopalian.

ROBERT NATHAN

Franz Roehn

was born on January 2, 1894, in New York City. He was educated in private schools in this country and abroad; he attended Harvard but did not take a degree. He worked in an advertising agency after college, and in 1924 and 1925 he taught at the Columbia School of Journalism. These are the only two positions that he has held, for his time since 1925 has been devoted exclusively to writing. He is a talented painter and also an accomplished musician and a composer of songs and a sonata. He is married to Janet McMillen. He is a member of the National Institute of Arts and Letters. *Journal for Josephine* (1943), a non-fiction book, contains observations on modern life.

Mr. Nathan has published several volumes of verse: *Youth Grows Old* (1922), *A Cedar Box* (1929), *Selected Poems* (1935), *A Winter Tide* (1940), *Dunkirk: A Ballad* (1942), *The Darkening Meadows* (1945), and *The Green Leaf* (1950). The poetic quality of his prose is notable. Delight in fantasy and whimsicality, tenderness and irony, humor and sharp intuitions—these qualities characterize his writing.

His first novel, *Peter Kindred* (1919), is semi-autobiographical and realistic, wholly unlike his succeeding work. *Autumn* (1921) is a sympathetic narrative, although not without irony, of an old man who has been relieved of his position as village schoolmaster because of his age. *The Puppet Master* (1923) concerns a marionette maker who expresses his philosophy of life through the creations of his own hands. *Jonah* (1925) relates a story based on the legend of the prophet. *The Fiddler in Barly* (1926) tells how a violinist and his dancing dogs bring joy to the life of a widow in a little village.

The Bishop's Wife (1928) concerns a cleric who needs an archdeacon; the angel Michael takes the job and in the process teaches the bishop that his wife needs love and understanding. *There Is Another Heaven* (1929) humorously satirizes a Jewish man who becomes a Protestant. The scene is in Heaven. *The Orchid* (1931) describes the unusual incidents that occur at the opening of a carrousel in Central Park in New York City and that provide a young lady with moral integrity. *One More Spring* (1933) illustrates what the proper attitude toward the seasonal rebirth of nature does for the victims of the depression who spend the winter in a toolshed in Central Park.

The Road of Ages (1935) is an allegorical treatment of the problem of displaced Jews. *The Enchanted Voyage* (1936) tells what occurs when a husband flees from his importunate wife. *The Barly Fields* (1938) is an omnibus volume, containing five early novels. *Journey to Tapiola* (1938) has an implicit moral which is deeper than the superficial story of a terrier, a canary, and a cat who seek adventure on a garbage scow. *Winter in April* (1938) is a sensitive and discerning account of the companionship between an elderly man and his young granddaughter.

Portrait of Jennie (1940), though it has as its theme the inspiration of a little girl seen but five times by a struggling young artist, is actually an application of John William Dunne's theory of time. *Tapiola's Brave Regiment* (1941) again introduces the little terrier and his friends in a parable which makes manifest Mr. Nathan's subtle understanding of the state of the world. *They Went On Together* (1941) presents a procession of war refugees in World War I; seen through the eyes of two bewildered children, it is a tragedy of futility. *The Sea-Gull Cry* (1942) relates the kindness that is extended to two refugee children.

But Gently Day (1943) is another time-fantasy in which a soldier, just before perishing in a plane crash, finds himself in the period directly after the Civil War. *Mr. Whittle and the Morning Star* (1947) is an account of a man who prepares himself and his friends for the coming of oblivion that the end of World War II seems to promise. *Long after Summer* (1948) describes the idyllic love of a fourteen-year-old orphanage girl and a Cape Cod boy. She nearly loses her mind when the boy drowns, but a former employer and a Catholic priest save her. *River Journey* (1949) tells of Minnie, who knows that she has only a short time to live and who wants to do something for Henry, her husband, something that he will remember always. *The Married Look* (1950) has a middle-aged man, a widower, find romance with "the girl in the hills."

ELIZABETH CUSTER NEARING

was born on January 9, 1900, in Philadelphia, Pennsylvania, the daughter of Edgar Alan Custer, a consulting engineer who invented the first sandless casting machine, painted water colors, and wrote novels. Her home overflowed with an individualistic family and talented guests who kept the house in an uproar the children loved. She would race home from school, desperately afraid she had missed something. She married Max Nearing in 1917. After World War I, while her husband was hospitalized for a service disability, she worked for the Philadelphia *Public Ledger* as a news reporter. Later she was managing editor of the Clifton, New Jersey, *Times*, and then became a news-feature writer for the New York *Telegram*. Her only son, a navy fighter pilot, lost his life in World War II. Her home is now in Cleveland, Ohio.

Under the pseudonym of "Sue MacVeigh" she published four mystery novels between 1939 and 1941. The first of these, *Grand Central Murder*, was based on material gleaned from the experience of Mr. Nearing, a railroad construction engineer, and on the life story of an editor of an encyclopedia who was mysteriously murdered in a New York hotel room on the evening after she had given him material for a biography of her father.

Elizabeth Custer Nearing writes about those subjects with which she has had intimate contact. Her inner life is devoted to the great spiritual force that is now sweeping the earth. In the face of war-mindedness and misunderstanding between rival nations, she strives for peace on earth.

The Lancasters (1947), her first serious novel, is the story of a woman's spirit. The book portrays the talented, noisy, and vital Lancaster family in Philadelphia, with close attention to the wife and mother, Norah. The family relationships are seen through the eyes of a doctor and a minister who quietly loved Norah for thirty years. The book was titled originally *From This My Hard Prison,* which gave a clearer indication of Norah's central position.

JOSEPHINA NIGGLI

was born in Monterrey, Mexico, of a half-Swiss and half-Alsatian father and a Virginia-born mother named Goldie Morgan. Miss Morgan was a concert violinist whose playing attracted the attention of Mr. Niggli. After ten years of correspondence, the two were married. Josephina's childhood was spent chiefly in Mexico. She had exactly five months of regular schooling before she entered the Main Avenue High School in San Antonio, Texas, but she had read widely and to good purpose. At the age of fourteen she entered Incarnate Word College in San Antonio and earned her bachelor's degree at eighteen. She became acquainted with Coates Gwynne, director of the San Antonio Little Theater, who coached her in the writing of plays. She moved to the University of North Carolina, where Professor Frederick Koch taught playwriting. She has held several fellowships and won the North Carolina Mayflower Cup in recognition of the play "Mexican Village." She has published a collection of her plays and textbooks on radio writing and on playwriting. Her first book of fiction was *Mexican Village* (1945), which contained ten stories of life in the village of Hidalgo, which is situated in the Sabinas Valley.

Step Down, Elder Brother (1947), her first novel, is a story of Mexican life and of a man who is suspended between changing generations. This book reveals Miss Niggli's deep interest in the impact of modernity upon Mexico and in that nation's future. *Farewell, Mama Carlotta* (1950) deals with two brothers and the legend of Mama Carlotta, symbol of Imperial Mexico kept alive by a small group of people so that the populace might be kept in subjection. The time is early in the twentieth century.

BLAIR NILES

Underwood & Underwood

was born in Charlotte County, Virginia, on a plantation which bordered on the Staunton River. She traces her family back to early Colonial days. Her grandfather was a general in the Confederate army and later was a supreme court justice in New York City. Her grandmother, Mrs. Roger A. Pryor, was the author of books of reminiscence and history who wrote her first book in her seventy-fourth year. In early life Blair Niles married the naturalist, William Beebe. She accompanied him on scientific expeditions to Mexico, Venezuela, British Guiana, Trinidad, Ceylon, India, Burma, Java, Borneo, the Malay States, China, and Japan. On these trips she lived a rugged and exciting life. The couple subsequently were divorced. Later she married Robert Niles of New York City. With him she traveled in Mexico, Guatemala, Haiti, Colombia, Ecuador, Peru, and French and Dutch Guiana. Mr. Niles supplied the beautiful photographs which illustrate her books of non-fiction, *Casual Wanderings in Ecuador* (1923), *Colombia, Land of Miracles* (1924), *Black Haiti* (1926), and others. Among the honors awarded her is the gold medal of the city of Lima, given in 1938; in 1941 she received the Constance Lindsay Skinner medal for achievement in the realm of books. In 1944 she was honored with the gold medal of the Society of Woman Geographers for her portrayal of the life history of the Americas.

Blair Niles writes because "she has an insatiable interest in human life and human motives." She has tried to see, and to show, what mankind has made of life in the fleeting, transient moment granted to human beings by their destiny. She has traveled and studied the original sources of history from this point of view. In both fiction and non-fiction it has been her inflexible rule never to take the smallest liberty with historical facts. It is a poor imagination, she feels, that cannot see the vivid, significant drama in man's life as he has, in truth and reality, lived it. She presents life as she studies and observes it.

In French Guiana she gathered the material for her spectacularly successful novel, *Condemned—To Devil's Island* (1928), the story of a prison. *Free* (1930) depicts the exiles in French Guiana whose terms of prison are over, but who must then serve terms of exile, often for life. *Strange Brother* (1931) is a study of the problems which confront the homosexual; Havelock Ellis called this "a fine book," showing "a firm and real grasp of the subject." *Light Again* (1933) has its setting in a private sanitarium for the insane. *Maria Paluna* (1934) describes the romance between an Indian girl and a Spanish caballero in sixteenth-century Guatemala. *Day of Immense Sun* (1936) is set in the period of the Spanish conquest of Peru. *East by Day* (1941) revolves about the famous case of the *Amistad,* a mysterious ship which put in at Montauk about a century ago, manned by a crew of Negro slaves who had overpowered their Spanish masters. The case of these men was appealed to the United States Supreme Court, where they were defended by John Quincy Adams; they won their freedom to return to Africa.

ANAIS NIN

Sunami

was born in 1914 in Paris of a Spanish father, who is a pianist and composer, and of a Cuban mother, who was a singer. Anais came to America at the age of eleven. At fifteen she ran away from public school, but she gained an education through reading extensively in public libraries. She wrote the first book by a woman on D. H. Lawrence. She married Ian Hugo, an engraver, and returned to France to live. When World War II started, she returned to America and, at first unable to find a publisher for her writings, learned to set type, bought a press, and published her own works for four years. Now her writings are issued by trade publishers.

Of her work Miss Nin has said: "I write as a poet in the framework of prose and appear to claim the rights of a novelist. I deal with characters, it is true, but the best way to appreciate my way of handling them is to act as one who accepts modern painting. I intend the greater part of my writing to be received directly through the senses, as one apprehends painting and music. The moment you begin to look at my writing in terms of modern painting, you will be in possession of one key to its meaning and will understand why I have left out so much that you are accustomed to find in character novels." She has also stated that "the richest source of creation is feeling, followed by a vision of its meaning. The medium of the writer is not ink and paper, but his body: the sensitivity of his eyes, ears, and heart. If these are atrophied, let him give up writing."

Her first book, *The House of Incest* (1936), is a prose poem on the theme that people are unable to love anyone but themselves. *Winter of Artifice* (1939) is a study of a relationship between father and daughter, and the analysis of the relationship reenacted before a psychiatrist; it was the first novel written on the theme of a psychoanalysis. *Under a Glass Bell* (1944) is a collection of short stories. Some are fantasies and some are realistic, like one which deals with the birth of a child or one concerned with a maid living on a houseboat. *This Hunger* (1945) contains three stories about the theme of relationship in its many manifestations; although the four main characters are women who fear men, the problem of this neurosis is enlarged to include both men and women. *Ladders to Fire* (1946) concerns three women who strive to understand their nature. *Children of the Albatross* (1947) is a study of adolescence, not only as evidenced in a boy of seventeen but as recurring in mature characters. *The Four-Chambered Heart* (1950) portrays a man of primitive and natural force who destroys himself. Rango, a guitar player from Guatemala, goes to Paris, where he marries a frigid, hysterical invalid although he loves a dancer. Inward experiences in visions and hallucinations give fullness of meaning to the outward events.

CHARLES BERNARD NORDHOFF

was born February 1, 1887, in London, England, of American parents. His grandfather and namesake was a well-known journalist and author during the Civil War; his mother came from an old Philadelphia family of Quaker stock. When he was three years old, his parents brought him to America, and he was educated in the schools of California. After his freshman year at Stanford University, he enrolled at Harvard and graduated in 1909. The next two years he spent on his father's ranch in Mexico. From 1911 to 1916 he was secretary and treasurer of a tile and firebrick manufacturing company in California. In 1916 he volunteered as an ambulance driver in France. Later he joined the Lafayette Flying Corps and in that organization met his collaborator, James Norman Hall. After Mr. Nordhoff's transfer to the American air service he was commissioned a first lieutenant. In 1920 he went with Mr. Hall to Tahiti, where he married a native lady, Pepa Teara; by this marriage there were six children, four daughters and two sons. In 1941 he married Laura Whiley. He died in Santa Barbara, California, on April 11, 1947.

Mr. Nordhoff said that he had two firm convictions regarding a novel: it should be dramatic, and the idea it presents should be constantly re-examined to insure a clear and cogent presentation. The first thing that he and Mr. Hall did before commencing a novel was to draw up a chart of characters to fit their idea; and since they were both capable of perfectly imitating each other's style, any embellishment of character or plot was made effortlessly.

Mr. Nordhoff was the sole author of three works of fiction. *The Fledgling* (1919) is his reminiscence in diary form of his experiences as an aviator. *The Pearl Lagoon* (1924) and *The Derelict* (1925) are adventure yarns of the South Seas; sharks and modern pirates combine to provide thrilling incidents. *Picaro* (1924) is the romantic tale of two Spanish brothers in Guadaloupe whose father is an American. Both enlist in the army; the one becomes famous as a war ace, the other as a mechanic and the inventor of a revolutionary airplane engine.

A summarization of the works on which he and James Norman Hall collaborated will be found under the latter's name. These books include the famous trilogy, *Mutiny on the Bounty* (1932), *Men Against the Sea* (1933), and *Pitcairn's Island* (1934).

KATHLEEN NORRIS

Ben Pinchot

was born on July 16, 1880, in San Francisco, California, the daughter of James Alden Thompson, a banker, who was born in Hawaii but whose family came from Boston. Her childhood was spent at "Treehaven," across the bay from San Francisco below the Tamalpais Mountain. She was educated by private teachers and by her parents. When she was nineteen, both her father and mother died, leaving her with three brothers and two sisters to care for. She went to work in a hardware store for thirty dollars a month. Following employment as a librarian and as a settlement worker, she became society editor of the San Francisco *Bulletin.* In the fall of 1903 she began a year's course in the English department of the University of California at Berkeley, but found it necessary to drop out when only half through the year in order to take care of the family. She then took a job on the San Francisco *Call,* where she met Charles Gilman Norris, brother of the novelist Frank Norris. They were married on April 30, 1909, in New York, where Mr. Norris was art editor of *The American Magazine;* they had three children, a son and two daughters, of whom only the son, a San Francisco physician, survives. Mr. Norris became a successful novelist; his *Salt* (1917), *Brass* (1921), *Bread* (1923), and other books became best-selling realistic novels. He died in 1945 in Palo Alto, California, where Mrs. Norris now resides.

Mrs. Norris' first successful effort at writing was a story called "The Colonel and the Lady," for which the San Francisco *Argonaut* paid her fifteen dollars. Later, the New York *Evening Telegram* ran a short-short-story contest, awarding a prize of fifty dollars to the writer of the best tale contributed each week. Her husband submitted three of her stories; all were accepted and one won the prize. Her real beginning came with the short story "What Happened to Alanna"; after twenty-six rejections it was accepted by *The Atlantic Monthly. Mother,* her first and very successful novel, was built up from this story because her husband was "profoundly, emotionally shaken by it."

Mrs. Norris' non-fiction books include *Noon* (1925), a brief autobiographical sketch giving encouragement to young writers; *Home* (1929), an inspirational essay on the home and the family; and *Hands Full of Living* (1931), essays on women's affairs. *One Nation Indivisible* (1942) is a poem on patriotism. Her two collections of short stories are *Poor, Dear Margaret* (1913) and *Over at the Crowleys* (1946). *These I Like Best* (1941) is an omnibus volume of her own novels and short stories.

Mrs. Norris has written seventy romantic novels. *Certain People of Importance* (1922), a serious novel, shows that she is essentially a realist with a passion for detail and truth. She makes her people and incidents come alive, and many of her characters are brimful of vitality and happiness. Most of her themes concern love and domestic experience, and her stories portray familiar situations. She extols the virtues of loyalty, kindness, charity, levelheadedness, and truthfulness. Her books possess depths of discernment, and their immensely popular appeal arises from the wise counsel she gives to readers in stories that maintain a rapid pace.

Her first novel, *Mother* (1911), is a tribute to the courageous struggle of a mother to prepare her children for the serious business of living. The story concerns chiefly the daughter, Margaret Paget, a teacher in a New York town, who wearies of a colorless life and then, with the assistance of her mother, foresees a happier future. *The Rich Mrs. Burgoyne* (1912) describes a sensible woman whose simplicity and womanliness lead her to live a normal life with varied interests and to reject the attractions of a fashion-crazy environment.

Saturday's Child (1914) is the psychological study of a girl's quest for happiness during the first few years of her own responsibility for her own life. *The Treasure* (1914) brings a domestic-science graduate into a home as a cook; her efficiency is excellent, but her employer seems to prefer the old hit-or-miss style of housekeeping. *The Story of Julia Page* (1915) is a character study of a girl who lifts herself above the sordid environment of her childhood and marries well. *The Heart of Rachael* (1916) is about a proud woman who divorces her husband because his drinking makes her life miserable. She marries a doctor and thinks all is well until a light-headed girl captures him. Rachael thinks seriously about marriage and divorce and averts another catastrophe.

Undertow (1917) describes a couple who cling together during adversity and then almost separate in prosperity; extravagance and a desire to follow fashion are the cause of their trouble. *Martie, the Unconquered* (1917) contrasts the lives of two sisters, the one ambitious and self-reliant, the other patient and resigned. In *Josselyn's Wife* (1918) Gibbs Josselyn becomes fascinated by his stepmother. When his father is found dead, Gibbs is held guilty, but Ellen Latimer stands by to prove him innocent.

Sisters (1918) concerns two married sisters and the complications which arise when the husband of one girl falls in love with the other. *Harriet and the Piper* (1920) shows that the ability to weather the storms of temptation ultimately provides happiness for Harriet Fields. *Beloved Woman* (1921) transplants Norma Sheridan from a humble home to one of wealth; it demonstrates that personal integrity is important in a successful marriage. *Lucretia Lombard* (1922) pictures a love triangle in which Lucretia finds a moral solution; a forest fire helps her to a decision.

Certain People of Importance (1922) chronicles the life of two generations of a New England family which seeks its fortunes in the Middle and Far West. Reuben Crabtree moves to California; there a new generation rises to carry forward, in good days and bad, the family enterprises. This novel has a seriousness and unmelodramatic lifelikeness which places it among the best family novels of the 1920's.

Butterfly (1923) relates the story of a gifted young girl musician who succumbs to the sterile attractions of luxury and ease. *The Callahans and the Murphys* (1924) describes in two long novelettes the joys and sorrows, successes and failures of two middle-class Irish families. *Rose of the World* (1924) concerns Rosalind Kirby, who is not socially acceptable as a daughter-in-law to Mrs. Talbot, but in the end holds a paper which would disgrace the Talbot family. *Little Ships* (1925) follows the trials and tribulations of five children—the "little ships"—who constitute the happiness of Molly and Peter Cunningham, an Irish-American Catholic family living in San Francisco.

The Black Flemings (1926) begins as a tangled and tragic family history in Massachusetts but ends happily. *Hildegarde* (1926) has the heroine, Hildegarde Sessions, despite her birth in the slums and an early seduction, achieve love and happiness. *The Sea Gull* (1926) proves that a firm love can triumph over the most bitter trials. *Barberry Bush* (1927) pictures the loves and friendships of a group of young people in a small California town, the youthful marriage of Barbara to an irresponsible poet, and their disagreement and eventual achievement of happiness. *The*

Fun of Being a Mother (1927) and *My Best Girl* (1927) show the kernels of their plots in their titles.

In *The Foolish Virgin* (1928) a young girl, Pamela Raleigh, compromises her reputation on a youthful lark and is compelled to work hard to clear herself. *Storm House* (1929) has a widowed writer marry the governess of his young daughter and, despite temptation, find peace and happiness. *Red Silence* (1929) tells how a blackmailer threatens the security of a happily married woman who has made a misstep. *Passion Flower* (1930) is the tragic narrative of a husband who divorces his wife to marry an unscrupulous woman possessed of wealth and beauty.

Margaret Yorke (1930) represents the conflict of will and ideals of two women; the protagonist of worldly ambitions comes out second best. *The Lucky Lawrences* (1930) shows how the five orphaned Lawrences, though born in poverty, avoid all moral and social pitfalls to achieve success and happiness. *The Love of Julie Borel* (1931) teaches the lesson that love is stronger than money in assuring a secure marriage through the experiences of Julie who, although poor, wins over an heiress. *Tree Haven* (1932) describes four sisters on a California ranch and Cynthia's hopeless love for a married man. *Second Hand Wife* (1932) recites the difficulties of a secretary who marries her divorced employer.

Wife for Sale (1933) concerns a desperate daughter who advertises for a husband in a newspaper in order to care for her invalid mother. *Angel in the House* (1933) is the story of a woman in her thirties who loves a man ten years younger than herself; a daughter with a pathological outlook also complicates the situation. In *Walls of Gold* (1933) a wealthy, elderly widower marries a beautiful young woman who thinks that big automobiles and yachts will make up for other things. *Maiden Voyage* (1934) concerns a society reporter who falls in love with her best friend's husband, but eventually realizes that her happiness must lie in another direction. *Manhattan Love Song* (1934) portrays four young Stanford University graduates, two boys and two girls, who find success and happiness during the depression in New York City.

Three Men and Diana (1934) finds only one man of the three true and faithful. *Woman in Love* (1935) is the story of a convent-bred girl and her near-tragic failure to achieve love and happiness. *Beauty's Daughter* (1935) pictures a woman who disdains romantic love but who remains undaunted when her marriage is threatened. *A Secret Marriage* (1936) is the tale of an unfortunate early marriage that interferes for a while with the course of true love. *The American Flaggs* (1936) has a daughter-in-law make a conquest of her husband's friends and relatives through her charm and loveliness.

Bread Into Roses (1937) portrays a jilted girl's unexpected happiness through marriage to a member of café society in New York City. *You Can't Have Everything* (1937) has romantic tensions supplied by divorce, remarriage, and young children. *Heartbroken Melody* (1938) is the romance of Honor Brownell, who finds her goal for happiness through an accident that brings out her better qualities. *The Runaway* (1939) is about a girl who goes to San Francisco and marries a shiftless husband, but sticks to her bargain and fights to avoid a divorce. *Lost Sunrise* (1939) concerns two sisters who find their lives and marriages curiously interwoven.

The World Is Like That (1940) involves the heartaches of a governess who falls in love with her widowed employer. *The Secret of the Marshbanks* (1940) shows that murder cannot restrain the irresistibility of love. *The Venables* (1941) is the chronicle of the Venable family in San Francisco during the years before and after the earthquake. Flo, the second daughter, provides for them after the father dies. *Dina Cashman* (1942) is about a poor girl who goes to parties with a rich youth; when she learns that she is to have an illegitimate child, she solves her problem in a novel way. *Apple for Eve* (1942) shows the influence of Quaker ancestry on the actions of Loveday Gurney, the heroine.

Corner of Heaven (1943) is the story of a sensible Maryland girl without formal education who meets successfully the competition of a heartless blonde. *Love Calls the Time* (1944) pictures the imperious role of love in the affairs of men. *Burned Fingers* (1945) concerns a beautiful girl who nearly brings ruin to her own life and that of a doctor who loves her because of a youthful lapse from rectitude. *Mink Coat* (1946) describes a wife who discovers her mistake after divorcing her husband to marry a playboy. *Secrets of Hilyard House* (1947) is a mystery story. *High Holiday* (1949) is the history of a San Francisco family from 1890 to the present day.

STERLING NORTH

was born on November 4, 1906, on a farm overlooking Lake Koshkonong in southern Wisconsin. He attended grade school and high school in Edgerton, Wisconsin, the "Brailsford Junction" of his novels. During his senior year in high school he sold poems to magazines, and while a student at the University of Chicago he contributed both poetry and prose to literary magazines and won several poetry prizes. He edited the college literary magazine, *The Forge,* and helped to direct a little theater.

In 1927 he married Gladys Buchanan, and then took a position as a cub reporter on the Chicago *Daily News.* Within three years he rose to be literary editor, a position he held for eleven years. He now conducts his own book-review syndicate and probably reaches through twenty newspapers more readers than any other reviewer. His first book, *The Pedro Gorino* (1929), was written in collaboration with an old Negro sea captain. His juveniles include *The Five Little Bears* (1935) and *Midnight and Jeremiah* (1943). Tales of fantasy and horror dealing with Satan are in *Speak of the Devil* (1945).

Plowing on Sunday (1934), his first novel, pictures the prosperity and optimism of the year 1913 in the life of a Wisconsin dairy farmer, Stud Brailsford, an egotistical and proud giant who is the strongest man in his area. He is troubled by the presence of a pretty hired girl, but he remains faithful to his wife of twenty-five years. *Night Outlasts the Whippoorwill* (1936) studies the effect of World War I on the people in the small town of Brailsford Junction, Wisconsin, in 1917–18. When Peter Brailsford goes off to war, Ann, his wife, moves to town and opens a store and has an affair that remains a secret after Peter returns home. *So Dear to My Heart* (1947) retells the story which was originally narrated in *Midnight and Jeremiah.* It concerns the year 1903 in Pumpkin Hollow in Fulton Corners, Indiana, where the boy, Jeremiah Kincaid, lives with his Granny Samantha and his Uncle Hiram. The lad has an enlightening experience that helps him grow up into a man's estate.

O'DELL *to* OSTENSO

SCOTT O'DELL

was born in Los Angeles in 1901. He was educated at Occidental College, Stanford University, and the University of Wisconsin. Except for several years of residence abroad and several years of service in the air corps during World War II he has made his home in California. He comes by his skill in writing historical novels naturally, for his great-grandmother was a first cousin of Sir Walter Scott, and his great-grandfather was also related to the father of the historical novel. Mr. O'Dell is book-review editor of the Los Angeles *Daily News*.

His first novel, *Woman of Spain* (1934), a story of pioneer life in early nineteenth-century California, is laid in the redwood country south of San Francisco and has as its principal characters a New England sea captain and a girl who was born in Spain. The story stresses the girl's efforts to hew a home out of the wilderness, to clear the land and plant it to wheat, to raise cattle, and eventually to sell the products of the rancho to the masters of the ships from Boston. *Hill of the Hawk* (1947) is based upon the historical events of 1846 and 1847: the Mexican War as it was fought in California, and the division of sympathies it caused among the state's people, Americans and Spaniards alike.

MARY KING O'DONNELL

was born on March 2, 1909, in Angleton, Texas, of Irish and Cherokee-Indian blood on her father's side and of Welsh and French Huguenot descent on her mother's. Her father was an oil driller in the tumultuous days following the discovery of petroleum in Texas. She attended the University of Texas for three years, and worked at various secretarial jobs in both Houston and New Orleans. In New Orleans she met her first husband, the late Edwin P. O'Donnell, a novelist, who helped her begin her career. She won a Houghton Mifflin fiction fellowship award for 1941. After Mr. O'Donnell's death in 1943, she went to live in San Francisco. Here she wrote her second novel and here she met and married the late Michael Quin, progressive journalist and radio commentator; they have a daughter. She now resides in Olena, California.

Quincie Bolliver (1941), her first novel published under her maiden name, is the story of a girl's upbringing in the sordid surroundings of a Texas oil town. *Those Other People* (1946) is the story of one day in the lives of a multitude of inhabitants of the French Quarter in New Orleans who cross and recross each other's paths during twenty-four hours. The central character, Leah, is looking for a red-haired sailor whom she had seen in a bar. She observes each passer-by and looks into his mind and heart on this hot June day in the 1930's.

ELISABETH OGILVIE

was born on May 20, 1917, in Boston, Massachusetts. She was educated in the Boston public schools until 1926, when the family moved to Quincy, Massachusetts; she graduated from North Quincy High School in 1934. She wanted to make writing her career, and, since it was impossible for her to go to college at the time, her family allowed her to concentrate at home on writing, with university extension courses as her one source of further study. It was while taking one of these courses that she met Donald MacCampbell, whose teaching shaped her talent and helped her find herself as a writer. He later became and remains her agent.

Miss Ogilvie writes about life on the coast and the small islands off the coast of Maine. She feels that the island existence, limited as it may appear, represents the world in microcosm and therefore provides an endless source of fresh, vital, and truthful material. Her sense of the importance in the American scene of Maine's islands and their people has been set forth in the *Tide* trilogy. The first of these and her first novel, *High Tide at Noon* (1944), describes life on a small island twenty-five miles off the Maine coast as a background for a study of Joanna Bennett's character. The story concerns her youth, marriage, widowhood, and return to the island she loved. *Storm Tide* (1945) shows Joanna learning the arduous position of a woman in a lobster-fishing community, and her difficult adjustment as the wife of the quietly immovable Nils Sorensen. *The Ebbing Tide* (1947) continues the story of Joanna after Nils enlists in World War II. Joanna still carries in her consciousness the psychic scar left by the sudden death of her first husband, for whom she never allowed herself to grieve; she feared that the depth of her sorrow would in some way injure her unborn child. Now, with Nils in battle, she suffers great terror for him, and this arouses intense emotions too long suppressed. These are complicated by the arrival of Dennis Garland, who bears a faint but unmistakable physical resemblance to the dead Alec. Joanna fights a hard battle against forces she cannot understand. She fears they are a symbol of weakness and possibly of evil deep within her, until through Garland's friendship she gains a new faith in herself.

Rowan Head (1949), with its scene set in a village on the coast, describes the renascence of an old shipbuilding family which had fallen into decadence. An attractive young girl, who comes to Rowan Head as a companion to an older woman, stirs jealousy and hatred among three brothers.

JOHN O'HARA

Dormand's

was born in Pottsville, Pennsylvania, on January 31, 1905. He was the eldest of seven children in the family of a physician. He attended Fordham Preparatory School, Keystone State Normal School at Kutztown, Pennsylvania, and graduated from Niagara Preparatory School in 1924. In the following years he was an engineer, boat steward, call boy, freight clerk, guard in an amusement park, laborer in a steel mill, Hollywood press agent, secretary to Heywood Broun, and critic and feature writer for many New York newspapers and magazines, notably the New York *Herald Tribune* and *The New Yorker* magazine. He was also the editor of the Pittsburgh *Bulletin Index* and a writer for Paramount Pictures. His short stories have been gathered in *The Doctor's Son* (1935), *Files on Parade* (1939), *Pipe Night* (1945), and *Hell Box* (1947).

As a short-story writer and a novelist Mr.

O'Hara is particularly skillful in reporting the conversation and the manners of the narrow segment of society of which he is historian—the Hollywood, country-club, and hotel-bar groups. His fiction is written in the "hardboiled" manner.

His first novel, *Appointment in Samarra* (1934), pictures derisively and sharply the fast set and one of its weaklings in a Pennsylvania country club. *Butterfield 8* (1935) anatomizes the superficial flask-toting era from 1925 to 1930 in a story of a fast girl who while drunk falls to her death from a boat. *Hope of Heaven* (1938) is about a Hollywood movie scenario writer and his unhappy love affair with a girl who works in a bookstore. *Pal Joey* (1940) is a series of letters written to a band leader by an aging nightclub singer, Pal Joey. His hopelessness symbolizes the dissolute society of which he is a part and on which he lives. *Here's O'Hara* (1946) is an omnibus volume of novels, containing *Butterfield 8, Hope of Heaven,* and *Pal Joey. A Rage to Live* (1949) is the story of Grace Tate, a beautiful, restless woman who is incapable of remaining faithful to one man. The setting is Fort Penn, near Harrisburg, Pennsylvania, in the period after 1917.

MARY O'HARA

was born at Cape May Point, New Jersey, on July 10, 1885. She received her early literary training by listening to the sermons of her Episcopal clergyman father. While traveling in Europe with her grandmother, she studied music. By the time she attained the age of eight, she was already the creator of voluminous diaries and dramatic stories. She spent the winters of her girlhood in the city atmosphere of Brooklyn Heights, New York, where her father had his parish; there she attended Packer Institute. Her summers were spent on her grandmother's Pennsylvania estate with horses, ponies, and cows. One of her earliest desires was for a colt which someone had promised but failed to deliver. The longing for that colt and the hope of some day acquiring it occupied her mind for many years, and undoubtedly influenced her later choice of subject matter when she began to write books and stories.

Soon after she was grown she went to California to live and there began to write for motion pictures. It was in this work, she feels, that she learned how to construct dramatic stories and paint vivid scenes. She also continued her interest in music by composing songs and arrangements for the piano. She is the author of such musical successes as "Esperan" (1943), "May God Keep You" (1946), "Wyoming Suite for Piano" (1946), and "Green Grass of Wyoming" (1946). Concerning this last name, it is interesting to note that both the song and the novel, in which the words of the song appear, stem from a poem of the same name written by Miss O'Hara one early Spring day when she first saw her beloved Wyoming green grass after a winter spent in New York City. It was her marriage to Helge Sture-Vasa, a Swedish-American, that took her to Wyoming and ranch life in 1931.

My Friend Flicka (1941), her first novel, tells the story of Ken McLaughlin, a dreamy boy growing up on a Wyoming ranch, and his colt. *Thunderhead* (1943) tells more about the attractive, hard-working McLaughlin family, and introduces Thunderhead, Flicka's ugly white colt, who grows up to become king of the wild horses, an incomparable race horse, and the center of a story of rushing adventure. *Green Grass of Wyoming* (1946) pictures the growth of young romance between Ken and Carey Marsh, the girl whose racing mare has run away and is suspected of joining Thunderhead in his remote hiding places; Thunderhead breaks out of his corral and steals mares from adjoining ranches for his harem.

LETITIA PRESTON OSBORNE

Leja Gorska

was born on August 9, 1894, in Union, West Virginia. Her ancestry is a blend of old Colonial stock, both southern and New England, but the fact that she is descended from Governor John Winthrop of Massachusetts was one of those things the family never spoke of until she came north. She spends her winters in New York City, where she has lived since the death of her husband in 1945. She is a lecturer; despite her profession, however, she maintains stoutly that women writers should be heard and not seen. Her lecture subjects are: "Are Men Here to Stay?", "Women are Dynamite," and "The Little Woman." She has traveled extensively in Europe, especially in Slavic countries and the Balkans, and to the West Indies and in both Central and South America. During World War II she was a WAC and was only a private; she spent all her time trying to get out of doing "K.P." and is proud of the fact that she succeeded.

In reading books, or writing them, Miss Osborne is much more interested in style and characterization than plot. She deplores the fact that morality seems to have declined and that the moral standards of the youth of today are being sadly influenced by cheap fiction, movies, radio programs, the comics, and the heavy accent on the quality of lure in advertising. She feels that a return to active participation in religion is the only hope for ameliorating the present condition of things and adds that the choice of dogma is unimportant so long as religion is practiced openly.

They Change Their Skies (1945), her first novel, is a story of the various foreigners who happened to dwell in a Latin *pension* in Tegucigalpa, the capital of Honduras; the novel emphasizes the love affair of an American girl. *Through Purple Glass* (1946) is a comedy of modern manners about the people who live in an apartment house on Beacon Hill, facing Boston Common. *The Little Voyage* (1949) is a love story, laid on a banana plantation, and tells the story of an American girl's search for love; it is filled with color, and with minor characters who are important to the narrative's development.

MARTHA OSTENSO

was born on September 17, 1900, on her grandfather's mountain farm near Bergen, Norway, but her childhood was spent in seven little towns in Minnesota and South Dakota. When she was fourteen, her family moved to the northern frontier of civilization in the wild brush-country of Manitoba, Canada, and there at seventeen she taught in a log-cabin school and later attended the University of Manitoba. Her writing career began in Winnipeg in 1920. During the year 1921–22 she took a course in the technique of the novel at Columbia University. For a time she was a secretary in a Brooklyn charity organization. Her first book was a volume of verse, *A Far Land* (1924). Miss Ostenso is married to Douglas Durkin, who is also a writer. They "commute," she says, between St. Louis Park, a suburb of Minneapolis, and New York City.

Miss Ostenso describes realistically the lives of immigrants and their descendants in the northwestern part of the United States and southwestern Canada. Her stories contain excellent pictures of the lonely toil of farmers, whose intense ambition and narrow religious feelings at times cause them to deal harshly with their wives and children. A romantic love story usually threads its way through these narratives.

Wild Geese (1925), her first novel, is a

tale of an Icelandic farming community in northern Manitoba; the central figure of the story is a dour Englishman who dominates his household and dies in the love of the earth he tills. This novel won the prize offered jointly by the Dodd, Mead Company, *Pictorial Review,* and the Famous Players-Lasky Corporation. *The Dark Dawn* (1926) is built upon the grim marriage of a young man to a woman much older than himself, and his final release from her. *The Mad Carews* (1927) concerns a family in northern Minnesota and the distaste for them taken by Elsa Bower. Yet she marries Bayliss Carew and struggles to retain her individuality and to hold him as her world appears to go to pieces. *The Young May Moon* (1929) describes the way Marcia Gunther suffers after the suicide of her husband, whom she had threatened to leave. She lives a life of self-sacrifice until the love of Paul Brule destroys the ghost of her past.

The Waters under the Earth (1930) pictures Matthew Welland dominating the lives of his seven children and causing them to lose their share of happiness. Only the youngest escapes, for she does not fight or rebel against her father. *Prologue to Love* (1932), set in the mountains of British Columbia, portrays a girl's return to her father's ranch after a nine-year-absence in Europe. Family feuds almost end her love affair. *There's Always Another Year* (1933) concerns a young farmer, Roderick Willard, in a small Dakota town. He must decide between his luxury-loving wife and Silver Grenoble, who owns his place.

The White Reef (1934), set on Vancouver Island, tells about a fisherman's proud daughter who runs away with a rich man's son. She returns unmarried with a child but re-establishes the good name of her family. *The Stone Field* (1937) describes three generations of the Hilyard family, with emphasis upon two grandsons. Young Ashbrooke, a carefree man who exploits his tenants, dies a violent death. Royce comes to love the soil and marries a tenant's daughter, Jobina Porte, who tells the story. *Love Passed This Way* (1942) is about Mary Holland, who leaves her beloved Dakota farm country after her half-crazy father's death to try to forget the stain of his conduct. She goes to New York City and under an assumed name becomes a famous writer. A secret regret gnaws at her heart and eventually takes her back to the man she has never forgotten.

O River, Remember (1943), a story of pioneers in the Red River Valley in Minnesota, describes two families from the 1870's to the 1940's. A grandmother keeps the Norwegian and Irish clans apart; after her death a grandson marries across the once-forbidden line. *Milk Route* (1948) gives the life stories of a cross section of a small midwestern town through Ben Start, the milkman, whose daily course brings him into relationship with all types of people. *Sunset Tree* (1949) concerns a lovely young girl in Minnesota dominated by a beautiful, neurotic mother who hides the truth of a past experience.

PACKER *to* PROUTY

PETER PACKER

Englishman by birth, American by choice, was born in London on January 22, 1908. He received very little formal education, and at the age of sixteen shipped as a cabin boy with the Union Castle Line plying between London and South Africa. A year later he enlisted in the British army for service in India, but was discharged when his parents disclosed his real age to the authorities. He then spent the next two years in the Canadian gold-mining country. It was at this time, during the long, desolate nights of the Canadian winter, that he first began to write in earnest. During the 1930's he returned to England and spent four years acquiring some of the academic training he had failed to receive in his youth. In 1937 he decided to visit the United States; he has been here ever since and has become an American citizen. At the beginning of World War II he enlisted as a private in the army, and was discharged with the rank of captain when the war ended.

White Crocus (1947), his first novel, is the sensitive psychological study of a girl on the threshold of adolescence whose normal development is crippled by war and the irresponsible selfishness of her parents. *The Inward Voyage* (1948) is the story of a young veteran torn between the conflicting responsibilities to his sick father and to his own future, told with a profound understanding of the basic clash between father and son.

JO PAGANO

Jane Smalley

was born on February 5, 1906, in Denver, Colorado, the youngest of five children; his parents were Italian immigrants who had come to the Colorado mining region. His interest in writing and art began early. When he moved to the West Coast, he first worked as a commercial illustrator. Soon he began to illustrate his short stories which California magazines published. "The Disinherited" (1934), a short story about the effect of the depression on homeless boys, was filmed by Hollywood. A number of other motion pictures are based on his original scripts.

The Paesanos (1940), his first book, is a series of sketches relating the adventures of a retired Italian merchant whose extravagances are symbolized by his gold-headed cane. He tyrannizes over his family. *Golden Wedding* (1943) chronicles fifty years in the married life of Luigi and Marietta Simone from their days in Italy to their years in Coalville, Colorado. *The Condemned* (1947) portrays the events leading Howard Tyler, a product of underprivileged upbringing, and Jerry Slocum, a man with a tumor on his brain, to murder a man seemingly without reason. It is a study of guilt that seems more social than personal and of a punishment that does not probe causes.

ELIZABETH PAGE

A. L. Schafer

was born at a summer cottage on Lake Bomoseen, Vermont, on August 27, 1889. During her early years she made trips with her mother to Oklahoma, where distant relatives were missionaries. When she was eleven her grandmother gave her a packet of letters written by a great-uncle during his journey across the plains in 1849. To prepare to write a book on this subject, Elizabeth Page read about the West as recorded by Bret Harte and Francis Parkman. She took her bachelor's degree at Vassar College in 1912 and a master's degree at Columbia University in 1914; her ambition was to become a college teacher. During World War I she worked with the YMCA at Camp Upton and then for nearly a year assisted in running a "Y" canteen near Bordeaux, France. Upon her return she took a year's training in the home-service department of the American Red Cross in order to work with Sir Wilfred Grenfell at White Bay, Newfoundland. During the winters of 1921 to 1925 she returned to the United States to sell the art work of the natives. She wanted to go to Labrador, but ill health prevented. In 1927 she became an assistant to a physician in Wyoming. On the death of her father in 1931 she went to New York to live with her mother; they moved to California in 1932.

Wagons Rest (1930), her first book, is a narrative of her great-uncle, Henry Page, who went to California over the Oregon Trail to retrieve his lost fortune in the gold fields. *Wild Horses and Gold* (1932) is a saga of adventure, perils, and hardship in an account of some horse wranglers who drove seventy-five animals overland from northern Wyoming to the Klondike gold fields in the autumn of 1897. *The Tree of Liberty* (1939) is a panoramic account of the growth of democracy from Braddock's defeat in 1755 to the Lewis and Clark Expedition in 1805, with pictures of almost every memorable episode occurring between those events. The story thread concerns the marriage of a freedom-loving frontiersman and an aristocratic tidewater girl. The episodes dramatize the conflict between the Hamiltonian and Jeffersonian theories of American democracy. *Wilderness Adventure* (1946) traces five men's experiences in leaving Virginia in 1742 to find Lisel Sailing, a girl captured by the Indians and taken to the Mississippi country. Their search carries them to Louisiana and France.

CHRISTINE WHITING PARMENTER

was born on December 21, 1877, in Plainfield, New Jersey, but moved to a New England country town near Boston when she was four years old. Her childhood, with a sister and three brothers as playmates, was exceptionally happy, and in 1901 she married a young doctor and settled down to what she expected to be a long life in her home town. However, the year 1917 found them in Colorado Springs where they intended to spend the winter; they remained for more than twenty years. Not until 1915 did Mrs. Parmenter consider writing, but after her first short story was immediately accepted by *The Woman's Home Companion,* she found it impossible to stop and has been writing ever since. Her present home is in Concord, New Hampshire, to which she moved after her husband's death in 1939 in order to be near her daughter and her family. Mrs. Parmenter is also the author of three juveniles, *Jean's Winter with the Warners* (1924), *The Real Reward* (1927), and *The Treasure at Shady Vale* (1925), as well as two short Christmas stories in book form, *Lights—And a Star!* (1941) and *David's Star of Bethlehem* (1930). *Stories of Courage and Devotion* (1939) contains nine short narratives.

The Unknown Port (1927), her first novel, is a chronicle of neighborly life in a New England seaport town. *One Wide River to Cross* (1928) tells of a family living on the wrong side of the river, and describes the people on both banks. *Silver Ribbons* (1929) is a tale of sturdy New England character, family loyalty, and passion for an ancestral home. *The Dusty Highway* (1929) is the love story of Nick and Gay Hastings, a married couple, and their desire for adventure. He is a bank teller. A lady from Boston enters his life and causes a melodramatic change. *So Wise We Grow* (1930) pictures three young fast-stepping couples and their worried parents.

Miss Aladdin (1932) has Nancy Nelson, a sub-deb whose father loses his fortune, go from Boston to a Colorado ranch and prove that pioneer blood still flows in her veins. *The Long Quest* (1933) concerns two orphan brothers who were separated in childhood and who seek each other when grown. *Shining Palace* (1933) is about a rich girl who is disinherited when she marries a penniless young man. An act of heroism cripples him, and then the father comes to the aid of them and their three children. *The Wind Blows West* (1934) is the saga of the Alden family which moved to Colorado in the 1860's and in three decades helped the state and Denver.

The Kings of Beacon Hill (1935) studies the relationship between the aristocratic King family of Boston and the ordinary Bowen family of Roxbury, beginning in 1900, when Robert King marries Sandra Bowen. She wins the good will of Robert's mother. *Swift Waters* (1935) is the story of a New England mill town and how the river in flood affects many of the inhabitants. *I Was Christabel* (1938) gives a picture of a New England childhood, mostly autobiographical. *As the Seed Is Sown* (1940) unites a boy from a divorced family with a motherly girl in a neighboring, happy home. *A Golden Age* (1942) portrays family life in a Massachusetts town in the 1880's and 1890's. *Fair Were the Days* (1947), a sequel, carries the story to the end of the nineteenth century. *Stronger Than Law* (1948) tells how a boy, brought up in luxury, develops a strong character after a hasty marriage and the loss of his wealth.

ANNE PARRISH

Leja Gorska

was born on November 12, 1888, in Colorado Springs, Colorado, where she spent her early childhood and attended the Misses Ferris' School. When she moved to her grandmother's home in Claymont, Delaware, she continued her education at the Misses Hebb's School in nearby Wilmington. She studied painting in Philadelphia. Both her father and mother were artists, and she was brought up in a studio atmosphere. Maxfield Parrish is a cousin, and her brother, Dillwyn Parrish (who died in 1941), was a painter, illustrator, and novelist. At the age of six months she began to travel in this country, Europe, England and Wales, the West Indies, Iceland, Norway, Sweden, Denmark, Turkey, Egypt, and the Orient. In 1915 she married Charles A. Corliss, who died in 1936. In the summer of 1930 she cruised around the Mediterranean, and rode camels in the desert and donkeys in the Holy Land. In 1938 she married the poet and novelist, Josiah Titzell; he died in 1943. With her brother, Dillwyn, she wrote and illustrated two books for children: *Knee-High to a Grasshopper* (1923) and *The Dream Coach* (1924), each doing half of the writing and half of the pictures. Brother and sister also collaborated on a group of short stories and sketches called *Lustres* (1924). She wrote and illustrated a book for children, *Floating Island* (1930), about the shipwreck of a house being moved to the Tropics.

A Pocketful of Poses (1923), her first novel, is the story of a girl who poses from childhood until affectation and romantic untruthfulness become second nature. *Semi-Attached* (1924) concerns a girl who has observed so much unhappy marriage that she is unwilling to wed. But in Switzerland she persuades a young man to dispense with the actual ceremony and return to the United States with her, apparently married. *The Perennial Bachelor* (1925), which was awarded the Harper prize, describes a man's life from his pampered childhood to the age of sixty, when he is still a beau who goes to young parties, unaware that everyone laughs at him. *Tomorrow Morning* (1926) concerns a widow who raises her son in an atmosphere of adoration and spoils him. His unsuccessful marriage for a time destroys her happiness, but she regains her cheerfulness.

All Kneeling (1928) pictures a vain, selfish young lady, Christabel Caine, who poses as a gentle and kindly person. She deludes all except her Uncle Johnnie, who sees through her. *The Methodist Faun* (1929) studies the inhibited and frustrated Clifford Hunter, whose mother's stern control made him pathetically incapable of finding pleasure anywhere except in trips to the woods. *Loads of Love* (1932) has a novelist become engaged to a young, intellectual woman, only to realize that he really loves a mountain girl. *Sea Level* (1934) pictures a group of people on a world cruise, where Mary Mallory hopes to reestablish her love for her husband. *Golden Wedding* (1936) concerns a poor boy who rises to great wealth despite an improvident wife. The four children are failures.

Mr. Despondency's Daughter (1938) traces the changes in a woman who alters from a clinging vine to a freed and freeing person. *Pray for a Tomorrow* (1941) is an allegorical tale of man's need for brotherhood. An English fisherman, Andrew, befriends and then betrays a Jewish refugee. Peter Fisher, really St. Peter, takes Andrew on a journey through the centuries to Calvary to teach what men have done to one another. *Poor Child* (1945) touchingly tells of a poor boy from the New York slums who is taken into a rich home and treated to superficial charity. *A Clouded Star* (1948) recounts the trek of nine slaves from the Carolinas to Canada under the inspiring leadership of Harriet Tubman, a Negro slave.

ALICE BEAL PARSONS

Bradford Bachrach

was born on October 8, 1886, in Rockford, Illinois, the daughter of Mart A. Beal. She was educated at Rockford High School and Bradford, Massachusetts, Academy and received her bachelor's degree from Rockford College in 1908. She then pursued special courses in literature at the University of Chicago. She has lived in the Midwest, in Vermont, where she managed a thousand-acre farm, and in New York City, where she did free-lance newspaper writing for one year and book reviewing for a dozen more. From 1922 to 1925 she was business manager of *The World Tomorrow,* a magazine. She married Hugh Graham Parsons in 1914; they have one daughter. Mrs. Parsons resides in the Hudson River Valley, about whose inhabitants she has written the short stories in *The Mountain* (1944) and *The World Around the Mountain* (1947).

Mrs. Parsons is primarily interested in observing and recreating the American scene with its highly individualistic people and the social and physical background in which they live.

The Insider (1929), her first novel, is a lyrical recreation of the lives of two dissimilar people. One is a woman novelist who becomes a legend in the 1920's for her love affairs and the stories that record them, who is an observer, exploiter, and intellectual parasite, and who lives outside the main stream of life. The other is the man who makes her success possible, but who in middle age is regarded by her with contempt because he is a "mere" businessman and has devoted his energies to building up a great industry. The story is set in New York City and in a Maine coast village. *John Merrill's Pleasant Life* (1930) is a study of two contrasting American types: Castle, a generous, abundant, creative spirit whose great factory reanimates the little Hudson River town in which he set it, and Merrill, his successor, an intellectually subtle, self-centered man, incapable of having created the Castle works, but quite able to carry it on for one comfortable lifetime.

A Lady Who Lost (1932) is a social comedy in which three codes of conduct—that of the conventional but spirited and magnanimous lady, that of a cynical intellectual, and that of an enthusiastic young labor leader—are brought into conflict by a mill strike and a murder in a charming Hudson River town. *The Trial of Helen McLeod* (1938) describes the hysteria which sweeps through an Illinois manufacturing city in 1919 when nine men and a woman are accused on "framed" evidence of criminal sedition because they have formed a branch of the Communist Labor party, which they have mistakenly assumed to be socialistic and democratic in its aims. The whole city takes sides for and against the accused in the sensational trial, which is eventually won by Clarence Darrow, the only non-fictional character in the book, which records in novel form an actual case. *I Know What I'd Do* (1946) is a dramatic and touching love story with a Hudson River Valley setting. The theme is that a whole community is responsible for a murder because the people continually say "I know what I'd do" about an emotional and deeply wronged young couple.

BELLAMY PARTRIDGE

was born in Phelps, New York, son of Samuel Selden and Frances (Bellamy) Partridge, one of a family of eight children. He was educated at the Norwalk Preparatory School, at Hobart College (which bestowed upon him the degree of Doctor of Literature in 1940), and Union University from which he graduated in 1901. He married Helen Lawrence Davis on October 22, 1928; they have two children. He was admitted to the New York bar in the year of his graduation and to the United States District Court soon afterward. After a period of practice in New York and California, he abandoned the law and in 1918 went to France as a war correspondent. In 1919 he was attached to the press delegation accompanying President Wilson to England, Italy, Belgium, and the peace conference at Versailles. After the war he served as a special correspondent of the United Press and during 1921 was on the editorial board of *Sunset* magazine. From 1923 to 1929 he was on the editorial staff of Brentano's, and from 1934 to 1936 he served as editor of Arcadia House Publications.

He is author of the following works: *Sube Cane* (1917), *Cousins* (1925), *Amundsen—The Splendid Norseman* (1929), *A Pretty Pickle* (1930), *Sir Billy Howe* (1932), *Pure and Simple* (1934), *Long Night* (under the *nom de plume* of "Thomas Bailey," 1935), *The Roosevelt Family in America* (1936), *Thunder Shower* (1936), *Horse and Buggy* (1937), and *As We Were* (with Otto Bettmann, 1946).

Country Lawyer (1939) is a well-seasoned portrait of a dignified, strongly individualistic and lovable personality such as could have been produced only by a country town as yet untouched by the automobile, the telephone, the motion picture, or the radio. *Big Family* (1941) deals principally with the out-of-the-office activities of the country lawyer. *Excuse My Dust* (1943) carries the country lawyer up to the turn of the century and the coming of the automobile.

January Thaw (1945) narrates the adventures of a young couple who buy and restore an ancient colonial house in Connecticut; the title thereto turns out to be spurious, and a former owner and his wife return, take up residence there, and remain until the flaw in the title is itself found to be false. In dramatized form the story reached Broadway for a successful run and has since been in great demand for summer theaters and amateur performances. *Big Freeze* (1948) is a novel of New York in the 1840's when the up-and-coming little town was planning to obtain its first city water through the construction of the then fabulous forty-five-mile Croton Aqueduct. *The Old Oaken Bucket* (1949), also placed in a Connecticut locale, is a novel with a garden-club setting and involves a dilapidated house with a slightly counterfeit historical background.

KENNETH PATCHEN

was born on December 13, 1911, in Niles, Ohio, of Scotch-French-English parentage. He grew up in Warren, Ohio, and attended high school there; at seventeen he went to work in the steel mills of the Mahoning Valley. After a short stay at Alexander Meiklejohn's Experimental College at the University of Wisconsin, he spent several years drifting around the country doing odd jobs. In 1936 he was awarded a Guggenheim fellowship. He paints individual pictures on the covers of limited editions of his books.

Mr. Patchen's first book was a volume of advance-guard poetry, *Before the Brave* (1936). This was followed by *First Will and Testament* (1939), which contains about one hundred poems, three surrealistic dramas, and the beginning of a projected epic. He has since written six more volumes of poetry, including *Selected Poems* (1947). His prose writings include *Sleepers Awake* (1946), a philosophical essay filled with great art and wisdom, and *They Keep Riding All the Time* (1947).

His first novel, *The Journal of Albion Moonlight* (1941), pictures the pain of the world and gives a terrifying history of a human mind in a style comparable with that of James Joyce's *Ulysses*. *The Memoirs of a Shy Pornographer* (1945) is, according to the title page, "an amusement," which retails a love story. *See You in the Morning* (1948), the story of a love that transcends the knowledge of death, concerns a young man who, knowing he has but a short time to live, falls in love with an idealistic girl who destroys his fear of death. The scene is on a beach at a resort.

ANNE PATERSON

is the pseudonym—her grandmother's name—employed by Anne F. Einselen, who was born in Philadelphia and educated in its public schools. In lieu of college she became a medical secretary to a urologist and gained an invaluable education from eminent specialists who teach as well as practice; she learned science, psychology, sociology, and economics in addition to office routine and research technique. With a psychiatrist she visited psychopathic wards and dispensaries; with an obstetrician, operating clinics, delivery rooms, and maternity wards. She attended lectures given to senior medical students. After her employer's death, she achieved perspective to see the experience for the rare thing it was; and she also found time to think about putting it on paper, to capture in particular the doctor and his group. She received a fellowship at the Bread Loaf conference in 1939. In February, 1944, she joined the editorial staff of *The Ladies' Home Journal,* where her particular job is advising and assisting beginning authors.

Take These Hands (1939), her first novel, is a psychological study of the education, disillusionment, and regeneration of a young obstetrician and his association with a great man. *Sleepless Candle* (1941) presents a brilliant and dynamic symphony cellist-composer who, going deaf and tormented into a breakdown, refuses to admit his dependence on his wife and best friend and thereby brings tragedy to his family. *Queen Street Story* (1949) concerns the struggle of medical science against superstition and ignorance in the 1880's, and the conflicts in the life of a young practitioner who is trapped into a marriage he never wanted.

LOUIS PAUL

was born on December 4, 1901, in New York City. His grandmother was a woodcarver and sculptor who emigrated from Paris, while his mother's ancestors were of pre-Revolutionary Dutch stock. After a public school education in New York, he enlisted in the army in World War I, although he was in reality too young to serve. There followed a period in which he did much traveling about the United States, making observations which were afterward incorporated in his early novels and short stories. His first short story appeared in *Esquire* and won the 1934 O. Henry Memorial award. In 1948 his play, "The Cup of Trembling," starring Elisabeth Bergner, was presented on Broadway. He is married and lives in New York.

Of himself he says: "It seems to me that the author functions best as an extension of his readers' own faculties. What I am trying to do in my books and stories is to impose a certain order and discipline upon the chaotic material of experience. Among other things I have worked as a laborer, as a movie extra, at mining, and on dam construction. I have worked as a teacher, both in a school for immigrants and in a university. I did some professional gambling, and some professional script-writing for Hollywood. These experiences are pertinent to the writer only if he is capable of ordering them into certain parts which illuminate and extend the reader's understanding. My novels in particular have been consistently designed to accomplish this purpose."

The Pumpkin Coach (1935), his first novel, pictures the strange mixture of cynicism and affirmation, of dishonesty and idealism in the United States as seen by a Samoan boy on a trip from San Francisco to New York. *A Horse in Arizona* (1936) describes the Rabelaisian wanderings in France and America of a soldier during and after World War I. *Emma* (1937) pictures a wife who leaves home to win personal success in New York as the owner of a chain of restaurants, only to want her husband back. *The Wrong World* (1938) is about Ernest Morrow, whose mother makes him study music. Although he makes his début in Carnegie Hall, he cannot find his niche in the world until he returns to San Francisco and achieves success as a vaudeville actor.

A Passion for Privacy (1940) pictures a rich family trying to avoid publicity because a polo-playing son marries a cook's daughter. His father-in-law's wise counsel helps the boy become a success. *The Reverend Ben Pool* (1941) has a young Presbyterian minister leave his small Missouri church to dwell among the frustrated tenants of a New York City boarding house. *This Is My Brother* (1943) tells, in the diary of one of them, the stories of five men captured on Bataan and executed as spies by the Japanese. *Breakdown* (1946) portrays the disintegration and recovery of a happily married newspaperwoman who has been an addict of alcohol. *Summer Storm* (1949) is a dramatic examination of jealousy, the story of a woman who tries to build an impregnable defense about herself in order to conceal a psychological weakness. *A Husband for Mama* (1950) describes a college professor's family's attempts to pay off its debts.

JOSEPH STANLEY PENNELL

Engstead

was born and brought up in Junction City, Kansas, a town which had, in earlier days, played host to Hickok, General Custer, Armistead, and Jeb Stuart. The son of a North Carolina photographer and his pioneer wife, Mr. Pennell traces his lineage back through an array of Civil War veterans, both Union and Confederate. After a conventional boyhood in Junction City, he attended the University of Kansas, from which he graduated in 1926, and then rounded out his education with three years of study at Pembroke College, Oxford. Returning to this country, he worked successively for newspapers in St. Louis, Los Angeles, and Huntington Park, where he was managing editor of the *Signal* until his return to Junction City. His career up to this time has included, also, teaching and a cub-reporting job on the Denver *Post;* he has also served as a continuity writer and announcer in radio, and was for a time heard twice a week as "Professor of Microphone English." Shortly after the completion of his first book, he enlisted in the army and became public-relations director for the entire anti-aircraft training center at Fort Bliss. He now resides in Seaside, Oregon.

The History of Rome Hanks (1944), his first novel, is a panoramic picture of America from 1860 to 1940 as seen through the eyes of Lee Harrington, who reviews the life of his great-grandfather and the men and women of the Civil War period. In *The History of Nora Beckham* (1948) Lee tells his own story and that of his vain and nagging mother, who dominated her husband, a photographer, and her son. The setting is in Fork City, Kansas, early in the 1900's.

GEORGE SESSIONS PERRY

Dmitri Kessel

was born in Rockdale, Texas, on May 5, 1910. He was educated at Allen Academy in Bryan, Texas; Southwestern University at Georgetown, Texas; Purdue University; and Houston University. In 1942 he became a war correspondent for *The New Yorker* and *The Saturday Evening Post.* Some of his short stories appeared in *Hackberry Cavalier* (1944).

His books include *Texas: A World In Itself* (1942), a biography of the state of Texas; *Thirty Days Hath September* (with Dorothy Cameron Disney, 1943), a mystery novel, which deals with some bizarre happenings during a long weekend in a small Connecticut summer resort; *Roundup Time* (1943), a collection of southwestern writing; *Where Away* (with Isabel Leighton, 1944), the story of the gallant cruiser *Marblehead,* which made its way home after being bombed and almost sunk in the Java Sea early in World War II; *Cities of America* (1947), a group of profiles of the larger and more colorful cities in the United States from New York to San Francisco, from Chicago to New Orleans, and as contrast to these cities, the author's home town, Rockdale, Texas; *My Granny Van* (1949), a biography of Mr. Perry's grandmother; and *Families of America* (1949), an account of nine families of Americans with varying ethnic backgrounds, temperaments, and means of earning their bread. Although they or their ancestors were born abroad, they are presented as neighbors.

Walls Rise Up (1939), his first novel, is an earthy, humorous tale of three hoboes arriving in a Texas community from California. Jimmy has schemes for getting food and drink; Eddie and Mike willingly follow his leadership through many adventures. *Hold Autumn in Your Hand* (1941) is about a "poor white," Sam Tucker, a Texas tenant farmer, who lives in a one-room cabin with his wife, three children, "Granny," and a hunting dog. After a poor year on his sixty acres and a summer-long duel with a catfish, he thinks that the next year will be better.

ANN PETRY

Edna Guy

was born on October 12, 1911, in Old Saybrook, Connecticut, the daughter of Peter and Bertha Lane. She graduated from the Old Saybrook High School in 1929 and received her degree in 1934 from the College of Pharmacy of the University of Connecticut. She then worked as a registered pharmacist in the drugstores owned by her family in Old Saybrook and Lyme and in spare moments wrote short stories. After her marriage to George Davis Petry on February 22, 1938, she moved to New York City. Deciding to seek a career as a writer, she took a position in 1939 in the advertising department of the Harlem *Amsterdam News.* Two years later she transferred to the Harlem *People's Voice* and edited the woman's page and wrote news stories. In this work she saw every phase of life in the Negro community, and it became her ambition to write about the Negroes of Harlem as people with feelings, problems, and abilities identical to those of the people of other races. She made a special study of the effects of segregation on children. In 1945 a Houghton Mifflin fellowship was awarded to her. Her first story appeared in 1943 in *The Crisis. The Drugstore Cat* (1949) is a juvenile.

Her first novel, *The Street* (1946), is the story of a young Negro woman who strives to lift herself and her eight-year-old son out of their unsatisfactory surroundings on 116th Street in Harlem. She distrusts the whites, but most of her struggle to maintain her moral integrity is against members of her own race. *Country Place* (1947) deals with the return of young Johnny Roane from four years in the army to his home in Lenox, Connecticut; in that small town during a hurricane the tension increases as a taxi driver gossips about John's wife.

ANN PINCHOT

Erich Hartmann

was born in New York City in 1910. Her first fifteen years were spent in Michigan, where she was educated, but after that she again lived in New York City and worked for Saks-Fifth Avenue. She has written short stories and serial novels for the leading women's magazines. She married Ben Pinchot, a graduate civil engineer who shifted to photography and who now collaborates with his wife. They have one child and live in Connecticut.

Hour upon the Stage (1929), her first novel, tells the story of Israel Challanty, who migrates from Poland to a Michigan lumber camp, where he rises from a peddler to be a successful merchant. His five children feel the effect of the care of a sensitive mother and a straightforward if uncouth father. *Shrine of Fair Women* (1932) portrays owners and employees of a stylish Fifth Avenue department store founded by Moses Marks, who began as a peddler and rose to eminence as a merchant. *Talk of the Town* (1941) is a story of civic corruption as seen in the dishonest building of a school, which collapses and kills the janitor. The contractor attempts to implicate an esteemed lawyer, but is foiled by his daughter and a newspaperman. *Hear This Woman!* (with Ben Pinchot, 1949) concerns a small-town newspaperwoman, Faith Holmes, who rises to prominence as a personality in radio and politics, because she organized women to achieve good government. She seems to some people to be a force for good and to others, a dangerous woman.

JOSEPHINE PINCKNEY

Arni

was born on January 25, 1895, in Charleston, South Carolina. She attended Ashley Hall in Charleston, and studied English at Charleston College, Columbia University, and Radcliffe College. Her literary career began with the writing of poetry; her poems on local themes gave a foretaste of the stories to come. She has been steeped in the peculiar and mysteriously haunting beauty of the Low Country of South Carolina: its moss-bearded live oak trees, its brooding cypress swamps, and its old houses on the rice rivers with their magnolia and azalea gardens, but her approach is not a sentimental one. She knows by heart the history of Charleston and she has been interested in the contrast between the survivors of the southern aristocracy and the new, vigorous generation engaged in trade and manufacturing. The folklore, the songs, and the superstitious beliefs of the people have been a special object of her study. In addition to her writing chores, she has found time to help found The Society for the Preservation of Spirituals and The Poetry Society of South Carolina. *Sea-Drinking Cities* (1927) is a volume of poems.

Hilton Head (1941) is an historical novel of a young surgeon who helps to colonize Charleston, South Carolina, in the seventeenth century amid suffering and hardship. *Three O'Clock Dinner* (1945), which portrays Charleston, shows the dismay of the Redcliffe family when Tat announces at a formal dinner party that he will marry Lorena Hessenwinkle. *Great Mischief* (1948) is a whimsical tale of a Charleston druggist, Timothy Partridge, who is dominated by his sister. He practices witchcraft, burns his shop, and makes a visit to Hell.

BENTZ PLAGEMANN

Axel

was born on July 27, 1913, in Springfield, Ohio; he was raised in Euclid, a suburb of Cleveland. He has worked in bookstores in Cleveland, Chicago, Detroit, and New York and has taught courses in journalistic style and short-story writing at New York University. While on duty in the navy in Africa during World War II he suffered an attack of poliomyelitis; the account of his treatment and cure at the Warm Springs Foundation in Georgia is given in *My Place to Stand* (1949).

The scene of his novels is Ohio; although the books differ widely in theme and treatment, Mr. Plagemann's preoccupation with changing social and religious forms is evident throughout. He is concerned not only with the struggle between good and evil but also with the questions raised by the development of the social and physical sciences in our time. He wants to examine the institutions of church, marriage, and home in this light. In his style he seeks simplicity, based on a study of the classic Latin writers.

William Walter (1941), his first book, is a biographical novel of a misunderstood genius who, unhappy himself, makes miserable everyone with whom he comes in contact because of his demands upon their understanding. *All for the Best* (1946), a satire intended as a modern *Candide* in the form of that novel, tells of a young man's search for the meaning of life. He is much concerned with the processes of democracy in America and examines them during his service as a physician in the navy during World War II. After a disillusioning episode with the wrong woman, he turns to the love of his youth. *Into the Labyrinth* (1948) deals with a young man's choice between the morality he feels dictated to him as a member of the Catholic Church and his natural impulses. The central theme is the spiritual conflict in a struggle between sacred and profane love. The story ends on a note of spiritual uplift.

ERNEST POOLE

was born on January 23, 1880, in Chicago, Illinois, and died in Franconia, New Hampshire, on January 10, 1950. He was educated in private schools in Chicago and graduated with honors from Princeton University in 1902. While living in the University Settlement House on the lower East Side of New York, he described tenement-house conditions and wrote magazine articles that were influential in anti-tuberculosis campaigns. *McClure's* magazine published some of his most potent "muckraking" articles. He was *The Outlook's* correspondent during the turbulent Chicago stockyard strike of 1904. He covered the Russian Revolution of 1905 and traveled among the peasants into the Caucasus Mountains. Married in 1907 in New York City, he lived in Greenwich Village, where many of his plays and novels were written. His plays—"A Man's Friends," with a political theme, and "None So Blind," which examined psychological traits—had short Broadway runs. In World War I he was a correspondent for *The Saturday Evening Post.* In 1917 he traveled through Russia, again reporting village life during the Lenin revolution. He wrote the story of his own life in *The Bridge* (1940), summing up his writings as a bridge between two periods of American development. *The Great White Hills of New Hampshire* (1945) is a non-fiction book about his adopted state.

Ernest Poole's first and most important novel, *The Harbor* (1915), pictures America as strong, turbulent, confident, able to solve the new problems confronting it, and worthy of the faith of the immigrants in their "promised land." William Dean Howells, then dean of American novelists, acclaimed it. Three decades later John Chamberlain, in his retrospect upon literature, characterized it as the outstanding American proletarian novel, partly because it pictures the America of the future as controlled by organized workers. The harbor, a symbol of the changing world of business, is both hero and villain as seen through the eyes of a Brooklyn boy brought up on the waterfront. The background came from the author's own observation and revealed an expanding, exuberant, dynamic America. The style was an innovation in novel writing, introducing journalistic crispness and a sense of urgent speed.

His Family (1917), a Pulitzer prize winner, has as its theme the new social forces arising out of the immigrant masses and impinging upon the life of an old New York family. The clash of old and new standards, aims, and cultures is brought into sharp relief; an impending change in American society is foreshadowed. The story concerns Roger Gale and his attempts to understand the bewildering currents of modern life as they are reflected in the activities of his three daughters.

Poole's next few novels were less deep and less popular. *The Village* (1917) concerns life in Russia. *His Second Wife* (1918) shows how the sister of a man's first wife revives his interest in his professional ideas and also marries him. *Blind* (1920) is the story of an

American correspondent who lost his eyesight in World War I. *Beggar's Gold* (1921) concerns a New York City schoolteacher who must wait thirty years to realize her dream of visiting China. *Millions* (1922) describes the attitudes of a sister, some uninvited relatives, and an actress who appear at the bedside of a supposedly dying millionaire. *Danger* (1923) is about morbid Maud Brewer, aged thirty-eight and an old maid, who wants to do well but who indirectly causes the death of her shell-shocked brother.

The Avalanche (1924) has the theme of a physician-healer overwhelmed by swarms of patients and by publicity that destroys his gift of healing. *The Hunter's Moon* (1925) is about the unhappy home life of a boy who escapes from his dominating grandmother and sings and dreams on an apartment roof. *The Little Dark Man* (1925) contains tales of old Russia and of the simple life of the peasants in the villages. *With Eastern Eyes* (1926) tells how a Russian astronomer on a visit to a fellow scientist in this country averts a tragedy developing between his friend and his friend's wife. *Silent Storms* (1927) has a forty-eight-year-old man marry a beautiful young French girl only to realize that he should have married her mother.

The Car of Croesus (1930) concerns an exiled Russian prince and a young lady who buy a Rolls Royce and rent it at a hundred dollars an hour. They play chauffeur and maid and listen to the passengers' stories. The book shows something of the folly and pretense of the 1920's. *The Destroyer* (1931) portrays an idealistic newspaper correspondent who sees the bitterness and disillusionment of Europe after World War I and who returns to New York, where he is bewildered by greed and hypocrisy. *Great Winds* (1933) deals with the theme of man's pursuit of material goods and his need to develop his soul to provide resources against a day of crisis. John Blake returns to his New Hampshire home, where the simple life is contrasted with that of city bankers and businessmen.

One of Us (1934) pictures some of the changes which have taken place in America through the record of a mountain village in New Hampshire as reported by Ted Gale, a storekeeper. Ted marries Leila, who goes to New York as a journalist. He feels that he has viewed life as fully as she. *The Nancy Flier, A Stagecoach Epic* (1949) is a vivid and accurate reconstruction of forty-five years of New Hampshire stagecoach history in the story of Bob Gale and other drivers who traveled through the New Hampshire hills. A stagecoach is the heroine in the same sense that the harbor was the hero of his first and most remembered novel.

EDITH POPE

was born in St. Augustine, Florida, on July 23, 1905. She was educated in the public schools; at Baldwin School in Bryn Mawr, Pennsylvania; at Florida State College for Women, where she received her bachelor's degree in 1928; and at Columbia University, where she earned a master's degree in 1931. A book of verse, *The Black Lagoon* (1926), and her first three novels, which were experiments in narrative writing, were published under her maiden name, Edith Everett Taylor. In 1933 she married Verle A. Pope of St. Augustine. *Biggety Chameleon* (1945) is a juvenile.

All of Mrs. Pope's books have had Florida as a locale. She considers her central interest to be the art of writing and not any specific subject, but the portrayal of the atmosphere and the nature of the country in which she was born concerns her more and more.

Not Magnolias (1928), her first novel, is about the love problem of Leigh Monroe, a southern college girl, who believes that she is morally obligated to marry her mentally ill cousin, Stephen, an inmate of a sanitorium, who sends her impassioned letters. She rejects another suitor until at Stephen's release she is freed to choose between duty and love. *Old Lady Esteroy* (1934), set in a Florida town in the years after 1835, is a psychological novel tracing the effect of an unhappy love affair upon a proud and masterful southern woman. At forty she had agreed to leave her husband, a general, for a livelier lover who changed his mind. Her disappointment causes her to become bitter in her old age and to tyrannize over her dependents and to use her money to further her malevolent ends. *Half Holiday* (1938) depicts the thoughts and feelings of three wives whose husbands presumably drown on a fishing trip.

Colcorton (1944), with the themes of miscegenation and the effect of sin upon later generations, is set in the jungle coastal region of northeast Florida near St. Augustine. Abby Claghearne and her brother, Jared, live in the mansion, "Colcorton," erected by their grandfather, who had married a Negress. Jared learns the secret after he marries, and Abby makes her peace with his wife after his death.

ZELDA POPKIN

Arthur Dobbs

was born July 5, 1898, in Brooklyn, New York. She has spent most of her life in Manhattan but nevertheless calls Wilkes-Barre, Pennsylvania, her "home town," because her diploma was issued by its high school and her first job was on the Wilkes-Barre *Times-Leader,* where at sixteen she became a specialist in reporting homicides. From 1919 until 1943 she was associated in the public-relations business with her late husband, Louis Popkin. During those years, while she was raising two sons and their animal pets, she wrote extensively for magazines and was the author of six mystery novels. She is a full-time writer but between books invariably undertakes something new. In 1944 she entered law school, but left the study of torts, crimes, and property when the American Red Cross asked her to go to the European theater of operations on special assignment. She traveled extensively in France, Germany, and Austria. In 1947 she collaborated on the writing of a play, and in 1948 boarded a ship for the battlefronts in Israel.

Zelda Popkin's novels have one central theme, the human capacity for growth in understanding and accepting life. *The Journey Home* (1945), her first novel, developed this theme through the meeting of a young air-force lieutenant on leave with a segment of America on a crack Florida train. *Small Victory* (1947) is the spiritual odyssey of an American college professor in post-war Germany. *Walk Through the Valley* (1949) tells of a woman's struggle for economic and emotional security in middle age.

DAWN POWELL

Glidden

was born on November 28, 1897, in Mt. Gilead, Ohio. Her mother died when Dawn was a small child; she and her two sisters were sent by their father from one aunt on a farm to another in a village, and then to one who ran a boarding house in a small factory town. Miss Powell learned about human nature from these relatives, whose codes varied from overstrictness to liberality. In 1909 her father married a second wife and brought the family together on her farm near Cleveland, Ohio. Miss Powell ran away with thirty cents in her pocket, a sum earned picking berries. She went to the home of an aunt in Shelby, Ohio, attended high school, edited the school paper, and worked on the town newspaper. She carried on journalistic enterprises while at Lake Erie College in Painesville, Ohio. After graduation in 1918, she went to New York, served as a yeoman in the navy, and then undertook publicity work. In 1920 she met and married Joseph R. Gousha, an advertising man. Several of her plays have been produced on Broadway, and her scenarios have been used in Hollywood.

Her earlier novels were realistic studies of small-town life, but in 1936 she began a series of novels satirizing the provincial people in New York City. Certain characters continue through several of these books. "Coming as I do from many generations of small-town American people," says Miss Powell, "I am basically interested in the problems of the provincial at home and in the world, in business, love, and art. I would like to portray these Americans as vividly as Balzac did his French provincials at home and in Paris."

Whither (1925), her first novel, is the story of Zoe Bourne, who leaves the dull, small town of her birth to follow a theatrical career in New York. She begins by writing short potboiler essays in preparation for composing a play. After hardship and disappointment, she finds romance. *She Walks in Beauty* (1928) pictures two girls, Linda and Dorrie, who grow up in a railroad boarding house run by their grandmother in a small Iowa town. One hopes for a place in local society, and the other has an imagination which finds beauty in her sordid surroundings. The wishes of each one come true. *The Bride's House* (1929) pictures rural Ohio aristocratic life in the 1890's in a story of Sophie Truelove, whose affair with another man jeopardizes her marriage.

Dance Night (1930) is a story of young aspirations and hope set against the tough factory and railroad town of Lamptown, Ohio. On Thursday evening Harry Fischer comes from Cleveland to teach a dancing class and to preside over the ball which follows. Here come the mill people, who are portrayed in their relationship to Jen, aged thirteen, who wants to be a Broadway dancer, and Morry, who hopes to be a famous New York architect. *The Tenth Moon* (1932) sets down in a setting of a small midwestern town the frustrations and hopes of Connie Benjamin, the wife of a cobbler, and Blaine Decker, a high-school music teacher. Their artistic interests draw them together into friendship and mutual assistance transcending tragic reality. *The Story of a Country Boy* (1934) traces the rise of a farm boy, Chris Bennett, to success as a steel-corporation manager. He and his wife, Joy, realize that they cannot be simple people as long as he remains an executive.

Turn, Magic Wheel (1936) satirizes the literary life in New York City in the story of a novelist who deserts his wife. Her loyalty is described as a life of "sterile lies" by another novelist in a book. *The Happy Island* (1938) tells about the small-time club entertainers, radio artists, dilettantes, professional beauties, and "doubtful men" in the tale of Prudence Bly, a magnetic night-club singer in Manhattan. *Angels on Toast* (1940) is about a group of high-pressure, selfish, morally unstable business people who have grown unhappy in marriage and have found solace in unfaithful mistresses. It is a commentary on the *nouveaux riches* in business life who spend their days in big deals and their nights in untangling their amorous adventures.

A Time To Be Born (1942) satirizes the career of a ruthless woman who uses love, marriage, friendship, and even the war itself to get what she wants. Amanda Keeler, a successful novelist, goes after what she desires and gets it. The incidental portraits of gaudy and shallow pretenders are excellent. *My Home Is Far Away* (1944) chronicles the struggle of a midwestern family in the early nineteenth century to keep together, and is the first of a trilogy about three motherless daughters who spend their time with one or another affectionate but uncaring relative. *The Locusts Have No King* (1948) satirizes the cultural charlatans and poseurs in New York City in a story of an intellectual scholar who loves the wife of a Broadway playwright.

THEODORE PRATT

was born in Minneapolis, Minnesota, April 26, 1901. When he was fourteen, his family moved to New Rochelle, New York. He spent two years at Colgate University and two more at Columbia University, but he was not interested in taking a degree; he simply studied subjects to his liking. After a year in Europe, he returned to work as a play reader, play reviewer, and play movie scout for motion-picture companies in New York City. On October 26, 1929, he married Belle J. Jacques and went with her to live for four years in Italy, France, and Spain. "Paradise Enjoys a Boom," his essay for *The American Mercury* about conditions in Spain, caused that country to request his departure.

In 1934 he moved to Florida, where he has made his home ever since. He says that Florida has furnished him with writing material he could find nowhere else in the United States, and he is grateful to the state for this. In return he has performed useful service, for an article, "Papa of the Everglades National Park," was instrumental in getting this park established. He wrote a large part of the Florida issue of *Holiday* magazine in 1947. "The Owl That Kept Winking" is in *Best Short Stories of 1945*.

Mr. Pratt has worked in Hollywood as a screen writer. One of his plays ran on Broadway for six months. His essays and stories appear in leading magazines; some of this material is in *Perils in Provence and Other Ticklish Places* (1944). Three of his murder mysteries, written under the name "Timothy Brace," have Florida settings: *Murder Goes Fishing* (1936), *Murder Goes in a Trailer* (1937), and *Murder Goes to the Dogs* (1938). A fourth mystery, *Murder Goes to the World's Fair* (1939), ended his work in this field, for it no longer interested him.

His main writing interest concerns the southeastern Florida coast. He has accumulated nearly a quarter of a million words of notes and regards himself as an authority on the history of the section from 1887 to the present time. He takes great pains to make his books authentic. He loves Florida, he says, but not blindly. He has pictured it as he has seen it. His essays, short stories, and eight novels probably make him the author who has written more about the state than any other.

His first novel, *Spring from Downward* (1933), concerns the depression. *Not Without the Wedding* (1934) describes expatriates in Spain. *Big Blow* (1936), a story about a Florida hurricane, tells the story of a Nebraska farmer who moves to Florida and makes a success with the aid of a back-country girl. *Mercy Island* (1941) is about the Florida Keys and the native conch people who befriend a small group seeking refuge after a shipwreck. In *Mr. Limpet* (1942) a man falls into the ocean and to his considerable astonishment discovers that he has been turned into a fish.

The Barefoot Mailman (1943), now recognized as a Florida classic, pictures the southeast Florida coast at the beginning of the settlement of the area between Miami and Palm Beach in the 1880's. The central figure is Steve Pierton, who on foot carries the mail between these two communities. *Mr. Winkle Goes to War* (1943) is about a mild little middle-aged man who leaves his bossy wife to become a soldier performing heroic feats in World War II. *Thunder Mountain* (1944) concerns a family which tries to retreat from the world on top of a lofty Colorado mountain. *Miss Dilly Says No* (1945) is the tale of a Hollywood movie secretary who refuses to sell her best-selling book to the movies.

Valley Boy (1946) pictures a neglected boy and his pet sea lion in the San Fernando Valley of California. *Mr. Thurtle's Trolley* (1947) has two old trolleymen take their street car along the railroad tracks from New York to California. *The Flame Tree* (1950) portrays the opening up of the southeast Florida coast when from 1893 to 1903 Henry Flagler and others built a luxurious playground out of the isolated settlement called Palm Beach. The title is derived from the royal poinciana, a tree with brilliant scarlet and orange flowers.

FREDERIC PROKOSCH

was born on May 17, 1908, at Madison, Wisconsin, of Austrian parents who had moved to the United States. His father was a renowned philologist. Frederic went to a convent school at the age of four and later to schools in Texas, Germany, Austria, and France. The family shuttled between Europe and America, and the boy traveled widely.

After receiving his degree from Haverford College, he did graduate work in English at the University of Pennsylvania and at Yale University, where he earned his doctorate in 1933. He was a research fellow in English literature at Yale from 1933 to 1935 and at King's College, Cambridge, from 1937 to 1939; he taught at New York University in 1936. Most of his time after 1936 was spent in Europe. His athletic prowess brought him in 1939 the squash-racquets championship of France. He was abroad during World War II, working for the Office of War Information and as attaché in the American Legation in Stockholm.

His several volumes of poems have, in general, a dark and brooding quality and deal with the theme of approaching disaster. His novels, which are set in the several parts of the world in which he has lived, are poetic and philosophical, though in form chiefly picaresque. The masters from whom he has derived guidance in various aspects of his art are the Grimm brothers, Chaucer, Chekov, Conrad, Cervantes, and to a lesser degree Thomas Mann.

Mr. Prokosch, in reply to a query about his philosophy, has said: "A good writer does not write to 'present a theme'; he writes because he loves to write, and of course the 'theme,' or philosophy, or vision of life creeps in little by little. I feel a need for continual movement in my books. I suppose my theme is 'search' or 'flight': *search* for a meaning in life, for peace, and for self-fulfillment; *flight* from stagnation, from imprisonment mental or spiritual. Aside from that, I am writing in order to produce something as moving and beautiful as I can—a work of art as revealing and as searching as it is in my nature to create, and craftsmanship as authentic and appropriate as I can master!"

The Asiatics (1935), his first book, is a first-person travel book and novel of a young American who journeys through Asia from Beirut, Lebanon, to the China Sea. In each of thirteen nations he has strange adventures, but the emphasis is on the interpretations of the Asiatic mind and spirit. *Seven Who Fled* (1937), winner of the Harper prize, tells of seven European men who hurriedly leave Kashgar in central Asia to go with Dr. Liu to Shanghai. They become separated and review their lives and philosophical opinions. The book contains mystical and antimaterialistic views. *Night of the Poor* (1939) is the story of a seventeen-year-old boy's hitchhiking journey from Wisconsin to Texas via the states along the Mississippi River. On the way he sees many aspects of American life and meets many people. His understanding is enlarged and his sympathy is aroused.

The Skies of Europe (1941) describes the mood and temper of Europe during the two months preceding the beginning of war in 1939 in a travel narrative of a wandering American writer. *The Conspirators* (1943) portrays Lisbon, Spain, during the civil war in 1940 and contrasts the old and new cosmopolitanism. Vincent, a man of good will, has escaped from prison and must kill the Nazi agent who betrayed him. *Age of Thunder* (1945) concerns a young soldier's night journey from the south of France on a secret mission to London to discover the traitors among the Maquisards. On the way he realizes the need for brotherhood among all men. *The Idols of the Cave* (1946) has the theme of moral decadence. Jonathan Ely returns to New York City in 1941 from the war in Europe and mingles with titled and aristocratic refugees. The emotional entanglements of five people cause them to blame society and willingly to be victims of a social circumstance they do not attempt to alter. He himself is charmed by a promiscuous ballerina. *Storm and Echo* (1948) follows four men making a journey into the heart of Africa. Each grows weary with civilization, and each changes his philosophy in the course of his travels. The theme is that "The wilderness inside a man is deeper and darker than the heart of the Congo."

OLIVE HIGGINS PROUTY

Bradford Bachrach

was born in Worcester, Massachusetts, the youngest child of Milton Prince Higgins, a professor at the Worcester Polytechnic Institute and later an educator of renown who became known as "the father of the trade school," and of Katharine Chapin Higgins, a speaker and organizer, who was one of the pioneers in founding the Parent-Teacher Association and one of its early presidents. Mrs. Prouty received her pre-college education in the Worcester public schools. She began writing verse and short stories in childhood. At Smith College, from which she graduated in 1904, she was the literary editor of the Smith College *Monthly* and she took a leading part in the literary clubs and activities of the college. In 1907 she married Lewis I. Prouty and went to live in Brookline, Massachusetts, where they still reside. Mrs. Prouty has had four children: one boy and three girls. Two of the girls have died.

Mrs. Prouty's novels reveal her familiarity with family life from the viewpoint of both the adult and the child. These novels, which are pervaded by New England atmosphere, portray that section's characteristics against backgrounds of both the privileged and unprivileged classes. Her chief interest is in character analysis and in the honest portrayal of the New Englander, his personality, and his background. She says: "I am more interested in character analysis than plot. The love story in my books is to me incidental to the problem it often presents. I am more interested in the cause and diagnosis of any problem than in its solution."

Bobbie, General Manager (1913), her first novel, is a unification of a series of incidents about one family; these episodes had appeared as short stories in *McClure's* magazine. *The Fifth Wheel* (1916) continues the story of the same family and pictures a woman who wants to support herself. *Star in the Window* (1918) is a love story with a World War I background about a girl starving for romance who breaks through her New England inhibitions and marries after a short acquaintance a man whom she meets by chance. *Good Sports* (1919) is a collection of short stories dealing with a variety of New England characters who show their good sportsmanship by coping successfully with various adversities.

Stella Dallas (1922), Mrs. Prouty's most widely-known novel, has as its chief character a New England woman of the underprivileged class who is cheap and ordinary but possesses "a heart of gold." Its theme is the sacrifice Stella makes to assure her daughter's happiness. This novel first appeared as a serial in *The American Magazine;* it was dramatized with Mrs. Leslie Carter as star, put into a silent movie which starred Belle Bennett, and then made into a talking picture which featured Barbara Stanwyck. For several years incidents about Stella Dallas have been related on the radio, but Mrs. Prouty has not written these serials and has no control over them.

Conflict (1927) is the story of a married woman's struggle between duty and desire. *White Fawn* (1931), the first in a series of novels dealing with the well-to-do Vale family living in Boston, gives an accurate picture of the life of a débutante in the late 1920's and tells of Fabia's rebellion against social restrictions and of her love for an Irish doctor from the wrong side of the railroad tracks. *Lisa Vale* (1938) tells of the conflicts and problems of Fabia's mother, Lisa, a woman in her forties, and how she deals with her secret love for a business associate of her elderly husband.

Now, Voyager (1941), which continues the Vale saga, tells the story of Charlotte Vale, a pitiable victim of mother domination, and relates her dramatic break from her New England background and her acquisition of independence. *Home Port* (1947) deals with another of the Vales, this time a male member of the family, a young man who is suffering not only from the domination of his New England conscience but from an inferiority complex caused by a brilliant older brother. He regains his self-confidence working as a guide in the Maine woods.

RAND *to* RYLEE

AYN RAND

was born in Petrograd, Russia. She decided to be a writer at the age of nine by inventing people who did things the neighbors would never do. She had no interest or enthusiasm for "people as they are." "I decided to become a writer—not in order to save the world, nor to serve my fellow men—but for the simple, personal, selfish, egotistical happiness of creating the kind of men and events I could like, respect, and admire."

She left home when quite young and has been independent ever since. She came alone to this country and is now an American citizen. This author never studied writing nor took any formal course in literature: she learned by herself in her own way. She worked at all sorts of odd jobs to make a living. "The Night of January 16th" (1935) is a play.

Ayn Rand stresses individualism as the basic theme of all her writing; it is her purpose to present the various aspects of this idea in everything she has written or will write. In regard to literary technique, she puts emphasis on the integration of plot and theme, a strong story line, and an abstract idea. Her work reflects a romantic realism.

We, the Living (1936), her first novel, has for its theme the conflict between the individual and the state. The action is laid in Soviet Russia; it is the story of three young people of independent spirit who cannot exist in slavery and are destroyed by a totalitarian dictatorship. *The Fountainhead* (1943) has as its theme a definition of a new code of ethics: the morality of individualism. The key statement is in Howard Roark's speech: "I wished to come here and say that I am a man who does not exist for others. It had to be said. The world is perishing from an orgy of self-sacrificing." The story, concerning the struggle and triumph of an architect who holds the integrity of his own ideas above all things and against all men, is a demonstration of how the principles of egoism and altruism work out in people and in the events of their lives.

MARJORIE KINNAN RAWLINGS

was born on August 8, 1896, in Washington, D.C., where her father, Arthur F. Kinnan, was a patent attorney. Following graduation from the University of Wisconsin in 1918, she became associated with the national headquarters of the Young Women's Christian Association to write publicity and to assist on the magazine *Home Sector*. From 1919 to 1923 she wrote features for the Louisville *Courier-Journal* and the Rochester, New York, *Journal*, and then for two years she wrote syndicated verse for United Features. In 1928 she purchased a seventy-two-acre grove at Cross Creek, near Hawthorne, Florida, and devoted her time to raising oranges and to writing. A short story, "Gal Young Un," won the O. Henry Memorial award in

1933. In the same year her first book became the choice of the Book-of-the-Month Club.

Her work is particularly notable for the fidelity with which she pictures the feeling of people who live close to nature in the scrub-pine and hammock country of Florida. These "Crackers," whose central Florida dialect she employs, are descendants of pioneer white settlers who shun urban and industrialized communities. The Big Scrub, where two of her novels are laid, is a nearly impenetrable, jungle-like country bounded by the St. Johns and Ocklawaha rivers and lying within the borders of Marion County. "It is profoundly stirring," she said of an early experience. "I became conscious of a peace, and isolation, and, strangely, a safety. The thought came to me then that human life in such a place must share the interest of its background."

Cross Creek Cookery (1942) is a chatty discussion of cooking as practiced in her village, as well as a compilation of more than two hundred recipes. *When the Whippoorwill* (1940) is a collection of stories and a novelette set in the Florida backwoods. *Cross Creek* (1942) is the story of the author's own life and her relationship with nature and her neighbors.

South Moon Under (1933), her first novel, describes the scrub country in the Florida backwoods where the hard conditions of pioneer life still existed in 1900. Lant Jacklin, the hero, is a hunter who retreats to the woods as the community enlarges. *Golden Apples* (1935), set in the 1890's, tells the story of an orphan brother and sister who take possession of an abandoned estate in the "cracker" country and raise oranges. Luke and Allie Brinley, orphaned when the boy is fourteen, move from their rented farm to an abandoned place near Orange Lake.

The Yearling (1938), set in the 1870's, portrays one year in the life of Jody Baxter, a sensitive twelve-year-old boy living in the Florida scrub country. Jody has a tame faun which persists in ruining the family crops; his parents insist that the animal be killed. Jody is frequently compared with Huckleberry Finn, and *The Yearling* is often classed with Mark Twain's novel as one of the important pieces of regional literature in America. It won the Pulitzer prize. Lloyd Morris stated that "within the terms of its intention this is as nearly a perfect work of art as American fiction can display."

ROBERT RAYNOLDS

was born on April 29, 1902, in Santa Fé, New Mexico, in the Governor's Palace, one of the old Spanish buildings in the town, and in the room where Lew Wallace is supposed to have written much of his novel, *Ben Hur*. Raynolds lived in Santa Fé until he was seven, and then moved to Omaha, Nebraska. He entered Princeton in 1919, stayed two years, and then spent a year working at a coal mine in Colorado. He came east and entered Lafayette College, where he alternated, one term in college and one term working in a cement mill, until he graduated in 1925. He went to Mexico, first going across that country from Vera Cruz to Manzanillo and later settling to work at a silver mine in the general region of Durango. At the end of 1929, after doing publicity and editorial work in New York City, he began to devote all his time to writing. After completing three novels, he devoted six years to seven plays. During 1942 and 1943 he worked in a war plant making tools; he is at present a teacher of advanced writing at Columbia University. He is married, has three children, and lives in Newtown, Connecticut.

The Ugly Runts (1935), a verse drama, deals with the struggle of coal miners to achieve a better life. *Summer Song* (1937), a comedy in verse, is a lyrical frolic of young love in the country. *Farewell, Villon,* a one-act comedy, is an imaginary scene occurring in the life of the French poet after he vanishes from Paris and from history. *Boadicea* (1940), a drama in verse, concerns that queen's struggle against Roman rule in Britain.

The statement Raynolds made to his workshop class in the novel at Columbia may well stand as a canon for his own writing: "I sometimes think that we are working to misinterpret life as well as we can, and that each new time we struggle once more to miss the truth by a narrower margin; and now, after all our failures from the beginning of our race on earth, we are still haunted by a living faith that there is truth and that we may find it. And I think that the artist, in whatever creative form, is one who openly devotes his life to this search and to a just expression of his findings, with reverence for the material universe, in humility of spirit and with compassion for his fellow men. For if he be not reverent, how shall he perceive the wonder of this world; and if he be not humble, how shall he receive understanding; and if he have not compassion for his fellow men, how shall he speak to their hearts?"

Brothers in the West (1931), his first novel, is the story of two brothers, bound by mutual love, who for many years roamed through the West and Southwest and died at last together; it is a story of man's fidelity to man in a wilderness world. This book won the Harper prize. *Saunders Oak* (1933) tells of a man's return to his family home in New England, after an absence of twenty years, in a determination to balance his life and achieve fulfillment. When a woman he has known in the past comes back into his life, in need of his protection, he faces the future happily. The scene of *Fortune* (1935) is laid in the Delaware River section between Philadelphia and New York, and the characters represent varying levels of the social scale in an industrial region, all knit together by human interdependence.

May Bretton (1944) is a story, told in simple human and spiritual terms, of May's efforts to make a life for herself in a Connecticut village in spite of severe pressure from fellow townspeople less devoted than she is to a creative vision of life. *The Obscure Enemy* (1945) pictures a man's struggle to find and hold the integrity of his spirit as violence reaches high intensity in an industrial city transformed to meet the demands of war. *Paquita* (1947) is a pre-nuptial comedy, set against a large background of Mexico's war for independence from Spain, and tells the story of a young and lovely daughter of a noble Spanish family brought by interest and affection into the midst of the people's army under the priest-liberator, Hidalgo.

ELMER RICE

Karsh

was born in New York City on September 28, 1892. After finishing high school, he studied law at night and worked during the day. He received his degree from New York Law School in 1912, and then devoted his time to writing plays. "On Trial" (1914), his first attempt, was a success on the stage and as an innovation, for it was the first play to employ the movie "cutback" technique. During the next nine years he wrote four New York productions and other plays which, for various reasons, were not produced. He also directed plays for such amateur organizations as the Morningside Players and the University Settlement Dramatic Society. "The Adding Machine" (1923) introduced the technique of expressionism in a play presenting the inner life of office workers engaged in work of a monotonously routine character. Following other successful plays, he wrote the Pulitzer prize play, "Street Scene" (1929), a picture of tenement dwellers in New York City. Between 1934 and 1938 he wrote no plays, but during that period he tried, unsuccessfully, to organize a repertory company, helped found the Federal Theatre Project, and served as its New York director for the better part of a year. In 1937 he organized, with Robert E. Sherwood, Maxwell Anderson, Sidney Howard, and S. N. Behrman, the Playwrights' Company.

Mr. Rice, an important American experimental dramatist, has been critical of producers who are unwilling to present plays containing liberal social ideas or representing experimental techniques. His entrance into the field of production has served to give new zest to the American theater. His novels reflect his opinions regarding the limited opportunities afforded creators of plays, and they also contain much of his social thinking. "There are certain subjects," Mr. Rice has stated, "that seem to lend themselves to fictional rather than dramatic treatment, and I see no particular reason why a dramatist must confine himself to the writing of plays."

Voyage to Purilia (1930), his first novel, is a satire on the art of the motion picture in a story about a voyage to the planet Purilia by DeWitt Johnson, an ethnologist. There the slightest reality causes a sensation of nausea, for this sweet, happy land knows no evil and always provides a compensating happiness to all who experience pain or suffering. Mr. Rice is concerned with the "art of the masses" and the extent to which it truly reflects the thoughts and ideals of the American people. *Imperial City* (1937) portrays the life of New York City in all its shining and shoddy aspects, but with particular attention to the deterioration of the Coleman family which controls an important Wall Street banking house. The mother, a former actress, becomes a dipsomaniac, and Greg, a son, is tried for murder. Gay is a liberal university professor, and Christopher is an aggressive businessman.

The Show Must Go On (1949) anatomizes the theatrical world and its management in New York City in the story of Eric Kenwood, a native Connecticut factory worker and ex-soldier, who without training or Broadway experience writes a play on the theme of incest. After a delayed opening, it closes because of a quarrel between the producer and the owner of the theater.

JENNINGS RICE

was born in Virginia on October 8, 1900. He graduated from Washington and Lee University in 1922 and expected to study law, but abandoned this plan after working for two years in a law office in a small town in the West Virginia coal fields. He moved to New York City to do free-lance writing in 1926 and has lived in New York and Newtown, Connecticut, ever since, except for several extended trips abroad. He taught creative writing courses at Columbia University in 1929–33 and again in 1946–49 and has also taught the same subject at St. Joseph's College in Brooklyn, New York. Mr. Rice has done book reviewing for various publications and has had short stories and critical articles published in American and British magazines. In addition, he has done editorial work and private criticism.

Mr. Rice's novels have dealt exclusively with the contemporary American scene as exemplified in the American small town. "I write with most confidence," he explains, "about those phases of life which I have known most intimately." Using the serio-comic approach, he places his emphasis on the anomalies of human behavior, specifically on the ironic contrast between motives and appearances, between what people are and what they wish to seem to be. These characters seem as real as the people next door.

The Man Who Insulted Somersville (1938), his first novel, pictures the effect on the town of Somersville of the return of the body of an unknown man to be buried under the direction of the Reverend Mr. Penny. Bewildered by this development, the minister sets out to solve the mystery and, as the story unfolds, most of Somersville becomes involved, from haughty old Miss Letitia to the town drunkard, Minnie Ball Somers; an ancient scandal is exhumed, false fronts are pulled aside, a snob is unmasked, and finally justice prevails in a manner never dreamed of either by Mr. Penny or Somersville. *Windmill Circle* (1943) centers in the feud between Florence Drew and Phyllis Webb, both of whom aspire to social dominance in the town of Guilford. One bone of contention between the women is a private lake which they own jointly, and this lake takes matters into its own hands in a curious way. There are also a broken love affair, a murder, an odd partnership—between Mrs. Adams, the town's only aristocrat, and a misanthropic carpenter—and, finally, a catastrophe that violently changes the face of Guilford.

CONRAD RICHTER

Nina Dean Webb

was born on October 13, 1890, in the small town of Pine Grove, Pennsylvania, the place that was later to provide the background for one of his novels. His ancestry is a mixture of south German, French, English, and Scots-Irish. At fifteen he finished high school and went to work. During the next few years he drove teams, served as a clerk, pitched hay, and was a bank teller, country correspondent, timberman, and subscription salesman. His first really interesting job was as reporter on the Johnstown, Pennsylvania, *Journal,* and at nineteen he edited the weekly *Courier* at Patton, Pennsylvania. Later he became a private secretary in Cleveland, Ohio, and it was there that he sold his first fiction story. He began writing children's stories for *John Martin's Book,* doing the first serial printed by this unique monthly. When he became a publisher, he launched his own children's magazine, *The Junior Magazine Book,* which he both edited and wrote. Using a dozen pen names, he composed everything in the various issues, including the poems and advertisements; the periodical was discontinued during World War I. In 1928 he sold his business and went west. During the next five years he collected first-hand notes from original sources on the history of the American Southwest, and it was in 1933 that he put this data to use, writing a volume of short stories and three novels on early American life. Mr. Richter is married, has one daughter, and lives alternately at Albuquerque, New Mexico, and Pine Grove, Pennsylvania.

Mr. Richter disclaims any desire to be historically accurate; indeed, he despises most historical novels. His aim is to try to give the reader the feel of life and color of a region and period as the reader himself might have experienced it had he lived at a given time. In *Early Americana* (1936), short stories, his effort was to portray the authentic background of the southwestern frontier; in *The Sea of Grass,* the feel of life and color on the vast green ranges; in *The Trees,* life under the oppressive shade of the great forests; in *The Freeman,* the peculiar manner of thought and dialect and the countryside of the early Pennsylvania Dutch; in *The Fields,* the sensations of woods folks emerging into open fields; and in *Always Young and Fair,* life in a small Pennsylvania town during and after the Spanish-American war.

The Sea of Grass (1937) traces the life of Lutie Brewton, a woman of noble qualities, who leaves her husband and three children for a lawyer in the East who betrays her. She returns to a ranch in the Southwest and to the man whose love never cooled. *The*

Trees (1940) tells the story of the pioneer, Worth Luckett, who with his wife and five children moves from a comfortable settlement in Pennsylvania to the Ohio wilderness. After the death of her mother, a daughter, Sayward, takes charge of the family. *Tacey Cromwell* (1942) pictures a woman's rise to respectability in Arizona in 1900's.

The Freeman (1943) concerns a Palatinate German who comes to Philadelphia in Colonial days and rises from an indentured servant to the status of a freeman. He fights as a Revolutionary soldier and marries his employer. *The Fields* (1946), a sequel to *The Trees,* pictures the young womanhood of Sayward and her marriage to Portius Wheeler, a lawyer, with whom she wrests a home out of the wilderness.

Always Young and Fair (1947), set in a Pennsylvania town in the Spanish-American War, studies the effect on Lucie Markie of her renunciation of love because of the death of her sweetheart. Later she turns to a spurned lover, only to have her marriage fail. *The Town* (1950) takes up and ties into a final knot several threads of ideas begun in *The Trees* and carried on in *The Fields.* One of these is the life of Sayward Luckett and that of her jurist husband, Portius Wheeler. A second is the story of the deep forests of Ohio and the gradual transformation of dense woods into an American city. The wild trees, at first hated and fought by the early settlers, are in the end tamed and beloved on the urban streets. Finally, this long novel is concerned with liberal American thought as expressed by Sayward's youngest son, Chancey Wheeler, in marked contrast to the older and harder philosophy of the pioneers. The author takes neither side but permits the reader to draw his own conclusions.

PEIRSON RICKS

was born on August 21, 1908, in Mayodan, North Carolina. The family moved to Winston-Salem, where he attended Reynolds High School. His one-act play, "Green Paint," won first prize in the annual playwriting contest for high-school students in the state. At the age of seventeen he shipped as messboy on a cattleboat to Scotland, and returned to attend the University of North Carolina. He and Lionel Stander (now of Hollywood) were the only freshman contributors to the campus literary quarterly during their first year. In his second year he was associate art editor of *The Carolina Buccaneer,* the college humor magazine. He dropped out to write a novel which was never published, and then went to the Yale School of Fine Arts to study oil painting, composition, and drawing. For three years he worked in a North Carolina cotton mill, simultaneously writing stories, poems, and plays. From 1936 through 1942 he worked as a copywriter for advertising agencies in Philadelphia and New York. He withdrew from this field to write free-lance magazine fiction. Rejected by the armed forces, he worked for the Office of Strategic Services in Washington during World War II.

Mr. Ricks is engaged in defining the American concept of democracy which developed from an amalgam of the theories of intellectual men of wealth and the rough, practical experience of the small farmers and traders of the yeomanry. He hopes to write many books exploring the American spirit, employing his native state as a background.

Bye-Bye Breeches (1936), his first novel, is a satire, which he has since regretted because of its callow immaturity; he has purchased all bound copies from the publisher and trusts that the work itself, if not the title, is now lost to posterity.

The Hunter's Horn (1947) has as its background an old plantation in the eastern Carolina lowlands a few decades after the Civil War. Here the old bachelor, Uncle Benjamin, a Civil War captain, with his hounds and his hospitality, struggles to preserve the aristocratic tradition amid a growing entanglement of debts. Grouped about him in the old house are all the elements which spin the social fabric of the period in the South: the poor whites; the Negroes, especially Aunt Tinzy, the old voodoo Negress who lives in the swamp; and, above all, the boy Conway, Uncle Benjamin's grandnephew, the central figure of the novel. The story develops around Conway's affair with Vonnie, the poor white girl whom he knows in his heart he can never marry. Over it all hangs the dank spirit of the swamp, symbol of the dark, hidden things that lurk in the corners of men's souls. The story reaches a tragic climax in the conflict between the mellow paganism of a dying order of living and the harsh Calvinism of a newer South; it is a novel of guilt, for, says Mr. Ricks, "the dominant American trait is such a feeling, born of the still unresolved struggle between the pagan spirit and the Puritan conscience."

MARY ROBERTS RINEHART

Phyfe

was born in 1876 in Pittsburgh, Pennsylvania. A left-handed child, she was forced to learn to write with her right hand because her left was tied behind her. In childhood she saw unforgettable story materials: the mute boy next door talking on his hands to his mother; the stern, gray walls of the penitentiary; her father rowing the family to safety in a flood; the butcher who ran amuck and killed his wife with a meat ax; and a frustrated inventor-father's suicide before a mirror in a hotel. At seventeen she entered the Pittsburgh Training School for Nurses and received a very thorough education in useful fundamentals of life. Four days after graduating in 1896 she married a physician, Dr. Stanley Marshall Rinehart; three sons were born to them. A financial disaster which engulfed the Rineharts in 1903 was responsible for Mrs. Rinehart's first venture into writing; it was to her simply a means to lift her family out of debt. At first the Rineharts lived in a large mansion in Sewickley, Pennsylvania, a suburb of Pittsburgh. In 1922 they moved to Washington, D.C. On the death of her husband in 1932, she moved to New York, where her three sons are actively conducting the publishing house of Rinehart & Company.

Asked to do a crime thriller with a love plot, she wrote *The Circular Staircase* (1908); it became a sensational best seller. *The Man in Lower Ten* (1909) also achieved wide popularity. She was immediately acclaimed as bringing to the crime story the most important innovation since Sir Arthur Conan Doyle invented Sherlock Holmes: she had created human and likelike characterization about normal, intelligent people entangled in real troubles. Popular, non-mystery fiction also came from her pen in the dryly humorous short stories written for *The Saturday Evening Post* about Letitia Carberry and two spinster companions. The "Tish" series is collected in five volumes: *The Amazing Adventures of Letitia Carberry* (1911), *Tish* (1916), *More Tish* (1921), *Tish Plays the Game* (1926), and *Tish Marches On* (1937). Mrs. Rinehart has also published eleven other books of short stories, four books of travel, two books based on her experiences as a war correspondent in World War I and, in collaboration with Avery Hopwood, four plays, the most famous of which is "The Bat." *My Story* (1931, revised 1948) is her autobiography.

As a novelist Mrs. Rinehart began to write joyful escape books. She was eager to share with others her ebullience, her feeling of excitement and strangeness; however, at her excellent best she is a realist. She is impatient with the back streets and main streets in America. She is troubled by a haunting conviction that happiness, security, even physical safety are somewhat tenuous possessions, and she points to personal experiences to bear out her generalization.

When A Man Marries (1909), her first non-mystery novel, is a comedy of a quarantined dinner party. *Where There's a Will* (1912) is about a young man who inherits a sanitarium with a mineral spring; also essential to the tale are a group of sulky and complaining people. *The Street of Seven Stars* (1914) tells the love story of an American girl in Vienna. *K* (1915) portrays a hospital nurse who brings back to the medical profession a surgeon who had deserted because of several unsuccessful operations. *Long Live the King* (1917) is a romantic adventure in southeastern Europe. *The Amazing Interlude* (1918) pictures a midwestern girl working in a canteen behind the battle line in France in World War I. *Dangerous Days* (1919) describes a marriage and its failure.

A Poor Wise Man (1920) is the saga of three great generations of a great house. *The Breaking Point* (1922) is a novel based on the strange ability of the mind to forget what it cannot bear to remember. *Lost Ecstasy* (1927) pictures the effort of a young eastern woman reared in wealth to adjust herself to marriage to a cowboy and the life of the West. *Two Flights Up* (1928) combines romance and mystery. *This Strange Adventure* (1929) is the story of a woman, Missie Colfax, from her sordid childhood in the 1880's to her unsuccessful attempt at suicide in her forties. Unwilling to hurt others, she has not dared to live her own life.

The State versus Elinor Norton (1934) is a psychological study of a sensitive and beautiful woman who is driven to commit murder. *The Doctor* (1936) describes the struggle of a physician to reconcile his professional career with his domestic life. *A Light in the Window* (1948) tells the story of the Wayne clan, New York publishers, from 1919 to 1948, and illuminates the alternating periods of prosperity and depression through which they pass.

HENRIETTA (SPERRY) RIPPERGER

was born in New England, brought up in the Middle West, and educated in the East; she is now a New Yorker by choice and marriage. She began her writing career with a weekly essay on foods for the New York *Times* Sunday magazine section, and thereafter for seven years her account of the Breton family appeared in monthly installments in *Redbook,* setting, the editors believe, a record for continuous appearance in any publication. Her husband, who wrote detective stories, could not understand why tales with such slight plots were so beloved by the public. Then one day he said, "I love that family of yours myself."

Mrs. Ripperger writes on subjects that have to do with everyday activities which show the beauty and rewards that come to parents and children in a happy home. "Like everybody else," she says, "I am trying to find out about life, and the way I do is to put down what I have discovered so far. I have never written a word of fact or fiction that I did not believe in from the ground up."

112 Elm Street (1943), her first novel, describes the Breton family and how the war strikes home to them in 1940. The father converts his toy factory to the making of shells. Dick, the eldest son, marries Eileen before he goes off to the army. Barbara learns to curtail her pleasures, and Freddie gets a playmate in a refugee boy from England. *The Bretons of Elm Street* (1947) continues the account of a typical American family during wartime and their experiences in solving their children's problems.

GARLAND ROARK

De Marler Studio

was born on July 26, 1904, in Groesbeck, Texas. His father was a surveyor, and his mother was a schoolteacher and artist. After completing high school, Garland Roark was forced to help support his widowed mother. Unsatisfied with his meager formal education, he studied intensely all college subjects, the favorites being history, English, and the history of English literature. After art study and an unsuccessful career as a water-color artist, he took up advertising and followed it with success for fifteen years. His first urge to write came in 1939; two novels about Texas resulted, but they have not been printed. Operating under the rule of writing about something you know, he tried again with the same results. Not to be outdone, he decided to write about one of his favorite water-color subjects, sailing ships. The result was *Wake of the Red Witch,* a Literary Guild selection.

"I have tried to write with conviction and genuine sincerity," Mr. Roark has said, "and have a desire that my readers look into the canvases I paint of ships, seas, and lush tropical islands, and view in detail what I see. Research, imagination, and an inherent attention to details are my tools of trade. The public is my goal; my job is to entertain." His stories contain vivid action, accurate details of sailing, and a love interest.

Wake of the Red Witch (1946) portrays human emotions in a wide range, building up in two powerful characters a conflict between men who are destitute of finer ideals. As in life, they sweep along to the cyclonic end the rational people who know love, pity, and honor. The scene could be set in any American city; the fact that it was placed in the South Seas with ships as pawns glazes the canvas with a final coat of strange adventure. The central theme of *Fair Wind to Java* (1948) is conflict: between ship and shipowner, captain and shipowner, and greed and contentment. Two competing shipowners and two sea captains attempt to get the jinx ship, *Gerrymander.* Before the dispute is settled the men distribute counterfeit money which the protagonist has created; it works with amazing results.

Rainbow in the Royals (1950) pits two sea captains against each other. Jim Quick of the *American Beauty* is tough and reliable; against him is his brother Bill, captain of the *Sea Star,* a boat owned by a rival line. Both men love Ellen Appleton, the daughter of the owner of Jim's ship. These clipper ships race from Boston around Cape Horn to the gold fields of California in 1850.

HAROLD ROBBINS

Henry L. Albert

was born in New York City on May 21, 1912. He was educated in the public schools of New York. He has had such jobs as soda puncher, short-order cook and counterman in a restaurant, cashier in various stores, salesman for a wholesale grocer, ice-cream vendor in Coney Island, packing and shipping clerk in a warehouse, fruit and vegetable clerk, and bookkeeper and general office clerk. In 1938 he went into business for himself, and then into bankruptcy in 1940. At this time he took a job with a major motion-picture company as a shipping clerk in their New York warehouse. Today he is employed there as a budget analyst and statistician, and as such is concerned with all phases of that company's activities.

Mr. Robbins began work on his first novel in June, 1943, and completed it in May, 1947. The book was written at night and at snatched moments over this four-year period. His life very much parallels the vicissitude that confronts the hero of his first book in that he has knocked about the streets of New York and other large cities. However, he denies the autobiographical nature of the work. He has not lived the life of the people about whom he writes, but he has observed them at close range.

Never Love a Stranger (1948), his first novel, traces the rise of Frankie Kane, a lonely orphan boy, into a boss racketeer in the year 1929 and after. He moves from an orphanage to an adopted home, to a bordello, to a period of service in the navy, and finally to leadership in organized crime. Quite notable is the description of the background of New York City's Harlem, with its poverty, race prejudice, and vice, and also with its decency and kindness. *The Dream Merchants* (1949) tells the story of the pioneer motion-picture makers and their eventual conflict with the bankers who struggle for control of the industry. Peter Kessler gives up his sound hardware business in Rochester to move to New York to make pictures. As the new business booms, he must turn to financiers for help. It is a tale of little people who get into a business that outgrows them, told with tenderness and pathos.

DOROTHY JAMES ROBERTS

Bradford Bachrach

was born on September 5, 1903, in Elizabeth, West Virginia. Her grandfathers were active in the founding of the state after secession, one as a surveyor, and the other as a delegate to the constitutional convention. Her mother was a musician, and her father an oil operator in Burning Springs, West Virginia, for more than fifty years. As a child she spent summers there, saw many wells drilled, and once was present when one came in. Her family moved to Marietta, Ohio, when she was seven; she attended public school there, and was graduated from Barnard College of Columbia University. She did graduate work in literature and language at the University of Wisconsin, and taught in a woman's college. After a year she collaborated with Kathleen Anne Smallzried in business and industrial writing; they wrote a study of the Studebaker Corporation, *More Than You Promise, A Business at Work in Society* (1942). For several years she has made her home in Westchester County, New York.

Asked about the central theme of her novels, Miss Roberts said: "It is that the individual is responsible for his pilgrimage through time, and must make the most of it himself, if the most is to be made. I try to show this individual coping with the circumstances that threaten or reduce his powers, and shaping in the struggle his own resources to meet them."

Miss Roberts' first novel, *A Man of Malice Landing* (1943), is the study of a man's conscience, and tells how Marius Robinson returned to the little town he had left to conquer the world. *A Durable Fire* (1945), which won the Ohioana Society fiction medal, is the portrait of a talented girl whose problems of life and work demand more of her than a woman's usual destiny. *The Mountain Journey* (1947) is the story of an oil operator's wife who, in the final days of her pregnancy, is cut off from the road to the hospital by a landslide. She and her husband walk over the mountain in an attempt to reach the highway; they become involved with several of the inhabitants of the region, and take an unwilling part in a mountain quarrel in which a child is about to be stoned. Though this is the least popular of the author's books, she and some critics consider it her best. *Marshwood* (1949) relates the changes in the lives of four sisters, and in their ancestral home, when they are faced with the necessity of adopting twin foundlings three weeks old.

EDITH ROBERTS

Paul Stone-Raymor

was born on August 4, 1902, in Marion, Indiana, and christened Edith Elizabeth Kneipple. Her father was born in a log cabin in Indiana where his pioneer grandfather had staked out a claim; he traces his ancestry to Bavaria and to the seventeenth-century Irish poet, Isaac Bickerstaff, on his mother's side. Her mother, Marie Antoinette Burgess, of Caledonia, New York, was descended through the Culbertson family on her mother's side from St. Cuthbert of Melrose Abbey in the eighth century. With this admixture of racial strains, Edith Roberts is not only a typical American, but has felt herself in sympathy with the peoples of all the many lands in which she has visited and lived, so that she has written with equal interest about life at home and abroad.

Graduating from the University of Chicago, where she took her advanced courses in writing under the novelist the late Robert Herrick, Edith Roberts went to Puerto Rico to teach English for one year and remained for ten. She married Richard J. Van Deusen, and, under the name of Elizabeth Kneipple Van Deusen, wrote several volumes of stories for children and a definitive book on Puerto Rico; she also acted as a correspondent for the International News Service for several years. In 1936 she married John Gaither Roberts of Chicago and went to live in the Austrian Tyrol. It was then that she adopted Edith Roberts as her permanent pen name. She left Europe just prior to World War II, carrying the manuscript of her second novel under her clothes to escape fascist detection. After the birth of their son, Christopher, the Roberts family lived for several years in the pine and lake region of northern Wisconsin. Subsequently, Mrs. Roberts held an editorial position with *Esquire* and *Coronet* magazines, during which period she married her present husband, George Wiswell, currently on the editorial staff of *Esquire*. The Wiswells live in Westport, Connecticut.

Candle in the Sun (1937), her first novel, tells of a young American college girl who marries into a prominent West Indian political family. Her first child has Negroid characteristics, and she awakens to the place of her husband's family in her life. *Reap the Whirlwind* (1938) shows how an American university student becomes interested in Marxist ideas and joins the underground revolutionary movement in Jugoslavia and then goes to fight in Spain. *Tamarack* (1940) describes the winter lull in a northwoods summer resort town, where gossip is the chief occupation. An illegitimate child is born out of desperation and ignorance, and a "legitimate" child is born out of weakness and hypocrisy; the central theme is the complicated community reaction to the two young mothers.

This Marriage (1941) is about a couple's prenuptial agreement that after marriage each will be free in work and love. Martin seeks affairs, and Clare wants fulfillment in the conventional way. A child merely increases their problems. *Little Hell, Big Heaven* (1942) is primarily a study of the evils and essential failure of charity; the scene is Chicago's "Gold Coast" and its contiguous slums.

That Hagen Girl (1946) tells of Janie Hagen, a supposedly illegitimate girl in a small midwestern town. Her struggles to establish her identity and integrity, and her final triumph over prejudice are the materials of the story. *The Divorce of Marcia Moore* (1948) describes the plight of a divorced mother, alone in the world, who is forced through the hostile attitude of other women and the attentions of men to adopt a common-sense attitude to achieve happiness. *That Loring Woman* (1950) shows how gossip inflames a small Minnesota town against the frustrated wife of a wealthy, domineering owner of a lumber mill when she has a platonic friendship with a physician.

KENNETH (LEWIS) ROBERTS

Harold Stein

was born on December 8, 1885, in Kennebunk, Maine. He graduated from Cornell University in 1908, and while there became editor-in-chief of *The Cornell Widow* in his sophomore year. He married Anna S. Mosser on February 14, 1911. From 1909 to 1917 he was reporter, special writer, and conductor of a humorous column and page for the Boston *Post*. During this time he also held editorial positions on *Puck* and *Life*. He was a captain in the intelligence section of the Siberian Expeditionary Force in 1918 and 1919. On his return to the United States he became a staff correspondent for *The Saturday Evening Post*. In 1928 he went to Italy with plans to write a series of novels bearing on the experiences of ancestors who were soldiers in the French and Indian Wars and in the American Revolution and who served as sea captains during the War of 1812. His home is in Kennebunkport, Maine.

Mr. Roberts has written fifteen non-fiction books, and together with Mrs. Roberts he translated *Moreau de St. Méry's American Journey, 1793-1798* (1947). His self-portrait, *I Wanted to Write* (1949), is a vivid account of the problems of authorship, the research necessary for the writing of accurate historical novels, the type of surroundings essential to a writer's best utilization of his abilities, and the inner meaning of writing to a serious author. He tells of the hard toil behind his success, the huge masses of source materials to be read with the passionate care of a scholar preparing a definitive monograph, and the agonizing struggles and painstaking effort to give dramatic surge to the inert facts of a diary record or to vivify events which have been recorded in dull chronologies. He states that once he starts a book he cannot tell its length until he has finished, nor can he stop until the picture is rounded and complete. Moods of doubt cloud day after day until there glows a certainty that the book will fill a niche in the public's esteem and be the artistically satisfying work which the author had planned.

His first novel, *Arundel* (1930), is a chronicle of the secret expedition against Quebec directed by Colonel Benedict Arnold up the Kennebeck River to the St. Lawrence River in 1775. *The Lively Lady* (1931) deals with Richard Nason of Arundel, Maine, who was the captain of a merchant ship in 1807 when Jefferson announced the Embargo. Nason set sail, was captured and imprisoned in Britain's notorious Dartmoor, and escaped to sail as a privateer against the British in the War of 1812. *Rabble in Arms* (1933) pictures the northern campaign in the American Revolution and shows General Benedict Arnold stopping Burgoyne's invasion with militiamen and armed farmers. *Captain Caution* (1934) concerns Daniel Marvin, nicknamed "Captain Caution," who while sailing home from China during the War of 1812 is captured by a British sloop.

Northwest Passage (1937) describes Major Robert Rogers' expedition to destroy the Indian town of St. Francis in the autumn of 1759 as a revenge for many atrocities. Not accomplished is his aim to find an overland route to the Northwest. On his return from the raid, he has many experiences arising largely from his strange personality. *Oliver Wiswell* (1940) portrays the Tory viewpoint in the American Revolution in an account of a Loyalist whose Americanism collides with that of the barnburning extremists. Oliver hates war as a waste, and he dislikes the terrorism and cruelties of civil war. *Lydia Bailey* (1947) details the adventures of Albion Hamlin, a young Maine lawyer, and Lydia Bailey from 1801 to 1805. He becomes embroiled in Toussaint L'Ouverture's attempts to resist the re-introduction of slavery into Haiti by the French, and he is captured by Tripolitan pirates. The climax describes Tobias Lear's plotting to foil an American victory over Tripoli.

WALTER ADOLPHE ROBERTS

was born on October 15, 1886, in Kingston, Jamaica, West Indies. He was educated entirely by private tutors. For a while he worked as a reporter on newspapers in Jamaica and then on the New York *Tribune* and Brooklyn *Daily Eagle*. He also was the editor of *Ainslee's Magazine* and the publisher and editor of *The American Parade*. From the eve of World War I in 1914 until January, 1917, he was a correspondent in France for the Brooklyn *Daily Eagle*. He had many close-up views of fighting on the Western Front. His home is in New Orleans, Louisiana. His first books were collections of verse, *Pierrot Wounded and Other Poems* (1919) and *Pan and Peacocks* (1928).

Mr. Roberts' aim in his novels is to use historical material accurately but in the romantic spirit. There is a marked preoccupation with the role of countries adjoining the Caribbean Sea and the Gulf of Mexico, as well as with the influence of French culture in that region.

His first novel, *The Moralist* (1931), characterizes Austin Bride, a man who experiments with love so much that he forgets to find true love; his life ends in loneliness. *The Pomegranate* (1941) is a tale set in the mythical republic of Caribbea, really a combination of Venezuela and Cuba. The hero strives for the overthrow of a despot, and is emotionally involved with an aging star of the Spanish dance and with her most promising pupil.

Royal Street, A Novel of Old New Orleans (1944) is an historical novel of the 1840's. There is a romance between the daughter of an aristocratic Creole planter and a descendant of *emigrés* from the French West Indies, a man accepted in the best circles but unfortunately "in trade." *Brave Mardi Gras, A New Orleans Novel of the '60's* (1946) describes events in the city and in the Red River campaign during the War between the States from a viewpoint sympathetic to the Confederate cause. *Creole Dusk, A New Orleans Novel of the '80's* (1948) tells the story of a young doctor and his two loves against the background of political intrigue in Louisiana, with an interlude in Panama during the French attempt to dig a canal there. The three last-mentioned novels form a trilogy of Creole life; the plots interlock and many of the characters appear in more than one of the books. In *Royal Street* there is secondary emphasis on the institution of the duel, in *Brave Mardi Gras* on the mysteries of the carnival, and in *Creole Dusk* on grand opera.

The Single Star (1949) is laid in the 1890's and deals with Cuba's struggle for independence, which culminated in the Spanish-American War. The hero is the son of a Confederate "irreconcilable" who loves a Cuban girl in the service of her country.

CONSTANCE NOYES ROBERTSON

was born on September 27, 1897, in Niagara Falls, Ontario, Canada. The grandchild of John Humphrey Noyes, who founded the Oneida Community, and daughter of Pierrepont Noyes, its present president, she grew up in Oneida, New York, in the home of the old Community. She was educated at Dana Hall in Wellesley, Massachusetts, and the University of Wisconsin. After her marriage she traveled widely in Australia and the Far East, lived in London for a year, and spent some time in Coblenz where her father was high commissioner of the Rhineland during the occupation after World War I. Her first stories were published while she was in her early twenties. Since then she has published occasional articles and stories but is interested chiefly in the novel. *Five Fatal Letters* (written under the pseudonym "Dana Scott," 1937) is a murder-mystery laid in the Adirondack region of New York state.

America's past, and particularly the past of her own native region, upper New York, has a deep attraction for her. "It has," in her own words, "at least the restful faculty of holding still while you look at it." To these historical circumstances she adds romantic incidents of young people in love in a simple, unaffected, and idealistic way. Yet most interesting to the reader is the faithful record of the quality of mind, as well as the color and drama, of the historical persons.

Enchanted Avenue (1931), her first novel, is an experiment in form, combining the actual events of a love story with the fantasy that supplements it in the heroine's mind. The events of the book take place in two worlds, one of reality and the other of dreams. The heroine loves a married man whom she sees occasionally; during the intervals she dreams of further meetings. The reveries are printed in italics, and thus there is differentiation in print as well as in actuality. A parallel use of subvocal speech appears in Eugene O'Neill's drama, *Strange Interlude* (1928).

Seek-No-Further (1938) portrays fully a spiritualistic community in New York state in the 1860's and its struggle against a group of charlatans who join it. The young hero, anxious to preserve the simple idealism of the original group, finds himself in a bitter fight with one of the fantastic spellbinders which that period so frequently produced, and the events of the story treat this battle for the control of the commune and for the love of an ardent young member, a girl who has been converted by the new messiah. The commune described is entirely fictional, but the material, including several theologies and their miracles, is taken from fact.

Salute to the Hero (1942) tells a story drawn from the life of a well-known Civil War general. It is told in a series of panels which repeat, on varying scales, the characteristic pattern of behavior of a liar, cheat, coward, and murderer who was still clever enough to capture the imagination of the public and become a national hero. The story opens with the murder, trial, and acquittal, which was a *cause célèbre* of the 1850's, and closes with the hero's final arrest and acquittal in 1913, at the age of 87—still the darling of the public.

Fire Bell in the Night (1944) describes the operation of the Underground Railroad in Syracuse, New York, ten years before the Civil War. Its theme is the violent division of opinion—pro- and anti-slavery—in the North. Well-known figures like Gerrit Smith, Rev. Samuel May, and others appear in the struggle which reached a climax locally in the riots and rescue by the Abolitionists of the fugitive slave, Jerry. The main character in the fictional love story is Mahala North, a worker on the Underground, who is torn between two lovers, a southern-born leader of the Underground and a northern-born enemy of the movement.

The Unterrified (1946) continues the theme of the contest between pro-southern and anti-southern feeling in the North during the Civil War. The story centers in the family of an elder statesman, Senator King, who at first opposes Lincoln and the war. His young and beautiful second wife is a Kentuckian, really working for the southern cause. Through her influence her two stepsons join her beliefs, and the older of the two, Ranyard, who is about her own age, translates this belief into action by helping to organize the Knights of the Golden Circle, the Copperhead secret society that worked against the war. He also finds himself enmeshed in a passion for his stepmother, and this guilt, together with his discovery of the traitorous purposes of the Circle, leads to his final desperate efforts to atone. The last section of the book deals with the Draft Riots in New York City, which were led and instigated by the Copperheads, the men of the North who hated Abraham Lincoln.

HENRY MORTON ROBINSON

Halsman

was born in Boston, Massachusetts, on September 7, 1898. After graduating from Columbia College in 1923, he remained there as an instructor in English until 1926. For two years, 1925–27, he edited the magazine *Contemporary Verse*. Thereafter for eight years he was a free-lance writer, and from 1935 to 1948 he was associated in an editorial capacity with *The Reader's Digest*.

He is the author of *Buck Fever* (1929), a book of poems; *John Erskine* (1928) and *A Skeleton Key to Finnegan's Wake* (with J. Campbell, 1944), literary criticism; *Stout Cortez* (1931), a biography of the conqueror of the Aztecs; *Science versus Crime* (1935), an account of modern ways of detecting criminals; and *Fantastic Interim* (1943), a survey of American fads and follies between 1919 and 1941. *Children of Morningside* (1924), is a novel in verse describing undergraduate life at Columbia College.

The Perfect Round (1945), his first novel, is about Wakefield O'Reilly, a psychoneurotic veteran, who struggles to rebuild his life which battle fatigue had nearly ended. His efforts to overcome a variety of difficulties are symbolized by his work in repairing an old merry-go-round. In the end he finds peace in the Roman Catholic Church. *The Great Snow* (1947) is an allegory of man's problems as symbolized in a great storm that menaces northeastern United States and causes a New York lawyer to be marooned on his estate along the Hudson River. *The Cardinal* (1950) pictures the Roman Catholic Church on both sides of the altar. The story concerns the rise of Stephen Fermoyle from a priest in a lowly parish to the office of Cardinal on the eve of World War II.

MABEL LOUISE ROBINSON

Artist: F. F. Maynard

was born in Waltham, Massachusetts. The summers of her childhood were spent near the ocean as it touches Boston harbor. She was educated in the public schools, at Radcliffe College, and at Columbia University from which she received her doctor's degree. From Radcliffe she went to Cincinnati to teach for one year, but she found the Middle West an arid spot with no sea and no islands. She returned to New England to teach at Wellesley College and then spent two years as an instructor at Robert College in Constantinople, Turkey. There she taught a great variety of girls and subjects, and spent her holidays sailing among the Greek islands in an English sailboat. For four years she did research work with the Carnegie Foundation, and then went to Columbia University, where she conducts a workshop in fiction writing.

The publications of Mabel Louise Robinson are varied both in subject matter and in the audience for which they are intended. Somewhere in all her books her love of the sea and of boats lends color to her writing. She has written many books for children, including the "Little Lucia" books, *Bright Island* (1937), now a classic for teen-age girls, and *Back Seat Driver* (1950). *Runner of the Mountain Tops* (1934) is a biography of Louis Agassiz. She has written two textbooks, *Creative Writing* (1932) and *Juvenile Story Writing* (1922); the latter was revised as *Writing for Young People* (1950).

Island Noon (1943), her first novel, is the story of a girl who salvaged her life through the infinite tenderness of the deformed man whose brother left her faced with desolation. *Bitter Forfeit* (1947) is the story of a girl of distinguished family who bears a child in secret and who, as she comes into maturity, discovers the profound tragedy of her loss.

BABETTE ROSMOND

Marcus Blechman

was born on November 4, 1918, in New York City. She studied at Wadleigh High School, and instead of attending college she went to work for a literary agent, criticizing manuscripts for eight dollars a week; she figured it still cost less than going to college. Until early in 1949 she was the editor of two magazines: one adventure, the other detective. "Hearty persons," she says, "were known to call up and ask to meet the red-blooded, he-man editor of these publications. It was embarrassing to admit that I did not own even a pearl-handled revolver. When I was not tied up with international spies, and/or ruthless killers, I wrote short stories. I have written small, unsung pieces for the radio, and once sold books in Macy's for two weeks—until they found me luring customers behind the counters to wrap their own packages." She is married and has a son.

In her novels Miss Rosmond deals mainly with contemporary metropolitan life. She has been called an author's author—meaning, probably, that while her books receive excellent reviews and enthusiastic critical comment, they sell only modestly. She has never been selected by a book club, although her books are witty and intelligent.

The Dewy, Dewy Eyes (1946), her first novel, carries an inexperienced Indiana girl to New York City, where she becomes a sophisticated editor of a "pulp magazine." *A Party for Grownups* (1948) details the marriage of a physician, Jim Burns, and witty Peg Harcourt, two nice people, who fall out because he becomes bored at her immaturity.

ISHBEL ROSS

Erich Hartmann

was born in Sutherlandshire, fifty miles north of Inverness, capital of the Highlands of Scotland, a picturesque old town where Highland chieftains still walk the streets in their tartans and where Gaelic is still spoken. Her own name is Gaelic for Isabel, but she says that does not mean that she can speak one word of the language.

She was educated in Scotland and is a graduate of Tain Royal Academy. When her school days were over, she moved to Canada and worked there for several years. She did publicity for the Canadian Food Board for a year and was with the Toronto *Daily News* for a year and a half. In 1919 she joined the staff of the New York *Herald Tribune*, for which she covered a wide variety of stories, including the Stillman divorce, the Hall-Mills murder, the death of Edison, and the Lindbergh kidnapping. She has interviewed scores of world celebrities. She left the *Herald-Tribune* in 1933 and was with the Office of War Information for three years, writing magazine articles on books, art, and music for the overseas division. In 1922, while working on the Stillman case, she met and married her newspaper husband, Bruce Rae of the New York *Times,* becoming an American citizen by marriage; they have one daughter.

Since 1933 Miss Ross has done fiction and magazine work. She is also an experienced globe-trotter and has been twice around the world. Her non-fiction books include *Through the Lich-Gate* (1931), a history of the Little Church Around the Corner in New York City; *Ladies of the Press* (1936), the story of women in journalism; and *Child of Destiny* (1949), a biography of Elizabeth Blackwell, the first woman doctor in England and America, who practiced in the mid-nineteenth century.

Promenade Deck (1932), her first novel,

portrays a group of people on a four-month cruise around the world. The characters include a husband who falls in love with a young girl and a dour Scotsman who is a woman-hater but who falls in love. *Marriage in Gotham* (1933) has the theme that the depths of the emotional life are more important than physical desires in a successful marriage. Hector Tullock discovers that his wife is unfaithful. After a much publicized divorce and her remarriage, she finds that she wants to be back with her husband and children, who now are alienated.

Highland Twilight (1934) is the story of Catriona Fraser, a Scottish girl, who goes to work in London for a cabinet minister and finds that he loves her. *Fifty Years a Woman* (1938) portrays through the life of Mary Leith, an actress, events in New York City in ten-year intervals from 1890 to 1930. She finds her triumphs flat and meaningless. *Isle of Escape* (1942) describes through the eyes of a reporter returning from England by ship to New York City the plight of refugees from Europe in the days just before the Japanese struck Pearl Harbor in 1941.

NANCY WILSON ROSS

was born in Olympia, Washington, on November 22, 1910. Her early years in the Pacific Northwest, she has said, account for her enduring interest in nature, the American Indian, and the Orient, although she has lived an equal amount of her life in the East, in upstate New York, New England, and Long Island, and has spent time in the Southwest—New Mexico, Arizona, and old Mexico. She has also traveled extensively in Europe and in the Orient in China, Korea, and Japan. She was educated at the University of Oregon and in Europe, chiefly at the Bauhaus, the famous modern German school which was one of Hitler's early targets. While still a student, Miss Ross published in *The Saturday Evening Post* some prophetic writings on a changing Europe and succeeded in getting herself on the Nazi blacklist. Upon her return from Germany she toured this country in a trailer house and out of this experience came her two nonfiction books of Americana: *Farthest Reach* (1941), a regional book on Oregon and Washington, and *Westward the Women* (1944), a study of women pioneers presented in modern terms. Miss Ross' interest in pioneer women led her to volunteer to write for the navy, during World War II, a book on the women in its service, *The Waves* (1943). Following her travels for the navy, she went abroad in the winter of 1945 with the army air corps and flew thousands of miles in Europe and northern Africa as a special war correspondent. She is married to Stanley Young, the playwright. They reside on Long Island, New York.

Friday to Monday (1932), her first novel, is a story of a week-end house party in an old conventional upstate New York town, where visitors from the outside create only a brief ripple, and where all emotions are so carefully muffled that no permanent impact is possible: Monday morning finds everyone back in the pre-Friday groove. *Take the Lightning* (1940) concerns the adjustment of young people to American life after years spent abroad. The three chief characters, in a university setting, are a psychologist, his young wife, and the "other" man. The psychologist is asked to apply his theories to his own marital life. The young woman, with his help, cures herself of a psychological difficulty, the roots of which lie deep in her childhood. The test for them both comes when the man with whom the wife has lived before her marriage reappears.

The Left Hand Is the Dreamer (1947) is a novel of family relationships in a typical upstate New York town brought to a climax by the war; the book stresses the contrast between the protected life of upper middle-class Americans and the tragedy of disoriented Europeans whose world has been shattered and destroyed through no fault of their own. The story hinges on the bitter choice that a woman must make between continuing her sheltered and secure existence and accepting a life of ever-increasing personal challenge with a man who has lost all the usual roots of home and country. *I, My Ancestor* (1950) examines the plight of a spiritually and intellectually bankrupt New Yorker who is propelled by an accident and a subsequent mental breakdown to seek a deeper intention and purpose in his life. He journeys to a remote western island and there is helped—with the aid of his long-neglected father, an elderly hermit, and a woman anthropologist—to discover equally difficult but potentially more sustaining meanings in his existence.

SAM ROSS

Erich Hartmann

was born on March 10, 1912, in the province of Kiev, Russia. A year later he came to the United States and grew up in the slum areas of Chicago. Athletics got him off the streets and made it possible for him to attend Northwestern University, where he received his degree in journalism. Prior to acquiring an interest in writing, he was the national high-school backstroke swimming champion and during his college years was selected as a member of the all-American intercollegiate swimming team. From college he went to work as reporter, radio writer, and publicity man, and spent several years on the Federal Writers' Project in Chicago. His radio dramas have been produced over the major networks and his short stories have been published both here and in England. During World War II he served both with the army and the merchant marine. In 1941 he married Charlotte Bergman, an artist who exhibits under her married name in this country's major museums; at present they live in New York City.

The central theme in Sam Ross' works is the effect of environment in the shaping of moral values, with tragic overtones of man's effort to grapple with society. Chicago, with its raw impact upon its people, is employed as a symbol of the American scene.

He Ran All the Way (1947), his first novel, is a psychological study of five people caught in a network of fear and terror. The book's overtones focus on the disjointed morale of today and its basic theme is the conflict between good and evil. It is the story of a killer, produced by the Chicago slums, who revolts against his environment and is eventually destroyed by violence.

Someday, Boy (1948) is the story of an adolescent who bases his values on the false glow of the prosperous 1920's and grows into manhood amid the ruins of the depression. The story embodies the conflict between illusion and reality. Rejecting the values and traditions of his foreign-born parents and frustrated by the limited horizons of his future, Benny Gordon creates his heroes from movies and success stories and bases his creeds on the over-publicized athlete, the easy money to be had from dupes, and the Midas touch of the gambler. Success is his dream, but with no understanding of the world he lives in he becomes the victim of his illusory values through the social forces which led to the financial crash of 1929. Benny Gordon is a symbol of the aspirations of the 1920's.

The Sidewalks Are Free (1950) tells about a boy who is brought to this country as an infant from the Ukraine and grows up into a true American in the northwest section of Chicago. The story explains how two cultures, two ways of life, combine to build a strong personality upon both hope and courageous despair.

FYNETTE ROWE

is an upstate New Yorker both by birth and inclination, for she was born on April 20, 1910, in Chatham, New York, and brought up in Canandaigua, a very old town in the Finger Lakes district. Her father's family came from the St. Lawrence Valley; her mother's from the rich heart of the state east of Syracuse. Mrs. Rowe recalls some of the brightest memories of her childhood which center on visits to the farms of her great-aunts and uncles, where the old Erie Canal skirted many an orchard and back pasture. At that time, she reports, life on a canal boat was her ideal. She is a graduate of Mount Holyoke College and holds a master's degree from the University of Michigan. She and her husband and their three children live in Scarsdale, New York.

The Chapin Sisters (1945), her first novel, describes fifty years in the frustrated lives of two upstate New York librarians. They quarrel over potential suitors who always lose interest. *The Burning Spring* (1947), set in the Finger Lakes district of western New York in World War I, tells of Jud Palmer and his sons, Ned and Harlow, who try to make a living from their hilly farm and to overcome the handicap of a bad reputation given the family by an ancestor.

MARGARET LEE RUNBECK

was born in Des Moines, Iowa. She first appeared in print a few weeks before her thirteenth birthday; she had won a prize contest sponsored by a Washington, D.C., newspaper. When she called at the newspaper office, the editor was surprised to discover that his prize winner was a child. Before the interview was over, he had agreed to run a weekly human-interest column which she was to write for his page of features. Because of her youth, the author was to remain anonymous and the column, which ran for two years, was merely signed by "The Scribe." Even the child's parents did not know of this secret enterprise in their household. While still only a sophomore at the University of Chicago, she won the McLaughlin award for excellency of prose.

Miss Runbeck began her adult writing career in Boston on *The Christian Science Monitor*. She then turned to advertising. "The first job was to learn how to write a lot of words at a moment's notice," Miss Runbeck explains, "and the second was to be able to write a valuable few." As soon as she felt she had learned her lesson, she resigned from her business position, purchased a tiny house in the country, and began to write fiction. For three and a half years she was a contributing editor of *The Christian Herald*. *Answer Without Ceasing* (1949) is a book giving evidence of God in everyday life. She has also written *The Great Answer* (1944), *Your Kids and Mine* (with Joe E. Brown, 1944), and *The Secret* (1946). *Our Miss Boo* (1942) and *Time for Each Other* (1944) contain short stories about a four-year-old girl.

People Will Talk (1929), her first novel, describes the joys of Peter and Sally Lauren in their early married years when they buy a home and stretch their modest budget to purchase occasional ornaments. *For Today Only* (1938) describes a dress sale in a department store and gives the secrets of manufacturing, buying, and selling to expose greed and ambition. *Hope of the Earth* (1947) concerns the Phelps family, which moves in 1837 from Philadelphia to Illinois, where they develop a religious and patriotic faith. *Pink Magic* (1949) is about adolescents, written for adult readers who collide with that alien race.

ROBERT RYLEE

was born on September 17, 1908, in Memphis, Tennessee. After attending public grammar school in Memphis, he went to Andover. He was graduated from Amherst College in 1929. Since college days he has lived in Mississippi, New York, Wisconsin, and for a number of years in Texas, his present home.

Deep Dark River (1935), his first novel, concerns a Mississippi Negro who, in spite of being sentenced to life imprisonment for a murder committed in self-defense, finds peace in religious mysticism. This was a Book-of-the-Month-Club selection. *St. George of Weldon* (1937) is the story of a young man's life in a small town in the Mississippi Delta examined from the point of view of deterministic psychology. *The Ring and the Cross* (1947) is the story of struggles for political power and of social and economic conflicts in a large fictional city in Texas during the early 1940's. The ring and the cross are symbols for the two age-old opposing rivers of human faith: worship of power and respect for human dignity and nobility.

SAMUEL *to* SYLVESTER

MAURICE SAMUEL

was born in Macin, Rumania, on February 8, 1895. He studied in the secondary schools and at Victoria University in Manchester, England. In 1914 he came to the United States and was naturalized in 1921. During World War I he served as a sergeant in the United States army and spent eighteen months in France. Immediately after the war he acted as interpreter at the peace conference, and still later was with the reparations commission in Berlin and Vienna. For ten years after 1929 he lived in Palestine; having had twenty-seven years of contact with practically every Jewish community between Jordan and the Golden Gate, between Manchester and Cape Town, Mr. Samuel has gained considerable insight into the Jewish problem. In 1944 *The Saturday Review of Literature* awarded him a prize for his book, *The World of Sholom Aleichem,* which was considered the best contribution of the year toward improving intergroup relations. Mr. Samuel is the author of more than a dozen books and the translator of books by Sholem Asch and others.

His work falls into two parts, one publicistic and belletristic, dealing with Jewish problems, with Zionism, anti-Semitism, and Jewish men of letters; the other novelistic and of a general nature. His non-fiction books include *You Gentiles* (1924), about the differences between Jews and Gentiles; *I, the Jew* (1923), an explanation of Zionism; *What Happened in Palestine . . . August, 1929* (1929), an eye-witness account of Arab-Jew conflict, a work expanded into *On the Rim of the Wilderness* (1931); *Jews on Approval* (1932), about Jewish accomplishments in the United States; *The Great Hatred* (1940), an analysis of anti-Semitism; *Harvest in the Desert* (1944), a record of the rebuilding of Palestine to 1942; *Prince of Ghetto* (1948), stories by, and a sketch of, Isaac Loeb Peretz, a Polish writer; and *The Gentleman and the Jew* (1950).

His first novel, *The Outsider* (1921), shows the attempt of an American soldier from the Midwest, demobilized in Paris in 1919, to adapt himself to the Bohemian life of that city; it tells how he fails because of his essentially puritanical upbringing. *Whatever Gods* (1923) presents the same theme against an American background: a young man revolts against the business career which his successful father tries to force on him, and likewise fails. *Beyond Woman* (1934) tells of a man who has given up an intellectual form of life, has achieved some success in business, and is unable to continue; he breaks with his wife and returns to his intellectual pursuits. The needs which drive him to make a large income are his relations with women; he passes beyond this need and beyond the control of his life by sexual relation. *Web of Lucifer, A Novel of the Borgia Fury* (1947) is a reconstruction of Italian life at the end of the fifteenth and the beginning of the sixteenth centuries, and describes the career of a youngster of good intentions who is lured into the service of Cesare Borgia and falls under the influence of Niccolo Machiavelli, the statesman and political philosopher.

WILLIAM SAROYAN

was born on August 31, 1908, in Fresno, California, where his father, an Armenian immigrant, was engaged in grape farming. As a boy Mr. Saroyan sold newspapers and pruned vines. He received his formal education in the public schools of Fresno. His first published story appeared in 1933 in an Armenian daily newspaper printed in Boston. A year later *Story* magazine accepted "The Daring Young Man on the Flying Trapeze." In 1934 he visited Armenia and Russia. In 1942 he directed the motion picture, "The Good Job," and also opened a theater in New York to produce his own plays. During World War II he served as a private in the European theater of operations. In 1944 the Office of War Information asked him to write something to help morale in the war; the result was *The Adventures of Wesley Jackson*. In February, 1943, Mr. Saroyan married Carol Stuart Marcus; they have two children. They were divorced in 1949.

Mr. Saroyan's books of short stories include *The Daring Young Man on the Flying Trapeze* (1934), *Inhale and Exhale* (1936), *Little Children* (1937), *Love, Here is My Hat* (1938), *The Trouble With Tigers* (1938), *Peace, It's Wonderful* (1939), *My Name is Aram* (1940), *Dear Baby* (1944), and *The Assyrian* (1950). Ninety-eight of these stories are collected in *The Saroyan Special* (1948). His plays include "My Heart's in the Highlands," "The Time of Your Life," and "Jim Dandy: Fat Man in a Famine."

Mr. Saroyan's short stories originally were plotless, subjective, and often sardonic accounts of everyday experience which took on overtones of universal meaning. His novels have something of this same quality, but the mood is more cheerful and the theme is an affirmation of the importance of the average person's contribution to society by living in friendship and harmony with all people.

The Human Comedy (1943), his first novel, is a group of related episodes in the life of a Postal Telegraph messenger boy, Homer Macauley, and his small brother, mother, and sister in the California town of Ithaca. The theme is the essential goodness of all human kind. *The Adventures of Wesley Jackson* (1946) tells the experiences of an ordinary enlisted man in the army during World War II. This nineteen-year-old son of a wonderful "Mom" and a drunken "Pop" is sent to England as a private. His many experiences with a great variety of people convince him that all men are brothers.

ALEXANDER SAXTON

was born in Great Barrington, Massachusetts, the son of an editor of a book-publishing house. He grew up in Manhattan and attended the Phillips Exeter Academy in New Hampshire. After two years at Harvard he went to the University of Chicago, from which he graduated in 1940. He started writing in school and shortly after leaving college finished his first novel while working as a railroad-yard switchman and fireman in Chicago. In 1943 he joined the merchant marine and became a radio operator on a liberty ship. He now lives in California with his wife and two daughters.

Grand Crossing (1943), his first novel, concerns Michael Reed, who cannot find answers to his problems at Harvard and so transfers to the University of Chicago. He forms friendships with a Negro student studying medicine and a Jewish boy studying philosophy. He is still uncertain whether he has learned the solution to the problem of principles and practice. *The Great Midland* (1948) is the story of a young railroad worker in Chicago who is sensitive to the social and economic issues of labor and capital, radicalism and reaction, and war and peace. He marries a railroader's daughter, who has an affair with a professor, and he becomes embroiled in racial strife when Negro car washers object to their status. The events occur just before the attack on Pearl Harbor by the Japanese on December 7, 1941.

MARK SAXTON

was born in Mineola, Long Island, on November 28, 1914, and grew up in New York City and New England. He studied at Friends Seminary in New York, then at the Berkshire School, and finally at Harvard College, from which he graduated in 1936. After that he spent an inconclusive two years working for newspapers, radio, and magazines, among the latter *The New Yorker,* and then in June, 1938, he became associated with a publishing house as assistant editor. There he stayed in various capacities until he entered the navy in 1943; he received a commission as ensign and served as an air-combat intelligence officer, first with the Atlantic fleet and, later, on the staff of Aircraft Seventh Fleet in the Philippines. Discharged as a junior lieutenant in February, 1946, he returned to the book-publishing business as executive editor of William Sloane Associates. In 1950 he became an editor of Whittlesey House. He was married in 1940 and has two children.

Following two mystery-adventure stories, *Danger Road* (1939) and *The Broken Circle* (1941), he wrote *The Year of August* (1943), which concerns Tom Holden's experiences in hunting for spies who disseminate rumors during World War II in New York night clubs. *Prepared for Rage* (1947) studies the psychological adjustment of Jerry Osgood, a Harvard graduate, to the intellectual confusion of the mid-1930's. He becomes a magazine writer and marries a fellow employee. He joins the army as an enlisted man and refuses an officer's commission because his principles will not let him accept it. The novel portrays some of the problems facing thoughtful young people in the depression.

JOEL SAYRE

was born on December 13, 1900, in Marion, Indiana, and spent most of his youth in Columbus, Ohio. During World War I he served with the Canadian Expeditionary Forces in Siberia; during World War II he was in Africa, the Middle East, and the European theater of operations. In the latter he served as a correspondent for *The New Yorker,* on which magazine he is a staff writer. *Persian Gulf Command* (1945) recounts the history of the United States army in that area, with full details of the strategic importance of that operation.

Rackety Rax (1932), his first novel, describes how a racketeer, Knucks McGloin, creates a football team for the nonexistent Canarsie University; he uses prize fighters as players and seeks profits only. A mob ends his career. *Hizzoner, the Mayor* (1933) pictures satirically the amazing actions of a playboy who becomes mayor of an American city with three million inhabitants. *The House Without a Roof* (1948) is the story of a German family who live in Berlin after their house is unroofed by a bomb. Their story pictures the German side of the war as told by ordinary people in terms of everyday incidents; it is fundamentally a study of a nation's physical and moral decay.

GLADYS SCHMITT

was born on May 31, 1909, in Pittsburgh, Pennsylvania. She graduated from the University of Pittsburgh with high honors in 1932 and for a year thereafter pursued advanced studies. In 1931 she won the Witter Bynner college poetry prize. Since 1933 she has been associated with *Scholastic* magazine. In 1939 she married Simon Goldfield and moved to New York City.

Her first novel, *The Gates of Aulis* (1942), winner of the Dial Press award, is in the style of Marcel Proust. It describes a German family in America, with emphasis on a youth's impersonal desire for social justice in Marxist terms and his sister's deep love for humanity. *David, the King* (1946) tells beautifully the life of the psalmist and his rise from shepherd boy to king. *Alexandria* (1947) is about an American girl's rise to fame as an actress; bored with success on Broadway, she returns to the scene of her childhood and falls in love with a clean-cut young painter. A Pittsburgh housewife is the narrator.

ISIDOR SCHNEIDER

was born on August 25, 1896, in Horodenko, a small town then in Austria-Hungary but now in the Soviet Ukraine. His parents moved to the United States when he was five years old. He earned his way through the College of the City of New York by teaching English to foreigners. Twice he held a Guggenheim fellowship and was in Europe in 1928 and again in 1937–38, staying mostly in the Soviet Union. He has worked for publishing houses, magazines, and newspapers. He married Helen Berlin in 1925; they have one daughter. He was one of the editors of *Proletarian Literature in the United States* (1936), and his several books of poetry include *The Temptation of Anthony* (1927) and *Comrade, Mister* (1934).

Dr. Transit (1925), his first novel, is a fantasy concerning a scientist who is idealized as a man capable of changing the world, satirized because he does not use his ability, and Satanized as one who looks too literally at things. *From the Kingdom of Necessity* (1935) portrays Isaac Hyman, who comes to America at the age of six and grows up during the first three decades of the twentieth century. *Judas Time* (1946) tells the story of Calvin Cain, a college professor of biology, who delights in attacking the heresy of others while engaged in left-wing activities. He reveals the names of the members of a communist group, and yet he goes to Mexico to visit Trotsky. This book reveals something of the conflict between the two factions of American adherents to communism.

LAWRENCE SCHOONOVER

Elliott Erwitt

was born in 1906 in Anamosa, Iowa. After attending Shattuck Military School in Faribault, Minnesota, he went for two years to the University of Wisconsin and then ran away to sea. A year as a sailor convinced him that he was grown up, and so he moved to New York City where he worked for an advertising agency. He subsequently became advertising manager for a photographic concern for ten years and then worked until 1947 as copy chief and account executive for advertising agencies. In 1938 he married Gertrude Bonn; they have four daughters and live in New Canaan, Connecticut.

The Burnished Blade (1948), his first novel and a Literary Guild selection, describes the adventures of an orphan boy, Pierre, in France and in Trebizond on the border of the Black Sea in Asia Minor. The story opens with the martyrdom of Joan of Arc in 1430 and proceeds with Pierre serving the financier, Jacques Coeur, rescuing a noblewoman from plague-stricken Paris, assisting the ruler of Trebizond, and finally returning to France as a wealthy man. He marries his beloved who had planned in his absence to become a nun.

The Gentle Infidel (1950) has a background of fifteenth-century Turkey and Constantinople. The hero is Michael, born a Venetian and a Christian, who is impressed into the service of the Sultan.

PRESTON SCHOYER

was born on June 13, 1911, in Pittsburgh, Pennsylvania. After graduating from Milton Academy in Massachusetts, he entered Yale where he became an editor of *The Yale Record* and one of William Lyon Phelps' group of Pundits. On graduation, he taught English at Yale-in-China from 1933 to 1935. During the next three years he worked at various jobs in this country, spending the bulk of his time trying unsuccessfully to put into writing his impressions of China. For a year he held a fellowship in the department of Oriental studies at Yale. In 1938 he was back in China doing relief work, driving an ambulance which was more often a hearse, dodging bombs, and helping overworked physicians patch up the wounded and the dying. In the midst of these experiences, sitting out air raids or on grave-covered hills, he began his first novel.

After Pearl Harbor he tried to enter a branch of military service that would take him to China, but two years passed before he was able to avoid the army's perverse desire to send him to Europe as a combat engineer. In 1943, then an air intelligence officer, he was finally sent to China where he laid the foundation of the army's air ground-aid section which rescued crashed airmen and other casualties from behind the enemy lines. Besides picking up American fliers, he gathered information from bandits, pirates, smugglers, and others who could supply valuable intelligence. One of his informants was a girl named Wei Teh-lien, an employee of a Shanghai newspaper. When the tempo of the war increased, she escaped to free China as a servant maid and worked with Mr. Schoyer. At the close of the war, he asked her to wait for him. When he had finished his second novel, he returned immediately to China and they were married on November 4, 1947. He now lives in Pittsburgh, where he is busy writing and lecturing.

The Foreigners (1942), his first novel, portrays the modern China scene, the odd types of people in that country, and the influence of the foreigner on China and of China on the individual from abroad. The story concerns Peter Achilles, an American, who teaches in a mission school at Showei, one hundred miles from Hangchow, when the Japanese strike in 1937. He and others go to the aid of the Chinese people, and he falls in love with a Chinese girl. *The Indefinite River* (1947) is about Captain David Russell, an American intelligence officer in eastern China, who is loved by his Chinese staff because he treats them like friends and who in 1944 runs afoul of the Kuomintang military bureaucracy. He is separated from his command and from the Chinese girl he loves. The theme concerns the effect of China's unsettled conditions upon a serious young outsider who tries to be helpful. *The Ringing Glass* (1950) has the China coast as its setting and deals with the complex problems arising from the meeting of the East and West. The story concerns the capture of a British steamer by pirates and the harsh experiences of the passengers; some of them are American tourists.

OTTO SCHRAG

Hilde Hubbuck

was born on October 11, 1902, in Karlsruhe, Germany, the son of a German father and an American mother who married the man she met on a trip to Europe. Otto Schrag studied at the universities of Freiburg and Munich, and after declining to take up his father's law practice and enter the malt-processing business of his grandfather, he received his doctorate from Heidelberg University in 1933. In 1927 he was married; the Schrags have a son, Peter.

When life in Hitler Germany became intolerable in 1935, Mr. and Mrs. Schrag visited the United States with the idea of perhaps moving here. He was deeply impressed by the grandeur of America and its people; however, they were forced to return to Europe to fetch Peter. Complications in receiving visas and permits delayed their departure to America, and they moved first to Luxembourg and then to Belgium, where they were at the outbreak of the German invasion in 1940. At that time Mr. Schrag was interned and sent to a concentration camp in France.

From here on the Schrags' life took on a story-book mold, filled with smugglers and Gestapo agents. In 1941 Mrs. Schrag, disguised as a nurse, went to France and helped her husband to escape and hide. Then she returned to Belgium, got Peter, and they were finally reunited in Lisbon in June, 1941, whence they came to the United States. At first Mr. Schrag, jobless, produced and sold blackout shades in New York, writing an account of his experiences in his spare time. He tried to sell this first book, but without success. Then he began a new book on a subject of which he had originally heard on his first visit in 1935, the locust plagues.

The Locusts (1943) describes the struggle of Kansas farmers in the 1870's against the plagues of insects that devoured their wheat fields. It is the story of Mormons and Mennonites, of gamblers and prospectors; Mr. Schrag likes to draw a parallel between the struggle against locust swarms and the fight of the people of Europe against totalitarian hordes. *Sons of the Morning* (1945) depicts the return of two veterans to a New England community. One of them brings with him a French girl. The two veterans are already somewhat bitter, but when the resentment of the town flares up against the girl, their bitterness reaches a climax; the book then goes on to tell how they readjust themselves to civilian life. *Bedrock* (1947) concerns a surgeon to whom the values and standards of modern life become worthless. He goes to the desert in Arizona and there reconciles himself to his world. Originally titled *The Desert,* its purpose is to portray the wasteland in which mankind now flounders and to show its helplessness against modern phenomena, specifically the atomic bomb.

BUDD SCHULBERG

Virginia F. Stern

was born in New York City on March 27, 1914. Raised in Hollywood, the son of a film producer, he was graduated from Los Angeles High School in 1931, Deerfield Academy in 1932, and Dartmouth College in 1936, each time serving as editor of his school publication. In addition to being included in Edward J. O'Brien's honor roll for 1939, his short stories have been reprinted in several anthologies. Mr. Schulberg has taught short-story writing at Columbia University, and in 1949 conducted a writers' workshop for wounded veterans at Valley Forge General Hospital. He lives with his wife and three children on a farm in eastern Pennsylvania.

What Makes Sammy Run? (1941), his first novel, a satire on Hollywood, is a study of a grasping, egocentric careerist who cheats and betrays his way to the top of the movie world. Sammy Glick begins as a copy boy in a New York newspaper, where his coarse language and hard, harsh, rough, and tough qualities begin to bring results.

The Harder They Fall (1947) presents at once an exposé of the racketeering element in the sport of professional boxing and an indictment of those who believe they can compromise with evil without becoming besmirched. Nick Latka, an unscrupulous fight promoter, builds up El Toro, an Argentinian peasant, to be the heavyweight champion. The story of the sleazy side of the business is climaxed by Latka's betrayal of the uncomprehending and wholly pathetic dupe.

The Disenchanted (1950) vividly contrasts two representative figures of the 1920's and the 1930's and continues Mr. Schulberg's search for the corruptive forces which, in his opinion, spawn wherever material success is emphasized to the detriment of genuine social service. This realistic story describes a genius whose novels in the 1920's had made those dizzy years seem wonderful but whose later life became tragically symbolic of events he was unable to understand.

NATALIE ANDERSON SCOTT

Robert C. Barry

was born on September 7, 1906, in Ekaterinoslov, Russia, the daughter of Boris Sokoloff. When she was a year old, her father, an old Russian liberal, moved his family to London. In 1912 he settled in the United States and his family joined him in 1915. Natalie Anderson Scott went to school in Dayton, Ohio, and in Montclair and Ridgefield Park, New Jersey. She has done considerable traveling throughout Europe and the Far East, and is now living in Westchester County in New York. In 1929 she sold her first story, which won a prize contest, and then wrote for *Adventure* magazine for four years, producing seven to nine stories a year. All of them were "starred" in O'Brien's short story anthologies. Her first novel won a Bread Loaf fellowship in 1935.

"The function of a novelist is not to preach or to write with a purpose," Natalie Anderson Scott believes. "A novelist must portray life as it is, objectively, with detachment, without disturbing the proportion of its components." She feels strongly that content and word-picture effects should never be sacrificed to form or the correctness of style. She believes that a novelist must have a creator's love for each one of his characters, good or bad, if he is to bring them to life.

So Brief the Years (1935), her first novel which was published over the name of Natalie B. Sokoloff, pictures the conflict between the Whites and the Reds after the Russian revolution in 1917; the story concerns a girl of noble birth who marries a Red official to save her mother from starving. *The Sisters Livingston* (1946) describes the eternal struggle between the spiritual and the emotional and the physical in man in a story of parent-children relationship. *The Story of Mrs. Murphy* (1947), a Book-of-the-Month-Club selection, grew out of Miss Scott's awareness of the strange, weird world of the alcoholics. She spent about four years in research, visiting (when necessary in the company of a friendly policeman) hangouts, saloons, and hospitals to find out whether alcoholism is a physical or mental disease. The story is that of a man hopelessly addicted to drink and of the three women who love him. *The Husband* (1948) is a story of a woman's enslavement in marriage. Laid in the Puritan Massachusetts of two centuries ago, it is an analysis of the power of sex in shaping conduct common to any marriage in any era. Cassie Harris becomes spiritually debauched as the wife of Ebenezer Rawson; she becomes cruel and scheming, justifying his tyranny and serving him almost blindly.

VIRGIL SCOTT

was born on August 1, 1914, in Vancouver, Washington, the son of a secondary-school teacher. During the next few years he lived in Pennsylvania, New York, and New Jersey. His family moved to Cleveland, Ohio, when he was ten years old, and he went through its public-school system and graduated from Cleveland Heights High School in 1932. For three years he attended Heidelberg College in Tiffin, Ohio, and then transferred to Ohio State University, where he received a bachelor's degree in education in 1936 and a master's degree in English in 1937. After four years of high-school teaching in Franklin, Ohio, he returned to Ohio State and completed his doctorate in 1945. He then taught for two years at the University of Minnesota and subsequently moved to Michigan State College to conduct courses in creative writing.

He grew up during the great depression and was forced, in common with most of his generation, to work at any job he could find during that bleak period. He started delivering newspapers when he was ten years old, got his own route on his twelfth birthday, and for a few months before he left for college was an inspector and assistant to the district manager in Cleveland Heights. Later he sold soap, painted houses, made deliveries for a Cleveland bootlegger, clerked in a grocery store, and worked in a munitions plant. In 1935 he married Justine Bittikofer, a schoolteacher; they have four children. He has prepared with Adrian Jaffe a textbook, *Studies in the Short Story* (1949).

His first novel, *The Dead Tree Gives No Shelter* (1947), is a fictionized case history of a juvenile delinquent by the name of Mike Brandon. This boy's father is a teacher and his upbringing is respectable, but by the time he is seventeen he is wanted by the police. At the age of twenty-one he associates with racketeers, bootleggers, and light women. *The Hickory Stick* (1948) is a story about Doug Harris, a young teacher who in the 1930's works his way through college, marries, and is glad to get a job in a small Ohio town. Doug experiences every type of difficulty and dishonesty. He meets lazy students and jealous colleagues, and although he has his moments of disillusionment, he makes a good recovery. The central theme is that man is noble until he is corrupted by society; each man must maintain his individuality and integrity if he is to preserve anything beyond that.

ALLAN SEAGER

D. D. Spellman

was born in Adrian, Michigan, on February 5, 1906. When he was eleven years old he moved to Memphis, Tennessee. He lived there until he went to college at the University of Michigan and, later, at Oriel College, Oxford, where he received his master's degree. On his return from England he served as an editor of *Vanity Fair* magazine for over a year. He has traveled in Europe and South America, and has a wife and two daughters. He now teaches at the University of Michigan. *The Old Man of the Mountain* (1950) contains short stories.

Equinox (1943), his first novel, expresses the tragic moral failure of a successful foreign correspondent who tries to make a home in New York with his seventeen-year-old daughter whom he has not seen for seven years. In his eagerness to escape the chaos of the world he has left, he unknowingly uses her devotion as a refuge and fails to recognize its unnatural intensity. When this is revealed to the daughter, she hangs herself.

The shock of her death forces her father to see that he is to blame. This novel, said Mary Ross, is "remarkable in candor, depth, and richness. The situation of Mary and her father is drawn with both dignity and delicacy; it has the spaciousness of true tragedy, the tragedy of persons whose very integrity and strength enmesh them in a coil from which there is no outcome but disaster."

The Inheritance (1948) portrays the struggle of a young man to restore the good name of his father, a small-town banker, wealthy and hated. After he is killed in an automobile wreck, it is discovered that his fortune has been dissipated and his reputation sinks. The son imitates his father, even tries to become his father in a long frenzied effort to avenge him before the town. In the end, after the son has insulted everyone, he rids himself of his father's ghostly presence, and a friend persuades him to make a fresh start in a new place.

MABEL SEELEY

was born at Herman, Minnesota, in 1903. She is of Norwegian descent. Her father, Jacob Hodnefield, is a librarian, and her mother, Alma Thompson Hodnefield, is a born teller of tales. Mabel Seeley was brought up on stories and began telling and writing them in the first grade. She attended the University of Minnesota, where she served as editor of the student literary magazine in her senior year. During her four years she took every course offered by Mary Ellen Chase, then teaching at Minnesota. After graduating in 1926, she married Kenneth Seeley, then a graduate student at the University of Chicago and now a professor of English at Western State College in Gunnison, Colorado; they have one son. She began to write advertising copy in Chicago and did research and copy on food and medical accounts. After two years she moved to Minneapolis, where she prepared large quantities of department-store advertising. She gave up this occupation in 1935 "to see," she has said, "if I could write other kinds of fiction."

She began with mystery novels designed to make horror more enthrallingly horrible and terror more terrifying by employing characters and places which seem to the reader to be real. The first was *Listening House* (1938). *The Crying Sisters* (1939) is an experiment with double plot. *The Whispering Cup* (1940) combines the regional with the mystery novel. *The Chuckling Fingers* (1941) unites the personal-development novel with the mystery. *Eleven Came Back* (1942) reflects political attitudes. *The Beckoning Door* (1950), set in a small town in Minnesota, may be her last mystery novel.

"I am antipathetic to anything that smells of 'art' in writing," Mrs. Seeley has stated; "writing to me is a craft—a careful, slow, disciplined construction, not especially of what I want to write, but the best I can produce of what I think people may want to read. Readers are warmly responsive to any value received. In a mystery that value means first-paragraph transportation to an emotion-charged, fast-moving other-life. In a more serious novel it may mean a more perceptive—or at least different—picture of living than the reader has seen for himself, one that satisfies him because it is in some way illuminating."

Woman of Property (1947), her first serious novel, studies some very ordinary aspects of the human hunger for acquisition—causes, effects, and results—in the story of Frieda Schlempke, a small-town, midwestern girl, who believes that money is the means to social emancipation and happiness. Reared in poverty in an immigrant home, she sets out to achieve social position through marriage. Her four husbands bring her money, but she loses the man she really loves. The characterization of Frieda is excellent, and the portrait of the late 1890's is particularly vivid.

ELIZABETH SEIFERT

was born in Washington, Missouri, on June 18, 1897. She attended public schools in St. Louis and graduated from Washington University in 1918. Thwarted by poor health and family disapproval in carrying out her ambition to study medicine, she did manage, without her family's knowledge, to take courses in anatomy, physiology, and medical dietetics, and later was employed as clinical secretary in a hospital. Her novels are based largely on observations made during her hospital career. In 1920 she married John Gasparotti, and she is the mother of four children.

Although she began writing when ten years old and always had an ambition to write, she did not publish her first book until 1938. "Raising four children, with the accompanying distraction of tonsils, teeth-bands, etc., and caring for a seven-room house," she has written, "did not leave any time or strength for writing until the children could take care of themselves so well that I could sometimes steal an hour or two in a day for it."

The difficulties facing the woman doctor, the problems of a young physician in a rural community, the ambitions and clashes of rival physicians in a great modern hospital, and the temptations of an astute drug magnate—these are some of the dramatic situations portrayed in Elizabeth Seifert's novels.

Young Dr. Galahad (1938), her first novel, winner of the Dodd, Mead prize, tells how Dr. Tony McNeill tries to bring good medical service to a Missouri town to replace low-grade doctors, quackery, and inadequate facilities. *A Great Day* (1939) portrays in the career of Stephen Blair the way an astute drug manufacturer can make a fortune by selling large quantities of harmless yet almost useless patent medicines to a gullible public. *Thus Doctor Mallory* (1940) pictures a young midwestern boy's determination to be a physician in spite of almost insurmountable handicaps.

Hillbilly Doctor (1940) takes to an underprivileged community in the Ozark Mountains the honor graduate in his class at medical school; there Bill Mulvaney gives the ignorant and superstitious people guidance in sanitation and personal hygiene. *The Bright Scalpel* (1941) has Dr. Jim Wyatt go to China as a medical missionary for two years and then return to his small home town to provide the complacent citizens with good medical service and some information on the needs of a war-torn world. *Army Doctor* (1942) pictures a young physician helping young civilians to understand their duties as soldiers.

Surgeon in Charge (1942) centers on Dr. Peter Mason's dissatisfaction with the management and personnel of a hospital and the steps he takes to improve conditions. *A Certain Doctor French* (1943) unravels the mystery of the long visit of a strange woman to a small community in her relationship to an unpopular physician. The murder of a woman by an overdose of drugs provides a clue. *Bright Banners* (1943) shows how Arnette, a pretty and youthful college instructor, overcomes the prejudice of the head of the faculty and marries the brilliant chairman of the chemistry department. *Girl Intern* (1944) sets forth the problems of a young woman physician, Chris Metcalf, in coping with the notion that medicine is for men alone. A fine young lawyer appreciates her qualities.

Doctor Ellison's Decision (1944) dramatizes the problems of wartime industrial medicine in the story of a physician who was disbarred for an alleged illegal operation and who after ten years clears his name. *Dr. Woodward's Ambition* (1945) portrays the domestic problems of a physician whose work and opportunity for advancement so engross him that he neglects family duties. *Orchard Hill* concerns Judy Quarles' discovery after marriage that she must live up to the Ballard family tradition in a mansion that also houses an attractive brother-in-law.

Old Doc (1946) probes the relationship between a medical man's personal life and profession in the story of Sam Lowry, who retires on his sixty-fifth birthday and discovers disquieting family problems at home. *Dusty Spring* (1946) illustrates the need for courage in everyday life and for deep tolerance between generations and between religious faiths in the story of the homecoming of a hero of World War I. *So Young, So Fair* (1947) centers in the problem of the postwar adjustment necessary in home folks when Rosalind Scott, a physiotherapist, returns from two years in an army hospital in England. *Take Three Doctors* (1947) characterizes three types of medical men: one filled with prejudice, one burned out and disillusioned, and the hero, Chris Johns, ambitious for his small yet stagnant town.

Hospital Zone (1948) details the conflict between a chief surgeon who is an idealist and his assistant who is an opportunist; it describes, also, an ambitious wife and a man who refuses to treat the ills of the body without due consideration for those of the spirit. *The Glass and the Trumpet* (1948) tells about a fine old French family living on the Mississippi River between St. Louis and New Orleans and about the spirited young English bride who is brought into the family. *The Bright Coin* (1949) examines the importance of an anesthetist in surgery and of the right girl in marriage. *Homecoming* (1950) concerns a returning military hero as the home town saw him, and his home-town life as he remembers it.

SHIRLEY SEIFERT

Jack Gould

was born in 1889 in St. Peters, Missouri, near St. Louis, and has lived all her life in that part of the country. She grew up along the Missouri River, and her early pleasures were square dances, old-style farm houses, cake in the kitchen, and good conversation around the open fire with her mother, father, and four younger sisters. She rode on government snag-boats and ferry-boats and packets on the Missouri River, and skated for miles on its frozen sloughs. Graduated from St. Louis High School at the top of her class, Miss Seifert won a scholarship at Washington University in St. Louis, where she earned Phi Beta Kappa honors and took leading roles in the plays of the campus dramatic society. She taught school for a short period, and then on America's entry into World War I took a business course and served until the midsummer of 1919 in the publicity division of the Liberty Loan organization. In that year *The American Magazine* bought one of her short stories. She purchased a typewriter and set herself seriously to writing, and has been engaged in it ever since.

Miss Seifert's interest is in the romance of history and the human side of men and women who have helped to shape it. "My romantic attitude toward history," she writes, "comes from two sources: my thorough enjoyment of a good story and my feeling that history is made by people living out their lives against a background of events. To take a figure of more or less prominence in history, who has remained to students and others only a figure, and to make a living man of him—or a living woman of her—gives me great delight. I think it also brings history to life."

Miss Seifert's first novel, *Land of Tomorrow* (1937), records the history of three generations of an aristocratic Kentucky family in the story of Geoffrey Ormond and his wife Helen, who move west after the Revolution. He kills an admirer of Helen and then commits suicide. An outcast son kills his sister, Jacqueline, and she and her son are killed. It is a story of a family which seems fated to meet violent death. *The Wayfarer* (1938), which is based on some of the adventures of Miss Seifert's maternal grandfather, tells about John Otis Cotter, who leaves New York state in the 1840's for a brief whaling voyage and then goes to the West and becomes a horse breeder. *River out of Eden* (1940), an historical novel of the years just before the American Revolution, tells the story of the founding of St. Louis. André Therriat at nineteen comes to America from France and joins a convoy of boats moving up the Mississippi River from New Orleans.

Waters of the Wilderness (1941) begins in 1778 when the Spanish royal governor brings to St. Louis his beautiful sister, Teresa de Leyba, with whom George Rogers Clark falls in love. The events concern American success in winning from the British the territory between the Ohio and Mississippi rivers. *Those Who Go Against the Current* (1943) tells the life story of Captain Manuel Lisa, a Spaniard born near New Orleans, who trades with the Indians in St. Louis and casts his lot with the Americans by helping the Lewis and Clark Expedition and fighting in the War of 1812. *Captain Grant* (1946) portrays the younger and lesser known years of Ulysses S. Grant, beginning with his entrance into West Point and ending in the summer of 1861, when he became commanding colonel of a regiment of Illinois volunteers. *The Proud Way* (1948) describes the courtship of seventeen-year-old Varina Howell by Jefferson Davis in 1843–44 and their eventual marriage in spite of intrigue, misunderstanding, and family interference.

The Turquoise Trail (1950) describes a trek by covered wagon from Independence, Missouri, to Sante Fé and El Paso. Susan Shelby of Kentucky was eighteen when she married Samuel Magoffin and accompanied him. The story reveals her part in the winning of the West.

JOHN ALLEN SELBY

Leja Gorska

was born in Gallatin, Missouri, on February 7, 1897. His father was a lawyer and an almost perfect "small-town gentleman." His mother was Swedish and "just barely reached America in time to be born." He attended Park College and then went to the University of Missouri. After service in the navy in 1918, he went to work for the Kansas City *Star* and remained there for eleven years. In 1928 he visited Europe and while in southern France wrote the first draft of *Sam,* the novel which in 1939 won the All-Nations contest. From 1933 to 1945 he was arts editor of the Associated Press. He wrote "Literary Guide Post," a daily column that appeared in more than three hundred newspapers; he also did most of the Associated Press news in the field of music. Since 1945 he has been editor of Rinehart & Company, book publishers. He resides in New York City.

His first novel, *Sam* (1939), traces the career of Sam Larsen, a midwestern American gambler and blackmailer, who wins a newspaper in a poker game and proceeds to use it to gain fame and fortune. Ironically he founds a university to bear his name. *Island in the Corn* (1941), the first volume in a trilogy, deals with the family of Archibald Trace, who loses his fortune in a Wisconsin town in the 1880's. His daughter marries Cornelius Starbuck and moves to a Missouri village, where he purchases a small hardware store with a thousand dollars and lives on an "island in the corn." *Starbuck* (1943) tells of Brant Starbuck, a gifted pianist, whose marriage fails when he enters the navy as a seaman and whose career ends in an accident at camp. *Elegant Journey* (1944) is chronologically first in the trilogy; it describes the journey of Sereno Trace westward in 1840. He voyages over the Erie Canal and the Great Lakes. With his wife and eight-year-old son he travels in fine style, taking china, linens, and silverware with them.

ANYA SETON

was born in New York City, the daughter of the two writers, Ernest Thompson Seton and Grace Gallatin Seton. Her father, who was born in England and emigrated to Canada, was cofounder of the Boy Scouts of America and a famous author-artist-naturalist. She graduated from the Spence School and lived for several years in France and England. Her first serious interest was medicine, and she intended to become a physician, but instead she married at eighteen. Her interest in medicine has led her to act as secretary of a mental-hygiene clinic and to work as a nurse's aide. Her mother's family is related to Albert Gallatin, the Secretary of the Treasury under Thomas Jefferson. While doing research work on family history, she became interested in Theodosia Burr and thus came to write her first novel. She is married to Hamilton Mercer Chase; they reside in Greenwich, Connecticut.

My Theodosia (1941) is the story of the life of Aaron Burr's daughter from the age of seventeen until her death at sea twelve years later. She marries a Carolina planter, Joseph Alston, to help her father secure campaign funds, but her loveless marriage causes a mental breakdown. *Dragonwyck* (1944) portrays the final days of the patroon system on the manor, "Dragonwyck," on the Hudson River. Nicholas Van Ryn, the owner, invites his farm-girl cousin, Miranda, to become a companion for his wife and child. The wife dies mysteriously, and Nicholas marries Miranda, who discovers to her horror the conditions she faces.

The Turquoise (1946) grew out of Miss Seton's visits to Santa Fé, New Mexico, where her father had a ranch in that land romantic with Indian and Spanish cultures. It is the story of Santa Fé Cameron, born in New Mexico in 1850, who is deserted by a traveling barker and then moves to New York as the fashionable wife of a Wall Street man. She finally returns to her first husband. *The Hearth and the Eagle* (1948) portrays ten generations of the Honeywood family in Marblehead, Massachusetts, with emphasis upon the daughter of the seventh owner of the inn, The Hearth and the Eagle, and her three tragic love affairs.

IRWIN SHAW

was born in 1913 in New York City. While a student at Brooklyn College, from which he graduated in 1934, he tutored children, worked in the school library, typed manuscripts, and played football. Many of these and subsequent experiences in the working world found their way into his writings. His first job after leaving college was in the field of radio, where he wrote the serials, "The Gumps" and "Dick Tracy," dramatizations of the comic strips. After the appearance in 1936 of Mr. Shaw's first play, "Bury the Dead," about dead soldiers rising from their graves and refusing to return, he went to Hollywood and wrote a number of screenplays. During World War II he served in the army signal corps as a private and warrant officer and saw action in such places as North Africa, the Middle East, Great Britain, England, France, and Germany. While in service he also wrote for *Yank* and *The Stars and Stripes*. He is married and lives in New York City.

Mr. Shaw's short stories, written in the "hard-boiled understatement" style, have appeared in O'Brien's *Best Short Stories* each year between 1939 and 1948, and in 1944 the author received the O. Henry Memorial award. His volumes of short stories include *Sailor Off the Bremen* (1939), about college undergraduates, taxi drivers, hooligans, fighting wives, middle-west college professors, western sheriffs, and farmers from Ohio; *Welcome to the City* (1942), about minor crises in the lives of secondary characters, little people with jobs and without them, and lonely persons; and *Act of Faith* (1946), with a war background. *Report on Israel* (with Robert Capa, 1950) is a text-and-camera picture of the new nation. *Mixed Company* (1950) collects his short stories in one volume.

The Young Lions (1948), his first novel, is the story of three soldiers in a concentration camp in Bavaria. An Austrian goes through all the excited frenzy of a Nazi who experiences joy in victory and bitterness in defeat. An American theatrical producer refuses a commission, and a Jewish filing clerk from California feels the sting of anti-Semitism. The Austrian shoots the Jew and then duels with the producer.

MARGARET SHEDD

Oggiano

was born in 1900 in Urumia, Persia, where her father and mother were Presbyterian missionaries and where her grandparents had followed the same vocation. At twelve she left Persia and went to boarding school in Switzerland, later to Manual Arts High School in Los Angeles, and graduated from Stanford University, where she instructed in the department of speech and dramatics for a time after graduation. At this point she wanted to go into the theater as an actress and director. Instead, she married Oliver Michael Kisich and they went to British Honduras, where her husband worked on and ultimately managed palm-oil plantations. There in the bush the absolute isolation and the need for creative occupation led her into writing. *Theatre Arts* magazine first published her articles. She went back and forth many times between British Honduras and New York and California, and also lived in Guatemala; Jamaica, British West Indies; and Mexico City, which she now considers her home equally with San Francisco, California. She and her husband have three children. Her short stories have been included in several anthologies. In 1950 she conducted a writers' conference in Mexico City.

Miss Shedd's drive in writing is to interpret her times as deeply as possible within the sphere of her own experience. She believes that a woman writer has a different problem from that of a man; because of a woman's more binding responsibility to children, she graduates somewhat later from the closely personal to the creative-general. But at that point, and because of the grind and absorption of detailed living, a woman writer is in a good position to test the general against the personal. Miss Shedd also believes that a writing life finds its own peculiar sequence, adapting itself steadily more to the needs of the artist, so that the second half has a multiplicity and excitement which the first half never knew existed.

Hurricane Caye (1942), her first novel, traces the course of three love affairs against the background of tropical Central America and brings them to their climaxes during and after a hurricane. It is an investigation of love with the fecundity and destructiveness of nature as counterpoint. *Inherit the Earth* (1944) portrays the struggle of Central American people against native and imported dictators as the background for the love story of an American woman with two children and an American man, recently blinded. This novel is a study of whether or not there is any belief or conviction with a pull stronger than that of personal attachment. *Return to the Beach* (1950) has an American background in Marietta, Ohio, and California. Its characters are the members of one family, from a great-grandfather one hundred and three years old who fought in the Civil War to a boy of twenty-one who fought in the

South Pacific, with the two intermediate generations involved in World War I. The theme is: What, if any, belief is worth dying for; does dying for something still serve a purpose? The story concerns the difficult problems posed by Paul Goode's return home after being in a veterans' hospital for two years.

VINCENT SHEAN

Pach

was born on December 5, 1899, in Pana, Illinois. He was educated at the University of Chicago. Afterwards he continued his education through a richly cosmopolitan service as journalist, foreign correspondent, and student of international affairs. Following a brief period as a reporter on the Chicago *Daily News* and the New York *Daily News,* he joined the Paris staff of the Chicago *Tribune.* He did on-the-spot reporting of Mussolini's march on Rome in 1922, and from that moment onward, and continuing through the succeeding turbulent years, exposed the dangers of fascism. He spent most of the period between the two world wars in Europe and the Middle East observing the growth of the inevitable storm. His nonfiction books are *An American Among the Riffi* (1926), *The New Persia* (1927), *Personal History* (1935), *Not Peace But a Sword* (1939), *Between the Thunder and the Sun* (1943), and *This House Against This House* (1946). *Lead, Kindly Light* (1949) is about Mahatma Gandhi and his philosophy. *The Pieces of a Fan* (1937) is a collection of short stories. He resides in New York City.

All his books, including his novels, have dealt with variations of the theme of man's emergence from bondage. "My work as a whole," he says, "concerns the region of experience in which man is related to society. That is, it does not concern private lives or individual relationships nearly so much as it does the connection between the individual and the generality of mankind."

In his first novel, *The Anatomy of Virtue* (1927), the frustrated life of Judith Arleigh as the wife of an English duke serves as a basis for an analysis of corrupt family traditions of love and politics in the days from Queen Victoria to the 1920's. *Gog and Magog* (1930) pictures a group of young people in Paris seeking happiness and an understanding of contemporary political philosophies. Sheila Rudd, an American who takes the husband of a Russian opera singer, turns communist. *The Tide* (1933) recounts the experiences of a Syrian Jew who for a time gains acceptance in America as a holy man striving for social justice.

Sanfelice (1936) is an historical novel of Naples in 1798 when Admiral Nelson after his victory on the Nile wreaks vengeance on the Jacobins who had gained power in the city through a revolution. The story revolves around the beautiful Luisa Sanfelice, the wife of a ruined noble, who wants to leave her husband to live with a lawyer's clerk. She symbolizes the responses of individuals to the forces of the time. *A Day of Battle* (1938) pictures the Battle of Fontenoy on May 11, 1745, and the victory by the French under Marshal Maurice de Saxe over the English in the War of the Austrian Succession. An account of "a battle of lost causes," the novel shows the paradoxes of life and history. Saxe had planned the battle for thirteen years, but he was so ill on the day of the conflict that he was not able to remain on the field.

Bird of the Wilderness (1941), set in the pre-war period of 1916 and 1917, is the story of a sensitive Illinois high-school boy, aged seventeen, whose disillusionment begins when he learns that his father is a drunkard. A teacher's attempt to befriend the lad leads to gossip, and a banker's daughter lays a shocking guilt at his door. *A Certain Rich Man* (1947) recounts the return of a multimillionaire from army service and his discovery that "inordinate wealth warps every relationship, public and private."

SAMUEL SHELLABARGER

was born on May 18, 1888, in Washington, D.C. He was educated at private schools there, at the Hill School, and at Princeton, where he received his degree. After a year of graduate study in Munich, Germany, he returned to this country to complete his doctorate at Harvard in 1917. In the wartime Spring of the same year, Dr. Shellabarger was assigned to duty in ordnance with the engineering division of the army; later he was transferred to military intelligence and appointed captain and assistant military attaché at the United States legation in Stockholm in the autumn of 1918. Following World War I, he was assistant professor of English at Princeton University for four years. Finding that he did not have enough time for creative writing, he resigned and with his family made his headquarters in Lausanne, Switzerland, for the next five years, traveling widely, meanwhile, in Italy and France. After two more years in Princeton, there followed a period of residence in France and England. The Shellabargers returned to America in 1931. From 1938 to 1946 he was headmaster of the Columbus, Ohio, School for Girls. He resides now in Princeton.

Under the pseudonyms of "John Esteven" and "Peter Loring," Dr. Shellabarger has written a number of detective stories and romances. He has published two scholarly biographies: *The Chevalier Bayard* (1928) and *Lord Chesterfield* (1935). The research required for the first of these has furnished much of the historical background of his Renaissance novels.

The immense popularity of Dr. Shellabarger's books arises, in part, from his sure handling of historical materials in a romantic manner. Although the facts and persons of history crowd his pages, the pace and verve of the narrative sweep the reader forward.

Captain from Castile (1945), his first novel, has for its underlying purpose the illustration of the various currents, medieval and modern, which characterized Spain and the formation of the Spanish empire in the sixteenth century. The story concerns Pedro de Vargas, who experiences the horrors of the Inquisition and who then escapes to Cuba, where he joins Hernando Cortes' expedition to invade and conquer Mexico. By harsh and treacherous conduct the Indians are defeated. Pedro falls in love with beautiful Catana Perez and returns to Spain as an envoy to the court of the emperor.

Prince of Foxes (1947) is about Andrea Orsini, a peasant-born man with skill in double-dealing, who assumes the airs of an aristocrat and attaches himself to Cesare Borgia as that cunning leader attempts to conquer the whole of Italy. Andrea goes to Cittia de Monte to betray it into Borgia's power. Dr. Shellabarger had a twofold purpose in writing this novel. He wanted to write a story sufficiently absorbing to hold the attention of his audience and also to guide the reader unobtrusively through an extended survey of Italy from 1500 to 1503, the period that witnessed the full bloom and the decay of the Italian Renaissance. The hero, Andrea Orsini, begins as a climber to whom the end justifies the means. Gradually, however, he learns that the means determine the end; that ruthless policy and deception are ultimately broken reeds both in public and private life, both for the state and the individual; and that the underpinnings of human society are truth, justice, and charity.

The King's Cavalier (1950), the last of the trilogy dealing with the Renaissance, pictures the plots and counterplots of the Bourbon conspiracy against Francis I. The story concerns the conflict between a young Frenchman, Blaise de Lallière, and the mysterious Englishwoman, the king's new favorite, whom Blaise loves and distrusts. The future of France depends on their adventures.

IRVING SHULMAN

was born on May 21, 1913, in Brooklyn, New York. He attended Ohio University and later received his master's degree in English literature from Columbia University in 1938. Work on his doctorate was interrupted by his acceptance of a government position, and he hopes to earn this degree "some day in the not too distant future." In Washington he held a variety of personnel, statistical, administrative, and information positions, and was a member of the English faculty at George Washington University from 1944 to 1947. Since publication of his first novel he has been employed upon several screen assignments in Hollywood.

As a writer Mr. Shulman's interests are sociological; he traces the impacts of our American culture on the various minority groups that make up so many bodies of our citizens. His descriptions of the causes of juvenile delinquency are forceful.

The Amboy Dukes (1947), his first novel, which begins a trilogy, is a story of a group of boys and girls who live in the Brownsville section of Brooklyn, New York, during the dramatic years of World War II. The youngsters, lacking proper home surroundings, are cited for various juvenile crimes and delinquencies. *Cry Tough* (1949), the second novel of the trilogy, concerns Mitchell Wolf, who on his release from a reformatory resolves to become a useful citizen and not to renew his relationships with former members of the Amboy Dukes. But his family's respectability seems drab and plodding; he resumes his friendship with his former companions in racketeering, and when he again determines to return to a life of respectability, he finds it impossible to give up the association with his former friends and new companions in crime.

MAX SHULMAN

was born in Saint Paul, Minnesota, on March 14, 1919. At the University of Minnesota, from which he graduated in 1942, he was editor of the campus humor magazine. Shortly after he became a free-lance writer in 1942, he entered the army air forces and served from May, 1942, to December, 1945. He is a frequent contributor to national magazines and is also active on Broadway and in Hollywood. He devotes himself exclusively to the writing of humor.

Barefoot Boy with Cheek (1943), his first novel, is a witty exposé of college life as experienced by Asa Hearthrug, a freshman in the University of Minnesota. Fun is poked at almost every aspect of academic routine. Asa is a boy with small intellectual power but with enough curiosity to dabble into every idea and nearly every organization on the campus. Especially lampooned are the "pink" liberals, the fraternities, and the faculty. *The Feather Merchants* (1944) satirizes civilian life on the home front during wartime. A soldier on leave is harassed by a welcoming committee, a women's club luncheon, a radio interview, and other events that unnerve him. He gladly goes back to camp to escape the talk of "war work."

The Zebra Derby (1946) brings Asa Hearthrug home from the army to a streamlined postwar world of not always sensible dreams and schemes. He tries to get himself readjusted to civilian life, seeks employment, and also returns to the university on the GI Bill of Rights. *Sleep Till Noon* (1950), a burlesque of middle-class morals and ethics, concerns Harry Riddle, a cafeteria busboy, who marries a rich girl, moves into her society, and finds his vistas broadened.

MARIAN (McCAMY) SIMS

Hoole Studios

was born October 16, 1899, in Dalton, Georgia, and received her bachelor's degree at Agnes Scott College. After graduation she taught history and French in the Dalton High School for three years, then became head copywriter for a Wisconsin advertising firm. In 1927 she married Frank K. Sims, Jr., also of Dalton. In 1929 she and her husband moved to North Carolina, spending a year in Greensboro and then moving to Charlotte, which is still her home. It was in her first years in North Carolina that she began to write fiction. During World War II, in which her husband served as a naval officer, she concentrated on magazine fiction "because it could be written more or less on the run, while I was waiting for instructions to set out for California—or heaven knows where." She wrote short stories and several magazine novels, all dealing with situations arising from the dislocation of war.

Feeling that her own social stratum had been neglected in southern fiction, that too much emphasis was being placed on sharecroppers, Negroes, and backward-looking aristocrats, she turned to writing novels in 1934. "It seemed to me," she says, "that southern novelists were presenting a distorted picture of the region, and that there was a need to round out the canvas. Not that the more prosperous and literate groups constituted *the* South (because the South has a thousand faces), but that they were certainly an integral part of the southern pattern." Therefore, with one exception, Marian Sims' novels have dealt with the upper-class and upper-middle-class South, a phase that has been almost completely neglected by other regional writers, with the result that she has been recognized as the spokesman for these groups.

She believes that more laughter is needed in southern literature. She has pondered the riddle of why the South, which is the most fun-loving and humor-full section of America, has produced only the grimmest and most medicinal literature. Her own work has vigor, gusto, sympathy, perspective, strong characterization, and a wry and rough and masculine sense of humor.

Morning Star (1934), her first novel, is the story of the revolt against her domineering mother by Emily Felton, a model child, who refuses to marry the man chosen for her and achieves happiness. *The World with a Fence* (1936) is about Coral Torrance's experiences in leaving her gracious Georgia home to find a more satisfying independent life in Atlanta. *Call It Freedom* (1937) describes what happens when an intelligent young woman divorces her husband in Reno and returns to her small North Carolina city where, like Noah's ark, the animals are expected to enter two by two. *Memo to Timothy Sheldon* (1938) portrays the duality in Lynn Sheldon's nature. After twelve years of happy married life, during which time she has suppressed that side of her nature which loves beauty and ideas, she meets an English professor and falls deeply in love, for he complements the other side of her nature.

The City on the Hill (1940) concerns the efforts of the Medbury family to improve the social and economic conditions in a small North Carolina city. *Beyond Surrender* (1942) is an historical novel of Reconstruction days on the theme of what it means to lose a war. Major Denis Warden returns to South Carolina and perceives the difficulties in the economic and political system. His unhappy marriage provides the story thread. *Storm before Daybreak* (1946) is the story of three average people caught in an emotional situation in the period after World War II. Paul Shannon, a battle-hardened Marine, returns home to find new responsibilities because of his mother's death and his worthless brother's desertion of wife and child. His mental and emotional growth forms the theme.

HAROLD SINCLAIR

Riegger

was born in Chicago, Illinois, on May 8, 1907. After finishing high school where in the third year he began to find himself, he wandered to Florida in time for the hurricane of 1926. He returned to Chicago, went on to Texas, and finally moved to Illinois. He worked at all sorts of jobs; he was a Western Union telegraph operator and a trumpet player in several dance orchestras. In 1933 he married Ethel Louise Moran; they have six children. He received in 1939 a Guggenheim fellowship; shortly before that he had been working in a Sears, Roebuck store in Bloomington, Illinois, where he still lives. He wrote a non-fiction book, *Port of New Orleans* (1942).

Journey Home (1936), his first novel, is about a thirty-year-old man who leaves his humdrum life in Jersey City during the depression in 1930 and wanders as a tramp. He builds roads in Ohio, becomes a rum runner, joins the bohemian set in Chicago, visits New Orleans, and finally settles down in California. He achieves an idea of what a better society might be like. *American Years* (1938), a Literary Guild selection, portrays the growth of Everton, Illinois, from 1830 to 1861. The book is particularly notable for its depiction of a wide variety of characters who reflect the moods of the era before the Civil War. *The Years of Growth* (1940), a sequel, carries the story to 1893. The main character is Blair Ransom, the son of the richest man in the community, who marries a poor girl. Emphasis is on the social and economic factors and not upon the Civil War.

Westward the Tide (1940) is an historical novel about Benedict Arnold's march on Quebec and George Rogers Clark's expedition to capture Vincennes in 1778. The central character is Philip Guard, a young officer. *Years of Illusion* (1941) continues the history of Everton to 1914 in the story of John Ransom's marriage to a professor's daughter and his work for the improvement of the town as the owner of a newspaper. Parnell McGuire, a son of immigrants, helps Blair.

JO SINCLAIR

Geoffrey Landesman

is the pseudonym of Ruth Seid who was born on July 1, 1913, in Brooklyn, New York. She was raised in Cleveland and graduated from the John Jay High School. Her first job was as clerk-typist; to relieve the monotony of her work, she studied playwriting at Cleveland College during the evenings. She worked for five years with the Works Projects Administration. Later she became an editor of the foreign-language newspaper digest project, which abstracted and recorded the history of Cleveland's many immigrant groups. Then, as America began to emerge from the depression, she worked in a bookbindery. During the time she spent with the WPA, Miss Sinclair had been writing continuously, and from her own experiences she was able to express the fears and poverty of those desperate years. In 1938 her first story was published in *Esquire*. In 1941 she began doing publicity for the Cleveland office of the American Red Cross and remained with that organization for the next five years.

Wasteland (1946), which received the Harper award, is a psychological character study of a Jewish man, Jake Braunovitz, who has denied his heritage by working for eighteen years as a newspaper photographer under the name of John Brown. His tormenting doubts lead him to a psychiatrist, before whom he pours out the story of his immigrant parents, his struggle for self-knowledge, and his effort to merge in the main stream of American life and his unhappiness.

UPTON SINCLAIR

was born on September 20, 1878, in Baltimore, Maryland. His family was southern, and his grandfather and seven uncles and cousins served in the Confederate navy. He was reared in a home of post-war poverty. In 1888 the family moved to New York, where he received his first schooling. In 1892, at the age of fourteen, he enrolled at the College of the City of New York and received his bachelor's degree in 1897. He studied at Columbia University until 1900, when he returned to the country and wrote a novel, *Springtime and Harvest* (1901), which failed to sell. It was reissued as *King Midas* (1901). In 1903 he moved to the country near Princeton, New Jersey, where he lived in a cabin and wrote for three years. In 1906 he founded a co-operative socialist venture, the Helicon Home Colony, at Englewood, New Jersey. When the building was destroyed by fire in 1907, Mr. Sinclair himself paid all the debts.

A lifelong vigorous socialist, during World War I he resigned from the Socialist party to protest against the anti-war position taken by its leaders in 1917. During 1918 and 1919 he was publisher of a magazine, *Upton Sinclair's,* which supported "a clean peace and the inter-nation." He founded the Intercollegiate Socialist Society in 1905; it later became the League for Industrial Democracy. He also founded the California branch of the American Civil Liberties Union in 1923. In 1906 he was the socialist candidate for Congress in New Jersey; in California he was the socialist candidate for Congress in 1920, for the Senate in 1922, and for governor in 1926 and 1930; in 1934 he was made the Democratic nominee for governor. In 1900 Mr. Sinclair married Meta H. Fuller, and in 1913, Mary Craig Kimbrough; he has one son, David, by his first marriage. He has lived in California since 1915.

Mr. Sinclair has written every form of prose composition and has published some seventy books and many volumes of uncollected essays and pamphlets. Possibly no other writer in the world in his generation has had equal acceptance and equal difficulty in finding a hearing. While his name was kept from American newspaper readers through suppression by editors, his books were best sellers in many other countries. *The Jungle* (1906) first brought him national fame, and soon that book and his other writings were translated into foreign languages, forty-seven in all. No other American fiction writer has been read as widely or possibly has been as influential in stirring up social and political, as well as literary, discussion.

As a socialist, Mr. Sinclair preaches a gospel of Christian brotherhood as the basis for the solution of mankind's social and economic difficulties. His concept of brotherhood has been dramatized again and again. He believes in state ownership of natural resources and utilities. Seldom does he miss an opportunity in his books to point out the contrast between conditions as they are at their worst under capitalism and as they could be at their best under socialism.

A series of book-length research essays, under the general title *The Dead Hand,* gave his indictment of the effect of capitalism on American institutions. *The Profits of Religion* (1918) dealt with the church, *The Brass Check* (1919) pictured the newspaper and publishing industry, *The Goose-Step* (1923) examined the control of American colleges, *The Goslings* (1924) reviewed the public-school system, *Mammonart* (1925) laid bare the world of the arts, and *Money Writes* (1927) dissected contemporary American literature. He also is author of a dozen published plays, including "Singing Jailbirds" (1924), "Marie Antoinette" (1939), and "A Giant's Strength" (1948), a dramatization of the effect of the atom bomb on an average American family.

Springtime and Harvest (*King Midas,* 1901) has a young girl marry her wooer's father. *Prince Hagen* (1903) is a fantasy satirizing American politics and finance. *The Journal of Arthur Stirling* (1903) is a young poet's lament that his work is not recognized. *Manassas* (1904), an historical novel, portrays southern social and political problems in the Civil War era in the story of a Boston-educated Mississippian who falls wounded at the Battle of Manassas. *The Jungle* (1906) speeded the Pure Food Act of 1906 because of its account of the unsanitary conditions in the packing industry in Chicago. The story concerns the economic problems of Jurgis Rudkus and his immigrant family.

The Overman (1906) pictures a man whose solitary life for twenty years on a South Sea island has brought him wisdom and mystical power. *The Metropolis* (1908) deals with the moral problem inherent in two brothers' accumulation of great wealth in New York City. *The Moneychangers* (1908), a sequel, shows power-mad capitalists' dishonest refinancing of steel companies and railroads. *Samuel the Seeker* (1910) shows a youngster learning his first lesson in socialism in a town with its manufacturing plant closed down. *Love's Pilgrimage* (1911) presents a frank discussion of the facts of courtship, marriage, and parenthood in the tale of an unhappily married writer. *Damaged Goods* (1913) is a novelization of Eugène Brieux's drama, *Les Avariés.*

Sylvia (1913) is about a southern girl who rejects a man she loves to marry a rich suitor provided by her family. *Sylvia's Marriage* (1914), a sequel, reveals the tragic effects of the union, for their child is born blind. Sylvia sets out to teach the truth about sex. *King Coal* (1917) puts a rich youth to work as a mule driver and miner's helper to get first-hand knowledge of the company-dominated life of the workers who went on strike in the Colorado coal fields in 1914–15. *Jimmie Higgins* (1919) is a pacifist novel about World War I and a machinist's socialist ideas on peace and conscientious objection to war; yet Jimmie joins the colors and fights in France. *100%, The Story of a Patriot* (1920) portrays a man who becomes a labor spy and false witness to help destroy men with unpopular opinions. The book is based on the Tom Mooney case.

They Call Me Carpenter (1922) has Christ visit a young rich man in a dream and teach the lesson that social injustice can be corrected. *Oil!* (1927) is a panoramic picture of life in southern California in the time of President Harding, with emphasis upon the oil business, the moving-picture industry, and the vogue of popular evangelism. The central character, Bunny Ross, is an oil operator's son who becomes interested in liberal ideas and espouses the cause of workingmen against capitalists. Paul Watkins, his friend who goes to Siberia with the American Expeditionary Force, returns with communist ideas. *Boston* (1928) is a two-volume fictional record of the Sacco-Vanzetti case. In 1920 two political radicals, Nicola Sacco and Bartolomeo Vanzetti, were arrested on the charge of murdering a shoe-factory paymaster. Their conviction was appealed unsuccessfully, and they were electrocuted on August 23, 1927. Through the eyes of an elderly aristocratic lady with liberal ideas there emerges a sympathetic portrait of the two men and a suggestion that justice was denied them. *Mountain City* (1930) satirizes money madness in the tale of Jed Rusher, the son of a handy man, who devotes himself wholly to becoming a financial titan.

Roman Holiday (1931) concerns a young man who, during three weeks of unconsciousness following an automobile accident, imagines himself living in ancient Rome under social and political conditions equivalent to those in present-day America. This situation serves to formulate an indictment of our civilization. In *The Wet Parade* (1931) no details are spared to show the social and political evils accompanying the illicit drinking of forbidden alcoholic beverages during prohibition. In this story of a sincere federal agent and his wife, prohibition fails because politics prevents its enforcement.

Co-op (1936) suggests that one solution to the problem of poverty and unemployment is found in Charlie Day's Self-Help Exchange, a co-operative, where labor is pooled and goods and produce are bartered. *Little Steel* (1938) is about Walter Quayle, owner of a small steel mill in Valleyville, who wants to do the right thing by his employees, but "industrial counselors" mislead him; his workers strike, and then a daughter helps him get straightened out. *Our Lady* (1938) is a fantasy of a visit of the Virgin Mary to Los Angeles, where some of the shortcomings of Christianity are made known to her.

In 1940 Mr. Sinclair began publishing a series of novels relating to the rise of the European dictators, Mussolini, Hitler, and Franco; the progress of events in their countries, Italy, Germany, and Spain; the purge of the Jews and the terrible devices of concentration camps and the death chamber; the gathering war clouds and the necessity for President Roosevelt to begin an armament program; the various diplomatic meetings and the dramatic "putsches" in one country after another; the start of World War II in September, 1939, and the events of that war; the embroilment of the United States; and finally the arrival of peace. No other novelist had ever developed so large a canvas nor portrayed so many events and people from the immediate past. In a sense Upton Sinclair has been the creator of a new type of historical novel, the novel of the immediate past as an interpreter of the present and the imminent future. The central character in this series is a young man named Lanny Budd. He is the illegitimate son of a Connecticut munitions millionaire. In the course of his journeys Lanny's socialist leanings make possible the most confidential relations with the world's chief political figures. His movements are such as to place him in the position of an eyewitness to each great event. These books explain World War II more simply and dramatically than most histories.

World's End (1940), the first in the series, pictures the youth of Lanny. He is born in Paris and educated in Europe, is wealthy, handsome, and gifted. The novel surveys 1913 to 1919, the period of World War I. Lanny gets the inside story of the peace conference and of munitions-makers' wiles. *Between Two Worlds* (1941) takes Lanny from the Treaty of Versailles through the stock-market crash in 1929. *Dragon's Teeth* (1942) covers the years between 1930 and 1934. Lanny lives part of this time in Germany and meets Hitler, Goering, and Goebbels. When the Nazi terror begins and a Jewish friend is imprisoned in Dachau, Lanny tries to rescue him but is imprisoned. The book closes with Lanny's release. *Wide Is the Gate* (1943) describes Lanny's anti-Nazi activities between the time of the blood purge and the Spanish civil war. In *Presidential Agent* (1944) Lanny assumes a new role, that of secret agent to President Roosevelt. The period covered is the year between the summer of 1937 and the Munich agreement of 1938. *Dragon Harvest* (1945) deals with "the terrifying days from Munich to the fall of Paris, while an apprehensive world watches Europe yield to the German war machine." *A World to Win* (1946) tells of the European crisis and war from 1940 to 1942. In this period Lanny is captured by the French patriots, is expelled from England, crashes in a plane, goes to Hong Kong on a yacht, travels through China and Siberia, and meets Stalin. *Presidential Mission* (1947) covers the time between the spring of 1942 and 1943; Lanny carries on during the African landing, sees Hitler and Goering, experiences the bombing of Berlin, and returns to America to tell the President all about it. In *One Clear Call* (1948) Lanny is assigned by the President to learn about German progress in developing the rocket bomb by quizzing an anti-Nazi German scientist. Lanny hoodwinks Hitler about America's plans for Italy, and the book ends with Franklin D. Roosevelt's election in 1944 for his fourth presidential term; he discusses his future plans with Lanny. The tenth and last volume, *O Shepherd, Speak!* (1949), covers the last months of the war and the following year. A friend has bequeathed Lanny a million dollars to be used in an effort to maintain world peace, and the money is employed to set up and maintain a radio program to advocate industrial democracy and an international government.

Another Pamela (1950), modeled upon Samuel Richardson's *Pamela* (1744), describes an innocent, religious heroine who works as a parlor maid for a wealthy family in California and who faces perils similar to those of her eighteenth-century prototype and meets them with equal courage.

ELSIE SINGMASTER

was born in Schuylkill Haven, Pennsylvania, on August 29, 1879, the daughter of a Lutheran clergyman who came of Pennsylvania Dutch stock. She grew up in Macungie, Pennsylvania; Brooklyn, New York; and Allentown, Pennsylvania, where she finished high school. Her college education was gained at the West Chester, Pennsylvania, State Normal School, Cornell University, and Wellesley College, from which she graduated in 1907. In 1912 she married Harold Lewars, who died three years later. She moved to Gettysburg, Pennsylvania, where her father was president of the Lutheran Theological Seminary.

Miss Singmaster began writing short stories at the age of eleven. The first of her many juvenile books appeared in 1909 and her first novel for adults in 1915. Most of her characters are Pennsylvania Germans, who are usually called Dutch from the word *Deitsch,* a dialect form of *Deutsch.* She began her work in the tradition of local color, which pictures the customs, manners, and speech of a group of people whose traditions are different from the main American pattern. Allentown, Gettysburg, and the Battle of Gettysburg in July, 1863, serve frequently as background for her stories. Her non-fiction books include *A Short Life of Martin Luther* (1917), *The Book of the United States* (1917), *The Book of the Constitution* (1926), and *The Book of the Colonies* (1927).

Katy Gaumer (1915), her first novel, tells how a Pennsylvania Dutch girl aspires to a college education which will train her for life in a larger world and how she adapts herself to a normal-school community. *Basil Everman* (1920) portrays the influence of Basil Everman, who never appears in the story, on a number of people who live in a small college town just north of the Mason and Dixon Line. *Ellen Levis* (1921) describes a girl who is cut off in her teens from a promised college education by the death of her father and the hostility of her narrow-minded grandfather and brother. She becomes a housemaid in the home of a wealthy physician whose wife is insane.

Keller's Anna Ruth (1926) relates the experiences of a young Pennsylvania Dutch girl who serves as a family drudge until she inherits a fortune and discovers her need for love and friendship. *What Everybody Wanted* (1928) tells of a beautiful forty-five-year-old woman who craves new clothes; her daughter, Marian, who wishes a career in music and an eligible bachelor; and the younger daughter, Arietta, who also wants the same young man. *The Magic Mirror* (1934) is about three eventful years in the life of a Pennsylvania German family, the Hummers, and particularly about the ambitions of Jesse to become a writer. *The Loving Heart* (1937) concerns a girl who lives with a grandmother engaged in conducting the underground railway just as the Battle of Gettysburg is about to take place. The climax comes with the great three-day battle.

A High Wind Rising (1942) recounts the heroic part played by the Pennsylvania Dutch and their leader, Conrad Weiser, in making this continent English during the French and

Indian Wars. The romantic interest occurs in the eight-year search of Bastian Schantz, a friend of Weiser, for the immigrant girl whom he had befriended. *I Speak for Thaddeus Stevens* (1947) is a fictionalized account of the lawyer and statesman who was a powerful figure in Congress in the Civil War period. *I Heard of a River* (1949) portrays the flight of a German Lutheran boy in company with a group of Swiss Mennonites to America in the seventeenth century and his attainment of happiness.

HOBERT DOUGLAS SKIDMORE

Marcus Blechman

was born in Webster Springs, West Virginia, on April 11, 1909. His identical twin brother, Hubert, was born fifteen minutes earlier. Both attended the University of Michigan; Hobert won the major Hopwood award for drama and Hubert for the novel. Hubert, who won distinction with four juveniles and an adult novel, *Hawk's Nest* (1941), served in the European theater of operations in World War II, he died tragically in a fire in his farmhouse on February 2, 1946. Hobert joined up as a private and went with the air force to the Pacific.

Valley of the Sky (1944), Hobert Skidmore's first novel, is the story of a bomber crew and tells their thoughts, emotions, and reactions as they fly the "Heartless Harpie" over the islands of the South Pacific. *More Lives Than One* (1945) describes the men of a ground crew in the air force and how they work, fight, and die in the South Pacific. *Disturb Not Our Dreams* (1947) is a fantasy written around an old ladies' home and the lovely little waif who was left on their doorstep by a carnival troupe. A disfiguring birthmark had caused the child to be treated cruelly on her first day at school. The dream world of the old ladies is rudely shattered through this experience, and a young doctor and the young woman supervisor find love while Lovely's birthmark is removed. *O Careless Love* (1949), "a singing novel of the West Virginia hills," concerns a hill girl who leaves her cabin home looking for love and who finds it after she experiences meanness, goodness, and indifference in her new associates.

CAROLINE SLADE

was born on October 7, 1886, at Minneapolis, Minnesota, the daughter of William G. McCormick. After completing high school, she went on to do special studies at Skidmore College in Saratoga Springs, New York. She married John A. Slade, a lawyer and instructor at Skidmore College. Later he became the president of the corporation of Yaddo, the creative artists' colony. Mrs. Slade organized and worked for the Saratoga County Board of Child Welfare and was an adviser in the Saratoga County Children's Court, doing probation and social work. She has taught students the methods of field work in sociology. She is now retired and devotes her time to writing. Mrs. Slade's novels are an outgrowth of her lifelong interest in the welfare of the average citizen.

Sterile Sun (1936), her first novel, is the account, in their own words, of the reasons why four young girls became prostitutes. *The Triumph of Willie Pond* (1940) analyzes the problems of people on relief and shows the unequal treatment accorded the same man when he is unemployed and when he is confined to a sanitarium. *Job's House* (1941) tells how an elderly couple refuse to apply for relief; instead, they sell their home and buy into a co-operative housing tenement. *Lilly Crackell* (1943) is about a woman with a gift for motherhood from 1918, when she is fourteen and having her first baby, until 1940. Poverty makes it impossible for her to provide for the children, and they are taken from her. The book is an indictment of the unsound methods of some social workers. *Margaret* (1946) is about a poor girl lured to her destruction by wicked men. *Susie* (1947) concerns a young girl who lives on relief. *Mrs. Party's House* (1948) examines the reasons why a respectable widow maintains a house of prostitution and defends her aims.

FRANK G. SLAUGHTER

Underwood & Underwood

was born on February 25, 1908, in Washington, D.C. He graduated from high school in Oxford, North Carolina, in 1922. In 1926 he received his bachelor's degree from Duke University at Durham, North Carolina, where, at the age of seventeen, he was elected to membership in Phi Beta Kappa. From Duke he went to Johns Hopkins Medical School and received his degree as a physician in 1930. In 1942 he entered the medical corps of the army as a major and rose to the rank of lieutenant-colonel before the end of the war. From 1946 to 1948 Dr. Slaughter lectured nationally, discussing socialized medicine, medical and surgical progress, and psychosomatic medicine. He is a Fellow of the American Medical Association, the American College of Surgeons, and a Diplomate of the American Board of Surgery. He has served as resident physician at Jefferson Hospital in Roanoke, Virginia, and as surgeon at the Riverside Hospital in Jacksonville, Florida. He has written one play and many short stories. On June 10, 1933, he was married to Jane Mundy; they have one son, Frank, Jr., and live in Jacksonville, Florida.

Dr. Slaughter has published three books of non-fiction. *The New Science of Surgery* (1946) is a popular review of surgical progress during the past several decades. *Medicine for Moderns* (1948) deals with psychosomatic medicine. *Immortal Magyar* (1950) is a biography of Dr. Ignaz Phillip Semmelweis, the discoverer of a method of antisepsis in obstetrics and a cure for childbed fever.

That Men Should Die (1941), his first novel, is about an idealistic young doctor whose attempt to end certain unsatisfactory medical practices leads to a realization that socialized medicine is not wise. *Spencer Brade, M.D.* (1942) goes behind the scenes of the medical profession to expose the unethical, money-seeking ways of physicians who mulct rich patients in expensive private hospitals. *Air Surgeon* (1943) is a romantic novel of two brothers, one a surgeon who falls in love with the wife of the other, a flying instructor. *Battle Surgeon* (1944) is about a hospital field unit which leaves England for service in Algiers, with an American surgeon using new techniques in handling casualties.

A Touch of Glory (1945) has a wounded veteran, Dr. Christopher Land, return to his Texas home town and dedicate himself to giving excellent medical care to war workers. *In a Dark Garden* (1946) is an historical novel about a Confederate surgeon, Julian Chisholm, who performs operations with modern techniques under battle conditions. *The Golden Isle* (1947) tells about an English physician, Dr. Michael Stone, who is shanghaied by the king of the slave traders, is brought to Florida, and is asked to choose between death and service on a slave ship. *Sangaree* (1948) describes an experiment in freedom involving land tenantry in post-Revolutionary Savannah, Georgia, and the efforts of Dr. Toby Kent to enforce it.

Divine Mistress (1949) portrays the conflict over human dissection between the early anatomists and the Church in the sixteenth century. *The Stubborn Heart* (1950), a sequel to *In a Dark Garden,* is set in the Cape Fear River Valley of North Carolina in the Reconstruction years following the Civil War. Julian Chisholm, a southern physician, is at first horrified at his northern wife's sympathy for both whites and Negroes, but at her instigation he turns his plantation into a hospital open to all.

CHARLES ALLEN SMART

was born on November 30, 1904, in Cleveland, Ohio. He was educated at Richmond Hill High School, near New York, and at Harvard College, from which he graduated in 1926. He did editorial work for three years for the publishing house of Doubleday, and then engaged in free-lance writing in New York and Europe. From 1932 to 1934 he taught English at the Choate School at Wallingford, Connecticut. On January 1, 1935, he married Margaret Warren Hussey of Plymouth, Massachusetts. From 1934 to 1942 he farmed and wrote at Oak Hill, Chillicothe, Ohio, and then for three years he served in the navy, enlisting as an apprentice seaman and being discharged as a lieutenant; he participated in the landings at New Guinea, Normandy, and Okinawa. Since 1946 he has been a writer-in-residence at Ohio University at Athens, Ohio. In 1949 he took a six-months' leave of absence to study at the Escuela Universitaria de Bellas Artes in Guanajuato, Mexico. He has written two non-fiction works. *R. F. D.* (1938) is a report of the adventures of the author and his wife as city-bred farmers. *Wild Geese and How to Chase Them* (1941) informally studies the art of living.

New England Holiday (1931), his first book, is a psychological novel about a house party in New England. Each of the fourteen guests—twelve young people and the mother and father of the host—writes down his emotional experiences and his reactions toward the others. *The Brass Cannon* (1933) is a modern love story. *Rosscommon* (1940) is a sociological novel presenting an imaginary utopian community in 1940, along the lines of the numerous American utopias of a century earlier. *Sassafras Hill* (1947) is a light novel which exhibits some depth.

BETTY SMITH

Blackstone Studios

was born December 15, 1906, in the Williamsburg section of Brooklyn, New York, the daughter of John C. Wehner. She went to work after graduating from the eighth grade and never attended high school. She married a young midwestern lawyer and had two children. When the children were old enough to go to school, she took special work at the University of Michigan, where in 1930 she won the Avery Hopwood award in drama. After studying playwriting under George F. Baker at the Yale Drama School for three years, she joined the Federal theater project. She is the author of seventy one-act published plays and editor of two volumes of dramas. In September, 1947, she joined the faculty of the University of North Carolina as play consultant and special lecturer on the drama. She has been married twice. Her first husband was named Smith, and her second one is Joseph Piper Jones, assistant editor of the Chapel Hill *Weekly*.

A Tree Grows in Brooklyn (1943), her first novel, describes the childhood and youth of Francie Nolan during the period preceding and following World War I. She grows up in the slums amid poverty and misery, but the stark realism of the book is softened by the author's wholesome philosophy. *Tomorrow Will Be Better* (1948) is the story of Margy Shannon, daughter of poor and defeated parents in Brooklyn, her marriage to a boy of similar background, and the gradual disintegration of that marriage. Yet always she hopes for a brighter future.

CHARD POWERS SMITH

was born in Watertown, New York, on November 1, 1894, the son of Justice Edward N. Smith of the New York Supreme Court. Almost all of his ancestry goes back to the earliest settlements in New England and, to the best of his knowledge, was all of an orthodox Congregational or Presbyterian cast. He received his primary education in public schools and at the Pawling School. He graduated from Yale College in 1916 and Harvard Law School in 1921. He subsequently did research in English at the Harvard Graduate School in 1925 and received a master's degree in history from Columbia University in 1949. At college Mr. Smith was managing editor of *The Yale News,* and his chief interest was in paleontology. He was a captain of field artillery in World War I. After practicing law for one year in 1921 and 1922, he abandoned it for writing. He has done field work in paleontology in America for the American Museum of Natural History, and privately in France and England.

Mr. Smith has devoted his life to the search for moral and religious absolutes, and to the restatement of them in contemporary idiom. His effort has been to reconcile a material environment to a metaphysical absolute. He early accepted self-expression as a rule of life, but he included the discovery of supernatural and social truth as essential to its realization. For fifteen years of his writing career the quest for self-expression was personal, and was recorded in poetry: *Along the Wind* (1925), *Lost Address* (1928), *The Quest of Pan* (1930), *Hamilton: A Poetic Drama* (1930), and *Prelude to Man* (1935). The last is an epic of evolution, the only comprehensive, poetic treatment of the subject. During the poetic period he wrote *Pattern and Variation in Poetry* (1932) and *Annals of the Poets* (1935). *The Housatonic* (1946), about a Connecticut valley, is a volume in the "Rivers of America" series.

Like many of his generation Mr. Smith discovered America in the 1930's. Self-expression became social self-expression, the expression of the impulse to serve the community, either directly or through indirect preachment in writing. He adopted the old-fashioned view that America's change since the Civil War, from concern with God and moral improvement to concern with the material world and material improvement, was a perilous alteration. He believed that unless moral responsibility could be restored, not on a scientific and temporal but on a mystical and eternal basis, the current competion for material self-aggrandizement would shortly dissolve the democratic experiment in ignorance, demagoguery, and the tyranny of the right, of the left, or both. Accordingly, Mr. Smith projected a series of novels to show the cycle of the country's swing from spiritual and selfless motivation downward into materialism and selfishness and, prophetically, back to spiritual and selfless action.

The first novel of the series, *Artillery of Time* (1939), is the story of the industrial revolution in the North, the shift from the agrarian to the urban-industrial economy. The second, *Ladies Day* (1941), portrays the decayed condition of the 1890's when religion was a dead stereotype and the most positive social service was material charity, carried on mostly by women. The composition of the third novel was interrupted by World War II. Some of the material was hurried into a small novel, *Turn of the Dial* (1943), which satirizes radio advertising in particular, and shows in general, with documentation, how Hitler and Goebbels took their methods of mass corruption from respected principles of American advertising. Another war novel, *He's in the Artillery Now* (1943), was one of a series similarly entitled. The theme concerns America's ideals and objectives.

LILLIAN SMITH

was born in 1897 in Jasper, Florida, a community the population of which was about equally white and Negro; she lived there until she graduated from high school. Her father, who had large lumber interests, was widely known in church and educational circles. In 1915 the family moved to Clayton, Georgia, the site of their summer home. This mountain community has only a few colored people.

Lillian Smith attended Piedmont College for a year, Peabody Conservatory of Music in Baltimore for four years, and Columbia University for a year. Then she taught for three years in a mission school at Huchow, China. She returned to Georgia and worked as executive secretary to a city manager. In 1925 she became the director and owner of Laurel Falls Camp, one of the best-known girls' camps in the United States. For almost ten years she was co-editor of *The South Today,* a magazine, and she wrote important pamphlets.

She was named in 1943 by the Schomburg nation-wide poll as one of the six white persons who had done most in the improvement of race relations. There is irony in the fact that in the five years following the publication of *Strange Fruit* she received no mention or award for her race-relations work by either white or colored groups. She received the Front Page award in 1944 and the Constance Lindsay award in 1945. Oberlin College awarded her a degree in 1950.

Lillian Smith believes that love for one's own region does not preclude deep loyalties to all people—black, brown, white, red, and yellow—wherever they may live. She is a southerner who wants to be a good world citizen, too. *Killers of the Dream* (1949), a non-fiction book, tells of man's hope for freedom and human dignity and how he kills this dream by his beliefs about the nature of sin, the shame and misery of the human body, and the sense of white superiority which abets those withdrawals which the word "segregation" describes.

Strange Fruit (1944), her first novel, brought Lillian Smith outstanding fame. The story concerns the love of an educated Negro girl and a white man in the South and the tragedy of murder and lynching resulting from that love. Named one of the ten best books of the decade of 1936–45, it has sold nearly three million copies in all American editions. Written with artistry, restraint, delicacy, and great power, it reveals the social and psychological forces underlying the heartbreaking southern race problem.

ROBERT PAUL SMITH

Eve Harrison

was born in New York City. While attending Columbia College, he edited *The Columbia Review*. Later he entered radio work with the Columbia Broadcasting Company. His first book was written in 1940 while he was in Mexico on an extended visit.

So It Doesn't Whistle (1941), his first novel, is about the rootlessness of young people in New York City in the 1930's and their preoccupation with jazz, alcoholic beverages, and marijuana. The story is about four men who share an apartment. *The Journey* (1943) describes a New York businessman's attempt to cleanse himself of pretense and artificiality. He goes to Mexico and there finds rest for his tired body and a cure for his tortured mind. *Because My Love* (1946) tells the story of the marriage of an ordinary couple, Joe Newman and Helen Straub, whose commonplace life ends when they move in with her father. When Mr. Straub dies through an accident for which Helen is responsible, Joe begins to wonder about his own welfare.

GEORGE SNELL

Jasmin

was born on April 4, 1909, in Caldwell, Idaho. He grew up in that and other small Idaho communities. His family moved to Salt Lake City when he was about sixteen, and he attended the University of Utah. While a junior in college he began what has turned out to be a career in radio. His actual vocation has always been in the production end of broadcasting, and his writing of serious books an avocation. For many years he was program manager at KDYL in Salt Lake City, Utah; in 1945 he joined the National Broadcasting Company in San Francisco as a producer. He has also been coeditor of *The Western Review* for eleven years. His special interests include classical music, record collecting, and his family of four sons. An interest in literary criticism has lately superseded his novel-writing career; *Shapers of American Fiction* (1947) is a study of American creative writing in prose since 1789.

The Great Adam (1934), his first novel, has as its theme the disintegration of a strong personality under the gradual impingements of family, economic, and personal misfortunes. It was modeled upon the framework of Greek drama; its locale is a small Idaho town on the "new frontier" of the early twentieth century. *Root, Hog and Die* (1936), an historical novel of the Mormon movement, anticipated the spate of such "Mormon novels" that was published in the years immediately following. Written in a realistic vein, it traces three generations of obscure men and women. *And If Man Triumph* (1938) is a fictional treatment of the experiences of John Manley, who traversed Death Valley with the historic Bennett-Arcane party in 1849. Two boys left the camp at Bennett's Well and rescued the group.

VIRGINIA SORENSEN

Thomas Hornsby Ferril

was born on February 17, 1912, in Provo, Utah. Descended from followers of Joseph Smith, she attended Mormon schools and graduated from Brigham Young University. In 1933 she was married to Frederick Sorensen, and they have two children, Elizabeth and Frederick Walter. The Sorensens have lived in California, where Mr. Sorensen received his doctorate from Stanford University, and in Indiana, Michigan, Colorado, and Alabama, where he is a professor of English in the Alabama Polytechnic Institute in Auburn.

"The critics who please me most," she has said, "are those who insist that I am not, properly speaking, a 'Mormon novelist,' even though I write mostly about Mormon people. I write of Mormons because they are the people I know and to whom I belong, and I believe they do not differ from other people in the general business of being and of keeping alive."

A Little Lower Than the Angels (1942), her first novel, pictures the Mormon settlement in Nauvoo, Illinois, and deals with the period of Mormon history just before and after the death of Joseph Smith and the beginning of the trek of his followers to Utah led by Brigham Young. It is a study of history from the viewpoint of the effect of large historical events on the lives of individuals, in this case a woman involved in the beginnings of polygamy. *On This Star* (1946) is a story of later Mormonism, set in a small enclosed Utah valley. It is concerned with some of the aftermath of polygamy and the general Mormon philosophy, spiritual and economic, again in individual terms; the story involves the love of two half brothers for the same girl.

The Neighbors (1947) describes the struggle between two families living on the same creek in the high country of Colorado. The necessity, for existence, of human co-operation is the theme of this book; here it is illustrated by the use of water, the great western symbol. *The Evening and the Morning* (1949) narrates the love stories of three generations of Mormon women, told from these different age levels during an anniversary celebration. It is an amalgamation of past and present toward whatever order it is possible for each individual to achieve. Like Mrs. Sorensen's other novels, it is concerned with the inescapable way in which historical events and beliefs affect the individual's supposedly private destiny.

DOROTHY SPEARE

Bruno

was born in Newton Center, Massachusetts, and received her bachelor's degree from Smith College in 1919. From 1919 to 1921 she did graduate work at Radcliffe College. Following her college years, Miss Speare sang in theaters and in opera in Italy, where she made her début in the title role of *Lucia di Lammermoor* in 1926. After filling engagements in France, she made her American début in *Mignon* in Washington, D.C., in 1927. For the succeeding three years she sang in concert and opera but was forced to abandon her career because of illness. She then did scenario writing in Hollywood, and since 1935 has been writing, lecturing, and teaching creative writing in the school of public relations of Boston University.

Dancers in the Dark (1922), her first novel, is about the frivolous young people of the 1920's in a story of three girls living together in Boston. *The Gay Year* (1923) describes the snappy, slangy, younger married couples who crave and get more excitement than the older folks in their suburban community think proper. Jerry Lancaster, a wiser wife than most, finds that a worthy project is the real solution to the art of keeping happy. *The Girl Who Cast Out Fear* (1925) concerns Miss Cecil King, a young novelist with one best seller to her credit, who wishes to retain her individuality after her marriage. *A Virgin of Yesterday* (1927) studies the character of Julie, an old-fashioned girl, who assumes that Bob is the right man for her until Steve turns up. Steve is married—or so it seems—and Julie takes time to find the truth. *The Road to Needles* (1937) is about a Broadway playwright who is in Hollywood and attempts to make over his wife, a New England girl. She seeks a divorce in the Arizona town of Needles. *Spring on Fifty-Second Street* (1947) is the story of a "lost lady," Anne Barclay, a girl once well known to café society, who committed suicide, as told eight years later by a friend and a cousin.

HARTZELL SPENCE

was born on February 15, 1908, in Clarion, Iowa, the son of a minister, and grew up in a number of communities. He began working at the age of twelve in a Denver, Colorado, candy store. The next year he carried three paper routes simultaneously, finally becoming a reporter on the Burlington, Iowa, *Hawk-Eye* at the age of fifteen while still a sophomore in high school. When he was eighteen he earned two dollars and fifty cents a week as city editor of a daily paper. In 1930 he graduated from the University of Iowa, where he was managing editor of the *Daily Iowan*. Except for six months in 1932, when he worked with George Gallup, Mr. Spence served the United Press for ten years.

Shortly after the beginning of World War II, he joined the army with the rank of captain, and was one of the founders of *Yank,* the army weekly. After the paper was successfully launched, he joined the staff of General Arnold, commander of the army air forces, in Washington, and was soon promoted to the rank of lieutenant-colonel. Mr. Spence was discharged from the army in 1945 and is now living on his farm near Somerset, Virginia, with his wife and two children. His non-fiction books include *One Foot in Heaven* (1940), the biography of a Methodist preacher; *Get Thee Behind Me* (1942), an evaluation of parsonage life as it affects a minister's children; and *Happily Ever After* (1949), an account of his pursuit of happiness after a war in which almost all his fundamental values required reappraisement in the light of an atomic-age civilization. Mr. Spence has also written for magazines a series of profiles of religious leaders who have developed techniques for successful ministry to a confused generation.

Radio City (1941), his first novel, is a kaleidoscopic picture of life in a giant city skyscraper dedicated chiefly to the forces that mold public opinion: radio, advertising, news magazines, and news commentators. The central character is an advertising-agency executive who discovers that a life successful economically is not necessarily successful spiritually. *Vain Shadow* (1947) is a novelized life of Francisco Orellana, the Spanish conquistador who discovered the Amazon River in 1541. For this book Mr. Spence went to South America and retraced the explorer's route.

CORNELIA SPENCER

Brooks

is a pseudonym employed by Mrs. Grace Sydenstricker Yaukey who was born in Chinkiang, China, on May 12, 1899. She is a sister of Pearl Buck. Her parents were missionaries; Grace grew up in a mission station, learned to speak the Chinese language, attended English-speaking schools, and then came to America for study at Maryville College and Columbia University. She resides near Washington, D.C.

Three Sisters (1939), about the famous Soong sisters of China, was her first book. It began a series of biographies which includes *Elizabeth: England's Modern Queen* (1942); *The Exile's Daughter* (1944), a life of Pearl Buck; *Nehru of India* (1948); and *Straight Furrow* (1949), a biography of Harry S. Truman for young readers. Other books presenting peoples of different countries with special emphasis on their contribution to world civilizations are *Made in China* (1943), *The Land of the Chinese People* (1945), *Made in India* (1946), and *Understanding the Japanese* (1949).

Cornelia Spencer's aim has been to present the influence of nations and their customs upon world understanding, and to show how the crosscurrents of contact, even though they spring from widely different sources, often flow in the same channels. She believes that the many different peoples of the world must become known to each other. "Peace," she says, "can never come by pronouncement or decree. It must come from the heart and have its roots in understanding." Every American must share in teaching and believing this truth.

Her first novel, *China Trader* (1940), is a story of the early trade between New England and China ports. At the end of the eighteenth century Nathan Hathaway takes his bride to Maceo, the Portuguese-held town, where foreigners are permitted to live. The story shows the development of their characters against the background of the struggle of the West for trade in the Far East. *The Missionary* (1947), with its setting in central China during the civil war, is concerned with the call to Christianize and the call to humanitarianism as reflected in the personalities of its leading characters.

ELIZABETH SPENCER

Walden S. Fabry

was born in Carrollton, Mississippi. She grew up in this north Mississippi hill town which lies just east of the Delta cotton country.

Fire in the Morning (1948), her first novel, is a story of two families in the little town of Tarsus. The Gerrards were mean and dishonest; they throve on violence and cruelty. The Armstrongs were gentlemen who were liked and respected. The feud between these two families develops the Hawthorne-like theme that evil persists through the generations and that no man can unload from his back the dark burden which his ancestors placed there.

JEAN STAFFORD

Arni

was born July 1, 1915, in Covina, California, and was reared and educated in Colorado. She spent a year in Germany after graduating from college, and then taught in Missouri for a year. Since that time she has lived in Massachusetts, Louisiana (where she worked on *The Southern Review*), Tennessee, Maine, and New York City. She held a Guggenheim fellowship in 1945 and again in 1948. The National Institute of Arts and Letters gave her an award in 1945, and early in 1948 the Women's National Press Club honored her for achievement in literature.

The theme of almost all her short stories and novels is the struggle out of childhood into maturity, and the ceaseless battle of all human beings against isolation.

Boston Adventure (1944), her first novel, is a character study in Proustian symbolistic style of Sonie Marburg, the daughter of a German father and Russian mother, who in extreme poverty dreams of better things. She becomes the secretary of Miss Pride, a rich Boston spinster. *The Mountain Lion* (1947) pictures the years of bitterness between childhood and adolescence of two children who escape from family feuds to an uncle's Colorado ranch: Ralph, aged eight, and Molly, aged ten.

WILBUR DANIEL STEELE

Doris Ulman

was born in Greensboro, North Carolina, on March 17, 1886, the son of a school principal. When the father went to Germany to pursue graduate study, the boy attended a kindergarten supervised by a niece of the eminent educator, Friedrich Fröbel. Wilbur continued his education in Denver, Colorado, where in 1902 his father became a professor of Biblical science in the university. At night and in the summer he studied art. On graduation from high school in 1907, he went to the Museum of Fine Arts in Boston and studied under Philip Hale. For a year Mr. Steele lived in Paris, Florence, and Venice, and for another in New York. Having been encouraged by Mary Heaton Vorse, who liked his short stories, he decided to make writing his career. In 1919 he was awarded second prize by the O. Henry Memorial Award Committee, and in 1921 he was given a special citation for sustained excellence in short-story writing during the preceding three years. He tied for first prize in 1925 and received first prize in 1926 and 1931. Meantime he had traveled in the Caribbean, Africa, and Europe, and during World War I served as a correspondent with the United States navy. He resides in Connecticut.

His short stories are published in *Land's*

End (1918), *The Shame Dance* (1923), *Urkey Island* (1926), *The Man Who Saw Through Heaven* (1927), *Tower of Sand* (1929), *Diamond Wedding* (1931), and *Best Stories* (1946). His plays include *The Giants' Stair* (1924), *The Terrible Woman* (1925), and *Post Road* (with Norma Mitchell, 1935).

Mr. Steele's short stories broke away from the popular style of Bret Harte's local-color devices and O. Henry's cleverness. He gave new twists to traditional forms by emphasizing psychological substance rather than plot. Although he has been noted primarily for his shorter fiction, his novels are effective for their character portrayal.

Storm (1914), his first novel, concerns Joseph Mantua who grows up in a Portuguese settlement on Cape Cod and fights big Jack Crimson for Allie Snow, the daughter of the town's wealthiest citizen. *Isles of the Blest* (1924) portrays the death of love between a couple living for a year on an island in the Caribbean; when each decides to escape from the other, they find themselves on the same boat, and through the good offices of another passenger they discover their mutual need. *Taboo* (1925) pictures the love which a man bears for a girl who he thinks is his daughter but who, it turns out, is the daughter of his best friend's wife, a woman he had loved passionately. The novel also studies the damaging effects of phobias.

Meat (1928) describes the changes which occur in the psychology of Anne India when she gives birth to a defective son. Her fierce protective instinct turns her from a person who worships strength and beauty to a guardian of the abnormally sensitive child; the effect is to ruin her husband's happiness and to darken the lives of an elder son and an adopted daughter. *Undertow* (1930) is a tale of love and sacrifice based upon a motion-picture script by Mr. Steele. *Sound of Rowlocks* (1938) is a psychological mystery story laid on Cape Cod. *That Girl from Memphis* (1945), with its setting in Beulah City, Arizona, during the first big silver boom, pictures the drama, color, and shifting social standards of a frontier settlement. The story concerns the love of a Kansas boy for a beautiful woman of easy virtue.

Diamond Wedding (1950) concerns Gowd Skinner, a dead-beat mountain wanderer, who meets and falls in love with young Hope Wheelock, an abandoned girl from the East. They form an unusual alliance and find happiness for themselves and their family in a struggle for survival and success. They are married on the diamond anniversary of their meeting. The setting is Colorado.

WALLACE EARLE STEGNER

was born on February 18, 1909, near Lake Mills, Iowa, and spent his childhood in a variety of places: Iowa, North Dakota, Washington State, Saskatchewan, Montana, Utah, Nevada, and California. It was the five years spent in Saskatchewan, however, that he considers the most valuable period of his life, inasmuch as he had opportunity to observe at first hand and to grow up with the last real frontier and to know its colorful collection of bad men, ranchers, bonanza farmers, cockney immigrants, and Texas cowpunchers. He went through high school and college in Salt Lake City, graduating from the state university in 1930. In the next five years, which included one year of graduate study at the University of California at Berkeley, he earned his master's and doctor's degrees at the University of Iowa. Since 1945 he has been professor of English and director of the Writing Center at Stanford University. On November 1, 1950, he and Mrs. Stegner left for a tour of India, Thailand, the Philippines, and Japan to conduct a series of seminars for writers in those countries.

His writing career began in 1937 with the winning of the Little, Brown novelette contest. *One Nation* (1945), about America's racial and religious minority groups, won the Houghton Mifflin Life-in-America award, and shared the *Saturday Review's* Anisfield-Wolf award. *Mormon Country* (1942) is a volume in the "American Folkways" series. *The Women on the Wall* (1950) contains short stories. In 1942 and again in 1948 Mr. Stegner was given second prize for short stories in the O. Henry Memorial award volume. In 1949 he was awarded a Guggenheim fellowship. He is married, has one child, a son, and lives in Palo Alto, California.

Remembering Laughter (1937) is a novelette set on an Iowa farm. Margaret Stuart discovers that her husband loves her sister, Elspeth, by whom he has a child. The three hide the truth and live together eighteen years in silence. *The Potter's House* (1938) deals with the tragedy of the deaf. *On a Darkling Plain* (1940) concerns a young Canadian, injured during World War I, who goes to Saskatchewan to recuperate and to get away from mankind. The human need for companionship draws him to a young girl in the influenza epidemic of 1918. *Fire and Ice* (1941) concerns a young student of the period of the great depression who is making his own way through college against bitter difficulties. He is a member of the Young Communist League, but an encounter with a wealthy girl shakes him loose from ready-made answers and throws him again upon himself in the hard search for equilibrium and self-respect.

The Big Rock Candy Mountain (1943) pictures a family which tries all the frontiers of the West after the real opportunities have passed; they seek their fortune within and without the fringes of the law. *Second Growth* (1947) develops the theme of the cultural antagonism which exists where two ways of life meet or merge. The setting is New Hampshire; the cultures are the static New England village life and the restless existence of the "summer people" from New York and Boston and Hartford. Some of the people caught at this border make the transition safely; others are destroyed in the attempt. *The Preacher and the Slave* (1950) portrays the waterfronts, railroads, and wheat fields of the far West as a background for the story of Joe Hill, a labor leader who was prominent in the I.W.W. and who nearly set the whole vast land aflame in the first quarter of the twentieth century.

JOHN STEINBECK

Breitenbach

was born on February 27, 1902, in Salinas, California. After graduating from Salinas High School, he attended Stanford University for four years as a special student rather than as a candidate for a degree. His interest at the time was science, particularly marine biology. Then, with writing in view as a profession, he worked at many jobs to gain experience; he was a ranch hand, carpenter, painter, bricklayer, fruit picker, newspaper reporter in New York City, caretaker of a Lake Tahoe estate, and chemist. In 1930 he married and settled down in Monterey, California. With *Tortilla Flat* (1935) his reputation was established as a distinguished writer. In 1937, the year of the successful dramatization of *Of Mice and Men,* he toured the Scandinavian countries and Russia. In 1938 a volume of short stories, *The Long Valley,* brought him acclaim as a writer of the highest distinction; in this collection are such favorites as "The Red Pony" and "Chrysanthemums." In 1940 he won a Pulitzer prize for *The Grapes of Wrath;* to escape the excitement created by this novel about migratory workers, he led a private research expedition to the Galapagos Islands off the coast of Ecuador. During World War II he was a foreign correspondent for the New York *Herald Tribune.* For the army air forces he wrote as a recruiting document *Bombs*

Away: The Story of a Bomber Team (1942), which traces the education molding six civilian boys into a plane crew. A non-fiction book, *Russian Journal* (1948), is a report on his journey through the Soviet Union with the photographer, Robert Capa. His other book of short stories is *The Pastures of Heaven* (1932). *The Portable Steinbeck* (1943, 1946) contains selections.

Mr. Steinbeck is a naturalistic writer whose men and women characters are usually unable to escape from the biological and environmental forces which mold their lives. Unlike most writers of this type of fiction, he reflects a mystical religious faith which often imparts cheer to characters who otherwise would not survive their difficulties. His writing is notable for clear, sharp pictures, a sardonic humor, and a direct, forceful style.

Cup of Gold: A Life of Henry Morgan, Buccaneer, with Occasional References to History (1929), his first novel, is a fictionized biography of the notorious pirate who captured Panama, the "cup of gold." The book reflects something of the mood of the roaring 1920's, for the excessive ambition, great personal power, and inordinate wealth of Morgan were characteristic of many people living in the United States in the third decade of the twentieth century. *To a God Unknown* (1933) takes a young Vermont farmer, Joseph Wayne, to California. He has a mystical feeling about the earth, and he thinks that his father's spirit hovers about the land and dwells in a giant oak tree. Because Joseph makes sacrifices to the tree, a brother kills it. Lean years come, and death, disease, and famine harass the community.

Tortilla Flat (1935) recounts the unmoral, carefree existence of some people of mixed Spanish, Indian, and white blood in the slums of Monterey, California. The central character is Danny, a *paisano* who comes home from World War I and gathers together in two recently inherited houses a group of his friends. *In Dubious Battle* (1936) tells the story of a strike among fruit pickers in a California community. The narrator—Jim Nolan, a radical in his outlook—explains why migratory workers revolt against the orchard owners. *Of Mice and Men* (1937) concerns two drifters, George and Lennie, who dream of owning ranches. Lennie, a simple-witted fellow of great strength who worships George, gets them in trouble when he unintentionally commits a murder.

The Grapes of Wrath (1939), which has been called "the twentieth-century *Uncle Tom's Cabin*" because of its picture of a serious economic and social problem, is a story of the thirteen members of the Joad family in the dust bowl of Oklahoma. Through no fault of their own they must leave their farm, which the family has owned for many years. Lured by the enticing advertising of fruit growers, the family decides to move to California. They convert an old automobile into a truck to carry the family and their few possessions. On the highway they learn that hundreds of other families are traveling in the same manner. Grandpa Joad dies first—he had not wanted to go—and then Grandma Joad passes away, but the goal must be reached so that the workers can get jobs. Hunger, heartbreak, disillusion, and exploitation are experienced on the road and in the workers' camps in California. So full of incident is the book that most of the motifs of the era of the depression are dramatized in scenes that are sometimes humorous and sometimes terrifying and horrifying.

The Moon Is Down (1942) portrays the heroic resistance of the Norwegian people to the invading Nazis in World War II. The central character is the mayor of the small city who goes to his death reciting Socrates' dying speech. Particularly interesting is the analysis of the psychology of brutality as practiced by the conquering German army. *The Red Pony* (1945) gives four episodes in the life of a boy on a California ranch. *Cannery Row* (1945) is a picture of the outcasts of society in a small canning town on the West Coast. Their kindly intentions and warmheartedness soften the sting of their vulgarity and immorality. *The Wayward Bus* (1947) describes a group of people who are stranded overnight at a roadside gasoline station in California; their experiences provide the basis for a study in human relationships. *The Pearl* (1948) concerns a gem that brings misfortune to a Mexican fisherman. *Burning Bright* (1950) is an allegorical play-novelette about the importance of the continuance of the human race; a sterile husband's wife seeks a baby by another man.

GENEVA STEPHENSON

Louis Neunhofer

was born in Portsmouth, Ohio. She graduated from Ohio State University and studied also at the American Academy of Dramatic Art at Columbia University. She has taught English and dramatics both at her alma mater and at Marietta College; she was program director of the Ohio School of the Air and, more recently, has been active in radio as lecturer, dramatic director, script writer, and program director on the national chains. She has given the creative-writing lecture series at New York's Town Hall and has appeared on the lecture platform in the Midwest and in eastern cities, speaking on literary and theatrical subjects.

Spring Journey (1939), her first novel, is a realistic account of England in the mid-eighteenth century in a romantic tale of Lady Bragdon, who, disguised as a serving boy, flees an unwelcome marriage by joining an artist on his spring painting expedition. The background includes a portrayal of gypsy life and glimpses of such notables as Hogarth the artist, Garrick the actor, and Fielding the novelist. *Melody in Darkness* (1943) is a romantic tale of an English musician who was blinded in the Battle of Falkirk in 1746 and who meets a Jacobite woman on his journey to London to consult an eye doctor. Their many adventures end in romance. The theme concerns the place of music in a world of war and crime; many well-known musicians of the period, including Bach and Händel, appear as important characters in the story. There is considerable detail of life in the theater and some dramatic scenes in the London underworld.

DAVID STERN

was born on September 2, 1909, in Philadelphia, Pennsylvania, the son of J. David Stern, II, a newspaper publisher. He graduated from Haddonfield, New Jersey, High School in 1928 and studied at the University of Pennsylvania and Harvard. His first jobs were in reporting and advertising work From September, 1939, to February, 1947, he was the publisher of the Camden *Courier Post*. During World War II, he served as co-officer in charge of the soldier newspapers, the *Midpacifican* and *Stars and Stripes of the Pacific*. He was discharged in August, 1945, with the rank of captain. Mr. Stern is married, has one son, and lives in Louisiana, where in July, 1949, he became president and publisher of the New Orleans *Item*. He has written a murder mystery, *Stop Press Murder* (1947), under the pseudonym of "Peter Stirling," and the movie scenario of "Francis."

Francis (1946), his first novel, is a satire on army life; Francis is a talking army mule who befriends a young lieutenant in the Burma Theater in World War II and helps him win fame and decorations. The officer is placed in a psychopathic ward for stating that he receives information from a mule. Finally, in a talk with the general, Francis proves his worth and agrees to use his talents to spur patriotism. *Francis Goes to Washington* (1948), a sequel, satirizes politics in general and current issues in particular.

PHILIP VAN DOREN STERN

was born on September 10, 1900, in Wyalusing, Pennsylvania. He was educated at Rutgers University, from which he received his bachelor's degree in 1924 and an honorary degree of Doctor of Letters in 1940. He spent the years from 1924 to 1933 in advertising work and became an expert in typographic design, writing his first book, *An Introduction to Typography* (1932), on that subject. He then entered the book-publishing business, first as a designer for Alfred A. Knopf and then for Simon & Schuster, whom he later served as editor. In 1941 he became the editor of Pocket Books, for which he edited many anthologies. In 1942 he took a leave of absence to join the Office of War Information. In 1943 he became the head of Editions for the Armed Services, a non-profit organization which printed and published over a hundred million paper-bound books for the armed forces overseas. He rejoined Pocket Books in 1945 and served as vice-president until November, 1946. After three years devoted to writing, he again entered business with a printing firm in New York City.

Although most of his work has been in American history, he is equally interested in general literature and has edited the writings of Thomas De Quincey, Edgar Allan Poe, Arthur Machen, and Abraham Lincoln. He has also specialized in stories of the supernatural and has edited three anthologies in that field.

His first novel, *The Man Who Killed Lincoln* (1939), was based on the life of John Wilkes Booth and his part in the famous assassination. It is thoroughly documented from primary sources and attempts to explain the workings of Booth's mind as he went about his plot to kill the President. *The Drums of Morning* (1942) deals with the abolitionist movement from 1837, the time of the killing of Elijah Lovejoy by mob violence, to the final freeing of the slaves at the end of the Civil War. *Lola* (1949) portrays an episode in the life of Lola Montez, the British dancer and adventuress, who died in New York in 1861. It covers the last years of her life and deals with her love affair with a fictional Boston hero.

JAMES STEVENS

was born on November 15, 1892, on a farm near Albia, Monroe County, Iowa. At the age of four he was taken to Appannoose County. When he was ten, he was placed with relatives in Idaho. At thirteen he started out to earn his own living, and for nine years he had many jobs requiring hard work; some of them involved handling horses and mules on construction jobs and in the forest industry. In 1917 he enlisted in the army and spent a year and a half in France as an infantry sergeant. After the armistice and his honorable discharge, he returned to the woods, camps, and mills. In 1923 H. L. Mencken suggested that Mr. Stevens write about his experiences, and soon autobiographical sketches and tales of Paul Bunyan, the folklore hero of the forests, brightened the pages of *The American Mercury*. Following the successful publication of his early books, Mr. Stevens became a public-relations counselor for the West Coast Lumberman's Association in Seattle.

Mr. Stevens gives much of his time to conservation and education. In 1939 he formed an organization that grew into the Keep Washington Green Association. In ten years this program of public education in forest-fire prevention has taken root in twenty-three other states. "In my novel, *Big Jim Turner,*" Stevens says, "I attempted to trace the influence of the free public library in our democracy. As a roving boy laborer in the Northwest I had invaluable help in self-education from libraries. The public library and the forests—here are the fields in which I try to contribute a little in return for the benefits that have come to me from life in America."

The plain purpose of James Stevens in his novels and tales is to project the soul of art which abides, he maintains, in the common ways of America. "America sings," he says. "America tells stories, dances, paints, and speaks in poetry on all occasions. America lives epics of romance and adventure. This is the American glory in my sight. Our best writing, that of Whitman, Twain, Sandburg, has been dedicated to revelation of this glory. I am satisfied to have a modest part in this enterprise of national art, to give literary form to a few of the things of the creative spirit which is everywhere in the life and lore of America."

Paul Bunyan (1925), his first book, is a collection of humorous tales about the legendary hero of the lumber camps. *Brawnyman* (1926) is an autobiographical novel which tells the story of a hobo laborer's travels from job to job. *Mattock* (1927) describes in the Kansas vernacular of Private Mattock the experiences of Company "F," an organization of draftees, from its first training period in France to its first convention as members of the American Legion. *Homer in the Sagebrush* (1928) contains thirteen short stories. *The Saginaw Paul Bunyan* (1932) is a book of Paul Bunyan stories drawn from material gathered in Michigan. *Timber!* (1943) sketches the life of the lumber camps for vocational study in high schools. *Paul Bunyan's Bears* (1947) has its source in Paul Bunyan stories told by forest guards and firefighters of high-school age in the northwest woods during World War II. *Big Jim Turner* (1948) tells about a young western boy in the early twentieth century who emerges from the labor troubles of the time with Walt Whitman's faith in America.

LOUIS STEVENS

Frew R. Archer

was born on January 6, 1899, in the South Ukraine of Russia. He arrived in San Francisco in 1905 at the age of six and still remembers the new-world excitement of the California city, which he lovingly considers his native home. A year later he was selling newspapers in the Horatio Alger tradition and gaining first-hand knowledge of the notorious Barbary Coast and the colorful San Francisco Bay area. One night he met Jack London, and the writer took an interest in the boy. Young Stevens became London's protégé. The novelist often invited the youngster to his ranch, encouraged his literary talent, and even gave him his American name. At sixteen Mr. Stevens was a reporter on the San Francisco *Bulletin.* He attended the University of California at Berkeley, quitting in his first year to resume newspaper work. In this period he boxed in amateur rings as an accredited member of the famous Olympic Club. After service in World War I Mr. Stevens did publicity work for the Southern Pacific Railroad and eventually migrated to Hollywood, where he became a script writer. He wrote motion-picture stories in Hollywood, London, and Munich. He traveled extensively throughout Europe, Mexico, and the Middle East. Now a resident of Beverly Hills, California, Mr. Stevens is married to a native Kansan who provided him with a son and the inspiration for the midwest setting of *Days of Promise,* his massive historical novel of the grass roots of American democracy.

When asked about the philosophic basis of his work, Mr. Stevens said: "The following is my credo and, in effect, will be, I feel sure, the tenor of all my future work: It is a faith in the hereditary principles of American democracy, specifically in parliamentary government; and in the dignity of the individual—this last possibly the most treasured possession of all. I feel that every individual in modern society, consciously or not, is basically, cruelly, and very often violently subject to the strains, tuggings, pressures, and uncertainties of his daily life; and his story is the story of his attempt to adjust himself to them, or to escape from them, or to justify himself as a human being. It is a story that makes, it seems to me, for intensive and realistic drama. That the novels of today are stark in content, often quite physical, more often brutal and violent, is due, I believe, to the new era upon which we have embarked. Yet, paradoxically, the violence, so-called, has not lessened but increased man's need for or dependence upon spiritual values or truths, all the Marxian philosophy to the contrary. And it will be spiritual faith in himself which, in the end, will make man worthy of his place as a decent human being in a civilized—if not the best possible—world."

All the King's Horses (1928), his first novel, tells the story of the disintegration of a ruling Hungarian social class in World War I, resulting in the collapse of the once-proud Austro-Hungarian empire. The narrative brings into brutal light the sparkling but unreal illusions of a life that had passed its time in history, and sets the stage for the new world, for better or for worse, that is to arise out of the ashes of both victory and defeat. *Here Comes Pancho Villa* (1932) recounts not so much the social or agrarian history of the modern Mexico, though it deals sketchily with both, as, in anecdotal form, the psychology of a killer in action, Pancho Villa, who arose out of the dust and misery of peonage and, after his fashion, helped to shape the Mexico of today. The story is told in an intimate and personalized manner and includes sketches of "off-beat" American personalities.

Days of Promise (1948) deals with four generations of the vigorous, high-minded MacAllister family of farmers, journalists, adventurers, doctors, and soldiers, each one of them testing his democratic heritage against the forces of his time and place. The time runs all the way from Appomattox Court House to the opening of World War II, and the scene shifts from Virginia to early-day Kansas, to all sections of America, and even to Europe.

ANN STEWARD

W. B. Poynter

was born in Cincinnati, Ohio, on August 29, 1898. At the University of Cincinnati and the University of Michigan she specialized in English and sociology. For several years after graduation she did social work, more with a writer's interest in the individual human being than in "cases." Later she worked on a newspaper, wrote plays for and acted with a little theater workshop, and did professional reading and lecturing. During this time she wrote stories, poems, and plays for children. Since 1935 she has lived on a Kentucky farm.

Mrs. Steward's main theme in fiction has arisen from a long inner search for a living knowledge and experience of a spiritual essence in the life of the earth and of man. Her words are meant to be pictorial images rather than intellectual representations of this theme. Her novels seek to give a universal, spiritual account of mankind's creative relationship with the earth through the lives of individuals.

Let the Earth Speak (1940), her first novel, is a twofold story combining realism and symbolism. Outwardly it describes life on a large Kentucky estate among a community of people whose destinies are related to each other and to Old Hayes, who founded the place on his passionate love of the land and who thereby dominated the lives of everyone after him. Inwardly it tells the earth's own story of man's spiritual relationship to it in as many manifestations as there are characters and events in the book. The earth as a living entity is presented as going through the yearly cycle of its life in a union with the human life upon it. *Take Nothing for Your Journey* (1943) continues the account of the deeply interrelated destinies of the people and place, and carries the inner story into a second stage of development in which the earth is threatened with destruction and is saved only by sacrifice. This book won the Ohio award in fiction in 1943.

GEORGE R. STEWART

M. Bridge & D. Leonard

was born on May 31, 1895, in Sewickley, Pennsylvania. In 1917 he received his bachelor's degree from Princeton University, in 1920 his master's degree from the University of California, and in 1922 his doctorate from Columbia University. He served in the army from 1917 to 1919. During the years 1920 to 1923 he was associated with the English departments of the University of California, Columbia University, and the University of Michigan. He has taught at the University of California at Berkeley since 1923, and been professor of English since 1942. In 1942–43 he was resident fellow in creative writing at Princeton, and in 1944 he was an editor in the University of California Division of War Research. He is married and has two children.

As a writer Mr. Stewart has always followed an uncharted course. His early books gave the first evidence of the independence and originality of his roving mind. Following two books on versification, *Modern Metrical Technique* (1922) and *Technique of English Verse* (1930), he wrote *Bret Harte: Argonaut and Exile* (1931), the authoritative biography of the founder of local-color fiction in America. *Ordeal by Hunger* (1936) is a nonfiction account of the Donner party of California immigrants who suffered indescribable hardships on being snowbound in the winter of 1846–47. *John Phoenix* (1937) is a biography of George Horatio Derby, the humorist. *Take Your Bible in One Hand* (1939) is a biography of William Henry Thomes. *Names on the Land* (1945), an historical account of place-naming in the United States, achieved effectively what had never been attempted in the field, and *Man: An Autobiography* (1946) tells the story of mankind, with man himself his own hero and narrator. *The Year of the Oath* (1950) deals with the loyalty tests at the University of California.

East of the Giants (1938), his first novel, is an historical tale of twenty-five years in the development of California after 1837. Judith Hingham, a New Englander, marries Don Juan Godoy, and they settle in Mexican California. The Gold Rush and immigration bring trouble, and Juan is killed. Judith moves to San Francisco. *Doctor's Oral* (1939) tells of Joe Grantland's struggle to complete his education and to get his degree of Doctor of Philosophy. The climax is the oral examination given by seven professors, whose conduct and motives provide a satiric commentary on graduate study. *Storm* (1941) is the story of twelve days during which a young meteorologist follows the path of a tempest from the time it begins on the China coast until it crosses the Pacific and sweeps over California. Its destructive force endangers the lives of millions of people. *Fire* (1948) describes the progress of a forest fire in the Ponderosa National Forest in northern California. It begins with a stroke of lightning and burns ten thousand acres of timber before rain helps to quell it. *Earth Abides* (1949) deals with the near-extermination of the human race by a virus, and with subsequent occurrences which lead toward the reconstitution of things in the coming seventy-five years.

HART STILWELL

Russell Lee

was born in 1902 in Texas. His grandparents moved there during the early days of the Anglo-American settlement. While at the University of Texas, where he took his degree in 1924, he did newspaper work, and for years afterward he worked as a free-lance writer. In 1942–43 he edited a newspaper. Many of his essays have dealt with outdoor life, as have two books, *Hunting and Fishing in Mexico* (1946) and *Fishing in Mexico* (1948).

For years Mr. Stilwell has been impressed with the pathetic condition of Latin Americans in Texas. He has consistently worked for liberalism, including equality and justice for people of all races, creeds, and nationalities. His plans include writing a novel about a Negro in Texas.

Border City (1945), his first novel, tells the story of the Latin Americans in Texas and the social and political discrimination they suffer. The central theme is that, even with an abundance of good will manifest on both sides, years must pass before the problem can be solved. *Uncovered Wagon* (1947), based largely on the story of Mr. Stilwell's father and mother, is about early times in Texas and shows the violent opposition of the pioneers to encroaching civilization and the toughness necessary to survive. *Campus Town* (1950) portrays life in a typical southern state university in the early 1920's, particularly the search of postwar youth to find a set of sound values in the face of prejudice and commercialism, and the intrusion of this commercialism into academic freedom at state universities. It outlines and attempts to analyze the way people live and the way they say they live.

IRVING STONE

Eric Schaal

was born on July 14, 1903, in San Francisco, California. During high-school days he worked at selling newspapers, driving a delivery wagon for a vegetable market, and as an errand boy and stock boy in stores. At the University of California at Berkeley, where he graduated with honors in 1923, he worked his way by playing saxophone in an orchestra for dances, and during the summer he picked fruit on ranches. Yet he found time to fight on the boxing team and serve on the debating team. In 1923–24 he taught economics and took a master's degree at the University of Southern California, and then for two years he taught at the University of California while studying for his doctorate.

In 1926 he decided that he wanted to fulfill a lifelong ambition to be a writer, a tendency that had led to the composition of short stories and one-act plays during his university days. For several years he lived in New York City, where he wrote eighteen full-length plays and saw two of them produced. While in Paris in 1930 he came upon the life and works of Vincent Van Gogh, about whom he wrote *Lust for Life* (1934). In 1937 he edited *Dear Theo: The Autobiography of Vincent Van Gogh.* For a time in Jersey City he directed a little theater, and later he made his living by writing for the pulp magazines. In 1934 he married Jean Factor. His first novel, *Pageant of Youth* (1933), was written while he worked in the potato locker of the steamship *Pennsylvania,* and he protected his manuscript by sleeping upon it. His nonfictional biographies include *Sailor on Horseback* (1938), about Jack London; *Clarence Darrow for the Defense* (1941); and *Earl Warren* (1948). *They Also Ran* (1943) is the story of the presidential nominees who were defeated. He edited *We Speak for Ourselves* (1950), an anthology of passages from American autobiographies.

Mr. Stone has specialized in the writing of fictionalized biographies. In these he retains the factual accuracy of the biographer while lending romantic interest to his characters by dramatizing their thoughts and achievements in their conversation. His early apprenticeship to playwriting is revealed by the effective manner in which he marshals his characters and keeps his central personages to the fore.

Lust for Life (1934) traces in fictional form the life story of Vincent van Gogh, the Dutch painter, whose mad genius first came to be widely appreciated in America through this book. Van Gogh began as an apprentice to an art dealer, served as a religious worker among miners, fell in love with several women, struggled to perfect his technique as a painter, and then committed suicide at thirty-seven. *False Witness* (1940) is about the bitter discord created in 1903 in Mission Valley, California, a hitherto idyllic community established by John Annester, when Widow Smithers says that fifty dollars was stolen from a flour barrel. An enemy of Annester spreads untruths and stirs hatred.

Immortal Wife (1944) is a biographical novel about Jessie Benton, daughter of a famous senator from Missouri and wife of General John C. Frémont, the explorer and geographer of the Southwest. This indomitable and ambitious woman urged forward her husband in his campaign for the presidency and in his other activities. *Adversary in the House* (1947) is the life story of Eugene V. Debs, the labor leader and organizer in 1897 of the Socialist party. He is here pictured as having within his own house an opponent in his wife, who continually tries by artifices and pressures to compel her husband to give up his agitation for socialism and settle down to a conventional life. The novel ends with the scene of Debs' departure in 1921 from the Federal Penitentiary in Atlanta where his love for his fellow man so captivates the other prisoners that they crowd the windows and cheer him through the bars.

The Passionate Journey (1949) is based on the tortured career of the Kansas painter John Noble who, having become discouraged with native indifference to American artists, goes to live in Paris during the fifty years preceding World War I and searches on his "passionate journey" for perfection as an artist and for spiritual meaning and religion.

PHIL (PHILIP DUFFIELD) STONG

was born on January 27, 1899, in Keosauqua, Iowa, where he grew up and attended local schools. He went to Drake University in Des Moines where he received his bachelor's degree in 1919; the same institution honored him with the degree of Doctor of Laws in 1947. He also studied at Columbia University and at the University of Kansas. From 1919 to 1923 he was a director of athletics and a teacher in high schools in Minnesota and Kansas. He returned to Des Moines, where he was editorial writer for the *Register* and taught the first journalism courses at Drake University. He moved in 1925 to New York as a wire editor for the Associated Press, and a year later he was copy editor for the North American Newspaper Alliance. In 1928 he transferred to the staff of *Liberty* magazine, and in 1929 he went with *Editor and Publisher,* the trade magazine of the newspaper industry. From 1929 to 1931, when the newspaper was sold, he directed the editorial feature section of the New York *World,* and then he did advertising writing until in 1932 the success of *State Fair,* his first novel, took him to Hollywood to work with Will Rogers, the famous cowboy wit and movie star, who played the lead in the first motion-picture version of the novel. At this time he purchased "with gold from California" the farm homestead in Keosauqua, Iowa, which his Grandfather Duffield, who had also been west, had originally purchased "with gold from California." Says Mr. Stong with an ironic twinkle, "But we didn't get the gold the same way; he worked for his." Mr. Stong lives in Washington, Connecticut, but frequently visits his Iowa farm.

In addition to his novels and a number of juvenile stories like *Farm Boy* (1934), he has written *Horses and Americans* (1939), a history of horses in America, with particular regard to their influence on American sociology and development; *Hawkeye* (1940), a biography of Iowa; *If School Keeps* (1940), a light autobiographical sketch containing his opinions on education; and *Marta of Muscovy* (1945), a biography of the wife of Peter the Great.

Mr. Stong employs the background of his Iowa home in his stories. "When I was in college," he has said, "there was a plague of midwest 'regional' writing in which the principal characters were all committing suicide with sheep-dip or being eaten by the hogs. This did not seem reasonable to me in view of my early farm experiences when we ate the hogs and virtually everything else, but not sheep-dip. It was a fairly full life, and I had vague ideas of correcting the 'regional' impression. Since then I have had a consciousness of the horrors that always stalk the world and of the duty of a man to enjoy as much pleasantry and pleasure as he can in his brief time. *Candide* and *The Mysterious Stranger* suit me as indicative texts."

State Fair (1932) is about the Frake family in Iowa and their year-long planning to attend the State Fair. Father has a boar, Blue Boy, which wins the prize, and Mother matches his success with a ribbon for pickles. Young Wayne takes all the prizes at a hoop-la stand. Wayne and Margy fall in love but decide to reject their new sweethearts; they have grown up during the week. *Stranger's Return* (1933) brings Louise Storr home to her grandfather's farm after an unhappy year of marriage to a New York newspaperman. She and Grandpa Storr achieve an understanding, but a cold, calculating cousin plans to win the farm away from Louise, who will inherit it. *Village Tale* (1934) pictures the trouble underneath the surface of the placid town of Brunswick, Iowa, whose one big event is the arrival of the 6:45 a.m. train from Keokuk. A postman attempts to shoot the town's rich man at the instigation of the town bully.

Week-End (1935) describes a house party of sophisticated New Yorkers in Connecticut and delves beneath the surface to expose the sham of these people who amuse themselves by hard drinking and triviality. *The Farmer in the Dell* (1935) is about Pa Boyer, an Iowa farmer, and his experiences as an actor in Hollywood. *Career* (1936) is a romantic novel set against the background of a bank failure and a storekeeper's efforts to conserve the life savings of his neighbors. *The Rebellion of Lennie Barlow* (1937) pictures a young southerner whose family has moved to Iowa and who will not be defeated by a Yankee.

Buckskin Breeches (1937), based in part on Mr. Stong's family history, tells about Jesse Ellison's decision to move from Ohio to the West in 1837 and his experiences during a year in Iowa. *The Long Lane* (1939) portrays the loneliness and disillusionment of a twelve-year-old boy on an Iowa farm when his mother runs away with his uncle. An actress comes into his father's life and takes charge of both. *Ivanhoe Keeler* (1939) is about a wandering violinist and two friends who are on a Mississippi River boat. *The Princess* (1941) portrays the drawbacks suffered by a motherless Iowa girl reared by an older brother and the hired man.

The Iron Mountain (1942) is about a town in the Mesabi iron region of Minnesota and portrays the effect of a Finnish woman on a community of Scandinavian and Balkan immigrants. Especially notable is the use of dialect. *One Destiny* (1942) describes the shock upon the Murdoch family in Iowa when news comes of Japan's attack on Pearl Harbor on December 7, 1941. Johnny enlists at once and Craig, who stays home, captures three escaped Nazi prisoners. *Jessamy John* (1947) is an historical novel about John Law, the Scottish financier, who was the world's first scientific gambler. In 1715 he organized the French banking system that flourished until the Mississippi Bubble scandal in 1720. He retired to Venice, Italy.

THELMA STRABEL

was born in Crown Point, Indiana. After graduating from the University of Illinois, she was successively a feature writer with Associated Editors in Chicago and New York City, a fashion writer for the Paris *Herald,* and an advertising writer for a New York City department store. She now resides in Washington, D.C.

Smart Woman (1933), her first novel, concerns a girl in New York City, her career as a fashion writer, and the failure of her effort to break away from the pattern she had made for herself. *Streamline Marriage* (1937) portrays the marriage and divorce of two smart young New Yorkers. Their second marriages are streamlined, but they too prove unsuccessful. *Reap the Wild Wind* (1941) is set in Key West, Florida, in 1923. It is a story of the colorful wreckers of the time. *Storm to the South* (1944) is an historical novel set in early nineteenth-century California and Peru in the time of Simón Bolívar. It is the story of the conflict of two cousins, one the daughter of a California trader and the other an ardent Peruvian revolutionist.

JAMES STREET

Mrs. Bernadette W. Hoyle

was born on October 15, 1903, in Lumberton, Mississippi, the southern frontier of its day—raw, beautiful, brutal. His father was John Street, a Roman Catholic lawyer in an ultra-Protestant community. His mother was William Thompson Scott Street, a name that always delighted her son because it gave him a chance utterly to confuse inquisitive people. As a boy James Street was in constant rebellion against the *status quo,* and he still is. After finishing three years of high school and three months of military school, he threw his textbooks away and became a newspaper reporter at seventeen. Although reared a Roman Catholic, at nineteen he became a Baptist preacher; he left the ministry after two years to associate himself with the freethinkers.

A newspaperman for fifteen years, constantly on the move, he was a restless reporter whose rebellious behavior usually led to disagreement with his employers. He worked for newspapers and the Associated Press all over the South and eventually in New York City, where he arrived with ten cents and a borrowed overcoat. Six weeks later he was one of William Randolph Hearst's "fair-haired boys." He covered all the big stories of his day, became a ship-news columnist, and wrote his first book while reporting the trial of Gerhard Hauptmann who was convicted of kidnapping the son of Colonel Charles A. Lindbergh. This book, *Look Away! A Dixie Notebook* (1936), contains sketches of life in Mississippi.

Mr. Street went to work for the New York *World Telegram* and, six months later, wrote his first short story, "Nothing Sacred," because he needed rent money. He left the newspaper business then to begin writing short stories for popular magazines, and was immediately successful. Of his scores of short stories, the best known are "The Biscuit Eater," "Weep No More, My Lady," "The Golden Key," and "I Am Not a Stranger";

fourteen are collected in *Short Stories* (1945). Awed by his material success and still not quite believing it, the Mississippi iconoclast moved to Connecticut. He became involved in so many outside interests that his writing production lapsed, and again he found himself without funds. Consequently in 1939 he contracted to write a history of the New York Police Department, about which he knew nothing. He never wrote it. Instead, he wrote *Oh, Promised Land* (1940), the first of his Dabney books. In 1945 he moved to Chapel Hill so his sons, both army veterans, and his daughter could attend the University of North Carolina.

A prodigious worker once he is spurred to work, James Street has two prides: his family and his farm, an organic farm that he has "brought back" from uselessness and where he experiments "with the benefit of ignorance and no prejudices." The lowly seek him, or he seeks them. He is a little man with a wild shock of white hair and owlish eyes. Sentimental and gregarious, he is a lover of good tobacco, comrades, and conversation. He is an electric-train enthusiast and a green-thumb farmer.

He calls himself a professional writer; when he speaks of his work, he never calls it art. He writes only when he needs money; then he spends it and writes again. James Street is often naïve, sometimes an indignant rebel, hating power and greed. He is a humanist, he hopes, believing man is capable of ethical greatness; he is convinced that man's only problem is to justify his own existence and the vanity that led him to create his god in his own image.

The Dabney books comprise a saga of life in Mississippi from 1794 to the present day. Each volume presents major historical episodes in the country's growth and the part played by members of the family in the military forces. These and other historical novels combine accurate insight into local and national events with swift-moving adventures. The books about London Wingo deal with religious faith in an age of uncertainty.

Oh, Promised Land (1940), his first novel, is an historical narrative of the old Southwest, from Georgia to the Mississippi, during the years from 1794 to 1817. The story follows the fortunes of Sam Dabney and his sister Honoria from the time they stand at the grave of their parents, who were killed by Indians, until they separate. *In My Father's House* (1941) pictures the Abernathy family in the cotton country of Mississippi and tells how the son brings trouble and tragedy to his parents and sister. *Tap Roots* (1942) describes the Dabney family in the anti-slavery section of Mississippi from 1858 to 1865 and how they begin life anew after a Confederate regiment destroys their possessions. *By Valour and Arms* (1944) is an historical novel of the early years of the Civil War. The central episode concerns the building of the ironclad *Arkansas,* which destroyed part of Farragut's fleet in 1862 and delayed the capture of Vicksburg.

The Gauntlet (1945) gives the life story of a Baptist minister, London Wingo, who in a small Missouri town experiences doubts and difficulties; in the end he realizes that he has chosen the right vocation and enjoys a rebirth of faith. *Tomorrow We Reap* (with James Childers, 1949) concerns the Dabney family in the 1890's in the valley of Lebanon, Mississippi, when absentee northern capitalists, acting through the Peninsula Lumber Company of Chicago, move into the virgin pine lands of Mississippi and collide with Dabney pride and courage. *Mingo Dabney* (1950) portrays the adventures of a high-spirited young Mississippian who loves Rafaela Galban, who as "La Entorcha" symbolized the Cuban people's revolt against the tyranny of Spain. To claim her he goes to the embattled island in 1895 and fights in defense of freedom. *The High Calling* (1950), a sequel to *The Gauntlet,* concerns London Wingo, who has accepted the pastorate of a small Baptist church in North Carolina, and his daughter who falls in love with and marries a Catholic. Sectarian differences are reviewed interestingly.

JESSE STUART

was born on August 8, 1907, near Riverton, Kentucky, of pioneer English and Scotch stock in the mountain country of Kentucky. He attended the country schools, but never finished more than two-thirds of a term during any year: he had to help plant and hoe and harvest the crop. As a compensation, he spent many days in the weed fields and briar thickets hunting rabbits, and nights in the woods hunting coons, foxes, and possums. At nine he began to hire out to well-to-do farmers for twenty-five cents a day. At eleven he quit school entirely to help the family, and until fifteen he cut corn in the Ohio River Valley during the season and cut timber and made crossties during the winter. At fifteen he spent sixty days in a country subscription school to improve his grammar, and then entered high school. A new world opened. "I cannot tell you the adjustments I had to make," he says; "I was like a mule in a new pasture." He finished in 1926 and then worked for eleven months in a steel mill as a blacksmith.

Admitted to Lincoln Memorial University at Harrogate, Tennessee, he earned his way, edited the school paper, and ran long-distance races on the track team. He finished in three years. He returned to his home country and taught school two years, the last as principal of Greenup County High School. Entering Vanderbilt University to do a year of graduate work on a budget of $130, he lived on eleven meals a week from September 22, 1931, to February 19, 1932. The dormitory burned, and all his possessions burned with it. He lost fifteen sonnets, some short stories, his thesis, and his dining-hall job. Thereafter until June 2, 1932, he lived on one meal a day. He finished his graduate work but he did not rewrite the thesis. He returned to schoolteaching. In 1934 the Jeanette Sewell Davis prize for poetry was awarded to him. On his return home from a trip to Europe in 1937, he started a small newspaper. In March, 1944, he enlisted as an apprentice seaman in the navy and rose to the rank of junior lieutenant. In 1946 he returned to Riverton, Kentucky.

His poems, which first attracted attention in 1932, have been published in *The Man with a Bull-Tongue Plow* (1934) and *Album of Destiny* (1944). His short stories are included in *Head o' W-Hollow* (1936), *Men of the Mountain* (1941), which received an award from the American Academy of Arts and Letters, and *Tales from the Plum Grove Hills* (1946). His autobiography is *Beyond Dark Hills* (1938). He held a Guggenheim fellowship in 1937, and won the Thomas Jefferson Southern award for *Taps for Private Tussie. The Thread that Runs So True* (1949) describes Mr. Stuart's experiences in secondary schools. *Clearing in the Sky* (1950) contains twenty-one stories about the backwoods country and the mountain people with their moments of joy and sorrow.

Trees of Heaven (1940), his first novel, contrasts two types of families in the Kentucky mountains. Anse Bushman owns his property and rents a portion on shares to Bolliver Tussie with the proviso that this shiftless squatter give up fishing and immoral conduct. The agreement leads to much difficulty between the two families. *Taps for Private Tussie* (1943) tells how the Tussie family squandered ten thousand dollars in government insurance money when Kim Tussie was killed overseas. Grandpa rents a pretentious house in town and forty-six relatives descend upon him. Soon he is evicted and all return to their former starvation existence. *Mongrel Mettle* (1944) is a dog's view of life in the Kentucky backwoods. He sets out to make a name for himself but returns to his first and only protector, a little girl. *Foretaste of Glory* (1946) reports the thoughts and actions of the people of a small Kentucky town who think the world is coming to an end in September, 1941. *Hie to the Hunters* (1950) is a story of a city boy who runs away to the Kentucky mountains and finds pleasure in fox hunting and tobacco growing.

RUTH SUCKOW

was born in Hawarden, Iowa, on August 6, 1892, the daughter of a Congregational minister. During her childhood and early youth she lived in places of various sizes, both small town and small city, in different parts of the state. Many of her vacations were spent on farms with relatives. She was educated at Grinnell College, the Curry School of Expression in Boston, and the University of Denver, where she taught for a year in the English department. While in Colorado she learned beekeeping, and for several years operated her own apiary in Iowa, raising and selling honey in the summer and writing in the winter. In 1929 she married Ferner Nuhn, author of *The Wind Blew from the East.* They have lived in New York City, Washington, D.C., Vermont, California, New Mexico, Iowa, and now in Arizona. *Iowa Interiors* (1926), *Children and Older People* (1931), and *Carry-Over* (1936) contain short stories.

"I feel strongly," Miss Suckow has said, "that, as a whole, the truth of a novel remains implicit within the pattern of human life shown. The quality of fiction lies in an evocation rather than in subject matter, viewpoint, theme, philosophy—although these must all be present in fiction's own terms." Her special concern is to see aspects of life and principles through the lives and life patterns of human beings. Place or setting is important as it affects and gives flavor to people's lives. She regards setting as secondary, however, and does not write merely to give a picture of the Middle West. It is not correct, therefore, to give a close-up over-"regional" interpretation of her writings. In her novels and short stories she makes use of the concrete instance, believing that the more truly seen, the wider the implications. She does not look first for an abstract theme which may be applied to human material or illustrated by it, but sees universality as growing out of concreteness. She sees material, theme, and method as all bound up together. Her stories concern the struggles of home-loving families, and she portrays simple, common lives with quiet accuracy of detail.

Country People (1924), her first novel, pictures three generations of a German-American family, the Kaetterhenrys, in a brief and concrete study. It follows the representative stages of this family life from early days to retirement. In style and method the book might be compared to a primitive painting or drawing of rural life. *The Odyssey of a Nice Girl* (1925) follows the career, both individual and representative, of Marjorie Schoessel, daughter of a business family in a small town, and herself a kind of cherished, small-town, American princess.

The Bonney Family (1928) recounts twenty years in the history of a minister's family and the rearing of four children. It is primarily a novel of character, and its theme and meaning lie in character and personal relationships. *Cora* (1929) tells the story of the Schwietert family and their slow change from Germans to Americans, first in an Iowa community and then in a midwestern city. The story focuses on Cora, the oldest daughter, who has strength and ambition, and on the losses and gains in her development into a successful business woman.

The Kramer Girls (1930) pictures three sisters. The two older sisters, held at home by custom and the needs of an invalid mother, center their efforts upon the youngest sister, Rose—particularly the oldest sister, Georgie, the most able of the three. The story lies in the nature and character of the three sisters, their situation, and the outcome of their efforts. *The Folks* (1934) presents the full-length portrait of the Ferguson family, prominent in the business, social, and church affairs of a midwestern town. It centers attention finally, however, upon the mother and father, Fred and Annie Ferguson, "the folks," and is essentially a story of parents and children, not only in an American town but the world over.

New Hope (1942) describes the two-year pastorate of a young "liberal" minister in the Puritan Church, which moved westward by way of New England, in a new town lying between East and West. The life of the young town, new and glowing with promise yet with older elements entering into its make-up and helping to determine its future, is seen through its effect upon two children: Clarence, son of a leading businessman and church member, and Delight, daughter of the minister. The time is the early 1900's. While told in concrete, realistic terms, the book is something of a parable and has the essential quality of being a study in joy.

RICHARD SULLIVAN

Priddy-Thompsett Studio

was born in Kenosha, Wisconsin, on November 29, 1908. He studied at the Art Institute of Chicago and at the University of Notre Dame; from the latter he graduated in 1930. He is married and has two daughters. Since 1936 he has taught literature and creative writing at Notre Dame. For English and American magazines he has written about fifty short stories; some of these are printed in *The Fresh and Open Sky* (1950). He has also composed a short play, "Our Lady's Tumbler."

"A novel rises out of a strong desire to pin down human experience in words," says Mr. Sullivan. "It is a desire to grab hold of reality and give it some close-up, firm, final shape." Mr. Sullivan is a Catholic. Asked to define a "Catholic novel," he replied: "Unfortunately, to many people the term suggests merely a pious tract in which many of the externals of Catholicism, such as rosaries, holy water, and novenas, are highly stressed, but in which the one thing necessary for a good novel—a feeling for reality—is completely ignored. Yet there is a sense in which the term may be used legitimately. Every work of fiction contains something of the mind behind it. If a novel reveals a habit of mind, a way of looking at reality which harmonizes with Catholic doctrine, it may justly be called a 'Catholic novel.' Such a mind would perhaps see the world as 'both fair and perilous'; it would view life as a journey, with an end; it would see man as a unit of body and soul. Such a novel would not ignore one of the most striking human realities—sin; it would not dodge the treatment of shabby characters or shocking events. It would be concerned with making 'something like the truth.' And the writer of such a novel might be a Catholic, a Quaker, a Jew, what you like—anyone who sees reality in this way."

Summer after Summer (1942), his first novel, pictures the anxious months while Eddie and Anna Nails, low-income, white-collar people, await the birth of their second child. *The Dark Continent* (1943) recounts a single day in the life of Francis Rafferty, a young teacher in a girls' college. He falls into an excavation, loses his memory, and achieves a wiser philosophy. *The World of Idella May* (1946) is the story of a contemporary American girl who—as a result of the glamorizing influences of radio, movies, and magazines—is never able to see herself as anything but a romantic heroine. *First Citizen* (1948) is a rendering, with stark, tragic overtones, of the career of an ambitious small-town businessman who wants to be a leader. He lies to an insurance company and collects a large sum of money to get a start, but just as he is about to become mayor, his wife incriminates him and his daughter turns to drink.

CID RICKETTS SUMNER

was born on September 27, 1890, in Brookhaven, Mississippi, the daughter of a college professor. She was tutored at home because her parents thought schools wasted time. She graduated in 1909 from Millsaps College in Jackson, Mississippi, and in 1910 received a master's degree from Columbia University, where she did further graduate work during 1912–13. She also completed the first year's program of the medical school of Cornell University. For a time she taught French and was dean of women in a Mississippi college. She spent a year in Brussels, Belgium, where one of her four children was born. During World War II she worked in a munitions plant and wrote her second novel to keep from worrying about her sons and sons-in-law who were overseas.

Ann Singleton (1938), her first novel, tells of a capable young woman scientist who takes a position in a laboratory in a small southern town where her self-sufficiency incites gossip. *Quality* (1946) is the story of a young Negro nurse, Pinkey Johnson, who has been passing in the North as a white person. She becomes engaged to a young physician from Boston who does not go through with the marriage. Back home in Mississippi, where she takes care of her grandmother, she is at first bitter and resentful; then she reviews the situation and finds a wise solution to her problem. *Tammy out of Time* (1948) is about a girl brought up "out of time" in a two-room shanty boat on the Mississippi River. At the age of seventeen she speaks an English similar to that of Elizabethan England in its robust simplicity and forthrightness. She represents the fundamental goodness of life and the spirit of the pre-Civil War South. Young Pete Brent falls in love with her. This novel, which was a selection of the People's Book Club, has been made into a musical play by Mrs. Sumner and Al Moritz. *But the Morning Will Come* (1949) lays bare the lives of a group of people caught in a web of deceit woven long before their time. It is the story of a girl who discovers that her child by the son of an old southern family has Negro blood.

NEIL HARMON SWANSON

was born on June 30, 1896, in Minneapolis, Minnesota, and brought up on a farm near Lake Minnetonka. He is the only living descendant of two Swedish immigrant pioneer families of the mid-nineteenth century; his maternal grandfather was a 'Forty-niner in California. His father left Marstrand, Sweden, at the age of eleven to come to America. To both of these families, America was the promised land of freedom, personal liberty, and individual dignity; and their early struggles and their deep love and appreciation of that promised land impelled Neil Swanson to intensive research in American history and profoundly influenced his writing.

The last Indian battle in Minnesota was fought when he was a boy there; the frontier was still a vivid memory in the minds of living men; he went to school in a little town, Wayzata, named for the Dacotah chief Wah-zah-to-hah; the neighbor on the adjoining farm had come west in a covered wagon. Neil attended the University of Minnesota with the class of 1917, leaving at the beginning of his junior year to earn money to graduate, a project interrupted and ended by World War I. He had also managed to fail in sophomore English: he was behind schedule because of his work as a night editor of the university newspaper.

His first job was on the Minneapolis *Journal* in 1915; when he left that paper in 1930, he was its managing editor. In the meantime he had volunteered for the army in 1917, was commissioned first lieutenant of infantry, went to France and served at the front with the 49th Battalion, Chasseurs à Pied, and as company commander in the 350th Infantry, 88th Division (Blue Devils). In 1930 he became managing editor of the Pittsburgh *Press* and the next year moved on to Baltimore and the *Evening Sun;* he has been executive editor and vice president of the Sunpapers since 1941; and in 1947–48 was in charge of establishing their television station WMAR.

The First Rebel (1937) and *The Perilous Fight* (1945) are factual historical narratives done, as Mr. Swanson says, "with the novelist's tools." They represent, he says, a "laboratory experiment to determine whether American history can be made as vivid, personal, intimate, human, and immediate as any novel by using the same techniques of descriptive detail, incident, character, motivation, and psychological reaction that produce a good novel.

In 1939 he conceived and signed the initial contracts for a series of thirty or more historical novels, biographies, and narratives. In these he plans, as he has said, to "recreate the life of Maryland and Virginia, Delaware, Pennsylvania and 'the Ohio country' during the critical years of the making of America. Each of these novels and narratives will be a complete story in itself, but all of them deal with one central, gradually expanding group of characters. The 'grand design' will emerge at last as one continuous narrative of the advance of the American frontier from the Atlantic to the Mississippi."

The Judas Tree (1933), his first novel, is an historical romance of the siege of Fort Pitt by the Indians in 1763. *The Phantom Emperor* (1934) tells the romantic tragedy of James Dickson, a white man who in 1836 proclaimed himself Montezuma II, Emperor of North America, and mustered an "army" at Buffalo to conquer a kingdom for himself in the Southwest. His scheme collapsed in a blizzard on the army's march across northern Minnesota to Winnipeg. *The Flag Is Still There* (1933) is a novel, for younger readers, telling of the defense of Baltimore in 1814 and the writing of "The Star Spangled Banner."

The Silent Drum (1940) continues the story begun in *The Judas Tree* and deals with the first armed uprising against British regulars, in the Cumberland valley of Pennsylvania, ten years before Lexington and Concord. *The Forbidden Ground* (1938) dramatizes a little-known episode of the Revolution involving the British fur trade at Detroit and in northern Minnesota. *Unconquered* (1947) returns to the scenes of the Pontiac War in the Allegheny Valley and at the Forks of the Ohio and introduces the Holdens, a new family in Mr. Swanson's projected series of interlocking narratives.

HARRY SYLVESTER

Walter Beebe Wilder

was born on January 19, 1908, in Brooklyn, New York. His maternal grandfather, Jeremiah Crimmins Curtin, was the first foreign editor of the New York *World*, editor of *Redpath's* magazine, and a translator of French and Italian novels. Harry Sylvester completed high school in Brooklyn and then took the degree of Bachelor of Arts in journalism at the University of Notre Dame in 1930. A year later he returned for graduate study in English; at the same time he was midwest correspondent for the New York *Evening Post.* He also served as a reporter for the New York *Herald Tribune* and the Brooklyn *Daily Eagle*. As an undergraduate he wrote short stories for literary and popular magazines. In 1935 he began to devote full time to the writing of fiction. In 1936 he married Rita Ryall Davis; they have four children.

Visits to Mexico are reflected in many of his short stories; seven of the fourteen in *All Your Idols* (1948) have Mexican backgrounds. He also wrote much correspondence from Mexico for magazines. In 1938 he went into Las Palomas, the stronghold of the rebel general, Saturnio Cedillo, and received an interview. Mr. Sylvester's report described the nature of the rebels' dissatisfaction. Cedillo died shortly afterward at the hands of Federal troops.

Mr. Sylvester's first three novels present a comprehensive treatment of the Roman Catholic Church in the United States. Strong elements of anti-clericalism mark his serious work, but his central and pervading theme has been that of growth, spiritual and intellectual, and the various ways and the events by which he feels it is sometimes achieved.

Dearly Beloved (1942), his first novel, is an ironic and realistic portrayal of the psychological and social problems of a young man, John Cosgrove, who allies himself with a Jesuit priest in an effort to improve the conditions of poor fishermen in St. Mary's County, Maryland. Racial intolerance and discrimination impede progress. *Dayspring* (1945) concerns Spencer Bain, an anthropologist, who visits New Mexico to study the Penitentes, a group of Roman Catholics who practice flagellation. He participates in their religious services with strong intellectual reservations, but comes to feel a steadying influence upon his life as a result. Some critics consider the book the first serious novel concerning "grace" by an American.

Moon Gaffney (1947) traces the career of the son of a Tammany Hall politician in New York City. The young man, who has been reared strictly as a Roman Catholic, is ambitious to become mayor. Yet his friends with social insight and liberal ideas lead him to take a vigorous stand for progress. *A Golden Girl* (1950) is a sharp departure from the earlier novels and reflects Mr. Sylvester's two visits and a period of residence in Peru. It concerns Therese Morley, an American girl of exceptional vitality and intuitive honesty, who has misused her talents. Four men, three Americans and a Spaniard, find in her the touchstone of their growth, and, although two of them die because of her, all find maturity and enlightenment from having known her.

ROBERT SYLVESTER

was born on February 7, 1907, in Newark, New Jersey. He grew up in Stonington and West Haven, Connecticut. After finishing high school, he spent two terms at Yale and Columbia. Then he worked as a reporter, rewrite man, feature writer for the New Haven, Connecticut, *Evening Register,* and in New York for *The Evening Post, The Evening World, The American,* and *The Daily News.* For two decades he wrote a column about the theater.

Mr. Sylvester believes that themes for novels run in cycles and that publishers are largely to blame for the absence of a system by which new and fresh writers are developed. He thinks that, economically, the writing of novels is a fool's business since, unless the movies or a magazine purchase it, even a good novel is almost certain to fail in giving a proper financial return for the amount of work involved. This is outweighed, however, by the fact that a finished novel is certainly the most satisfactory form of creative writing.

In *Dream Street* (1946), his first novel, the show business and Broadway supply background for the story of Jake Harkness, a theatrical agent, and Penny Farmer, a nightclub singer. Under his direction she becomes very successful and has an opportunity to go to Hollywood if she leaves Jake behind, but she refuses to go back on her partner. *Rough Sketch* (1948) portrays in the reminiscences of four people the character and inside life of Tony Ferrer, a wealthy and powerful New York theatrical magnate. A reporter gathers data for a magazine article and in doing so hears the truth. China Valdes, his Cuban sweetheart, tells of his youthful days and his part in causing a revolution. Three others reveal how Tony's drive for money and position causes the loss of friendship. In *The Second Oldest Profession* (1950) Ned Gorse begins his career as a crusading reporter and, as his fame and talents grow, confuses the freedom of the press with its power until he wrecks not only the lives of two innocent people, but also his own. Gorse does, however, manage to atone partly for his past with one final "last-edition" job of "killing" a scandal story with which he planned to ruin an old friend. Ned comes to understand his weakness.

TABER *to* TURNBULL

GLADYS TABER

was born on April 12, 1899, in Colorado Springs, Colorado, the daughter of Rufus M. Bagg. However, as both of her parents were New Englanders, she early developed a love for Massachusetts and graduated from Wellesley College in 1920. She received a master's degree from Lawrence College at Appleton, Wisconsin, in 1921. From 1921 to 1926 she taught English at Randolph-Macon College. She married Frank A. Taber, Jr., in 1922. In addition to taking care of her household duties at "Stillmeadow," her home near Southbury, Connecticut, Mrs. Taber commutes to New York City to teach short-story writing at Columbia University and to engage in her activities at *The Ladies' Home Journal* office, where she has been a regular staff editor since May, 1946. Her monthly column, "Diary of Domesticity," has been running in the *Journal* since 1937. This is an informal essay on country living, dogs, cats, children, gardens, books and music, cooking and people. Her favorite place is the home, and from there has come the rich store of experience so helpful to millions of American women. A pleasing humor graces her commentaries.

Her non-fiction books include *Especially Spaniels* (1945); *Flower Arranging for the American Home* (with Ruth Kistner, 1947); *The Book of Stillmeadow* (1947); *Stillmeadow Kitchen* (1947), a cookbook of traditional and special recipes; *Especially Father* (1949), a biography of American family life with the father as the central character; *Stillmeadow Seasons* (1950); and three juveniles.

Late Climbs the Sun (1934), her first novel, portrays the growth in character of Katherine Allen, a shy girl whose father abruptly ends her engagement to a young man during World War I. For a time she teaches in a Virginia college and out of boredom marries a Latin professor, only to learn that she can not stifle her personality. *Tomorrow May Be Fair* (1935) is about Oliver Heron, an unemployed professor of English, who takes a position as tutor in the home of a former sweetheart, Helen Carlyle, now married. She finds his poverty a barrier to their renewed love interest. *The Evergreen Tree* (1937) chronicles events in the lives of a Wisconsin family from pre-World War I until the depression brings home two married daughters, their children, and their bankrupt husbands.

This Is for Always (1938) is about Karl, a football hero from the wrong side of the tracks, who loves Ann, the daughter of a mill-owner. There are fights with crooked loggers before Karl wins Ann. *A Star to Steer By* (1938) is about a union organizer in a Wisconsin pulp mill and his love for the wife of the owner. *Nurse in Blue* (1943) concerns the love problems of a girl in the Brooklyn Navy Yard hospital. *Give Us This Day* (1944) tells how Livia Warren, a New England housewife, works out in a buoyant way the problems of her three adolescent children, the threat of sudden economic disaster, and the danger implicit in her husband's interest in a widow. *The Heart Has April Too* (1944) is about Julie York, whose sweetheart is unable to attend college with her because he must support his family. *Give Me the Stars* (1945) pictures against the background of women of all classes working in a war plant Leslie March's lesson of loyalty and love. *The Family on Maple Street* (1946) describes the changes in attitude of members of a family during World War II, especially as each is affected by food rationing and calls to the colors.

ROBERT TALLANT

was born on April 20, 1909, in New Orleans, Louisiana, where he attended the public schools and continues to make his home. All his books have dealt with life there. He thinks there has been too much unreal pseudo-romantic writing about the city, and he is weary of the "moonlight and magnolias" school of southern literature. He feels that New Orleans and its people are sufficiently colorful and interesting as they are, and he tries to depict them that way. Although he has written non-fiction, Mr. Tallant feels he is essentially a novelist and that his principal interest is in fiction. He collaborated with Lyle Saxon and Edward Dreyer in the final writing and editing of *Gumbo Ya-Ya, A Collection of Louisiana Folklore* (1945), and he wrote *Voodoo in New Orleans* (1946), *Mardi Gras* (1948), and *The Romantic New Orleanians* (1950).

• His first novel, *Mrs. Candy and Saturday Night* (1947), tells of the events of a night in Mrs. Candy's rooming house in a poor quarter of New Orleans: the ghost of her husband appears and suggests a party. *Angel in the Wardrobe* (1948) pictures a once-wealthy, aristocratic New Orleans lady in her struggle to keep her children and grandchildren bound to the old rules of New Orleans society. *Mr. Preen's Salon* (1949) is another comedy of manners in which a southern gentleman of plantation stock, but residing in the New Orleans French Quarter, strives to avoid marriage to a lonely divorcée and an eccentric lady novelist, while surrounded and harassed by a group of peculiar acquaintances whose problems become his own, much against his will. *A State in Mimosa* (1950) with satirical humor pictures events in the complacent southern town of Mimosa, where foreigners are disliked, when two Polish refugees are sponsored by the unconventional John Caliph.

ROSEMARY TAYLOR

was born in Phoenix, Arizona, on May 8, 1899, the daughter of Mose Drachman. She attended the Tucson, Arizona, public schools and the University of Arizona, and graduated with Phi Beta Kappa and *cum laude* honors from Stanford University in 1922. Her career has been divided between being a free-lance writer and a housewife, with a few years spent in travel and secretarial work. She counts as extremely valuable the time she spent as secretary to Miss Edith R. Mirrielees, who teaches creative writing at Stanford. Mrs. Taylor makes her home in Tucson with her husband, John Winchcombe-Taylor.

At one time she thought her forte was the romantic and exotic love story, but she never sold a single one of the hundreds she wrote. Her right vein did not appear until she turned to her own background and in *Chicken Every Sunday* (1943) told of the harum-scarum doings of an Arizona family in the early nineteen hundreds. A sequel, *Ridin' the Rainbow* (1944), is about her father and his attempts to get on "Easy

Street." *Bar Nothing Ranch* (1947) describes the dude doings of the famous 76 Cattle and Dude Ranch, near Willcox, Arizona. In these non-fiction books Mrs. Taylor says she is an exponent of "keyhole literature." She finds it easy to "tell all" about herself and her relatives and friends, and thinks her success is due to the fact that at heart most people are inquisitive and enjoy knowing intimate and embarrassing details.

Mrs. Taylor now feels she prefers writing fiction to non-fiction. In fiction she is not confined to truth, and relatives are not irritated because she has made them less than perfect. If she has any basic philosophy, it is summed up in five words: Good food and some fun. Since well-fed and amused people certainly do not start wars, she wishes she could figure out some way to give more people more meals and more laughs. She likes a sharp focus on small doings and enjoys relating amusing and revealing anecdotes.

Come Clean, My Love (1949) is her first novel although it was begun as a factual story of her brother and his struggles with a decrepit laundry he had inherited. However, the brother decided he did not want to be written up, and so Mrs. Taylor made the book into a light novel about a young lad and his trials and tribulations in a similar situation. A love interest is included, and the hero does not know until the end of the book which girl to choose. The theme is that there should be more fun in work.

ROSS McLAURY TAYLOR

was born on December 29, 1909, at Snyder, Oklahoma. He is a descendant of John Taylor of Caroline, Virginia, and the blood of the Cherokee Indians is also in his veins. Although he was born in Oklahoma, his family on both sides are Texan. After graduating from the University of Oklahoma in 1930, he spent a year at Harvard University studying creative writing. In 1938 he earned his doctorate in creative writing at the State University of Iowa. He has taught English and dramatics at Centre College in Kentucky, George Washington University, the University of Wichita, and other universities. During World War II, from 1943 to 1946, he was a major in army military intelligence on staff duty in Washington, D.C., and for nearly two years in China and Southeast Asia. With Douglas Bement he wrote *The Fabric of Fiction* (1943), a study of the basic elements of creative prose composition. He is now professor of English and chairman of the department of American Civilization at the University of Wichita.

Long a student of southwestern and western history, Mr. Taylor has applied his interest in the art of literary composition to the fashioning of historical fiction around these areas, firm in the belief "that it is possible to make history entertaining and palpable for the reader without making it pedestrian in execution." Since 1946 his interest has shifted from purely historical fiction toward fiction generally, but on subject matter laid in the Southwest.

Brazos (1938), his first novel, is an historical tale of the Southwest in the 1870's and 1880's. Brazos Bolton leaves his ranch home at the age of sixteen on a picaresque journey to see the world and has many adventures while driving cattle to Kansas. Imprisoned for four years in Indian Territory, he starts life over again as a boss of a railroad construction gang on his return to frontier Texas. *The Saddle and the Plow* (1942) continues the story of Brazos Bolton and tells of his marriage to Mary Sullivan. At first they have a difficult time to make a success of their Texas ranch, but soon their breed of horses becomes the most sought after at the Fort Worth Horse Fair, and their reputation spreads throughout Texas along the Red River and into Indian Territory.

VAL TEAL

was born in Bottineau, North Dakota, on St. Valentine's Day, from which she derives her name. The family soon moved to Bagley, Minnesota, then to Hettinger, North Dakota, and later to Renville, Minnesota, where she went to high school. She attended the University of Minnesota, majoring in writing, but she left before graduation to marry Clarence W. Teal, an electrical engineer.

Her father was born in Sweden and her mother's parents were born in the same country. She lived among Scandinavians in little towns where her father was in the flour-milling business. Life was slow and wholesome and good, and family life was a taken-for-granted, happy thing. To girls of her time and station in life, marriage and children seemed a fine and worthy career.

Second on her list of desirable things came writing. She made up stories even before she could write; these she sang and they were all very sad. When she had children, she began making books for them—writing them, illustrating them, and binding them herself—just for the fun of it, so that the children could themselves be in books and could have stories about themselves. Her husband sent one of these to a publisher, who issued it. She then started writing for children's magazines, and finally worked into the adult field. Her play, *With Sirens Blowing,* was produced by the Omaha Community Playhouse in January, 1949. Mrs. Teal also paints portraits and makes braided rugs. Mr. Teal is inventory and costs engineer for the Northwestern Bell Telephone Company. They have four living children: John, who is on a National Scholarship at Harvard; Peter, in high school; Thomas (always called "Topper"), in grade school; and a daughter, Alison, not yet in school. With her husband, who is an amateur photographer, and her boys, one of whom is an ardent nature student, another a collector of rock specimens, and a third a budding actor, she leads a busy and often exciting life. Their lives are full of hobbies: Little Theater, museums, botany, and gardening.

She writes about family life, ordinary, happy family life. She makes it sound fine and good and worth while and happy; many young people write to her to say that they had been waiting to start families until the day when they could afford it, but that now they realize that they already have everything necessary to offer children, and so do not intend to wait longer.

Her first book, *The Little Woman Wanted Noise* (1943), tells about a little woman who lives in a city where she hears all sorts of delightful noises, street cars clanging, whistles shrieking, machinery rumbling, children shouting. But when she moves to the country she has no rest or peace of mind because it is so quiet. "Get some animals with voices to them," a neighbor advises, and she does so. The noisier the farm becomes, the better she likes it; it is still too quiet, however, and she has no rest or peace of mind until at last she adds the noisiest thing of all to her ménage: two boys—then, at last, she has peace of mind but no rest.

Angel Child (1946) is about Peter and Patty, children and neighbors, who find a little angel in a tree in their garden and play with it through the day until they push it too high in a swing and it flies off to its home. Patty's mother has a baby that autumn, and the children recognize it as the angel child, even though it does not have wings. *It Was Not What I Expected* (1948) is Mrs. Teal's autobiographical account of her experiences as a wife and a mother and of the humorous incidents, unexpected crises, surprises, pleasures, and rewards which the rearing of children brings. It is a cheerful, happy account of days full of little moments that bring throbs to the heart.

DARWIN TEILHET

Chas. W. Miller

was born on May 20, 1904, at Wyanette, Illinois. On his mother's side he is Johnson and Courtelyou of pre-revolutionary stock; his father was half French and half English. Darwin Teilhet studied one year at Drake University in Des Moines, Iowa, but graduated from Stanford University in California. A year of post-graduate work at the Sorbonne in Paris was followed by a year at the University of Heidelberg in Germany. From 1929 to 1937 he was an executive of an advertising agency; from 1937 until 1942 he was a consultant in public-opinion and marketing research for Hawaiian and San Franciscan interests. In World War II he was an intelligence officer for the 8th Air-Support Command, with British training at Highgate, London, and afterwards he was assigned to the planning staff of the Office of Strategic Services. Since the war, Mrs. Teilhet and he have been free-lance writers.

He has lived or traveled in Hawaii, Japan, China, Singapore, most of the European countries, Mexico, and Central America, and after his war-service years found that he and his wife wished nothing more than to live in Los Altos, California, and stay there until their three daughters had finished their schooling.

He has written two boys' books, *The Avion My Uncle Flew* (1946) and *Ab Carmody's Treasure* (1948), under the name of "Cyrus Fisher."

Bright Destination (1935), his first novel, is a satirical comedy of morals and describes the adventure of a young American with a circus while he is in France in pursuit of his wife. *Journey to the West* (1938) is a picaresque novel of the wanderings on the Pacific Coast of Rufus Cobbs, an advertising agent, who becomes a communist in the depths of the depression when out of a job, and ends as a staunch Republican, after having at last obtained a very remunerative position. *Trouble Is My Master* (1941) is an historical novel about the adventures of a young boy in the Philadelphia of 1804 and about Oliver Evans, one of America's greatest inventors. *Fear Makers* (1944) is about dishonest polls and wicked propaganda, wrapped up in the disguise of a thriller. *My True Love* (1945) is a satirical comedy about a returning war veteran. *Something Wonderful to Happen* (1947) is a farce of manners concerning the adventures of a young newspaper owner who falls into a political snare which threatens his integrity.

The Happy Island (1950) is a study of the downfall of a man. Park Mattison, who poses as an amateur artist, is playing for high stakes and cutting corners to win. With a bit of luck his Happy Island Morale Operation will provide a fortune. He becomes involved in a conspiracy to destroy several Hawaiian labor leaders and comes to his own ruin.

JOHN UPTON TERRELL

Gerry

was born on December 9, 1900, in Chicago, Illinois. Among his ancestors are Lord Tyrel, Irish leader; John Upton, famed British engineer who built the great forts of Sevastopol; and noted but largely unsung Scotch-Irish pioneers who crossed the Allegheny Mountains in pre-revolutionary days. He was educated in Chicago's public schools. Before and immediately after World War I he spent several years exploring and working in the western wilderness areas, and during the war he was attached to a Red Cross unit as an ambulance driver. In the early 1920's he entered magazine and newspaper work in Chicago. He was a Washington correspondent for several years, and served during World War II as a correspondent for *Newsweek* in Europe. *Jean Blue* (1929) is a collection of sketches and poems which had appeared first in Chicago newspapers.

"The study of the West has always fascinated me," he has said, "and I have spent a great deal of time seeing it first hand as well as finding it in various libraries throughout the country. My first stories were about the West and appeared in a number of literary magazines. Newspaper work was more suited to my restless nature than anything else, and periods of writing were interspersed with work as a reporter."

Adam Cargo (1934), his first novel, pictures the Southwest in the period immediately following the Civil War and concerns a renegade Confederate cavalryman who is a reckless outlaw. *The Little Dark Man* (1934) is about an outlaw in New Mexico. *Sunday Is the Day You Rest* (1939) characterizes a woman of easy virtue in the rough New Mexico environment of the cattle and Indian country. *Plume Rouge* (1942) is a long novel of mountain men and fur traders who were the first to explore and open the West following the Lewis and Clark expedition. It extols pioneer courage and fortitude.

ELSWYTH THANE

Blackstone Studios

was born in Burlington, Iowa. She has done newspaper work and has written for motion-picture studios. Her summers during the years 1928 through 1939 were spent in London where she did historical research in the British Museum. On September 22, 1927, she was married to William Beebe, the naturalist and writer.

Riders of the Wind (1926), her first novel, is the story of Alexandra Marley, a girl too much alive to be bent to the will of her elderly husband; she meets Blaise Dorin, an adventurer, with whom she escapes her humdrum life. *Echo Answers* (1927), set alternately in the London of society and of artists' lives, is the story of an English author who tries to recapture the ardor of his youthful love. *His Elizabeth* (1928) is a half-humorous little love story in which a poet searches for the little girl of his childhood. *Cloth of Gold* (1929) is a continuation of the adventure of Blaise and Alexandra, the characters of *Riders of the Wind.*

In *Bound to Happen* (1930) a young member of parliament and his wife, Charles and Cicely, fall violently in love with Nancy and Richard, respectively; they sacrifice Charles' political career for their mutual happiness. *The Tudor Wench* (1932) is a fictionized biography of Queen Elizabeth in the time of Shakespeare. The real hero of *Queen's Folly* (1937) is an old house in Worcestershire which had been presented to her loyal subject, Anthony Brand, by Queen Elizabeth. For four centuries the Brand family remains faithful to the home, which it maintains as a shrine for a picture of Elizabeth. In *Tryst* (1939) the heroine falls in love with the ghost of a British secret-service officer who died on the desert in India and has come back to haunt his home. *Remember Today* (1941) concerns a lonely boy from the East who is in love with a girl from a western ranch. It is told from the viewpoint of the girl's "guardian angel." *From This Day Forward* (1942) is the love story of a famous American ornithologist and a famous dancer of lowly birth.

In 1943 Elswyth Thane began publishing a series of historical novels picturing Williamsburg, Virginia, from Revolutionary days to the present time. *Dawn's Early Light* (1943) portrays events from 1774 to 1779 and tells of Julian Day's political conflict as a background for his wooing. *Yankee Stranger* (1944) deals with civilian life behind the lines during the Civil War in an account of Eden Day's love for a Yankee rebel, Cabot Murray. *Ever After* (1945) pictures the late

1890's, when Bracken Murray goes to Cuba during the Spanish-American War. *The Light Heart* (1947) concerns the period between the coronations of Edward VII in 1901 and World War I and narrates two intermarriages. The setting includes London and New York as well as Williamsburg. *Kissing Kin* (1948) brings the saga from 1914 down to 1934 with the Richmond twins, Calvert and Camilla, as the central characters. *Homing,* which is in preparation, will carry the narrative to 1940. *Melody* (1950) is a modern romance about a London portrait painter.

BENEDICT THIELEN

was born on April 29, 1902, in Newark, New Jersey. After taking his bachelor's degree in 1923 and his master's degree in 1924 at Princeton, he spent eight years in Europe, mostly in France. He has traveled in Europe, Central America, the West Indies, and the western United States. In addition to his novels he has written some seventy short stories, some of which have been included in three O. Henry collections, in four volumes of Frederick O'Brien's *Best Short Stories,* and in others. He lives in Key West, Florida, and in Chilmark on Martha's Vineyard, Massachusetts.

Deep Streets (1932), his first novel, unfolds the story of twelve people who are affected by Dr. Bodley's gift of five dollars to his servant, Katy Schultz. In *Women in the Sun* (1933) a New York lawyer, who had lost his loved one, hires out to an Italian with a vineyard and becomes enmeshed in the lives of his employer and his two daughters. The theme is the unwisdom of allowing events to destroy one's life through maintaining a detached view of life. *Stevie* (1941) contains eleven stories about Stevie and his pal Joe, the narrator, and their wives, a quartet of business people who at work or in play imbibe too much alcohol. *The Lost Men* (1946) pictures the veterans of World War I who were driven from the Anacostia flats near Washington, D.C., and went on construction work to Key West, Florida. A hurricane completes their destruction on Labor Day in 1935, and a rescue train does not arrive. The life story of each man appears from flashbacks suggested by their present difficulties. *Friday at Noon* (1947) characterizes each of five members of a mother-dominated family as their household goods are auctioned after her death. Ruth is a spinster; Judith is an artist; Irene is a war widow; Perry is their brother, and Isabel is his wife.

HELEN TODD

R. Standiger

was born on August 23, 1912, in St. Louis, Missouri. She was privately educated, and studied English literature, political science, and music at Washington University in St. Louis and at the New School for Social Research in New York City. For a time she worked on the administrative staff of the New School, but her central interest has always been in writing. Her books are particularly concerned with character; plot and theme are both governed by the nature of the character she has chosen. She has written a biography of Ulysses S. Grant, *A Man Named Grant,* which won the Houghton Mifflin Fellowship for non-fiction in 1939. Her interests are varied and elastic, centering chiefly in history, political theory, natural science, music, art, and fiction; she says that to her, reading is a business, a recreation, an art, and sometimes almost a vice. She lives at present in Falls Church, Virginia.

So Free We Seem (1936), her first novel, is a story of the Missouri frontier. It deals with two inseparable and incompatible desires which affect the marriage of Ann Wingate and Blaize Ormandy. He wishes to build a firm future in a new land, and she wants to see what is beyond the horizon. *The Roots of the Tree* (1944) is a study of Reinhard Eysen, a German novelist, who has always believed that he had no relationship to politics. He leaves Nazi Germany to teach in a midwestern American university, and there finds a new significance in the ideas of exile and of homeland. *High Places* (1947) is laid in the city hospital of an eastern mill town, and concerns Dr. Drew Fraser, the director of the hospital; Kay Eliot, the assistant pathologist; and others of the hospital staff. Its theme is the problem of compromise: how far it is necessary to achieve an essential purpose, and at what point compromise destroys the purpose itself.

BORIS TODRIN

Morris Gordon

was born on May 1, 1915, in Brooklyn, New York, and was raised in that borough which, he insists in his writings, is a province unto itself. He took his bachelor's degree with honors at Columbia College, where he was editor of *The Columbia Review* and won three major undergraduate awards for poetry: the Van Rensselaer, Boar's Head, and Philolexian prizes. He received his master's degree from Columbia in 1938 and has held various editorial positions since that time. During the summers of 1938, 1947, and 1949 he was a fellow at the MacDowell Colony in Peterborough, New Hampshire. For a number of years Mr. Todrin was a newspaperman in New York City and for five years was a reporter and department head of the newspaper *PM*. During the spring and summer of 1948 he was an accredited war correspondent in the new state of Israel. Since then he has been devoting his full time to writing.

He has been writing poetry since he was fifteen years of age. After the publication of his first book of poems, *First Furrow* (1932), issued when he was still a senior at Thomas Jefferson High School, he won the recognition and friendship of Edwin Arlington Robinson. His other volumes of poetry include *The Room by the River* (1936), *5 Days* (1936), *7 Men* (1938), and *At the Gates* (1944).

In response to a query, Mr. Todrin has this to say of his own work: "A novel, any work of art, must say something. I have tried always to wed craftsmanship, held in such slight regard these days, to the thing said. What I have been trying to say in all of my work is that there are certain basic tenets of human character and behavior which can make for better living among individuals and, consequently, among peoples. Understanding of one another, love, tenderness, and gentleness must be reinstated as precepts of our daily living. Perhaps the simplest thing would be to quote Stendhal's definition of good books: 'They widen the horizon, abolish barriers, and lead men to understand and love more and more.' "

Out of These Roots (1944), his first novel, gives a portrait of a young American of Russian-Jewish antecedents, together with his family background. Nicky grows up on the East Side of New York and becomes the friend of a famous poet. The theme is that "the strength of America resides in the absorption of different racial strains and the blending of nationalities into an independent American type." *Paradise Walk* (1946) is laid in Greenwich Village and the Williamsburg section of Brooklyn in 1937. The story concerns Nick Gordon, a poet and newspaperman, who marries Jerry. She leaves him for another man and then returns. Nick, who loves her, finds that he is equally attached to Martha. Nick's dilemma lies in being required to make a decision. *The Plundered*

Heart (1948) pictures Nick Gordon after Jerry dies in childbirth. His love for Ellen Swan, a co-worker on a tabloid newspaper, seems to him to be treachery to Jerry's memory; he struggles with his desire to be faithful and his need for happiness.

LIONEL TRILLING

Sylvia Salmi

was born on July 4, 1905, in New York City. He was educated in the New York public schools and at Columbia University, where he is now Professor of English. He is an advisory editor of *The Kenyon Review,* a member of the advisory board of *The Partisan Review,* one of the editors of the "American Men of Letters" series, and one of the three Senior Fellows of the Kenyon School of English at Kenyon College, Gambier, Ohio. His literary criticism has appeared in leading magazines, and he is the author of a volume of critical essays, *The Liberal Imagination* (1950). He has written several short stories and two critical biographies, *Matthew Arnold* (1939) and *E. M. Forster* (1943).

Mr. Trilling's critical work reflects a concern with what he calls the "moral imagination," the faculty that seeks to discern the real as against the fancied consequences of acts deriving from the commitment to morality and the real as against the fancied motives of moral action.

The Middle of the Journey (1949), his first novel, has been called a novel of detection in which the reader must discover for himself which of the author's characters are guilty, and why they are guilty, and of what they are guilty. Those who are guilty use moral and political virtue to mask their fierce, coercive wills. The time of the novel is in the late 1930's; the scene is chiefly rural Connecticut. John Laskell, recuperating from a nearly fatal illness that has subtly but decisively changed his view of many things, goes to stay in the country with his closest friends, Arthur and Nancy Croom. He involves himself in the dangerous situation of another friend, Gifford Maxim, a former communist who fears the vengeance of his party. This provides the political actuality of the chief characters' relations and establishes the theme, which is the relation of personal emotions to the ultimate issue of politics. The novel, though original in form, is in the classic tradition.

AUGUSTA TUCKER

R. A. Taylor Harrison

was born in 1904 in Saint Francisville, West Feliciana Parish, Louisiana. She is half New England Yankee, although all of her male forebears fought for the Confederacy. For five generations her paternal grandfathers have been ministers; while clearing out a rectory, she packed five barrels of manuscript written by her grandfather, seven barrels written by her father, and one barrel written by herself. The second of five children, she has lived in thirteen different towns and cities all the way from Seattle to Mobile, and from Baton Rouge to Baltimore. She went to work at the age of seventeen as a schoolteacher and has been a stenographer, an insurance salesman, a hospital historian, and a writer of feature articles for the Baltimore *Sunday Sun* and a book reviewer for the New York *Times Book Review.*

Her chief interest has always been medicine. She worked for six years on her first novel; during part of that time she lived at a medical boarding house, attended autopsies and operations with the students, rode ambulances on week ends and helped to deliver babies while doing so, stood all night in accident rooms, and haunted Johns Hopkins Hospital. She says that she likes the medical profession because it always tries to reply to the word, "Why?"

Miss Susie Slagle's (1939), her first novel, pictures The Johns Hopkins University Medical School in Baltimore, Maryland, and the people in the boarding house run by a prim spinister for students, beginning in September, 1912. Portrayed are the student life, the classroom activity, and the laboratory work as assigned by the famous physicians, Sir William Osler, William Henry Welch, Howard Atwood Kelly, and William Stewart Halsted. *The Man Miss Susie Loved* (1942) recounts Miss Susie Slagle's youth in 1866 and her ill-fated romance with Major Christopher Beverly of the Confederate Army. He died in London of an infection caused by unsterilized surgical instruments. She helped Mr. Johns Hopkins overcome local prejudice as he established the famous university and hospital.

AGNES SLIGH TURNBULL

Howard Somers

was born on October 14, 1888, in New Alexandria, Pennsylvania, of Scots-Irish ancestry, the daughter of Alexander H. Sligh. Her childhood and girlhood were passed in the horse-and-buggy-days, which meant sleigh rides in winter and drives all over the countryside to strawberry festivals in summer; they were "the slow days of those calm and sunny years." She attended the school on the village green, as it was then called. In due time she graduated from a teachers' college, attended the University of Chicago for a year, and then taught in various high schools until she married James Lyall Turnbull in 1918. They now live in Maplewood, New Jersey, and have one daughter.

Mrs. Turnbull's first short story appeared in *The American Magazine* in 1920, and for about fifteen years she wrote nothing but stories. When she finally began to write novels, she realized that in spite of the infinitely harder and more wearing work, their composition brought much greater satisfaction; however, she still is partial to the short story as a medium.

Her books include *Far Above Rubies* (1926), stories about women in the Bible; *The Wife of Pontius Pilate* (1928), about Procla, the reputed wife; *In the Garden* (1929), a story of the first Easter; *The Four Marys* (1932), about Mary of Nazareth, Mary of Magdala, Mary of Bethany, and Mary of Capernaum; *Old Home Town* (1933), nine short stories; *The Colt That Carried a King* (1933); *Elijah, the Tishbite* (1940); and *Dear Me* (1941).

The Rolling Years (1936), her first novel, describes three generations of a family on a farm in a Scots-Irish community in western Pennsylvania. The theme is the liberalization of religion from the hard Calvinism of the past. *Remember the End* (1938) is the success story of Alex MacTay, a young Scot, who migrated to America in the 1890's and rose from a farm hand to a magnate in the coal and steel industry just before World War I. The book contains a careful study of the soft coal industry.

The Day Must Dawn (1942) is about Scots-Irish pioneers, Sam Murray and his wife Martha, set in the 1770's in the western Pennsylvania wilderness in Hannastown, near Pittsburgh, against a background of the Revolutionary War and the dangers of marauding Indians. Hugh, their adopted son, falls in love with their daughter, Violet. This book is one of the few historical novels written from the woman's point of view. *The Bishop's Mantle* (1947) is a study of an honest, sincere, brilliant young Episcopal minister, Hilary Lawrens, and his struggle to reconcile his idealistic approach to his ministerial duties with the more materialistic philosophy of his parishioners.

VANCE *to* VIERTEL

ETHEL VANCE

Blackstone Studios

is the pseudonym of Mrs. Grace Zaring Stone, who was born on January 9, 1896, in New York City. She is a great-great-granddaughter of Robert Dale Owen, the founder of the New Harmony Community, and all her childhood summers were spent at the site of this early nineteenth-century social experiment. After studying under private tutors and in the Sacred Heart Convent in New York, she took lessons in music and dancing in Paris. A few days before the United States entered World War I, she married Ellis S. Stone, an officer in the United States navy. She traveled extensively over the world with her husband, who remained in the service through World War II.

The passionate interest in social problems which is traditional in her family and implicit in a Roman Catholic upbringing have been the sources of the two strongest themes in Mrs. Stone's work.

Letters to a Djinn (1922), her first book, is a series of letters written by an American girl, the social secretary of a lady in Australia who goes to Singapore. The girl has a romance with an explorer. *The Heaven and Earth of Doña Elena* (1929) studies the conflict within the soul of a mother superior in a convent in the days of the Conquistadores in the Caribbean. Late in life she entertains doubts, and thrice Captain Dyke appears to tempt her. *The Bitter Tea of General Yen* (1930) is the story of a provincial governor and a Massachusetts girl. She is knocked unconscious at a railroad station, and the general rescues her. In his home emerges the difference between the Chinese concept of excellence and the Christian idea of universal brotherhood. *The Almond Tree* (1931), set in Washington, D.C., portrays the characters of the three middle-aged Gentry sisters and the daughter of one of them. *The Cold Journey* (1934) deals with the Deerfield massacre in 1704, when the French and Indians swooped down upon the village.

Escape (1939) became a sensationally successful anti-Nazi story of the experiences of a German actress who leaves America to return to Germany. There she is imprisoned, condemned to death, and finally is helped to escape. It was on the publication of this book that the pen name "Ethel Vance" was adopted by Mrs. Stone. Her daughter, Eleanor, was at this time living in Budapest; the pseudonym was a device to obviate Nazi reprisals. Even after her daughter, the Baroness Perenyi, was safe, Mrs. Stone continued to use the pseudonym.

Reprisal (1942) describes the difficulties of Occupied France in World War II in the story of a kindly official living in Brittany who learns that twenty hostages are to be shot because a German sergeant has been killed. *Winter Meeting* (1946) is the love story of a naval officer and a young poetess. *The Secret Thread* (1948) tells of a college president, returned from a special mission in Berlin, who comes upon gangsters in a house in Manhattan and during thirty hours of captivity gains a clearer understanding of himself and of his duties to society.

FREDERIC FRANKLYN VAN DE WATER

was born on September 30, 1890, at Pompton, New Jersey. His mother, grandmother ("Marion Harland"), aunt, and uncle (Albert Payson Terhune) were authors, and he probably was influenced by their example in choosing to become a professional writer. His early education was acquired in the public schools of New Jersey and New York City. From 1910 to 1912 he was a student at New York University, and then he transferred to Columbia University, where he took his degree in 1914. He became a reporter on the New York *American* in 1914 and in the following year moved to the *Tribune* as reporter, special writer, night city editor, and book critic; he remained until 1924. From 1922 to 1928 he was a staff writer on *The Ladies' Home Journal*. From 1928 to 1932 he was book critic on the New York *Evening Post*. In 1934 he moved to a farm in West Dummerston, Vermont. He has written essays, biography, and history, as well as magazine stories and articles.

Mr. Van de Water has made the history of Vermont his special province. His historical novels and essays picture with sympathetic accuracy the people and the landscape of the Green Mountain State. He works into his novels personages from history and imaginary characters whose conversation is spiced with happy figures of speech and attractive gusts of humor. His tales have a rapid pace and strongly developed romantic plots.

After writing several stories about the New York state mounted police and a number of other adventure and mystery books, he wrote his first serious piece of fiction, *Thundershield* (1933), an historical novel of the Indian wars in the 1870's in the West; it ends with the annihilation of Custer and his men by the Sioux under Laughing Horse at Little Big Horn in 1876. *Mrs. Applegate's Affair* (1944), set in a Vermont village, concerns a woman who suggests to her army-officer husband that they reconsider their dull marriage during his absence in Washington, D.C. *Fool's Errand* (1945) deals with a middle-aged artist and his wife who buy a farm in Vermont and try unsuccessfully to blend into the community. *The Sooner to Sleep* (1946) details the love problems of several women in a Vermont village during World War II when the eligible men are away.

Reluctant Rebel (1948) is an historical romance about the land grants in Vermont that culminates in the capture of Fort Ticonderoga by Ethan Allen and the Green Mountain Boys on May 10, 1775. Adam Corlaer of Albany, a young man with Loyalist notions, joins the Vermonters and falls in love with Delight Royden, a rebel. *Catch a Falling Star* (1949) portrays the heroism of a loyal Vermonter who plays an important part in holding off the British by negotiation in the last years of the Revolutionary War.

DOROTHY GRAFFE VAN DOREN

was born in San Francisco, California, on May 2, 1896, but she has spent most of her life in and around New York City. After graduating from Barnard College in 1918, she joined the staff of *The Nation* as assistant editor and then served as associate editor from 1925 to 1935. From 1942 to 1946 she was a member of the radio staff of the Office of War Information (later incorporated into the Department of State) in charge of English-language broadcasts to Europe. In private life she is Mrs. Mark Van Doren, wife of the poet, critic, and professor of English at Columbia University. *The Country Wife* (1950) pictures rural pleasures.

Strangers (1926), her first novel, concerns two well-educated couples whose long-term friendship leads to a quadrangle of interwoven adultery when love crosses the lines. *Flowering Quince* (1927) is a psychological study of the relationship between a minister's wife and her daughter. The girl grows up detached from life, leaves home for a career, but is so incapable of human contacts that she returns to find comfort in the cold affection symbolized by the mother's quince bush. *Brother and Brother* (1928) is an account of two normal, decent boys in the Downing family who inherit the honest, hard-working traits of the father and the wisdom of the mother. Ellery's marriage to a girl living in their home is unhappy, but John, his younger brother, stands by him. *Those First Affections* (1938) sensitively portrays an American middle-class family in Brooklyn from 1897 to 1910 from the point of view of the small daughter of Dan Tower, a former newspaperman. *Dacey Hamilton* (1942) analyzes the character of Candace Fenn, who marries a famous artist. When he dies in Hawaii, she goes to New York with her five children to work on a newspaper and there marries a lame man whose bitterness she softens.

DALE VAN EVERY

was born in Levering, Michigan, on July 23, 1896. He attended school alternately in Michigan and California, but his education at Stanford University was interrupted by World War I, during which he served as ambulance driver with the French army and transport officer in the American. In 1920 he returned to Stanford to graduate with a major in history. After a brief bout with the publishing business, Mr. Van Every joined the staff of the United Press; his assignments at Harrisburg, New York City, and Washington, D.C., included covering the White House during the Coolidge era. During this period he wrote two non-fiction books, *Charles Lindbergh* (1927) and *The A. E. F. in Battle* (1928).

Visiting Hollywood in connection with a news project, he remained to work directly for pictures in various capacities, as a writer, scenario editor, and associate producer. During the next twelve years he was connected in one way or another with the production of "Trader Horn," "Spirit of Notre Dame," and some hundred-odd other motion pictures. In 1940 he retired from motion-picture-making to live on his ranch, which lies well north of Los Angeles, between the mountains and the sea. There Mr. Van Every raises cattle, rides, fishes, collects Americana, and writes.

His novels have dealt with the early American frontier and in particular with the effect of the wilderness upon the first men and women who came to claim it. Each book so far has used as its immediate historical background some phase of the extraordinary services to the westward advance contributed by George Rogers Clark and his younger brother, William. The novels contain vivid pictures of the dark mountains and sky-piercing peaks at the head of the Missouri River.

Westward the River (1945), his first novel, is the story of the involuntary association on an Ohio River flatboat of a young frontiersman and an aristocratic Englishwoman whose personal conflict becomes entangled with General Clark's amazing design to capture New Orleans from Spain in 1794. *The Shining Mountains* (1948) follows the career of a farm boy who, when disappointed in his desire to join the Lewis and Clark expedition, feels the compulsion for years thereafter to struggle westward on his own, though the effort costs him everything else he values. *Bridal Journey* (1950) deals with the fate of a woman made captive by the Indians on her wedding day and the way in which this incident affects Clark's last desperate attempt to take Detroit in 1781.

ROBERT VAN GELDER

was born on October 19, 1904, in Baltimore, Maryland. Reading was his greatest pleasure in early childhood, and the first dollar he ever spent went to a widow who was willing to dispose of a library of forty-five volumes that had been the property of her husband for that price. Finding most of these books too dull for his taste, he innocently decided to write books that would please him more, not realizing that it is practically impossible for a writer to enjoy a book that he himself has written. An illness when he was ten years old made it necessary for him to drop out of school for a year, and he spent that time in the futile business of trying to write for pleasure.

At sixteen he met an elderly man who was also ambitious to write and who lamented that he had spent forty years in business when he, had he not been influenced by his father, might have become first a newspaperman and then a professional writer. Accepting this tip at full value, Mr. van Gelder went the next day to the editor of the New Haven, Connecticut, *Times-Leader* and talked himself into a reporting job. He worked in New Haven as a reporter, and then as an advertising copywriter until, at twenty, he decided that he was ready to make his way in New York.

Partly supported by writing biographical sketches of prominent men for lodge magazines, he attended the Columbia School of Journalism from 1926 to 1928. For six months after graduation he wrote short stories without making a sale, and then he joined the staff of the New York *Times.* He remained on that newspaper as reporter, rewrite man, daily book critic, and, from 1943 to 1946, editor of the Sunday *Book Review.* While with the *Times* he wrote a number of books for boys; edited, with Dorothy van Gelder, his wife, an anthology, *American Legend* (1946); and produced *Writers and Writing* (1946), a volume of interviews with authors. While lunching with W. Somerset Maugham one day, and attempting to persuade Mr. Maugham to write some reviews for the *Times,* that wily expert on human relations, who did not want to write reviews, turned the subject to the idea of Mr. van Gelder's writing a novel. Mr. Maugham has never reviewed for the *Times,* but Mr. van Gelder did write the novel, *Important People,* resigning from the *Times* to do it.

Important People (1948) tells how young Dixon West returns from service in World War II with the hope of doing a real job in his grandfather's publishing firm. Dixon attends a cocktail party, runs down a Negro boy while driving in an alcoholic haze to Harlem, and becomes disillusioned at he realizes that people in his class are fascist at heart.

LILLA VAN SAHER

was born in Budapest, Hungary, the seventh child of a philosopher. She received her preliminary education in Switzerland and then studied philosophy at the Sorbonne and medicine at the École de Médecine, Paris. Seeking a more glamorous and feminine profession than that of medicine, Mrs. Van Saher became a model, and later embarked on a successful motion-picture career. As an actress, she played several starring roles, one of them for a French company as Jean Gabin's leading lady. It was only after she came to the United States that Lilla Van Saher chose writing as a profession.

Her first novel, *The Echo* (1947), a Basic Book Club selection, is a portrait of one woman's soul laid bare by the scalpel of psychoanalysis. The story concerns the love life of Louise de Faivres, a Parisian aristocrat.

Macamba (1949) draws its title from a word in the Papiemento language meaning white man and foreigner, and its setting is on the island of Curaçao in the Netherlands West Indies. The story is about Paul, the illegitimate son of a Jewish banker and a native woman of humble Indian birth. He rebels against the world of the *macambas* and engages in many strange adventures which teach him native secrets of black magic. When he meets Doerga den Uyl, a girl from Java, he understands the basis of his unrest, and through her love he learns the true meaning of his existence.

ALFRED E. VAN VOGT

was born on April 26, 1912, in Manitoba, Canada. He is the son of an attorney-at-law, and spent his youth in Saskatchewan and Manitoba. Later he moved to Toronto, and finally took up permanent residence in Los Angeles, California. He sold his first story at the age of twenty, and has made writing his profession ever since. In 1939 he married Edna Mayne Hull, who has written and published a number of science-fiction and fantasy stories under the name of E. Mayne Hull. *Out of the Unknown* (1948) is a collection of fantasy stories. *Away and Beyond* (1950) is a large collection of the best science-fiction stories of Mr. van Vogt.

He turned to science fiction as a medium of expression to free himself from the humdrum present, so that he could search for the answer to the riddle of himself without being hampered by a lack of basic information.

Slan (1946), Mr. van Vogt's first novel, takes place some hundreds of years in the future. The Slan, a human-like race who have mutated from present-day men, are forced to live an underground existence in order to survive. The story tells of the adventures of Jommy Cross, a Slan, who has knowledge of a decisive scientific principle. *The Weapon Makers* (1947) is the romance of an immortal man and Innelda, Empress of Isher, seven thousand years hence. *The Book of Ptath* (1947) is a story of an age so far in the future that gigantic geologic convulsions have created new continents.

The World of Ā (1948) looks forward to the operation of the new science of general semantics into the year 2560 A. D. To insure that all men shall be treated fairly, human beings have for generations depended on a gigantic electronic brain. To this machine every year come students to compete for ruling posts on Earth or Venus. Gilbert Gosseyn attends the games and discovers that he has a false memory of the past. *The Voyage of the Space Beagle* (1950) is the story of a strange journey through the reaches of outer space. *The House That Stood Still* (1950) concerns a group with a space ship and their amazing power.

GORE VIDAL

Otto Fenn

was born on October 3, 1925, at West Point, New York, into a family of southern descent. He grew up in Washington, where his grandfather was a senator, and where he attended elementary school. A month after his graduation from the Phillips Exeter Academy in New Hampshire, he enlisted in the army and served from 1943 to 1946. He was first mate of an army freight-supply ship in the Aleutians when at nineteen he wrote his first published novel. After leaving the service, he worked for a time as assistant editor in a publishing house. He has written articles and poetry for literary magazines. His work is somewhat in the manner and mood of that of Tennessee Williams, the dramatist, and Carson McCullers.

Williwaw (1946), his first novel, describes a storm, called a williwaw, in the Aleutian Islands and the wreck of a freight steamer. Each of the passengers is characterized in terms of his response to his predicament. *In a Yellow Wood* (1947) deals with a day and a night in the life of Robert Holton, a returned war veteran, who must decide between a conformity that may lead to stagnation and a freedom that portends instability. *The City and the Pillar* (1948) pictures sympathetically a young Virginia boy, Jim Willard, whose homosexuality places him in conflict with normal people. His search for understanding is climaxed by his murder of an early associate. *The Season of Comfort* (1949) portrays the difficulties of a young man breaking away from his selfishly possessive mother. *A Search for the King: A Twelfth-Century Legend* (1950) tells how Blondel, a faithful troubador of Richard the Lionhearted, travels across Europe, defying magic spells and real dangers, to rescue his beloved king from prison. *Dark Green, Bright Red* (1950) concerns an American army officer, Peter Nelson, who participates in a Central American revolution designed to make a deposed military dictator the president.

PETER VIERTEL

Caskey

was born on November 16, 1920, in Dresden, Germany. He was an Austrian by birth and became an American by naturalization. He completed high school, spent two years at Dartmouth College, and then graduated from the University of California at Los Angeles. In 1942 he enlisted in the United States Marine Corps and served until December, 1945. He saw action both in the Pacific theater and in Europe. *The Survivors* (1948) is a play written in collaboration with Irwin Shaw, and he has written a few motion pictures.

The Canyon (1940), his first novel, describes the adolescence of a California boy, George, who works for a realtor and learns something about race prejudice, the struggle for survival, and the greed for property. *Line of Departure* (1947) portrays the experiences of Pat Dimick, a young American lieutenant, during his years in army camp and overseas in World War II, with emphasis on the tensions created by his own and his wife's infidelity during his absence. At the end comes news of his return to the United States.

WAKEMAN *to* WYLIE

FREDERIC WAKEMAN

was born on December 26, 1909, in Scranton, Kansas, a small village near Topeka. His father was a newspaperman who went into politics and from there into government service with headquarters in Kansas City, Missouri. After finishing high school, Frederic Wakeman worked throughout the Southwest for the Santa Fé Railroad and in the Kansas City, Missouri, railway mail terminal. He attended Park College at Parkville, Missouri, and there edited the school paper and literary magazine. During summers he hoboed around, working on newspapers, hauling ice, and shocking wheat. When he graduated in 1933, his first position was as a writer for the Kansas City *Journal-Post.* On the side he did some free lancing for radio stations in that area. In 1934 he began to prepare advertising for department stores and then for an agency, meanwhile continuing his radio writing. That same year he married Margaret Keys, a fellow-student at Park College; they now have three children. New York beckoned in 1937, and for a period he worked in an advertising agency as copy chief. From there he went into radio production and became an account executive. Early in World War II he enlisted in the navy and trained for air combat intelligence. While on active duty in the Pacific and in naval hospitals, he picked up the material for his first novel. A medical discharge separated him from the navy, and he re-entered advertising as a writer of radio shows and other programs. In July, 1945, he resigned. Because of ill health he went to live in Cuernavaca, Mexico, where he remained until the following Spring. Since then he has lived in Bermuda and Cuba, but New York remains his home.

Politically, he believes in individualism and feels that mass movements of any kind hamper writers. He feels that he can write only about his contemporaries to help clarify problems of the immediate moment. He broods about what to write until it is clear and complete in his mind. Thereupon he writes quickly, first with pencil, then with typewriter.

Shore Leave (1944), his first novel, describes five war-weary, bewildered, and frustrated naval officers, veterans of the South Pacific, on leave in San Francisco. This story was dramatized as "Kiss Them for Me" (1945). *The Hucksters* (1946) is a satire on radio advertising, with particular attention to the head of a soap business. Against this background there is played a love story in which the hero grows progressively disillusioned with the advertising industry; at the same time he discovers the difference between true love and infatuation. *The Saxon Charm* (1947) concerns the mix-ups which result when a successful novelist and playwright, Eric Busch, begins doing business with Matt Saxon, a producer. *The Wastrel* (1949) portrays Duncan Bell's fight to save his own life and that of his young son when cast adrift at sea by an explosion on their boat. He relives the events which have made him a rich idler and wrecked his marriage.

MILDRED WALKER

was born on May 2, 1905, in Philadelphia. She spent her childhood in Scranton, Pennsylvania, and in Grafton, Vermont. After graduation from Wells College at Aurora, New York, in 1926, she taught briefly in Philadelphia and then went to work at Wanamaker's. There she progressed to copywriting in the advertising department; this career was interrupted permanently on October 25, 1927, by her marriage to Dr. Ferdinand Ripley Schemm. Her husband was a young surgeon in a mill town in upper Michigan, and her life for the next three years became that of wife to a country doctor. She received a master's degree in 1933 from the University of Michigan, where she studied while her husband was associated with its medical school. In 1934 she won an Avery Hopwood prize. Dr. and Mrs. Schemm now live in Great Falls, Montana; they have three children.

Fireweed (1934), her first novel, is laid in a small lumber town on the isolated peninsula of upper Michigan, where a new generation follows the pioneers, as the purplish pink fireweed follows the tall pine. Celie Henderson and Lin Linsen are of this generation. Celie wants to get away to the city but instead she marries Lin, bears him children, and measures her days by the mill whistle, missing it when the factory shuts down. Lin makes a living and traps and fishes and calls his soul his own. Their lives are not without meaning, although they never escape from the mill town. *Light from Arcturus* (1935) is the story of a woman's revolt against the crudeness and limitations of life in a frontier town. In the mind of Julia Hauser, the three World's Fairs of 1876, 1893, and 1933 symbolize the "larger life"; that they also symbolize escape she is unwilling to admit. To that "larger life" she sacrifices her husband's happiness for the sake of what she feels she is doing for her four children. By 1933, in her seventies, she is able to see the effect on her children's lives, her husband's, and her own, but she is still bemused with the glamour of the symbol. *Dr. Norton's Wife* (1938) studies the effect of the hopeless illness of his wife on a doctor in a medical school and on the group of young men working under him. It poses the question of how much love can endure and answers it in terms of the relationship of one man and one woman.

The Brewers' Big Horses (1940) is about a gently bred young girl in the 1880's who marries the son of a German brewer from the other side of town and undertakes, at his death, to run the brewery herself. It is the story of a woman fighting against tradition, prejudice, and social intolerance and depicts the effect of that struggle on her own nature. *Unless the Wind Turns* (1941) concerns a man who spent his boyhood in Montana and now returns for a pack trip in the mountains with his wife and a few friends from New York in the hope that the experience may draw his wife and himself closer together. A forest fire confronts them with tragedy and personal danger, and throws their relationships and characters into a new perspective. *Winter Wheat* (1944) depicts the growth of a girl's understanding of life. While still embittered by her first experience with love, Ellen Webb learns the circumstances of the marriage between her Russian mother and Vermont father and believes that only hatred can exist between her parents. A lonely winter spent as a teacher in Montana brings her, through the miracle of another spring, not only to an understanding of the true nature of that relationship but to a new faith in life.

The Quarry (1947) describes life in a Vermont village from 1857 to 1914 as a background for the story of Lyman Converse. He lives out his whole life in that narrow valley, loses the woman he loves, marries his dead brother's sweetheart, runs the soapstone quarry, and has for a friend a Negro slave. In this friend Lyman finds the understanding and strength that help him maintain his own spiritual integrity. *Medical Meeting* (1949) portrays the crisis in the lives of a man and his wife when the announcement of the discovery to which they have devoted twelve years is anticipated by others. Under the impact of this blow they are forced to analyze themselves and their motives and decide what they desire most in life. In the end they ally themselves with other research scientists. The action takes place, for the most part, in three days in the impersonal atmosphere of a medical convention.

LESLIE WALLER

Louise Barker

was born on April 1, 1923, in Chicago, Illinois. He attended the University of Chicago before World War II while working as a police reporter and rewrite man for the Chicago City News Bureau. During the war he served as a public-relations specialist with the army air forces, writing newspaper articles, radio scripts, and speeches and contributing short stories to *Yank* and *Our Army*. Returning to the University of Chicago after the war, he continued his studies for more than a year before moving to New York, where he is currently working as a free-lance writer while taking courses at Columbia University. He is on the book-reviewing staff of the Chicago *Sun-Times*. He is married to the former Louise Hetzel, also of Chicago.

The central theme of Mr. Waller's novels is the interaction of principle and practice in man's existence. Even the man to whom principles are consciously, deliberately alien must act from an inner philosophy created out of the world in which he lives. Although mankind has evolved a fantastic variety of philosophies as a guide, Mr. Waller considers them extensions or perversions of two basic principles: progress and the denial of progress.

Mr. Waller has become increasingly concerned in his writing with those characters to whom the fundamental problems of existence are paramount. Such questions as fate, the impingement of the supernatural on man, the mystical undercurrents of personality, and the sterility of neurotic introspection have become for him subsidiary to and apart from the material problems of real life. In his view, food, peace, achievement, security, love, and happiness are the problems basic to man's existence; the actions of men revolve around these questions. To be useful, fiction must serve that widest of audiences, the masses of people, by helping them to push forward into the greatness of the future as seen in historical perspective.

Three Day Pass (1945), his first novel, written while in the service, concerns a young American soldier from a North Carolina camp who spends three days in New York with a Canadian WAC. They wander the streets and bars of the city during the hectic summer of 1944 trying to find some certainty in their confused lives. But to the girl, confusion is the final summation of existence, while to the soldier there must be something worth living and fighting for. Reacting to her confusion, the soldier eventually decides that the anti-fascist war is, after all, primary, and he returns to camp and goes overseas, understanding the task he must perform.

Show Me the Way (1947) concerns Wally Blanchard, a combat veteran returned from active service to a midwestern army camp. Fundamentally a man of good will without any fixed ideology, Blanchard meets anti-Semitic discrimination overseas and intolerance in the small American town when a Negro soldier he knows slightly is the focal point of violence. Out of such experiences and the things he has learned from army companions and a local girl, Blanchard forges a personal philosophy for the first time in his life. He decides that there is no longer room in society for the man without convictions; one must choose sides or be cut down by cross fire. Blanchard chooses the side of the people and leaves the army with hope and determination for the struggle ahead.

DOROTHY WALWORTH

Dorothy Wilding

was born on March 15, 1900, in Cornwall-on-the Hudson, New York, the daughter of a Methodist minister. Her early religious training instilled in her a lifelong faith that permeates everything she writes. After graduating from Vassar College in 1920, she married Allan Carman; they had one child. In 1931 she married Merle Crowell, a senior editor of *The Reader's Digest,* and they live in Chappaqua, New York.

Feast of Reason (1941), her first novel, has its setting in a small, exclusive women's college in Connecticut and deals with Susan Laird, who as dean attempts to correct the errors of its "progressive" curriculum. *Nicodemus* (1946) pictures four people, whose lives never cross, in search of proof of the existence of God and the proof of His work on earth. The Reverend Job Tatum does not believe a word of his Easter sermon, but achieves an answer by Christmas. The others in this fashionable New York Church also find the direction they need.

MARY JANE WARD

was born on August 27, 1905, in Fairmount, Indiana, but grew up in Peru, Indiana, and Chicago and Evanston, Illinois. After graduating from Evanston, Illinois, Township High School, she spent four semesters between 1923 and 1926 at Northwestern University, where she majored in Latin. Between college and her marriage to Edward Quayle on March 7, 1928, she attended art school, was a tutor in English, worked as a commercial artist, and served as an instructor in a summer art camp. She began writing shortly after her marriage. In addition to her novels, she has written short stories and articles on mental health. The Women's National Press Club in 1949 gave her its annual award for distinguished service in behalf of mental health.

The Tree Has Roots (1937), her first novel, is a series of character studies of several people, janitors, a waitress, a stenographer, and others employed by a university. A fire set by a psychopathic janitor destroys the university's chapel and in various ways affects the lives of all the characters in the book. *The Wax Apple* (1937) is a tragedy set in a duplex house occupied by two lower-middle-class Chicago families. The story is the result of the long, unwitting collaboration of the two mothers whose ambitions differ sharply, but who are both quite successful in directing the courses of their children's lives.

The Snake Pit (1946) concerns the experiences, both real and imaginary, of a young woman who spends a year in a mental hospital. The story is written entirely from the viewpoint of the mentally ill protagonist. Toward the end this character is recovering normal insight, but at no time is the novel entirely free of the distortion that accompanies schizophrenia.

The Professor's Umbrella (1948) is about a teacher who has been as indifferent to the growing anti-Semitism of his university's administration as he has been to the occasional personal annoyances anti-Semitic attitudes have caused him in the past. However, when in middle life he is dismissed from his school on a trumped-up morals charge, he is forced to realize that his Christian background and lifelong association with Gentiles have not separated him from a minority that has special occupational and social problems.

ROBERT PENN WARREN

was born in Guthrie, Kentucky, on April 24, 1905. He was educated in public schools and at Vanderbilt University, where he was one of the group contributing to *The Fugitive,* a magazine devoted to poetry. He subsequently held fellowships at the University of California, where he took a master's degree in 1927, and at Yale. He was a Rhodes scholar and in 1930 was awarded the degree of Bachelor of Letters at Oxford. He is professor of English at the University of Minnesota. Mr. Warren was one of the founders and an editor of *The Southern Review.* In 1936 he received the Levinson prize of *Poetry: A Magazine of Verse,* and in 1936, 1937, and 1938 was awarded the Caroline Sinkler prize by the same publication. He was given a Houghton Mifflin literary fellowship, and was awarded Guggenheim fellowships in creative writing in 1939 and 1947. In 1942 he won the Shelley Memorial award. *All the King's Men* won the Southern Authors' annual award as the most distinguished book of 1946 by a southern author on a southern subject, and received the 1947 Pulitzer prize for fiction. He is the author of *John Brown: The Making of a Martyr* (1929), *Thirty-Six Poems* (1936), *Eleven Poems on the Same Theme* (1942), and *Selected Poems* (1944). He wrote in 1946 a critical study of Coleridge's "Rime of the Ancient Mariner." Mr. Warren has edited several volumes, and is the author of college textbooks in literature and rhetoric.

Mr. Warren draws the themes for his books from historical incidents in the South. He has said that he cannot understand why some writers have difficulty in finding new subjects; in Kentucky courthouses alone is buried in old records enough material for a whole generation of writers. His novels are crammed with blood and thunder in the tradition of historical fiction, but his stories take on the depth and universality of a parable, because the characters seek to learn the causes of their plight, the reasons for the rules of society, and the philosophical ideas which seem tenable in a morally, politically, and economically confused world. Malcolm Cowley has stated: "He is, I think, more richly endowed than any other American novelist born in the present century."

Night Rider (1939), his first novel, describes the tobacco war in Kentucky in the early 1900's as the growers and manufacturers quarrel; the basic problems in the novel are moral rather than social. *At Heaven's Gate* (1943) is a study of the struggle for economic and political power in the story of the daughter of an aristocratic but unscrupulous financier. She rebels against her father, leaves home, and through her tragic death provides public sympathy to save her father. *All the King's Men* (1946), which has more to do with the meaning of life than with Louisiana politics, is the story of a southern demagogue who, like Huey Long, rises to an incredible success and then goes to his death. *The Circus in the Attic* (1948) is a collection of two novelettes and twelve short stories written over a period of seventeen years. Each story is set in the country or in a small town. The significance of the ordinary individual forms the theme.

World Enough and Time (1950) portrays a man of tragic grandeur, a young lawyer in the Kentucky of the 1820's, whose wife demands that he kill her former lover. Jeremiah Beaumont, a lonely man searching for the meaning of life, goes to study law with his spiritual father, Colonel Cassius Fort, a successful attorney and politician. Jeremiah falls in love with Rachel Jordan, and her consent to wed carries with it the injunction, "Kill Fort." Following his act, which is committed in a mood of romantic idealism, Jeremiah suffers agony because he erred in not achieving a compromise. This philosophical novel, which was a Literary Guild selection, is based on an actual occurrence, the murder in 1825 of Colonel Solomon P. Sharp by Jereboam O. Beauchamp; Edgar Allan Poe in *Politian,* William Gilmore Simms in *Beauchampe,* and other writers employed the same material in plays and novels, but Mr. Warren has given the most satisfying interpretation and most artistic presentation.

FRANK WATERS

John Collings

was born on July 25, 1902, at the foot of Pike's Peak in Colorado Springs, Colorado. As a boy he lived some time in the mining camp of Cripple Creek, Colorado, and on the Navajo reservation. He majored in physics and engineering at Colorado College, and worked for a while as an engineer for the Pacific Telephone and Telegraph Company, being variously stationed at Imperial Valley, California, on the Mexican border; San Bernardino County, California, in the Mojave Desert; at Las Vegas, Nevada, during the Colorado River survey for Boulder Dam; and at Los Angeles, California. During World War II he was in Washington, D.C., as a writer in the office of the Co-ordinator of Inter-American Affairs.

His main interest has been the West, its history and peoples: Indians, Mexicans, and whites. He has made several trips into the peninsula of Lower California and the mainland of Mexico, including one five-month horseback trip through the Sierra Madre Mountains. A special interest of Mr. Waters is the significance of ancient man's intuitive ceremonial magic and modern man's rational magic of atomic fission. His non-fiction books include *Midas of the Rockies* (1937), a biography of Winfield Scott Stratton, who discovered gold on the south slope of Pike's Peak and founded the camp of Cripple Creek which led the world in gold production; and *The Colorado* (1946), a volume in the "Rivers of America" series. *Masked Gods* (1950) is on Indian life and ceremonials.

His first novel, *Fever Pitch* (1930), is a story of a Mexican dancing girl's obsession for gold in the deserts of Lower California and its effect on an American engineer. *The Wild Earth's Nobility* (1935), *Below Grass Roots* (1937), and *The Dust within the Rock* (1940) form a Colorado mining trilogy centering in the Pike's Peak region. The story covers the period from 1870 to 1925, from the Golconda boom days when silver was discovered in Leadville and gold at Cripple Creek, and concerns three generations of the Rogier family. The main story is that of Joseph Rogier, a southern gentleman impoverished by the Civil War, who comes west by wagon train. Making a small fortune as an architect and builder, he finally succumbs to the gold fever, loses his fortune, ruins his family, and becomes a crackpot epileptic still digging for gold in his back yard. His search for gold is an allegorical search for the meaning of life.

Three novels constitute a trilogy of the major minority types found in the Southwest: Mexicans, Indians, and those of mixed blood. *People of the Valley* (1941) is set in a remote hidden valley in the Sangre de Cristo Mountains of New Mexico. The people of the valley are isolated and inbred descendants of the Spanish-Colonial settlers of the sixteenth and seventeenth centuries and the last survivors of the Penitente cult. The story concerns their conflict with government reclamation engineers who open up the valley and construct a dam, thus flooding their ancient homes and farmlands. It is told through the life of old Maria, a blind herb doctor and midwife. *The Man Who*

Killed the Deer (1942) is a novel of Pueblo Indian ceremonialism, portraying the esoteric meanings of the various kiva rituals, myth-dramas, and tribal dances. It is told through the efforts of Martiniano, a young Pueblo Indian, to redeem himself for having killed a deer, thus sinning against the official white laws pertaining to the government's national forest and the ritual Indian laws prescribed by ancient ceremony. *The Yogi of Cockroach Court* (1947) is a story laid in the cantinas, casinos, cribs, and opium dens of a slum area on the American-Mexican Border. Here are contrasted the western physical concept of power and wealth, and the eastern metaphysical concept of non-attachment. "Cockroach" is Mexican slang for "prostitute"; hence the residents of the court are streetwalkers, pimps, thieves, Chinese, whites, Negroes, and half-breeds. The Yogi is an old Chinese shopkeeper who gives refuge to a half-breed boy and a Mexican percentage girl, through whom the story is related.

In collaboration with Houston Branch, Mr. Waters is co-author of two Civil War historical novels, *River Lady* (1942) and *Diamond Head* (1948). The first is about lumber shipping on the upper Mississippi, and the second chronicles the world cruise of the famous Confederate cruiser *Shenandoah,* which destroyed the last whaling fleet.

JOHN D. WEAVER

was born on February 4, 1912, in Washington, D.C., where his father was an official reporter of debates in the House of Representatives. The first twenty-one years of his life were divided between Washington and the Shenandoah Valley of Virginia, where his family has lived for nearly two hundred years. The Blue Ridge hill country outside of Front Royal, Virginia, has been the setting of much of his work. He was graduated from William and Mary College in 1932 with a bachelor's degree and from George Washington University the following year with a master's certificate. He worked for various government agencies in the early years of the New Deal, then joined the staff of the Kansas City *Star* in 1936. He married a fellow-writer, Harriett Sherwood, in Kansas City in 1937, and three years later they moved to Los Angeles to begin free-lancing. With the exception of three years in the army from 1943 to 1946, he has been writing steadily ever since. His short stories have appeared in leading magazines here and abroad, and in such collections as *Cross-Section,* O'Brien's *Best American Short Stories,* and the *O. Henry Memorial* collection. He now resides in Hollywood, California.

Mr. Weaver's work has been profoundly influenced by his childhood in Washington, where he played in the Capitol corridors, and by the Blue Ridge country, where he fished and hunted with young hill farmers trying desperately to scratch a living out of their rocky slopes. As a result, the theme which recurs most often in his work involves poverty and prejudice, and the connecting link between them.

His first novel, *Wind Before Rain* (1942), deals with the increasing industrialization of the Virginia hill country, which had formerly been devoted primarily to farming and small-scale manufacturing enterprises. *Another Such Victory* (1948), based on the Bonus March of 1932, concerns Lorry and Park Hoyt, who with their small child join other veterans in their expedition to Washington, camp on the outskirts of the city, and experience failure as troops disperse these unemployed soldiers of World War I. The Hoyts, however, retain their faith in their country. Mr. Weaver wrote this novel because in 1946, on being mustered out of the army, he watched the beginning of the economic readjustment which followed World War II, and became deeply disturbed at the dangerous parallels of the two post-war periods. This novel was written, the author has stated, "not as an indictment of any individual or any political party, but simply as a warning against the possible consequences of another economic disaster. I wanted to say as Pyrrhus did when, after losing thirty-five hundred men in winning the battle of Asculum, he replied to his congratulators, 'Another such victory and we are undone.' "

BARBARA WEBSTER

Leja Gorska

was born in St. Louis, Missouri, on April 5, 1900, the eleventh generation of a family that is noted for its legal talent. Her father was a well-known corporation lawyer, and her maternal grandfather was a judge of the Supreme Court of Missouri. Daniel Webster is a collateral ancestor. On both her mother's and father's sides of the family, her ancestors have fought in all the country's wars, and they have had a considerable part in building up its institutions.

After study at Mary Institute in St. Louis, Miss Webster in 1918 entered Wellesley College, where her major interest was the history of art. For a closer study of painting she entered in 1920 the Academy of Fine Arts in Philadelphia and during four years there won two Cresson traveling scholarships. From 1924 to 1926 she lived and studied in Europe. On returning to this country, she gradually became interested in writing; a number of her short stories were published in *Scribner's* magazine. In 1930 she married Edward Shenton, who has become known as a writer, illustrator, and editor; they have one son.

Miss Webster has stated that she has only one aim in writing: "To express my views on life, its truths, and men's reactions thereto. I have chosen the novel as a medium because it seems best fitted to this end."

Shadows on the Valley (1940), her first novel, is a study of the mutual impact of a pair of wanderers with liberal ideas and of an inbred community of old county families. *The Magic Water* (1942) concerns the attractions and repulsions between age and youth, and the fortunes of a young girl who comes as a companion to a house full of eccentric characters. *Mrs. Heriot's House* (1945) describes a woman, a house, and the maid who goes with it; the underlying and inevitable relations of master and servant picture a sort of slavery in microcosm. *The Color of the Country* (1947) is an attempt to realize the actual flavor of country life in Pennsylvania and of one particular family's reactions. The wife loves solitude enough to fight for it, and the husband, a worker in the city, delights to return each night to the joys of his rural home.

JEROME WEIDMAN

was born in New York City on August 4, 1913. He studied at the College of the City of New York, New York University, and the New York Law School, where he graduated in 1937. Although he was admitted to the bar, he never practiced. He traveled around the world, and upon his return in 1939 entered the publishing business. During World War II he was a writer for the Co-ordinator of Information and other government agencies. He married Peggy Wright in 1943; they have two children. His books include *The Horse that Could Whistle "Dixie"* (1939) and *The Captain's Tiger* (1948), short stories, and *Letter of Credit* (1940), an account of his trip around the world.

Mr. Weidman is chiefly interested in the depiction of certain types of New Yorkers who have been called "heels," and he dissects these unpleasant people with the skill and objectivity of a surgeon. He shows indignation at the way in which ruthless and unprincipled persons take advantage of gentle or kindly human beings. He belongs in the "hard-boiled" school of fiction, but unlike some writers in this school he directs his shafts of ridicule at wrongdoers.

I Can Get It for You Wholesale (1937), his first novel, pictures an unscrupulous and ambitious shipping clerk in a New York garment firm who rises to become a successful dress manufacturer by consistently trying to outsmart his competitors. *What's in It for Me?* (1938), a sequel, continues Harry Bogen's experiences as he follows his career as a garment maker. This book was withdrawn from circulation because of its unfavorable picture of men engaged in this industry. *I'll Never Go There Any More* (1941) details the experiences of a young man from Albany who goes to New York as an accountant and experiences so many trials with peculiar people that he is glad to return to his native city.

The Lights Around the Shore (1943) tells about Peter Landor, a son of Hungarian immigrants, who accompanies his aunt to Europe when he is fifteen. Some of his problems are solved on the journey, and the greatest one is cleared up when she is on her deathbed. *Too Early to Tell* (1946) satirizes the men who are employed in a government agency called the Bureau of Psychological Combat. *The Price Is Right* (1949) describes the manner in which Henry Cade, an employee in a newspaper feature business in New York, works his way up to become sales manager and then through ambition and fear struggles to get to the top. It is a tale of the moral terror and the relentless self-destruction of ambition that lie in wait for all people.

PAUL I. WELLMAN

was born on October 14, 1898, in Enid, Oklahoma, of pioneer stock who had moved to the Indian Territory just when that region was emerging from the Indian hunting-ground stage. When he was less than a year old he was taken by his parents to Angola, the Portuguese colony in West Africa, where his father, Dr. Frederick C. Wellman, later widely known as an expert on tropical medicine, as well as a scientist, artist, and writer—the last two under the name of "Cyril Kay-Scott"—was health officer for a chain of mission stations.

Paul Wellman spent most of his first ten years in Africa, and in England and Portugal when the family was on brief furloughs. Sent back to the United States for his education, he received his early schooling in Utah, part of the time living in the heart of the Ute-Uintah reservation. From these boyhood experiences arises his interest in primitive peoples, and their life and customs, out of which grew his early books.

Later he spent several years in western Kansas and Oklahoma, working as a cowhand and learning much of the story of the old West from grizzled frontiersmen who had played a part in it. Following his graduation in 1918 from Fairmount College, now the University of Wichita, he served in the United States army during World War I. On his return from the service in 1919 he became a reporter on the Wichita *Beacon;* in 1928 he was made city editor. A year later he moved to the Wichita *Eagle,* and after a period on the Chicago *American* he went in 1936 to the Kansas City *Star.* In this period he became one of the West's best-known newspaper feature writers.

His first books were histories. *Death on the Prairie* (1934) and *Death in the Desert*

(1935) have become classic histories of the Indian wars of the West and Southwest respectively, and have since been republished in one volume as *Death on Horseback* (1948). *The Trampling Herd* (1939) is a chronological history of the western cattle industry. Mr. Wellman was called upon to assist with the compilation of *The Dictionary of American History,* to which he contributed more separate items than any other historian, and *The Atlas of American History,* for which he supervised the western Indian war maps. From 1944 to 1946 he wrote screen plays in Hollywood, but since the last date he has devoted himself wholly to novels, for which he has attained a wide public following.

Broncho Apache (1936), his first novel, concerns an outlaw Apache Indian who escapes from a prison train in Illinois when Geronimo and his band are being taken to exile at Fort Marion, Florida, in 1886. Although he makes his way back to Arizona, his own people betray him. He escapes a second time and becomes untamable, a broncho, and begins and conducts a one-man war against Mexicans, Americans, and his own people.

Jubal Troop (1939) deals with the West and its dramatic changes in the thirty years starting in 1886, as told through the career of a man who in his own life typifies the country. Jubal Troop has adventures in the Dakotas, Texas, Mexico, and Oklahoma; beginning as a boy in a sheepherder's camp, he runs the gamut to acquire millions as an oil man as the West changes from a wilderness to a settled and in places even industrialized country. *Angel with Spurs* (1942) is an historical novel based on a little-known episode of the War between the States: the march of Confederate General Jo Shelby and a thousand "no-surrender" officers and men into Mexico to establish new homes for themselves.

The Bowl of Brass (1944) is a study of the passions and politics of frontier Kansas in 1889, involving a county-seat war, in which any method, however questionable, is used by the rival towns to gain their end of becoming the county capital. The book is also an examination of the slow deterioration of the mind of a man crazed by a combination of religious fanaticism, greed, and jealousy. It is important in Wellman's writing as the first of the "Jericho" books, this one dealing with his famous fictitious town in its inception. *The Walls of Jericho* (1947) is the second of the series. It tells the story of two men, once the closest of friends, whose friendship is poisoned by an ambitious woman, and who become bitter enemies in a political feud, fought against the background of post-Populist Kansas. This novel was a Literary Guild selection. *The Chain* (1949), the third of the "Jericho" books, was a Literary Guild selection. The novel deals with an uncompromising young minister of an Episcopal Church who seeks to conduct his mission along the truest principles of the Christian teaching and who encounters the inevitable prejudices of the world, including parish politics, with tragic results.

EUDORA WELTY

Louise Dahl-Wolfe

was born on April 13, 1909, in Jackson, Mississippi, where she has lived ever since, except for a few pioneering trips into the Middle West and New York. She attended the Mississippi State College for Women from 1925 to 1927, the University of Wisconsin from which she received her bachelor's degree in 1929, and the Columbia University School of Advertising in 1930–31. She has worked in publicity and advertising, has written feature stories and radio scripts, and has taken publicity photographs. In 1942 and 1943 she received the O. Henry Memorial prize for the best stories of each year. In 1944 she won the award of the American Academy of Arts and Letters "in recognition of her artistry in the subtle portrayal of character." She held a Guggenheim fellowship in 1949. Her collections of short stories include *A Curtain of Green* (1941), largely concerned with the abnormal and grotesque; *The Wide Net* (1943), dealing with southern white aristocracy fallen from glory; and *The Golden Apples* (1949), a book of connected short stories covering forty years in a small town in Mississippi.

The Robber Bridegroom (1942), her first novel, tells in a setting of New Orleans and the bayous the events of an old ballad. Jamie Lockhart, an outlaw by night and a gentleman by day, runs away with Rosamund, the daughter of a Mississippi planter. Into this fantasy are introduced Mike Fink and other heroes of American folklore. *Delta Wedding* (1946) is a series of pictures of three generations of the Fairchild family, which gathers in 1923 on a Mississippi plantation to witness the wedding of Miss Dabney to Troy Flavin. *Music from Spain* (1949) is a short tale of a Mississippian and a day's adventures in San Francisco.

GLENWAY WESCOTT

Geo. Platt Lynes

was born in Kewaskum, Wisconsin, on April 11, 1901. He went to high school in West Bend and Waukesha, Wisconsin, and then attended the University of Chicago from 1917 to 1919. His family wished him to become a minister, but he had hoped to become a musician. He lived for a year each in New Mexico and in Germany, where he wrote the greater part of his first novel. He spent the year 1924 in New York, and in 1925 went to France where he made his home for the next eight years. Since 1934 he has lived on the family farm in Hunterdon County, New Jersey. *Like a Lover* (1926) and *Goodbye, Wisconsin* (1928) contain short stories. *The Bitterns* (1920) and *Native of Rock* (1925) are books of poems.

The Apple of His Eye (1924), his first novel, has a Wisconsin farm setting and tells of the conflicting influences shaping a boy's view of sex. *The Grandmothers* (1927), which won the Harper prize, is the chronicle of a pioneer Wisconsin family told from the viewpoint of a young man whose curiosity was aroused when as a child he had looked at the old family photograph album and had begun to piece together their various life stories.

The Babe's Bed (1930) tells about a young man who meditates on the future of his sister's baby boy. *The Pilgrim Hawk* (1940) describes two Americans resident in France who receive as callers an Irishman and his wife, the owners of a falcon. *Apartment in Athens* (1945), a selection of the Book-of-the-Month Club, describes the effect of the German occupation upon the Helianos family in Athens, Greece. The father is executed, and the children avenge his death.

JAN WESTCOTT

Michael Denning

was born in Philadelphia, Pennsylvania. Her father, Dr. Nicholas P. Vlachos, a native of Holland, was a distinguished classical and historical scholar. She grew up in Swarthmore, Pennsylvania, and attended Swarthmore College. Her interest in history, especially that of the Elizabethan period, is of long standing, but she first began writing in 1944. While working on a book, she writes from nine to one in the morning and from seven-thirty to eleven in the evening, six days a week. Despite this drastic schedule she manages to supervise a large household, which includes two sons.

The Border Lord (1946), her first novel, is an historical romance of Scotland in the sixteenth century about the adventures of

Francis Hepburn, Earl of Bothwell, and a nephew of the Bothwell who was Mary Stuart's third husband. *Captain for Elizabeth* (1949) is an account of the third circumnavigation of the world, the hero being Captain Thomas Cavendish. *The Hepburn* (1950), with its setting in England and Scotland in the fifteenth century, is a story about Patrick Hepburn, third Earl of Bothwell, and the intrigues of James IV of Scotland and Henry VII of England to conquer each other.

DAVID WESTHEIMER

Ellis Sweatte

was born in 1917 in Houston, Texas. After graduating from Rice Institute of Technology with a major in chemistry in 1937, he worked at odd jobs before joining the staff of the Houston *Post* two years later. He entered the army air force in May, 1941, and in July of the following year was sent overseas as a navigator of a bomber. During World War II and in the course of duty he was in North Africa, the Near East, and Europe. He was shot down over Italy in December, 1942, and was held a prisoner of war in Italian and German camps until April, 1945. On his discharge in 1946 as a captain and with a Distinguished Flying Cross and an Air Medal he returned to the *Post*. In October of that year he decided to devote full time to writing.

Summer on the Water (1948), his first novel, has for its locale the Gulf of Mexico bayshore district, twenty-five miles from Houston, an area abounding with live oaks and mockingbirds. One summer day Mrs. Carably wonders who is the father of her Negro maid's eight-year-old son, a boy with the hands of a white child. The inquiry leads to tragic conclusions. *The Magic Fallacy* (1950) tells of Pershing Williams, a teen-age boy, who grows up in the belief that nothing in life is ugly, but who loses his youthful illusions when his twenty-year-old stepmother seduces him. Told by Joe Albert, a neighbor boy, the story has the theme that "the innocence of one child cannot reach out to save the innocence of another."

JUNE WETHERELL

Robert Campbell Barry

was born in Bellingham, Washington, on June 8, 1909. She received her education at the Western Washington College of Education and the University of Washington, where she served as associate editor of her college annual and of the campus humor magazine. After graduation she engaged in newspaper work in Seattle and Bellingham. In 1933 she married Daniel Frame, and moved with him to Minnesota. She served on the staff of *The Family Circle* magazine in New York City from 1945 to 1946, and was an instructor in the English department of the Michigan State Normal College in Ypsilanti in 1947 and 1948 while her husband was studying for his master's degree at the University of Michigan. She has two sons. Mr. and Mrs. Frame now reside in New York City.

Every Ecstasy (1941), her first novel, has for its theme: "If you had your life to live over, would you do it differently?" *Run With the Pack* (1942), written under the pseudonym of "Patricia Frame," deals with the evil effects of gossip. *But That Was Yesterday* (1943) concerns a happily married woman who relives in retrospect her college years and her broken romance with a world-famous correspondent scheduled to lecture where her husband teaches. The theme is that individual integrity is of greater importance than social approval, and that the sorority system is bad.

Shut the Door Behind You (1944) tells how Alexandra Brainerd outgrew her childhood and the college sweetheart for whom she had promised to wait; the target for attack in the novel is nostalgia. *Dead Center* (1946) is a story of marriage, and of what happens when a man takes his wife and baby home to his big possessive family. It is a criticism in particular of the Scandinavian Middle West and of the people who consider a wife and food the two indispensables of life. *Run Sheep Run* (1947) concerns the generation that was old enough to have suffered the depression and young enough to be drafted into World War II. It is a picture of young people whose lives would have been different had they been born at another time.

CATHARINE WHITCOMB

Hans van Nes

was born on December 13, 1911, in Philadelphia, Pennsylvania. She is descended from William Brewster, one of the original members of Plymouth Colony, who came over on the *Mayflower*. Among her ancestors is Captain Charles Fanning, who served through the American Revolution and who was an original member of the Sons of the Cincinnati. In youth she wished to be an actress, but she started to write while living in Paris at the age of nineteen. She has one son, John Cyrus Cort II, from her first marriage, and she did not write for a number of years following his birth. She is now married to Daniel A. Davis.

I'll Mourn You Later (1936), her first novel, is a psychological novel of family life whose interest arises from the portrayal of the moods, thoughts, and actions of the characters. *The Grown-Ups* (1937) delineates the theme of children against adults and the effect of divorce on a growing child. It is a character study of Camilla Madden from the age of three to seventeen. *In the Fine Summer Weather* (1938), set in a New Hampshire summer colony, concerns three married couples: a writer whose stories do not sell and his wife who drinks; a wealthy philanderer and his childless wife; and a young, happy pair and their small son. The arrival of a bogus countess hastens solutions to some of their problems.

The Malfreys (1944) is about a pair of people who are pathologically unsuited to one another but morbidly inclined to stay together and to be miserable together. *The Door to the Garden* (1949) is a story about the roots and beginnings of a young girl who feels unloved and unwanted, and an account of her tempestuous search for her own identity. *The Hill of Glass* (1950) deals with the theme of the search for an ideal, with the ultimate discovery that the ideal, in the long run, turns out to be quite different from the original conception.

HELEN CONSTANCE WHITE

was born on November 26, 1896, in New Haven, Connecticut. She studied at Radcliffe College and at the University of Wisconsin, where she has been a teacher since 1919 and a professor of English since 1936. She has also taught at Smith College, at Barnard College, and at Columbia University in the summer session. She has held a Guggenheim fellowship and a Huntington Library fellowship; in 1942 she received the Laetare medal from the University of Notre Dame. She has been very active in the American Association of University Women, of which organization she was president from 1941 to 1947. In the summer of 1946 she served as a member of the United States delegation to the fifth meeting of the Preparatory Commission for UNESCO in London and later went to Germany as a member of the United States Education Mission. She is also a member of the United States National Commission for UNESCO and of the National Board of Foreign Scholarships. She has said, "I have a passion for history, and I revel in research." Her scholarly books include *The Mysticism of William Blake* (1927), *English Devotional Literature (Prose), 1600–1640* (1931), and *The Metaphysical Poets* (1936).

A Watch in the Night (1933), her first novel, which presents the conflict between inspiration and order, is an historical novel based upon the life of Jacopone de Todi, the famous lawyer and poet of the Middle Ages, who turns to the church and joins the Franciscans to help unfortunate people when his young wife dies. *Not Built with Hands* (1935) concerns an episode in the struggle between church and state, and is the life story in fictional form of Matilda, Countess of Tuscany, who ranks with the first heroines of history, and of Gregory VII, who has been called the greatest of the popes. *To the End of the World* (1939) portrays the struggle between loyalty to religious tradition and enthusiasm for social reform, and the reconciliation between the two in a young priest who exemplifies both. The time is the Reign of Terror in the French Revolution. *Dust on the King's Highway* (1947) treats the great problems of human understanding involved in the contact of different kinds and levels of civilization in colonial and missionary effort. It is an historical novel of the winning of the far West for God and the King of Spain. The central character is Father Garces, a Franciscan missionary priest, who works among the Indians of California and Mexico and ends his life in martyrdom.

MAX WHITE

Hilda Reis

is the pseudonym of Charles William White, who was born in 1906. He has always been reluctant to give biographical data about himself, believing that writers should be read and not heard or known about. Educated in New England and France, he early became a cosmopolitan and now resides in France and Italy. His love of good food appears in *How I Feed My Friends* (1947), a book of recipes for Sunday night suppers.

Anna Becker (1937), his first novel, is a story of New England small-town life showing the clash between real and artificial education. The heroine, who is a graduate of the local college and who has stayed on to run a tea room, is confronted by a man who painfully teaches her that living is something quite different from what she believed it to be. *Tiger, Tiger* (1940) describes twenty years in the life of an imaginary modern painter. A story of genius and how it meets the world, the tale explores the nature of genius.

In the Blazing Light (1946) is a novelized version of forty years in the life of the eighteenth-century Spanish painter, Francisco de Goya y Lucientes, running from his second trip to Madrid to the invasion of the city by Napoleon's troops. The story pictures Goya against the Spanish court during his lifetime. *The Midnight Gardener* (1948), a novel about the French poet Charles Baudelaire, shows that his life does not explain his genius but that his genius explains his life. *The Man Who Carved Women from Wood* (1949) pictures a strange group of people in the French Quarter of New Orleans and chiefly concerns a young sculptor with a high and rigid ideal who meets with experience in his love for a doctor's wife and is thereby killed. The theme is that living is not what it is usually believed to be; it is something more complicated and both better and worse.

NELIA GARDNER WHITE

Bradford Bachrach

was born in Andrews Settlement, Potter County, Pennsylvania, on November 1, 1894, the daughter of a Methodist minister. She was educated in New York and Pennsylvania high schools, at Syracuse University, and at the Emma Willard Kindergarten School in Syracuse, New York. On August 11, 1917, she was married to Ralph L. White, a lawyer, and she began her writing career about that time. During World War II she was one of several American women writers invited to England to describe the wartime spirit there. She has written several books for girls.

"All my books," Mrs. White has stated, "even the earlier and more sentimental ones, have as their theme man's essential loneliness, his struggles toward communication, and the necessity for the acceptance of loneliness before he can begin to know himself and, thus, others. Personal integrity and growth are my chief concern."

David Strange (1928), her first novel, is a simple chronicle of country life. *Tune in the Tree* (1929) expresses through the life of an orphan girl the theme that the melody is in the listener rather than in the bird. *Hathaway House* (1931) pictures a charming family whose friendly cheer is not upset by the arrival of an elderly aunt. *Mrs. Green's Daughter-in-Law* (1932) portrays incidents in the home of an aging mother who looks after her four children and their families during a summer visit. *This, My House* (1933) shows how Martin Brereton helps his three nearly grown children to gain direction in life. *Family Affair* (1934) concerns Joel and Mary Goodspeed, their three daughters, his mother and her father. Mary feels slightly misunderstood, but Grandmother Goodspeed helps to give her a vital cheer.

The Fields of Gomorrah (1935) is about a minister's wife who for years trod the fields of Gomorrah, "the place of doubt, the region of no faith," because of hypocritical congregations, but who emerges triumphantly because of her love for her husband. *Daughter of Time* (1941) portrays in fictional form the life of Katherine Mansfield, the New Zealand author of brilliant short stories, from the age of six until her death in 1923, at thirty-four. *Brook Willow* (1944) brings an ill lady pianist and a thwarted physician together to find mutual support and readjustment. *No Trumpet Before Him* (1948), winner of the Westminster Press Award, portrays the problems of a spiritually minded young preacher, Paul Phillips, whose difficulties with his congregation arise from his disturbing idealism and unwillingness to merchandize Christianity in bazaars and lectures. *The Pink House* (1950) is a psychological study of a crippled child growing up in a New England family full of meanness and cruelty and becoming a courageous woman.

OLIVE BERNARDINE WHITE

was born on May 28, 1899, in New Haven, Connecticut. She is a younger sister of Helen C. White, the historical novelist and scholar. Olive was educated in Boston and at Radcliffe College. She taught for a year at Wellesley College, and since 1927 has been at Bradley University in Peoria, Illinois, where she is now professor of English, dean of women (since 1940), and dean of Laura College (since 1946).

Her novels are by-products of her research centering in the literary and intellectual history of sixteenth-century England. Of the imaginative approach to this material she has written: "Between and beneath and beyond the events worthy of commemoration in the formal records of the age must have lain a crowded text of human reality—the comprehension and the darkening or the clarity and the beauty of the spirit of man—a text which we can retrieve by applying the reagents of thought to the shadowy interstices between the lines of the documents."

The King's Good Servant (1936), her first novel, is based on the last six years of the life of Sir Thomas More, and describes his heroic struggle against political dictatorship in matters of religion. Its focus is upon both Sir Thomas' public career and his family life in the large household of children and young friends during the critical years of 1529 and 1535. His arrest, imprisonment, trial, and condemnation to death are presented in major scenes of the book. *Late Harvest* (1940) deals with the dilemma of the Roman Catholics in England under Queen Elizabeth during the troubled years of political and religious antagonism between 1580 and 1603. In spite of persecution Alice and Hugh Winbourne still believe that as loyal Englishmen they can win peace, if not for themselves, at least for their children. The effects on ordinary lives of such events as the threatened invasion by the Spanish Armada in 1588 shape the action of the novel. The background of ordinary life in England is portrayed well.

DAN WICKENDEN

Helen Williams

was born on March 24, 1913, in Tyrone, Pennsylvania. The better part of his first fourteen years was spent in Flushing, New York, which at that time contained large tracts of comparatively untrodden wilderness. After he graduated from the eighth grade, he and his family spent nine months in England, a good many of them in London. After returning to America, the family moved farther out on Long Island to Manhasset, where Dan went to high school. His years at Amherst coincided with the depth of the depression. For the college drama club he wrote a three-act play about certain abuses then prevalent in the fraternity system, with particular stress on race prejudice. It was produced for two nights in his senior year. Six months after graduation in 1935, he found a job as writer of trade publicity with the Columbia Broadcasting System. Meantime he had a one-act play accepted by *Stage* magazine and a short story by *Vanity Fair*. Subsequently he appeared in *Story* with a novella called "Journey Through Sunlight." By the time his first novel was published in 1937, he had left CBS to become a free-lance writer. During the summer of 1940, he motored through the United States and Mexico, and the following year he became a newspaper reporter in the Middle West. After eighteen months he moved to Connecticut where, except for two extended visits to Guatemala, he has since lived.

About the writing of novels Mr. Wickenden has said: "It is my belief that a good novel should be, on whatever level, an entertainment: not primarily a social tract, a work of political propaganda, a psychological or clinical study, or simply an expression of the author's own aesthetic sensibilities. It may be any or all of these things incidentally, but first it must tell an interesting story about characters who seem alive and move in a world which seems as vivid as actuality, and in doing this it should provide the reader with enjoyment. If it fails to be enjoyable, it fails as a novel. And life, no matter how tragic and chaotic it is nowadays, remains remarkably rich and various; I think a good novel should at least suggest some of this richness and variety. Even a light novel, however, is better for having a central core of meaning, for expressing a viewpoint." His first four novels were about family life.

The Running of the Deer (1937), his first novel, tells how a roving uncle comes to the home of a Long Island family just as the father loses his job and rescues the adolescent boy, Mel, from the drabness of his parents' lives. The theme is summed up in Uncle Christopher's final remark to Mel: "Keep your excitement." *Walk Like a Mortal* (1940) tells the story of a marriage that fails. The viewpoint is that of the adolescent boy, Gabe Mackenzie, who in the summer after his third year in high school sees trouble brewing between his parents. By the end of his senior year Gabe acquires understanding and looks forward to a normal life. The theme is summed up in the title itself, which implies that one cannot expect human beings to behave as other than human beings and that it is wise to bear in mind that one is oneself a mere mortal.

The Wayfarers (1945), a meditation on love in all its aspects, is a story about an American family in the days just before the beginning of World War II. Ten years have elapsed after the wife's death; the husband begins to test himself and endeavors to develop a full understanding of his children. *Tobias Brandywine* (1948), which was designed as an entertainment pure and simple, a kind of fairy tale without resort to outright fantasy, is basically concerned with the process of growing up and suggests that there is inevitably a moment when the fully mature adult cuts the bond with his parents. The story concerns the arrival of Tobias Brandywine, a starving adult waif, at the home of the aged and aristocratic Senator Windrow in Wanhope and of the way in which the newcomer tackles and solves the many problems which trouble the community and the senator. After a nine-year sojourn he slips away as quietly as he came.

A Dry Season (1950), with its setting in Guatemala in a postwar winter, presents the experiences, past and present, of two young women and three young men from the United States, and their relations with the members of a small foreign colony. The book contrasts a highly mechanized society, the supreme achievement of which is the atom bomb, with a social pattern which even now remains virtually untouched by the machine. From this contrast the author attempts to derive certain basic, positive values concerned with man's relationship to the earth, to his God, and to his fellow men.

MARGARET WIDDEMER

Underwood & Underwood

was born in Doylestown, Pennsylvania, of parents whose stock migrated to America in Colonial days. Her father was a clergyman. She was educated privately at home, and graduated from the Drexel Institute Library School in Philadelphia. In 1931 she received the degree of Doctor of Literature from Bucknell University; Middlebury College awarded her a master's degree in 1933. She began writing in childhood; her poem "Factories" was reprinted and discussed widely. From 1928 to 1932 she lectured at the Middlebury College Writers' Conference at Bread Loaf, Vermont, and in 1933 she was a lecturer at the University of Colorado Writers' Conference. Since 1947 she has been in charge of fiction at the Chautauqua Writers' Conference. In 1936 she delivered a series of broadcasts, "Do You Want to Write?", over the blue network of the National Broadcasting Company; the next year these talks were included in a book by the same title.

She prepared an anthology, *The Haunted Hour* (1920). Her most notable books of poetry are *Factories* (1917), *The Old Road to Paradise* (1918), *The Road to Downderry and Other Poems* (1932), *Hill Garden* (1936), and *Collected Poems* (1928). She has written one play, "The Singing Wood" (1926).

Miss Widdemer's principal interest in her prose fiction has been the romance of young people in normal, gay American life. Until her last two books, her backgrounds have been principally American small towns, ranging from Asbury Park, New Jersey, where part of her childhood was spent, to Westchester County and its environs in New York. Since 1948 she has taken a wider field for her own, and has written carefully documented historical novels. She considers her poetry the most important part of her work; her various volumes have ranged from the social interest of *Factories,* which expresses her abiding and deep interest in social service, to the satire on American poets in *A Tree with a Bird* (1923). She occupies an important place among the American poets of her time.

Her first work of prose fiction was a best seller, *The Rose Garden Husband* (1915), the story of a young librarian. *You're Only Young Once* (1918) is a romantic tale of gay love affairs in a family of eight children. *Charis Sees It Through* (1924) recounts the struggles of a young American wife, married to a brilliant Czech engineer, to adjust herself to the idiosyncrasies of his immigrant relatives. In *Gallant Lady* (1926) a first wife, believed to be dead, appears to harass the woman who is now happily married to the husband. *More Than a Wife* (1927) has as its theme the adjustment of a career woman to married life.

Rhinestones (1929) is the story of a girl who forsakes the tinsel existence of sophisticated society for small-town life. In *All the King's Horses* (1930) a jilted bride, under pressure of added responsibilities, readjusts her life by forgetting her pride. *Loyal Lover* (1930) is the story of an American girl reared in England who, through her return to her American relatives, finds love and happiness in her native land. *The Truth about Lovers* (1931) points the lesson that no one will ever know that verity.

In *Pre-War Lady* (1932) a beautiful woman, clad in the style of other years, sings to a night-club audience and by her nostalgic songs causes innumerable complications in love. *Golden Rain* (1933) projects a woman's discovery that ideals are worth more than the sophisticated world of money. *The Years of Love* (1933) proves the old adage that no one ever escapes the subtle onslaught of the tender passion. *Back to Virtue* (1934) is a comedy relating the efforts of an older girl to keep her rash younger sister from becoming a common-law wife.

Other Lovers (1934) has as its chief character a charming old lady who has the insight of a Dorothy Dix into the problems of the heart. *Eve's Orchard* (1935) illustrates the theme that country community life may be preferable to a city existence. *Marriage Is Possible* (1936) tells the story of three marriages and how two of them failed. *This Isn't the End* (1936) relates the rise to fame and wealth of a radio broadcaster, with the subsequent breakup of his marriage. *Hand on Her Shoulder* (1938) makes ancestral memories the impulse behind a happy love affair. *Ladies Go Masked* (1939) is another variation on the Dorothy Dix perceptions of the old lady of *Other Lovers.*

She Knew Three Brothers (1939) tells the story of a young female explorer who finds more excitement in meeting three brothers than she does in her scientific discoveries. *Some Day I'll Find You* (1940) concerns a pretty college girl who experiments with a career and with love, only to find that the former is an empty thing. *Let Me Have Wings* (1941) treats the successful struggles of a rich girl to escape from the domination of her grandmother.

Lover's Alibi (1941) indicates that listening to other people's stories may straighten out one's own difficult life. *Angela Comes Home* (1942) has a girl return after a long residence in France simultaneously to fall in love with her own country and a young American. *Constancia Herself* (1945) is the romance of a girl in the Social Register who, on the eve of her marriage, discovers that she is an adopted daughter and so seeks to learn her true identity and find the right man.

Lani (1948) is an historical novel set in the 1890's in the South Pacific and in Hawaii in that significant period when the major nations were competing for the Hawaiian Islands; the story concerns the life of missionaries. *Red Cloak Flying* (1950) is an historical romance of upstate New York in the 1740's, ten years before the French and Indian Wars, in the early days of Sir William Johnson. It pictures vividly eighteenth-century life in the colonies, and tells the story of a girl whose red cloak of courage carries her through the dangers to which her beauty and a dangerous gift of clairvoyance subject her. Its locale is Miss Widdemer's own summer home, the Adirondack foothills near Johnstown, New York.

ROBERT WILDER

was born on January 25, 1901, in Richmond, Virginia. He was educated at John B. Stetson University in De Land, Florida, and at Columbia University. For a time in New York City he was a soda clerk in a drug store, and then he worked in a boatbuilding concern in New Jersey. Moving to Cincinnati, he became an usher in a theater and later an employee of a soap-manufacturing firm. As soon as he was established in the city, he became a copy boy on the *Commercial Tribune*. On returning to New York City, he wrote publicity for eight years for famous actors and actresses like Walter Huston and Claudette Colbert. After a period of service on Station WOR, where he persuaded Mahatma Gandhi to make his first radio broadcast, he joined, in 1934, the staff of the New York *Sun,* for which newspaper he wrote during five years a daily column, "On the Sun Deck." His journalistic experiences provided the basis for *Out of the Blue* (1944), a series of sketches and short stories. He wrote two plays, *Stardust* (with Frances Starr, 1935) and *Sweet Chariot* (with Frank Wilson, 1946). He left the newspaper business in 1944, lived for a time in Florida, and now resides in Los Ranchos de Taos, New Mexico.

God Has a Long Face (1940), his first novel, tells the life story of a young Ohio giant, Basil Wallace Burgoyne, who deserts four days after Appomattox, spends five years returning to Cincinnati, and then migrates to Florida, where he becomes a powerful political leader and land developer in the boom days on the east coast. *Flamingo Road* (1942) is a romantic tale of local and state politics in Florida in the bootleg era. Titus Semple, a sheriff, grooms young Fielding Carlisle to be governor, and then has his life altered by Lane Ballou, a waif in a bankrupt circus. *Mr. G. Strings Along* (1944) is an amusing tale of a manufacturer of metal jumping frogs who wants to be useful in the war effort. After a series of tribulations in Washington, he converts his factory, only to learn that his original product is essental to the nation's war activity.

Written on the Wind (1946) deals with the family of Andrew Whitfield, a North Carolina tobacco planter, whose children deteriorate. A sharecropper's son, brought in to nurse the worst of the lot, falls in love with the young man's actress wife. *Bright Feather* (1948) portrays the life and times of Osceola, the Seminole Indian chief, in Florida in the 1830's when the white man was ruthlessly taking Indian lands. The story centers in Clayfield Hammond, a crippled and embittered plantation owner, and his thoughtful grandson who knows and appreciates the attitude of the red men. *Wait for Tomorrow* (1950) deals with an ex-king, his mistress, and his financial adviser who are in Mexico City scheming to enter the United States with the aid of an American oilman and a cynical reporter.

THORNTON WILDER

Petrelle

was born on April 17, 1897, in Madison, Wisconsin, the son of Amos Parker Wilder, editor of *The Wisconsin State Journal.* He spent his youth in China where his father was American Consul General at Hong Kong for three years and at Shanghai for five years. The education which Thornton had begun in a high school in Chafoo, China, was continued in 1914 in Berkeley and Ojai, California. He was a student at Oberlin College from 1915 to 1917. During World War I he served as a corporal in the Coast Artillery Corps at Narragansett Bay. His work for the bachelor's degree was completed at Yale in 1920, and then he studied at the American Academy in Rome.

In 1921 he was housemaster at the Lawrenceville School in New Jersey, where he taught French in order to leave himself ample time for reading and writing; at this time he made up his mind not to write for commercial success. He received a master's degree at Princeton in 1925, and from 1930 to 1936 served on the faculty of the University of Chicago. Although he had written one-act plays since the age of sixteen and had his play, "The Trumpet Shall Sound," produced in a little theater in 1926, it was the novel, *The Bridge of San Luis Rey,* that brought fame and a Pulitzer prize. During World War II he was an intelligence officer with the army air force in the Tunisian and Algerian campaigns and later in Caserta, Italy. He was honorably discharged as a lieutenant-colonel in September, 1945. He lives in Hamden, Connecticut, and is unmarried.

"The art of literature," Mr. Wilder has written, "springs from two curiosities, a curiosity about human beings pushed to such an extreme that it resembles love, and a love of a few masterpieces of literature so absorbing that it has all the richest elements of curiosity." He believes that a writer gets his best training through "the passionate assimilation of a few masterpieces written from a spirit somewhat like his own." His own early enthusiastic reading included all the writings of Cardinal Newman and Jonathan Swift. Mr. Wilder infuses a spiritual quality into his work, and many of his plays and his novels are based on great religious themes.

He has published two collections of short plays: *The Angel That Troubled the Waters* (1929) and *The Long Christmas Dinner.* His extremely successful and original plays are "Our Town" (1938), a warmly human account of life in the village of Grover's Corners, New Hampshire, in the early 1900's, and "The Skin of Our Teeth" (1942), an allegory of man's progress from the Ice Age to the time of his ultimate destruction.

The Cabala (1925), his first novel, is an urbane portrayal of a group of people who represent the sophisticated aristocracy of Rome, but whose lives are fundamentally shallow. *The Bridge of San Luis Rey* (1927) tells the life stories of five characters who fall to their death when a bridge collapses in Peru in 1714; through the providence of God each person reaches a great decision just before crossing the structure. *The Woman of Andros* (1930) appraises certain ethical values in life through the beauty and wisdom of a Greek hetaera on the island of Brynos; she brings a new concept of woman to the crude young men who visit her home, and she brings the cheer of hope to minds darkened with pessimism.

Heaven's My Destination (1935) is a realistic and comic tale about a traveling salesman, George Brush, whose practical application of religious principles gets him into difficulties. He is beaten for being a pacifist, and he marries a waitress whom he had seduced some years earlier. The book clarifies a number of problems facing converts to religion in an age of irreverence, and its picture of society hints that an age of moral regeneration is coming. *Ides of March* (1948) describes Julius Caesar's actions and thoughts in the months preceding his assassination in 45 B. C. The story is told through a series of imaginary documents, private letters, diary entries, and police reports.

GALE WILHELM

was born on April 26, 1908, in Eugene, Oregon. All her life except one year in New York has been spent on the Pacific Coast, in Washington, Oregon, and California. She enjoys cities but prefers to live in the country. She likes to cook and to work with wood. She says that she writes very slowly or very swiftly, but that the biggest part of the job is done before she puts her hand to paper. This first draft is always done in longhand, and there is virtually no revision in the two or three typescripts that carry it toward a completed work. She is most interested in the short story as a form of writing.

We Too Are Drifting (1935), her first novel, tells of the unhappy triangular love affair among three women, one of whom is an artist famous for her woodcuts. *No Letters for the Dead* (1936) portrays Paula, who becomes a prostitute in order to earn her living when her lover goes to prison for the supposed murder of his wife, but in her letters to him, which form the core of the book, she gives no hint of the life that is leading her to tragedy. *Torchlight to Valhalla* (1938) has Morgen, a sensitive and talented girl of twenty-one, looking in vain for a reflection in herself of Royal's love, and finding what she needs in Toni, a seventeen-year-old girl.

Bring Home the Bride (1940) pictures the love, marriage, and brief happiness, before tragedy intervenes, of a sophisticated girl with an unconventional past and of a man younger in years and experience. *The Time Between* (1942) brings an American soldier back to his California home where he marries the girl he loves and receives a citation for bravery beyond the line of duty. *Never Let Me Go* (1945) concerns a beautiful and wealthy young woman who goes into a business office to escape from a jealous mother. When the girl marries, her mother tries to destroy her happiness, and what the mother is not able to do is almost accomplished by a sister-in-law.

BEN AMES WILLIAMS

was born in Macon, Mississippi, on March 7, 1889; he is a grandnephew of James Longstreet, the Confederate general who figures prominently in *House Divided.* Eventually the Williams family moved northward to Ohio. Ben attended school in Massachusetts and then went to Cardiff, Wales, where his father was the United States Consul. After graduating from Dartmouth College in 1910, Ben worked as a reporter on the Boston *American;* in his spare time he wrote short stories. In 1912 he married Florence Trafton Talpey of York, Maine; her father, grandfather, and great-grandfather had been captains of ships in the trade between New England and China. In December, 1916, he decided that he could support his family as a free-lance writer and resigned from the newspaper. Spectacularly successful as a short-story writer, he found that, while magazines were demanding shorter and shorter stories, he wanted to write longer and longer ones, and so he began composing novels. Mr. and Mrs. Williams, who have two sons and a daughter, live in the winter at Chestnut Hill, Massachusetts, and in the summer at "Hardscrabble," Searsmont, Maine.

Some of Mr. Williams' five hundred short stories have been collected in *Thrifty Stock* (1923) and *Fraternity Village* (1949). His mystery stories include *The Silver Forest* (1926), *The Dreadful Night* (1928), *Death on Scurvy Street* (1929), *Touchstone* (1930), *An End to Mirth* (1931), *Money Musk* (1932), *Mischief* (1933), *Pascal's Mill* (1933), *Hostile Valley* (1934), and *Crucible* (1937).

Mr. Williams is a large, athletic man with a great fondness for hunting, fishing, and outdoor life. His friend and neighbor, Kenneth Roberts, who accompanied him on trips to Canada, New Mexico, and Colorado, describes him as being "tolerant, wise, the best of sportsmen and the best of friends—qualities that shine out from every paragraph that he writes."

More than thirty novels have come from the pen of Mr. Williams. "To write a book which seeks to interweave fact and fiction," he says, "is something like the work of a detective." He has been a painstaking student of social history and a wide traveler, always for the purpose of gaining insight into human nature. Even though on occasion he speaks of himself as a mere storyteller, a man who likes to write and who composes with an amazing fluency and rapidity, hard work lies behind his success.

His books range in style from magazine serials to serious historical novels; at least half a dozen of the latter have shed new light on incidents in the Revolution, the War of 1812, the Civil War, and the recent past. It is for these notable books that he will ultimately be judged as a contributor to American fiction, for they are crowded with vivid details of everyday life and animated with action exemplifying the problems of people responding to the forces operating in their day. Yet in the shortest and lightest of his tales there is something of his affirmative attitude that mankind can work its way upward steadily in spite of handicaps or difficulties.

All the Brothers Were Valiant (1919), his first novel, is an adventure story involving pirates and mutiny at sea; the youngest of five Shore brothers demonstrates traditional family courage. *The Sea Bride* (1919) tells of a young bride of an old whaling captain who goes mad on a three-year voyage. In *The Great Accident* (1920) a seemingly worthless son of a politician becomes an honorable man when elected mayor of his city. *Evered* (1921) portrays the remorse of a Maine farmer-butcher who stood by as his wife was killed by an enraged bull. *Black Pawl* (1922) pictures love and hate aboard a whaling schooner captained by Black Pawl, an embittered man who scorns all mankind. *Audacity* (1924) has an ex-convict replace, for a time, a rich young Bostonian, Perry Danton, in his home and in his relations with the latter's sweetheart.

The Rational Hind (1925) concerns the deterioration of the Dillard family in Fraternity, Maine, a small community, in the years after 1900. *Longings* (1927) takes wealthy, nostalgic Walter Overlook home to Maine and to an old love after his success in New York *Splendor* (1927) is a detailed, authoritative picture of an American family and of life in the United States from 1872 to 1916 as seen through the experiences of a newspaper employee, Henry Beeker, the son of a Boston blacksmith, who begins as an office boy. *Great Oaks* (1930) traces the Kirk family's rule of a tropical island off the coast of Georgia through three generations from the time of Blackbeard, the pirate, to the Civil War. *Pirate's Purchase* (1931) is about a house party on an island off the coast of Georgia.

Honeyflow (1932) recounts the rise of Sophie Randle from her childhood in a New England orphan asylum to her success as a famous singer in the Metropolitan Opera Company. *Small Town Girl* (1935) tells of Kay Brannon's desire to escape from a dull New Hampshire town and her marriage to a Boston physician. *The Strumpet Sea* (1938) details the experiences of several missionaries in the Fiji Islands in the 1860's. *Thread of Scarlet* (1939) is an historical novel about

Nantucket Island in the War of 1812 when that whaling center was being starved by the British blockade. Because help did not come from the mainland, the islanders seceded and signed a neutrality pact with England. The romantic action centers in the flirtatious Quaker girl, Damaris Coffin, who is loved by an American seaman and a British officer.

Come Spring (1940) pictures everyday life in Sterlington, now Union, Maine, during the Revolutionary War. Joel Adam comes home after three years of fighting and marries Mima Robbins. The story of their life together supplies the narrative thread for the portrayal of community activities on the northern frontier as early settlers created permanent homes out of the wilderness. The war itself is distant and seldom mentioned. *The Strange Woman* (1941) analyzes the character of Jenny Hager, a woman who in Maine from 1814 to 1865 surrounded herself with an air of saintly rectitude but whose evil nature became known. *Time of Peace* (1942) is a contemporary historical novel covering the period from September 26, 1930, to December 7, 1941, in a story of Mark Worth, a composite American. He is an anti-F. D. Roosevelt isolationist as a result of the cynicism following World War I. His analysis of European events leads him to approve American foreign policy.

Leave Her to Heaven (1944) portrays the two dissimilar sisters whom Richard Harland marries. Ellen murders her crippled brother-in-law and then commits suicide. Ruth, though accused of murdering Ellen, brings Richard great happiness. *It's a Free Country* (1945) concerns a young couple who spend their inheritance, have many children, and come to grief in the depression. *House Divided* (1947) is a long historical novel about the Currain family in Virginia before and during the Civil War. Five major characters typify traditional southern attitudes. The events concern civilians rather than soldiers, and especially notable is the account of the effect of war upon their lives. *Owen Glen* (1950) is the life story of a youngster who at thirteen in 1893 digs his first ton of coal and joins the United Mine Workers. A year later he is secretary of the local, and at nineteen he is vice-president of the southern Ohio district. The richly detailed background portrays the social conditions lying behind the American labor movement: company villages, broken political promises, mine disasters, violent strikes, and unsafe working conditions.

THAMES ROSS WILLIAMSON

was born on February 7, 1894, on the Nez Percé Indian Reservation near Genesee, Idaho. His ancestry is Welsh-Norwegian on his father's side and French-Irish on his mother's. When he was fourteen years of age, he ran away from home. He worked as a circus hand, cabin boy, laborer, reporter, secretary to the warden of the Iowa State Prison, and interpreter at the Hull House in Chicago. He graduated with high honors in 1917 from the University of Iowa, and a year later took his master's degree at Harvard. From 1920 to 1921 he taught economics at Smith College.

Mr. Williamson has written voluminously. *Civics at Work* (1928) and *Introduction to Economics* (1936) are two of his textbooks. *Far North Country* (1944) traces the history of Alaska from prehistoric times through the battles of Attu and Kiska. His children's books include *Opening Davy Jones's Locker* (1930) and *The Flint Clipper* (1940).

Mr. Williamson's novels are romantic and swift-paced in historical settings. His main characters are analyzed in terms of their psychological responses.

His first novel, *Run, Sheep, Run* (1923), portrays the experiences of a shepherd in the Lost Mountains of California. *Gypsy down the Lane* (1926) is a picaresque romance of modern Romany life and a loving portrayal of nature. *The Man Who Cannot Die* (1926) is a fantasy based on a Philadelphian's morbid fear of death in 1781 and his drinking an elixir of life which helps him survive into modern times. *The Stride of Man* (1929) portrays the development of America in the story of a man who begins life in an Oregon log cabin and lives to see the conquest of the air by the Wright brothers. *Hunky* (1929), a Book-of-the-Month-Club selection, is a psychological study of the giant, Jencic, whose strength comes to the rescue of Teena, a girl in a bakery. *The Earth Told Me* (1930), with its setting in the Alaskan tundra, pictures Taliak regaining his wife after she has fallen in love with a youth educated in a mission school. *In Krusack's House* (1931), a sequel to *Hunky,* probes into the inner life of Jencic, whose marriage to Teena is a failure.

The Woods Colt (1933) is the story of an illegitimate child in the Ozarks who grows into manhood plagued by the sin of his birth. He kills an officer and escapes to the woods. This book was a choice of the Book-of-the-Month Club. *D for Dutch* (1934) is about a Pennsylvania German farmer who covets his neighbor's farm and uses a pow-wow book and *hexerei* to gain his end. *Under the Linden Tree* (1935) and *Beginning at Dusk* (1935) treat of superstition and its effects on gullible people. *Christine Roux* (1945) concerns a deeply religious novice who is compelled to leave a French convent and adjust herself to secular life. Despite the hazards of Paris and an unscrupulous suitor, she retains her innocent outlook and an abiding faith. *The Gladiator* (1948) is a novel that has as its setting the times of Nero and his corrupt court; the hero is converted to Christianity and escapes from the burning city of Rome.

DOROTHY CLARKE WILSON

Bradford Bachrach

was born in Gardiner, Maine, on May 9, 1904. When she was ten, she suddenly felt an urge to write, and immediately began, "Old Mrs. Witch in her very best gown. . . ." From then on, her mother and father, a Baptist minister, encouraged their only child in everything she did and were far prouder of her new-found talent than she herself was. Although she graduated from Bates College with highest honors and a Phi Beta Kappa key, one of her lifelong regrets is losing the women's college tennis championship by one point. The silver cup, she thinks, would improve her standing in the eyes of her children.

At Bates she also met her future husband, Elwin L. Wilson, whom she married while he was a student at Princeton Theological Seminary. Later they returned to New England, where her husband, a graduate of the Boston University School of Theology, has served as pastor and district superintendent in the Maine Methodist Conference. While her husband was serving one of his first rural churches, a religious play was needed, and a suitable one could not be found; Dorothy Clarke Wilson wrote one and has been writing them ever since. At present she has fifty-four plays in print, and had the distinction of having more plays under production in 1949 than any other playwright in the world. She is the author of a collection of plays, *Twelve Months of Drama for the Average Church* (1933). In addition to her innumerable duties as a minister's wife, housekeeper, and mother of two adopted children, Harold and Joan, her chief avocation outside of writing is music. In 1947 Bates College conferred on Mrs. Wilson the degree of Doctor of Letters.

The Brother (1944), her first novel, is a portrait of James, the brother of Jesus, who joined Peter as the head of the church in Jerusalem and was the first to die a martyr's death. *The Herdsman* (1946) is the story of Amos, one of the lesser prophets but the first to discover God as love and justice rather than vengeance. While much of the story is of necessity imaginary, the background is as true to historical fact as careful research can make it, and presents an accurate picture of Biblical times.

Prince of Egypt (1949), winner of the Westminster Press award for a novel best portraying a fundamental human problem, is a story of Moses. Of its purpose the author says: "To me the important thing about this novel is not its recreation of a historical character in a realistic setting but its delving into the origin of the principles of democracy and human rights."

MITCHELL WILSON

Lotte Jacobi

was born on July 17, 1913, in New York City. He attended the public schools of that city and of Long Beach, Long Island, New York, where he spent a considerable portion of his boyhood, the third of four children in a middle-class family of comfortable circumstances. Toward the end of his college career he became interested in science, and he holds degrees from both New York University and Columbia University. Until 1945 he was a professional research physicist, writing fiction in his spare time. He married Helen Weinberg in May, 1941, and is the father of two girls. He has written two mystery novels, *Footsteps Behind Her* (1941) and *Stalk the Hunter* (1943).

Mr. Mitchell began as a writer of mystery stories, and, although he continues to employ the same tightness of plot required by this form of fiction, he has deepened the psychological and character elements in his novels. He has moved steadily to sever his interest from the technique and content of melodramatic writing.

None So Blind (1945) is a tightly knit triangle of human relations. A wife fears her blind and sinister husband, a war veteran. A police lieutenant comes to assist her and try to win her love. *The Panic-Stricken* (1946) is a suspense story of a cruise on the yacht *Gara,* whose millionaire owner is murdered. *The Kimballs* (1947), with a theme of parental tyranny, is about a Long Island millionaire whose wife, Connie, died under strange circumstances twelve years earlier. Believing she had been unfaithful, he has destroyed the love of his daughter, Ann, for Connie. Steve La Farge, a returned war veteran, who had accidentally killed Connie with an arrow, sets out to help Ann, his sweetheart.

Live With Lightning (1949), a Literary Guild selection, traces the career of an ambitious young physicist who, encouraged by the devotion of his wife, becomes more and more successful until he runs the risk of letting money and fame destroy his devotion to science.

WILLIAM E. WILSON

was born in Evansville, Indiana, on February 12, 1906, of pioneer stock that emigrated from New England and South Carolina and that was of Scottish, English, and French origin. He was brought up against a background of political campaigning, his father, William E. Wilson, Sr., being at one time a member of the House of Representatives from southern Indiana. Young Wilson attended the public school of Evansville and later went to Harvard, graduating with a bachelor's degree in 1927 and receiving a master's degree in 1930. His employment has been divided between newspapers and schoolrooms. During World War II he served three and a half years in the naval reserve. He is now director of the writers' conference and a professor of English at the University of Colorado. He is married and has three sons.

His non-fiction books include *The Wabash* (1940), a volume in the "Rivers of America" series; *Big Knife* (1940), a biography of George Rogers Clark for adolescents; and *Shooting Star* (1942), a biography of Tecumseh written for young readers.

Mr. Wilson is interested in people, as individuals and in groups, and in the timeless quality of the spiritual problems with which they are confronted in any age. Although he has written on themes drawn from events in America, he does not consider himself an historical novelist.

His first novel, *Yesterday's Son* (1941), with its setting in a New England college town, concerns John Corey and Jessica Pindar, the youthful wife of a banker fifteen years older than she is. For a week during a summer vacation they were deeply in love. Twenty years later Larry Pindar, Jessica's son, is a member of a class taught by John at college, and John realizes that the boy is his own child. *Crescent City* (1947) recounts the history of an Ohio town from 1912 to 1946 through the flashback memories of a White House correspondent, Stephen Holt, during his train ride home to attend the funeral of his father, Jay Holt, editor of the *Gazette*. The events include murder, fights, a lynching, marital infidelity, arson, and crookedness in politics. Through the son's eyes the father emerges as a man of integrity, great strength, and social usefulness.

Abe Lincoln of Pigeon Creek (1949) is a fictionized treatment of the few known facts concerning Lincoln's fourteen formative years in southern Indiana from 1816 to 1830. The boy begins school, becomes an apprentice to his father, and experiences an unsuccessful romance which sends him on a brief trip to New Orleans where he sees slavery in action.

PERCY WINNER

Arni

was born in New York City on October 16, 1899. He attended Columbia University from 1916 to 1918 and then went to Paris, where for three years he studied at the Sorbonne. He earned his way by working at night for the Paris editions of the New York *Herald* and the Chicago *Tribune*. In 1923 he joined the Associated Press, serving as correspondent in London, Paris, and Rome. After four years in Italy he had had enough of fascism. For the next five years he was news and foreign editor of the New York *Evening Post*. Then he was chief correspondent for North America of the Havas News Agency of France and foreign commentator for the Columbia Broadcasting System, speaking in French to Europe. For a year he was director of the international division of the National Broadcasting Company. From 1939 until the autumn of 1941 he was director of the International News Service in Rome.

Joining the Office of Strategic Services, Mr. Winner went to London and from 1941 to 1944 served as chief of liaison with the British political warfare organization, special assistant to the American Ambassador to Great Britain, deputy director of the Office of War Information, chief of the psychological warfare section of Allied Force Headquarters in North Africa, and special field representative in Spain. He left government service in the autumn of 1944. Since 1948 he has been an editor of *The New Republic*.

His first novel, *Dario, 1925–1945* (1947), is an accurate political and historical account of Fascist Italy as reported by a newspaper correspondent whose acquaintance with Dario Duvolti, a writer, brings knowledge of the corrupt and cynical Mussolini government. *Scene in the Ice-Blue Eyes* (1947) is also about an American newspaperman in Italy who places his knowledge at the disposal of the

British secret service in order to hunt spies. He becomes involved in a murder. *The Mote and the Beam* (1948) concerns an American writer in Europe who flees from an orgy in a rich Spaniard's home in Paris and then associates with a woman of great sexual passion. She is a leader of a fascist gang, but a Frenchman comes to the rescue of the writer.

ANNE GOODWIN WINSLOW

was born in Memphis, Tennessee, in the last quarter of the nineteenth century. She did not attend school; her father, a lover of the classical languages and literatures, supervised her education. Until her marriage she lived in the country at Raleigh, near Memphis. Her husband, Eveleth Winslow, of the distinguished naval family of Boston, was an officer in the corps of engineers of the army, and her life with him took her into many lands and places. After his retirement they returned to her old home to live, and there, since her husband's death and the marriage of her two children, she continues to lead her contentedly rural existence. Her first writings were poems, and these were collected into *The Long Gallery* (1925). *The Dwelling Place* (1943) gives her reminiscences of her years of wandering as the wife of an army officer. Her first book of fiction contains seven short stories, *A Winter in Geneva* (1945); it has some of the qualities of Henry James and Katharine Mansfield.

Cloudy Trophies (1946), her first novel, is a study of the meaning of love, death, and sacrifice in the story of a woman's inconsolable sorrow over the death of her only child. *A Quiet Neighborhood* (1947) discusses the way of life in the South as discovered by a northern girl on a visit early in the 1900's. *The Springs* (1949) portrays the emotional coming of age of a young southern girl; medicinal springs are found near her home and cause an influx of visitors. *It Was Like This* (1949) deals with the theme of the enrichment of life through love in a story of a mother, two sons, and an adopted daughter on a Mississippi plantation.

KATHLEEN WINSOR

The Brockway Studios, Inc.

was born on October 16, 1919, in Olivia, Minnesota. She grew up in Berkeley, California, and received her bachelor's degree from the University of California in 1938. Two years earlier she had married Robert J. Herwig, a star football player. She contributed stories on football to the Oakland *Tribune.* When her husband was required to do a class exercise on the death of Charles II of England, she became fascinated by the Restoration period. Beginning in 1938 she read extensively in the history of the years in England following 1660 and especially of the lives of courtiers. She then wrote the best-selling novel *Forever Amber.* Of her approach to writing of the Restoration period, Miss Winsor says: "In my research I tried to become so immersed in the customs, manners, morals, language, and other aspects of the time that I would see it not as a twentieth-century American, but as one who lived in the seventeenth century. Many of my central characters are imaginary—I haven't put anyone I know into the novel—but they could have lived, and if they had, I think they would have behaved just as they do in the book and recorded history would still be exactly the same. I have made them people of their own time, not of ours, and hope they will be judged accordingly." She is now married to Arnold Robert Krakower, a New York lawyer engaged in general practice.

Forever Amber (1944) is an historical romance in which sixteen-year-old Amber St. Clare is taken from a country village to London and becomes involved in affairs with a variety of persons of importance. The immorality of the Restoration is pictured with frankness. *Star Money* (1950) concerns a modern girl who achieves phenomenal success in her twenties as a novelist, has love affairs while her husband is away at war, and then calmly faces the break-up of her marriage.

SOPHUS KEITH WINTHER

Witter

was born in Denmark on June 24, 1894. His parents in 1897 brought him to their first home in the United States at Hampden, Massachusetts. This stony soil provided a poor place for a Danish farmer to till, and the family moved after two years of failure to Nebraska. There, in spite of many difficulties, they prospered in a mild, farmer-like manner. "But the destiny of the emigrant farmer is west," Mr. Winther writes, "so we followed that drive and finally settled in Oregon." He received his bachelor's degree from the University of Oregon in 1918 and his master's degree in 1919. His doctorate came in 1927 from the University of Washington, where he is now professor of English literature.

Dr. Winther's first three novels comprise a trilogy dealing with the immigrant theme in American life. It is not just a story of Danes, but a story of Americans who from the days of the Puritans to the last caravan moving west to conquer the Pacific slopes of the continent have been an emigrant people. They have always lived in two worlds: the one of the past involving thoughts returning over the ocean to the old countries, or over the Alleghenies to the East, or over the plains and mountains back to the Ohio Valley; and the other of the practical world where they made their living, built their homes, raised their families, and lived their daily lives. This trilogy dramatizes the greatest single influence in American culture: the conflict between the longing for the place "back home" and the new location on the frontier where success may be achieved.

Take All to Nebraska (1936), his first novel, tells how Peter Grimson, a small farmer in Denmark, comes to America with his wife and children and settles on a farm in Massachusetts. After three unsuccessful years, he moves again, this time to Nebraska. There the story develops the inner conflict of the immigrant and his children with the culture of the new world. The ever-present longing for the old country in contrast to the growing acceptance of the new is dramatized in suffering and sorrow. The parents' decision to give up the struggle and return to Denmark is brought to a climax when the discovery is made that the children are at heart Americans. The parents thereupon abandon their plan and take a new lease on life in this country. *Mortgage Your Heart* (1937) continues the story of the family life on a rented farm. As the six sons of the Grimsons grow up to be American they rebel against old-country customs and manners. This conflict is intensified by poverty and the extreme physical hardships of farm life. As a modicum of material success develops, one of the boys realizes his hope to go on through high school and ultimately to the university. *This Passion Never Dies* (1938) describes the family's rise to momentary success and then the loss of their farm in an economic depression. The father dies, the children scatter to the cities, and the mother lives on alone. She mortgaged her heart to the new world, a debt contracted that for her will never be settled.

Beyond the Garden Gate (1938) portrays a young man who suddenly finds that the innocent love which leads to serious consequences for the girl is no measure of life for him. He deserts her to marry a woman his equal in education and interests. The price he pays is the realization that the rational solution of a moral problem does not end the heartache and sense of doom that traditional moral patterns impose on life. His retribution is well portrayed.

IRA WOLFERT

was born on November 1, 1908, in New York City. During his years at the Columbia University School of Journalism he worked as a taxi driver and streetcar motorman. Taking his degree in 1930, he became associated with the North American Newspaper Alliance, an organization which syndicates his writings to newspapers. During World War II he prepared in 1941 an exclusive report on the seizure by the Free French of St. Pierre and Miquelon. From 1942 to 1943 he was a war correspondent in the South Pacific, and on June 6, 1944, he was present at the invasion of Normandy. In 1943 he received a Pulitzer prize for reporting. His non-fiction books are *Battle for Solomons* (1943), *Torpedo 8: The Story of Swede Larsen's Bomber Squadron* (1943), *One-Man Air Force* (with Don Gentile, 1944), and *American Guerrilla in the Philippines* (1945).

Tucker's People (1943), his first novel, deals with the love of men and women for one another and the destructive shapes this love assumes under the pressures of the society in which it must find expression. The society is the one formed by monopoly capitalism as it developed from Rockefeller to Hitler. Its anguishes are described at their fever point in the depression of the 1930's, and in their least ameliorated manifestations in the numbers-racket monopoly.

An Act of Love (1948) demonstrates the triumph of human will over evil as it exists in the modern world which the human will has created. The scene is an island in the South Pacific, a Garden of Eden from which man has been driven by himself. Its hero is a naval pilot, wrecked and thrown ashore by the sea, a man fallen from the angels to be cast up to the animals. He tests himself against a wide range of perils in peace and war until in the end he develops enough strength to assert himself for what he is, a being with the wisdom to love.

WILLIAM WOODS

Kesslere

was born in 1916 in Port Chester, New York. He attended school in Vienna, and then after graduating from the University of North Carolina he engaged in 1937 in free-lance newspaper work in Europe. Among other things during this time he smuggled Jews out of Germany and was banned from that country by the Nazis. Most of World War II was spent in England; he barely escaped being torpedoed off the coast of Scotland and being killed in a Norwegian plane in the Shetlands. He married Kato Havas, the Hungarian violinist; they have three children and now live in New Hampshire.

The Edge of Darkness (1942), his first novel, is a moving story of a Norwegian fishing village and its resistance to the Nazi garrison placed there to crush patriotic feelings. It is a parable of man's fortitude. *The Street of the Seven Monks* (1948) concerns a French composer from Haut-Savoie who has been imprisoned in a German concentration camp. The story portrays what happens in the musician's home after the Germans surrender, and studies the emotional conflicts created in a sensitive people by war and its aftermath. The form is a modern Odyssey of the spiritually disoriented soul.

HERMAN WOUK

Editta Sherman

was born in New York City on May 27, 1915, of immigrant parents, both of whom came to America in their teens in 1905. His father became an owner and manager of a large power laundry. Herman Wouk went to public schools in New York and to Columbia College, where he edited *The Columbia Jester* and wrote the varsity shows in 1933 and 1934. He graduated in 1934 with general honors, and went to work in radio as a script writer, collaborating with Arnold M. Auerbach, who has since become the author of the Broadway musical shows "Call Me Mister" and "Inside U.S.A." The writing team assisted Fred Allen in preparing his weekly comedy scripts for the five years from 1936 to 1941.

In June, 1941, Herman Wouk left this position to volunteer his services as a dollar-a-year expert for the United States Treasury, writing and producing radio shows to sell defense bonds. At the outbreak of the war he joined the navy, and served as a deck officer for four years, three of these at sea aboard destroyer-minesweepers, and saw action in the Rendova, Kwajalein, Eniwetok, Saipan, Guam, and Okinawa invasions. At the war's end he was executive officer of the destroyer-minesweeper *Southard,* which was wrecked in the Okinawa typhoon of October, 1945. Herman Wouk climbed off the wreck with the half-finished manuscript of his first novel, *Aurora Dawn,* in the ship's mail pouch; he had been writing the novel in spare hours at sea.

Aurora Dawn was his first writing for publication, although he had ground out a great many words for radio. It was a Book-of-the-Month-Club selection for May, 1947. Thereupon he undertook a literary career, and has since written plays, "The City Boy" and "The Traitor" (1949); a motion picture, "Slattery's Hurricane; and short stories.

Herman Wouk has pursued literary work for too short a time to estimate the trend of his writings. He seems to be primarily a humorist. Thus far he has used clear-cut plots in the familiar story-telling tradition and has avoided modern innovations of excessively frank language and formless narratives. His tales are optimistic, the style aims at precision and grace, and the tone is pleasant.

Aurora Dawn, or the True History of Andrew Reale (1947) is a chatty and urbane satire on the advertising industry in general and radio salesmanship in particular. The title names a soap, and the hero is a radio-time salesman who has gay and harried moments. He finds a hillbilly preacher who delivers remarkable sermons. The book is mainly a *tour-de-force* in style, telling a streamlined modern story in the eighteenth-century manner of Fielding.

The City Boy (1948) is the story of eleven-year-old Herbie Bookbinder, fat, "brainy little guy" living in The Bronx in New York City. His adventures occur during school days and at a summer camp with an Indian name in the 1920's, when he is passing from the seventh to the eighth grade. An athletic classmate accuses him of actually liking grammar. He feels betrayed when his teacher, with whom he has been in love, marries an assistant principal. He finds consolation in little, red-haired Lucille Glass, a charmer of his own age, who lives in a private house, not an apartment, on Mosholu Parkway. His parents send him and a sister to a camp in the Berkshires, where he is annoyed by the chirping of crickets, the pretended enthusiasm of the management, and the synthetic friendliness of the singing hour. He comes to despise the way the sense of fear is created in youngsters. This humorous book evokes nostalgic memories of the joys and brief sorrows of childhood, the exhilarating effect of love, the dark if momentary despair of losing a sweetheart, and the dawning of doubts about one's elders.

RICHARD WRIGHT

was born on September 4, 1908, on a plantation near Natchez, Mississippi, where his father worked as a farmhand and teacher in a Negro school. The father deserted his family when Richard was only five, and the mother moved to Memphis, Tennessee, and later to Helena, Arkansas. The boy shuttled from relative to relative, and spent some time in an orphans' home. An aunt who was a teacher made it possible for him to attend a Seventh Day Adventist school in Jackson, Mississippi. At the age of fifteen he went to Memphis, Tennessee, and there engaged in odd jobs. Happening to come upon H. L. Mencken's *Book of Prefaces,* he conceived the idea of becoming a writer. He wandered all over the United States and worked at odd jobs until he arrived in Chicago in 1934. He joined the labor commission, published some free-verse poems, and in 1935 became associated with the Federal Writers' Project, one of the New Deal activities designed to give work to writers during the depression. In 1937 he moved to New York City, where he wrote the *Guide to Harlem* for the Writers' Project. For a time he contributed to *The New Masses* magazine. In 1938 he won a prize of five hundred dollars offered by *Story* Magazine, and a year later he was awarded a Guggenheim fellowship. In recent years he has lived in Paris where he says the environment is congenial for writing. *Black Boy* (1945) is an autobiography of Wright's childhood and youth.

Mr. Wright portrays the plight of Negroes who are poor, inadequately sheltered, and often victimized by white people. His major theme has been the degrading effect of segregation and racial discrimination. He portrays the Negro's sordid poverty in some parts of the nation, the feeling of social imprisonment, and the physical and spiritual cruelty resulting from unfriendliness and, at times, from well-meant kindness.

His first book, *Uncle Tom's Children* (1938), contains four long stories which deal with conflicts between whites and Negroes in the South. The first story, "Big Boy Leaves Home," describes the tragedy resulting from the prank of four Negro boys who go swimming in a pond reserved for white people. "Down by the Riverside" recounts the experiences of a Negro, Mann, who during a Mississippi River flood borrows a boat stolen from a white man to row his wife, in labor with child, to a Red Cross hospital. He kills the owner in self-defense. "Long Black Song" concerns the tragic outcome of a Negro's discovery that his wife has been seduced by a white traveling salesman. "Fire and Cloud," a picture of starvation and unemployment in a small southern city, has a Negro preacher, Dan Taylor, lead a bi-racial parade to protest against unfair distribution of food and jobs. "Bright and Morning Star," added to the second edition, portrays Negro and white sharecroppers uniting to seek equality and justice from landowners.

Native Son (1940), a title designed to show that the chief character is an authentic American, is the story of a young Chicago Negro, Bigger Thomas, who finds no outlet for his abilities and ambition because of his race. Insults, injury, and segregation give him the impression that he does not belong to society. He reads cheap magazines, goes to exciting movies, and soon is a petty thief. Environment warps him. When he takes home his employer's drunken daughter and tries to hide her presence from her blind mother, he unwittingly strangles her to death and then burns the corpse in a furnace. He is caught and electrocuted. The story is based in part on the case of Robert Nixon, a Negro who was electrocuted in Chicago in 1938 for murdering a white woman. This book was a Book-of-the-Month-Club selection, and Paul Green dramatized it.

PHILIP WYLIE

was born on May 12, 1902, in Beverly, Massachusetts. His father was a Congregational minister. His mother, who wrote popular novels and magazine serials, died in 1907, soon after the family had moved to Cleveland, Ohio. Four years later Dr. Wylie married again. In 1914 he accepted a call to the Central Presbyterian Church in Montclair, New Jersey. There Philip finished high school and then went on to spend three years at Princeton University from 1920 to 1923. He left college because he concluded that money and social position made undergraduate competition so unfair that life under such conditions was intolerable. The examining methods were the last straw, for, ironically, a teacher failed Mr. Wylie in English not for wrong answers to questions, but for the manner in which answers were phrased. In college he published a book of poems, and by this time he had decided to become a professional writer. With boyhood friends in medical school, he went to classes, read their textbooks, and sat through hundreds of hours of internship. This training supplemented a considerable college training in the basic sciences.

He went straight from Princeton to a job with Edward L. Bernays, a public-relations expert. In 1924 Mr. Wylie entered the publicity business for himself, but late that year worked as press agent for *The New Yorker* magazine, which was first published in February, 1925. In 1925 he joined the staff in the art and editorial departments. He wrote verse, fiction, notes and comment, and satirical pieces. With the publication of his first novel in 1928 he devoted his whole time to writing as a contributor of stories and articles to the leading magazines. For considerable periods he lived in France. Up to 1934 he was interested in general ideas and in classical English literature in the manner of a liberal-minded, caustic, intellectual aesthete. After 1934 he became interested, through psychoanalysis, in the study of psychology.

In 1936 he went abroad and there contracted a serious illness. His earlier interests in medicine and psychology were deepened by this experience. Especially did he make a deep study of certain ideas of Carl Gustav Jung of Zurich, Switzerland. Mr. Wylie has devoted three books not so much to an exposition of Jungian psychology as to the deliberate attempt to tear up false premises in present thinking and belief. His purpose is to prepare the minds of as many readers as possible for future calm and logical expositions of the new theory of instinct. *Generation of Vipers* (1943) and *An Essay on Morals* (1947) explain the Jungian concepts. Feeling it to have been premature, he produced *Opus 21* (1949) as a further preparation. It is his hope to have a large audience of readers sufficiently jarred out of the common orientations of modern men so that they will be prepared for later, quieter books of exposition.

For a number of years Mr. Wylie has lived during the winter in Miami Beach, Florida, and during the summer he travels in the North. He has done many things other than writing. He has on occasion actively entered politics, and has held several posts in conservation organizations. He has long been a director of Angler's Incorporated, which runs Miami's fishing tournaments. He spent about three years, in all, working as a writer for Paramount Pictures and Metro-Goldwyn-Mayer. He was one of the chief executives of Dade County Civil Defense during World War II. He worked at sea and elsewhere for the government during the war as an air-sea rescue and survival expert. For a time, he headed an air-force writing unit which collected an official history of the Twentieth Air Force, the B29's. He served in Washington in the Office of Facts and Figures.

Mr. Wylie is one of the fastest and most productive writers in the country. *Generation of Vipers* was written in eight weeks. *Babes and Sucklings,* a fairly long novel, was completed on a nine-day boat trip. He has written a twenty-five-thousand-word novelette in a day, between an early breakfast and late retiring. A six-thousand-word short story, such as his "Crunch and Des" *Saturday Evening Post* fishing stories, often takes only a day, often two mornings, and sometimes only a single morning to write. He corrects his manuscripts, but never rewrites them. If he dislikes them, he discards them, and he has laid aside countless articles, short stories, novelettes, and novels. He has probably published in more different magazines than any other American author; his output includes hundreds of short stories, scores upon scores of serials, hundreds of articles, scores of syndicated newspaper columns, movies, verse, radio programs, hundreds of thousands of words of advertising copy, maybe a million of publicity, and so on. He has written for the "slicks," the "pulps," technical journals, religious publications, journals of opinion, literary publications, and newspapers. Once he even wrote a comic strip.

Of his outlook on life, Mr. Wylie has said: "I do have a serious, coherent, hopeful, scientific theory of life and of man, toward the final expression of which I am steadily blasting a series of steps in the rocky cliff of tradition and convention. If I succeed in expressing, at long last, what it is that I know, and what it is that I believe in, I shall consider my work decently done. For I believe that the theories for which I am hewing the way are those upon which the better destinies of unborn billions will ultimately be founded."

Some of his short stories about Crunch and Des, two young fishermen who have adventures with their rehabilitated boat off the coast of Miami, Florida, appeared in *The Big Ones Get Away!* (1940); *Salt Water Daffy* (1941), which takes the men to Hollywood; and *Fish and Tin Fish* (1944).

Heavy Laden (1928), his first novel, contrasts the new and old generations in a story of Ann MacGregor's conflict with her father, a minister. *Babes and Sucklings* (1929) tells of a couple who dwell together in free love in the 1920's and then fall genuinely in love. *Gladiator (*1930) portrays the effect on Hugh Danner of his superman quality as a result of his biologist father's prenatal experiment. *Footprints of Cinderella* (1931) is a romantic tale of a resentful sister who substitutes a French baby girl for her brother's child. *The Savage Gentlemen* (1932) concerns a rich man's son who is reared to the age of thirty on an island in the Indian Ocean and who then goes to New York City to meet social perils.

Finnley Wrenn (1934), the novel which attracted attention to Mr. Wiley as a thought-provoking commentator on the follies of his generation, is about a New York advertising man who detests the modern world and talks and acts in a Rabelaisian fashion. *As They Reveled* (1936) deals with four gay young couples involved in a complex set of emotions of love and jealousy, feelings they thought they were too sophisticated to have. *Too Much of Everything* (1936) studies the effect on a newly rich family of its loss of fortune in the depression. *An April Afternoon* (1938) is about four children in the Sheffield family and their modern ways of making and taking love where they find it. *The Other Horseman* (1942) presents a warning against isolationism in the reactions of a midwestern boy who was in England during the blitzkrieg. *Night unto Night* (1944) deals with the threat of doom to contemporary society as symbolized by the thoughts of living people about death.

Opus 21 (1949), a title indicating that this is Mr. Wylie's twenty-first important book, is devoted to a presentation in fictional form of the ideas of the author. One of the characters, who is purely fictional, is named Philip Wylie. The theme of the book is the need for people to accept some fundamental truths and to live in accordance with them as a form of moral discipline.

YATES *to* YOSELOFF

ELIZABETH YATES

was born on December 6, 1905, in Buffalo, New York. After graduation from the Franklin School, she spent one year at Oakmere and another in Paris and London. When school days were over, she settled in New York to earn her living by any sort of writing she could do. New York offered her many opportunities in book reviews, special articles, and interviews, but not enough entirely to pay her way. She therefore undertook other occupations, ranging from work with Macy's to teaching girls to ride horseback in a summer camp. In 1929 she married William McGreal, an American whose business was in London. Ten years in England followed, with frequent travel in the British Isles and on the continent. During those years she did considerable writing and editorial work, but it was not until 1938 that she published her first book, *High Holiday,* a story of mountain climbing in the Swiss Alps. In 1939 the McGreals moved to New Hampshire where, just outside Peterborough, they maintain a small farm. She is on the staff of the University of New Hampshire's Writers Conference held every summer at Durham. Mr. McGreal is executive director of the New Hampshire Association for the Blind.

Since her first story was published in England, a rich sequence of books has followed, several of them for children, including *Patterns on the Wall* (1943) which won the New York Herald Tribune Spring Festival award. It is the story of a journeyman stenciler plying his trade in the early days of New Hampshire. *Mountain Born* (1943) is the lovely pastoral tale of a small boy's growing into his place on a mountain farm. Elizabeth Yates has edited, and arranged for publication, the work of the nearly forgotten Cornish writer, Enys Tregarthen: *Piskey Folk* (1940), *The Doll Who Came Alive* (1942), *The White Ring* (1949), and *Children of the Bible* (1950).

Serenity and idealism pervade her work as do an honest and courageous facing of issues. Whatever her subject, she enriches it with hope and leavens it with wisdom. Life to her is a quest, and its meaning is spiritual conquest. Her husband says of her that "usefulness seems to be the yardstick of her philosophy—beginning at home, then in the community, and through her writing broadening into an ever-wider field."

Her first novel, *Wind of Spring* (1945), is a quiet and beautifully composed story of the life of Susie Minton who, going into service in Victorian England while barely out of childhood, lives through the changes wrought by three wars. *Nearby* (1947) tells of a young teacher's struggle to make her place in a small New England community and to do away with elements of smugness and prejudice. *Beloved Bondage* (1948) is a warm and very human story of the marriage of John and Althea and of the maturing of their love from emotional romanticism into richness and force. *Guardian Heart* (1950), set in a New Hampshire village, pictures love, faith, and understanding.

JULIA TRUITT YENNI

Ben Pinchot

was born on February 21, 1913, in Birmingham, Alabama. She is a granddaughter of Julia Truitt Bishop, southern writer and newspaperwoman for forty years in various towns in Texas and in New Orleans, Louisiana. For one year she attended Lincoln Memorial University at Harrogate, Tennessee. She is married to Charles R. Hikes and is the mother of two daughters. Her main interest as a writer is the depiction of character. She resides in Pine Grove, Pennsylvania.

Never Say Goodbye (1937), her first novel, describes the life of a large family as seen from the viewpoint of a child of five; its purpose is to show that a child's life, far from being carefree and simple, is complicated by its own tragedies and misunderstandings. *This Is Me, Kathie* (1938) is the story of a young girl, allowed to grow up more or less as she pleases while her mother concentrates on making a belle of a beautiful older sister, who is brought abruptly to face the problems of maturity. While she learns, with difficulty, to realize and conquer the problems of adult life, she retains always the charm and innocent enthusiasms of her childhood. *House for the Sparrow* (1942) portrays the amusing difficulties and near-tragedies encountered by an irresponsible family living in a conservative small-town neighborhood. Clara, the oldest daughter, struggles to become accepted by the community at its own conventional and ordinary standard of value.

FRANK (GARVIN) YERBY

was born on September 5, 1916, at Augusta, Georgia. While he was attending secondary school at Haines Institute in Augusta, James Weldon Johnson approved some of his verses and thus stimulated his interest in writing. At Paine College in Augusta he majored in English and languages and received his bachelor's degree in 1937. The following year he achieved his master's degree at Fisk University in Nashville, Tennessee. In 1939 he studied education at the University of Chicago. At this time he worked on the Federal Writers' Project of the Works Progress Administration, a federal agency which was providing employment during the depression. For a year he taught at the Florida Agricultural and Mechanical College in Tallahassee and spent the next year teaching at Southern University at Scotlandville, Louisiana. During World War II he worked at Dearborn, Michigan, and at Jamaica, Long Island. His short story, "Health Card," won the O. Henry Memorial Prize award in 1944; it is about an unjust act committed upon a Negro couple by military police. His other short stories describe Negro people of Georgia and neighboring states. On March 1, 1941, he married Flora Helen Claire Williams at New Orleans. They have three children: Jacques, Nikki, and Faune.

Mr. Yerby's novels have been written for their value as entertainment rather than as serious literature. "My literary interest at present," he said in 1949, "is gradually to move away from the costume-historical novel toward books having more enduring worth, regardless of the period in which they are laid."

The Foxes of Harrow (1946), his first novel, employs the familiar characters and situations of southern romantic fiction. The story is about Stephen Fox, a gambler, who goes to New Orleans in 1825 and makes a fortune in sugar. He marries a Creole girl and dreams of establishing a great family, but by the end of the Civil War the great house and plantation, "Harrow," is in ruin and he is bankrupt. *The Vixens* (1947) is about New Orleans in the Reconstruction days of carpetbaggers, scalawags, and klansmen. Laird Fournois, who returns home after fighting in the Union army, takes over his plantation, marries an insane beauty, and falls in love with a Creole lady. His enemy, Hugh Duncan, pursues him.

The Golden Hawk (1948) is a tale of adventure and exotic love in the West Indies in the seventeenth century. Christopher Giradeux, the hero, captains a pirate ship and seeks to gain revenge upon a Spanish nobleman who tortured and killed his mother. *Pride's Castle* (1949) portrays early nineteenth-century high finance in the "Robber Baron" era of Gould, Vanderbilt, and their associates. The story concerns the rise and fall of Pride Dawson, who wrecks several lives in order to achieve his towering ambitions. *Floodtide* (1950) pictures Natchez, Mississippi, in the slavery days of the 1850's. Ross Parry, who was born in the water-front slums, rises to live among the wealthy people. Morgan Brittany, the evil wife of a middle-aged man, impedes his progress, and Conchita, a Cuban girl, assists him.

MARTIN YOSELOFF

was born on July 26, 1919, in Sioux City, Iowa, and spent most of his childhood in Mason City, Iowa. He began his writing career, he says, when at twelve he won a contest sponsored by an ice-cream company for a composition on the theme, "Why the Three Bears Eat Higley's 'Luxus' Ice Cream." At fifteen he was writing articles for his school publication and at seventeen he was doing reportorial work for a newspaper. At the University of Iowa he wrote feature stories for the *Daily Iowan*, the school paper. After graduating in 1941 he went to New York and worked in the editorial departments of several publishing houses until 1943. Then he was inducted into the army, where he served in the transportation corps until 1946, writing technical manuals covering such subjects as "How to Lift a Bag of Cotton" and "How to Construct a Field Kitchen." While in the service, he wrote his first book. He returned to New York in 1946 and again worked in a publishing house, but with the publication of his first work, it became increasingly hard for him not to spend his time writing. Consequently, in September, 1946, he began using his days to write, working under the self-employment program of the G.I. Bill of Rights. His second novel was completed the following year.

No Greener Meadows (1946) is the autobiographical story of a childhood spent in Iowa in the late 1920's and the early 1930's. His father dies, and the family revolves around the mother, who somehow manages every emergency and holds the children together in love, even as they establish their own households. *The Family Members* (1948) is a moving story of the ever-widening effects of an innocent young girl's mistake. At seventeen Lorraine Hollenbeck, the daughter of the YMCA secretary, falls in love with a high-school boy and becomes pregnant. The novel centers on the effect—on each member of her family, as well as on the people of her town—of the birth of her illegitimate baby. *The Girl in the Spike-Heeled Shoes* (1949) describes Maybelle Reardon, who grew up in Iowa in the 1930's and early 1940's, and delineates her poor childhood, her seduction, her brief whirl as a traveling dancer, her marriage, and the decision she is brought to make when she learns of her husband's transgression.

ZARA

LOUIS ZARA

was born on August 2, 1910, in New York City, of immigrant parents who had come to this country from eastern Europe. His mother's family was occupied with trade, and his father's was devoted to learning and theology. The home was bilingual, with Yiddish as the chief spoken language. When Louis Zara was a child, the family moved to Buffalo and from there to Chicago, where he received his public-school education. At Crane Technical High School he edited the school paper and wrote fictional sketches, a humor column, editorials, and news articles. During high-school days he also attended a theological seminary, since his parents hoped that he would enter the ministry, but he was reluctant to continue in that field, for authorship had already attracted him.

Upon leaving high school he went to work in a law printshop, where he worked five nights a week from five o'clock in the evening to three o'clock in the morning. During the day he attended Crane Junior College and carried a full program. Later he attended the University of Chicago; he left in 1932 in his senior year. He sent his first story, "Travail," to *The American Mercury;* the editor, H. L. Mencken, not only published it, but also offered lively encouragement. Subsequently Mr. Zara set to work on a story of Jewish-American immigrant life; when this novel was one-third completed, a publisher offered a contract and a modest advance. In spite of the depression he gave up his printshop job and undertook writing as a profession. With two novels completed, he was called to Hollywood, but there he had no opportunity to do anything he felt worth while. He was so stunned by this strange world that he felt his integrity would be endangered if he remained, so he returned to Chicago, where he continues to make his home.

"My chief concern as a writer," Mr. Zara has stated, "is to express the feelings of the individual, as far as possible to extol the dignity of man, and, at the same time, to portray how far below his own potential man still lives. As for the art of writing, I am convinced that he who says most in the fewest words creates the greatest effects. I have no patience with obscurities and am convinced that writings requiring handbooks and special keys and essays to explain them are on a lower plane than works whose emotional, if not intellectual, content is at once apparent to the reader. In brief, I believe that Homer and Shakespeare live today, not because persons of high intellectual perception help to keep them alive, but because their messages and styles are so clear, and offer so much, that masses of people have found in them the echoes of their own trials and tribulations, and so have conferred upon them the only immortality that counts: continuity in the hearts of people."

Blessed Is the Man (1935), his first novel, tells the story of Jake Krakauer, a Jewish immigrant, who comes to this country to avoid military servitude under the Czar. In Chicago he begins as a peddler and, by dint of hard work, rises in the world. He purchases one store, acquires a second, and finally becomes a banker. The style of the book echoes, in American prose, the laughter and tears of Yiddish idiom. The book was selected by *The Nation* as one of its fifty "notables" of the year. *Give Us This Day* (1936) is a story about a baker. The theme is bread, the staff of life, and how it affects the lives of ordinary people. *Some for the Glory* (1937) concerns the role which politics plays in the American community. Michael Hawks begins life as an orphan boy and fifty years later goes down to defeat as a presidential candidate.

This Land Is Ours (1940), an historical novel on the winning of the old Northwest Territory from the time of Braddock's defeat to the beginnings of Chicago as a village, covers eighty years in the life of Andrew Benton, who grows up on the frontier, lives as a captive with the Shawnee Indians, fights with George Rogers Clark, and survives the Fort Dearborn massacre. This novel received the award of the Chicago Foundation for Literature. *Against This Rock* (1943) is a psycho-biographical novel of the life of Charles V, the Emperor of the Holy Roman Empire and King of Spain, in the sixteenth century. A deeply religious man who loved justice and peace, but whose life was marked by continuous warfare, he struggled with Martin Luther, Francis I of France, and Moritz of Saxony, and ultimately abdicated his crown to retire to a monastery in Spain.

The first volume of a trilogy, *Ruth Middleton* (1946), is the story of the life of an American girl from birth to adolescence. Later volumes are planned to make this a triptych on the role of womanhood from the turn of the century to the present. *In the House of the King* (1950), a psycho-biographical novel of Philip II of Spain, gives new insight into the character of a monarch who was formerly regarded as an enigma and a tyrant.

INDEX OF MARRIED NAMES AND PSEUDONYMS